Research, Innovation, and Industry Impacts of the Metaverse

Jeetesh Kumar
Taylor's University, Malaysia

Manpreet Arora
Central University of Himachal Pradesh, India

Gul Erkol Bayram
Sinop University, Turkey

A volume in the Advances in Social Networking
and Online Communities (ASNOC) Book Series

Published in the United States of America by
　　IGI Global
　　Information Science Reference (an imprint of IGI Global)
　　701 E. Chocolate Avenue
　　Hershey PA, USA 17033
　　Tel: 717-533-8845
　　Fax: 717-533-8661
　　E-mail: cust@igi-global.com
　　Web site: http://www.igi-global.com

　　　　　　　　Library of Congress Cataloging-in-Publication Data

CIP DATA PROCESSING

Research, Innovation, and Industry Impacts of the Metaverse
　Jeetesh Kumar, Manpreet Arora, Gul Erkol Bayram
　　2024 Information Science Reference

ISBN: 9798369326077(hc) | ISBN: 9798369351994(sc) | eISBN: 9798369326084

This book is published in the IGI Global book series Advances in Social Networking and Online Communities (ASNOC) (ISSN: 2328-1405; eISSN: 2328-1413)

British Cataloguing in Publication Data
A Cataloguing in Publication record for this book is available from the British Library.

For electronic access to this publication, please contact: eresources@igi-global.com.

Advances in Social Networking and Online Communities (ASNOC) Book Series

Hakikur Rahman
Ansted University Sustainability Research Institute, Malaysia

ISSN:2328-1405
EISSN:2328-1413

MISSION

The advancements of internet technologies and the creation of various social networks provide a new channel of knowledge development processes that's dependent on social networking and online communities. This emerging concept of social innovation is comprised of ideas and strategies designed to improve society.

The **Advances in Social Networking and Online Communities** book series serves as a forum for scholars and practitioners to present comprehensive research on the social, cultural, organizational, and human issues related to the use of virtual communities and social networking. This series will provide an analytical approach to the holistic and newly emerging concepts of online knowledge communities and social networks.

COVERAGE

- Networks as Institutionalized Intermediaries of KC
- Performance Evaluation and Benchmarking of Deployed Systems
- Epistemology of Knowledge Society
- E-capacity Building Programmes to Ensure Digital Cohesion and Improved E-Government Performance at Local Level
- Strategic Management and Business Process Analysis
- Leveraging Knowledge Communication in Social Networks
- General Importance and Role of Knowledge Communities
- Local E-Government Interoperability and Security
- Leveraging Knowledge Communication Networks – Approaches to Interpretations and Interventions
- Methodologies to Analyze, Design and Deploy Distributed Knowledge Management Solutions

IGI Global is currently accepting manuscripts for publication within this series. To submit a proposal for a volume in this series, please contact our Acquisition Editors at Acquisitions@igi-global.com or visit: http://www.igi-global.com/publish/.

Titles in this Series

For a list of additional titles in this series, please visit: http://www.igi-global.com/book-series/advances-social-networking-online-communities/37168

Exploring the Use of Metaverse in Business and Education
Jeetesh Kumar (Taylor's University, Malaysia) Manpreet Arora (Central University of Himachal Pradesh, India) and Gül Erkol Bayram (Sinop University, Turkey)
Information Science Reference • copyright 2024 • 332pp • H/C (ISBN: 9798369358689) • US $245.00 (our price)

Creator's Economy in Metaverse Platforms Empowering Stakeholders Through Omnichannel Approach
Babita Singla (Chitkara Business School, Chitkara University, India) Kumar Shalender (Chitkara Business School, Chitkara University, India) and Nripendra Singh (Pennsylvania Western University, USA)
Engineering Science Reference • copyright 2024 • 287pp • H/C (ISBN: 9798369333587) • US $315.00 (our price)

Critical Roles of Digital Citizenship and Digital Ethics
Jason D. DeHart (University of Tennessee, Knoxville, USA)
Information Science Reference • copyright 2023 • 296pp • H/C (ISBN: 9781668489345) • US $235.00 (our price)

Global Perspectives on Social Media Usage Within Governments
Chandan Chavadi (Presidency Business School, Presidency College, Bengaluru, India) and Dhanabalan Thangam (Presidency Business School, Presidency College, Bengaluru, India)
Information Science Reference • copyright 2023 • 353pp • H/C (ISBN: 9781668474501) • US $215.00 (our price)

Social Capital in the Age of Online Networking Genesis, Manifestations, and Implications
Najmul Hoda (Umm Al-Qura University) and Arshi Naim (King Kalid University, Saudi Arabia)
Information Science Reference • copyright 2023 • 301pp • H/C (ISBN: 9781668489536) • US $215.00 (our price)

Advanced Applications of NLP and Deep Learning in Social Media Data
Ahmed A. Abd El-Latif (Menoufia University, Egypt & Prince Sultan University, Saudi Arabia) Mudasir Ahmad Wani (Prince Sultan University, Saudi Arabia) and Mohammed A. El-Affendi (Prince Sultan University, Saudi Arabia)
Engineering Science Reference • copyright 2023 • 303pp • H/C (ISBN: 9781668469095) • US $270.00 (our price)

Community Engagement in the Online Space
Michelle Dennis (Adler University, USA) and James Halbert (Adler University, USA)
Information Science Reference • copyright 2023 • 364pp • H/C (ISBN: 9781668451908) • US $215.00 (our price)

Handbook of Research on Bullying in Media and Beyond
Gülşah Sarı (Aksaray University, Turkey)

701 East Chocolate Avenue, Hershey, PA 17033, USA
Tel: 717-533-8845 x100 • Fax: 717-533-8661
E-Mail: cust@igi-global.com • www.igi-global.com

Editorial Advisory Board

MD Tariqul, *Taylor's University, Kuala Selangor, Malaysia*

Rajesh Verma, *Mittal School of Business, India*

Chia Kei Wei, *School of Hospitality, Tourism and Events, Faculty of Social Sciences and Leisure Management, Taylor's University, Malaysia*

Table of Contents

Foreword xvii

Preface... xix

Acknowledgement xxv

Chapter 1
Dive Into Metaverse: Concept, Evolution, Framework, Technologies, Opportunities, and Trends 1
    Joana Raquel Neves, CEOS.PP, Polytechnic Institute of Coimbra, Coimbra, Portugal
    Lara Mendes Bacalhau, CEOS.PP, Polytechnic Institute of Coimbra, Coimbra, Portugal

Chapter 2
Historical Context and Evolution of Metaverse... 27
    Meenu Sharma, The Assam Royal Global University, India
    Arpee Saikia, The Assam Royal Global University, India

Chapter 3
Exploring the Factors Impacting the Intention to Use Metaverse in the Manufacturing Industry
Through the Lens of Unified Technology Acceptance Theory... 43
    Mohammad Imtiaz Hossain, Multimedia University, Malaysia
    Yasmin Jamadar, BRAC University, Bangladesh
    Md. Kausar Alam, BRAC University, Bangladesh
    Tanima Pal, BRAC University, Bangladesh
    Md. Tariqul Islam, Taylor's University, Malaysia
    Nusrut Sharmin, University of Chittagong, Bangladesh

Chapter 4
Metaverse Perspectives: Unpacking Its Role in Shaping Sustainable Development Goals - A
Qualitative Inquiry 62
    Monika Chandel, Central University of Himachal Pradesh, India
    Manpreet Arora, Central University of Himachal Pradesh, India

Chapter 5

Human Resource Management in the Metaverse Era: A Bibliometric Analysis and Future
Research Agenda..76
> *Sahil Sharma, Central University of Himachal Pradesh, India*
> *Anu Sohal, Central University of Himachal Pradesh, India*

Chapter 6

From Clicks to Virtual Realms: Exploring Metaverse-Driven E-Commerce and Consumer Shifts 93
> *Animesh Kumar Sharma, Lovely Professional University, India*
> *Rahul Sharma, Lovely Professional University, India*
> *Rajesh Verma, Lovely Professional University, India*

Chapter 7

Metaverse: Transforming the User Experience in the Gaming and Entertainment Industry..............115
> *Pooja Swami, Chaudhary Devi Lal University, India*

Chapter 8

Integration of the Metaverse in the Healthcare Industry: A Catalyst for Profound Change..............129
> *Sabyasachi Pramanik, Haldia Institute of Technology, India*

Chapter 9

Navigating the Metaverse: A Comprehensive Guide to Marketing, Branding, and Innovation 146
> *Harleen Pabla, I.K. Gujral Punjab Technical University, India*
> *Harmeen Soch, I.K. Gujral Punjab Technical University, India*

Chapter 10

The "Metaverse Society": Transformative Effects of Metaverse on Society 167
> *Irfan Nawaz, Ministry of Human Rights, Pakistan*
> *Nazirullah, Universiti Sultan Zainal Abidin, Malaysia*
> *Sabeeha Rahman, Alama Iqbal Open University, Islamabad, Pakistan*
> *Alia Shaheen, Social Welfare and Baitul Mall, Pakistan*

Chapter 11

Navigating the Metaverse in Business and Commerce: Opportunities, Challenges, and Ethical
Consideration in the Virtual World...183
> *Pooja Shukla, Amity University, Ranchi, India*
> *Bhavna Taneja, Amity University, Ranchi, India*

Chapter 12

The Metaversal Shift: A Bibliometric Analysis of Industry Transformation 197
> *Navneet Kaushal, Central University of Himachal Pradesh, India*
> *Anshu Duhoon, Central University of Himachal Pradesh, India*

Chapter 13
Transformation of Marketing Strategy by Metaverse in the Hospitality Industry Facing Crisis........ 213
    Asik Rahaman Jamader, Pailan College of Management and Technology, India
    Santanu Dasgupta, Pailan College of Management and Technology, India
    Mushtaq Ahmad, The Neotia University, India

Chapter 14
Unlocking the Potentials and Constraints of Metaverse Implementation in Manufacturing Firms.... 223
    Mohammad Imtiaz Hossain, Multimedia University, Malaysia
    Yasmin Jamadar, BRAC University, Bangladesh
    Nurunnesa Begum Momo, BRAC University, Bangladesh
    Nusrat Hafiz, BRAC University, Bangladesh
    Rufaida Nurain Saiba, BRAC University, Bangladesh

Chapter 15
Unleashing the Power of Research, Innovation, and Industry Impacts: Exploring the
Transformative Role of the Metaverse in Business and Commerce 247
    Paramjeet Kumar, North Eastern Hill University, India

Chapter 16
Exploring Safe Hedging Options for Blockchain Assets in the Face of COVID-19-Induced
Volatility 254
    Himani Gupta, Jagannath International Management School, India
    Rupinder Katoch, Lovely Professional University, India
    Manisha Gupta, Sharda University, India

Chapter 17
Metaverse Metamorphosis: Bridging the Gap Between Research Insights and Industry
Applications 275
    Manpreet Arora, School of Commerce and Management Studies, Central University of
       Himachal Pradesh, India

Compilation of References 287

About the Contributors 329

Index 334

Detailed Table of Contents

Foreword xvii

Preface xix

Acknowledgement xxv

Chapter 1

Dive Into Metaverse: Concept, Evolution, Framework, Technologies, Opportunities, and Trends 1

Joana Raquel Neves, CEOS.PP, Polytechnic Institute of Coimbra, Coimbra, Portugal
Lara Mendes Bacalhau, CEOS.PP, Polytechnic Institute of Coimbra, Coimbra, Portugal

The ever-changing environment of the Metaverse claim for a study that leads to a captivating journey for readers of this chapter in which the current condition of this digital space is explained, its historical roots and evolution up to the present day, the novel prospects it offers and the revolutionary forces advancing its virtual worlds that leads to the transformative potential of this digital frontier. Through an interdisciplinary lens, this research clarifies the Metaverse by examining its fundamental elements and supporting technologies and highlighting important challenges that deserve further research. It thoroughly examines and investigates several aspects of this new paradigm in detail, providing a spotlight on everything from the functioning of virtual markets to the nuances of digital identities. The purpose of this chapter is to serve scholars, business professionals, and enthusiasts alike, a set of guidelines for a deep understanding of the current Metaverse environment and predicting its bright future highlighting its boundless opportunities.

Chapter 2

Historical Context and Evolution of Metaverse 27

Meenu Sharma, The Assam Royal Global University, India
Arpee Saikia, The Assam Royal Global University, India

The use of the metaverse in various periods is explained, including its use in novels and movies, video games, social media, industries, businesses, and headsets. This chapter is divided in to five sections: section one provides the introduction, literature review and ancient concept of metaverse; section two explains the use of term metaverse and historical context and evolution of metaverse; section three is related with use of metaverse in different sectors/fields: movies, novels, gaming, education, industry, retail, architecture, medical care and social media; section four provides a insight into prolific ways in which the metaverse was used during the Covid-19 pandemic times with special reference to the financial sector; section five describe managerial or practical applications and future research directions for the use of metaverse.

Chapter 3
Exploring the Factors Impacting the Intention to Use Metaverse in the Manufacturing Industry Through the Lens of Unified Technology Acceptance Theory...43

Mohammad Imtiaz Hossain, Multimedia University, Malaysia
Yasmin Jamadar, BRAC University, Bangladesh
Md. Kausar Alam, BRAC University, Bangladesh
Tanima Pal, BRAC University, Bangladesh
Md. Tariqul Islam, Taylor's University, Malaysia
Nusrut Sharmin, University of Chittagong, Bangladesh

This study accordingly explores the factors impacting the adoption of a metaverse in the manufacturing industry and develops a new model based on the Unified Theory of Acceptance (UTAT). Gender, age, and education were control variables. 235 questionnaire responses from employees of Malaysian manufacturing firms were collected through convenience sampling techniques and analyzed by Smart-PLS software. The findings reveal effort expectancy, perceived risk, and perceived technology accuracy have a significant relationship with intention to use a metaverse. Moreover, attitude to use evidenced mediating with perceived risk, perceived technology accuracy and intention to use a metaverse. The control variables did not evidence any impact on the intention to use a metaverse. This study provides insights to metaverse technology developers and manufacturing practitioners to explore and focus on the factors impacting the adoption of a metaverse in the manufacturing industry, as well as theoretical contributions for academia to progress further.

Chapter 4
Metaverse Perspectives: Unpacking Its Role in Shaping Sustainable Development Goals - A Qualitative Inquiry 62

Monika Chandel, Central University of Himachal Pradesh, India
Manpreet Arora, Central University of Himachal Pradesh, India

The metaverse, a virtual realm, has drawn considerable attention from academicians as well as policymakers in recent years. In this chapter, we explored the metaverse's social, economic, and environmental effects, which align with various UN Sustainable Development Goals (SDGs), using an interdisciplinary perspective to show how it might transcend geographical borders and promote sustainability. This study adds to the ethical and sustainable development of digital technologies by analysing the opinions about the metaverse's influence on the SDGs. It will help administrations, corporations, and communities use the metaverse to make the world more inclusive, equitable, and sustainable. We are still learning how the metaverse fits into sustainable development, and scholars are examining the positive and negative aspects. This area must balance technical innovation and global sustainability as it progresses towards a more sustainable future.

Chapter 5
Human Resource Management in the Metaverse Era: A Bibliometric Analysis and Future Research Agenda...76

Sahil Sharma, Central University of Himachal Pradesh, India
Anu Sohal, Central University of Himachal Pradesh, India

The advent of the metaverse offers human resource management both new opportunities and challenges as digital technologies continue to progress. To examine the state of HRM research in the metaverse era and pinpoint significant themes and gaps in the body of literature, this study conducts a bibliometric analysis. The authors examine the distribution of articles, authors, journals, and keywords associated with HRM in the context of the metaverse through a methodical examination of scholarly publications from the Scopus database. This research indicates an increasing amount of interest in this field, with studies concentrating on digital leadership, people management, remote work, and virtual collaboration. The authors offer a research agenda for the future to fill in these knowledge gaps and improve comprehension of HRM in the metaverse era. This study adds to the expanding corpus of research on HRM in digital contexts and offers insightful guidance on how to navigate the potential and difficulties presented by the metaverse for scholars, practitioners, and policymakers.

Chapter 6

From Clicks to Virtual Realms: Exploring Metaverse-Driven E-Commerce and Consumer Shifts 93
Animesh Kumar Sharma, Lovely Professional University, India
Rahul Sharma, Lovely Professional University, India
Rajesh Verma, Lovely Professional University, India

This study conducts a comprehensive bibliometric analysis using the preferred reporting items for systematic reviews and meta-analyses (PRISMA) model to explore the convergence of e-commerce, customer experience, and virtual environments in the evolving metaverse. Utilizing Scopus database data from 2010 to 2023, this research aims to map the trends, patterns, and emerging themes surrounding augmented reality (AR), virtual reality (VR), and immersive technologies, shaping consumer behaviour within virtual realms. Initial screening resulted in a substantial corpus of scholarly articles, conference papers, and reviews. Moreover, utilizing visualization tools like VOSviewer, this study provides insightful graphical representations, revealing clusters and connections among keywords, and offering a deeper understanding of the interdisciplinary nature of Metaverse in e-commerce. The analysis focuses on quantifying publication trends, identifying influential authors, institutions, and countries, and mapping key themes and connections within the domain. The analysis encompasses a range of bibliometric indicators, including publication trends, prolific authors, influential journals, and co-occurrence networks of keywords It investigates how virtual environments affect purchasing decisions, brand interactions, and loyalty-building strategies, emphasizing personalized experiences, social interactions, and gamification. The analysis also uncovers emerging research trends and gaps, suggesting avenues for further exploration, including the integration of artificial intelligence, blockchain technology, and spatial computing in enhancing e-commerce in virtual spaces. This research contributes to understanding the impact of the metaverse on e-commerce, customer experience, and engagement, providing valuable insights for academics, practitioners, and policymakers navigating this dynamic field.

Chapter 7

Metaverse: Transforming the User Experience in the Gaming and Entertainment Industry.............. 115
Pooja Swami, Chaudhary Devi Lal University, India

The concept of the metaverse is not new, as it dates back to 1992, but it is an interesting area that is receiving increased attention from researchers and marketers. This chapter provides insight into how the emerging virtual world of the metaverse is significantly enhancing the user experience in the gaming and entertainment industries by leveraging the latest technologies such as augmented reality (AR), virtual reality (VR), artificial intelligence (AI), blockchain technology, NFT, and others. This chapter aims to provide insight into the current developments in metaverse entertainment and gaming applications and how they will affect our user experience in the future. The approach used in this study is based on a comprehensive literature review on the subject of metaverse applications and their potential future in the gaming and entertainment industries. This chapter also discusses the various opportunities for the metaverse in the near future, as well as the challenges involved with it, such as privacy, security, and inclusivity.

Chapter 8
Integration of the Metaverse in the Healthcare Industry: A Catalyst for Profound Change 129
    Sabyasachi Pramanik, Haldia Institute of Technology, India

This chapter explores the connection of the metaverse and healthcare, investigating whether this integration signifies a significant shift or is just a passing trend. The chapter begins by explaining the notion of the metaverse and its ramifications in the healthcare environment, setting the stage for the next discussion. The chapter examines the possible catalyst impact by exploring several options. This text discusses the potential of the metaverse to transform medical teaching, enhance telemedicine, enable therapeutic interventions, and promote worldwide collaborative networks in healthcare. This investigation aims to ascertain whether the metaverse has the capacity to revolutionize healthcare methodologies, improve patient treatment, and overcome geographical obstacles. However, there are significant obstacles that need to be addressed in order to successfully integrate the metaverse, as outlined in the next section. The chapter examines the long-term viability of the metaverse's influence on healthcare by analyzing technological complexities, ethical considerations, and barriers to adoption. The chapter showcases real-world case studies that illustrate how metaverse technologies have shown to be valuable and enduring in the healthcare industry, in contrast to the fleeting nature of fads. This supports the premise that the metaverse has the potential to go beyond being a temporary fad and establish a significant presence in healthcare procedures. By analyzing historical similarities, this chapter investigates whether the metaverse has the characteristics of long-lasting change or whether it is prone to being quickly outdated. As the chapter approaches its end, it presents a prospective view on the development of the metaverse in the healthcare sector. The text compiles the acquired insights from the investigation and provides a detailed assessment of whether the metaverse has the potential to be a powerful catalyst or a temporary trend in the field of healthcare. This chapter examines the possible impact of integrating the metaverse into healthcare, examining whether it will be a driving force for long-term change or a passing trend.

Chapter 9
Navigating the Metaverse: A Comprehensive Guide to Marketing, Branding, and Innovation 146
    Harleen Pabla, I.K. Gujral Punjab Technical University, India
    Harmeen Soch, I.K. Gujral Punjab Technical University, India

Delving into the dynamic intersections of augmented reality, artificial intelligence, blockchain, and spatial computing, this chapter offers strategic insights for brands seeking to establish a meaningful presence. From the evolution of brands in virtual environments to future trends, technological predictions and challenges, this chapter acts as a strategic roadmap. It addresses the needs of academic researchers, students, executives, and practitioners by synthesizing current research, offering practical applications, and proposing solutions. The chapter bridges the gap between theory and application, fostering a deeper understanding of the metaverse's impact on marketing, branding, and innovation. Aiming to be a valuable resource, the chapter equips a diverse audience with insights into the evolving metaverse landscape, providing a foundation for academic exploration and practical application.

Chapter 10

The "Metaverse Society": Transformative Effects of Metaverse on Society 167

Irfan Nawaz, Ministry of Human Rights, Pakistan
Nazirullah, Universiti Sultan Zainal Abidin, Malaysia
Sabeeha Rahman, Alama Iqbal Open University, Islamabad, Pakistan
Alia Shaheen, Social Welfare and Baitul Mall, Pakistan

The term metaverse originated from the "Snow Crash" novel by Neal Stephenson in 1992. The term underwent massive evolution from a speculative concept into an immersive digital ecosystem. Technological advancement unveils the metaverse's potential in shaping the digital future more transformative and promising. The rapid growth of the metaverse extends beyond social interaction and entertainment. Metaverse has started contributing to education, commerce, and professional collaboration. The scope of this chapter is to provide a secondary analysis of the influence of metaverse in individual's lives and societal structures, using the embodied social presence theory and relying on key thematic areas (access and adoption; wellbeing; diversity and inclusion; sustainability; and empowerment) discussed by the World Economic Forum.

Chapter 11

Navigating the Metaverse in Business and Commerce: Opportunities, Challenges, and Ethical
Consideration in the Virtual World... 183

Pooja Shukla, Amity University, Ranchi, India
Bhavna Taneja, Amity University, Ranchi, India

Trade and consumer interactions with goods and services could be drastically changed by the convergence of the metaverse and commerce. Blockchain technology is used in the metaverse to facilitate the production, ownership, and exchange of virtual products and digital assets. This opens up new business opportunities and includes digital stuff such as in-game items, digital art, virtual real estate, and other digital goods. The idea of " Metaverse" and the role played by Metaverse in business and commerce are intended to be explained in this chapter. The chapter aims to address the genesis, requirements, advantages, opportunities and challenges in the area of Metaverse . It also intends to highlight the ethical considerations and the actions necessary to make the associated practices robust, viable, and effective.

Chapter 12

The Metaversal Shift: A Bibliometric Analysis of Industry Transformation 197

Navneet Kaushal, Central University of Himachal Pradesh, India
Anshu Duhoon, Central University of Himachal Pradesh, India

Metaverse has emerged as an immersive digital environment, capturing widespread attention owing to its significant impact on industrial growth. This study aims to explain the evolution of research focused on the metatarsal shift in industries. This study offers a bibliometric analysis of industrial transformation research from 2007 to 2024. The finding shows a tremendous rise in publication over time. The objective of this analysis is to extract valuable insights and trends and to shed light on the key challenges and opportunities associated with digital transformation in the industrial sector. This study provides thorough coverage of existing literature on the implications of metaverse-enabled digital transformation for the industrial revolution and explores the interplay of various factors such as technology adoption, organizational culture, and strategic planning. The study contributes to understanding the ongoing discourse on digital transformation and its impact on the industrial landscape.

Chapter 13

Transformation of Marketing Strategy by Metaverse in the Hospitality Industry Facing Crisis........ 213

    Asik Rahaman Jamader, Pailan College of Management and Technology, India
    Santanu Dasgupta, Pailan College of Management and Technology, India
    Mushtaq Ahmad, The Neotia University, India

The hospitality industry is one of the largest manpower-driven industries and hence generates huge employment. Strategies evolved and applied till 2019 transformed greatly facing the crisis in 2020 to cope with the prevailing circumstances for sustenance. The use of technology came greatly into effect on the Metaverse. Hence a drastic change has taken place in hospitality marketing strategy using the Tourism Marketing Union Model (TMUM). People are becoming more and more technophiles, and desire to have as much data as possible before starting the tour hoping for a hindrance-free, comfortable, and enjoyable expedition. Therefore, a complete transformation occurred in every phase of the industry, especially in the marketing sector. Cost reduction and Time-saving became the aims of new strategies and for that, Metaverse Marketing Technology (MMT), influencer marketing, and targeting the right audience through Metaverse Visual Marketing are extensively used by marketers.

Chapter 14

Unlocking the Potentials and Constraints of Metaverse Implementation in Manufacturing Firms.... 223

    Mohammad Imtiaz Hossain, Multimedia University, Malaysia
    Yasmin Jamadar, BRAC University, Bangladesh
    Nurunnesa Begum Momo, BRAC University, Bangladesh
    Nusrat Hafiz, BRAC University, Bangladesh
    Rufaida Nurain Saiba, BRAC University, Bangladesh

This research investigates the potentials and constraints of metaverse technology within Malaysian manufacturing companies underpinned by the technology-organization-environment (TOE) theory. Firm size, firm age, annual revenue, and ownership structure were control variables. 240 questionnaire responses from Malaysian firms collected through convenience sampling techniques and analyzed by Smart-PLS software. The findings reveal technological limitations, poor diffusion through the network, lack of collaboration, and low perception of value by customers are significant constraints for the failure of metaverse technology implementation. The control variables did not evidence any impact on implementation. This study provides insights to metaverse technology developers and manufacturing practitioners besides theoretical contributions.

Chapter 15

Unleashing the Power of Research, Innovation, and Industry Impacts: Exploring the
Transformative Role of the Metaverse in Business and Commerce 247

    Paramjeet Kumar, North Eastern Hill University, India

The notion of the metaverse has garnered substantial attention in recent years, captivating the imagination and piquing the interest of researchers, inventors, and industry executives alike. This chapter, "Unleashing the Power of Research, Innovation, and Industry Impacts: Exploring the Transformative Role of the Metaverse in Business and Commerce," seeks to investigate the potential of the metaverse and its impact on several facets of business and commerce. This proposal aims to examine the present patterns in metaverse research, which are influenced by applications that exploit the merging of interdisciplinary technologies. The advancement of developing technologies presents diverse prospects for the use of the metaverse in the realms of industry and commerce.

Chapter 16
Exploring Safe Hedging Options for Blockchain Assets in the Face of COVID-19-Induced
Volatility 254

Himani Gupta, Jagannath International Management School, India
Rupinder Katoch, Lovely Professional University, India
Manisha Gupta, Sharda University, India

This chapter examines the transfer of daily volatility returns from one block-chain asset to another and hedging alternatives. The technique is based on adequately modelling of the dynamic conditional correlation of generalised autoregressive conditional heteroscedasticity (DCC GARCH) and the hedging ratio. The results reveal that the volatility spillover impact from Etherium to other block-chain assets exists both in the short and long run. There are also hedging possibilities available between the selected block-chain assets. This implies that, prior to investing, policymakers, regulators, and investors should be aware of volatility, spillover effects, and hedging alternatives in the constituent variables.

Chapter 17
Metaverse Metamorphosis: Bridging the Gap Between Research Insights and Industry
Applications 275

*Manpreet Arora, School of Commerce and Management Studies, Central University of
Himachal Pradesh, India*

The incorporation of the metaverse into the world of business has brought about a significant and fundamental change, altering conventional frameworks and methods while presenting unparalleled prospects for expansion and creativity. This chapter examines the significant influence of the transformation of the metaverse on the worldwide economy, emphasising its ability to generate fresh prospects for work, labour, and employment. In addition, an attempt has been made to explore the economic consequences of the metaverse, encompassing the emergence of fresh sectors, markets, and sources of income, as well as the promotion of economic expansion and employment generation. This chapter examines the impact of the metaverse on economic development, innovation, and quality of life globally, highlighting its revolutionary capabilities. Furthermore, the author explores the significance of closing the divide between research discoveries and industrial implementations, highlighting the necessity of cooperation and information sharing to convert academic discoveries into tangible advancements that have a tangible effect on the real world. This chapter examines the impact of the metaverse on economic development, innovation, and quality of life globally.

Compilation of References 287

About the Contributors 329

Index 334

Foreword

In an era defined by rapid technological advancement and digital transformation, the concept of the metaverse stands as a testament to humanity's boundless creativity and innovation.

The metaverse, a term first popularized by Neal Stephenson's science fiction novel "Snow Crash" and further conceptualized by subsequent thinkers and technologists, represents a convergence of virtual and physical realities. It encapsulates a vast digital dominion where users can interact, create and transact in immersive and interconnected virtual environments. From virtual reality simulations to augmented reality overlays, from blockchain-based economies to AI-driven interactions, the metaverse promises to revolutionize how we perceive, interact with, and shape our world.

This edited collection, crafted by esteemed scholars and practitioners at the forefront of their respective fields, serves as a comprehensive exploration of the multifaceted dimensions of the metaverse. Through a series of insightful chapters, readers are taken on a journey that traverses the theoretical foundations, technological innovations and practical applications of the metaverse across a spectrum of industries. One of the remarkable aspects of this edited volume is the spectra of contributors who have lent their expertise and insights to its pages. Hailing from Malaysia, Pakistan, Sri Lanka, Mexico and various states across India, the contributors represent a rich tapestry of cultural, geographical and academic backgrounds. This diversity not only enriches the scholarly discourse within the volume but also reflects the global significance and appeal of the metaverse phenomenon. By bringing together voices from different corners of the world, the volume offers a truly comprehensive and inclusive examination of the research, innovation, and industry impacts of the metaverse. Such a global perspective not only enhances the breadth and depth of the discussions but also underpins the universal relevance and applicability of the insights shared within this collection. One of the most compelling aspects of this volume is its emphasis on the intersectionality of disciplines and perspectives. By bringing together contributions from diverse fields such as; management, tourism, hospitality, sociology, psychology, economics, and beyond, the editors have created a treasure of insights that reflect the interdisciplinary nature of the metaverse phenomenon. This interdisciplinary approach not only enhances our understanding of the metaverse but also underscores the importance of collaboration and knowledge exchange in driving meaningful innovation across academia and industry. From entertainment and gaming to education and healthcare, the potential applications of the metaverse are as vast as they are transformative. By providing an in-depth analysis, the contributors have offered valuable perspectives on how the metaverse is reshaping consumer experiences, business models and societal dynamics.

At the helm of this groundbreaking volume are three distinguished editors, each bringing their unique expertise and perspectives to the fore. Dr. Jeetesh Kumar, from Taylor's University, Malaysia, is a visionary scholar whose research spans the intersections of tourism, technology, society and culture.

With a keen understanding of the global digital landscape, Kumar brings invaluable insights into the multifaceted dimensions of the metaverse phenomenon. Dr. Manpreet Arora, representing the Central University of Himachal Pradesh, India embodies a commitment to interdisciplinary scholarship and practical applications. Her intensive and extensive background in research and education uniquely positions her to navigate the complexities of the metaverse and its implications for various industries. Dr. Gül Erkol Bayram, hailing from Sinop University in Turkey, brings an international perspective to the editorial team. Her expertise in tourism, hospitality, emerging technologies and digital innovation adds depth and breadth to the discussions within the volume, ensuring a truly global perspective on the research, innovation and industry impacts of the metaverse. Together, these editors have curated a collection that not only reflects the cutting edge of scholarship but also sets the stage for meaningful dialogue and collaboration in this rapidly evolving field.

As we stand on the precipice of this new digital frontier, it is incumbent upon us to embrace the opportunities and challenges that the metaverse presents. As Vice Chancellor of the esteemed Central University of Himachal Pradesh in Dharamshala, India, it is my distinct pleasure to introduce the edited volume *Research, Innovation, and Industry Impacts of the Metaverse* published by IGI International, USA which will act as a roadmap and a call for action for the researchers, innovators, policymakers, academicians and industry leaders to collectively navigate and shape the future of the metaverse. I commend the editors and contributors for their dedication, scholarship and foresight in producing this seminal work, and I am confident that it will serve as a beacon of inspiration for generations to come.

Sat Prakash Bansal
Central University of Himachal Pradesh, Dharamshala, India

Preface

In the dynamic landscape of modern technology, few concepts have captured the imagination and attention of scholars and innovators quite like the metaverse. Its emergence marks a significant inflection point, signaling the convergence of virtual and physical realities, and offering tantalizing prospects for societal transformation. As editors of *Research, Innovation, and Industry Impacts of the Metaverse*, we are delighted to present this comprehensive volume exploring the multifaceted dimensions of the metaverse phenomenon.

The metaverse, with its roots extending into science fiction lore, has now become a tangible realm of exploration and innovation. Its relevance spans diverse domains, from the realms of academia to the corridors of industry and commerce. What sets this book apart is its endeavor to dissect the metaverse from various angles, shedding light on its technological underpinnings, academic research frontiers, real-world applications, and attendant challenges.

In the opening chapters, readers are introduced to the foundational concepts of the metaverse, tracing its historical trajectory and envisioning its future potential. Through meticulous examination, the book elucidates the intricate tapestry of metaverse technologies and frameworks, unraveling the threads that weave together virtual environments and immersive experiences.

A central focus of this volume is the exploration of academic research in the metaverse. Scholars from diverse disciplines converge to probe the boundaries of virtuality, offering insights into metaverse development, human-computer interaction, security, privacy, and ethical considerations. Their contributions not only enrich our understanding of the metaverse but also pave the way for responsible innovation and development.

Beyond academia, the book delves into the practical applications and societal impacts of the metaverse. From its role in reshaping business models and commerce to its implications for education, society, and the economy, each chapter offers invaluable perspectives on how the metaverse is reshaping our world.

Looking ahead, the book ventures into future directions and challenges, charting the course for continued exploration and growth in the metaverse. As we navigate the ethical, regulatory, and technological frontiers of this nascent domain, the insights contained within these pages will serve as beacons guiding our path forward.

In assembling this volume, our aim has been to provide a comprehensive resource that not only captures the current state of the metaverse but also stimulates further inquiry and innovation. We extend our gratitude to all the contributors whose expertise and dedication have made this endeavor possible.

It is our sincere hope that this book will serve as a catalyst for dialogue, collaboration, and discovery, inspiring readers to embark on their own journeys of exploration within the boundless realms of the metaverse.

Chapter 1: Dive Into Metaverse: Concept, Evolution, Framework, Technologies, Opportunities, and Trends

Neves and Bacalhau lead readers on an immersive journey through the current landscape of the Metaverse, tracing its historical roots, and illuminating its transformative potential. Through an interdisciplinary lens, this chapter clarifies the Metaverse's fundamental elements, technological frameworks, and emerging trends, offering insights into its functioning, virtual markets, and digital identities. Scholars, business professionals, and enthusiasts will find a comprehensive guide to understanding the Metaverse's current environment and its boundless opportunities.

Chapter 2: Historical Context and Evolution of Metaverse

Sharma and Saikia delve into the historical origins and evolution of the Metaverse, from its conceptualization in science fiction to its realization in digital realms. Exploring pivotal moments and milestones, this chapter examines the cultural, literary, and technological influences that have shaped the Metaverse's development, including its depiction in novels, movies, video games, and social media platforms.

Chapter 3: Exploring the Factors Impacting the Intention to Use Metaverse in the Manufacturing Industry Through the Lens of Unified Technology Acceptance Theory

Hossain et al. investigate the factors influencing the adoption of the Metaverse in the manufacturing industry, utilizing the Unified Theory of Acceptance. Through empirical research, they uncover significant relationships between factors such as effort expectancy, perceived risk, and technology accuracy, offering insights for developers and practitioners to enhance Metaverse adoption in manufacturing contexts.

Chapter 4: Metaverse Perspectives: Unpacking its Role in Shaping Sustainable Development Goals: A Qualitative Inquiry

Chandel and Arora explore the Metaverse's potential to advance sustainable development goals, examining its social, economic, and environmental impacts. Through qualitative inquiry, they demonstrate how the Metaverse can transcend geographical boundaries and promote sustainability, offering insights for policymakers, corporations, and communities to leverage digital technologies for inclusive, equitable, and sustainable development.

Chapter 5: Human Resource Management in the Metaverse Era: A Bibliometric Analysis and Future Research Agenda

Sharma and Sohal conduct a bibliometric analysis of human resource management in the Metaverse era, identifying key themes and gaps in the literature. Their research offers valuable insights for scholars, practitioners, and policymakers seeking to navigate the opportunities and challenges presented by the integration of digital technologies in HRM practices.

Chapter 6: From Clicks to Virtual Realms - Exploring Metaverse-driven E-commerce and Consumer Shifts: Metaverse in E-commerce and Consumer Behavior

A comprehensive bibliometric analysis by Sharma, Sharma, and Verma explores the intersection of e-commerce, consumer behavior, and the Metaverse. Mapping trends and emerging themes, their research sheds light on how immersive technologies are shaping consumer behavior within virtual environments, offering actionable insights for academics, practitioners, and policymakers in the evolving digital landscape.

Chapter 7: Metaverse: Transforming the User Experience in the Gaming and Entertainment Industry

Swami investigates how the Metaverse is revolutionizing user experiences in the gaming and entertainment sectors. By leveraging technologies such as AR, VR, AI, and blockchain, this chapter explores current developments and future opportunities, highlighting challenges such as privacy and security while envisioning a more immersive digital future.

Chapter 8: Integration of the Metaverse in the Healthcare Industry: A Catalyst for Profound Change

Pramanik explores the integration of the Metaverse in healthcare, examining its potential to transform medical education, telemedicine, and therapeutic interventions. By navigating opportunities and challenges, this chapter offers insights into leveraging digital technologies to overcome geographical barriers and enhance patient care in a globalized world.

Chapter 9: Navigating the Metaverse: A Comprehensive Guide to Marketing, Branding, and Innovation

Pabla and Soch provide strategic insights into leveraging the Metaverse for marketing, branding, and innovation. From understanding evolving consumer behaviors to predicting future trends, this chapter equips readers with practical strategies for establishing a meaningful presence in virtual environments and driving business growth.

Chapter 10: The 'Metaverse Society': Transformative Effects of Metaverse on Society

Nawaz et al. analyze the transformative effects of the Metaverse on society, drawing on theories of social presence and thematic areas outlined by the World Economic Forum. By exploring access, wellbeing, diversity, sustainability, and empowerment, this chapter offers a comprehensive understanding of how digital technologies are reshaping individual lives and societal structures.

Chapter 11: Navigating the Metaverse in Business and Commerce: Opportunities, Challenges, and Ethical Considerations in Virtual Worlds

Shukla and Taneja examine the role of the Metaverse in business and commerce, addressing its genesis, requirements, advantages, challenges, and ethical considerations. By exploring opportunities for virtual commerce and navigating ethical dilemmas, this chapter offers a roadmap for businesses to thrive in virtual environments while upholding responsible practices.

Chapter 12: The Metaversal Shift: A Bibliometric Analysis of Industry Transformation

Kaushal and Duhoon conduct a bibliometric analysis of the Metaverse's impact on industrial transformation, exploring trends, insights, and challenges. By synthesizing existing literature, their research provides valuable insights into the implications of digital transformation in various industries, guiding stakeholders in navigating the evolving landscape of technological innovation.

Chapter 13: Transformation of Marketing Strategy by Metaverse in Hospitality Industry Facing Crisis

Jamader et al. analyze the transformation of marketing strategy in the hospitality industry, leveraging the Metaverse to navigate crises and embrace technological innovations. By exploring new strategies such as Metaverse Marketing Technology and influencer marketing, this chapter offers insights for marketers seeking to adapt to changing consumer behaviors and preferences.

Chapter 14: Unlocking the Potentials and Constraints of Metaverse Implementation in Manufacturing Firms

Hossain et al. investigate the potentials and constraints of Metaverse implementation in Malaysian manufacturing firms, utilizing the Technology-Organization-Environment theory. By identifying technological limitations and organizational challenges, this research offers insights for developers and practitioners to enhance Metaverse adoption and implementation in manufacturing contexts.

Chapter 15: Unleashing the Power of Research, Innovation, and Industry Impacts: Exploring the Transformative Role of the Metaverse in Business and Commerce

Kumar explores the transformative role of the Metaverse in business and commerce, examining current research patterns and technological applications. By synthesizing interdisciplinary technologies and exploring emerging trends, this chapter offers insights into harnessing the potential of the Metaverse to drive innovation and industry impacts in a rapidly evolving digital landscape.

Chapter 16: Exploring Safe Hedging Options for Blockchain Assets in the Face of Covid-19-Induced Volatility

Gupta et al. examine safe hedging options for blockchain assets amidst Covid-19-induced volatility, utilizing dynamic conditional correlation modeling. By analyzing volatility spillover effects and hedging alternatives, this research offers insights for policymakers, regulators, and investors navigating blockchain markets in uncertain times.

Chapter 17: Metaverse Metamorphosis: Bridging the Gap Between Research Insights and Industry Applications

Arora delves into the transformative impacts of the Metaverse on research advancements and industry landscapes, examining technological, sociological, and psychological dimensions. By exploring research insights and translating them into tangible impacts, this chapter offers a comprehensive understanding of the Metaverse's implications for various industries, guiding stakeholders in navigating ethical, regulatory, and technological challenges.

In concluding this comprehensive exploration of the metaverse, we are reminded of the profound impact that digital technologies continue to have on our lives, societies, and industries. The journey through the diverse chapters of this book has illuminated the multifaceted dimensions of the metaverse, from its historical roots to its present-day applications and future potential.

As we reflect on the insights shared by esteemed contributors from around the globe, it becomes clear that the metaverse is more than just a technological phenomenon—it is a catalyst for societal transformation, innovation, and collaboration. From its role in reshaping industries such as healthcare, manufacturing, and hospitality to its implications for marketing, branding, and human resource management, the metaverse presents boundless opportunities for exploration and growth.

However, amidst the excitement and promise of the metaverse, we must also confront the challenges and ethical considerations that accompany its development and adoption. Issues such as privacy, security, inclusivity, and digital equity demand our attention as we navigate this rapidly evolving digital landscape. By addressing these challenges with foresight and responsibility, we can ensure that the metaverse serves as a force for positive change and empowerment.

As editors, we extend our deepest gratitude to all the contributors whose expertise, dedication, and passion have made this volume possible. Their scholarly contributions have enriched our understanding of the metaverse and inspired us to continue exploring its potential for research, innovation, and industry impacts.

It is our sincere hope that this book will serve as a valuable resource for scholars, practitioners, policymakers, and enthusiasts alike, sparking dialogue, collaboration, and discovery in the dynamic realm of the metaverse. As we embark on this journey of exploration and innovation, let us remain mindful of the transformative power of the metaverse and its capacity to shape the future of our digital world.

Editors:

Jeetesh Kumar
Taylor's University, Malaysia

Manpreet Arora
Central University of Himachal Pradesh, Dharamshala, India

Gül Erkol Bayram
Sinop University, Turkey

Acknowledgement

As editors of the edited volume *Research, Innovation, and Industry Impacts of the Metaverse*, we extend our heartfelt gratitude to the individuals who have supported us throughout this endeavor.

First and foremost, we express our deepest appreciation to our parents and family members for their unwavering love, encouragement, and understanding. Their steadfast support has been the cornerstone of our academic pursuits and professional endeavors, and we are profoundly grateful for their endless sacrifices and guidance.

Additionally, we would like to extend special thanks to specific individuals whose contributions have been instrumental in shaping this volume. Dr. Manpreet Arora extends her sincere gratitude to **Professor Sat Prakash Bansal**, the Honorable Vice Chancellor of Central University of Himachal Pradesh and **Dr Sunita Bansal**, (Mrs. HVC) for their unwavering support and mentorship. She also expresses heartfelt appreciation to her father, **S. Surinder Singh Arora**, for his boundless love, wisdom, and encouragement throughout her academic journey, she remembers fondly her mother Late Arvind Arora who acted as a pillar and guiding star in her life and career at this moment where this academic venture adds up to her career.

Dr. Gül Erkol Bayram extends her gratitude to Professor Marco Valeri from Niccolò Cusano University, Italy, and Associate Researcher at Magellan Research Center, Iaelyon Business, for his invaluable guidance and collaboration. She also extends her thanks to Mohammad Nawaz Tunio from the University of Sufism and Modern Sciences, Bhitshah, Pakistan, for his insightful contributions and support.

We are truly grateful to all the contributors, reviewers, colleagues, and friends who have generously shared their expertise, feedback, and encouragement throughout the development of this book. Your collective efforts have enriched the scholarly discourse and made this volume possible.

Finally, we express our appreciation to the publishers, editors, and staff involved in the publication process for their professionalism, dedication, and support.

Thank you all for your invaluable contributions and unwavering support.

Sincerely,

Jeetesh Kumar
Taylor's University, Malaysia

Manpreet Arora
Central University of Himachal Pradesh, Dharamshala, India

Gül Erkol Bayram
Sinop University, Turkey

Chapter 1
Dive Into Metaverse:
Concept, Evolution, Framework, Technologies, Opportunities, and Trends

Joana Raquel Neves

CEOS.PP, Polytechnic Institute of Coimbra, Coimbra, Portugal

Lara Mendes Bacalhau

(iD) https://orcid.org/0000-0001-9674-4167

CEOS.PP, Polytechnic Institute of Coimbra, Coimbra, Portugal

ABSTRACT

The ever-changing environment of the Metaverse claim for a study that leads to a captivating journey for readers of this chapter in which the current condition of this digital space is explained, its historical roots and evolution up to the present day, the novel prospects it offers and the revolutionary forces advancing its virtual worlds that leads to the transformative potential of this digital frontier. Through an interdisciplinary lens, this research clarifies the Metaverse by examining its fundamental elements and supporting technologies and highlighting important challenges that deserve further research. It thoroughly examines and investigates several aspects of this new paradigm in detail, providing a spotlight on everything from the functioning of virtual markets to the nuances of digital identities. The purpose of this chapter is to serve scholars, business professionals, and enthusiasts alike, a set of guidelines for a deep understanding of the current Metaverse environment and predicting its bright future highlighting its boundless opportunities.

INTRODUCTION

The dawn of the Metaverse heralds a paradigm shift in our conception of digital spaces, presenting a transformative vision of interconnected virtual environments that transcend the boundaries of traditional media and communication platforms. Rooted in Virtual Reality (VR), Augmented Reality (AR), and Spatial Computing, the Metaverse represents a convergence of technological innovation, social interaction, and cultural expression, offering boundless opportunities for exploration, creativity, and collaboration.

DOI: 10.4018/979-8-3693-2607-7.ch001

The authors of this chapter sought to carry out academic research on the Metaverse to unravel its complexities, understand its implications, and contribute to the academic discourse around this emerging digital phenomenon. To write this chapter, the authors have drawn on a diverse range of scholarly works, including those by Burlington (2021), Bhattacharya et al. (2023), Sullivan & Tyson (2023), and Lv et al. (2022), among others, which provide an interdisciplinary perspective and valuable insights into the technological, socio-economic, and ethical considerations of data governance in the Metaverse. The study sought to cover the breadth and depth of this emergent digital phenomenon.

At its core, the Metaverse represents a fusion of virtual and physical realities, blurring the boundaries between the digital and the physical. It offers users a gateway to immersive and interactive experiences, where they can traverse virtual landscapes, engage with digital artifacts, and interact with other users in real time. From virtual marketplaces and entertainment venues to educational platforms and social networks, the Metaverse offers a kaleidoscope of possibilities of virtual environments that cater to its inhabitants' diverse interests and preferences. The Metaverse can be applied in numerous fields such as videogame industry, art, event industry, manufacturing, retail, financial services, fashion, media and communication, hospitality, tourism, healthcare, workspace, education, among others (Athar et al., 2023; Bruni et al., 2023; Cali et al., 2022; Chen, 2023; Fazio et al., 2023; Gao & Braud, 2023; Jung et al., 2024; Kaddoura & Al Husseiny, 2023; Mogaji, 2023; Mogaji et al., 2024; Mohamed & Naqishbandi, 2023; Nuñez et al., 2024; Profumo et al., 2024; Wong et al., 2023; Yang & Wang, 2023; Yaqoob et al., 2023; Zainurin et al., 2023).

Technologically, the Metaverse is underpinned by a sophisticated infrastructure of computational systems, networking protocols, and immersive interfaces. Scholars such as Bhattacharya et al. (2023) have delved into the intricacies of VR technology, exploring its capabilities, limitations, and potential applications in the context of the Metaverse. By understanding the technological foundations of the Metaverse, we can better appreciate its evolution and anticipate future developments in this dynamic digital landscape.

Moreover, the Metaverse holds profound socio-economic implications, shaping the way we work, play, and interact with one another. As Sullivan & Tyson (2023) have highlighted, privacy, security, and digital rights loom large in the Metaverse, raising important ethical questions about data governance, identity management, and algorithmic bias. By critically examining these ethical considerations, we can foster a more inclusive and equitable Metaverse that prioritizes the well-being and autonomy of its users.

With these considerations in mind, this chapter aims to contribute to a deeper understanding of the Metaverse, informed by interdisciplinary inquiry and scholarly rigor. By drawing on insights from diverse fields such as computer science, sociology, economics, and ethics, it seeks to highlight the multifaceted nature of the Metaverse and offer insights into its potential impact on individuals, communities, and society.

In short, the authors of this study invite readers to embark on a voyage of exploration and discovery into the Metaverse. Through rigorous analysis, critical reflection, and interdisciplinary dialogue, the research has endeavored to deepen the understanding of this transformative digital landscape and chart a course toward a more informed and inclusive future.

In the following chapters, a comprehensive exploration of the Metaverse will be attempted, delving into its conceptual underpinnings, historical evolution, and the technological frameworks that enable its immersive experiences. The dynamics of metamarkets will be analyzed, opportunities in various sectors will be identified and the emerging trends shaping the Metaverse landscape will be examined. Additionally, it will examine the complexities of digital identities and propose future research directions. This structured investigation aims to offer readers a deeper understanding of the Metaverse and its potential implications for individuals and society.

CONCEPT OF METAVERSE

The term 'Metaverse' was coined by Neal Stephenson in his science fiction novel, 'Snow Crash' (1992), where he envisioned a computer-generated universe accessed through goggles and earphones, describing it as 'the Metaverse.' This term combines the prefix 'meta,' meaning 'beyond,' with 'verse,' evoking the concept of the universe (Bale et al., 2022; Cheng et al., 2022; Hackl, 2020; Ng, 2022; Park & Kim, 2022).

The Metaverse has roots in video game infrastructures developed over decades (Faraboschi et al., 2022), with pioneering platforms like There (1998), RuneScape (2001), and Second Life (2003) laying the groundwork for online virtual worlds where users socialize as avatars (Clement, 2023). Second Life is often regarded as the first iteration of the Metaverse, facilitating interactions between consumers and businesses (Dwivedi et al., 2022). Recent advancements in AR and VR technologies have further enhanced the immersive nature of these platforms (Cipresso et al., 2018; Trevor, 2022).

The Cambridge Dictionary defines the Metaverse as a virtual world where humans, as avatars, interact with each other in a three-dimensional space that mimics reality' (*Metaverse*). In essence, the Metaverse can be conceptualized as a social structure (Novak, 2022) that embodies the principles of Web 3.0 (Xu et al., 2022) and integrates blockchain and computer interfaces (Ahn et al., 2022), allowing users to establish virtual identities and socialize in digital environments (Zyda, 2022), blurring the boundaries between the virtual and real worlds (Al-Ghaili et al., 2022).

According to Trevor (2022), the Metaverse is an open, collective virtual space that bridges the gap between physical and virtual realities, offering immersive experiences and hosting diverse activities within isolated environments. Table 1 presents alternative definitions of the Metaverse.

EVOLUTION OF METAVERSE

The evolution of the Metaverse is intricately linked to technological advancements and shifts in online paradigms. The emergence of decentralized networks, the introduction of cryptocurrencies, and the rise of digital collectibles like Non-Fungible Tokens (NFTs) have spurred a renewed focus on the concept of the Metaverse (Golf-Papez et al., 2022). Major technology companies, game publishers, and brands have converged to create immersive digital spaces, exemplified by Meta's Horizon platform and Microsoft's Mesh platform announced in 2021 (Bonetti et al., 2018; Zyda, 2022).

Significant milestones have propelled the evolution of the Metaverse. The widespread adoption of virtual worlds since the turn of the millennium laid the groundwork for the Metaverse's emergence, while advancements in VR and AR technologies have enhanced user immersion and interaction (Neves et al., 2024). Blockchain technology, particularly through the utilization of NFTs, has enabled the creation and ownership of unique digital assets within the Metaverse, while generative agents have facilitated the development of virtual societies.

Understanding the evolution of the Metaverse necessitates a historical perspective on internet technologies, particularly the evolution of the web. The transition from Web 1.0 to Web 2.0 marked a shift towards user-generated content and social connectivity, facilitated by advancements in mobile internet

Table 1. Metaverse concepts

Authors	Concept of Metaverse
Acevedo Nieto (2022)	A Metaverse is an online universe in permanent mutation, change, and development. Similarly, a Metaverse is a virtual, online world in which different avatars interact, but which, unlike massively multiplayer online role-playing games (MMORPGs), does not have a single competitive purpose: it is a virtual world in which avatars interact with each other, with the objective-based exclusively on a system of levels.
Afrashtehfar and Abu-Fanas (2022)	The Metaverse is a virtual environment that simulates the natural world through multisensory interactions with 3D objects. In other words, the Metaverse ecosystem is a simulation of the 3D world or twin world.
Bibri et al. (2022)	The Metaverse is an idea of a hypothetical set of "parallel virtual worlds" that embody ways of living in virtual credible cities as an alternative to data-driven smart cities in the future.
Golf-Papez et al. (2022)	The Metaverse is an ecosystem of interconnected, shared digital and physical environments that can be experienced synchronously, persistently, and interoperably, in which physical and technological realities are harmoniously enhanced.
Kim et al. (2022)	With the development of immersive experience technology, the Metaverse is a cyberspace, which will establish itself as an expanding reality of the physical world.
Lv et al. (2022)	The spread of digital twins to other domains, such as people and society, is what the Metaverse is all about.
Kim (2021)	[The Metaverse] is an interoperable network of shared virtual environments where people can interact synchronously through their avatars with other agents and/or objects.

Source: Self Elaboration

access and the proliferation of social media platforms (Hester et al., 2016; Oliveira, 2023). This era witnessed the dominance of platforms like Facebook, Instagram, and Twitter, driving significant economic growth and reshaping online business models (Nath, 2022).

Web 3.0 represents the latest phase in the evolution of the web, characterized by decentralization and personalized content delivery. Cryptoeconomic networks like Bitcoin underpin Web 3.0, offering users greater control over their data and privacy (Ashmore & Venz, 2023). Artificial intelligence (AI) and natural language processing (NLP) technologies enable intelligent content distribution tailored to individual preferences, revolutionizing advertising strategies and communication (Goel et al., 2022).

Table 2 provides a comparative overview of the key phases in the evolution of the web, highlighting the progression from static web pages to decentralized, AI-driven platforms in Web 3.0.

The evolution of the web has revolutionized online interactions, shifting from simple messaging to encompassing e-commerce and immersive virtual experiences that transcend physical boundaries. Games within the Metaverse have surged in popularity, paralleling the evolution of the web, and enabling the creation of virtual worlds that mirror physical reality (Novak, 2022).

Web 3.0 represents a significant leap forward, characterized by immersive realities such as VR, AR, mixed reality (MR), and extended reality (XR). These technological advancements, coupled with the development of AI, have empowered brands to deliver unique, personalized, and interactive virtual experiences, capturing consumers' attention and fostering engagement (Goel et al., 2022).

As technology continues to advance, the evolution of the web is propelling us toward Web 4.0, heralded as the era of AI (Oliveira, 2023). In this new phase, complete decentralization of processes is anticipated, facilitated by blockchain technology, to create a secure and transparent online environment where users can interact and transact without intermediaries (Chaves, 2023). This transition holds the promise of reshaping digital interactions and further blurring the boundaries between physical and virtual realms, with technologies that have been improved shown in the next section.

Table 2. Evolution of the web

	Web 1.0	**Web 2.0**	**Web 3.0**
Timeline	1990-2004	2004-2016	2016 - now
Interaction	Read	Read and write	Read, write, and own
Support	Static text	Interactive content	Virtual economies
Organization	On-prem servers	Cloud	Blockchain
Infrastructure	Centralized	Centralized	Decentralized
Virtual Worlds	Second Life	Minecraft	Decentraland
Browers		Google Chrome	Brave
Payment Platforms		Paypal	Metamask
Operating Systems		Windows, Mac OS, Android	Ethereum, EOS
Social Networks		Facebook, Youtube	Steem

Source: Adaptation of Kujur and Chhetri (2015); Sandal et al. (2023)

TECHNOLOGIES POWERING THE METAVERSE

In the dynamic environment of the Metaverse, the confluence of immersive technologies, virtual economies, and interactive games represents a transformative paradigm in digital spatial computing. In this way, the dimensions of the technologies that underpin the Metaverse are Immersive Realities, Markets in the Metaverse, and Gamification in the Metaverse. Immersive realities represent an integration of VR, AR, and MR technologies, facilitating deep levels of immersion and presence in virtual environments, as is possible to seen in Figure 1.

Markets in the Metaverse outline complex virtual economies where digital goods, assets, and services are traded, signifying a fundamental evolution in digital commerce and interaction paradigms. On

Figure 1. Metaverse technologies
Source: Self Elaboration

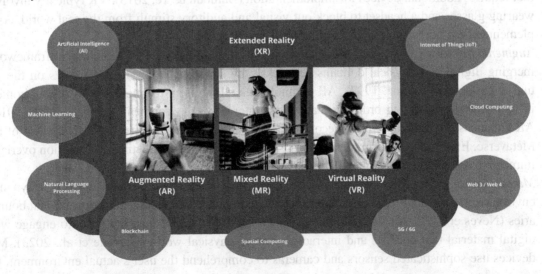

the other hand, gamification in the Metaverse takes advantage of gamified mechanics and incentives to optimize user engagement and interactivity, promoting nuanced and rewarding experiences in virtual realms. Collectively, these technological foundations form the fundamental structure of the expansive and multifaceted Metaverse, heralding new modes of expression, commerce, and socio-cultural interaction in the digital realm.

To understand the technological dimensions of Metaverse, we should see in detail the components of Immersive Realities, Markets in the Metaverse, and Gamification in the Metaverse, that are explained in the next subsections.

1. Immersive Realities

Immersive realities are gaining prominence as they enable brands to offer interactive products and services, facilitating immersive experiences in shopping, gaming, and social environments (Cheng et al., 2022; Kumawat et al., 2020). Various definitions of immersive virtual realities exist, with Taçgın and Dalgarno (2021) describing it as a 3D environment generated by a computer that affects users' perception of reality. Srikanth Vemula (2020) defines immersive VR as the perception of being physically present in a non-physical world created through images, sounds, or other stimuli. In essence, immersive VR aims to fully immerse users in a generated world, providing the sensation of presence in a synthetic environment ("Immersive Virtual Reality," 2008). Immersive realities include virtual reality, augmented reality, and mixed reality that can be joined under the extended reality "umbrella". Which of these realities can be briefly defined as follows:

- *Virtual Reality (VR):* VR is characterized as modeling and simulation that allows interaction with a three-dimensional, artificial visual environment (Harley, 2022). It enables users to immerse themselves in a simulation of reality using interactive devices. VR applications provide an illusion of telepresence, allowing users to have real-time experiences such as picking up and manipulating objects and visiting virtual environments (Lowood, 2022). VR technologies have evolved over the years, categorized into three main types: non-immersive, immersive, and semi-immersive. Non-immersive systems, known as desktop VR systems, enable interaction with the virtual environment from a computer, while semi-immersive systems extend immersion by providing a visual experience without physical sensations. Immersive systems offer a realistic virtual experience that requires additional devices for implementation (Bamodu & Ye, 2013). VR typically involves wearing glasses and a headset to block out visual and auditory stimuli from the real world, complemented by other technologies for enhanced experiences.

- *Augmented Reality (AR):* AR is a core component of the Metaverse's technological framework, merging digital and physical domains seamlessly by superimposing virtual features on the actual environment (Azuma, 1997). AR technologies allow users to interact with digital content in real-time, transforming ordinary places into interactive environments (Bonetti et al., 2018). AR enhances the ordinary world, becoming a crucial component of the immersive fabric of the Metaverse. Examples of AR implementation include interactive marketing, information overlays, immersive navigation, and contextualized data.

- *Mixed Reality (MR):* MR coordinates virtual and real worlds within the Metaverse's dynamic environment, providing users with an immersive experience that transcends conventional boundaries (Neves et al., 2024). MR combines aspects of VR and AR, enabling users to engage with digital material that coexists and interacts with the physical world (Calzone et al., 2023). MR devices use sophisticated sensors and cameras to comprehend the user's actual environment, facilitating a dynamic and context-aware digital overlay. Users can interact with digital elements in real-world contexts more naturally and intuitively, enhancing immersion and participation in the digital world (Guan et al., 2023). Spatial computation plays a crucial role in MR within the Metaverse, enabling the provision of dynamic and context-aware digital overlays.

The Extended Reality (XR) serves as an umbrella term for all immersive technologies within the Metaverse, including VR, AR, and MR, extending the limits of human perception and interaction in digital contexts (Abrash, 2021). By integrating various immersive technologies, XR offers users a wide range of experiences, from fully virtual to augmented and everything in between (Berglund et al., 2018). XR blurs the boundaries between real and virtual worlds within the Metaverse, providing users with a seamless and flexible digital environment (Koohang et al., 2023). Users can interact with digital information in ways that mimic and enhance interactions in the real world, redefining their perception and interaction with digital environments within the Metaverse (Bhattacharya et al., 2023).

2. Markets in Metaverse

The intricate web of technologies within the Metaverse orchestrates the functionality and dynamism of digital markets, reshaping traditional commerce and value exchange (Bhattacharya et al., 2023). The Metaverse, characterized by a fusion of AR, VR, blockchain, and decentralized technologies, emerges as a multifaceted marketplace, transforming economic paradigms. Lets see these technologies:

- *Decentralized Ledger Technologies (DLT) and Blockchain:* At the core of the Metaverse's economic environment lies the revolutionary impact of decentralized ledger technology, led by blockchain. Blockchain technology ensures transparency and immutability, addressing concerns about the ownership and legitimacy of digital assets (Massaro, 2023). In the Metaverse, blockchain creates decentralized markets where users can securely exchange virtual products, digital assets, and NFTs, with provenance guaranteed by cryptography (Huynh-The et al., 2023).
- *Smart Contracts:* Smart contracts play a pivotal role in the dynamics of the Metaverse's markets by enabling self-executing agreements. These programmable contracts automate and uphold transaction rules, ensuring transparency and reducing the need for intermediaries (Wu & Liu, 2023). Smart contracts facilitate smooth digital asset exchange in the decentralized markets of the Metaverse, minimizing counterparty risks and enabling efficient and trustless transactions (Koohang et al., 2023).
- *Tokenization of Assets:* Tokenization, enabled by blockchain technology, converts intangible digital assets into marketable tokens, including virtual real estate, collectible digital items, and representations of real-world assets (Vidal-Tomás, 2023). In Metaverse marketplaces, tokenization enhances accessibility, liquidity, and divisibility, fostering fractional ownership and democratizing participation in the digital economy (Lee et al., 2023).
- *Non-fungible tokens (NFTs) and the Digitalization of Value:* NFTs serve as the foundation of individualized value in the Metaverse, reflecting ownership of distinct digital goods. NFTs redefine ownership, scarcity, and value attribution in a transparent, decentralized framework, encompassing art, virtual real estate, and technological objects as prominent digital assets (Wu & Liu, 2023). By redefining concepts of value, NFTs drive a paradigm shift in the Metaverse's markets, empowering creators and collectors alike (Sung et al., 2023).
- *Virtual Economies and Digital Exchange Platforms:* Dynamic virtual economies thrive within the Metaverse, supported by digital currencies exclusive to virtual environments. Digital exchange

platforms serve as market intermediaries, facilitating the seamless conversion of various digital assets and currencies (Vidal-Tomás, 2023). These platforms integrate liquidity pools, advanced trading methods, and decentralized finance (DeFi) components, enhancing the liquidity and efficacy of Metaverse markets (Koohang et al., 2023).

The Metaverse's marketplaces evolve as complex ecosystems in the fusion of decentralized technology, revolutionizing digital commerce. The Metaverse heralds a new era of economic interactions, where traditional boundaries dissolve, and the digitization of value becomes integral to this emerging digital frontier.

3. Gamification in Metaverse

Gamification within the expansive Metaverse transcends mere amusement to become a ubiquitous force that modifies user engagement, behavior, and interaction. This section explores the technologies supporting gamification in the Metaverse, shedding light on the interplay between immersive technologies, AI, and game mechanics that redefine digital experiences. These technologies can be defined as:

- *Game Mechanics:* The core of Metaverse gamification comprises a complex set of game mechanics designed to elicit user behaviors (Thomas et al., 2023). Elements such as points, badges, leaderboards, and quests act as behavioral catalysts, encouraging active engagement, cooperation, and exploration within the Metaverse. A robust technology foundation is essential to coordinate various gameplay elements seamlessly (Arya et al., 2023).
- *AI and Dynamic Gameplay:* AI advancements drive gamified experiences in the Metaverse, enabling automatic adjustment and customization of games based on user data and behavior. AI systems enhance Metaverse environments by facilitating interactions between non-player characters (NPCs) and generating procedural content (Pérez et al., 2023). These environments adapt in real-time to user actions and preferences, enriching immersion, and personalization (Proelss et al., 2023).
- *Social Dynamics and Collaborative Gamification:* Gamification fosters communication and teamwork within the Metaverse, a social and cooperative environment. Gamified social dynamics promote alliances, group challenges, and collaborative content creation. Technological frameworks such as shared virtual spaces, AI-driven matchmaking systems, and communication tools facilitate collaborative gamification, enhancing engagement and interaction (Park & Kim, 2022; Wanick & Stallwood, 2022).

In summary, a symbiotic integration of game mechanics, AI, immersive technologies, blockchain, and cooperative frameworks drives gamification in the Metaverse. Together, these elements create a vibrant online environment where users actively shape the Metaverse's narrative, fostering engagement and community participation, from the same frameworks, as seen next section.

FRAMEWORK OF METAVERSE

1. Immersive Realities

Immersive realities, bridging the digital and physical realms, form the cornerstone of the Metaverse's architecture. AR and VR seamlessly intertwine within the Metaverse, offering interactive experiences that redefine digital engagement (Al-Ghaili et al., 2022).

In the Metaverse, users seamlessly transition between AR and VR experiences, crafting a continuous digital narrative. AR enhances real-world interactions, seamlessly integrating with fully immersive VR environments. This versatility enables a wide array of activities within the Metaverse, ranging from social interactions to entertainment and collaborative workspaces (Bale et al., 2022).

Immersive realities in the Metaverse extend beyond mere entertainment. Organizations leverage AR to create interactive product showcases, while VR revolutionizes remote work and learning through virtual conferences and training environments. As immersive technologies converge within the Metaverse, distinctions between the real and virtual blur, usher in a new era of creative exploration (Hackl, 2020), leading to new engagement and entertainment experiences, like gamification.

2. Gamification as a strategy in Metaverse

Gamification emerges as a pivotal element within the Metaverse, driving consumer engagement and brand differentiation (Park & Kim, 2022). It permeates the consumer experience, fostering brand collaboration and elevating exclusivity through mechanisms like NFTs (Faraboschi et al., 2022).

Game development companies wield significant influence beyond traditional gaming domains, impacting various social and economic facets, including AI and entertainment media (Carew, 2022). The gamification trend extends beyond gaming, with emerging technologies incorporating gaming mechanisms to enhance user interactions (Smith & Shakeri, 2022).

Incorporating gaming elements within the Metaverse fosters user enjoyment, creativity, and loyalty, driving sustained engagement (Jungherr & Schlarb, 2022). Advergaming, where brands integrate into gaming environments, blurs the lines between advertising and entertainment, presenting both advantages and challenges (Daimiel et al., 2022).

Global brands such as Nike, Gucci, and Hyundai are actively embracing gamification within the Metaverse, leveraging immersive virtual worlds to engage consumers (Daimiel et al., 2022). These initiatives underscore the Metaverse's evolution into a decentralized marketing ecosystem, where brands navigate immersive realities to enhance consumer experiences and foster brand loyalty (Joy et al., 2022) in the metamarkets as can be seen in the next section.

METAMARKETS

Consumer perceptions of brands transcend traditional mediums, encompassing all experiences across physical and digital realms (Keller, 2001). Understanding these experiences is crucial in the Metaverse, where 85% to 95% of consumer actions are driven by subconscious, emotional impulses (Lindstrom, 2009). In this expansive digital landscape, influencing positive consumer experiences and fostering brand interaction and retention is paramount (Kim, 2021).

Customizable experiences reign supreme in the Metaverse, with consumers seeking immersive, multi-dimensional encounters (Panda, 2022). Virtually replicating real-world activities—from sports to commerce—underscores the Metaverse's versatility and appeal (Jeon, 2022).

Luxury brands capitalize on consumer desires for exclusivity and personalization within the Metaverse, with limited-edition products driving avatar differentiation. For example, Balenciaga has partnered with

Fortnite, personifying avatars with their clothing and establishing a dedicated department for virtual realities (Dobre et al., 2021; Jeon, 2022; Rauschnabel et al., 2022).

Immersive technologies, particularly AI, enhance consumer interactions with products and services, bolstering online commerce retention (Trevor, 2022). Experiential immersion is paramount in guiding consumers through the purchasing journey, heightening brand engagement and perceived value (Schnack et al., 2021; Solomon, 2018).

Younger generations, steeped in technology and novelty, are predisposed to immersive experiences, with Millennials and Generation Z driving Metaverse engagement. For instance, Samsung, Gucci, and Louis Vuitton are actively establishing a Metaverse presence, leveraging partnerships and immersive experiences to engage consumers (Joy et al., 2022). While Generation X exhibits less enthusiasm, younger cohorts embrace immersive social networks and gaming platforms, positioning them as key players in Metaverse interactions (Jackson, 2023).

Brands across various sectors, notably fashion, and technology, are actively establishing Metaverse presence, leveraging partnerships and immersive experiences to engage consumers. For example, Volvo virtual showrooms and training platforms, reshaping production, and consumer engagement paradigms (Bidar, 2022; Volvo, 2022). Table 3 shows more brands incorporated in the Metaverse world.

Investments in Metaverse branding underscore its significance, with companies prioritizing immersive experiences to capture consumer attention. In the first quarter of 2022, notable brands like Nike and Atari invested significantly in branding and positioning within the Metaverse (Clement, 2022). As Metaverse adoption surges, marketing strategies emphasize emotional connections and gamification to foster brand engagement across diverse consumer experiences (Arya et al., 2023; Berlo et al., 2021; Nevelsteen, 2018). Another example is the Coca-Cola company strategy in the metaverse, which sells NFTs in platforms like Decentraland, which is exploring opportunities to engage with consumers and provide a decentralized cycle economy (Kim, 2021).

While gamification trends show promise, particularly in enhancing brand engagement, further research is needed to understand its impact on the Metaverse and its influence on consumer-brand relationships (Thomas et al., 2023). In other words, gamification is an opportunity in the Metaverse, which some brands are already implementing, but is possible to see other opportunities.

Table 3. Sample of brands on metaverse

Categories	Brands
Experience	Fortnite, Minecraft, EA, Nintendo, Netflix, Second Life, Zoom, Youtube, Twitch, Twitter, Gather (…)
Discovery	Unity, Discord, Google, Steam, Epic Games, (…)
Economic developers	Roblox, Adobe, Microsoft, Sandbox, Decentraland, Shopify, Rokoko (…)
Computing	Unity, Autodesk, Matterport, Google AI, Open AI, Descartes Labs (…)
Decentralization	Ethereum, Microsoft, ubuntu, IBM, OpenSea, Polygon (…)
Human Interfaces	Apple, Oculus, Xbox, PlayStation, Samsung, Huawei, Neurolink, Razer, Magic Leap, Amazon Alexa (…)
Infrastructure	Aws, Azure, NVidia, Dfinity, AMD, Intel, Sony, At&T, Akamai, Qualcom (…)

Source: Adaptation of Zyda (2022)

OPPORTUNITIES IN THE METAVERSE

The Metaverse, as an evolving virtual realm, presents boundless opportunities for creativity across diverse domains. From economic innovation to educational transformation, the following opportunities are poised to reshape various industries within the Metaverse:

- *Economic aspects:* The Metaverse serves as an expanding economic frontier, offering novel avenues for entrepreneurship, innovation, and value generation. Virtual marketplaces, decentralized finance (DeFi) infrastructures, and asset tokenization present uncharted economic landscapes ripe for exploration. Organizations can delve into digital entrepreneurship, virtual real estate development, and the creation of virtual goods and services, fostering a dynamic Metaverse economy (Vidal-Tomás, 2023). For example, the Nike brand has created virtual sneakers and clothing that users can purchase and wear in their virtual worlds, like Roblox and Fortnite, as well as played events and experiences on these platforms.

- *Skill Development:* With the Metaverse's growth comes a demand for diverse skill sets, ranging from blockchain engineering to virtual experience design. This surge in demand translates into increased job opportunities and avenues for skill enhancement, enabling individuals to contribute to the Metaverse ecosystem while gaining valuable expertise in cutting-edge industries (Al-Ghaili et al., 2022). For example, the company Mango Excellent Media Co. is exploring exquisite VR content, digital identities, and NFT trading platforms to build the Mango Planet Metaverse. Another example is the investment of Meta group in VR/AR technologies and the aim to cover around 1 billion of people in the metaverse, with the assistance of VR gaming (Qi, 2022).

- *Virtual Marketing and Commerce:* Businesses can engage with customers in novel ways through virtual commerce in the Metaverse. By establishing virtual storefronts, hosting virtual events, and leveraging immersive advertising, brands can reach a global audience. The Metaverse presents opportunities for innovative storytelling, brand experiences, and consumer engagement in dynamic virtual environments as digital marketing strategies evolve (Lee et al., 2023). For example, the Samsung brand has been exploring the Metaverse reality through the creation of virtual showrooms for their products and hosting events, allowing the leveraging of this virtual reality technology to enhance consumer engagement and allow the presentation of their products in innovative ways.

- *Educational Transformation:* The Metaverse revolutionizes education by offering immersive and interactive learning experiences. Virtual classrooms, collaborative educational platforms, and simulations enhance the educational landscape, providing educators, content providers, and edtech developers with opportunities to advance digital education (Al-Adwan et al., 2023; Vemula, 2020; Wu & Liu, 2023). For example, related to virtual classrooms, platforms like EngageVR enable educators to create immersive virtual classrooms where students can attend lectures, collaborate on projects, and participate in interactive learning experiences from anywhere in the world (Engage, 2024). Another example is the company edX which partnered with Meta to launch a learning ecosystem, that includes immersive learning materials and training sessions (Podmurnyi, 2022).

- *Entertainment and Cultural Experiences:* The Metaverse offers a platform for entertainment beyond conventional boundaries, allowing creators to reimagine gaming, storytelling, and cultural events. Artists, musicians, and storytellers can leverage virtual platforms to reach global audiences, while virtual events and performances serve as innovative venues for artistic expression and collaboration (Wanick & Stallwood, 2022). For example, the pop star and songwriter Ariana Grande performed in the Metaverse inside the hit video game Fortnite, where millions of gamers assisted her (BBC, 2021).

- *Healthcare Improvements:* Virtual simulations, telemedicine, and digital therapies redefine healthcare experiences within the Metaverse. Opportunities abound for healthcare professionals, developers, and innovators to contribute to virtual health services, patient care simulations, and therapeutic interventions within immersive digital environments (Koohang et al., 2023). For example, the telemedicine platform such as XRHealth leverages virtual reality to facilitate remote consultations, allowing healthcare professionals to diagnose and treat patients in immersive virtual environments (Orr, 2022).
- *Social Impact:* The Metaverse provides avenues to address social challenges and promote inclusivity. Virtual spaces can foster community building, support social activism, and create accessible environments for individuals with diverse abilities. Initiatives focused on social impact, cultural exchange, and global collaboration find new avenues for realization within the Metaverse (Davis et al., 2009; Sowmya et al., 2023).

Based on these opportunities, some trends are now beginning to emerge in the Metaverse, which we'll look at in the next section of this chapter.

TRENDS SHAPING THE METAVERSE

The Metaverse is rapidly evolving, shaped by key trends that merge technological, social, and ethical dimensions. These trends include the rise of DAOs and NFT integration, convergence with real-world applications, AI-driven personalization, sustainability considerations, and the push for Metaverse interoperability. In other words, decentralized technologies promote interoperability between different platforms and virtual worlds inside the Metaverse, allowing for seamless integration of advertising campaigns, data sharing, and cross-platform interactions from brands to users, as presented by Kim (2021).

- *DAOs:* Decentralized Autonomous Organizations (DAOs) are reshaping the Metaverse by facilitating group decision-making and resource distribution through smart contracts, challenging traditional governance models (Calzada, 2023).
- *Integration of NFTs:* NFTs represent ownership and individuality in the Metaverse, impacting virtual economies by reinventing concepts of scarcity and provenance across various digital assets (Bhattacharya et al., 2023).
- *Convergence with physical world applications:* The Metaverse is increasingly integrated with practical applications in industries like healthcare, education, and remote work, transforming how we interact and learn (Bhattacharya et al., 2023).
- *AI-driven personalization and user experience:* AI plays a key role in personalizing user experiences in the Metaverse by analyzing behavior and interactions to customize virtual environments, enhancing immersion and user-centricity (Fu et al., 2023). As referred by Kim (2021) AI technologies can enhance personalization and improve targeting in virtual environments and with NLP

can facilitate natural interactions between users and brands, leading to more engaging and effective communication in Metaverse, providing, for example, through virtual assistants.

- *Emergence of Metaverse Interoperability:* Interoperability efforts aim to enable seamless communication and engagement across multiple Metaverse platforms, allowing users to move between virtual worlds effortlessly (Naderi & Shojaei, 2023; Park et al., 2023).
- *Sustainable Environmental Practices and Ethical Issues:* Rising awareness of ethical issues and environmental impacts prompts the development of sustainable practices and ethical frameworks to mitigate the negative effects of Metaverse expansion (Bale et al., 2022). Given the relevance of ethical issues in Metaverse, an exclusive section has been included in this chapter to highlight dimensions such as privacy concerns, data governance, and algorithmic biases.

Understanding these trends is crucial for predicting the Metaverse's trajectory and adapting to its evolving landscape and the new user identity – data identity.

DIGITAL IDENTITIES

The transition of human existence into the digital realm is epitomized by the emergence of the Metaverse, highlighting the evolving nature of identities over time (Burlington, 2021). Within this expansive digital frontier, the concept of self takes on a new dimension, transcending the physical constraints of our tangible world. At the heart of this transformative journey lies the development of digital identities, where avatars serve as conduits for self-expression within the infinite expanse of VR.

Avatars, as representations of users in the Metaverse, liberate individuals from the constraints of physical appearance. Through the creation of these virtual personas, individuals enter a realm of customization and personalization that extends beyond the boundaries of the physical realm. Digital identities are molded to reflect cultural influences, aspirational narratives, and personal preferences, fostering a journey of self-expression and discovery (Han et al., 2023). Kim (2021) states that digital identities play a crucial role in the metaverse, for brands and companies to understand how the users communicate, establish relationships, present themselves, and purchase behavior within virtual spaces to advertisers and marketers operating in this reality, with authentical strategies.

The concept of digital twins - virtual counterparts intricately linked to identity verification—underscores the critical importance of security and trust within this digital landscape. Operating in conjunction with authentication technologies such as voice recognition and biometrics, digital twins safeguard the integrity of digital identities, providing users with confidence and assurance as they navigate the Metaverse (Lv et al., 2022).

The consistency of identities across platforms in the Metaverse defines this online environment as distinctive. Users seamlessly traverse a variety of virtual environments while maintaining consistency in their presence. This continuity fosters a connected experience that enables collaboration across platforms and the establishment of a unified digital identity spanning different virtual worlds (Rad & Far, 2023).

However, privacy and security concerns loom large in this expansive canvas of digital identities. Robust frameworks safeguard personal data, empower users with control over data access, and ensure ethical handling of consent within the dynamic ecosystem of the Metaverse (Sullivan & Tyson, 2023). Striking a balance between the imperatives of security and privacy becomes a complex endeavor in this evolving landscape.

As digital identities evolve, they transcend mere representations to acquire social capital and reputations. A user's contributions, interactions, and behavior within online communities coalesce to shape their digital reputation, measuring their authority and reliability. Redefining social interactions in the Metaverse, these reputational dynamics introduce a novel dimension of digital sociality that both echoes and diverges from its physical counterpart (Kim et al., 2023).

Conventional notions of selfhood are challenged by the Metaverse in this exploration of digital identities. It offers individuals a blank canvas for exploration, reinvention, and expression of their digital selves beyond the confines of the real world. The interconnectedness and interoperability of these digital identities paint a complex yet captivating portrait of the evolving human experience within the dynamically evolving Metaverse. There are countless opportunities and advantages within the Metaverse, however, it also carries risks and ethical considerations to be considered, as with digital identities and as will be explained below.

ETHICAL CONSIDERATIONS AND RISKS IN THE METAVERSE

In any technological scenario, there is a greater concern with matters relating to virtual security, transparency of models, clarity in the provision of data, and security in the often-personal data provided. As it is a virtual world, made up of decentralized processes, it is essential to check the ethical considerations and risks that this reality can entail for companies and users. This study will be focused on three dimensions: privacy concerns, data governance, and algorithmic biases.

- *Privacy concerns:* Data privacy is the right of users to have control over how the information is collected, used, and shared about them. In practical scenarios, the law generally protects Personal Identifiable Information (PII), which implicates non-public information and can be tied back to an "identified" or "identifiable" person, on a sub-set of personal information is sensitive information, which may have additional stricter privacy rules (such as social security numbers, financial information, and others).

As users immerse themselves in virtual worlds, the metaverse poses so far unseen concerns to individual privacy rights. The massive gathering and use of personal data by virtual world providers and metaverse platforms is one of the most urgent issues. The ubiquitous monitoring present in these settings, which includes user behavior tracking and preference profiling, presents serious concerns regarding data security and privacy. Users may have trust breaches and worries about data misuse if they are uneasy about how much their interactions and behaviors are being watched and evaluated (Han et al., 2022).

Users' privacy worries are further compounded by the lack of openness surrounding data-gathering procedures, which leaves them unsure of how their information is shared and used (Han et al., 2022; Munn & Weijers, 2023). People can be used and manipulated in the metaverse environment if there aren't any explicit rules and accountability systems in place. To defend user rights and rebuild confidence in virtual environments, it is imperative to provide strong privacy measures and encourage greater transparency in data management procedures. This is because there is still a lack of regulation in the metaverse as, for example, a commercial enterprise, due to the lack of adequate legal protections or resources in cases of privacy breaches, and disputes, among other events (Munn & Weijers, 2023). This vulnerability leads to other security breaches, such as data leaks and privacy violations, putting users' information at risk.

Another situation that can raise privacy considerations is the lack of recognition of virtual goods as private property, ownership of assets, and the security of end users in virtual spaces that need standardized legal protection (Munn & Weijers, 2023).

- *Data governance:* Ensuring the responsible governance and utilization of user data in the metaverse requires effective data governance (Han et al., 2022). Regulating and safeguarding data across many platforms and experiences is a huge difficulty, though, because many virtual environments are decentralized (Munn & Weijers, 2023). These difficulties are made worse by the lack of established procedures and control frameworks, which leaves openings for potential data breaches and abuse.

Stakeholders must work together to create thorough data governance frameworks that give user consent, data protection, and accountability the highest priority to address these problems. To reduce the possibility of unauthorized access or data infringements is necessary the implement strong security measures in addition to procedures for transparent data collection and processing (Munn & Weijers, 2023). Furthermore, encouraging data independence and giving users more control over their data can support the development of trust and confidence in metaverse platforms, which will increase user involvement and engagement.

- *Algorithmic biases:* The metaverse's user experiences and interactions are greatly shaped by algorithms, which have an impact on everything from social interactions to content recommendations. These algorithms are not impervious to prejudices, though, and prejudice can still exist in virtual environments where it is tolerated (Ariel Gendler, 2023). Inadvertent reinforcement of societal biases and exclusionary behaviors via algorithmic decision-making processes, for instance, may result in unequal representation and access inside the metaverse. In other words, the term "algorithmic bias" describes the unfair or discriminating results that algorithms generate because of faulty programming or biased input. This may result in decision-making processes that reinforce past biases, stereotypes, and injustices (Carter & Egliston, 2023).

A multimodal strategy that includes locating, reducing, and fixing discriminating algorithms is needed to address algorithmic biases. In addition to encouraging diversity and inclusion in data collecting and algorithm training procedures, this calls for continual research and development efforts to identify and address biases in algorithmic systems (Carter & Egliston, 2023). All users can benefit from a more inclusive and equitable metaverse by reducing the influence of biases and implementing principles of justice, transparency, and accountability in algorithm design and implementation (Han et al., 2022; Munn & Weijers, 2023).

IMPLICATIONS AND FUTURE RESEARCH

As the Metaverse continues its expansion, the exploration of future research avenues becomes imperative to unravel its intricacies and anticipate emerging challenges. Several promising directions beckon academic inquiry, each offering a unique lens through which the Metaverse's evolution can be comprehensively understood.

First, investigations into the ethical considerations surrounding digital identities within the Metaverse stand as a crucial avenue. Examining the subtleties of security, privacy, and data utilization might help to clarify the moral dilemmas raised by the gathering and handling of user data, offering important new perspectives on ethical Metaverse activities.

Second, the evolving landscape of human-computer interaction within the Metaverse warrants investigation. An analysis of how people engage with avatars, immersive technology, and virtual environments provides ways to improve user experiences, ensure accessibility, and promote diversity in the digital world.

Third, research into the cultural and social impacts of the Metaverse offers a wealth of opportunities. Determining how the Metaverse affects distinct cultures on a cultural and socioeconomic level provides insights into broader societal ramifications. Understanding how digital identities impact cultural expression, representation, and standards within virtual environments is crucial, particularly in educational contexts.

The transformative potential of the Metaverse in education opens a promising frontier for research. Investigating the effectiveness of virtual classrooms, collaborative learning environments, and the influence of digital identities on learning outcomes contributes to ongoing discussions about the future of education.

Additionally, exploring the relationship between extended Metaverse activity and mental health and well-being is insightful. Studies in this field can shed light on the effects on individuals and offer tactics to ensure a healthy and fulfilling virtual experience.

Fourth, analyzing the impact of decentralized technologies, such as blockchain, on the virtual economy and digital identities is essential. This includes examining governance structures, decentralized identity solutions, and the effects of blockchain on security and vulnerability in the Metaverse.

Moreover, studying the impact of AI-driven customization on user engagement, social dynamics, and ethical considerations contributes to a nuanced understanding of evolving virtual interactions.

Finally, directing future research toward Metaverse interoperability and cross-cultural perspectives is crucial. Understanding how smooth transitions between virtual environments affect user experiences and exploring the technological, social, and economic elements of building a more integrated Metaverse provides valuable insights. Additionally, studying digital identities in the Metaverse from a cross-cultural perspective offers important insights into how different cultures view and interact with virtual representations.

By delving into these subjects, researchers can enhance the understanding of the Metaverse's multiple elements and ensure that academic research remains aligned with this constantly evolving digital frontier.

CONCLUSION

In reviewing the Metaverse comprehensively, this piece has delved into its foundational elements, explored virtual worlds, examined technological underpinnings, and delineated new directions and trends. Rather than offering prescriptive directives, the suggested future research directions serve as scholarly guideposts, grounded in ethical considerations, human-computer interaction, and societal impacts.

As elucidated in this chapter, the Metaverse is not a static entity but a multifaceted and dynamic subject deserving of ongoing scientific inquiry. The proposed research avenues represent ripe areas for exploration, guided by a commitment to rigorous research methodologies, ethical scrutiny, and a steadfast dedication to advancing academic discourse.

This chapter invites the academic community to discuss the future evolution of Metaverse. The outlined future research trajectories do not signify uncertainty but rather reflect an evolving scholarly dedication to unraveling the complexities of this digital realm. As scholars, it is incumbent upon us to uphold rigorous research standards and contribute substantively to the unfolding narrative of the Metaverse.

In summary, this chapter serves as both a culmination and a prologue - a culmination of collective endeavors to shed light on various facets of the Metaverse and a prologue to the next phase of scholarly inquiry. As we navigate the scholarly landscape of the Metaverse, the trajectory is one of continuous exploration, with the shared pursuit of understanding and discovery propelling scholarly pursuits forward. The Metaverse, with its expansive terrain, awaits further scholarly scrutiny, and it is through collaborative efforts that the narrative of this digital frontier will unfold.

ACKNOWLEDGMENT

The authors are grateful for the support to this research given by the Polytechnic Institute of Coimbra, Coimbra Business School, Quinta Agrícola - Bencanta, 3045-231 Coimbra, Portugal, and the CEOS. PP, ISCAP, Polytechnic of Porto, Portugal.

REFERENCES

Abrash, M. (2021, Dec 11-16). Creating the Future: Augmented Reality, the next Human-Machine Interface. *IEEE International Electron Devices Meeting*. IEEE International Electron Devices Meeting (IEDM), San Francisco, CA. 10.1109/IEDM19574.2021.9720526

Acevedo Nieto, J. (2022). Una introducción al metaverso: conceptualización y alcance de un nuevo universe. *adComunica,* (24), 41-56. doi:10.6035/adcomunica.6544

Afrashtehfar, K. I., & Abu-Fanas, A. S. H. (2022). Metaverse, Crypto, and NFTs in Dentistry. *Education Sciences*, *12*(8), 538. https://www.mdpi.com/2227-7102/12/8/538. doi:10.3390/educsci12080538

Ahn, S. J., Kim, J., & Kim, J. (2022). The future of advertising research in virtual, augmented, and extended realities. *International Journal of Advertising*, 1–9. doi:10.1080/02650487.2022.2137316

Al-Adwan, A. S., Li, N., Al-Adwan, A., Abbasi, G. A., Albelbis, N. A., & Habibi, A. (2023). Extending the Technology Acceptance Model (TAM) to Predict University Students' Intentions to Use Metaverse-Based Learning Platforms. *Education and Information Technologies*, *28*(11), 15381–15413. doi:10.1007/s10639-023-11816-3 PMID:37361794

Al-Ghaili, A. M., Kasim, H., Al-Hada, N. M., Hassan, Z. B., Othman, M., Tharik, J. H., Kasmani, R. M., & Shayea, I. (2022). A review of Metaverse's definitions, architecture, applications, challenges, issues, solutions, and future trends. *IEEE Access : Practical Innovations, Open Solutions*, *10*, 125835–125866. doi:10.1109/ACCESS.2022.3225638

Ariel Gendler, M. (2023). De la cibernética al metaverso: Una genealogía de características, transparencias y opacidades algorítmicas. *Disparidades. Revista de Antropologia*, *78*(1), e001b. doi:10.3989/dra.2023.001b

Arya, V., Sambyal, R., Sharma, A., & Dwivedi, Y. K. (2023). Brands are calling your AVATAR in Metaverse-A study to explore XR-based gamification marketing activities & consumer-based brand equity in virtual world. *Journal of Consumer Behaviour*. doi:10.1002/cb.2214

Ashmore, D., & Venz, S. (2023). *A brief history of Web 3.0*. Forbes Advisor. Retrieved May 20th, 2023 from https://www.forbes.com/advisor/au/investing/cryptocurrency/what-is-web-3-0/

Azuma, R. T. (1997). A Survey of Augmented Reality. *Presence (Cambridge, Mass.)*, *6*(4), 355–385. doi:10.1162/pres.1997.6.4.355

Bale, A. S., Ghorpade, N., Hashim, M. F., Vaishnav, J., Almaspoor, Z., & Agostini, A. (2022). A comprehensive study on Metaverse and its impacts on humans. *Advances in Human-Computer Interaction*, *2022*, 1-11. *Article*, *3247060*. Advance online publication. doi:10.1155/2022/3247060

Bamodu, O., & Ye, X. (2013). Virtual Reality and Virtual Reality System Components. *Advanced Materials Research*, *765-767*, 1169–1172. doi:10.4028/www.scientific.net/AMR.765-767.1169

BBC. (2021). *Ariana Grande sings in Fortnite's metaverse*. BBC. https://www.bbc.com/news/av/technology-58146042

Berglund, Å. F., Gong, L., & Li, D. (2018). Testing and validating Extended Reality (xR) technologies in manufacturing. *Procedia Manufacturing*, *25*, 31–38. doi:10.1016/j.promfg.2018.06.054

Berlo, Z. M. C., Reijmersdal, E. A., & Eisend, M. (2021). The Gamification of Branded Content: A Meta-Analysis of Advergame Effects. *Journal of Advertising*, *50*(2), 179–196. doi:10.1080/00913367 .2020.1858462

Bhattacharya, P., Saraswat, D., Savaliya, D., Sanghavi, S., Verma, A., Sakariya, V., Tanwar, S., Sharma, R., Raboaca, M. S., & Manea, D. L. (2023). Towards Future Internet: The Metaverse Perspective for Diverse Industrial Applications. *Mathematics*, *11*(4), 941. doi:10.3390/math11040941

Bibri, S. E., Allam, Z., & Krogstie, J. (2022). The Metaverse as a virtual form of data-driven smart urbanism: Platformization and its underlying processes, institutional dimensions, and disruptive impacts. *Computational Urban Science*, *2*(1), 24. doi:10.1007/s43762-022-00051-0 PMID:35974838

Bidar, M. (2022). *Companies race to build "digital twins" in the metaverse*. CBS News. https://www.cbsnews.com/news/metaverse-amazon-bmw-lockheed-martin-adobe-digital-twin/

Bonetti, F., Warnaby, G., & Quinn, L. (2018). Augmented Reality and Virtual Reality in Physical and Online Retailing: A Review, Synthesis and Research Agenda. In T. Jung & M. C. tom Dieck (Eds.), *Augmented Reality and Virtual Reality: Empowering Human, Place and Business* (pp. 119–132). Springer International Publishing., doi:10.1007/978-3-319-64027-3_9

Bruni, R., Piccarozzi, M., & Caboni, F. (2023). Defining the Metaverse with challenges and opportunities in the business environment. *Journal of Marketing Theory and Practice*, 1–18. Advance online publication. doi:10.1080/10696679.2023.2273555

Burlington. (2021). *Searching for utopia: from dinosaurs to the metaverse*. Burlington. https://www.burlington.org.uk/archive/editorial/searching-for-utopia-from-dinosaurs-to-the-metaverse

Cali, U., Kuzlu, M., Karaarslan, E., & Jovanovic, V. (2022). *Opportunities and Challenges in Metaverse for Industry 4.0 and Beyond Applications.* IEEE 1st Global Emerging Technology Blockchain Forum - Blockchain and Beyond, (IGETblockchain), Irvine, CA. https://doi.org/ doi:10.1109/iGETblockchain56591.2022.10087104

Calzada, I. (2023). Disruptive Technologies for e-Diasporas: Blockchain, DAOs, Data Cooperatives, Metaverse, and ChatGPT. *Futures, 154,* 103258. doi:10.1016/j.futures.2023.103258

Calzone, N., Sileo, M., Mozzillo, R., Pierri, F., & Caccavale, F. (2023). Mixed Reality Platform Supporting Human-Robot Interaction. Advances on Mechanics, Design Engineering and Manufacturing IV, Cham. doi:10.1007/978-3-031-15928-2_102

Carew, A. (2022). A whole new world: Metaverse as fairytale in Belle. *Metro*(212), 92-97. https://search.informit.org/doi/abs/10.3316/informit.938183067792285

Carter, M., & Egliston, B. (2023). What are the risks of Virtual Reality data? Learning Analytics, Algorithmic Bias and a Fantasy of Perfect Data. *New Media & Society, 25*(3), 485–504. doi:10.1177/14614448211012794

Chaves, A. (2023). *O que é Web 5.0 e qual a diferença da web3?* Be(in)Crypto. https://br.beincrypto.com/aprender/o-que-e-web-5-0/

Chen, Z. S. (2023). Beyond Reality: Examining the Opportunities and Challenges of Cross-Border Integration between Metaverse and Hospitality Industries. *Journal of Hospitality Marketing & Management, 32*(7), 967–980. doi:10.1080/19368623.2023.2222029

Cheng, R. Z., Wu, N., Chen, S. Q., & Han, B. (2022, Mar 12-16). Reality check of metaverse: A first look at commercial social virtual reality platforms. *2022 IEEE Conference on Virtual Reality and 3D User Interfaces Abstracts and Workshops.* IEEE. 10.1109/VRW55335.2022.00040

Cipresso, P., Giglioli, I. A. C., Raya, M. A., & Riva, G. (2018). The Past, Present, and Future of Virtual and Augmented Reality Research: A Network and Cluster Analysis of the Literature. *Frontiers in Psychology, 9,* 2086. doi:10.3389/fpsyg.2018.02086 PMID:30459681

Clement, J. (2022). *In what type of projects does your company invest in the metaverse?* Statista. https://www.statista.com/statistics/1302200/metaverse-project-investment-businesses/

Clement, J. (2023). *Video game industry - statistics & facts.* Statista. https://www.statista.com/topics/868/video-games/#topicOverview

Daimiel, G. B., Estrella, E. C. M., & Ormaechea, S. L. (2022). Analysis of the use of advergaming and metaverse in Spain and Mexico. *Revista Latina De Comunicacion Social, 80*(80), 155–178. doi:10.4185/RLCS-2022-1802

Davis, A., Khazanchi, D., Murphy, J., Zigurs, I., & Owens, D. (2009). Avatars, People, and Virtual Worlds: Foundations for Research in Metaverses. *Journal of the Association for Information Systems, 10*(2), 90–117. doi:10.17705/1jais.00183

Dobre, C., Milovan, A. M., Dutu, C., Preda, G., & Agapie, A. (2021). The Common Values of Social Media Marketing and Luxury Brands. The Millennials and Generation Z Perspective. *Journal of Theoretical and Applied Electronic Commerce Research, 16*(7), 2532–2553. doi:10.3390/jtaer16070139

Dwivedi, Y. K., Hughes, L., Baabdullah, A. M., Ribeiro-Navarrete, S., Giannakis, M., Al-Debei, M. M., Dennehy, D., Metri, B., Buhalis, D., Cheung, C. M. K., Conboy, K., Doyle, R., Dubey, R., Dutot, V., Felix, R., Goyal, D. P., Gustafsson, A., Hinsch, C., Jebabli, I., & Wamba, S. F. (2022). Metaverse beyond the hype: Multidisciplinary perspectives on emerging challenges, opportunities, and agenda for research, practice and policy. *International Journal of Information Management, 66*, 102542. doi:10.1016/j.ijinfomgt.2022.102542

Engage. (2024). *Engage Studio*. EngageVR. https://engagevr.io/engage-studio/

Faraboschi, P., Frachtenberg, E., Laplante, P., Milojicic, D., & Saracco, R. (2022). Virtual worlds (Metaverse): From skepticism, to fear, to immersive opportunities. *Computer, 55*(10), 100–106. doi:10.1109/MC.2022.3192702

Fazio, G., Fricano, S., Iannolino, S., & Pirrone, C. (2023). Metaverse and tourism development: Issues and opportunities in stakeholders' perception. *Information Technology & Tourism, 25*(4), 507–528. doi:10.1007/s40558-023-00268-7

Fu, Y. C., Li, C. L., Yu, F. R., Luan, T. H., Zhao, P. C., & Liu, S. (2023). A Survey of Blockchain and Intelligent Networking for the Metaverse. *IEEE Internet of Things Journal, 10*(4), 3587–3610. doi:10.1109/JIOT.2022.3222521

Gao, Z., & Braud, T. (2023). VR-driven museum opportunities: Digitized archives in the age of the metaverse. *Artnodes, 0*(32). Advance online publication. doi:10.7238/artnodes.v0i32.402462

Goel, A. K., Bakshi, R., & Agrawal, K. K. (2022). Web 3.0 and Decentralized Applications. *Materials Proceedings, 10*(1), 8. https://www.mdpi.com/2673-4605/10/1/8

Golf-Papez, M., Heller, J., Hilken, T., Chylinski, M., de Ruyter, K., Keeling, D. I., & Mahr, D. (2022). Embracing falsity through the metaverse: The case of synthetic customer experiences. *Business Horizons, 65*(6), 739–749. doi:10.1016/j.bushor.2022.07.007

Guan, J., Morris, A., & Irizawa, J. (2023). *Extending the Metaverse: Hyper-Connected Smart Environments with Mixed Reality and the Internet of Things*. 30th IEEE Conference Virtual Reality and 3D User Interfaces (IEEE VR), Shanghai. 10.1109/VRW58643.2023.00251

Hackl, C. (2020). The Metaverse is coming and it's a very big deal. *Forbes*. https://www.forbes.com/sites/cathyhackl/2020/07/05/the-metaverse-is-coming--its-a-very-big-deal/

Han, D.-I. D., Bergs, Y., & Moorhouse, N. (2022). Virtual reality consumer experience escapes: Preparing for the metaverse. *Virtual Reality (Waltham Cross), 26*(4), 1443–1458. doi:10.1007/s10055-022-00641-7

Han, E., Miller, M. R., DeVeaux, C., Jun, H., Nowak, K. L., Hancock, J. T., Ram, N., & Bailenson, J. N. (2023). People, places, and time: A large-scale, longitudinal study of transformed avatars and environmental context in group interaction in the metaverse. *Journal of Computer-Mediated Communication, 28*(2), zmac031. doi:10.1093/jcmc/zmac031

Harley, D. (2022). "This would be sweet in VR": On the discursive newness of virtual reality. *New Media & Society, 17*, 14614448221084655. doi:10.1177/14614448221084655

Hester, A. J., Hutchins, H. M., & Burke-Smalley, L. A. (2016). Web 2.0 and Transfer: Trainers' Use of Technology to Support Employees' Learning Transfer on the Job. *Performance Improvement Quarterly, 29*(3), 231–255. doi:10.1002/piq.21225

Huynh-The, T., Gadekallu, T. R., Wang, W. Z., Yenduri, G., Ranaweera, P., Pham, Q. V., da Costa, D. B., & Liyanage, M. (2023). Blockchain for the metaverse: A Review. *Future Generation Computer Systems, 143*, 401–419. doi:10.1016/j.future.2023.02.008

Immersive Virtual Reality. (2008). In B. Furht (Ed.), *Encyclopedia of Multimedia* (pp. 345–346). Springer US., doi:10.1007/978-0-387-78414-4_85

Jackson, R. (2023). *Young users favor immersive media over social media. Why it matters?* TipRanks. https://www.nasdaq.com/articles/young-users-favor-immersive-media-over-social-media.-why-it-matters

Jeon, Y. A. (2022). Reading Social Media Marketing Messages as Simulated Self Within a Metaverse: An Analysis of Gaze and Social Media Engagement Behaviors within a Metaverse Platform. *Proceedings - 2022 IEEE Conference on Virtual Reality and 3D User Interfaces Abstracts and Workshops, VRW 2022*. IEEE. 10.1109/VRW55335.2022.00068

Joy, A., Zhu, Y., Pena, C., & Brouard, M. (2022). Digital future of luxury brands: Metaverse, digital fashion, and non-fungible tokens. *Strategic Change, 31*(3), 337–343. doi:10.1002/jsc.2502

Jung, T. M., Cho, J. S., Han, D. I. D., Ahn, S. J., Gupta, M., Das, G., Heo, C. Y., Loureiro, S. M. C., Sigala, M., Trunfio, M., Taylor, A., & Dieck, M. C. T. (2024). Metaverse for service industries: Future applications, opportunities, challenges and research directions. *Computers in Human Behavior, 151*, 108039. Advance online publication. doi:10.1016/j.chb.2023.108039

Jungherr, A., & Schlarb, D. B. (2022). The extended reach of game engine companies: how companies like epic games and unity technologies provide platforms for extended reality applications and the Metaverse. *Social Media + Society, 8*(2), 12. doi:10.1177/20563051221107641

Kaddoura, S., & Al Husseiny, F. (2023). The rising trend of Metaverse in education: Challenges, opportunities, and ethical considerations. *PeerJ. Computer Science, 9*, e1252. doi:10.7717/peerj-cs.1252 PMID:37346578

Keller, K. L. (2001). *Building Customer-Based Brand Equity: A Blueprint for Creating Strong Brands* (01-107). (Working Paper). M. S. Institute. http://anandahussein.lecture.ub.ac.id/files/2015/09/article-4.pdf

Kim, D., Lee, H. K., & Chung, K. (2023). Avatar-mediated experience in the metaverse: The impact of avatar realism on user-avatar relationship. *Journal of Retailing and Consumer Services, 73*, 103382. doi:10.1016/j.jretconser.2023.103382

Kim, J. (2021). Advertising in the Metaverse: Research Agenda. *Journal of Interactive Advertising, 21*(3), 141–144. doi:10.1080/15252019.2021.2001273

Kim, J., Hwang, L., Kwon, S., & Lee, S. (2022). Change in Blink Rate in the Metaverse VR HMD and AR Glasses Environment. *International Journal of Environmental Research and Public Health, 19*(14), 8551. https://www.mdpi.com/1660-4601/19/14/8551. doi:10.3390/ijerph19148551 PMID:35886402

Koohang, A., Nord, J. H., Ooi, K. B., Tan, G. W. H., Al-Emran, M., Aw, E. C. X., Baabdullah, A. M., Buhalis, D., Cham, T. H., Dennis, C., Dutot, V., Dwivedi, Y. K., Hughes, L., Mogaji, E., Pandey, N., Phau, I., Raman, R., Sharma, A., Sigala, M., & Wong, L. W. (2023). Shaping the Metaverse into Reality: A Holistic Multidisciplinary Understanding of Opportunities, Challenges, and Avenues for Future Investigation. *Journal of Computer Information Systems*, *63*(3), 735–765. doi:10.1080/08874417.2023.2165197

Kumawat, V., Dhaked, R., Sharma, L., & Jain, S. (2020). Evolution of Immersive Technology. *Journey of Computational Reality*.

Lee, C. T., Ho, T. Y., & Xie, H. H. (2023). Building brand engagement in metaverse commerce: The role of branded non-fungible toekns (BNFTs). *Electronic Commerce Research and Applications*, *58*, 101248. Advance online publication. doi:10.1016/j.elerap.2023.101248

Lindstrom, M. (2009). *Buy.ology: A ciência do Neuromarketing*. Gestão Plus.

Lowood, H. E. (2022). *virtual reality*. Encyclopedia Britannica. https://www.britannica.com/technology/virtual-reality

Lv, Z., Qiao, L., Li, Y., Yuan, Y., & Wang, F. Y. (2022). BlockNet: Beyond reliable spatial Digital Twins to Parallel Metaverse. *Patterns (New York, N.Y.)*, *3*(5), 100468. doi:10.1016/j.patter.2022.100468 PMID:35607617

Massaro, M. (2023). Digital transformation in the healthcare sector through blockchain technology. Insights from academic research and business developments. *Technovation*, *120*, 102386. doi:10.1016/j.technovation.2021.102386

Mogaji, E. (2023). Metaverse influence on transportation: A mission impossible? *Transportation Research Interdisciplinary Perspectives*, *22*, 100954. doi:10.1016/j.trip.2023.100954

Mogaji, E., Dwivedi, Y. K., & Raman, R. (2024). Fashion marketing in the metaverse. *Journal of Global Fashion Marketing*, *15*(1), 115–130. doi:10.1080/20932685.2023.2249483

Mohamed, E. S., & Naqishbandi, T. A. (2023). Metaverse! Possible Potential Opportunities and Trends in E-Healthcare and Education. *International Journal of E-Adoption*, *15*(2), 1–21. doi:10.4018/IJEA.316537

Munn, N., & Weijers, D. (2023). The real ethical problem with metaverses. *Frontiers in Human Dynamics*, *5*, 1226848. doi:10.3389/fhumd.2023.1226848

Naderi, H., & Shojaei, A. (2023). Digital twinning of civil infrastructures: Current state of model architectures, interoperability solutions, and future prospects. *Automation in Construction*, *149*, 104785. doi:10.1016/j.autcon.2023.104785

NathK. (2022). Evolution of the Internet from Web 1.0 to Metaverse: The Good, The Bad and The Ugly. TechRxiv. doi:10.36227/techrxiv.19743676

Nevelsteen, K. J. L. (2018). Virtual world, defined from a technological perspective and applied to video games, mixed reality, and the Metaverse. *Computer Animation and Virtual Worlds*, *29*(1), 22, Article e1752. doi:10.1002/cav.1752

Neves, J., Bacalhau, L. M., & Santos, V. (2024). *A Systematic Review on the Customer Journey Between Two Worlds: Reality and Immersive World.* Marketing and Smart Technologies.

Ng, D. T. K. (2022). What is the metaverse? Definitions, technologies and the community of inquiry. *Australasian Journal of Educational Technology, 38*(4), 190–205. doi:10.14742/ajet.7945

Novak, K. (2022). Introducing the Metaverse, Again! *TechTrends, 66*(5), 737–739. doi:10.1007/s11528-022-00767-0

Nuñez, J., Krynski, L., & Otero, P. (2024). The metaverse in the world of health: The present future. Challenges and opportunities. *Archivos Argentinos de Pediatria, 122*(1). doi:10.5546/aap.2022-02942. eng PMID:37171469

Oliveira, C. M. (2023). *Humantech Marketing: o marketing molecular e humano.* Conjuntura Actual Editora.

Orr, E. (2022). The Metaverse Can Create A Boundless Healthcare Experience. *Forbes.* https://www.forbes.com/sites/forbestechcouncil/2022/01/26/the-metaverse-can-create-a-boundless-healthcare-experience/?sh=1b21c0ab2340

Panda, T. K. (2022). In the world of Metaverse. *NMIMS Management Review, 30*(03), 03-05. doi:10.53908/NMMR.300210

Park, A., Wilson, M., Robson, K., Demetis, D., & Kietzmann, J. (2023). Interoperability: Our exciting and terrifying Web3 future. *Business Horizons, 66*(4), 529–541. doi:10.1016/j.bushor.2022.10.005

Park, S., & Kim, S. (2022). Identifying world types to deliver gameful experiences for sustainable learning in the Metaverse. *Sustainability, 14*(3), 14. doi:10.3390/su14031361

Pérez, J., Castro, M., & López, G. (2023). Serious Games and AI: Challenges and Opportunities for Computational Social Science. *IEEE Access : Practical Innovations, Open Solutions, 11*, 62051–62061. doi:10.1109/ACCESS.2023.3286695

Podmurnyi, S. (2022). Business Insights On The Opportunity For The Educational Metaverse. *Forbes.* https://www.forbes.com/sites/forbestechcouncil/2022/08/05/business-insights-on-the-opportunity-for-the-educational-metaverse/?sh=240d59874a3f

Proelss, J., Sévigny, S., & Schweizer, D. (2023). GameFi: The perfect symbiosis of blockchain, tokens, DeFi, and NFTs? *International Review of Financial Analysis, 90*, 102916. doi:10.1016/j.irfa.2023.102916

Profumo, G., Testa, G., Viassone, M., & Ben Youssef, K. (2024). Metaverse and the fashion industry: A systematic literature review. *Journal of Global Fashion Marketing, 15*(1), 131–154. doi:10.1080/20932685.2023.2270587

Qi, W. (2022). The Investment Value of Metaverse in the Media and Entertainment Industry. *BCP Business &amp. Management, 34*, 279–283. doi:10.54691/bcpbm.v34i.3026

Rad, A. I., & Far, S. B. (2023). SocialFi transforms social media: An overview of key technologies, challenges, and opportunities of the future generation of social media. *Social Network Analysis and Mining, 13*(1), 42. doi:10.1007/s13278-023-01050-7

Rauschnabel, P. A., Babin, B. J., tom Dieck, M. C., Krey, N., & Jung, T. (2022). What is augmented reality marketing? Its definition, complexity, and future. *Journal of Business Research*, *142*, 1140–1150. doi:10.1016/j.jbusres.2021.12.084

Sandal, M. M., Taner, T., Firat, B. B., Ünal, H. T., Ulucan, S., & Mendı, A. F. Ö, Ö., & Nacar, M. A. (2023, 8-10 June 2023). *WEB 3.0 Applications and Projections*. *2023 5th International Congress on Human-Computer Interaction, Optimization and Robotic Applications (HORA)*. IEEE. 10.1109/HORA58378.2023.10156728

Schnack, A., Wright, M. J., & Elms, J. (2021). Investigating the impact of shopper personality on behaviour in immersive Virtual Reality store environments. *Journal of Retailing and Consumer Services*, *61*, 102581. doi:10.1016/j.jretconser.2021.102581

Smith, A. H., & Shakeri, M. (2022). The future's not what It used to be: Urban wormholes, simulation, participation, and planning in the Metaverse. *Urban Planning*, *7*(2), 214–217. doi:10.17645/up.v7i2.5893

Solomon, P. R. (2018). Neuromarketing: Applications, Challenges and Promises. *Biomedical Journal of Scientific & Technical Research*, *12*(2). doi:10.26717/BJSTR.2018.12.002230

Sowmya, G., Chakraborty, D., Polisetty, A., Khorana, S., & Buhalis, D. (2023). Use of metaverse in socializing: Application of the big five personality traits framework. *Psychology and Marketing*, *40*(10), 2132–2150. doi:10.1002/mar.21863

Stephenson, N. (1992). Snow Crash (Spectra, Ed.). Bantam Books.

Sullivan, C., & Tyson, S. (2023). A global digital identity for all: The next evolution. *Policy Design and Practice*, *6*(4), 433–445. doi:10.1080/25741292.2023.2267867

Sung, E., Kwon, O., & Sohn, K. (2023). NFT luxury brand marketing in the metaverse: Leveraging blockchain-certified NFTs to drive consumer behavior. *Psychology and Marketing*, *40*(11), 2306–2325. doi:10.1002/mar.21854

Taçgın, Z., & Dalgarno, B. (2021). Building an Instructional Design Model for Immersive Virtual Reality Learning Environments. In *Designing* (pp. 20–47). Deploying, and Evaluating Virtual and Augmented Reality in Education. doi:10.4018/978-1-7998-5043-4.ch002

Thomas, N. J., Baral, R., Crocco, O. S., & Mohanan, S. (2023). A framework for gamification in the metaverse era: How designers envision gameful experience. *Technological Forecasting and Social Change*, *193*, 122544. Advance online publication. doi:10.1016/j.techfore.2023.122544

Trevor, A. (2022). *Metaverso 360 - La guida più completa su Metaverse e investimenti, web 3.0, NFT, DeFi, augemented reality (AR), cryptoassets, digital real estate e future networking*. Independently published.

Vemula, S. (2020). Leveraging VR/AR/MR and AI as Innovative Educational Practices for "iGeneration" Students. In Handbook of Research on Equity in Computer Science in P-16 Education (pp. 265-277). doi:10.4018/978-1-7998-4739-7.ch015

Vidal-Tomás, D. (2023). The illusion of the metaverse and meta-economy. *International Review of Financial Analysis*, *86*, 102560. doi:10.1016/j.irfa.2023.102560

Volvo. (2022). *The Volvoverse: Volvo Cars launches first car in the metaverse.* Volvo. https://www.volvocars.com/au/news/technology/The-Volvoverse/

Wanick, V., & Stallwood, J. (2022). *Brand storytelling, gamification, and social media marketing in the "Metaverse": a case study of The Ralph Lauren winter escape.*

Wong, L. W., Tan, G. W. H., Ooi, K. B., & Dwivedi, Y. K. (2023). Metaverse in hospitality and tourism: A critical reflection. *International Journal of Contemporary Hospitality Management.* doi:10.1108/IJCHM-05-2023-0586

Wu, C. H., & Liu, C. Y. (2023). Educational Applications of Non-Fungible Token (NFT). *Sustainability (Basel), 15*(1), 7. Advance online publication. doi:10.3390/su15010007

Xu, M., Ng, W. C., Lim, W. Y. B., Kang, J., Xiong, Z., Niyato, D., Yang, Q., Shen, X. S., & Miao, C. (2022). A Full Dive into Realizing the Edge-enabled Metaverse: Visions, Enabling Technologies, and Challenges. *IEEE Communications Surveys and Tutorials, 1.* doi:10.1109/COMST.2022.3221119

Yang, F. X., & Wang, Y. (2023). Rethinking Metaverse Tourism: A Taxonomy and an Agenda for Future Research. *Journal of Hospitality & Tourism Research (Washington, D.C.).* doi:10.1177/10963480231163509

Yaqoob, I., Salah, K., Jayaraman, R., & Omar, M. (2023). Metaverse applications in smart cities: Enabling technologies, opportunities, challenges, and future directions. *Internet of Things : Engineering Cyber Physical Human Systems, 23,* 100884. doi:10.1016/j.iot.2023.100884

Zainurin, M. Z. L., Masri, M. H., Besar, M. H. A., & Anshari, M. (2023). Towards an understanding of metaverse banking: A conceptual paper. *Journal of Financial Reporting and Accounting, 21*(1), 178–190. doi:10.1108/JFRA-12-2021-0487

Zyda, M. (2022). Let's rename everything "the Metaverse!". *Computer, 55*(3), 124–129. doi:10.1109/MC.2021.3130480

KEY TERMS AND DEFINITIONS

Augmented Reality (AR): Technology that covers digital content into the physical world, enhancing the user's perception of reality by adding virtual elements to their surroundings.

Decentralized Autonomous Organizations (DAOs): Operate without centralized control, governed by smart contracts and member decision-making for resource distribution.

Digital Identity: Representation of an individual or entity in the digital realm through avatars or online profiles, reflecting personal characteristics, preferences, and interactions.

Ethical Considerations: Reflecting on the societal impact of technological advancements ensures that digital innovations respect privacy, security, and human rights while considering moral implications.

Gamification: The process of adding game elements such as points, rewards, and challenges to non-game contexts to increase engagement and motivation.

Human-Computer Interaction (HCI): Studies the interaction between people and digital technologies, focusing on user interface design, usability, and user experience.

Interoperability: Ability of different systems or platforms to communicate, exchange data, and operate seamlessly together enabling users to move between virtual environments with ease.

Metaverse: A digital space where users can interact and engage with others through immersive technologies, such as virtual reality and augmented reality, overreaching physical boundaries.

Non-fungible tokens (NFTs): Unique digital assets stored on a blockchain representing ownership of digital or physical items and enabling secure verification of authenticity and ownership.

Virtual reality (VR): Immerses users in a simulated environment allowing them to interact with a computer-generated world as if it were real.

Chapter 2
Historical Context and Evolution of Metaverse

Meenu Sharma
ⓘD https://orcid.org/0000-0003-0493-556X
The Assam Royal Global University, India

Arpee Saikia
The Assam Royal Global University, India

ABSTRACT

The use of the metaverse in various periods is explained, including its use in novels and movies, video games, social media, industries, businesses, and headsets. This chapter is divided in to five sections: section one provides the introduction, literature review and ancient concept of metaverse; section two explains the use of term metaverse and historical context and evolution of metaverse; section three is related with use of metaverse in different sectors/fields: movies, novels, gaming, education, industry, retail, architecture, medical care and social media; section four provides a insight into prolific ways in which the metaverse was used during the Covid-19 pandemic times with special reference to the financial sector; section five describe managerial or practical applications and future research directions for the use of metaverse.

METAVERSE: LITERATURE REVIEW AND ANCIENT CONCEPT OF METAVERSE

Introduction

The current technological world is going through monumental changes over the past few years. The year 2015 marked the beginning of the Industry 3.0 phase. This phase saw the advent of a massive proportion of data conversion into bytes being uploaded into the cloud servers around the world. Following this transformative stage was Industry 4.0 which witnessed the exponential rise of artificial intelligence or AI. The world was connected even better due to the billions of devices being added to the deluge of data. It was virtually impossible to handle such huge amount of data manually and therefore machine-

DOI: 10.4018/979-8-3693-2607-7.ch002

intervention was the need of the hour. The colossal amount of data needed to be handled to meet the demands of the big-tech world. The metaverse's enabling technologies have been developed over many years. Enterprise-focused metaverses has figure out how to accommodate digital twins that are more intricate and modular, enhancing design, testing, and expert collaboration. In the interim, the design, construction, and operation of buildings, transit networks, and smart cities are already being optimized with the use of digital twins and digital threads (Ritterbusch & Teichmann, 2023). Virginie Maillard, head of Siemens U.S. technology, has explained that these technologies will soon have a significant impact on how businesses operate in the simulation and digital twin spaces. There is still more room for advancement in other groundbreaking metaverse technologies like 5G connectivity, AI, machine learning, 3D engines, cloud, edge computing, and extended reality (Ball, 2022). The future is here, in many senses, according to PwC vice chair Emmanuelle Rivet "The metaverse is an evolution and convergence of technologies that businesses are currently using and experimenting with today."

Literature Review

Children with attention deficit hyperactivity disorder can benefit from using 3D virtual worlds to improve their language communication skills (LCS) (Lan, 2024). According to the study, children with ADHD significantly improved their LCS and learning behavior.

To reap the benefits of diversification, investors and portfolio managers ought to think about including NFTs into their S&P 500 or Bitcoin portfolios (BenMabrouk, 2024).

"Digital health" is described by the World Health Organization as using information and communication technology to enhance one's health. The use of these digital tools has increased significantly in recent years, which has significantly altered conventional healthcare paradigms (Joia Nuñeza, 2024).

The financial management pre-alarm model of neural network's random parameter selection and local extremum phenomena cause the forecast results to be highly erratic. In the standard BPNN, a genetic algorithm (GA) with ergodic properties is added. When it comes to forecasting the financial status of virtual currency in the online game Metaverse, the financial management model performs better (Li, 2024). This gives each particle ergodic properties, regulates the degree of particle aggregation, prevents the occurrence of local extremum, finds the global optimal value, and guarantees the model's pre-alarm outcomes.

The predominant pattern of media development in the modern era has long been the integration of media due to the ongoing advancements in science and technology. The metaverse is a new area for video game development from the standpoint of media integration (Chen, 2024). For the decentralized dynamic database of security cloud storage, it performs security certification using the blockchain's Myrtle tree optimization method. to guarantee the security of video game play within the meta-universe.

With Facebook's formal name change to Meta in October 2021, social networks and three-dimensional (3D) virtual worlds have adopted the metaverse as the new standard. Through the application of numerous relevant technologies, the metaverse seeks to provide consumers with 3D immersive and individualized experiences. How to secure users' digital material and data in the metaverse is a natural question, notwithstanding its popularity and advantages (Huynh-The T. T., 2024). The study demonstrated how blockchain affects major metaverse-enabling technologies such as digital twins, big data, artificial intelligence, multi-sensory and immersive applications, and the Internet of Things.

The idea that there is no difference between one's online and offline identities is the foundation of Generation Z society and the metaverse. Owing to advances in technology in deep learning-based high-precision recognition models and natural generation models, the Metaverse is being upgraded in several ways, including mobile-based always-on access and connectivity with reality through virtual money (Park S. M., 2022). The application of fundamental techniques is necessary for the realization of the Metaverse into three components: user interaction, implementation, and application. These components are hardware, software and contents.

Considering the opportunities that today's post-digital techno-cultures bring, Virtual Museum (VM) considers the processes and semantic models that it uses to realize its Metaverse (Maurizio Unali, 2024). Since the 1980s, when the multidisciplinary concept of virtual reality (VM) first emerged in response to the era's technical advances, it has experimented with a range of online and offline interaction modes as well as many conformative dimensions of digital space.

As an emerging platform for improving customer satisfaction experiences almost identical to those in physical businesses, marketing practitioners and academics are still interested in technological metaverse and NFTs (Olaleye, 2023). Through the lens of bibliometric analysis using R Bibliometrix, the effects of combining the metaverse and NFTs in marketing are investigated.

In the sphere of education, virtual reality techniques are employed because they have the potential to make learning more interesting, immersive, and enjoyable. Virtual reality has the potential to be a useful tool for raising student motivation for learning and has a good impact on the educational process. The learning process can be accelerated by combining standard teaching and learning methods with augmented reality and virtual reality (Kumar, 2024). The usage of virtual reality (VR) can improve student engagement and learning. In our highly digitalized world, virtual reality-based education has the power to totally change the manner that educational content is presented.

This qualitative study used systematic Literature review to lay down it's arguments and theories.

Ancient Concept of Metaverse

The concepts of Multiverse and metaverse have existed in several stories, tales and folklores which discusses about the idea of an alternate world. The concept of an alternate universe has found its presence in Hindu mythology, which depicts infinite universes. The whole idea and premises of parallel universes is a question to modern scientists but is quite natural to Indian traditions. During the epic battle of Kurukshetra between paternal cousins Pandavas and Kauravas, Lord Krishna had agreed to be an ally of the Pandavas.In one episode when the famous warrior Arjuna was contemplating his decisions and choices pertaining to war,Lord Krishna took his "Viswaroop" and showed Arjuna a scene of multiple cosmic creations and destructions.In his narration which is compiled in the form of Bhagwad Gita,he explains to Arjuna thatthere lies different universes in different parts of the former's body. He explains to his friend Arjuna that there aremany powerful creators or Brahmas and many more enormous universes than this universe, the existence of a hypothetical self-contained plane of existence, co-existing with each other thereby establishing the concept of parallel universes in the psyche of his friend (Jana, 2023).

In Hindu philosophy and texts, "Maya" refers to the illusion, temporary and destructible nature of the material world that humans live in. It can be considered as an earlier manifestation of the digital metaverse, where reality may be far from what human minds can imagine it to be. The ancient Indian texts talk about various "lokas" or realms.These realms were characterized by different features and residents. The residents reflected the essence of the realms namely Swarglog or heaven where the gods, demi gods and celestial beings resided,Naraklok where the demons, or rakshases existed and finally the Earthly realm i.e the dhartilok where the mortals resided.The mythology also mentions about a prominent figure,Naradmuni who had the power of travelling to all the loks or realms was a "Realm traveller". The fact that there are realms beyond what the human eyes can see was established way before modern scientific brains proposed the same.In Hinduism, the Vedas are regarded as the oldest sacred texts.These texts provide insight into different areas including rituals, medicine, science music to name only a few areas. References to a concept resembling the modern day metaverse is found in both the Vedas and the Puranas.In the Vedas, Akasha is depicted as a realm where the human mind connects with universal consciousness, providing a glimpse into infinite dimensions of existence. Akashais often translated as "ether," "space," or "sky.". Akasha is described as a space where consciousness surpasses the limitations of time and matter. The mind is limitless and goes beyond any boundary. This concept reflects the idea of an alternative, virtual space where individuals can interact, coexist, and explore without physical constraints. 'Maya' is another prominent word which features in the ancient Hindu texts.The idea of "yugas"or cycles of time or epochs, each with a reincarnation of Lord Vishnu could be metaphorical or an indication for the evolution of digital realities. Like how the world transitions through different yugas, the digital realm has evolved through various stages or timelines. Rooted in ancient philosophy spanning across nations and modern technology, the metaverse is an amalgamation of ancient wisdom and modern-day innovation. Metaverse blurs the lines between the past and future and provides unimaginable opportunities for the human minds to imagine and explore.

The year 1956 witnessed the infamous rivalry between the United States of America and the Union of Soviet Socialist Republics. The year saw an American scientist Morton Heilig transforming his Brooklyn motorcycle ride into a shared experience through the Sensorama, the first Virtual Reality machine which helped the audience to feel what he felt while riding. This lead to an immersive experience characterized by a 3D video with surrounding sounds, scents, and a vibrating chair recreating the real life bike riding experience.

METAVERSE: HISTORICAL CONTEXT AND EVOLUTION

Use of Term Metaverse

The term metaverse was phrased by Neal Stephenson in the year 1992 in his seminal work *Snow Crash*. In his book he describes a 3D virtual collective shared space created by converging virtually enhanced digital and physical reality. Another literary work that has inspired the creation of the metaverse is Ernest Cline's Ready Player One which was published in 2011 and was so successful that renowned director Steven Spielberg adapted it into a blockbuster Hollywood film in 2018. In 2017, a digital space Decentraland enabled anyone to own an estate on the blockchain and, as such, to start a new virtual business and earn continuously. The Metaverse is an evolution of the internet into an immersive augmented reality experience that integrates all societal activities, from work to sleep to entertainment, into a unified virtual world. The blockchain technology brings Web 3.0 and Metaverse on to a similar platform. People can experience the large virtual space in an organic way because of advancements made in virtual and augmented reality technology.AI is widely used in the metaverse. AI tracking systems have the capability of following and copying human motions and expressions, they can enhance the naturalness and realism of our avatars. Since all works are protected by copyright and are difficult to tamper with, blockchain offers a safe platform for artists in the metaverse. The gaming world is not new to the world of Metaverse, Numiverse, the first anime metaverse on the Venom blockchain has come into existence which provides an "Utopian Escape" to its users (Robertson, 2021).

Historical Context and Evolution of Metaverse

During the nineteenth century in 1838, Sir Charles Wheatstone, a physicist, presented the idea of "binocular vision," which required producing a single three-dimensional view. This was the first instance of virtual reality. The results of this early study led to the creation of stereoscopes, which employ the same technology as modern virtual reality headsets: the illusion of depth to produce an image.

American science fiction author Stanley Weinbaum introduced readers to the idea of virtual reality with Pygmalion's Spectacles, which was first published in 1935. The protagonist of the novel totally immerses himself in a made-up world, creating the illusion that it is real, by donning goggles that mimic every sense experienced by a human. The term "virtual reality," also known as "la réalité virtuelle," was used in 1938. Antoine Artaud, a French writer and poet, is frequently cited as its creator. In his collection of writings, The Theater and its Double, he talked about how theaters might stage people, things, and images to create other worlds.

In 1962, American director Morton Heilig created a device that gave users the impression that they were riding a motorcycle in a different place. The Sensorama was a gadget that combined effects including a moving seat, fragrances, and 3D screens to immerse its users in a virtual environment. Despite never making it past the prototype stage, the machine showed that it was possible to make it harder to distinguish between truth and illusion. Director Morton Heilig of the United States created the Sensorama system, which uses a 3D video, a vibrating chair, a fan, and fragrances to replicate the feeling of riding a motorcycle throughout Midtown Manhattan. John Licata, chief innovation foresight strategist and vice president of SAP New Venture Technologies Future Hub, stated that "the Sensorama was by far the ultimate advancement that laid the groundwork for what the immersive virtual environment could become."

The Aspen Movie Map, created in the 1970s by the Massachusetts Institute of Technology, lets visitors explore Aspen, Colorado, through computer-generated imagery. This was the first time they had used virtual reality to transport clients to a different area. Multi-User Dungeon1, released in 1978, was the first multiplayer virtual environment to be played in real time. Jaron Lanier and Thomas G. Zimmerman, pioneers in virtual reality, founded VPL Research, Inc. in 1984. They were among the first to build and market virtual reality headsets and data gloves, also known as wired gloves. It provides situations of how virtual reality can be applied in business and creative settings."While there's a host of prior thinking and experiments (including a great 1965 paper by Ivan Sutherland imagining an 'Ultimate Display' that recognizably describes this sci-fi staple), Jaron Lanier's VPL Research started to commercialize goggles and gloves to facilitate augmented reality and virtual reality interactions," as stated by Alex Weishaupl, managing director of Protiviti Digital

The first draft of the World Wide Web was written in 1989 by British computer scientist Tim Berners-Lee when he was working at CERN. Information could be transferred globally between universities and other institutions back when the web was initially invented. This was a major improvement over earlier text-based sharing platforms like Gopher and proprietary bulletin board systems. The public was able to access a client and server for a network of linked web pages with text, images, and audio.

SEGA debuted popular virtual reality arcade devices in the early 1990s, such as the SEGA Virtual Reality-1 motion simulator, which was put in many arcades. The term "metaverse" was initially used in

1992 in Neal Stephenson's fantasy novel Snow Crash. The American science fiction author imagined a dystopian future society in which people may utilize computer avatars to travel to a better reality. The author used the phrase to describe a virtual environment where each person has an avatar, or a digital representation of their real identity. The name was derived from combining the words "meta" and "universe".

As people purchase, construct, and refurbish virtual real estate, the alternate reality grows from its initial 65,536 km road around a man-made planet. In this perspective, all people are connected to a single world. Avatars are controlled by the individual and can range from highly customized beautiful works of art to generic Walmart products referred to as "Clints" and "Brandys."

If the term has been around for many years, why did it suddenly gain popularity in 2021, primary causes are: a few metaverse-related technologies, like HTC's VR headsets, have developed over time, a growing number of individuals are starting to understand the idea of blockchain and Blockchain creates and stores enormous amounts of difficult-to-tamper-with transaction data using cryptography and other technology. The growth of the metaverse is propelled by blockchain due to "unhackability" and "immutability."

Platform security is essential in virtual environments since hacker assaults and data leaks happen often. The metaverse's evolution has accelerated due to the COVID-19 pandemic. The epidemic has drastically altered people's lives, requiring most of them to work remotely. This has led to a huge rise in the need for virtual world connection. The proof-of-work (PoW) concept was developed in 1993 by computer scientists Moni Naor and Cynthia Dwork to stop service abuses such as network spam and denial-of-service assaults. To use the software, users must complete a difficult but easily verifiable cryptography task. Afterward, the fundamental ideas are codified and serve as the foundation for Bitcoin.

Renowned video game developer Richard Garriott originally used the term in 1997 while working on Ultima Online, an online role-playing game that was released a year later and is widely regarded as the first Massively Multiplayer Online game.

The practice of superimposing graphics on top of real-world views was quickly copied by other sports broadcasters after Sportsvision showed the first National Football League game live in 1998, complete with a yellow yard marker.

Five years before Apple released its first iPhone, in 2002, HTC created the first smartphone in history using the Microsoft operating system. But in the last few years, it has transformed into a metaverse business, launching the first virtual reality glasses, HTC VIVE, in 2016.

Second Life is a multimedia platform that Linden Lab launched in 2003 and marked the beginning of the twenty-first century. Users can connect to shared virtual spaces with their computers and explore, interact, and create there—even if it's not immersive because there are no goggles or gloves required. More than just a game, Second Life is an online community where everyone may create a new online persona. Introduced by Linden Lab, Second Life is a shared 3D virtual world where users may build things, explore, interact with others, and exchange virtual goods. Almost 70 million Second Life accounts are active at the moment. What a shared virtual world should seem like was established by the virtual space.

The year 2006 saw the launch of the Roblox gaming platform by Roblox Corporation, which lets users play a variety of multiplayer games. Users can also create their own games to play and share with others. In addition to offering free gameplay, Roblox has an in-game store where users can purchase virtual cash called Robux. Google introduced Street View in 2007 as an extension to its Maps product. Users can turn a map into a realistic image of the real world with the aid of Street View. A street can be viewed by anyone in real time on a computer or mobile device.

The first widely used decentralized blockchain and cryptocurrency, Bitcoin, was originally made public by Satoshi Nakamoto in 2008. He subsequently mined the first Bitcoin in 2009. Under the pseudonym Satoshi Nakamoto, the first public blockchain and Bitcoin were established via a proof-of-work technique. It eventually ascended to the top of the bitcoin value list, demonstrating that decentralized ledgers can secure volume transactions. Excessive speculation fuels interest in a range of alternative cryptocurrencies and in novel approaches to establishing decentralized markets that are not dominated by one party. The Oculus Rift virtual reality headset prototype was developed in 2010 by 18-year-old inventor and entrepreneur Palmer Luckey. The cutting-edge headset offers a 90-degree field of vision and leverages computer processing power to entice people to experience virtual reality (Rosenblum & Cross, 1997).

The Gacha model for video games is presented. By using a combination of skill and luck, players can earn currency and in-game rewards by playing toy vending machines or gachas.

Ready Player One, written by Ernest Cline, was published in 2011. It offered us yet another look at a fully realized world where we may escape from reality. Following the novel's immediate popularity, director Steven Spielberg turned it into a movie in 2018. The shared virtual environment idea became well-known after Steven Spielberg's 2018 film adaption.

In 2012, entrepreneur Palmer Luckey launched Oculus on Kickstarter, the first low-cost VR headgear with hardware that lets users interact with a 3D virtual environment for work, play, and leisure. Facebook purchased Oculus in 2014, two years later, in an effort to make the technology available to more people. Israeli entrepreneur Yoni Assia introduced Colored Coins in 2012 with a blog post titled "Bitcoin 2. X (aka Colored Bitcoin) - initial specs." This creates the framework for a brand-new method of creating, purchasing, selling, and owning assets on top of a public blockchain.

In 2014, Kevin McCoy and Anil Dash created Quantum, the first non-fungible token (NFT) ever created. It included a picture of an octagon with pixels on it. It was minted on the Namecoin blockchain and was referred to as "monetized graphics" rather than an NFT. Facebook paid $2 billion to acquire Oculus Virtual Reality in 2014. The first Cardboard gadget and Google's augmented reality glasses were released in 2014, making it a significant year for XR. In the same year, Samsung and Sony each released their own virtual reality headsets. Cardboard is a low-cost cardboard virtual reality viewer designed by Google for cellphones. The first non-fungible token was created by American internet entrepreneur Anil Dash and artist Kevin McCoy. It is a unique virtual asset that is protected by encryption. This offers chances for virtual creative experiments, concert tickets, and novel play-to-earn experiences. Digital engineering company Virtusa's executive vice-president and head of technology, Frank Palermo, said, "The fast growth and general acceptance of the paradigm was a critical milestone for the metaverse."

The idea of Ethereum was first proposed by Vitalik Buterin in a blog post titled Ethereum: The Ultimate Smart Contract and Decentralized Application Platform, which was published in 2013.

Then in 2015, Ethereum, a decentralized computer platform, was introduced. With Ethereum, developers can use smart contracts to experiment with their own code to construct DApps. Ethereum is introduced by English computer scientist Gavin Wood and Canadian programmer Vitalik Buterin. It has characteristics that allow users to create decentralized applications on a blockchain. "Ethereum introduced a practical take on smart contracts, which is the foundation for offerings like NFTs and the ability to 'own' assets in a distributed environment," Weishaupt stated.

Back in 2015, during the height of the social media boom on the internet and as the world began to become aware of decentralized technology, the idea for the first metaverse was conceived.

Decentralized autonomous organizations and Pokémon GO both made their debuts in 2016. The concept behind the Ethereum launch of the first Decentralized autonomous organizations, was that any member could be a part of the organization's governing body. Pokémon GO, an augmented reality game that links to a 3D map of the real world, is one of the most played smartphone games ever. It was one of the most widely used and lucrative smartphone apps globally by the end of the year, having been downloaded over 500 million times (Needleman, 2021).

With the advent of Microsoft's HoloLens headsets in 2016, mixed reality which combines virtual and augmented reality became widely accessible. via HoloLens, we can create a holographic picture in front of us that we can then place in the real world and control via augmented reality. In 2016, players of Pokémon GO, an augmented reality game, raced into their neighborhoods all over the world in an attempt to catch Pokémon. The world is first introduced to augmented reality games through Pokémon GO. Players locate, seize, and engage in combat with virtual animals linked to real-world locales using their phones.

In 2016, Based on the Ethereum blockchain, the DAO became the first decentralized autonomous organization to solicit venture capital money. Within one month of its launch, hackers embezzle a third of company funds. This destroys the business, but the concept generates new ways to jointly acquire assets and manage businesses.

IKEA made a metaverse debut in 2017 with their Place App, which lets people choose furniture and visualize how it might look in the home or place of business.

In 2018 A video game that can be played for money Axie Infinity, developed by the Vietnamese company Sky Mavis, expands the application of NFTs linked to the Ethereum network. It peaked in 2021 with over 2.7 million users, having the highest cumulative value of any play-to-earn game. Hackers had pilfered about $600 million in 2022.

In 2019, with over 250 million active players, Epic Games' Fortnite surpassed all previous records for popularity as a shared virtual environment. In order to accommodate additional virtual games and experiences, the company improves the platform. In 2020, rapper Travis Scott emceed a webcast event that attracted more than 12 million people. Subsequently, Epic integrates the platform with popular enterprise tools like geographic information systems, design, and infrastructure. In 2020, Lidar (Light Detection and Ranging) was added to the iPhone and iPad lineup, opening the door for future mixed-reality headsets and facilitating enhanced depth sensing for better images and augmented reality (Boletsis, 2017).

The year 2021 saw Facebook change its name to Meta, which solidified the metaverse's reputation as a real place rather than just a sci-fi idea. Since then, the business has spent billions of dollars creating and acquiring resources linked to the metaverse, including software, headsets for augmented and virtual reality, and metaverse content. Businesses are being courted by Microsoft "Mesh" and Facebook (Meta) Worlds to employ virtual reality (VR) and meetings for workshops, conferences, and other purposes (Brown, 2021).

Two other companies have released highly portable virtual reality headsets (HTC's Vive Flow) and smart glasses (Ray-Ban Stories).

A joint partnership between NVIDIA and Siemens to create the Industrial Metaverse was announced in 2022. The collaboration leverages Siemens' well-known proficiency in industrial automation and software, infrastructure, building technology, and transportation, along with NVIDIA's leadership in accelerated graphics and Artificial Intelligence. Video games played online already have access to metaverse technologies. Though historical claims of metaverse development started soon after the term was coined, Second Life, a virtual world platform that launched in 2003 and integrated many elements of social media into a persistent three-dimensional world with the user represented as an avatar, is frequently referred to as the first metaverse. Among the first conceptions were Active Worlds and The Palace. Among the well-known games included in the metaverse include Roblox, the game creation platform, Fortnite, World of Warcraft, Minecraft, Habbo Hotel, and Virtual Reality Chat. Since then, Roblox has heavily utilized the term in its marketing. In a January 2022 interview with Wired, Second Life developer Philip Rosedale defined metaverses as a three-dimensional Internet populated by real people.

The evolution of the metaverse and the possibilities for virtual and augmented reality events are demonstrated by the upcoming "Grand Slamming" of the Australian Open tennis tournament in the metaverse, which took place in June 2022 and was hosted by Decentraland.

USE OF METAVERSE IN DIFFERENT SECTORS/FIELDS

Metaverse in Movies and Novels

The idea of the Metaverse has gained a lot of traction in literature, video games, and film. We witness a fully developed metaverse where people can explore new realms and live out their fantasies in movies like Tron Legacy and Ready Player One. Novelists such as Neal Stephenson and Ernest Cline have written a great deal about the Metaverse. Novels: "Neuromancer" (1984) by William Gibson; "Snow Crash" (1992) by Neal Stephenson; "Altered Carbon" (2002) by Richard K. Morgan; "Ready Player One" (2011) by Ernest Cline; and "A Frayed New World" (2021) by Damini Rana. Films include The Wachowski Brothers' 1999 film "The Matrix," Steven Lisberger's 1982 film "Tron," David Cronenberg's 1999 film "eXistenZ," Josef Rusnak's 1999 film "The Thirteenth Floor," Steven Spielberg's 2018 film "Ready Player One," and Shawn Levy's 2021 film "Free Guy."

In addition to having the ability to personalize our avatar and digital assets, we may imagine ourselves to be "in" a virtual world and sense the presence of others. The 2009 film "Avatar" features a representation of the metaverse. Jake, the main character in the film, is paralyzed, but upon arriving in Pandora, he transforms into a Na'vi and gains the ability to walk and run. But he still has his awareness, which is a hybrid of reality (his consciousness) and virtuality (Na'vi's body).

Metaverse in Gaming

For many years, games have made substantial use of Augmented Reality/Virtual Reality and metaverse elements. With the development of this technology, game developers will be able to produce visually stunning games that enhance player interaction with their surroundings. To give customers the impression that they are in a real-world setting, the images and visuals will only get better. It is impossible to overlook this market's anticipated expansion. The global market for metaverse gaming is predicted to grow to a value of over $660 billion. The comparison between the metaverse and a video game has been made by some. That might be the case (Rajan, et al., 2018).

We see the metaverse in gaming as a collection of social and personal identities. A single game or platform is now frequently referred to by businesses as a "Metaverse." By this concept, everything can be considered a metaverse, including internet games and VR music concerts. In summary, although metaverses are not merely games, games can be thought of as part of them.

A gaming firm called Roblox was founded on the idea of the metaverse. Users of the platform can play other people's games in addition to creating their own using the Roblox Studio engine. Additionally, trading on the platform is possible using the virtual currency Robux. In March 2021, Roblox effectively went public in the US.

Metaverse technology has the potential to increase the diversity and intrigue of sports. In addition, Meta's "Virtual Gym" opened, enabling customers to work out at home and maintain their fitness levels without having to purchase flywheels or treadmills. Additionally, Mark Zuckerberg posted a video of him fencing in the metaverse alongside Olympic gold medalist Lee Kiefer.

Metaverse in Education

The education system has been utilizing the aid of the metaverse and Augmented Reality/Virtual Reality. Additionally, it would improve their learning outcomes by maintaining students' focus on the material they are studying. Virtual reality and augmented reality are already being used in education because of resources like Google Arts & Cultures.

The application of metaverse in education is one of the key areas. Creating a 3D interactive learning environment, the gaming business Roblox has also entered the education sector, hoping to serve over 100 million students by 2030. Education has become more engaging and dynamic with the use of the metaverse. For instance, students studying ancient Egyptian civilization used to be limited to viewing the picture of the pyramids in their history textbooks (Pellas, Mystakidis, & Kazanidis, 2021).

Students can discover the culture of ancient Egypt by going straight into the pyramid and even getting a virtual reality look at the mummy because of the metaverse. Furthermore, with the Metaverse platform, students can collaborate to build rockets and tour space stations and experiences that are not possible with books.

Students' involvement with a variety of courses can be improved by creating immersive educational experiences with the help of the metaverse. Making concepts tangible in the virtual world is especially helpful for subjects like anatomy and physics, which are difficult to visualize. It also offers a perfect setting for role-playing, which improves the efficacy of training activities. As stated by Aji Abraham of Armia Systems Inc. The metaverse is an immersive environment designed for one-to-one or one-to-many instruction using interactive 3D models, remote video conferencing, and other technologies. According to Sean Barker, cloud EQ Academic simulations in colleges are one real-world use for the metaverse. This is an option for students, particularly in hybrid or virtual learning environments, to obtain "hands-on experience" without having to leave the classroom. Before ever working on their first deal, novice analysts may, for instance, go through an M&A process and comprehend all the key processes according to Deal Room's Kison Patel

Metaverse in Industry

Using the industrial metaverse, digital twins of actual physical infrastructure and products are created. Workers can use these digital twins to fuel risk-free trial and error experiments, identify issues before they arise. Metaverse facilitate early-level Product Development. It enables the design team to quickly change course and make pertinent and appropriate design decisions. For industries, using the metaverse to develop products at an early stage would be a profitable "low-hanging fruit" use case, according to Bosch Global Software Technologies Pvt Ltd., Srinivasulu Nasam.

Metaverse and Property: The real estate market is quite profitable, and this also applies to the virtual world. This refers to the selling of digital land in a virtual environment. As an illustration, the primary asset of the decentralized Ethereum blockchain network is Decentraland Island. Plots of land are exchangeable for NFTs. 34,356 lots of land, with a combined market value of over $30 million at the time, were up for bid at Decentraland's inaugural auction held in late 2017. Microsoft concentrates on its core competencies—services associated with "work." For remote work and virtual meetings, it offer a more engaging and customized experiece (Park, 2022).

In addition to participating in online meetings, exchanging data and documents, and holding lengthy lectures, we may host huge seminars on the Mesh for Microsoft Teams space. Its most notable feature is the ability to build customized avatars—a digital representation of yourself that can even imitate your motions and facial expressions. Instruction and Upkeep for Industrial Systems Within the industrial sector, the metaverse presents opportunities to increase efficiency. The display and monitoring of vital indicators, as well as practical instruction, are made simpler by the visual depiction of complicated systems.

Metaverse in Retail

Brands might be promoted through the metaverse in ways that have never been seen before. Customers will be able to interact with potential customers more deeply and receive a higher response rate thanks to these technologies. Virtual reality experience booths are another tool that shops may employ. This is essential to raise customer response rates, which can lead to increased revenue.

Ikea is one of the many outstanding examples. The Ikea Place App allows users to virtually "position" furniture in their own spaces. The item is automatically resized by the software to fit the customer's room's proportions. Metaverse provides Virtual Marketplace. Virtual Reality Chat is a massively multiplayer virtual reality game in which users can engage and converse with one another via virtual characters.

Nike and other brands from all areas of life might decide to join the Virtual Reality and Non-Fungible Token industry. Maybe in the future, Nike's virtual world will show us sparks flying between these two ideas. Online Shops Virtual business, or "v-commerce," is one real-world use for the metaverse. Companies may design dynamic, three-dimensional virtual storefronts that provide customers with a distinctive and captivating shopping experience. Before making a purchase, customers can engage with goods or services in a lifelike digital setting, giving merchants useful data and possibly increasing consumer happiness, according to Hello Data AI's Marc Rutzen. It facilitate in linking Brands and Consumers. There is a brand issue with the metaverse. When people hear the term "metaverse," many immediately think of virtual reality or the virtual world. However, the theories underlying the metaverse are far more expansive, opening up new avenues for connecting not just people but also brands and consumers. Metaverse promotes Customized Internet Purchasing means prefer to study things before buy them, whether it's a couch or an item of apparel. The metaverse facilitates the customization of the customer's experience, making it both realistic and virtual. Retailers can save money and time by using it to manage a physical shop and process returns. Working remotely is one scenario where the metaverse is put to use. This combines the freedom of working remotely with in-person office companionship, according to EZ Cloud's Andrew Blackman

Metaverse in Architecture

Architects can visualize their work in a 3D environment by using AR/VR and the metaverse. This would entail making a virtual environment and populating it with structures, vegetation, and other natural features. Using this technology, they can build objects and interact with the real environment. It would also make it easier to show clients what they have made or will build. Virtual reality is used by New York-based Ennead Architects to help clients visualize data and space in three dimensions.

Metaverse in Medical Care

Physicians can develop 3D clinical devices using Augmented Reality/Virtual Reality and the metaverse. They can enhance a patient's experience by engagingly using this technology. After that, they can keep an eye on a patient's vital signs virtually. They can also give patients apps to track their blood pressure, weight, and other parameters and make tests more user-friendly. The metaverse can bring about several significant changes in the field of medicine. Here are a few illustrations. Remote health care: When people were unwell in the past, they visited the hospital or clinic to see a doctor.

Phone conversations or video chats might be utilized to finish the consultation for certain straight-forward illnesses. Patient can wear virtual reality equipment and attend the doctor's office, for instance, if patients are in other place but the finest specialist for patients' ailment is in the other place. Local medical institutions offer scans and examinations, real-time data transmission to the doctor allows the other doctor to provide patient with remote consultation assistance. Managing personal health information and medical records is a particularly safe usage for this capability. Creating a "virtual twin" of any item, procedure, or system is referred to as a digital twin (Huynh-The, 2023). When used in the context of metaverse medicine, it entails creating a virtual patient duplicate in order to assess the patient's reaction to various drugs following surgery, recuperation, etc. Safer for the actual patient is the Media and the Social media sector can benefit from the creation of virtual worlds through the metaverse.

Metaverse in Social Media

Instant Messaging Virtual Universe, an online social network game that was developed in 2004 and allows users to create 3D avatars and communicate with one another, has become more and more well-known in the social media space. Additionally, one of the largest social media companies globally, Facebook, changed its name to Meta in 2021, a sign of the direction social networks are taking. Meta is the tech company most committed to building the metaverse. The fundamental idea of Facebook is "connections between people." These days, people communicate with family and friends on Facebook through posting and like content, messaging via Messenger, participating in live broadcasts, and other primarily text-based, passive activities. "Connections between people" is still at the center of Facebook's metaverse, but the environment is now three dimensions, allowing for more varied and realistic interaction.

Anyone can play cards, have conversations, and have coffee in this area as if the others were actually at their side. Anyone can use their phone to make video calls to their family.

USE OF METAVERSE IN COVID-19 PERIOD AND IN FINANCIAL SECTOR

Metaverse and COVID-19

COVID-19 pandemic's effects on remote work can be lessened more effectively in the metaverse. Colleagues who work remotely communicate with each other via conference calls, messaging apps, or emails. While it reduces commute time, there is less social interaction and the employer cannot monitor the status of the workers. Because of this, several managers requested that staff members come back to work following the pandemic.

Facebook launched a service dubbed "Workrooms" in August 2021, which enables remote work using virtual reality technologies. Colleagues can meet, communicate, by creating virtual offices using Facebook Workrooms anywhere, even on beaches and in the mountains. Businesses will benefit from lower office rental costs and reduced commute times as a result, which will boost productivity.

Metaverse and Non-Fungible Token

The term "fungible tokens" describes tokens with a fixed value that are divisible. All digital crypto-currencies are fungible tokens, including Ether (ETH) and Bitcoin (BTC). Digital crypto-currencies also come in the form of "non-fungible tokens," which are distinct, non-divisible, and irreplaceable tokens. Any digital artwork, including images, audio files, videos, etc., can serve as examples. In the past, it was simple to copy these digital data, but now NFTs allow ownership. It is also extremely hard to duplicate. It can therefore be auctioned off like actual artwork, regardless of whether it is a short film, meme, or article. The digital artist Beeple sold his artwork for $69 million in a Non-Fungible Token auction in 2021. The same year, an Iranian cryptocurrency entrepreneur purchased Jack Dorsey's first-ever tweet, which was turned into an Non-Fungible Token and sold for $2.9 million. This Non-Fungible Token was to be sold by the business owner in April 2022. His first bid was $48 million, but he only placed a winning bid of $280 in the end. Non-Fungible Tokens are blockchain-based ownership certificates that hold the key to the virtual world's economy. An unchanging, duplicable, and unbreakable encryption key safeguards each Non-Fungible Token, enabling it to validate a person's digital assets and virtual identity, a crucial function for the metaverse.

MANAGERIAL OR PRACTICAL APPLICATIONS OF METAVERSE AND FUTURE RESEARCH DIRECTIONS

Managerial or Practical Applications of Metaverse

The metaverse can be used practically for online instruction and training. Many companies are searching for ways to provide remote training to their staff as remote work becomes more common. Training can be given in a novel method that is immersive, interactive, and engaging thanks to the metaverse. Virtual conferences and gatherings are among the most useful uses for the metaverse. The pandemic has made many events virtual, but the metaverse provides a special means of bringing people together virtually. Product demonstrations and virtual showrooms can also be made with the metaverse. A vehicle manufacturer might, for instance, design a virtual showroom where clients can view and test drive their newest models in a lifelike three-dimensional setting.

Many companies are looking for ways to train their staff remotely as remote work becomes more common. A novel approach to providing immersive, interactive, and interesting instruction is through the metaverse. Creating virtual homes that may be rented or sold to anyone worldwide is made possible by the metaverse in a distinctive fashion. Virtual marketing and advertising includes the metaverse. Virtual advertising can be a fresh approach to get customers' attention in light of the rise of ad blockers and the growing difficulties of reaching audiences through traditional media.Businesses can design immersive, interactive ads in the metaverse that let customers interact with their brand in a special way. The metaverse presents a novel approach to providing healthcare services in a virtual setting, especially with the advent of telemedicine.

Future Research Directions

The Metaverse may eventually offer incredibly lifelike virtual worlds that appeal to all of our senses, including sight, sound, touch, taste, and smell. Virtual tourism and training simulations, in addition to gaming and entertainment, would be revolutionized by this immersive experience. The Metaverse is expected to rely even more heavily on blockchain technology. Decentralized ledgers are perfect for handling digital assets, virtual property, and in-game money because they provide unmatched security and transparency. Anticipate a growing convergence of blockchain technology and the Metaverse, allowing users to transact in and really own digital assets within virtual environments, ranging from virtual real estate to uncommon rarities.

The future Metaverse will be significantly shaped by artificial intelligence. Virtual experiences will be customized to each user's preferences and requirements thanks to AI-driven customisation. AI is going to transform the Metaverse into a highly personalized environment, whether it be through content curation, learning material adaptation, or the creation of innovative gaming challenges. The impact of the Metaverse will go beyond work and entertainment to include additional real-world uses. The Metaverse will be a vital tool for teaching, testing, and experiencing real-world events in a secure and regulated digital environment. Applications ranging from urban planning and design to healthcare simulations and disaster preparedness drills will rely on it. The Metaverse will unavoidably run across moral and legal issues as it develops.

The protection of virtual identities, digital ownership rights, and data privacy will all become more important issues. Ensuring the responsible and ethical development of the Metaverse will need policymakers, corporations, and users to adeptly manage these intricate concerns.

CONCLUSION

Corporate world has been experiencing a huge rise in the use of AR/VR and the metaverse. The metaverse will give businesses a means of customer communication that will significantly improve workers' productivity and management process. A concept rooted in ancient texts and books of religion spanning across various nations and centuries, metaverse has transformed into an indispensable part of modern day's technological advancements. With the potential to completely change how we interact with technology and the virtual world, metaverse is positioned at a turning point in our digital history. It is the result of years of technical progress, combining social connectivity, blockchain, artificial intelligence, and augmented and virtual reality into a seamless digital fabric. It is impossible to overestimate the importance of the Metaverse since it signifies a radical change in how we view, engage with, and use the digital world. Services in the metaverse provide an immersive, networked, and interactive environment where the lines between the real and virtual worlds are blurred. People can go across a variety of virtual environments there, mingle, work, learn, and amuse themselves in ways that were previously only possible in science fiction. There is no denying the advantages, which range from better digital experiences to fresh business prospects and better healthcare. It is very important to tread very carefully while navigating the world of technology consumption. Integrating metaverse into the very fabric and essence of how humans function, one must be conscious while using Artificial Intelligence (AI) in any form. It becomes very easy to depend on modern technology like metaverse, however, we need to make a conscious decision as to what extent the lines between the virtual and real world can be blurred. Hence, it is important to go cautiously, addressing privacy, ethical, and legal issues as one moves ahead.

Funding

This research received no external funding.

Conflicts of Interest

The author declares no conflict of interest.

REFERENCES

Ball, M. (2022). *The Metaverse: And How it Will Revolutionize Everything*. Liveright Publishing. doi:10.15358/9783800669400

BenMabrouk, H. S., Sassi, S., Soltane, F., & Abid, I. (2024). Connectedness and portfolio hedging between NFTs segments, American stocks and cryptocurrencies Nexus. *International Review of Financial Analysis*, *91*, 102959. doi:10.1016/j.irfa.2023.102959

Boletsis, C. (2017). The New Era of Virtual Reality Locomotion: A Systematic Literature Review of Techniques and a Proposed Typology. *Multimodal Technologies and Interaction*, *1*(4), 24. doi:10.3390/mti1040024

Brown, D. (2021). "What is the 'metaverse'? Facebook says it's the future of the Internet. *The Washington Post*.

Chen, N. C. (2024). Analysis on the Development of the Meta Universe to the Generation of Electronic Games from the Perspective of Media Convergence. *Computer-Aided Design and Applications*.

Huynh-The, T. G., Gadekallu, T. R., Wang, W., Yenduri, G., Ranaweera, P., Pham, Q.-V., da Costa, D. B., & Liyanage, M. (2023). Blockchain for the metaverse: A Review. *Future Generation Computer Systems*, *143*, 401–419. doi:10.1016/j.future.2023.02.008

Huynh-The, T. T. (2024). Blockchain for the metaverse: A Review. *Future Generation Computer Systems*.

Jana, K. (2023, June 17). Metatext and metaverse. *The Telegraph Online*.

Joia Nuñeza, L. K. (2024). The metaverse in the world of health: The present future. Challenges and opportunities. *Archivos Argentinos de Pediatria*. PMID:37171469

Kumar, M. (2024). Virtual Reality in Education: Analyzing the Literature and Bibliometric State of Knowledge. In Transforming Education with Virtual Reality (pp. 379-402). Wiley Online Library.

Lan, Y. J. (2024). 3D immersive scaffolding game for enhancing Mandarin learning in children with ADHD. *Journal of Educational Technology & Society*.

Li, J. J. (2024). Virtual Currency and Smart Financial Management in Immersive Online Games in the Metaverse Environment. *Computer-Aided Design and Applications*.

Maurizio Unali, G. C. (2024). Towards a Virtual Museum of Ephemeral Architecture: Methods, Techniques and Semantic Models for a Post-digital Metaverse. In M. R. Andrea Giordano, Beyond Digital Representation. Springer Nature Switzerland.

Needleman, S. E. (2021). The Amazing Things You'll Do in the 'Metaverse' and What It Will Take to Get There. *The Wall Street Journal*.

Olaleye, S. (2023). The Bibliometric Commingling of Metaverse and Non-fungible Tokens in Marketing. In J. R. Reis, Marketing and Smart Technologies. Springer Nature Singapore.

Park, S. M., & Kim, Y.-G. (2022). A Metaverse: Taxonomy, Components, Applications, and Open Challenges. *IEEE Access : Practical Innovations, Open Solutions*, *10*, 4209–4251. doi:10.1109/AC-CESS.2021.3140175

Park, S. M., & Kim, Y.-G. (2022). A Metaverse: Taxonomy, Components, Applications, and Open Challenges. *IEEE Access : Practical Innovations, Open Solutions*, *10*, 4209–4251. doi:10.1109/AC-CESS.2021.3140175

Pellas, N., Mystakidis, S., & Kazanidis, I. (2021). Immersive Virtual Reality in K-12 and Higher Education: A systematic review of the last decade scientific literature. *Virtual Reality (Waltham Cross)*, *25*(3), 835–861. doi:10.1007/s10055-020-00489-9

Rajan, A., Nassiri, N., Akre, V., Ravikumar, R., Nabeel, A., Buti, M., et al. (2018). *Virtual Reality Gaming Addiction*. Fifth HCT Information Technology Trends (ITT).

Rosenblum, L., & Cross, R. (1997). Challenges in Virtual Reality. In *In Visualization and Modelling*. Academic Press.

Chapter 3
Exploring the Factors Impacting the Intention to Use Metaverse in the Manufacturing Industry Through the Lens of Unified Technology Acceptance Theory

Mohammad Imtiaz Hossain
iD https://orcid.org/0000-0002-9637-3201
Multimedia University, Malaysia

Yasmin Jamadar
BRAC University, Bangladesh

Md. Kausar Alam
iD https://orcid.org/0000-0002-9748-5862
BRAC University, Bangladesh

Tanima Pal
BRAC University, Bangladesh

Md. Tariqul Islam
iD https://orcid.org/0000-0002-7367-2989
Taylor's University, Malaysia

Nusrut Sharmin
University of Chittagong, Bangladesh

ABSTRACT

This study accordingly explores the factors impacting the adoption of a metaverse in the manufacturing industry and develops a new model based on the Unified Theory of Acceptance (UTAT). Gender, age, and education were control variables. 235 questionnaire responses from employees of Malaysian manufacturing firms were collected through convenience sampling techniques and analyzed by Smart-PLS software. The findings reveal effort expectancy, perceived risk, and perceived technology accuracy have a significant relationship with intention to use a metaverse. Moreover, attitude to use evidenced mediating with perceived risk, perceived technology accuracy and intention to use a metaverse. The control variables did not evidence any impact on the intention to use a metaverse. This study provides insights to metaverse technology developers and manufacturing practitioners to explore and focus on the factors impacting the adoption of a metaverse in the manufacturing industry, as well as theoretical contributions for academia to progress further.

DOI: 10.4018/979-8-3693-2607-7.ch003

INTRODUCTION

The metaverse, a fully immersive virtual environment where users engage with each other and digital entities, has attracted considerable attention due to its potential to reshape industries (e.g., Smith & Jones, 2023). Manufacturing, a sector poised for significant transformation, has received limited attention in previous research regarding metaverse adoption, particularly in understanding user perceptions. This study addresses this gap by investigating factors influencing metaverse adoption in manufacturing, aiming to contribute to the field by developing a new model based on the Unified Technology Acceptance Theory (UTAT) (Davis et al., 1989).

The metaverse, a term coined by Neal Stephenson in his 1992 science fiction novel "Snow Crash," has evolved from conceptual origins to a sophisticated virtual environment (Stephenson, 1992). Types of metaverses include social, gaming, and enterprise-oriented, each catering to diverse user needs (Villalonga-Gómez et al., 2023). This evolution is marked by a rich tapestry of activities and applications, spanning entertainment, education, and business (Huang et al., 2021).

Within business, the metaverse facilitates virtual meetings, collaborative product development, and immersive training simulations (Huang et al., 2021). In manufacturing, its potential lies in streamlining processes, enhancing collaboration, and optimizing supply chain management. These applications underscore the transformative potential of the metaverse in redefining traditional business operations.

Despite its potential, implementing the metaverse in manufacturing poses challenges including technical hurdles, security concerns, and the need for an organizational cultural shift (Yao et al., 2024). Overcoming these challenges requires a nuanced understanding of the factors influencing the intention to use the metaverse in the manufacturing sector. The research domain of metaverse is new and there is a dearth of research on influencing factors on intention to use the metaverse in manufacturing industry and how do these factors drive or affect metaverse adoption attitude.

The implementation of the metaverse in manufacturing faces several technical hurdles that could impact its widespread adoption. One significant challenge is the current limitations in hardware and software for Virtual Reality (VR) and Augmented Reality (AR) technologies (Smith & Jones, 2023). These technologies may lack the necessary power and affordability to enable immersive experiences and smooth interaction in factory settings (Smith & Jones, 2023).

Additionally, the reliance on reliable and high-speed internet connectivity is crucial for real-time data transmission and low latency within the metaverse. However, deficiencies in existing network infrastructure, particularly in remote areas, pose a potential hindrance to seamless metaverse operation (Gupta & Singh, 2022). The integration of metaverse technologies with existing manufacturing systems and data platforms is vital for efficient workflows. However, complexities in integrating diverse data formats and protocols can create obstacles, leading to information silos (Li & Zhang, 2021). Furthermore, interoperability issues between different metaverse platforms could hinder collaboration between partners and suppliers, especially when using incompatible systems. The lack of standardized protocols may limit the full potential of the metaverse ecosystem (Huang et al., 2021).

Security concerns represent another critical challenge in metaverse implementation within manufacturing. Protecting sensitive manufacturing data and intellectual property is paramount, as data breaches and unauthorized access can have severe consequences (Chen et al., 2022). The susceptibility of virtual environments to cyberattacks, such as malware injection and data manipulation, underscores the need for robust cybersecurity protocols and user authentication systems (Yu & Fang, 2020). Ensuring the physical safety of workers interacting with virtual elements within the manufacturing environment is also crucial, considering potential hazards like collisions with physical objects or virtual reality sickness (Lee et al., 2023).

Apart from technical challenges, an organizational cultural shift to adopt new technologies is necessary for successful metaverse adoption in manufacturing industry. Change management becomes crucial, requiring organizations to adapt and train employees to embrace new workflows and technologies in manufacturing industry. Resistance to change, stemming from concerns about job displacement, privacy, or the unknown, can hinder adoption and necessitate effective communication and addressing of concerns (Smith & Jones, 2023). Moreover, addressing the skills gap is essential, as upskilling and reskilling the workforce may be necessary to meet the demands of working in a metaverse manufacturing environment. New skills, including virtual collaboration, data analysis, and digital problem-solving, may become imperative for employees (Lin & Huang, 2022) in manufacturing firms.

A comprehensive literature review reveals studies employing various methodologies exploring factors such as user experience, perceived usefulness, and perceived ease of use (Davis, 1989). However, a gap exists in understanding the unique challenges faced by manufacturing companies. Previous studies serve as a foundation but underscore the necessity of tailoring insights to the manufacturing context. Previous studies highlight the multifaceted nature of metaverse adoption, revealing both positive and negative aspects (Lin, 2019). However, gaps emerge when considering the industry-specific nuances of manufacturing. These gaps prompt the need for a dedicated exploration of factors influencing metaverse adoption within Malaysian manufacturing companies. Thus the objective of this study is to examine the impact of performance expectancy, effort expectancy, perceived risk, resistance to accept, and perceived technology accuracy on intention to use a metaverse and the mediating role of attitude to use metaverse on these associations in Malaysian manufacturing industry.

This research aims to contribute to the growing body of knowledge on metaverse adoption by providing a comprehensive understanding of factors influencing intention to use in the manufacturing industry. The development of a new model based on the Unified Technology Acceptance Theory (Davis et al., 1989) will offer practical insights for manufacturing companies navigating the intricate landscape of metaverse adoption.

LITERATURE REVIEW

Unified Technology Acceptance Theory

The metaverse, a fully immersive virtual environment, has garnered significant attention across industries due to its potential transformative impact (Smith & Jones, 2023). In the manufacturing sector, where processes, collaboration, and supply chain management are crucial, understanding the factors influencing the intention to use the metaverse is essential for successful integration (Huang et al., 2021). This literature review delves into the Unified Technology Acceptance Theory (UTAT) as a framework for comprehending the variables influencing metaverse adoption in manufacturing (Davis et al., 1989).

UTAT, proposed by Davis et al. in 1989, is an extension of the original Technology Acceptance Model (TAM) (Davis et al., 1989) and TAM posits that perceived ease of use and perceived usefulness are crucial determinants of users' acceptance of technology (Lin, 2019). UTAT builds upon this foundation by incorporating additional factors that influence technology acceptance. It emphasizes the role of external variables such as social influence, facilitating conditions, and cognitive instrumental processes (Lin, 2019).

UTAT emerged in response to the limitations of TAM, aiming to enhance the model's explanatory power and predictive capability (Yao et al., 2024). TAM primarily focused on individual perceptions, overlooking the broader contextual factors influencing technology adoption. UTAT addressed this limitation by incorporating external variables, providing a more comprehensive understanding of the complex nature of technology acceptance and exploring the variables in UTAT and how these are relevant to adopt Metaverse (Chen et al., 2022).

Performance Expectancy (PE)

PE refers to users' perceived ability of the technology to achieve desired tasks (e.g., Davis et al., 1989). In the context of manufacturing metaverse adoption, PE assesses how users perceive the metaverse's capability to enhance collaboration, streamline processes, and optimize supply chain management. Positive perceptions of these benefits contribute to a higher intention to use (Davis et al., 1989).

Effort Expectancy (EE)

EE represents the perceived ease of using a technology (e.g., Venkatesh et al., 2003). Manufacturing professionals are more likely to adopt the metaverse if they perceive it as user-friendly and easily integrated into their workflows. Low effort expectancy can be a barrier to adoption (Venkatesh et al., 2003).

Resistance to Accept (RA)

RA gauges the degree of resistance to adopting a new technology (e.g., Tornatzky & Fleischer, 1990). Manufacturing employees might resist the metaverse due to concerns about work routine changes, job displacement, or uncertainties. Understanding and mitigating resistance is crucial for successful implementation (Tornatzky & Fleischer, 1990).

Perceived Risk (PR)

PR assesses users' perception of potential negative consequences associated with technology adoption (e.g., Taylor & Todd, 1995). Manufacturing professionals might perceive risks related to data security, privacy issues, and metaverse reliability. Addressing and minimizing perceived risks is vital for fostering positive adoption intentions (Taylor & Todd, 1995).

Perceived Technology Accuracy (PTA)

PTA reflects users' perception of technology accuracy and reliability (e.g., Lee et al., 2023). In manufacturing, accurate and reliable data within the metaverse is crucial for decision-making. High PTA contributes positively to the intention to use the metaverse (Lee et al., 2023).

HYPOTHESIS DEVELOPMENT

Performance Expectancy and Attitude and Intention to Use Metaverse

In general, users are more likely to embrace a new system if they perceive it as useful, efficient, and capable of enhancing their performance (Venkatesh et al., 2003). High-performance expectancy often fosters positive attitudes towards technology adoption, as users tend to assess potential benefits and advantages before committing to using technology.

Within the context of the metaverse, performance expectancy becomes a key determinant of user attitudes and intentions (Venkatesh et al., 2003; Li et al., 2021). A positive attitude towards the metaverse is more likely when users perceive it as a platform that can fulfill their expectations and enrich their overall virtual experience. The immersive and interactive nature of the metaverse makes performance expectancy critical in shaping user perceptions.

The relationship between performance expectancy and technology adoption has been explored in several studies. For instance, Davis (1989) introduced the Technology Acceptance Model (TAM), emphasizing the significance of perceived usefulness and ease of use. Venkatesh et al. (2003) extended TAM with the Unified Theory of Acceptance and Use of Technology (UTAUT), highlighting performance expectancy as a critical factor. In the context of the metaverse, recent studies by Li et al. (2021) and Kim et al. (2022) provide valuable insights into the complex dynamics of metaverse adoption through their exploration of performance expectancy's role in shaping user attitudes and intentions.

H1: Performance Expectancy has significant impact on Intention to Use Metaverse

H2: Attitude to use mediates between Performance Expectancy and Intention to Use Metaverse

Effort Expectancy and Attitude and Intention to Use Metaverse

Beyond perceived benefits (performance expectancy), users also consider the perceived effort required to utilize a technology, known as effort expectancy. This factor, along with attitude, plays a crucial role in shaping their intention to use new technologies. Studies like Venkatesh et al. (2003) have shown that low effort expectancy, alongside high perceived usefulness, often leads to positive attitudes and increased technology adoption.

In the context of the metaverse, effort expectancy becomes another critical lens through which users judge it's potential. A complex virtual environment can be daunting if navigating it requires significant effort or mastering intricate interfaces. Conversely, intuitive controls, seamless interactions, and user-friendly interfaces can drastically reduce perceived effort, fostering a more positive attitude toward adoption.

The connection between effort expectancy and attitude towards technology adoption has been explored in various studies. For instance, Agarwal and Prasad (2000) found that low effort expectancy significantly diminished users' willingness to adopt e-commerce platforms. More recently, Kim et al. (2022) investigated the metaverse specifically, highlighting the importance of user-friendly interfaces and intuitive controls in shaping positive attitudes and intentions. Their findings suggest that minimizing perceived effort within the metaverse is crucial for attracting and retaining users.

Understanding the interplay between effort expectancy, attitude, and intention to use the metaverse is critical for developers and designers aiming to foster its widespread adoption. By prioritizing user-friendliness, intuitiveness, and seamless interaction, they can reduce perceived effort, cultivate positive attitudes, and ultimately encourage users to explore the vast potential of the metaverse.

H3: Effort Expectancy has significant impact on Intention to Use Metaverse

H4: Attitude to use mediates between Effort Expectancy and Intention to Use Metaverse

Resistance to Accept and Attitude and Intention to Use Metaverse

Resistance to accept the metaverse, characterized by individuals' reluctance or hesitation towards embracing virtual environments, is a significant factor influencing their intention to use this emerging technology. Users may harbor concerns, skepticism, or preconceived notions that hinder their willingness to fully engage with the metaverse (Rogers, 2003; Venkatesh and Davis, 2000).

Within the metaverse, users may exhibit resistance stemming from various factors, including unfamiliarity with virtual interactions, concerns about the impact on real-world relationships, or apprehensions regarding the value proposition of virtual experiences. Overcoming this resistance is crucial for fostering widespread adoption and encouraging users to explore the diverse possibilities within the metaverse.

Barriers to overcoming resistance may include a lack of understanding about the metaverse's potential, misconceptions about its purpose, or concerns about the societal impact of virtual interactions. Developers and advocates of the metaverse can address these barriers through informative campaigns, educational initiatives, and highlighting the positive aspects of virtual engagement. Clear communication about the benefits and addressing misconceptions can help alleviate resistance (Rogers, 2003; Venkatesh and Davis, 2000).

Building trust in the metaverse involves addressing users' concerns and establishing credibility in the technology's capability to enhance rather than diminish real-world experiences. Transparent communication, user testimonials, and success stories within the metaverse can contribute to building trust and mitigating resistance to acceptance.

Research in the field of technology adoption has explored the concept of resistance to new technologies. Studies by Rogers (2003) in the Diffusion of Innovations theory and Venkatesh and Davis (2000) in the context of the Technology Acceptance Model provide insights into overcoming resistance through effective communication and demonstrating the value of innovations. While specific studies on metaverse resistance may be limited, lessons from technology adoption research remain relevant.

Addressing and mitigating resistance to accept the metaverse is essential for its successful integration into mainstream culture. Developers, educators, and influencers should collaborate to provide accurate information, showcase positive experiences, and emphasize the metaverse's potential benefits. By navigating skepticism and fostering a positive narrative, stakeholders can encourage users to overcome resistance and embrace the metaverse for its diverse and transformative offerings (Rogers, 2003; Venkatesh and Davis, 2000).

H5: Resistance to accept has significant impact on Intention to Use Metaverse

H6: Attitude to use mediates between Resistance to accept and Intention to Use Metaverse

Perceived Risk and Intention to Use Metaverse

Perceived risk, the apprehension individuals feel regarding potential negative consequences associated with technology, is a critical factor influencing their intention to use the metaverse (Dinev and Hart,

2006). Users assess risks related to privacy, security, and unforeseen challenges, which can significantly impact their willingness to adopt and engage with the metaverse.

In the metaverse, users grapple with concerns related to the security of personal information, potential identity theft, or unauthorized access to virtual spaces: the fear of experiencing adverse consequences, both within the virtual realm and in connection with real-world implications, can create hesitancy and resistance to metaverse adoption (Dinev and Hart, 2006).

Barriers to addressing perceived risk may include a lack of transparent privacy policies, instances of cyber threats within the metaverse, or the potential for misinformation (Dinev and Hart, 2006). Developers and platform providers can mitigate these concerns by implementing robust security measures, transparent data handling practices, and fostering a culture of trust within the metaverse community.

Factors such as reputation, reliability, and transparent communication about security measures play a crucial role in building trust and reducing perceived risk (Dinev and Hart, 2006; Siponen and Vance, 2010). Collaborative efforts within the metaverse community to address and rectify security concerns contribute to a more positive environment, encouraging users to embrace the metaverse with greater confidence.

Research by Dinev and Hart (2006) has explored the connection between perceived risk and online technologies, emphasizing the importance of trust-building mechanisms. Additionally, studies in the context of virtual worlds, like the work of Siponen and Vance (2010), underscore the significance of mitigating perceived risks for user adoption.

Effectively managing perceived risks is essential for the sustained growth and adoption of the metaverse. Developers and stakeholders must prioritize transparent communication, robust security measures, and community collaboration to address and alleviate concerns related to perceived risk (Dinev and Hart, 2006; Siponen and Vance, 2010). By fostering a secure and trustworthy metaverse environment, users are more likely to feel confident in their intention to explore and engage with the diverse possibilities offered by virtual spaces.

H7: perceived risks has significant impact on Intention to Use Metaverse

H8: Attitude to use mediates between perceived risks and Intention to Use Metaverse

Perceived Technology Accuracy and Attitude and Intention to Use Metaverse

Perceived technology accuracy, reflecting users' confidence in the reliability and precision of metaverse technologies, is a fundamental factor shaping their intention to use the metaverse. Users' assessments of the technology's effectiveness and accuracy significantly influence their attitudes and willingness to invest time and effort in virtual experiences (Lee et al., 2012; Li et al., 2021).

In the metaverse, users seek assurance that the technology accurately represents their actions, interactions with others, and the immersive environment itself. Concerns about glitches, inaccuracies, or technological limitations may deter individuals from fully embracing the metaverse experience.

Barriers to perceived technology accuracy may include frequent technical glitches, limitations in graphical representation, or inconsistencies in user experiences. Developers can enhance accuracy by continuously refining algorithms, addressing technical challenges promptly, and ensuring a seamless and consistent metaverse environment.

User confidence in the metaverse's technological accuracy directly impacts their engagement and intention to use the platform. A reliable and accurate representation of the virtual world fosters trust and encourages users to explore, create, and interact within the metaverse with a sense of confidence and satisfaction.

Research by Lee et al. (2012) has delved into the relationship between perceived technology accuracy and user satisfaction in virtual environments. Similarly, studies by Li et al. (2021) emphasize the importance of continuous technological advancements and accuracy in shaping positive attitudes toward metaverse adoption.

Ensuring and communicating the accuracy of metaverse technologies is paramount for sustained user trust and adoption. Developers should prioritize technological advancements, address glitches promptly, and provide users with a consistently reliable virtual experience. By establishing a foundation of trust through accurate representation, the metaverse can attract and retain users, driving positive attitudes and intentions toward immersive virtual engagement (Lee et al., 2012; Li et al., 2021).

H9: Perceived technology accuracy has significant impact on Intention to Use Metaverse

H10: Attitude to use mediates between perceived technology accuracy and Intention to Use Metaverse

METHODOLOGY

The study applies positivism philosophy, quantitative survey method, cross-sectional time horizon and deductive approach. Data was collected through structured questionnaire to get more data in a quick time frame. The items were adapted from the previous studies and applied a five-point likert scale. Measurement items are provided in Table 1. Three (3) academicians and three (3) industry players checked the item's relevancy and quality. The sentence structures of the items were revised in accordance with the

Figure 1. Conceptual model

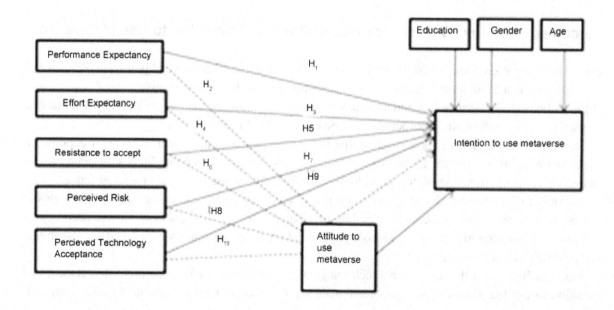

feedback provided by experts and respondents. The researchers considered dropping few questions to ensure relevancy of the items with the context.

The study is of a cross-sectional nature as data was obtained at a singular point in time. A pilot study was performed consists 30 respondents. The respondents were employees of manufacturing firms. The non- probability sampling method and convenience sampling technique were employed as the sample frame was not available. By using the G-power software, based on the six (6) predictors in this study's framework, 146 sample sizes are suggested (Figure 2). However, 240 responses were received after distributing questionnaire through a Google form link in various sources such as social media groups of manufacturer and email sending personally. 235 questionnaires were found usable for final analysis.

FINDINGS AND DISCUSSION

Non-Response Bias (NRB) and Common Method Bias (CMB)

This study employs the Wallace & Cooke (1990) approach to examine NRB. NRB guarantees that the survey accurately reflects the desired study population. The researchers analysed the mean and standard

Table 1. Measurement scales of constructs

Constructs	Items	Sources
Performance Expectancy	PE1 I think metaverse is helpful for manufacturing industry. PE2 I think metaverse could solve manufacturing related problems. PE3 I think metaverse can manage manufacturing related issues quickly. PE4 I think metaverse can increase the capability of manufacturing -management.	Venkatesh et al. (2003), Venkatesh et al. (2012)
Effort expectancy	EP1 I think I can easily learn to use metaverse. EP2 I can understand the service information on metaverse. EP3 I can easily use metaverse. EP4 I can get the skill of using metaverse.	Venkatesh et al. (2003), Venkatesh et al. (2012)
Resistance to accept	RA1 I have a negative opinion about metaverse RA2 I will refuse even if someone recommends using metaverse RA3 I feel reluctant to us metaverse RA4 I have something to criticize about using metaverse	Ju & Lee (2021)
Perceived Risk	PR1 I am concerned about cheating of metaverse information. PR2 I worry about problems of metaverse information PR3 I worry that my consumption will not provide value for my money.	Efendioğlu (2023).
Perceived Technology Accuracy	PTA1 I can rely on the services provided by metaverse. PTA2 My metaverse services offer consistent results over time. PTA3 I think metaverse have good working standards continuously. PTA4 I think the metaverse services are reliable. PTA5 I feel confident that metaverse services are offering error-free results.	Yang et al. (2022)
Attitude to use metaverse	AU1 I am interested in using metaverse AU2 I am likely to use metaverse because of its attractiveness AU3 I feel my work overall will be better with metaverse	Albayati (2024).
Intention to Use metaverse	IUES1 I intend to use metaverse to manage my business in the future. IUES2 I will always try to use metaverse to manage my day to day business operation in the future. IUES3 I plan to use metaverse frequently to manage my business in the future. IUES4 I would be willing to develop a habit of using metaverse soon. IUES5 I predict I will use metaverse to manage my health information.	Yang et al. (2022)

Figure 2. Sample size determinations using G-power software

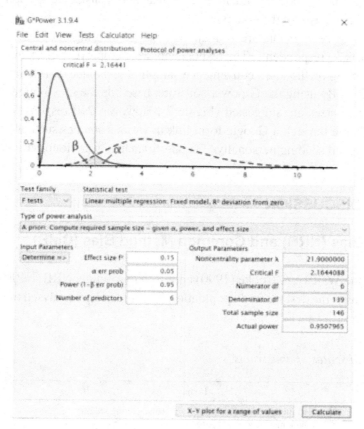

Table 2. Demographic data (n = 235)

Sample characteristics	Categories	Frequency
Gender	Male	165
	Female	64
	Prefer not to say	6
Age	20- 25 years	37
	26 - 31 years	60
	32 - 37 years	47
	38-43 years	49
	More than 43 Years	42
Education	No formal education	12
	Vocational	7
	Foundation	1
	SPM	10
	STPM	3
	Diploma	42
	Bachelor	83
	Masters	63
	PhD	14

deviation for the first 30 and final 30 respondents. They found no significant differences between the two groups, confirming the absence of NRB in the study.

Based on (Kock, 2015), if all VIFs in the inner model resulting from a full collinearity test are equal to or lower than 5.0, the model can consider free of CMB. The model is free from CMB because the VIFs are lower than 5.0 (Table 5).

Demographics Data

Table 2 showed that majority of the responses were male (165). Most of the respondents are 26-31 years old (60), and bachelor degree holder (83).

Measurement Model

Figure 3. The measurement model

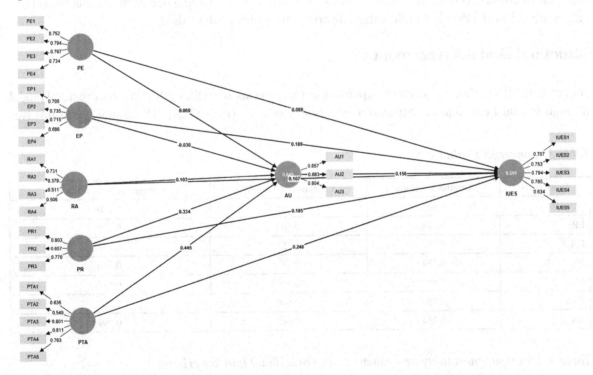

Convergent Validity

Convergent validity, as defined by Bagozzi et al. (1981), pertains to the degree of correlation among multiple indicators or measures of the same construct. The calculation of the Average Variance Extracted (AVE) involves squaring the loading of each indicator on a construct and computing the mean value, following the approach outlined by Hair et al. (2019). Internal consistency, or reliability, is assessed using Cronbach's alpha coefficient, a measure introduced by Cronbach (1951) to evaluate the reliability of a set of survey items. Composite reliability, akin to Cronbach's alpha, serves as a gauge of internal consistency in scale items, as proposed by Netemeyer et al. (2003).

The outcomes presented in Table 3 demonstrate that all the items' except RA's Average Variance Extracted (AVE) values surpass the 0.5 thresholds recommended by Hair et al. (2019). Additionally, constructs except RA's Cronbach's alpha and composite reliability exceed the 0.6 threshold, as suggested by Shi et al. (2012). These findings indicate that the measures exhibit acceptable reliability and high internal consistency, supporting the convergent validity of the study.

Discriminant Validity

Fornell & Larcker (1981) criteria and Heterotrait-Monotrait (HTMT) ratio were applied to confirm discriminant validity. Table 4 demonstrates that the square root of AVE is higher than its correlation with other variables, confirming discriminant validity.

Henseler et al. (2015) proposed the HTMT method, which confirms discriminant validity between each pair of constructs if the correlation values are less than 0.90. Table 5 below shows that the HTMT values are below the threshold value, thus, discriminant validity established.

Structural Model Assessment

Hair et al. (2019) outlined a systematic approach comprising six steps for evaluating the structural model through Partial Least Squares Structural Equation Modeling (PLS-SEM). The initial phase involves

Table 3. Convergent Validity

Constructs	Cronbach's alpha	Composite reliability	Average variance extracted
AU	0.805	0.885	0.720
EP	0.674	0.803	0.505
IUES	0.782	0.852	0.537
PE	0.759	0.847	0.580
PR	0.602	0.789	0.557
PTA	0.760	0.840	0.517
RA	0.234	0.618	0.299

Table 4. Discriminant validity assessment using Fornell and Larcker criteria

Constructs	AU	EP	IUES	PE	PR	PTA	RA
AU	0.849						
EP	0.410	0.710					
IUES	0.650	0.530	0.733				
PE	0.512	0.256	0.487	0.762			
PR	0.709	0.451	0.647	0.490	0.746		
PTA	0.747	0.518	0.691	0.553	0.679	0.719	
RA	0.514	0.400	0.517	0.392	0.506	0.509	0.547

Table 5. Discriminant validity assessment using Heterotrait-Monotrait (HTMT)

Constructs	AU	EP	IUES	PE	PR	PTA	RA
AU							
EP	0.557						
IUES	0.815	0.723					
PE	0.652	0.362	0.626				
PR	0.898	0.706	0.836	0.718			
PTA	0.846	0.735	0.893	0.728	0.800		
RA	0.822	0.898	0.843	0.852	0.796	0.850	

addressing latent collinearity issues. Subsequently, the examination of the significance and relevance of relationships within the structural model is undertaken. This is followed by the assessment of the variance explained by the dependent variable (R^2), the effect size (f^2), and the predictive relevance (Q^2predict). Finally, an evaluation of the corresponding t-values of the path coefficients is conducted through bootstrapping, employing 5,000 resamples with a two-tailed test at a significance level of 0.05. The results encompassing R^2, f^2, inner and outer model's Variance Inflation Factor (VIF), and Q^2predict are presented in Table 6 below.

The coefficient R^2 signifies the proportion of variance in the endogenous variable attributed to all exogenous variables. Ranging from 0 to 1, a higher R^2 indicates enhanced predictive accuracy. The conventional benchmarks for R^2 values categorize them as weak (0.25), moderate (0.50), and substantial (0.75) levels of predictive accuracy (Hair et al., 2019). In this study, the model prediction exhibited strong, as evidenced by R^2 value of 0.637 and 0.580.

Assessing the effect size of predictor constructs using Cohen's f^2 (Cohen, 2013) provides insight into their relative impact on an endogenous construct. Cohen defines effect sizes as high (0.35), medium (0.15), and small (0.02) based on f^2 values. The current study's results, presented in Table 6, indicate small effect sizes for the exogenous variables.

The examination of collinearity in Table 6 reveals no multicollinearity concerns in the current study. Both inner model's Variance Inflation Factor (VIF) and outer model's VIF values fall below the threshold of 5.

In PLS version 4, Q^2-Predicts systematically remove and predict each data point of indicators within the reflective measurement model of the endogenous construct. This test evaluates the predictive ca-

Table 6. Quality of the structural model

Endogenous Variables	R^2	Q^2predict	Exogenous Variables	f^2	VIF
AU	0.637	0.620	AU	0.021	2.818
IUES	0.580	0.547	EP	0.060	1.449
			PE	0.013	1.539
			PR	0.035	2.380
			PTA	0.051	2.971
			RA	0.018	1.530

pabilities of items related to endogenous variables in the structural model. As indicated in Table 6, a Q^2-Predict value exceeding 0 signifies the model's predictive capacity (Hair et al., 2019), establishing a higher level of predictive relevance in the study.

The researchers evaluated the association between constructs in the structural model based on the p-value and t-statistics value. The hypothesized relationship was perceived as significantly accepted when p values were less than 0.05 and T statistics were above 1.96 (Hair *et al.*, 2019). Table 7 indicates

Table 7. Path coefficient result for hypotheses

Paths	Original sample	T values	P values	Result
PE -> IUES	0.089	1.350	0.17	Not supported
EP -> IUES	0.189	3.060	0.00	Supported
RA -> IUES	0.107	1.856	0.06	Not supported
PR -> IUES	0.185	2.464	0.01	Supported
PTA -> IUES	0.248	2.869	0.00	Supported
PE -> AU -> IUES	0.011	1.065	0.28	Not supported
EP -> AU -> IUES	-0.005	0.581	0.56	Not supported
RA -> AU -> IUES	0.016	1.283	0.19	Not supported
PR -> AU -> IUES	0.052	1.924	0.05	Supported
PTA -> AU -> IUES	0.069	2.081	0.03	Supported

Figure 4. The structural model

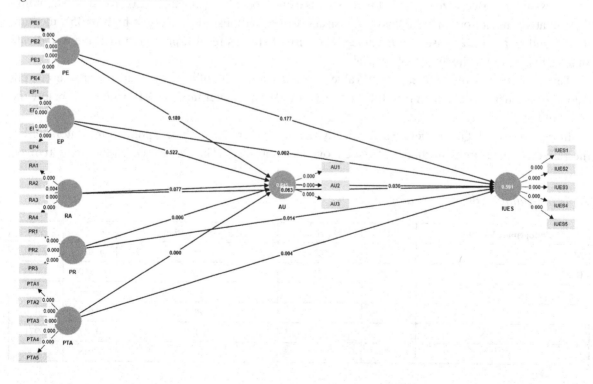

that EP, PR, PTA have a significant relationship with IUES. Moreover, AU evidenced mediating with PR-IUES and PTA-IUES. Control variables did not show any influence in intention to use metaverse.

Performance expectancy is not significant in predicting intention to use metaverse technology in the manufacturing industry in Malaysia due to factors such as limited awareness and understanding, lack of relevance or fit, resource constraints, technological complexity and risk, cultural and organizational factors, and external pressures and market dynamics.

Effort expectancy is significant in predicting intention to use metaverse technology in the manufacturing industry in Malaysia due to factors such as user-friendly interfaces, availability of training and support resources, compatibility with existing systems, perceived usefulness and relevance, peer influence and social norms, and perceptions of complexity and technical skills.

Resistance to accept new technology often stems from a lack of awareness or understanding of its potential benefits and implications. However, if professionals in the manufacturing industry in Malaysia are adequately informed about the capabilities and applications of metaverse technology, they may be less resistant to adopting it. Education and awareness-building efforts can help mitigate resistance by addressing misconceptions and highlighting the value proposition of metaverse technology.

Metaverse technology encompasses a wide range of advanced and cutting-edge technologies, including virtual reality (VR), augmented reality (AR), artificial intelligence (AI), and blockchain. Professionals in the manufacturing industry in Malaysia may perceive metaverse technology as complex and unfamiliar, leading to concerns about their ability to understand, implement, and use it effectively. The perceived technological complexity can increase perceived risk and hesitation towards adopting metaverse technology.

Perceived technology accuracy is significant in predicting intention to use metaverse technology in the manufacturing industry in Malaysia due to its potential impact on operational efficiency, quality control, safety, risk management, product design, decision support, strategic planning, and customer satisfaction. Addressing concerns about technology accuracy requires ensuring that metaverse technology platforms deliver reliable, precise, and trustworthy information and experiences that meet the needs and expectations of professionals in the manufacturing industry.

Moreover, AU evidenced no mediating influence with PE-IUES, EP-IUES and RA-IUES. In manufacturing firms, individuals may primarily focus on how metaverse technology helps them perform specific tasks or achieve organizational goals rather than forming attitudes towards the technology itself. Their intention to use the technology may be driven more by practical considerations such as perceived usefulness and ease of use rather than subjective evaluations or attitudes towards the technology.

Individuals in Malaysian manufacturing firms may have neutral or ambivalent attitudes towards metaverse technology, meaning they neither strongly favor nor strongly oppose its use. In such cases, attitudes may not play a significant mediating role in influencing intention to use the technology, as individuals may base their decisions more on objective assessments of the technology's utility and feasibility.

Contributions

Explaining the impact of performance expectancy, effort expectancy, resistance to accept, perceived risk, and perceived technology accuracy on intention to use a metaverse extends the Unified Theory of Acceptance (UTAT) by incorporating additional factors and contextual considerations relevant to the adoption of emerging technologies like the metaverse. This enhanced model allows researchers and practitioners to better identify, measure, and address the multifaceted determinants of technology adoption, thereby contributing to more effective strategies for promoting the adoption and use of the metaverse in various domains.

Understanding the intricate relationship between performance expectancy, attitude, and intention to use the metaverse is essential for designers, developers, and policymakers aiming to enhance the adoption and acceptance of this evolving technology. Understanding those factors can help manufacturing companies tailor their adoption strategies. For instance, if perceived risk is identified as a significant barrier, strategies to mitigate these risks can be developed, such as offering training programs or providing guarantees on the performance of the metaverse technology. Insights gained from the study can aid in the allocation of resources towards areas that are identified as crucial influencers of intention to use a metaverse. This could involve investing in technologies that enhance performance expectancy or efforts to minimize perceived risks associated with metaverse adoption. Companies can prioritize technologies with a proven track record of accuracy and reliability, thereby increasing confidence among users and enhancing their intention to use. Insights from the study can also inform the development of organizational policies related to metaverse adoption. This might include policies addressing data security and privacy concerns, as well as guidelines for acceptable use of metaverse technologies within the manufacturing context. Early adoption of metaverse technologies can provide manufacturing companies with a competitive advantage in the market.

Limitations and Future Research Directions

Despite significant theoretical and empirical contributions, this study acknowledges a few limitations. First, a single survey method can cause CMB issues. However, statistical post-hoc procedures were taken into account to eradicate this issue. Secondly, this study examines a single country (Malaysia) and single industry (Manufacturing). Service firms from other regions can be explored. Thirdly, this study used single method and cross-sectional quantitative survey. Other researchers can use comparative, qualitative, mixed or longitudinal studies to enhance generability. Other moderating or mediating variables, such as social influence, facilitating conditions etc., can be considered with this model.

REFERENCES

Agarwal, R., & Prasad, J. (2000). The role of e-commerce success factors in customer satisfaction. *Journal of the Academy of Marketing Science, 28*(1), 18–25. doi:10.1177/0092070300281002

Albayati, H. (2024). Investigating undergraduate students' perceptions and awareness of using ChatGPT as a regular assistance tool: A user acceptance perspective study. *Computers and Education: Artificial Intelligence, 6*, 100203. doi:10.1016/j.caeai.2024.100203

Bagozzi, R. P., Yi, Y., & Phillips, L. W. (1991). Assessing construct validity in organizational research. *Administrative Science Quarterly, 36*(3), 421–458. doi:10.2307/2393203

Chen, X., Li, H., Zhao, J., & Li, H. (2022). Security and privacy issues in the metaverse: A survey. *ACM Computing Surveys, 55*(2), 1–41.

Cohen, J., Cohen, P., West, S. G., & Aiken, L. S. (2013). *Applied multiple regression/correlation analysis for the behavioral sciences*. Routledge. doi:10.4324/9780203774441

Cronbach, L. J. (1951). Coefficient alpha and the internal structure of tests. *psychometrika, 16*(3), 297-334.

Davis, F. D. (1989). Perceived usefulness, perceived ease of use, and user acceptance of information technology. *Management Information Systems Quarterly, 13*(3), 319–340. doi:10.2307/249008

Davis, F. D., Bagozzi, R. P., & Warshaw, P. R. (1989). User acceptance of computer technology: A comparison of two theoretical models. *Management Science, 35*(8), 982–1003. doi:10.1287/mnsc.35.8.982

Dinev, T., & Hart, P. J. (2006). An empirical examination of the deLone and McLean model of information systems success. *Management Information Systems Quarterly, 30*(3), 691–721.

Efendioğlu, İ. H. (2023). The Effect Of Information About Metaverse On The Consumer's Purchase Intention. *Journal of Global Business and Technology, 19*(1), 63–77.

Fornell, C., & Larcker, D. F. (1981). Evaluating structural equation models with unobservable variables and measurement error. *JMR, Journal of Marketing Research, 18*(1), 39–50. doi:10.1177/002224378101800104

Gupta, R., & Singh, S. (2022). Network infrastructure for the metaverse: Requirements and challenges. *IEEE Internet of Things Journal, 9*(12), 13298–13310.

Hair, J. F., Risher, J. J., Sarstedt, M., & Ringle, C. M. (2019). When to use and how to report the results of PLS-SEM. *European Business Review, 31*(1), 2–24. doi:10.1108/EBR-11-2018-0203

Henseler, J., Ringle, C. M., & Sarstedt, M. (2015). A new criterion for assessing discriminant validity in variance-based structural equation modeling. *Journal of the Academy of Marketing Science, 43*(1), 115–135. doi:10.1007/s11747-014-0403-8

Huang, Y., Wu, S., & Zhao, X. (2021). The metaverse for business: Opportunities and challenges. *Journal of Management Information Systems, 38*(3), 1089–1111.

Ju, N., & Lee, K. H. (2021). Perceptions and resistance to accept smart clothing: Moderating effect of consumer innovativeness. *Applied Sciences (Basel, Switzerland), 11*(7), 3211. doi:10.3390/app11073211

Kim, Y., Park, J., & Sohn, D. (2022). Understanding user acceptance of the metaverse: Integrating the technology acceptance model and the flow theory. *Journal of Information Technology Management, 13*(2), 357–377.

Kock, N. (2015). Common method bias in PLS-SEM: A full collinearity assessment approach. [ijec]. *International Journal of e-Collaboration, 11*(4), 1–10. doi:10.4018/ijec.2015100101

Lee, J., Park, H., & Song, J. (2023). Safety assessment of augmented reality and virtual reality in the metaverse: A review. *International Journal of Occupational Safety and Health, •••,* 1–10.

Lee, Y., Kim, J., & Lee, Y. (2012). The role of perceived realism and trust in the continued usage of virtual worlds. *Computers in Human Behavior, 28*(2), 346–352.

Li, H., Li, Z., & Zhang, X. (2021). Understanding users' acceptance of the metaverse: An extended UTAUT model and empirical test. *International Journal of Information Management, 59,* 102495.

Li, H., & Zhang, Y. (2021). Data integration challenges and technologies in the metaverse. *IEEE Access : Practical Innovations, Open Solutions, 9,* 149696–149709.

Lin, C. C., & Huang, Y. (2022). The impact of metaverse technology on human resource development: A review of the literature. *Journal of Human Resources Development, 41*(4), 599–618.

Lin, H. (2019). The acceptance of virtual worlds: A meta-analysis. *Computers in Human Behavior, 93,* 113–122.

Netemeyer, R. G., Bearden, W. O., & Sharma, S. (2003). *Scaling procedures: Issues and applications.* Sage publications.

Rogers, E. M. (2003). *Diffusion of innovations.* Simon and Schuster.

Shi, J., Mo, X., & Sun, Z. (2012). Content validity index in scale development. *Zhong nan da xue xue bao. Yi xue ban= Journal of Central South University. Medical Science, 37*(2), 152–155.

Siponen, M., & Vance, A. (2010). User trust in information systems: A critical review of the literature. *Management Information Systems Quarterly, 34*(2), 339–368.

Smith, J., & Jones, A. (2023). The metaverse: A potential game-changer for industries. *Journal of Emerging Technologies, 12*(3), 45–62.

Stephenson, N. (1992). *Snow Crash.* Bantam Books.

Taylor, S. E., & Todd, P. A. (1995). Understanding information technology use as a process: A conceptual model of user acceptance and use. *Management Information Systems Quarterly, 19*(4), 197–217.

Tornatzky, L. G., & Fleischer, M. (1990). *The process of technological innovation.* Lexington Books.

Venkatesh, V., Brown, S. A., & Bala, H. (2013). Bridging the qualitative-quantitative divide: Guidelines for conducting mixed methods research in information systems. *Management Information Systems Quarterly, 37*(1), 21–54. doi:10.25300/MISQ/2013/37.1.02

Venkatesh, V., & Davis, F. D. (2000). A theoretical extension of the technology acceptance model: Four longitudinal field studies. *Management Science, 46*(2), 186–204. doi:10.1287/mnsc.46.2.186.11926

Venkatesh, V., Morris, M. G., Davis, G. B., & Davis, F. D. (2003). User acceptance of information technology: Toward a unified view. *Management Information Systems Quarterly, 27*(3), 425–478. doi:10.2307/30036540

Villalonga-Gómez, C., Ortega-Fernández, E., & Borau-Boira, E. (2023). Fifteen years of metaverse in Higher Education: A systematic literature review. *IEEE Transactions on Learning Technologies, 16*(6), 1057–1070. doi:10.1109/TLT.2023.3302382

Wallace, R. S. O., & Cooke, T. E. (1990). The diagnosis and resolution of emerging issues in corporate disclosure practices. *Accounting and Business Research, 20*(78), 143–151. doi:10.1080/00014788.1990.9728872

Yang, Q., Al Mamun, A., Hayat, N., Salleh, M. F. M., Jingzu, G., & Zainol, N. R. (2022). Modelling the mass adoption potential of wearable medical devices. *PLoS One, 17*(6), e0269256. doi:10.1371/journal.pone.0269256 PMID:35675373

Yao, X., Ma, N., Zhang, J., Wang, K., Yang, E., & Faccio, M. (2024). Enhancing wisdom manufacturing as industrial metaverse for industry and society 5.0. *Journal of Intelligent Manufacturing*, *35*(1), 235–255. doi:10.1007/s10845-022-02027-7

Yu, X., & Fang, B. (2020). *Cybersecurity challenges and opportunities in the metaverse*. Research Gate.

Chapter 4
Metaverse Perspectives:
Unpacking Its Role in Shaping Sustainable Development Goals – A Qualitative Inquiry

Monika Chandel

https://orcid.org/0000-0001-8179-6175

Central University of Himachal Pradesh, India

Manpreet Arora

https://orcid.org/0000-0002-4939-1992

Central University of Himachal Pradesh, India

ABSTRACT

The metaverse, a virtual realm, has drawn considerable attention from academicians as well as policy-makers in recent years. In this chapter, we explored the metaverse's social, economic, and environmental effects, which align with various UN Sustainable Development Goals (SDGs), using an interdisciplinary perspective to show how it might transcend geographical borders and promote sustainability. This study adds to the ethical and sustainable development of digital technologies by analysing the opinions about the metaverse's influence on the SDGs. It will help administrations, corporations, and communities use the metaverse to make the world more inclusive, equitable, and sustainable. We are still learning how the metaverse fits into sustainable development, and scholars are examining the positive and negative aspects. This area must balance technical innovation and global sustainability as it progresses towards a more sustainable future.

INTRODUCTION

The term "metaverse" has attracted attention as a possible accelerator for global sustainability as the world becomes more digitally linked. The metaverse, a virtual shared area that merges physical and digital worlds, may help fulfil Sustainable Development Goals in many ways. The metaverse, a virtual realm has drawn considerable attention from academicians as well as policymakers in recent years. This is due to the integration of platforms like Facebook, Instagram, and WhatsApp under the term "Meta",

DOI: 10.4018/979-8-3693-2607-7.ch004

to encompass all types of digital communication and virtual environments. The COVID-19 epidemic has further added to this phenomenon since the need for online social engagement has increased because of the cancellation of face-to-face gatherings (Maden & Yücenur, 2024). It is not just about online gaming and browsing anymore; people are envisioning it as a potential new dimension of the internet that can contribute to creating a more inclusive society.

The concept of sustainable development has been subject to several interpretations, with the most often cited definition being from "Our Common Future", commonly referred to as the Brundtland Report (WCED, 1987): *"Sustainable development is the development that meets the needs of the present without compromising the ability of future generations to meet their own needs."* The 2030 Agenda for Sustainable Development and its Sustainable Development Goals (SDGs) are the primary global framework for international cooperation, with sustainability as its core principle. Modern technologies are crucial in attaining the three fundamental aspects of sustainable development: the environment, the economy, and society. These technologies might potentially have both beneficial and detrimental effects on sustainable development (Al-Emran, 2023). Sustainable entrepreneurial and environmental activities prioritise overall well-being, which extends beyond financial considerations, by emphasising wellness and spirituality. Integrating such sustainable initiatives can enhance spirituality, and wellness which can foster and bolster entrepreneurship as well as the economy. The cultivation of an inventive and creative mindset can be fostered through the prioritisation of values, awareness, and connectivity (Arora et al., 2023).

The metaverse is an integral component of the fourth industrial revolution, sometimes known as "Industry 4.0." The Industry 4.0 enabling technologies encompass a range of distinct advancements, such as the Internet of Things (IoT), Cloud Computing, Edge Computing/Fog Computing, Big Data Analytics, Artificial Intelligence (AI), Machine Learning (ML), Blockchain, Augmented Reality (AR), Virtual Reality (VR), Mixed Reality (MR), Digital Twin, Metaverse, and Robotics (Pachouri et al., 2024). These technologies are being implemented across various industries, including finance, retail, logistics, manufacturing, education, healthcare, business and management, telecommunication, tourism and hospitality, agriculture, smart cities etc. The implementation of these technologies differs throughout industries, and several sectors are actively investigating how to use these advances to enhance efficiency, production, and creativity, while also prioritizing the creation of a more sustainable environment which aligns with the UN Sustainable Development Goals. VR has the potential to augment student learning and involvement. Virtual reality-based education has the potential to revolutionise the delivery of educational content in our highly digitalized society. Virtual reality is based on the idea of generating a virtual environment, whether it is actual or imagined, and enabling people to not only observe it but also engage with it (Arora, 2024). There is a growing demand for skilled people in this field due to a range of global developments, including the excessive use of technology, demographic transitions, changes in labour requirements, a strong reliance on digitalization, and the adoption of disruptive technologies. Investing in technical skill-building activities can enhance the economic prospects of a country. In a more competitive economic landscape, the optimal investment strategy entails the cultivation of a diverse set of abilities aimed at enhancing the overall skill set of the general populace (Arora & Chandel, 2023).

Currently, there is little research that specifically examines the connection between the Sustainable Development Goals (SDGs) outlined in the United Nations 2030 Agenda and the subject of the metaverse. We explored the metaverse's social, economic, and environmental effects using an interdisciplinary perspective to show how it might transcend geographical borders and promote sustainability. This study adds to the ethical and sustainable development of digital technologies by analysing the opinions about the metaverse's influence on the SDGs. It helps administrations, corporations, and communities use the metaverse to make the world more inclusive, equitable, and sustainable. We must comprehend the metaverse's effects on sustainable development to create a future where technology drives good global change.

Research Questions

1. How do individuals perceive the metaverse's impact on the Sustainable Development Goals (SDGs) and what connections do they make between metaverse activities and SDG achievement?
2. In what ways do participants see the metaverse influencing social inclusion, economic development, and environmental sustainability, and how do these perceptions align with established SDG principles?
3. What recommendations do participants provide for positive contributions to SDGs within the metaverse, and how can these insights inform ethical guidelines and best practices in the metaverse ecosystem?

Metaverse Across Various Industries

The Metaverse is a conceptual notion of a theoretical "parallel virtual world" that embodies different methods of living and working in the virtual world as an alternative to the future's smart cities. Emerging new technologies, like Artificial Intelligence, Big Data, the Internet of Things (IoT), and Digital Twins, provide extensive datasets and powerful computational insights into human behaviour (Allam et al., 2022). The Metaverse is expected to provide an array of possibilities across various sectors (Arpacı et al., 2022). Despite being in its initial phases of research and application, the metaverse holds the potential to significantly change how companies engage with consumers across both the virtual and physical worlds. Service businesses are actively investigating the potential of the metaverse to enhance client experiences by offering more immersive, interactive, and captivating interactions (Jung et al., 2024). Technological breakthroughs have significantly disrupted the banking industry. The metaverse's influence on the financial industry has become very significant (Ooi et al., 2023). Understanding the evolving banking industry and the influence of technological progress is essential for banks to effectively handle the difficulties and possibilities brought out by digital transformation.

Digital travellers may experience space travel and other unthinkable things in the metaverse, creating an astounding future. After the pandemic, COVID-19 travel anxiety has increased interest in virtual settings like metaverse travel. The 'new normal' has revived travellers' cost-conscious and tech-savvy behaviour, influencing their choices for innovative, engaging, and rewarding travel experiences (Zaman et al., 2022). Go and Kang (2022) performed research to provide a clear definition of metaverse tourism and to offer insights and future directions for studying the potential of metaverse tourism in the context of sustainable tourism. The study examined the capacity of the metaverse to support sustainable tourism, drawing on reports from the United Nations World Tourism Organization (UNWTO), data from Google Trends, and prior research in the fields of human-computer interactions, virtual reality, and cognitive studies. This study discovered that metaverse goods and experiences have the potential to enhance the variety of tourism resources and promote sustainable tourism by offering alternative and viable options. Developing licensed and viable metaverse tourism goods and experiences has the potential to enhance profitability for tourist destinations and should be aligned with the Sustainable Development Goals (SDGs) set by the United Nations World Tourism Organization (UNWTO). Utilizing metaverse tourism goods and experiences is a novel strategy for achieving the overall Sustainable Development Goals (SDGs).

The COVID-19 epidemic has caused significant disruptions to the education system, prompting a strong emphasis on the urgent need to speed up digitalizing education. The impact of AI and big data on contemporary enterprises is significant. Due to the vast amount of different information included in big data, modern businesses rely on AI-assisted technologies, tools, and gadgets to process it efficiently and meaningfully. Hence, business leaders and entrepreneurs must prioritise many viewpoints to effectively address a wide array of challenges and issues, especially considering the recent crises triggered by the COVID-19 epidemic (Arora & Sharma, 2022). The Metaverse offers a potential option for social engagement and further development of educational activities (Arpacı & Bahari, 2023). The metaverse has the potential to bring the imagination to life by incorporating diverse technologies, serving as a platform for sustainable education that transcends the limitations of space and time. This can ensure that all learners have the same educational opportunities by establishing inventive educational atmospheres. Thus, enabling the achievement of SDG 4 (quality education) (Park & Kim, 2022). Non-fungible tokens (NFTs) which is a blockchain technology have enabled educational institutions to incentivize students by using NFTs as rewards. This is achieved via the automated processing of transaction information and the execution of buying and selling activities employing smart contract technology. The system facilitates the creation of recognition tiers and motivates students to earn NFT recognition awards (Wu & Liu, 2022). The educational applications of NFTs comprise, "textbooks", "micro-certificates", "transcripts and records", "scholarships and rights", "master classes and content creation", "learning experiences", "registration and data collecting", "patents", "innovation", and "research, art, payment, and deposit" (Wu & Liu, 2022).

The global fashion sector is valued at approximately US $1 trillion, making it one of the most environmentally unfriendly industries worldwide. The emergence of digital fashion offers the possibility to separate some essential elements of the fashion business from their physical dependencies. Given the surging interest in the metaverse, nonfungible tokens, the swift advancement of augmented reality (AR) and virtual reality (VR) technology, and the increasing involvement of prominent fashion brands in gaming, comprehending the commercial viability of digital fashion is becoming gradually essential (Schauman et al., 2023). Fashion brands use the metaverse to create brand credibility and attract new customers by generating and/or extending product ideas in virtual reality. Brand interest in the metaverse as an alternative channel rises with paid digital marketing prices. The metaverse offers the fashion industry a limitless online format for product and brand concept development, reaching new customer groups, a new multi-channel approach, more space for testing new products, developing the customer experience, holding their attention, etc (Alexandrova & Poddubnaya, 2023). This can significantly help in achieving SDG 12 (responsible production and consumption) and SDG 9 (industry, innovation, and infrastructure)

Metaverse implementations are beginning to appear in several sectors, offering improved industrial services and contributing to the development of a more sustainable society (Society 5.0). Simultaneously, there are numerous obstacles to the use of the metaverse (Tlili et al., 2023). Although the Metaverse encourages social engagement among users, there is a lack of understanding of the factors that impact its social viability (Arpacı et al., 2022). Nevertheless, there are still ethical, human, social, and cultural concerns about the impact of the Metaverse on the quality of human social relationships and its potential to transform the overall quality of life (Allam et al., 2022). The use of the metaverse in industries is still at an early stage, with most of the research being implemented in the education and health sectors.

Furthermore, there is an uneven spatial dispersion of research on the metaverse across many sectors, necessitating further international cooperation to promote the global adoption of the metaverse (Tlili et al., 2023).

METHODOLOGY

This study utilizes a qualitative research approach with an exploratory design to examine people's opinions of the metaverse and its possible influence on Sustainable Development Goals (SDGs). The research used a convenience sample method, specifically targeting about 10 to 15 people from various backgrounds, including academia, industry, and the public. The questionnaire aims to evaluate participants' comprehension of the metaverse, their knowledge of SDGs, and their perspectives on the potential impact of the metaverse on sustainable development.

A primary investigation was conducted, which was intentionally sent to students, researchers, academics, and professionals from several disciplines. The questionnaire aimed to examine participants' perspectives and viewpoints about the following topics: Metaverse awareness by formulating inquiries to evaluate participants' understanding of the metaverse. along with, presenting inquiries aimed at eliciting participants' viewpoints on how the metaverse impacts sustainable development, either by supporting it or hindering it. The process of data analysis will include content and narrative analysis, with a specific emphasis on discerning repetitive patterns, themes, and insights within the qualitative replies. The responses were not hampered and presented as it is. The findings are put together at the end of the discussion section. The study recognizes some limitations, such as the presence of sample bias and the inherent subjectivity of qualitative research.

RESULTS

Metaverse Understanding

In this section, the opinions of the participants about their understanding of the term metaverse and its applicability in various sectors are stated. The participants are asked to describe what they think when they hear the term "Metaverse" and what is its applicability in various sectors.

P1. "Metaverse is hypothetical reality stimulated with the help of the internet. It has its potential in the sectors like hospitality industry, marketing sector, and most significantly manufacturing firms."

P2. "Virtual 3D space"

P3. "The metaverse is a hypothetical, immersive 3D environment where we can experience life in ways, we would not be able to in the physical world. It is believed to be the next iteration of the internet, and it is taking AR/VR to the next level."

P4. "A communal virtual shared area that blends elements of social networking, online gaming, augmented reality, and virtual reality is referred to as the "metaverse". It is envisioned as an immersive, networked virtual world where users can communicate in real-time with virtual settings and one another."

P5. "Metaverse is a virtual world created using virtual and augmented reality. application in various sectors such as education, entertainment, real estate, shopping etc"

P6. "Metaverse is helpful in the achievement of 3D virtual space where humans experience life in ways they could not in the physical world."

P7. "My own digital world where I can interact with various people and can create our own virtual space. this can help in faster transmission of sensitive information as well as provide a secure space."

P8. "Metaverse is the virtual reality where you can create your virtual avatar and execute activities. Metaverse is the upcoming future and its application can be seen in various sections such as banking, gaming, real estate, healthcare sector etc."

P9. "Access points for the metaverse include general-purpose computers and smartphones, augmented reality, mixed reality, and virtual reality. Dependence on VR technology has limited metaverse development and wide-scale adoption."

P10. "The metaverse is like a big, shared digital space where you can play games, learn, work, and hang out with others using virtual reality. It could change how we do things online, making it more immersive and interactive in areas like gaming, education, work, and socializing."

Many of the respondents described the metaverse as a digital world where they can create their virtual world with the help of augmented reality and various other technologies. It was seen that the metaverse can be useful in almost all industries today be it technology-oriented or human-oriented like sports and healthcare.

SDG and Metaverse Linkage

This section highlights the linkages between the SDGs and metaverse technologies and the participants apprehension as specifically what SDGs can be achieved with the help of metaverse technologies

P1. "Yes, the metaverse will positively relate to SDG-9,11,12. Like usage metaverse will lead to industry, innovation, and infrastructure growth in terms of as creation of stimulations and will have less wastage in terms of actual concrete materials. Likewise, the metaverse will inculcate sustainability in terms of longer use of tools. Lastly, SDG-12 will benefit by creation of the products which are environmentally friendly and easy to use."

P2. "It will create a revolution in the education process by giving a real-life experience via online platforms."

P3. "Digital technologies have the potential to revolutionize education by making it more accessible, interactive, and personalized. The metaverse has the potential to contribute to the achievement of quality education in SDG 4."

P4. "There are various Sustainable Development Goals (SDGs) that the metaverse may help achieve. For example, it could improve accessibility to education through immersive learning, support environmental sustainability by eliminating the need for physical travel through virtual meetings, and promote international cooperation in the face of obstacles."

P5. "Quality education, life on land, affordable and clean energy"

P6. "Metaverse is helpful in achieving all SDGs"

P7. "Almost all the SDGs can be benefitted from the adoption of metaverse technologies. specifically, it can help in achieving the SDG 4, SDG 5, SDG 7, SDG 8, SDG 9, SDG11, SDG 12 and SDG 17 the most."

P8. "By providing virtual education, it can lead to quality education. By reducing a little of carbon footprint, it may also contribute to climate action."

P9. "Metaverse technology can accelerate the transmission of information. This accelerated speed can be directed towards the field of environmental research in general and towards research for carbon-neutral fuels in specific. This would create a sustainable world."

P10. "SDG 9"

From the opinions gathered it is quite clear that almost all the SDGs can be achieved with the help of metaverse technologies. Such as using metaverse in education for SDG 4, in the healthcare sector for SDG 3, and in industries such as manufacturing, hospitality, banking and commerce for SDG 8, SDG 9 and SDG 12.

Social, Environmental, and Economic Aspects

Further to highlight the three pillars of sustainability i.e., Social, economic and environmental participants were asked to provide their insights on how the metaverse influences social inclusivity, impacts the environment and promotes economic growth.

SOCIAL INCLUSIVITY THROUGH METAVERSE

P1. "Metaverse will adhere to inclusivity by managing the solving the conflicts among the diversity of the people. Moreover, through the metaverse, people can relate to the common problem and can empathize by helping others."

P2. "I don't think it can be of that much help to fill the gap. As people require proper training to utilize any kind of platform effectively and without any personal willpower, it's very difficult to get people of different sociocultural backgrounds on the same page."

P3. "The metaverse has the potential to play a significant role in promoting social justice and creating a more inclusive world. Through virtual experiences, people can interact with others from different backgrounds and cultures, learn about social issues, and participate in advocacy and activism."

P4. "The metaverse presents an opportunity to promote social inclusion and diversity by providing a virtual space where people from different socioeconomic origins and cultural backgrounds can interact and work together without being physically bound. It might present chances for international cooperation, language acquisition, and cross-cultural exchange."

P5. "The Metaverse could revolutionize social interactions, offering a novel platform for meaningful connections and reshaping the way people engage with each other."

P6. "The metaverse has the potential to enhance social inclusion by providing a platform for diverse cultural"

P7. "Metaverse can help in reducing the gaps among people which are the result of their cultural backgrounds and various socioeconomic factors by providing an equitable platform to all."

P8. "In my opinion, the metaverse will influence social inclusion and diversity making individuals interact with people with different cultural backgrounds and socio-economic factors in virtual reality by creating their avatars. It may be positive or negative."

P9. "Metaverse technology or any other technology for that matter, technology by nature is not inclusive. This is the truth because technology is never inclusively distributed. Rich people always have better technology at their disposal. Therefore, metaverse technology like any other technology would not create social inclusion and would not increase the acceptance of diversity in the society."

P10. "Metaverse provides a platform for different backgrounds and different cultures to interact with each other that is not possible in physical conditions."

Influence on the Environment

P1. "Metaverse will be like two sides of a coin having both negative and positive impacts on the environment. The overuse of it will lead to radiation and harm the environment. On the flip side, virtual designing likewise will help in decreasing the waste."

P2. "No, it will help the environment by reducing offline storage and reducing document work."

P3. "Metaverse could lead to an influx of greenhouse gas emissions. Virtual reality technology and data centres use AI and cloud services, which require quite large amounts of energy."

P4. "The development and broad application of the metaverse may give rise to environmental issues, especially when it comes to the higher energy requirements of data centres that host virtual worlds. The SDGs about environmental sustainability may be challenged by this increased demand for computer resources. To achieve these objectives, initiatives such as increasing awareness about reducing the carbon footprint connected to digital activities, investigating sustainable technologies, and optimizing energy efficiency in metaverse infrastructure should be undertaken."

P5. "Environmental impact of the Metaverse raises concerns, particularly in terms of increased energy consumption for server infrastructure and hardware production."

P6. "The metaverse could pose environmental concerns, particularly if the infrastructure supporting it relies heavily on energy-intensive technologies."

P7. "It can reduce paper waste, carbon emissions and industrial waste to some extent as people can meet and share in a virtual world thus helping in achieving environmental sustainability."

P8. "The potential environmental impact of the metaverse raises concerns about increased energy consumption, electronic waste, and resource usage. Balancing the development of the metaverse with sustainability goals outlined in the SDGs requires careful consideration of energy-efficient technologies, responsible resource management, and eco-friendly practices to minimize negative environmental effects. Achieving alignment involves prioritizing sustainable development practices, renewable energy sources, and circular economy principles within the metaverse infrastructure."

P9. "Symbolic one-rupee amounts have been allocated by the politicians towards environmental research. They do not give a fuck about the environment. But they should. The answer to your question is that as long as metaverse technology or any other technology runs on hydrocarbon fuels and not carbon-neutral fuels, the environment of our earth will not improve."

P10. "It will increase the emission of greenhouse gas that will challenge to achieve SDG goal 13."

CONTRIBUTION TO ECONOMIC DEVELOPMENT, JOB CREATION, AND ENTREPRENEURSHIP

P1. "It will have a increase the employability of people."

P2. "It will take away job of millions of people who have manual work like data entries, enquiries, front office jobs etc."

P3. "Economic empowerment is addressed through discussions on virtual economies within the Metaverse, highlighting opportunities for entrepreneurship, job creation, and financial inclusion. This exploration corresponds to SDG 1 (No Poverty), SDG 8 (Decent Work and Economic Growth), and SDG 10 (Reduced Inequality)."

P4. "The metaverse has the ability to boost the economy by opening up new doors for entrepreneurship and the creation of jobs. Jobs in virtual economies such as content creation, tech assistance, and virtual real estate development can be created within the metaverse. It might also make remote work and teamwork easier, advancing SDG 8 (Decent Work and Economic Growth). In line with SDG 9 (Industry, Innovation, and Infrastructure), metaverse platforms can help foster entrepreneurship and innovation in the ICT sector."

P5. "Metaverse has the potential to boost economic development by creating jobs, fostering entrepreneurship, and promoting innovation. This aligns with Sustainable Development Goals 8 and 9, focusing on decent work, economic growth, and industry, innovation, and infrastructure."

P6. "This can lead to the growth of a digital economy, creating jobs and supporting entrepreneurial ventures."

P7. "Metaverse require certain IT skills and innovation which can lead to job creation requiring such skills in various industries. as innovation often creates entrepreneurship which further leads to more jobs hence overall economic development will benefit from it."

P8. "The metaverse has the potential to contribute significantly to economic development, job creation, and entrepreneurship in alignment with Sustainable Development Goals (SDGs) 8 and 9. It can facilitate remote work, enabling a global talent pool, fostering inclusivity, and reducing geographical constraints. Virtual economies within the metaverse can stimulate entrepreneurship through innovative business models, creating diverse employment opportunities. Developments in virtual infrastructure can support sustainable urban planning and reduce environmental impact, aligning with SDGs focused on industry, innovation, and sustainable cities."

P9. "Metaverse technology like any other technology is being built by the big private companies. The leader is Microsoft. But not counting the IIT and IIM class companies, the normal private companies would continue to run the status quo. The answer to your question about SDG 8 and the phrase decent work would remain an ideal only achieved after death. The normal sons and daughters would still not find decent work. I do not consider Rs. 30,000 jobs with 24-hour by seven days disrespect towards the employee as jobs. You have a job on paper. The dark truth is that you are a contract labour."

P10. "The distorting of actual and virtual boundaries will lead to increased purchases and language in the metaverse, which will accelerate global economic development. The experiences that society has with virtual professions that offer significant value will be preserved by a virtual economy."

The participants provided some positive and some negative perspectives on the influence of metaverse technologies in creating a more inclusive society which is environmentally sustainable and promotes economic growth which are discussed in the findings section of this chapter in detail.

What Can Be Done for the Future

When the participants were asked what could be done in the future they thought of some specific actions or initiatives within the metaverse that they believe individuals and organizations should undertake to contribute positively to the SDGs following were their answers.

P1. "All the educational certificates and libraries can be in one single place for easy access all around the world."

P2. "The public sector, the private sector, and the academicians must work together to raise awareness in this area. It is clear that when all of these activities come together, they create a more substantial impact."

P3. "No, the Sustainable Development Goals (SDGs) can be favourably impacted by encouraging digital inclusivity, virtual space education, and sustainable metaverse activities."

P4. "Metaverse promotes diversity and creates virtual spaces aligned with social and environmental goals. This involves supporting ethical virtual businesses, developing educational platforms, and fostering global collaborations within the virtual realm. Integrating sustainability principles into the Metaverse design and operation is key for a meaningful impact on SDG achievement."

P5. "To provide more security guidelines and regulations so that by wrong persons these technologies should not be misused. Another thing that requires attention from various relevant authorities and organizations is to act regarding the awareness among people about metaverse and different usage and application of metaverse."

P6. "1. Inclusivity: Ensure equitable access to the metaverse, addressing digital divides and making virtual spaces accessible to diverse populations.

2. Educational Initiatives: Promote digital literacy and skills development programs within the metaverse to empower individuals and communities, aligning with SDG 4 (Quality Education).

3. Sustainable Practices: Implement environmentally conscious measures in the development and maintenance of virtual worlds, supporting SDG 13 (Climate Action).

4. Diversity and Inclusion: Foster diverse representation in virtual environments, promoting inclusivity and combating discrimination, contributing to SDG 5 (Gender Equality) and SDG 10 (Reduced Inequality).

5. Social Impact Ventures: Support or create virtual projects and businesses that address social and environmental challenges, contributing to SDGs such as SDG 1 (No Poverty) and SDG 3 (Good Health and Well-being).

6. Data Ethics: Prioritize user privacy and data ethics in metaverse development, aligning with SDG 16 (Peace, Justice, and Strong Institutions)."

P7. "Organisations have never, do not and would never give a damn about environment, sustainability and such other ideals."

P8. "No Idea."

P9. "Metaverse will contribute to increasing the global economy which will help to reduce poverty, increase jobs, and increase technological infrastructure."

P10. "Metaverse can help in building more resilient societies and can promote peace and prosperity."

The respondents urged to focus on ethical issues and data privacy which are big concerns regarding the use of AI technologies such as metaverse itself. Furthermore, the environmental impact of these machinery should also be looked at. Strict laws and regulations adhering to the production and usage of these technologies should be implemented.

INTEGRATION OF FINDINGS

The "metaverse" is a shared virtual world created by combining physical and virtual reality, which includes Virtual meetings, gaming, education, social interactions, business, and other digital activities. Metaverse has the potential to achieve almost all the 17 sustainable development goals. The goals which can benefit the most from the emergence of metaverse technologies are SDG 3 (good health and wellbeing) by incorporating metaverse in healthcare, SDG 4 (quality education) by bringing virtual reality to the classrooms, SDG 7 (Affordable and green energy) through technological advancements focused on enhancing energy efficiency in server facilities and overall infrastructure that supports virtual experiences. Further, it can also help in achieving SDG 8 (Decent Work and Economic Growth) and SDG 9 (Industry, Innovation, and Infrastructure) by fostering more job opportunities and innovations in almost every industry be it finance, retail, manufacturing, commerce, healthcare, agriculture, and business etc. lastly, metaverse can help in achieving SDG 10 (Reduced Inequality) by providing equitable access to digital experiences and SDG 17 (partnership for goals) as collaboration between public and private organizations is often necessary for the advancement of the metaverse. Collaboration among governments, technology corporations, and other stakeholders in developing the metaverse could support both the inclusivity and sustainability of virtual worlds.

When we talk about the three pillars of sustainability that is social inclusion, environmental sustainability, and economic growth all three of them can be achieved through metaverse technologies. Metaverse provides a safe and sound platform which is free from any discrimination and cultural barriers and hence can support social inclusivity. As we are approaching a world where more environmentally conscious practices are appreciated and needed in almost every industry and even in day-to-day life metaverse can be very helpful. However, teaching people these technologies and getting them to use them in real life is still a challenge that requires attention from policymakers and practitioners in the field of metaverse.

Metaverse plays a very crucial role in the environmental aspect of sustainable development. On the positive side where using these technologies such as virtual meetings and interactions has the potential to decrease the need for actual travel, which results in decreased carbon emissions linked with travel and transportation. Metaverse can also provide remote work opportunities which can lower the need for huge office buildings and associated environmental expenses. On the negative side, the creation and maintenance of virtual worlds, notably those that need detailed visualizations and computational aspects, may lead to high consumption of energy. Additionally, the manufacturing of hardware components for virtual reality equipment and other technologies used in the metaverse may include the extraction and utilization of materials that have environmental consequences and can create electronic waste if not handled appropriately. to overcome these developers should prioritize the use of renewable energy sources and the integration of energy-efficient technology while building and managing metaverse infrastructure. The focus should be on promoting virtual collaboration and interactions to minimize the need for physical travel. The authorities should Implement and make sure that everyone is following strict environmental regulations in the creation and operation of metaverse technologies which could help in reducing negative impacts. The contribution of the metaverse to economic development, job creation, and entrepreneurship is multifaceted. Metaverse enables economic development by facilitating the emergence of new industries and markets. These can include virtual properties, virtual goods and services, digital artwork, and many more. The metaverse necessitates ongoing technological advancement, resulting in increased demand for research and development projects. Consequently, this attracts investments and develops a culture of technical progress, which is crucial for economic growth. Metaverse can create more tech-savvy job opportunities as it requires software developers, graphic designers, UX designers, and others to build and maintain the metaverse. Metaverse virtual currencies, markets, and assets may provide finance, economics, and analytics professionals with new job opportunities as well. Virtual experiences, gaming, art, and events fuel the metaverse. Creative professionals like content creators, 3D modellers, animators, and authors get employment opportunities which overall helps in economic development. Metaverse is primarily dependent on technology, which offers the potential for businesses to innovate and create new apps, platforms, and tools to improve the virtual experience. Entrepreneurs can create and operate businesses within the metaverse by producing virtual goods, services, and experiences.

It is crucial to acknowledge the obstacles such as digital inequality, data privacy concerns, and regulatory issues which need attention so that equitable distribution of the positive aspects of the metaverse can be guaranteed. Furthermore, the long-term effects of the metaverse on employment and business creation are going to depend on how societies adapt and handle these new technologies. Like any other research, ours is also not free from any limitations. First, the sampling technique chosen for the following research is convenience sampling to get the results which can lead to sample bias. Another, limitation of the research is purely qualitative hence it adheres to the limitation of qualitative research as well. Additionally, the limitation of qualitative research can impact the output of this research, as it is based on people's opinions which can vary from place to place and time to time.

Future Directions and Policy Implications

The metaverse has the potential to improve social inclusion by offering a platform for people from different backgrounds to engage with one another, regardless of their geographical location. Nevertheless, there may be difficulties in guaranteeing accessibility, tackling cultural complexes, and minimizing the possibility of excluding certain groups of people. Efforts must be taken to actively encourage inclusion, diversity, and cultural sensitivity in the planning and management of metaverse environments. The environmental implications of the metaverse revolve around heightened energy usage in data centres, device production, and electronic trash accumulation. Green data centres and sustainable technology practices are going to be crucial to mitigate negative impacts. The metaverse can enhance economic growth by establishing fresh markets, generating employment opportunities, and assisting in entrepreneurial endeavours. Nevertheless, it is essential to thoroughly analyse and tackle the possibility of job loss and skill deficiency, while also guaranteeing equitable economic participation, particularly for vulnerable communities. Virtual volunteering, educational courses, and responsible digital citizenship initiatives may bolster the metaverse's contribution to accomplishing the Sustainable Development Goals (SDGs). To summarize, the development and acceptance of the metaverse provide a multitude of possibilities and difficulties in many aspects, necessitating a deliberate and all-encompassing strategy to assure compatibility with the Sustainable Development Goals.

CONCLUSION

As discussed above metaverse can be proved a very useful tool in attaining so many SDGs such as SDG 4 (quality education), SDG 5(women's empowerment), SDG 8 (decent work and economic growth), SDG 12 (responsible production and consumption) and SDG 17 (partnership for achieving all goals) etc. metaverse can not only provide a platform for people from all around the world to gather at one platform but also share their experiences, knowledge and create a community from which everyone can benefit. It was also found in the study that most of the participants just limited the term metaverse to virtual reality. But it is an umbrella term which encompasses much more. The respective organizations and authorities should focus more on educating the people about the uses of metaverse technologies in various sectors so that their full potential can be harnessed to create a sustainable environment. We are still learning how the metaverse fits into sustainable development, and scholars are examining the positive and negative aspects. This area must balance technical innovation and global sustainability as it progresses for a more sustainable future.

REFERENCES

Al-Emran, M. (2023). Beyond technology acceptance: Development and evaluation of technology-environmental, economic, and social sustainability theory. *Technology in Society, 75*, 102383. doi:10.1016/j.techsoc.2023.102383

Alexandrova, E., & Poddubnaya, M. (2023). Metaverse in fashion industry development: applications and challenges. *E3S Web of Conferences, 420*, 06019. doi:10.1051/e3sconf/202342006019

Allam, Z., Sharifi, A., Bibri, S. E., Jones, D. S., & Krogstie, J. (2022). The Metaverse as a virtual form of smart Cities: Opportunities and challenges for environmental, economic, and social sustainability in urban futures. *Smart Cities, 5*(3), 771–801. doi:10.3390/smartcities5030040

Arora, M. (2024). Virtual Reality in Education Analyzing the literature and bibliometric state of knowledge. In *Transforming Education with Virtual Reality* (pp. 379–402). Wiley. doi:10.1002/9781394200498.ch22

Arora, M., & Chandel, M. (2023). SDGs and Skill Development: Perspectivizing future insights for the tourism industry. In Springer international handbooks of education (pp. 1–20). Springer. doi:10.1007/978-981-99-3895-7_26-1

Arora, M., Dhiman, V., & Sharma, R. L. (2023). Exploring the Dimensions of Spirituality, Wellness and Value Creation amidst Himalayan Regions Promoting Entrepreneurship and Sustainability. *Journal of Tourismology*. doi:10.26650/jot.2023.9.2.1327877

Arora, M., & Sharma, R. L. (2022). Artificial intelligence and big data: Ontological and communicative perspectives in multi-sectoral scenarios of modern businesses. *Foresight, 25*(1), 126–143. doi:10.1108/FS-10-2021-0216

Arpacı, İ., & Bahari, M. (2023). Investigating the role of psychological needs in predicting the educational sustainability of Metaverse using a deep learning-based hybrid SEM-ANN technique. *Interactive Learning Environments*, 1–13. doi:10.1080/10494820.2022.2164313

Go, H., & Kang, M. (2022). Metaverse tourism for sustainable tourism development: Tourism Agenda 2030. *Tourism Review, 78*(2), 381–394. doi:10.1108/TR-02-2022-0102

Jung, T., Cho, J., Han, D. D., Ahn, S. J., Gupta, M., Das, G. D., Heo, C. Y., Loureiro, S. M. C., Σιγάλα, M., Trunfio, M., Taylor, A., & Dieck, M. C. T. (2024). Metaverse for service industries: Future applications, opportunities, challenges and research directions. *Computers in Human Behavior, 151*, 108039. doi:10.1016/j.chb.2023.108039

Maden, A., & Yücenur, G. N. (2024). Evaluation of sustainable metaverse characteristics using scenario-based fuzzy cognitive map. *Computers in Human Behavior, 152*, 108090. doi:10.1016/j.chb.2023.108090

Ooi, K., Tan, G. W., Aw, E. C., Cham, T., Dwivedi, Y. K., Dwivedi, R., Hughes, L., Kar, A. K., Loh, X., Mogaji, E., Phau, I., & Sharma, A. (2023). Banking in the metaverse: A new frontier for financial institutions. *International Journal of Bank Marketing, 41*(7), 1829–1846. doi:10.1108/IJBM-03-2023-0168

Pachouri, V., Singh, R., Gehlot, A., Pandey, S., Akram, S. V., & Abbas, M. I. (2024). Empowering sustainability in the built environment: A technological Lens on industry 4.0 Enablers. *Technology in Society, 76*, 102427. doi:10.1016/j.techsoc.2023.102427

Park, S., & Kim, S. (2022). Identifying world types to deliver gameful experiences for sustainable learning in the metaverse. *Sustainability (Basel), 14*(3), 1361. doi:10.3390/su14031361

Schauman, S., Greene, S. K., & Korkman, O. (2023). Sufficiency and the dematerialization of fashion: How digital substitutes are creating new market opportunities. *Business Horizons, 66*(6), 741–751. doi:10.1016/j.bushor.2023.03.003

Tlili, A., Huang, R., & Kinshuk, K. (2023). Metaverse for climbing the ladder toward 'Industry 5.0' and 'Society 5.0'? *Service Industries Journal, 43*(3–4), 260–287. doi:10.1080/02642069.2023.2178644

World Commission on Environment and Development (WCED). (1987). *Our Common Future (Brundtland Report)*. United Nations. https://sustainabledevelopment.un.org

Wu, C., & Liu, C. (2022). Educational Applications of Non-Fungible Token (NFT). *Sustainability (Basel), 15*(1), 7. doi:10.3390/su15010007

Zaman, U., Koo, I., Abbasi, S., Raza, S. H., & Qureshi, M. G. (2022). Meet your digital twin in space? Profiling international expat's readiness for metaverse space travel, Tech-Savviness, COVID-19 travel anxiety, and travel fear of missing out. *Sustainability (Basel), 14*(11), 6441. doi:10.3390/su14116441

Chapter 5
Human Resource Management in the Metaverse Era:
A Bibliometric Analysis and Future Research Agenda

Sahil Sharma
https://orcid.org/0000-0002-0139-254X
Central University of Himachal Pradesh, India

Anu Sohal
https://orcid.org/0000-0003-4737-0992
Central University of Himachal Pradesh, India

ABSTRACT

The advent of the metaverse offers human resource management both new opportunities and challenges as digital technologies continue to progress. To examine the state of HRM research in the metaverse era and pinpoint significant themes and gaps in the body of literature, this study conducts a bibliometric analysis. The authors examine the distribution of articles, authors, journals, and keywords associated with HRM in the context of the metaverse through a methodical examination of scholarly publications from the Scopus database. This research indicates an increasing amount of interest in this field, with studies concentrating on digital leadership, people management, remote work, and virtual collaboration. The authors offer a research agenda for the future to fill in these knowledge gaps and improve comprehension of HRM in the metaverse era. This study adds to the expanding corpus of research on HRM in digital contexts and offers insightful guidance on how to navigate the potential and difficulties presented by the metaverse for scholars, practitioners, and policymakers.

INTRODUCTION

Recent years have seen remarkable growth in technology, which has completely changed many aspects of human life, including how we communicate and work together. The rise of the Metaverse, a virtual

DOI: 10.4018/979-8-3693-2607-7.ch005

environment where users may communicate in real-time with digital items and each other, is one of the most exciting advances in this field. As it presents previously unheard-of chances for cooperation, invention, and creativity, this virtual environment is becoming a more interesting subject for interdisciplinary study (Bennet & McWhorter, 2022). Given the increasing attention being paid to the metaverse, its implications must be investigated for several fields, one of which is human resource management (HRM). Managing an organization's most precious asset, its people, is the responsibility of HRM. HRM procedures must adapt as technology continues to change the workplace (Arora, 2020).

Technological advancements have increased learning capacity and performance, which has changed how workers interact with one another and their jobs (Chaudhary et al., 2023). Within this framework, the metaverse offers HRM new and exciting opportunities for hiring, development, teamwork, and employee engagement. However, to fully utilise the metaverse in HRM, it is imperative to comprehend the existing state of study in this field, identify important themes and trends, and suggest possible directions for further investigation.

The metaverse is set to transform many elements of management and the workplace, including human resource management. It will profoundly transform how people interact and operate in virtual settings, affecting the recruitment, training, and performance review processes. The metaverse will demand new methods of staff training and assistance, supplied through fresh channels. This transition will also transform workplace productivity and engagement tactics. Onboarding and training in the metaverse will take place in remote, risk-free environments, giving managers hands-on experience and allowing them to resolve concerns more efficiently. Overall, Bloomberg Intelligence predicts that the metaverse will generate a major business opportunity, with revenues reaching USD 800 billion by the end of 2024 (Koohang et al., 2023).

As research into human resource management and the metaverse evolves, advanced research approaches will be required to meet the expectations of both industry and academia. Currently in its early phases, research in the area is projected to progress, resulting in a better understanding of the metaverse's impact on HR management. The ability for users to enter virtual office settings while interacting with digital avatars of employees constitutes a major change in HR management, providing a more personalized experience and insight into organizational culture. The metaverse's ability to recreate real-world surroundings makes it useful for a variety of HR services such as recruitment, training, employee relations, and regulatory compliance, big corporate firms will benefit from this optimal utilisation of human resources (Arora & Sharma, 2023). This innovative approach to working in the metaverse has the potential to alter hybrid work patterns by allowing for remote collaboration and true participation.

Metaverse

Metaverse, a term first coined by Neal Stephenson in 1992, is the 3D iteration of the internet which is facilitated by VR (Virtual Reality) and AR (Augmented Reality) technologies. The metaverse architecture is composed of different technologies like machine learning, blockchain, and 3-D graphics and is usually used via VR-enabled headsets like *Apple Vision Pro* and *Meta Oculus*. Initially developed as a concept for playing interactive video games, the metaverse has split into many contours (Yilmaz et al., 2023). Started with interactive meetings, the metaverse technology has now applications in productivity, learning environments, e-commerce, healthcare, and but not limited to, real estate. The COVID-19 situation triggered the need for exponential development of virtual technologies. Though already in existence, the companies' view towards virtual technologies tilted positively, after the pandemic. *Meta* is pioneering the haptics technology as well which will enable users to feel texture, pressure, and movement as well.

The concept of the metaverse has roots dating back to Stephenson's novel "Snow Crash" (1992), where the term was first introduced almost 30 years ago. Over time, various scholars have attempted to define the metaverse, with definitions shaped by the technological landscape of their era. Dickey (1999) defines the metaverse as "The ultimate 3D interactive world in which users interact (by way of realistic-looking avatars) in a fully immersive virtual world" (p. 40). This definition emphasizes the immersive and interactive qualities of the metaverse, wherein users navigate and engage with virtual environments using avatars. Schlemmer & Backes (2015) provide a definition stating that "The word metaverse is a compound word with "meta", meaning "beyond", and "verse" as an abbreviation for "universe", thus constituting a virtual reality universe" (p. 49). This definition highlights the metaverse's vast and comprehensive nature, suggesting it as a realm beyond traditional conceptions of reality. The latest definition is given by Kevin (2022) explaining the metaverse as "a network of interconnected experiences and applications, devices and products, tools and infrastructure".

Some individuals perceive the metaverse as simply a rebranding of VR or AR. However, it encompasses far more than these technologies alone (Park & Kim, 2022). The framework for a metaverse (see Figure 1), explaining that the metaverse varies from traditional VR or AR systems in three important ways: "shared," "persistent," and "de-centralized." Sharedness refers to user interactions in a virtual environment, whereas persistence refers to the ability to live, work, study, and create in the virtual world continuously. Decentralization, as enabled by technology such as blockchains, assures the security and integrity of economic activity and personal property. These capabilities need the use of artificial intelligence (AI) to enforce creator-defined rules and provide immersive experiences. Systems that lack these traits, such as single-user VR training systems, are not considered part of the metaverse, which stresses multi-user interactions and persistent virtual life (Hwang & Chien, 2022).

Figure 1. The framework of a metaverse
Source: *Hwang & Chien (2022)*

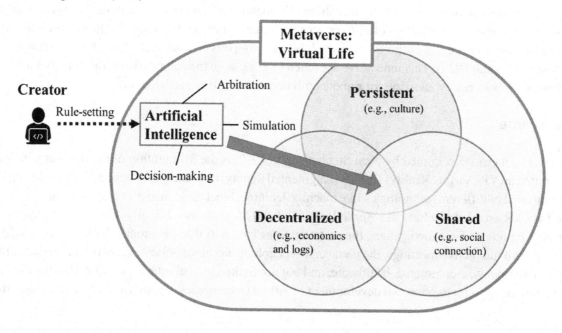

Metaverse and Human Resources

Metaverse seems to be a boon to employee productivity with enhanced teamwork and collaboration. *Accenture* uses the metaverse for onboarding and convening remote work, *BMW* for creative collaboration, *Hyundai* for training the workers, etc. The concept of 'digital human' is being researched for better collaboration between human resources (Yu et al., 2022). The training component of human resource management is witnessing a revolution through the metaverse, especially in the medical field among other domains. The use of metaverse in training increases the efficacy of the training programs to a greater extent (Hajjami & Park, 2023). Immersive reality platforms have gained attraction due to a lack of engagement on 2D interactive platforms like *Google Meet*. By creating a digital avatar for employees, companies can simulate real-life scenarios, thus creating more engagement. Metaverse also solves the loss of informal and spontaneous conversations in 2D virtual platforms.

In any organization, human capital is an important factor for adopting new technologies. As the metaverse continues to grow, conventional professions like real estate companies, professionals in event management, designers, content creators, and architects are transitioning into virtual realms by adapting and acquiring new skills relevant to operating in the metaverse (Vig, 2023). The metaverse also offers a dynamic learning environment where employees can engage in immersive training programs, simulations, and virtual classrooms (Arora, 2024; Dutta et al., 2023). Moreover, with the help of the metaverse, teams can come together in virtual environments to brainstorm ideas, work on projects, and solve problems in real-time, regardless of geographic boundaries. Virtual meeting places can be customized to replicate various work settings, from boardrooms to casual coffee shops, allowing for natural and spontaneous interactions that boost team cohesion and innovation. The metaverse also improves employees' well-being by providing a virtual office environment that aids in time management and work-life balance, fostering a sense of community among employees, and providing positive experiences through virtual spaces for relaxation and socialization, thereby reducing feelings of isolation (Arora & Rathore, 2023; Park et al., 2023).

The principal aim of this study is to present a comprehensive summary of the existing body of research on the relationship between the metaverse and human resources. The purpose of this study is to investigate the scope and depth of this topic by addressing the following questions:

RQ1. In what ways has scholarly inquiry assessed the connection between human resource management and the metaverse?

RQ2. Which studies are important and what research themes are most prevalent in this field?

RQ3. Which conceptual frameworks or structures serve as the foundation for the research done in this area?

By answering these questions, we hope to shed light on the status of the metaverse and HRM research at the moment, point out areas that still need to be investigated and suggest a path forward for future studies in this emerging subject. In the end, this research aims to further knowledge about how the metaverse might transform HRM procedures and result in more creative and successful methods of managing human resources in the digital era.

RESEARCH METHODOLOGY

Search Strategy and Data Retrieval Process

Figure 2 illustrates the data retrieval process extracted from the Scopus database, highlighting the systematic approach used to retrieve relevant literature for analysis. The data extracted from the Scopus database were analyzed using the R 4.03 package programme "Biblioshiny", which is an R-based package and web application designed specifically for bibliometric analysis (Nazma et al., 2023). Unlike other traditional literature reviews, bibliometric reviews emphasize the visualization and analysis of substantial amounts of literature-specific data, providing deeper thoughts into research trends and patterns (Donthu et al., 2021).

Analysis Method

A bibliometric analysis was performed to analyse the dynamics of human resources in the metaverse world. The bibliometric analysis is a useful technique for academics to systematically investigate and analyse large volumes of literature, as it provides insights into the dynamics and trajectory of scholarly discourse within a given area (Dhiman & Arora, 2024). The final search was realized in February 2024 on the Scopus database using the keywords "metaverse" AND "human resource management" OR "HRM" OR "human resource". To achieve the objectives outlined in the study, the science mapping method was used, which is the combination of "classification and visualization" (Boyack & Klavans, 2014) using the RStudio software (Aria & Cuccurullo, 2017). Classification methods are used to categorize and organize information (such as publications, documents, countries, and journals), whereas visualization tools are used to represent the classified data in a graphical format (Zupic & Cater, 2015).

Figure 2. Data retrieval process
Source: *Created by the authors*

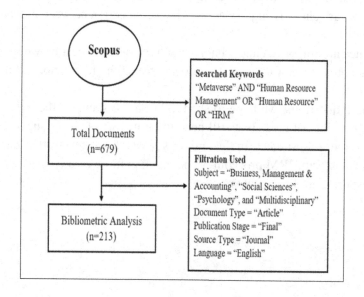

In the present study, the objectives will be addressed through the application of performance analysis techniques using bibliometric methods.

RESULTS

Figure 3 provides a brief overview of the bibliometric analysis conducted on a dataset comprising 213 selected documents spanning from 2009 to 2024. The analysis reveals that research on the intersection of the metaverse and human resources has garnered considerable attention, with 131 distinct journals showing receptivity to this area of study. There has been an annual growth rate of 26.75% in publications on this topic, highlighting its increasing significance over time. These journals collectively feature a total of 706 authors, 898 authors' keywords, and 16,987 references. Out of 213 documents, 36 documents are solo-authored, depicting a prevalent trend of collaboration among researchers in the field. Moreover, this overview represents that there is 43.66% international co-authorship, highlighting the collaborative efforts among researchers across different geographical locations. As of February 2024, the average number of citations per document stands at 6.023, indicating the impact and influence of research in this burgeoning field.

Performance Analysis

3.1.1. Publication Trends

Figure 4 illustrates the annual distribution of publications spanning from 2009-2023. It was found that the first article related to this topic was published back in 2009, followed by a significant gap until 2012. Figure 4 represents that up to 2020, there was a dearth of publications in this domain. However, in 2022, there was a substantial increase in the number of published articles (34). The reason could be the increase in the trend of application of metaverse in human-computer interaction (Hwang & Chien,

Figure 3. Descriptive summary of 213 documents for bibliometric analysis
Source: *Extracted from RStudio*

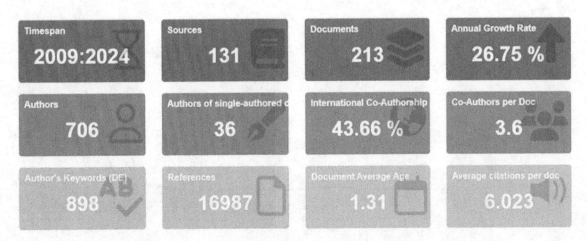

2022). The year 2023 was the most productive in terms of total production count (134). As for 2024, the published articles were not depicted due to non-completion of the year, but it is worth noting that around 35 research articles were published in January-February 2024.

3.1.2. Publication Outlets

Table 1 provides an overview of the top 10 leading journals publishing articles related to metaverse and human resources. The most prominent journal in this field is the *Contemporary Readings in Law and Social Justice,* which is a US-based journal having the highest number of published articles (29) on the subject of social sciences. It was followed by the Switzerland journal *Sustainability,* with a total number of 10 publications, and the US-based *Technological Forecasting and Social Change,* with 6 publications.

Figure 4. Annual publication trend between period 2009-2023. Data for 2024 (January-February) is not depicted for the publication trend due to the non-completion of the year.
Source: *Authors' compilation (Data retrieved from Scopus on February 2024)*

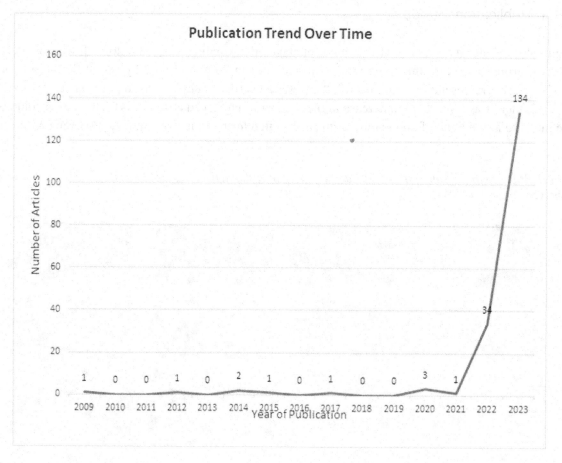

Table 1. The top ten leading journals

Source Title	Country	h-index	NP	Subject Area
Contemporary Readings in Law and Social Justice	United States	16	29	Social Sciences
Sustainability (Switzerland)	Switzerland	136	10	Computer Science, Energy, Environment Science, Social Sciences
Technological Forecasting and Social Change	United States	155	6	Psychology and Business, Management, and Accounting
Computers in Human Behavior	United Kingdom	226	5	Psychology, Arts and Humanities, and Computer Science
Journal of Cleaner Production	United Kingdom	268	4	Business, Management, and Accounting, Energy, Engineering, Environmental Science
Journal of Open Innovation: Technology, Market, and Complexity	Switzerland	38	4	Social Sciences, Economics, Econometrics and Finance
Journal of Business Research	United States	236	3	Business, Management, and Accounting
Psychology and Marketing	United States	133	3	Psychology and Business, Management, and Accounting
International Journal of Contemporary Hospitality Management	United Kingdom	113	2	Business, Management, and Accounting
Organizational Psychology Review	United States	36	2	Psychology and Business, Management, and Accounting

Note: NP = Number of publications (among a pool of 213 articles)
Source: Authors' compilation from SCOPUS database

3.1.3. Most Cited Articles

Table 2 presents the top 10 highly cited articles in the field of metaverse and human resources based on global citations. "Global Citation" is the total number of Scopus citations for a publication, whereas "Local Citation" is the number of times a manuscript has been cited by other papers within the 213 documents network (Fahimnia et al., 2015). As per global citations, article by Dwivedi et al. (2023) titled ""*So what if ChatGPT wrote it?" Multidisciplinary perspectives on opportunities, challenges and implications of generative conversational AI for research, practice and policy*" is the most cited article, with a total number of 474 citations. It is followed by Buhalis et al. (2023) titled *"Smart hospitality: from smart cities and smart tourism towards agile business ecosystems in networked destinations"* and Lăzăroiu et al. (2022), titled *"Artificial intelligence-based decision-making algorithms, Internet of Things sensing networks, and sustainable cyber-physical management systems in big data-driven cognitive manufacturing"*, with a total global citation of 54 and 50 respectively.

3.1.4. Most Cited Countries

Table 3 presents the leading countries in the realms of metaverse and human resources. According to total citations, the United Kingdom emerges as the most cited country, boasting the highest count of 595 citations, with an average annual citation of 22.0 and 76 published articles. It was followed by Romania with the second-highest citation count of 115, with an average annual citation of 7.20 and 32 published articles. According to the number of published articles, China, India, the UK, and the USA, stand out as the leading countries. China has dominated the research field with the highest production, contributing 87 research articles, followed closely by India with 80 articles, the UK with 76 articles, and the USA with 71 articles.

Table 2. The top ten most cited articles

Author(s)	Article Title	Local Citations*	Global Citations**
Dwivedi et al. (2023)	"So what if ChatGPT wrote it?" Multidisciplinary perspectives on opportunities, challenges and implications of generative conversational AI for research, practice and policy	15	474
Buhalis et al. (2023)	Smart hospitality: from smart cities and smart tourism towards agile business ecosystems in networked destinations	0	54
Lăzăroiu et al. (2022)	Artificial intelligence-based decision-making algorithms, Internet of Things sensing networks, and sustainable cyber-physical management systems in big data-driven cognitive manufacturing	0	50
Pellas & Kazanidis (2015)	On the value of Second Life for students' engagement in blended and online courses: A comparative study from the Higher Education in Greece	0	45
Polas et al. (2022)	Artificial Intelligence, Blockchain Technology, and Risk-Taking Behavior in the 4.0IR Metaverse Era: Evidence from Bangladesh-Based SMEs	3	33
McKenzie et al. (2012)	User-generated online content 1: Overview, current state and context	0	32
Kraus et al. (2023)	From moon landing to metaverse: Tracing the evolution of Technological Forecasting and Social Change	0	26
Tlili et al. (2023)	Metaverse for climbing the ladder toward 'Industry 5.0' and 'Society 5.0'?	1	25
Novak et al. (2022)	Big Data-driven Governance of Smart Sustainable Intelligent Transportation Systems: Autonomous Driving Behaviors, Predictive Modeling Techniques, and Sensing and Computing Technologies	3	23
Sharifi et al. (2023)	Progress and prospects in planning: A bibliometric review of literature in Urban Studies and Regional and Urban Planning	0	20

*Local Citation: citation within the 213 documents
**Global Citation: actual citation of SCOPUS
Source: Authors' compilation from the SCOPUS database

Table 3. The top ten highly cited countries

Country	TC	AAC	TP
United Kingdom	595	22.00	76
Romania	115	7.20	32
China	73	3.60	87
Canada	64	8.00	20
Italy	60	12.00	17
USA	59	3.30	71
Bangladesh	36	12.00	8
India	28	1.90	80
Australia	27	5.40	17
Japan	20	20.00	1

Note: TC = Total Citation; AAC = Average Annual Citation; TP = Total Publication
Source: Extracted from RStudio

Conceptual Structure Through Science Mapping

3.2.1. Co-Occurrence Network Analysis

Figure 5 presents the network analysis of authors' keywords, which are selected and created by the authors of the research articles to reflect the important content provided in the publication. Co-occurrence analysis finds a discipline's overarching themes by creating thematic connections with other keywords (Dhiman & Arora, 2023). This analysis provided a dataset of 36 keywords which were divided into six clusters, each representing different thematic areas within the research domain:

Cluster 1 (purple) – The first cluster has a total of 11 keywords such as artificial intelligence (AI), human, article, learning, humans, human experiment, adult, education, female, male, and controlled study. The most frequent keywords that appeared within the cluster are "human", "articles", and "learning" which suggests a focus on exploring how AI and human-centric learning methodologies intersect within the context of the metaverse.

Cluster 2 (green) – The second cluster has a total of 7 keywords such as virtual reality (VR), human computer interaction, behavioural research, design, marketing, business research, and communication. The most frequent keywords that appeared within the cluster are "virtual reality" and "human computer interaction". This cluster indicates a focus on understanding user experiences, behaviour, and interactions within virtual environments.

Cluster 3 (red) – The third cluster has a total of 6 keywords such as sustainable development, innovation, sustainability, literature review, commerce, and knowledge management. The most frequent keywords observed within the cluster are "sustainable development" and "innovation". This cluster suggests an interest in exploring how the metaverse can contribute to sustainable innovations and knowledge-sharing practices.

Cluster 4 (blue) – The fourth cluster has a total of 7 keywords that include metaverses, augmented reality (AR), computation theory, decision making, consumer behaviour, and decisions making. The most frequent keyword observed within the cluster is "metaverses". This cluster indicates a focus on the technological aspects of the metaverse, particularly how AR and decision-making algorithms impact human interactions and experiences.

The other two clusters are comparatively small in size. The fifth cluster (yellow) has a total of only 3 keywords that include block-chain, blockchain, and digital storage. The last and smallest cluster has only 2 keywords, supply chain management and efficiency. Despite limited keywords, these two clusters point towards a focused inquiry into the role of blockchain and supply chain management within the field of metaverse.

Moreover, the various keywords in all the clusters, the keywords such as "human", "articles", "learning", "virtual reality", metaverses", "innovation", and "sustainable development" exhibit high frequencies of occurrence. This suggests that these keywords serve as a research hotspot within the realm of the nexus of metaverse and human resources. Further, they demonstrate strong connections with other keywords, as indicated by their large circle size, underscoring their high relevance in the field.

3.2.2. Thematic Map and Future Scope

The authors conducted an additional analysis to strengthen the findings and provide guidance for future research. The "bibliometrix" package in RStudio software provides an evolution of themes and thematic

Figure 5. Co-occurrence network
Source: *Extracted from RStudio*

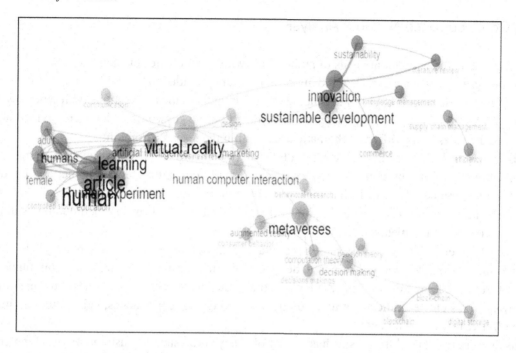

maps (Dhiman & Arora, 2023). The themes in the map are divided into four quadrants based on their centrality and density (see Figure 6). According to Cobo et al. (2011), the bottom right and left quadrants show emerging or underlying and crucial themes, whereas the top right and left quadrants are categorized as specialized and developed themes.

The upper left quadrant of the analysis represents the niche themes that have been developed but remain somewhat isolated within the research landscape. The themes covered in the first quadrant are human resource management practice, resource management, least squares approximations, and organizational, and theoretical framework. While these themes have been explored to some extent, there is room for improvement by incorporating new and insightful content that expands upon these existing themes. On the other hand, the upper right quadrant of the analysis represents motor themes that have grown substantially and are considered fundamental pillars shaping the research area. The topics covered in the second quadrant are sustainable development, metaverses, virtual reality, augmented reality, commerce, big data, blockchain, computation theory, decision-making, human resource management, knowledge management, technology adoption, innovation, resource management, human-computer interaction, human experiment, artificial neural network, personnel training, behaviour management, supply chain management, efficiency etc. These topics are not only foundational but also serve as base studies for further research and are considered important topics for research in the field of metaverse and human resources.

The lower left quadrant of the analysis represents the emerging or declining themes within the research landscape. The topics covered in the third quadrant are performance, structural equation models, climate change, and software. While these themes have received some attention, their importance and relevance in the field of metaverse and human resources are less pronounced than those in the upper right quadrant. Researchers may explore these themes with different constructs to identify their potential. Conversely, the lower right quadrant represents basic themes that are underexplored and have a very high level of relevance in the research. The topics covered in the fourth quadrant are economic and social effects, consumption behaviour, and social media. Despite their high relevance, these themes have received less attention. Therefore, the researchers are encouraged to focus on these particular themes to enhance the existing studies related to metaverse and human resources. By delving into these underexplored areas, researchers have the opportunity to uncover new insights and address gaps in the literature.

DISCUSSIONS

The metaverse and human resource management (HRM) intersection bibliometric analysis has yielded important insights into the present and future orientations of this developing field of study. The identification of significant themes, trends, and patterns in scholarly publications has provided a thorough overview of the body of literature. The bibliometric analysis reveals that there has been a notable surge in research on the subject, especially in the last several years. This is indicative of the growing understanding of the possible influence of the Metaverse on HRM procedures and organisational dynamics. The examination of the domain covered a wide range of subjects, such as talent manage-

Figure 6. Thematic evolution map
Source: *Extracted from RStudio*

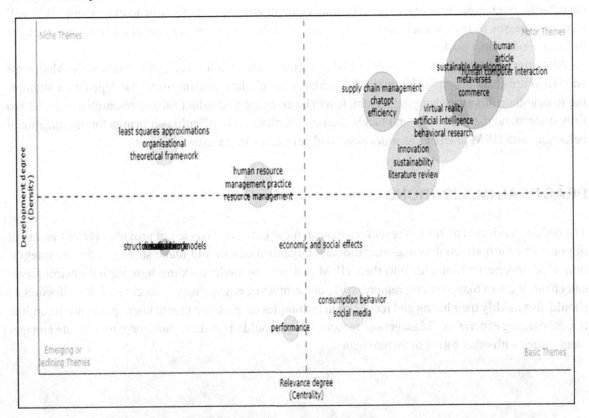

ment, employee engagement, virtual teams, and remote work, demonstrating the complex interplay between HRM and the Metaverse.

The analysis also emphasised how multidisciplinary this field of study is, with contributions from management, computer science, psychology, and sociology. This multidisciplinary method emphasises how difficult it is to research how technology and human behaviour interact in the workplace. The analysis also revealed important research gaps and areas that warrant further study. For example, despite a wealth of study on the potential advantages of the Metaverse for HRM, such as increased flexibility and collaboration, additional practical studies are required to support these assertions and examine any potential disadvantages or difficulties. Furthermore, the analysis identified patterns in research output related to geography and institutions, pointing to possible areas of collaboration and regions of focus for researchers and institutions. Future research projects and collaboration between various academic institutions and geographical areas may benefit from this.

The Metaverse can have AI-powered human-like bots for assistance. The separation of work and home life provides clarity to the employees. With the growing reliance of industries on technology, the metaverse will make its presence felt in almost all industries. For example, the concept of "Metaversity" has traction among academics, but the national boundaries will be blurred in terms of talent. The research on metaverse has accelerated after the COVID-19 pandemic. With industries looking for alternatives at similar times, the research trend on the topic is expected to remain positive. As Metaverse is still in its nascent stage, there are to be many research iterations till we get a product viable enough to replace the traditional scheme of things. Human resource management as well as other facets of management will be affected by this change in business but as hybrid work is the new reality, it's time for the companies to contemplate their future in the metaverse. As a result, there will be substantial changes in human resource management and other aspects of management. This will force businesses to review their approaches and seize the opportunities that the Metaverse presents in the age of hybrid work.

All things considered, the results of our bibliometric analysis help us comprehend how the Metaverse and HRM are changing and offer insightful guidance to scholars, practitioners, and legislators attempting to negotiate this ever-changing terrain. It will be essential to conduct further research in this field to fully understand the Metaverse and tackle the opportunities and difficulties it brings for organizational behaviour and HRM practices as it develops and permeates more areas of society.

PRACTICAL IMPLICATIONS

The review conducted on human resources management in the metaverse era provides various practical implications for both scholars and practitioners. Organizations should make strategies for the integration of Metaverse technologies into their HRM practices by understanding how virtual environments can enhance talent management, remote work, and employee engagement. Moreover, HR professionals should also modify their hiring and recruitment techniques to reach the global talent pool and streamline the onboarding experience. Managers of remote teams should upgrade to metaverse to mitigate engagement issues with other forms of virtual teams.

LIMITATIONS

While our study on bibliometric analysis of the metaverse and human resource management makes a unique and valuable contribution to the current literature, certain limitations need to be addressed in future research. Firstly, our data was sourced solely from a single database, Scopus, which may limit the generalizability of the results, suggesting the need to explore additional databases like Web of Science, EBSCOhost, ProQuest, Lens, Dimensions etc. to enhance the breadth of future studies. Moreover, since the concept of the metaverse is relatively dynamic and continually evolving, bibliometric analyses may struggle to capture the diversified source and lack relevant findings. Lastly, this review exclusively focused on published articles, perhaps ignoring valuable insights from other document types such as websites, white papers, newspaper articles, book chapters, and discussion notes. Future studies can explore these document types to enrich the studies. Despite these limitations, this literature review provides a comprehensive overview of the continue practices of human resources in the metaverse era.

CONCLUSION

The bibliometric analysis based on the HRM practices in the metaverse era offers both opportunities and challenges. This study highlights the multidisciplinary nature of this field and key trends. As the metaverse evolves, organizations must adapt their HRM practices to fully leverage its potential. By understanding the practical implications, organizations can effectively integrate metaverse technologies into their strategies, focusing on global talent acquisition, immersive training programs, virtual collaboration, and employee well-being. Addressing limitations and gaps in research is crucial for a comprehensive understanding of this rapidly evolving landscape. By leveraging insights from this study, organizations can capitalize on the metaverse's opportunities while managing its challenges, leading to more innovative and inclusive HRM practices in the digital age.

REFERENCES

Aria, M., & Cuccurullo, C. (2017). Bibliometrix: An R-tool for comprehensive science mapping analysis. *Journal of Informetrics*, *11*(4), 959–975. doi:10.1016/j.joi.2017.08.007

Arora, M. (2020). Post-truth and marketing communication in technological age. In *Handbook of research on innovations in technology and marketing for the connected consumer* (pp. 94–108). IGI Global., doi:10.4018/978-1-7998-0131-3.ch005

Arora, M. (2024). Virtual Reality in Education: Analyzing the Literature and Bibliometric State of Knowledge. *Transforming Education with Virtual Reality*, 379-402. doi:10.1002/9781394200498.ch22

Arora, M., & Rathore, S. (2023). Sustainability Reporting and Research and Development in Tourism Industry: A Qualitative Inquiry of Present Trends and Avenues. In International Handbook of Skill, Education, Learning, and Research Development in Tourism and Hospitality (pp. 1-17). Singapore: Springer Nature Singapore. doi:10.1007/978-981-99-3895-7_33-1

Arora, M., & Sharma, R. L. (2023). Artificial intelligence and big data: ontological and communicative perspectives in multi-sectoral scenarios of modern businesses. *Foresight, 25*(1), 126-143. doi:10.1108/FS-10-2021-0216

Bennett, E. E., & McWhorter, R. R. (2022). Dancing in the paradox: Virtual human resource development, online teaching, and learning. *Advances in Developing Human Resources, 24*(2), 99–116. doi:10.1177/15234223221079440

Boyack, K. W., & Klavans, R. (2014). Including cited non-source items in a large-scale map of science: What difference does it make? *Journal of Informetrics, 8*(3), 569–580. doi:10.1016/j.joi.2014.04.001

Buhalis, D., O'Connor, P., & Leung, R. (2023). Smart hospitality: From smart cities and smart tourism towards agile business ecosystems in networked destinations. *International Journal of Contemporary Hospitality Management, 35*(1), 369–393. doi:10.1108/IJCHM-04-2022-0497

Chaudhary, M., Jaswal, N., & Sohal, A. (2023). Demystifying the Relationship Between Emotional Intelligence and Leadership Effectiveness: Focusing on Mental Health and Happiness. In AI and Emotional Intelligence for Modern Business Management (pp. 113-133). IGI Global. doi:10.4018/979-8-3693-0418-1.ch008

Cobo, M. J., López-Herrera, A. G., Herrera-Viedma, E., & Herrera, F. (2011). Science mapping software tools: Review, analysis, and cooperative study among tools. *Journal of the American Society for Information Science and Technology, 62*(7), 1382–1402. doi:10.1002/asi.21525

Dhiman, V., & Arora, M. (2023). How foresight has evolved since 1999? Understanding its themes, scope and focus. *foresight.* doi:10.1108/FS-01-2023-0001

Dhiman, V., & Arora, M. (2024). *Exploring the linkage between business incubation and entrepreneurship: understanding trends, themes and future research agenda.* LBS Journal of Management & Research., doi:10.1108/LBSJMR-06-2023-0021

Dickey, M. D. (1999). *3D virtual worlds and learning: an analysis of the impact of design affordances and limitations in active worlds, blaxxun interactive, and onlive! Traveler; and a study of the implementation of active worlds for formal and informal education.* [Doctoral dissertation, The Ohio State University].

Donthu, N., Kumar, S., Mukherjee, D., Pandey, N., & Lim, W. M. (2021). How to conduct a bibliometric analysis: An overview and guidelines. *Journal of Business Research, 133*, 285–296. doi:10.1016/j.jbusres.2021.04.070

Dutta, D., Srivastava, Y., & Singh, E. (2023). Metaverse in the tourism sector for talent management: A technology in practice lens. *Information Technology & Tourism, 25*(3), 331–365. doi:10.1007/s40558-023-00258-9

Dwivedi, Y. K., Kshetri, N., Hughes, L., Slade, E. L., Jeyaraj, A., Kar, A. K., Baabdullah, A. M., Koohang, A., Raghavan, V., Ahuja, M., Albanna, H., Albashrawi, M. A., Al-Busaidi, A. S., Balakrishnan, J., Barlette, Y., Basu, S., Bose, I., Brooks, L., Buhalis, D., ... Wright, R. (2023). "So what if ChatGPT wrote it?" Multidisciplinary perspectives on opportunities, challenges and implications of generative conversational AI for research, practice and policy. *International Journal of Information Management*, *71*, 102642. doi:10.1016/j.ijinfomgt.2023.102642

Fahimnia, B., Sarkis, J., & Davarzani, H. (2015). Green supply chain management: A review and bibliometric analysis. *International Journal of Production Economics*, *162*, 101–114. doi:10.1016/j.ijpe.2015.01.003

Hajjami, O., & Park, S. (2023). Using the metaverse in training: Lessons from real cases. *European Journal of Training and Development*. Advance online publication. doi:10.1108/EJTD-12-2022-0144

Hwang, G. J., & Chien, S. Y. (2022). Definition, roles, and potential research issues of the metaverse in education: An artificial intelligence perspective. *Computers and Education: Artificial Intelligence*, *3*, 100082. doi:10.1016/j.caeai.2022.100082

KevinsJ. (2022) Metaverse as a New Emerging Technology: An Interrogation of Opportunities and Legal Issues: Some Introspection (SSRN paper 4050898). doi:10.2139/ssrn.4050898

Koohang, A., Nord, J. H., Ooi, K. B., Tan, G. W. H., Al-Emran, M., Aw, E. C. X., Baabdullah, A. M., Buhalis, D., Cham, T.-H., Dennis, C., Dutot, V., Dwivedi, Y. K., Hughes, L., Mogaji, E., Pandey, N., Phau, I., Raman, R., Sharma, A., Sigala, M., & Wong, L. W. (2023). Shaping the metaverse into reality: A holistic multidisciplinary understanding of opportunities, challenges, and avenues for future investigation. *Journal of Computer Information Systems*, *63*(3), 735–765. doi:10.1080/08874417.2023.2165197

Lazaroiu, G., Androniceanu, A., Grecu, I., Grecu, G., & Neguriță, O. (2022). Artificial intelligence-based decision-making algorithms, Internet of Things sensing networks, and sustainable cyber-physical management systems in big data-driven cognitive manufacturing. *Oeconomia Copernicana*, *13*(4), https://doi.org/. doi:1047-1080

Nazma, R. B., & Devi, R. (2023). Sustainable Development Using Green Finance and Triple Bottom Line: A Bibliometric Review. *Management*, *1*, 22. doi:10.1177/ijim.231184138

Park, H., Ahn, D., & Lee, J. (2023). Towards a Metaverse Workspace: Opportunities, Challenges, and Design Implications. In *Proceedings of the 2023 CHI Conference on Human Factors in Computing Systems* (pp. 1-20). ACM. 10.1145/3544548.3581306

Park, S. M., & Kim, Y. G. (2022). A metaverse: Taxonomy, components, applications, and open challenges. *IEEE Access: Practical Innovations, Open Solutions*, *10*, 4209–4251. doi:10.1109/ACCESS.2021.3140175

Schlemmer, E., & Backes, L. (2015). The metaverse: 3D digital virtual worlds. In *Learning in Metaverses: Co-Existing in Real Virtuality* (pp. 48–81). IGI Global., doi:10.4018/978-1-4666-6351-0.ch003

Stephenson, N. (1992). *Snow Crash: A Novel*. Bantam Books.

Vig, S. (2023). Preparing for the New Paradigm of Business: The Metaverse. *Foresight and STI Governance (Foresight-Russia till No. 3/2015)*, *17*(3), 6-18. doi:10.17323/2500-2597.2023.3.6.18

Yilmaz, M., O'Farrell, E. & Clarke, P. (2023). Examining the training and education potential of the metaverse: results from an empirical study of next generation SAFe training. *Journal of Software: Evolution and Process*. doi:10.1002/smr.2531

Yu, F., Jian, S., Shen, C., Xue, W., & Fu, Y. (2022). On the Issue of "Digital Human" in the context of digital transformation. In *2022 International Conference on Culture-Oriented Science and Technology (CoST)* (pp. 258-262). IEEE. 10.1109/CoST57098.2022.00060

Zupic, I., & Čater, T. (2015). Bibliometric methods in management and organization. *Organizational Research Methods, 18*(3), 429–472. doi:10.1177/1094428114562629

Chapter 6
From Clicks to Virtual Realms:
Exploring Metaverse–Driven E–Commerce and Consumer Shifts

Animesh Kumar Sharma

https://orcid.org/0000-0002-6673-319X

Lovely Professional University, India

Rahul Sharma

https://orcid.org/0000-0001-8880-7527

Lovely Professional University, India

Rajesh Verma

Lovely Professional University, India

ABSTRACT

This study conducts a comprehensive bibliometric analysis using the preferred reporting items for systematic reviews and meta-analyses (PRISMA) model to explore the convergence of e-commerce, customer experience, and virtual environments in the evolving metaverse. Utilizing Scopus database data from 2010 to 2023, this research aims to map the trends, patterns, and emerging themes surrounding augmented reality (AR), virtual reality (VR), and immersive technologies, shaping consumer behaviour within virtual realms. Initial screening resulted in a substantial corpus of scholarly articles, conference papers, and reviews. Moreover, utilizing visualization tools like VOSviewer, this study provides insightful graphical representations, revealing clusters and connections among keywords, and offering a deeper understanding of the interdisciplinary nature of Metaverse in e-commerce. The analysis focuses on quantifying publication trends, identifying influential authors, institutions, and countries, and mapping key themes and connections within the domain. The analysis encompasses a range of bibliometric indicators, including publication trends, prolific authors, influential journals, and co-occurrence networks of keywords It investigates how virtual environments affect purchasing decisions, brand interactions, and loyalty-building strategies, emphasizing personalized experiences, social interactions, and gamification. The analysis also uncovers emerging research trends and gaps, suggesting avenues for further exploration, including the integration of artificial intelligence, blockchain technology, and spatial computing

DOI: 10.4018/979-8-3693-2607-7.ch006

in enhancing e-commerce in virtual spaces. This research contributes to understanding the impact of the metaverse on e-commerce, customer experience, and engagement, providing valuable insights for academics, practitioners, and policymakers navigating this dynamic field.

INTRODUCTION

Digital technology development has had a profound impact on how businesses interact with their customers, constantly changing the face of commerce (Silitonga et al., 2024). A new age is about to begin, driven by developments in immersive technologies such as augmented reality (AR), virtual reality (VR), and others (Gasmi and Benlamri, 2022). In this new era, e-commerce is going to be significantly impacted by the idea of the Metaverse (Toraman and Geçit, 2023). In his 1992 novel "Snow Crash," science fiction writer Neal Stephenson first introduced the term "Metaverse," which describes a communal virtual area made up of linked virtual worlds, augmented reality settings, and the internet (Zakarneh et al., 2024). Here, users can engage, create, transact, and explore in fully virtual surroundings, symbolising the confluence of the physical and digital worlds. The Metaverse has gained traction in recent years as both startups and industry titans in technology have made significant investments in creating immersive digital experiences (Jeong et al., 2022). These encounters go beyond the confines of conventional e-commerce, giving customers a new way to interact and engage with goods and services. Metaverse has the power to completely transform e-commerce in several ways, including by improving customer interaction, changing the way people shop, and creating new avenues for companies to thrive in a society where everything is connected by technology (Periyasami and Periyasamy, 2022). Comparing the Metaverse to conventional e-commerce platforms, one can have a more engaging and dynamic buying experience. Thanks to augmented reality (AR) and virtual reality (VR) technology, users can browse products in 3D, explore virtual storefronts, and even try them on. Customers' levels of engagement and happiness can rise when they have an immersive experience that mimics what it feels like to be in a physical store (Baskaran, 2023). Massive volumes of user data are gathered and analysed by the Metaverse to provide highly customised product recommendations and customisation possibilities based on unique needs and preferences. Businesses may improve their conversion rates and the shopping experience considerably by implementing this degree of personalisation.

Through virtual surroundings, users can shop with friends, relatives, or other like-minded persons in the Metaverse, which promotes social connections and community participation (Oh et al., 2023). To foster a feeling of community and belonging around brands and products, social shopping experiences can incorporate live streaming, virtual events, and interactive discussions. By employing storytelling tactics, businesses may utilise the Metaverse to create virtual brand experiences and narratives that captivate people closer (Sutherland and Barker, 2023). A company can stand out in a competitive market by using interactive storytelling, virtual brand activations, and immersive product launches to strengthen emotional connections with its target audience. Branded virtual items, in-game advertising, virtual events, and virtual real estate sales are just a few of the new revenue streams and monetization opportunities that the Metaverse offers start-ups (Mancuso et al., 2023). Enterprises can expand their sources of income and reach untapped markets and consumer groups by capitalising on these prospects. Huge volumes of data about user behaviour, interactions, and preferences are produced by the Metaverse; this data provides businesses with important insights to improve their customer experiences, product offers, and marketing campaigns. To help organisations make data-driven decisions and remain ahead of market trends, advanced analytics tools and machine learning algorithms can analyse this data in real time.

The metaverse overcomes geographic boundaries, giving companies access to a worldwide customer base without being constrained by physical locations or distribution routes (Allam et al., 2022). Access to markets and possibilities is made more democratic by this worldwide accessibility, which puts independent producers and small enterprises on an even playing field with larger organisations. Exciting opportunities for e-commerce are presented by Metaverse, which redefines the shopping experience, boosts customer engagement, and creates new opportunities for companies to prosper in a linked digital environment (Dwivedi et al., 2022). Businesses may stay ahead of the curve and provide their clients with unique, immersive, and personalised experiences by embracing Metaverse and utilising its potential (Yemenici, 2022). In this chapter, we conduct a bibliometric study using the Preferred Reporting Items for Systematic Reviews and Meta-Analyses (PRISMA) methodology to investigate previous studies and the relationship between virtual reality, e-commerce, and the growing metaverse. This chapter provides an understanding of how the Metaverse might affect e-commerce, examining how it might change the way people buy, improve customer interaction, and open up new business prospects in a digital world where everything is connected. Additionally, this chapter attempts to explain future directions regarding the incorporation of the metaverse into online shopping procedures.

REVIEW OF LITERATURE

In recent years, the idea of the metaverse, a virtual reality environment where users can communicate with other users and a computer-generated world has drawn a lot of interest. Furthermore, because of modifications in consumer behaviour and technological improvements, the e-commerce landscape has changed. The idea of the metaverse a shared virtual environment for all—was born out of the convergence of augmented reality (AR), virtual reality (VR), and other digital platforms in recent years (Cappannari and Vitillo, 2021). In addition to changing the entertainment and gaming industries, this virtual world is also having a big impact on e-commerce and consumer behaviour. The concept of metaverse, a virtual realm where users interact with digital things in real-time, has emerged from the confluence of virtual reality (VR), augmented reality (AR), and numerous immersive technologies (Bibri and Jagatheesaperumal, 2022).

Metaverse and Virtual Reality (VR) Technologies

The metaverse's evolution has been made possible by the rise of virtual reality technologies. Slater and Sanchez-Vives (2016) emphasise immersive virtual reality (VR) and how compelling virtual environments can be made with it. Furthermore, Dincelli and Yayla (2022) talk about how technology is advancing to create connected virtual worlds, which are the foundation of the metaverse. Online shopping experiences can take on additional dimensions thanks to the metaverse's connection with e-commerce systems. To improve sensory experiences and boost purchase intentions, Liberatore and Wagner (2021) contend that immersive technologies like virtual reality (VR) and augmented reality (AR) allow users to interact with items in virtual settings. The immersive quality of the metaverse encourages a sense of presence and interaction, which lowers the anxiety that comes with making purchases online and increases customer confidence (Han et al., 2022). Furthermore, metaverse-powered e-commerce sites enable customised and engaging buying experiences. Rana et al. (2022) claim that AI-powered assistants installed in virtual shops may adjust to user preferences and make customised product recommendations, simulating the kind of individualised customer care found in physical retail establishments. Likewise, Allam et al. (2022) underscore the significance of social interactions in the metaverse, stressing how peer recommendations and social validation impact buying choices in virtual spaces.

Evolution of E-Commerce in the Metaverse

With the increasing accessibility of virtual reality technologies, e-commerce companies are investigating prospects in the metaverse. Companies are using virtual environments to provide realistic shopping experiences that let customers browse products in a simulated context (Xi and Hamari, 2021). Furthermore, Billewar et al. (2022) talk about how e-commerce platforms can include augmented reality (AR) and virtual reality (VR) technologies to improve the entire purchasing experience for customers. Thanks to developments in virtual reality (VR), augmented reality (AR), and mixed reality (MR) technologies, Kraus et al. (2022) describe how the metaverse has transformed from a theoretical idea to an actual platform. With immersive and engaging experiences that go beyond standard web interfaces, e-commerce within the metaverse offers a fresh take on online buying. The potential of virtual reality commerce (VRC) is that customers visually browse products and make purchases in a simulated setting (Dong et al., 2021). Businesses now face both new opportunities and challenges as e-commerce becomes more metaverse-driven. Some of these challenges include developing compelling virtual shops and incorporating seamless payment systems (Koohang et al., 2023).

Consumer Behaviour in the Metaverse

The changing preferences and behaviour of consumers are impacted by the metaverse. Consumers may be more influenced to make purchases by the immersive experiences provided by virtual environments (Lombart et al., 2020). Furthermore, as shoppers try to interact with people in virtual places as they shop, the study highlights the significance of social interactions within the metaverse (Hennig-Thurau et al., 2023).

Challenges and Opportunities

The metaverse offers chances for innovative e-commerce but also has drawbacks for both customers and companies. In their discussion of privacy and security concerns in virtual environments, Kim et al. (2023) emphasise the importance of taking strong precautions to safeguard user data. Furthermore, Yaqoob et al. (2023) emphasise how critical it is to remove technological obstacles to guarantee the smooth integration of e-commerce platforms with the metaverse. Notwithstanding its possible advantages, metaverse-driven e-commerce presents some difficulties. Widespread adoption may be hampered by technical issues including bandwidth and hardware requirements (Zawish et al., 2024). Furthermore, protecting data security and privacy in virtual environments continues to be a worry for both companies and customers. These difficulties do, yet also offer chances for development and innovation. Businesses that can successfully negotiate the metaverse's intricacies stand to benefit from a competitive advantage by providing distinctive and customised purchasing experiences.

Technical constraints, privacy problems, and regulatory obstacles are some of the challenges that metaverse-driven e-commerce faces, despite its potential benefits. Torous et al. (2021), found the complicated issues with data security and trust when real-world data is integrated with virtual environments. It is anticipated that to overcome these obstacles and realise the complete potential of the metaverse for e-commerce, experts stress the significance of interdisciplinary partnerships (Bibri and Jagatheesaperumal, 2023). Retailers and marketers face difficulties with metaverse-driven e-commerce, despite the great prospects it offers. In the metaverse, for example, users traverse virtual worlds with real-world ramifications, raising privacy and security problems (Ali et al., 2023). Furthermore, concerns regarding brand legitimacy and intellectual property rights are brought up by the growth of virtual markets (Hamza and Pradana, 2022). To increase engagement and loyalty, astute brands are utilising gamification and immersive storytelling to take advantage of the metaverse's ability to create closer ties with customers (Mittal and Bansal, 2023).

Exploring the possibilities of metaverse-driven e-commerce and its influence on customer behaviour is becoming more and more popular in the future. Wedel et al. (2020) predict that virtual environments will see a growing number of personalised shopping experiences and immersive product demos. Shen et al. (2021) also suggest doing further research on the psychological components of consumer behaviour in the metaverse, including how virtual interactions affect buying decisions.

Metaverse and E-Commerce Integration

The term "metaverse" refers to a network of virtual environments where people can communicate in real-time with one another and digital items. E-commerce sites are progressively connecting with the metaverse to produce immersive buying experiences as a result of technological advancements. For example, customers can browse and buy things using virtual avatars in virtual reality stores (Alzayat and Lee, 2021). In addition to improving the purchasing experience, this integration gives companies new opportunities to interact creatively with their customers. The metaverse is a virtual environment where people can communicate in real-time with one another and digital items. Using this immersive environment, e-commerce in the metaverse creates virtual shops where customers may browse, buy, and engage in new ways with goods and services (Enache, 2022). Businesses may now create virtual identities and interact with customers in incredibly immersive settings thanks to platforms like Roblox and Decentraland, which are leading the way in metaverse-driven e-commerce (Dwivedi et al., 2022).

Consumer Engagement and Immersion

The emphasis on consumer participation and immersion is one of the fundamental features of e-commerce powered by the metaverse. According to research, customers may be more engaged and satisfied when they have immersive experiences provided by the metaverse (Bousba and Arya 2022). Customers can see products in a virtual environment thanks to VR and AR technologies, which help them make better-educated purchases. Additionally, the metaverse's social component promotes a sense of community and belonging by enabling users to communicate with one another, ask for advice, and discuss their buying experiences. Social relationships, sensory experiences, and digital identities are some of the variables that influence consumer behaviour in the metaverse. Purchase intentions and brand perceptions are influenced by consumers' feelings of presence and immersion in virtual environments (Huang et al., 2024). Furthermore, Horng and Wu (2020) found that virtual communities and social networks have a big impact on how consumers choose to behave. In the metaverse, companies can improve customer engagement and loyalty by employing gamification and personalised experiences (Arya et al., 2023).

Consumer Shifts and Behavior

There have been significant changes in customer behaviour because of the metaverse's integration with e-commerce platforms. Bag et al. (2022) found in the study that traditional metrics used to measure online buying, like website traffic and conversion rates, may not be an effective indicator of customer engagement today. Instead, key indications of consumer behaviour are measurements like the amount of time spent in virtual environments and social interactions within the metaverse. Furthermore, the blending of real and virtual worlds has given rise to new ways for consumers to express themselves and define their identities, which has an impact on their purchasing behaviour and brand loyalty (Wongkitrungrueng and Suprawan, 2023). A fundamental shift in how customers interact with online buying is brought about by the convergence of e-commerce and the metaverse. Businesses must adjust as virtual reality technologies develop to satisfy the changing demands and tastes of customers in virtual settings. Businesses can take advantage of new chances to improve online purchasing and propel growth in the digital marketplace by comprehending the junction of consumer movements and metaverse-driven e-commerce.

The emergence of the metaverse has led to significant changes in consumer behaviour, which has prompted scholars to explore novel consumption patterns and reasons. Barrera and Shah (2023) studied that virtual world immersion promotes a feeling of escape by enabling users to explore alternative identities and satisfy aspirational desires through the customisation of their avatars and virtual belongings. Cheng et al. (2023) provide additional evidence in support of this escapism, arguing that people can experiment with self-expression and fantasy consumption without fear of repercussions in the actual world because of the anonymity provided by the metaverse. Consumer behaviour has undergone significant changes because of the metaverse's development. Customers are interacting with products in three dimensions and exploring virtual places, which leads to higher degrees of personalisation and engagement (Hollebeek et al., 2020). Customers can see how things fit and seem in real-time via virtual try-on experiences, for instance, which decreases purchase reluctance and improves the whole shopping experience (Hwangbo et al., 2020). Furthermore, community-driven commerce is encouraged by the metaverse's social aspect, allowing users to recommend, evaluate, and transact with other users (Chen et al., 2023). Moreover, e-commerce powered by the metaverse blurs the lines between online and offline experiences, resulting in the emergence of "phygital" consumption. Romano et al. (2021) studied that buyers are looking for smooth transitions between digital and physical worlds, and they are using augmented reality to see things in real life before deciding to buy them. The increasing significance of omnichannel strategies in metaverse-driven retailing is highlighted by this merging of digital and physical channels.

RESEARCH METHODOLOGY

This research adopts a systematic approach to explore and analyze the existing literature on consumer engagement in the metaverse from 2010 to 2023. The methodology involves several sequential steps, including data collection, bibliometric analysis, and data interpretation (Dhiman and Arora, 2024).

Research Design

The study employed a bibliometric analysis approach to examine the trends, patterns, and themes in the literature related to consumer engagement in the metaverse. Bibliometric analysis allows for a quantitative assessment of scholarly publications, facilitating the identification of key authors, journals, and research themes (Dhiman and Arora, 2024).

Data Collection

The selection of keywords is crucial for retrieving relevant literature from the Scopus database. Selecting appropriate keywords is paramount for effectively retrieving relevant literature from the vast repository of the Scopus database, which encompasses a diverse array of scholarly works. Considering this, a meticulous approach was undertaken to pinpoint keywords that directly correlate with the research topic. The chosen keywords were meticulously curated to encapsulate various facets of the subject matter. These keywords include "metaverse," representing the evolving virtual space where digital interactions occur; "e-commerce," denoting the electronic trading of goods and services; "customer experience," emphasizing the quality of interactions between consumers and businesses; "customer engagement," highlighting the active involvement of consumers with brands or products; "virtual realms," delineating the immersive digital environments within the metaverse; "consumer shift," elucidating the changing preferences and behaviours of consumers; and "metaverse in e-commerce," underscoring the intersection between virtual reality and online commerce. By strategically incorporating these keywords, the search process aims to yield comprehensive insights into the dynamics of the metaverse within the realm of e-commerce, facilitating a deeper understanding of consumer behaviour, market trends, and technological advancements in this burgeoning domain. These keywords were selected to ensure comprehensive coverage of the literature related to consumer engagement in the metaverse and its intersection with e-commerce.

The primary data source for this study is the Scopus database, which is a comprehensive repository of scholarly publications across various disciplines. Scopus provides access to a vast collection of peer-reviewed journals, conference proceedings, and other scholarly documents, making it an ideal resource for bibliometric analysis. A comprehensive study has been conducted with meticulous attention to inclusion and exclusion criteria. In the process of selecting relevant studies, certain parameters were established to ensure the quality and relevance of the data. The inclusion criteria comprised publications written exclusively in English, articles published within the timeframe spanning from 2010 to 2023, articles explicitly centring on consumer engagement within the metaverse, and those available in full-text format. Conversely, publications in languages other than English, articles published before 2010 or after 2023, articles not directly addressing consumer engagement in the metaverse, and inaccessible or incomplete publications were excluded from the study. This rigorous selection process aimed to gather a focused and comprehensive dataset for analysis, thereby enhancing the validity and reliability of the study's findings.

Bibliometric Analysis

Scopus is utilized as the primary database for retrieving relevant literature on consumer engagement in the metaverse. Scopus offers advanced search functionalities and citation analysis tools, enabling a comprehensive bibliometric analysis of the research output in this domain. This analysis is focused on articles published between 2010 and 2023 to capture the recent developments and trends in consumer engagement in the metaverse. The selected keywords are used to construct search queries tailored to the research topic. Boolean operators (AND, OR, NOT) are employed to refine the search queries and enhance the relevance of the retrieved results. The Preferred Reporting Items for Systematic Reviews and Meta-Analyses (PRISMA) framework will be employed to ensure transparency and rigour in the data extraction and analysis process. PRISMA provides a structured approach for conducting systematic literature reviews, thereby minimizing bias, and enhancing the reproducibility of this study. VOSViewer, a widely used software tool for bibliometric analysis, will be utilized to analyze and visualize the bibliographic data obtained from Scopus. VOSViewer enables the generation of bibliometric maps, co-authorship networks, and keyword co-occurrence networks, facilitating a comprehensive understanding of the research landscape. The retrieved publications are screened based on the inclusion and exclusion criteria outlined earlier. Duplicate records were removed, and the remaining articles underwent a thorough review to identify relevant studies focusing on consumer engagement in the metaverse. Key metrics such as publication year, authorship patterns, citation counts, journal impact factors, and keyword frequencies are extracted from the selected articles using Scopus and VOSViewer. The extracted data is synthesized to identify trends, patterns, and gaps in the literature on consumer engagement in the metaverse. The findings will be interpreted considering the research objectives and theoretical frameworks, providing insights into the evolving nature of consumer behaviour in virtual environments.

Research Questions

RQ1: What are the publication trends in the intersection of metaverse and e-commerce over the past decade, and how have they evolved?

RQ2: Who are the most influential authors, which institutions are leading in research output on virtual realms and consumer shifts and which key themes and connections are identified through co-occurrence networks of keywords in publications discussing customer engagement and metaverse in e-commerce?

RQ3: How do publication trends differ across countries concerning the integration of metaverse technologies into e-commerce platforms, and which countries are emerging as key contributors in this domain?

RESULTS AND DISCUSSIONS

The results of the study are summed up here. One other method for examining the intellectual structure of a study topic is bibliometric mapping, which appeared recently. Investigating this structure involves looking at the co-occurrence of author keywords and the bibliographic coupling of nations. With the help of the VOSviewer programme (University of Leiden, Netherlands), two-dimensional (2D) bibliometric networks that are easy to use and analyse in any study area may be created, explored, and visualised. Many different scientific domains have made use of this program. Below are the sections where the findings are shown. Analysis was conducted on 132 documents, of which 72 (54.54%) were categorised as journal publications (articles), and 60 (45.46%) as conference papers. The results are summarised in Fig 1 showing the PRISMA technique used in this study.

Figure 1. PRISMA

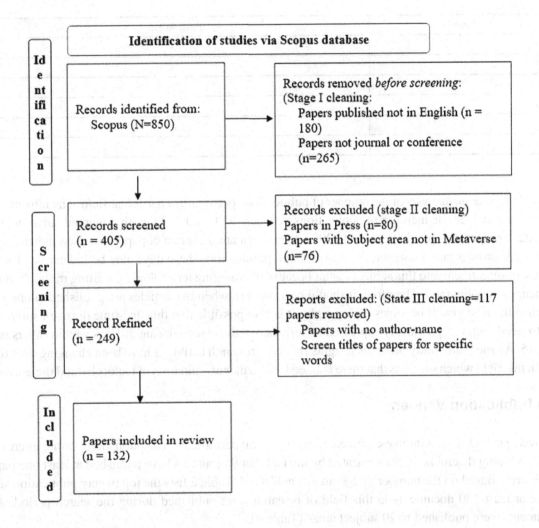

Trends in Publications

We found that the most often occurring keywords in technology for research on sustainable healthcare include metaverse, e-commerce, customer engagement, customer experience, consumer shifts, virtual realms and metaverse in e-commerce. The prevalence of "metaverse in e-commerce" indicates a rise in interest in the application of algorithms for data analysis and prediction in patient monitoring, treatment planning, and illness diagnosis. The terms "consumer shift" and "virtual realms" highlight the emphasis on leveraging modern technology in e-commerce.

Table 1 displays the year of publication and the most referenced publications (titles). This is quite useful for figuring out the themes that scholars in a field concentrate on. Examining superior articles could aid future scholars in developing their writing skills. These were the most often produced pieces in the region.

Table 1. Year wise publication

Year	Publications
2023	88
2022	38
2021	2
2016	1
2015	1
2010	2

Table 1 gives an analysis of the number of publications per year in a particular field. The information displays a considerable increase in publications between 2010 and 2023, with a marked surge in 2022 and 2023 compared to previous years. In 2023, there is an amazing rise of papers up to 88 indicating an impressive growth rate. However, the sharp rise in publications these days may be indicative of more interest or investment into this subject matter because of emerging technologies, shifting research trends or changes in policy(ies). Therefore, it should be a concern when two articles are published in one year and then the next year it becomes eighty-eight. It is also possible that this one-time dormant spike was due to steady interest previously expressed in periods like those seen during 2010 as well as others such as 2015. As such, this study provides insights into how research activities have been changing over time within this field which suggests that there is a need for further examination of factors behind these trends.

Top Publication Venues

Metaverse is highly popular in e-commerce across several periodicals. The publishers' strong interest in this developing discipline is demonstrated by the fact that 95 journals have published at least one paper in this area. Based on the number of documents published, Table 2 lists the top twenty publication sites where at least 180 documents in this field of research were published during the search period. 267 documents were published in 20 subject areas (Table 3).

In table 2, an analysis of publications across different venues is presented to provide an understanding of research output distribution. Significantly, "Linguistic and Philosophical Investigations" has the highest number of publications, which suggests its focus on linguistic and philosophical issues. After this, four articles were published in "Review of Contemporary Philosophy," "ACM International Conference Proceeding Series," "Influencer Marketing Applications within the Metaverse" as well as "Lecture Notes in Computer Science," thus indicating different interests from current philosophy to computer science and metaverse related subjects. Besides, the table often reveals several publication locations such as academic journals and conference proceedings that highlight the interdisciplinary nature of research space. The way that publications are distributed across different outlets gives insight into what scholarly communities value most among other things in linguistics, philosophy, computer sciences and emerging areas like metaverse studies.

Table 3 presents the analysis of publications across various subject areas. It shows that Computer Science has the highest number of publications with 68 articles while Business, Management, and Accounting have 45 publications. Engineering and Social Sciences are tied for third position with 27 publications each. Besides, other subject areas such as Economics, Arts and Humanities, Decision Sciences, Mathematics,

Table 2. Publication venue and number of publications

Publication Venue	No. of Publications
Linguistic And Philosophical Investigations	7
Review Of Contemporary Philosophy	5
ACM International Conference Proceeding Series	4
Influencer Marketing Applications Within the Metaverse	4
Lecture Notes in Computer Science Including Subseries Lecture Notes in Artificial Intelligence and Lecture Notes in Bioinformatics	4
Analysis And Metaphysics	3
Studies In Computational Intelligence	3
2023 International Seminar on Application for Technology of Information and Communication Smart Technology Based on Industry 4 0 A New Way Of Recovery From Global Pandemic And Global Economic Crisis Isemantic 2023	2
Business Horizons	2
Cyberpsychology Behavior and Social Networking	2
Developments In Marketing Science Proceedings of The Academy of Marketing Science	2
Electronic Commerce Research	2
Frontiers In Artificial Intelligence and Applications	2
Handbook Of Research on Consumer Behavioral Analytics in Metaverse and The Adoption of a Virtual World	2
Journal Of Cosmetic Dermatology	2

Energy etc., exhibit a reducing trend in publication volume over the years as indicated by this analysis. From this data, one can deduce that some fields such as medicine have relatively low publishing levels compared to other fields like computer science or business which have many researchers working on them. In turn, this could be crucial for informing scientists about where research is happening most and thereby, they would be able to make informed decisions regarding their studies in addition to providing information on where academic resources should be allocated.

The Most Prolific Nations and Institutions

A total of 182 countries have contributed to the journal and conference publications of works on health-care technology. The dispersion of papers among various countries is indicative of the diversity and international scope of research on the metaverse and e-commerce. It suggests that scholars are actively working on this topic and bringing their diverse viewpoints and methods to the table. Finding the most inventive and active locations in a research field can have an impact on future international partnerships among researchers. Table 4 shows the top fifteen (15) countries with the largest research output in metaverse, regions, and institutions. In terms of metaverse technology, the India and US have the most documents (20), followed by the United Kingdom (15 documents), South Korea (13), China (9), Italy (9), Slovakia (8), Romania (7), Australia (6), Malaysia (6), Canada (4), and other countries that also contribute. It is crucial to remember that this does not always imply the highest degree of network participation or worldwide impact in Metaverse technology. The findings show that the US is actively contributing significantly to developments and breakthroughs in e-commerce technology. Furthermore,

Table 3. Subject area and number of publications

Subject Area	No. of Publications
Computer Science	68
Business, Management and Accounting	45
Engineering	27
Social Sciences	27
Economics, Econometrics and Finance	20
Arts and Humanities	18
Decision Sciences	14
Mathematics	13
Energy	7
Materials Science	6
Psychology	6
Physics and Astronomy	5
Chemical Engineering	2
Environmental Science	2
Medicine	2
Agricultural and Biological Sciences	1
Biochemistry, Genetics and Molecular Biology	1
Earth and Planetary Sciences	1
Multidisciplinary	1
Nursing	1

the fact that the UK, Canada, India, Australia, and China are among the top contributors shows that there is interest worldwide and that efforts are being made to work together to use technology to overcome the difficulties associated with metaverse e-commerce. The findings once more highlight how important international cooperation and knowledge sharing are to e-commerce technology research. Finally, the presence of several nations contributing to the corpus of knowledge suggests the possibility of global collaborations, the exchange of effective strategies, and joint efforts to progress the area.

Co-Authorship Analysis

The co-authorship analysis of the reviewed manuscript using VOSviewer is displayed in Fig. 2. The plot was limited to writers who had at least 500 citations across five co-authored works. The arrows show the co-authorship connections between them. The size of each node in the dataset corresponds to the number of publications a researcher has co-authored. We saw a high dynamic of information exchange, cross-disciplinary teamwork, and idea flow in the field of technology for sustainable research. The result confirms the preliminary findings (see Table 5). In the field of metaverse in e-commerce technology, we have noted that Kwon, K.H. has several works. One more time, the clones between authors suggest that authors in this discipline collaborate more frequently.

Table 4. Countries and respective publications

Country	No. of Publications
India	20
United States	20
United Kingdom	15
South Korea	13
China	9
Italy	9
Slovakia	8
Romania	7
Australia	6
Malaysia	6
Canada	4
Germany	4
Morocco	4
Taiwan	4
United Arab Emirates	4

Table 5. Authors and number of publications

Author Name	No. of Publications
Kwon, K.H.	3
Lee, J.	3
Grupac, M.	2
Horak, J.	2
Korbel, J.J.	2
Lee, C.C.	2
Popescu, G.H.	2
Riva, G.	2
Valaskova, K.	2
Zarnekow, R.	2
Ahmed, E.	1
Ahn, S.J.	1
Al-Adaileh, A.	1
Al-Kfairy, M.	1

Table 5 presents the analysis of authors and their number of publications. Kwon, K.H. and Lee, J. have the highest number of publications, with three each. Following closely are Grupac, M., Horak, J., Korbel, J.J., Lee, C.C., Popescu, G.H., Riva, G., Valaskova, K., and Zarnekow, R., each with two publications. Other authors such as Ahmed E., Ahn S.J., Al Adaileh A. and Al-Kfairy M. have one publication each. Such distribution propounds that Kwon's inclusion in the list shows him as a highly productive author within this dataset where his input may be for instance significant than others or he was focused on it extensively in this field leading to multiple articles published under his name over time while some others whom we do not know well were only able to bring out one title per person thus trying to explain many things but this is hard since they can also produce highly valuable research output just like anybody else who could perhaps think that they are still new in this area compared to him or her at least until further research is done about them through which case any conclusions might come out later than expected should any findings be found by researchers concerning their work; however, no enough information has been given regarding these issues yet, therefore, our point remains valid enough before considering all aspects together again?. Additionally? a few more names appear alongside several authors who underlie series works and put together really many texts. Further on – there's another issue: other investigators' names have similar counting. This table provides a snapshot of author productivity within the field of study, highlighting both individual contributions and collaborative efforts. Deeper insights into the research landscape as well as potential avenues for future investigation can be gained from an examination of these publications themselves through further analysis of them would yield insightful knowledge about what is happening academically and how such work could be taken on in the future.

Co-Occurrence of Keywords

The current study investigated how knowledge is distributed in this field using keyword analysis. In addition, we were able to find new research directions because the links among the different themes were clear. Keyword co-occurrence in the documents this study examined is displayed in Table 6 and Fig. 2. The 182 documents examined in this paper contained a total of 557 keywords. The density-based spatial clustering was utilised in conjunction with the full counting strategy during the network development. The circles for the terms "metaverse," "virtual reality," "augmented reality," "customer experience," "electronic commerce," "immersive" "e-commerce," and other terms linked to making decisions are noticeably larger than the circles for the other categories.

Table 6 analyses the frequency of each keyword within the group of keywords extracted from the publication. As it can be seen, "Metaverse" exists the most, 60 times, and its derivative "Metaverses" exists 34 times. This signals high interest in the research related to the Metaverse concept. The terms directly connected with virtual and augmented reality, like "Virtual Reality" or "Augmented Reality," are also strong, which proves that these technologies are becoming relevant. Other important keywords were "Customer Experience," "Electronic Commerce," and "Sales," thereby assuming an important thematic focus to be around the area of overlap of immersive technologies with consumer behaviour and commerce applications. Interestingly, there are variances within the isolation of terms like "E- Commerces" and "E-commerce," meaning probably some form of mismatch of keywords within the literature. All in all, this table of information shows valuable results within the thematic landscape of the research and reflects what has been outlined and the possible avenues for further investigation. That demonstrates a huge focus with immense research having been put into vast fields of research interests, ranging from immersive technologies to economics, virtual environments to e-commerce, and other technological advancements that are involved in this, such as blockchain and digital twin technologies. "The big new rise of 'Metaverse' and 'Virtual Reality' suggests that interest associated with digital experiences and virtual environments was growing.

Table 6. Keywords and number of publications

Keywords	No. of Publications
Metaverse	60
Metaverses	34
Virtual Reality	25
Augmented Reality	19
Customer Experience	12
Electronic Commerce	11
Immersive	11
Sales	10
E- Commerces	9
E-commerce	9
Block-chain	8
Blockchain	8
Digital Twin	7
Consumer Behavior	6
Human	6
Internet Of Things	6
Marketing	6
Retail	6
Virtual Worlds	6
Avatar	5

Future Trends of Metaverse in E-Commerce

The future trends of the metaverse in e-commerce are likely to revolutionize the way we shop, interact, and experience online retail. Here are some potential trends to watch out for:

Virtual Stores and Marketplaces: E-commerce systems will build online shops and marketplaces in the metaverse where customers can peruse merchandise in fully immersive three-dimensional spaces. Compared to conventional e-commerce websites, these virtual storefronts will provide a more dynamic and interesting shopping experience.

Virtual Try-On and Product Visualization: Customers will be able to virtually try on clothing, see furniture in their homes, and test out products before making a purchase thanks to advances in virtual reality (VR) and augmented reality (AR) technologies. This will make physical storefronts less necessary and improve the online shopping experience.

Social Shopping Experiences: Users will be able to shop in virtual locations with friends, family, or online communities thanks to the integration of social aspects within the metaverse. This social element will strengthen the feeling of community and create a more joyful and cooperative shopping environment.

Personalized Recommendations and AI Assistants: Virtual assistants with AI capabilities will offer tailored product recommendations based on users' tastes, past web surfing activity, and metaverse

Figure 2. Co-occurrences of keywords

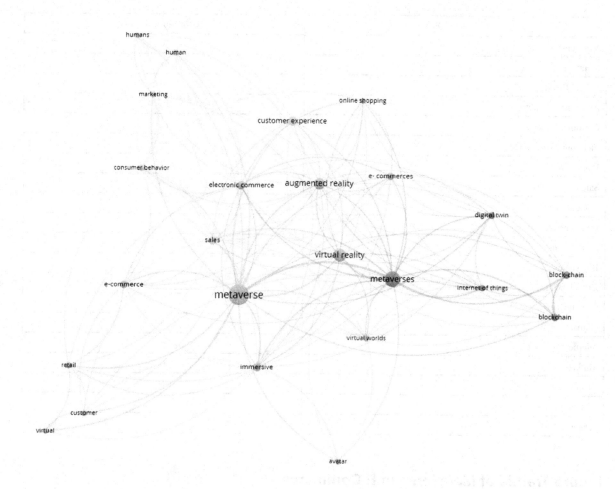

behaviour. When a user needs help or support, these AI assistants will help them along the way through their purchasing experience.

Virtual Events and Experiences: Stores and brands will use the metaverse to hold virtual events like interactive shopping, fashion shows, and product releases. A worldwide audience will be drawn to these events, which will also open new avenues for interaction and brand promotion.

Digital Assets and NFTs: In the metaverse economy, which enables users to purchase, sell, and exchange virtual products, collectables, and limited-edition items, NFTs and digital assets will be important components. Platforms for e-commerce will incorporate NFT markets and let users make money off their digital works.

Decentralized and Blockchain-based Commerce: With the use of blockchain technology, decentralised e-commerce platforms will be possible in the metaverse, providing an increased level of security, transparency, and confidence for online transactions. To ensure equitable and effective trade, smart contracts, and decentralised finance (DeFi) solutions will simplify payments.

Virtual Real Estate and Retail Spaces: Brands and merchants will make investments in virtual real estate within the metaverse to develop distinctive retail spaces and establish their presence. Customers from all around the world will be drawn to these virtual retail venues, which will act as pop-up shops, flagship stores, and experience marketing hubs.

Ultimately, by offering immersive, interactive, and customised buying experiences that surpass the constraints of conventional online retail, the metaverse will transform the future of e-commerce. We anticipate that as technology develops further, many more creative opportunities and solutions will present themselves in this quickly expanding digital environment.

IMPLICATIONS

Managerial and theoretical implications of the current research study are discussed below.

Managerial Implications

The emergence and exploration of the metaverse in e-commerce present several significant managerial implications for both retailers and marketers. Retailers and marketers need to invest in understanding how consumers interact within the metaverse environment. This includes studying user preferences, browsing patterns, purchase behaviour, and engagement metrics specific to virtual environments. Retailers should focus on creating immersive and engaging shopping experiences within the metaverse. Marketers should focus on maintaining brand consistency across virtual and physical channels while also adapting messaging and content to suit the unique characteristics of the metaverse environment. This research study of the metaverse in e-commerce underscores the transformative potential of virtual environments for retailers and marketers.

Theoretical Implications

The emergence of the Metaverse as a significant platform for various activities, including e-commerce, has sparked interest in understanding its implications for consumer behaviour. This research explores the theoretical underpinnings and implications of Metaverse-driven e-commerce on consumer shifts. By applying these theoretical frameworks, researchers can gain insights into the complex dynamics of Metaverse-driven e-commerce and its impact on consumer behaviour. Understanding these implications is essential for businesses, marketers, and policymakers seeking to navigate the evolving landscape of digital commerce in virtual worlds.

CONCLUSION

Our research sheds light on the transformative potential of the metaverse in shaping the landscape of e-commerce and consumer behaviour. Through an in-depth analysis of emerging trends, technological advancements, and consumer preferences, we have elucidated the profound impact of virtual environments on the way individuals interact, transact, and perceive products and services. The metaverse presents unprecedented opportunities for businesses to create immersive and personalized shopping experiences, fostering deeper engagement and loyalty among consumers. Moreover, it has the potential to democratize access to markets, particularly for small and medium-sized enterprises, by reducing barriers to entry and enabling innovative business models. However, amidst the promises of the metaverse, challenges such as privacy concerns, digital inequality, and regulatory uncertainties must be addressed to ensure its equitable and sustainable development. As we navigate this evolving landscape, businesses, policy-makers, and stakeholders must collaborate proactively in harnessing the full potential of the metaverse while mitigating its risks. By embracing innovation responsibly and prioritizing user-centric design principles, we can unlock new frontiers in e-commerce and consumer engagement, ushering in a future where virtual and physical worlds seamlessly converge for the benefit of all.

LIMITATIONS AND SCOPE OF FUTURE RESEARCH

The study's temporal scope is confined to the years 2010-2023, utilizing only the Scopus database. This limitation may overlook earlier seminal works or recent developments in Metaverse-driven e-commerce and consumer behaviour, potentially constraining the comprehensiveness of the analysis. Future research should extend beyond the confines of the Scopus database and encompass a broader range of scholarly repositories such as Web of Science, JSTOR, ERIC, ScienceDirect, IEEE Xplore, and others. This broader search strategy would enhance the inclusivity and diversity of the literature reviewed, providing a more comprehensive understanding of Metaverse-driven e-commerce and consumer shifts. Future research should adopt a cross-cultural perspective to investigate how cultural differences influence consumer behaviours and preferences within the Metaverse. By examining diverse cultural contexts, researchers can uncover nuanced insights into the adoption, usage patterns, and impact of Metaverse-driven e-commerce on consumer behaviour worldwide. Complementing quantitative studies with qualitative approaches such as interviews, focus groups, or ethnographic research would provide deeper insights into the subjective experiences, motivations, and perceptions of consumers engaging with Metaverse-based platforms and virtual environments.

REFERENCES

Ali, M., Naeem, F., Kaddoum, G., & Hossain, E. (2023). Metaverse communications, networking, security, and applications: Research issues, state-of-the-art, and future directions. *IEEE Communications Surveys and Tutorials*, 1. doi:10.1109/COMST.2023.3347172

Allam, Z., Sharifi, A., Bibri, S. E., Jones, D. S., & Krogstie, J. (2022). The metaverse as a virtual form of smart cities: Opportunities and challenges for environmental, economic, and social sustainability in urban futures. *Smart Cities*, 5(3), 771–801. doi:10.3390/smartcities5030040

Alzayat, A., & Lee, S. H. M. (2021). Virtual products as an extension of my body: Exploring hedonic and utilitarian shopping value in a virtual reality retail environment. *Journal of Business Research*, 130, 348–363. doi:10.1016/j.jbusres.2021.03.017

Arya, V., Sambyal, R., Sharma, A., & Dwivedi, Y. K. (2023). Brands are calling your AVATAR in Metaverse–A study to explore XR-based gamification marketing activities & consumer-based brand equity in virtual world. *Journal of Consumer Behaviour*. doi:10.1002/cb.2214

Bag, S., Srivastava, G., Bashir, M. M. A., Kumari, S., Giannakis, M., & Chowdhury, A. H. (2022). Journey of customers in this digital era: Understanding the role of artificial intelligence technologies in user engagement and conversion. *Benchmarking*, *29*(7), 2074–2098. doi:10.1108/BIJ-07-2021-0415

Barrera, K. G., & Shah, D. (2023). Marketing in the Metaverse: Conceptual understanding, framework, and research agenda. *Journal of Business Research*, *155*, 113420. doi:10.1016/j.jbusres.2022.113420

Baskaran, K. (2023). Customer Experience in the E-Commerce Market Through the Virtual World of Metaverse. In *Handbook of Research on Consumer Behavioral Analytics in Metaverse and the Adoption of a Virtual World* (pp. 153–170). IGI Global. doi:10.4018/978-1-6684-7029-9.ch008

Bibri, S. E., & Jagatheesaperumal, S. K. (2023). Harnessing the potential of the metaverse and artificial intelligence for the internet of city things: Cost-effective XReality and synergistic AIoT technologies. *Smart Cities*, *6*(5), 2397–2429. doi:10.3390/smartcities6050109

Billewar, S. R., Jadhav, K., Sriram, V. P., Arun, D. A., Mohd Abdul, S., Gulati, K., & Bhasin, D. N. K. K. (2022). The rise of 3D E-Commerce: The online shopping gets real with virtual reality and augmented reality during COVID-19. *World Journal of Engineering*, *19*(2), 244–253. doi:10.1108/WJE-06-2021-0338

Bousba, Y., & Arya, V. (2022). Let's connect in metaverse. Brand's new destination to increase consumers' affective brand engagement & their satisfaction and advocacy. *Journal of Content. Community & Communication*, *15*(8), 276–293. doi:10.31620/JCCC.06.22/19

Cappannari, L., & Vitillo, A. (2022). XR and Metaverse Software Platforms. *Roadmapping Extended Reality: Fundamentals and Applications*, 135-156. doi:10.1002/9781119865810.ch6

Chen, H., Duan, H., Abdallah, M., Zhu, Y., Wen, Y., Saddik, A. E., & Cai, W. (2023). Web3 Metaverse: State-of-the-art and vision. *ACM Transactions on Multimedia Computing Communications and Applications*, *20*(4), 1–42. doi:10.1145/3630258

Cheng, X. U. (2023). From Fiction to Reality: Harnessing the Power of Imaginative Narratives to Shape the Future of the Metaverse. *Journal of Metaverse*, *3*(2), 108–120. doi:10.57019/jmv.1277525

Dhiman, V. & Arora, M. (2024). Exploring the linkage between business incubation and entrepreneurship: understanding trends, themes and future research agenda. *LBS Journal of Management & Research*. doi:10.1108/LBSJMR-06-2023-0021

Dhiman, V., & Arora, M. (2024). How foresight has evolved since 1999? Understanding its themes, scope and focus. *Foresight*, *26*(2), 253–271. doi:10.1108/FS-01-2023-0001

Dincelli, E., & Yayla, A. (2022). Immersive virtual reality in the age of the Metaverse: A hybrid-narrative review based on the technology affordance perspective. *The Journal of Strategic Information Systems*, *31*(2), 101717. doi:10.1016/j.jsis.2022.101717

Dong, Y., Sharma, C., Mehta, A., & Torrico, D. D. (2021). Application of augmented reality in the sensory evaluation of yogurts. *Fermentation (Basel, Switzerland)*, *7*(3), 147. doi:10.3390/fermentation7030147

Dwivedi, Y. K., Hughes, L., Baabdullah, A. M., Ribeiro-Navarrete, S., Giannakis, M., Al-Debei, M. M., Dennehy, D., Metri, B., Buhalis, D., Cheung, C. M. K., Conboy, K., Doyle, R., Dubey, R., Dutot, V., Felix, R., Goyal, D. P., Gustafsson, A., Hinsch, C., Jebabli, I., & Wamba, S. F. (2022). Metaverse beyond the hype: Multidisciplinary perspectives on emerging challenges, opportunities, and agenda for research, practice and policy. *International Journal of Information Management*, *66*, 102542. doi:10.1016/j. ijinfomgt.2022.102542

Enache, M. C. (2022). Metaverse Opportunities for Businesses. *Annals of the University Dunarea de Jos of Galati: Fascicle: I. Economics & Applied Informatics*, *28*(1), 67–71. Advance online publication. doi:10.35219/eai15840409246

Gasmi, A., & Benlamri, R. (2022). Augmented reality, virtual reality and new age technologies demand escalates amid COVID-19. In *Novel AI and Data Science Advancements for Sustainability in the Era of COVID-19* (pp. 89–111). Academic Press. doi:10.1016/B978-0-323-90054-6.00005-2

Hamza, R., & Pradana, H. (2022). A survey of intellectual property rights protection in big data applications. *Algorithms*, *15*(11), 418. doi:10.3390/a15110418

Han, D. I. D., Bergs, Y., & Moorhouse, N. (2022). Virtual reality consumer experience escapes: Preparing for the metaverse. *Virtual Reality (Waltham Cross)*, *26*(4), 1443–1458. doi:10.1007/s10055-022-00641-7

Hennig-Thurau, T., Aliman, D. N., Herting, A. M., Cziehso, G. P., Linder, M., & Kübler, R. V. (2023). Social interactions in the metaverse: Framework, initial evidence, and research roadmap. *Journal of the Academy of Marketing Science*, *51*(4), 889–913. doi:10.1007/s11747-022-00908-0

Hollebeek, L. D., Clark, M. K., Andreassen, T. W., Sigurdsson, V., & Smith, D. (2020). Virtual reality through the customer journey: Framework and propositions. *Journal of Retailing and Consumer Services*, *55*, 102056. doi:10.1016/j.jretconser.2020.102056

Horng, S. M., & Wu, C. L. (2020). How behaviors on social network sites and online social capital influence social commerce intentions. *Information & Management*, *57*(2), 103176. doi:10.1016/j.im.2019.103176

Huang, W., Leong, Y. C., & Ismail, N. A. (2024). The influence of communication language on purchase intention in consumer contexts: The mediating effects of presence and arousal. *Current Psychology (New Brunswick, N.J.)*, *43*(1), 658–668. doi:10.1007/s12144-023-04314-9

Hwangbo, H., Kim, E. H., Lee, S. H., & Jang, Y. J. (2020). Effects of 3D virtual "try-on" on online sales and customers' purchasing experiences. *IEEE Access : Practical Innovations, Open Solutions*, *8*, 189479–189489. doi:10.1109/ACCESS.2020.3023040

Jeong, H., Yi, Y., & Kim, D. (2022). An innovative e-commerce platform incorporating metaverse to live commerce. *International Journal of Innovative Computing, Information, & Control*, *18*(1), 221–229. doi:10.24507/ijicic.18.01.221

Kim, M., Oh, J., Son, S., Park, Y., Kim, J., & Park, Y. (2023). Secure and Privacy-Preserving Authentication Scheme Using Decentralized Identifier in Metaverse Environment. *Electronics (Basel)*, *12*(19), 4073. doi:10.3390/electronics12194073

Koohang, A., Nord, J., Ooi, K., Tan, G., Al-Emran, M., Aw, E., & Wong, L. (2023). Shaping the metaverse into reality: Multidisciplinary perspectives on opportunities, challenges, and future research. *Journal of Computer Information Systems*. doi:10.1080/08874417.2023.2165197

Kraus, S., Kanbach, D. K., Krysta, P. M., Steinhoff, M. M., & Tomini, N. (2022). Facebook and the creation of the metaverse: Radical business model innovation or incremental transformation? *International Journal of Entrepreneurial Behaviour & Research, 28*(9), 52–77. doi:10.1108/IJEBR-12-2021-0984

Liberatore, M. J., & Wagner, W. P. (2021). Virtual, mixed, and augmented reality: A systematic review for immersive systems research. *Virtual Reality (Waltham Cross), 25*(3), 773–799. doi:10.1007/s10055-020-00492-0

Lombart, C., Millan, E., Normand, J. M., Verhulst, A., Labbé-Pinlon, B., & Moreau, G. (2020). Effects of physical, non-immersive virtual, and immersive virtual store environments on consumers' perceptions and purchase behavior. *Computers in Human Behavior, 110*, 106374. doi:10.1016/j.chb.2020.106374

Mancuso, I., Petruzzelli, A. M., & Panniello, U. (2023). Digital business model innovation in metaverse: How to approach virtual economy opportunities. *Information Processing & Management, 60*(5), 103457. doi:10.1016/j.ipm.2023.103457

Mittal, G., & Bansal, R. (2023). Driving Force Behind Consumer Brand Engagement: The Metaverse. In *Cultural Marketing and Metaverse for Consumer Engagement* (pp. 164-181). IGI Global. doi:10.4018/978-1-6684-8312-1.ch012

Oh, H. J., Kim, J., Chang, J. J., Park, N., & Lee, S. (2023). Social benefits of living in the metaverse: The relationships among social presence, supportive interaction, social self-efficacy, and feelings of loneliness. *Computers in Human Behavior, 139*, 107498. doi:10.1016/j.chb.2022.107498

Papagiannidis, S., Pantano, E., See-To, E. W., Dennis, C., & Bourlakis, M. (2017). To immerse or not? Experimenting with two virtual retail environments. *Information Technology & People, 30*(1), 163–188. doi:10.1108/ITP-03-2015-0069

Periyasami, S., & Periyasamy, A. P. (2022). Metaverse as future promising platform business model: Case study on fashion value chain. *Businesses, 2*(4), 527–545. doi:10.3390/businesses2040033

Pizzi, G., Scarpi, D., Pichierri, M., & Vannucci, V. (2019). Virtual reality, real reactions?: Comparing consumers' perceptions and shopping orientation across physical and virtual-reality retail stores. *Computers in Human Behavior, 96*, 1–12. doi:10.1016/j.chb.2019.02.008

Rana, J., Gaur, L., Singh, G., Awan, U., & Rasheed, M. I. (2022). Reinforcing customer journey through artificial intelligence: A review and research agenda. *International Journal of Emerging Markets, 17*(7), 1738–1758. doi:10.1108/IJOEM-08-2021-1214

Romano, B., Sands, S., & Pallant, J. I. (2021). Augmented reality and the customer journey: An exploratory study. *Australasian Marketing Journal, 29*(4), 354–363. doi:10.1016/j.ausmj.2020.06.010

Shen, B., Tan, W., Guo, J., Zhao, L., & Qin, P. (2021). How to promote user purchase in metaverse? A systematic literature review on consumer behavior research and virtual commerce application design. *Applied Sciences (Basel, Switzerland), 11*(23), 11087. doi:10.3390/app112311087

Silitonga, D., Rohmayanti, S. A. A., Aripin, Z., Kuswandi, D., Sulistyo, A. B., & Juhari. (2024). Edge Computing in E-commerce Business: Economic Impacts and Advantages of Scalable Information Systems. *EAI Endorsed Transactions on Scalable Information Systems*, *11*(1). Advance online publication. doi:10.4108/eetsis.4375

Slater, M., & Sanchez-Vives, M. V. (2016). Enhancing our lives with immersive virtual reality. *Frontiers in Robotics and AI*, *3*, 74. doi:10.3389/frobt.2016.00074

Sutherland, K. E., & Barker, R. (2023). The Future of Transmedia Brand Storytelling and a Model for Practice. In Transmedia Brand Storytelling: Immersive Experiences from Theory to Practice (pp. 247-271). Singapore: Springer Nature Singapore. doi:10.1007/978-981-99-4001-1_12

Toraman, Y., & Geçit, B. B. (2023). User acceptance of metaverse: An analysis for e-commerce in the framework of technology acceptance model (TAM). *Sosyoekonomi*, *31*(55), 85–104. doi:10.17233/sosyoekonomi.2023.01.05

Torous, J., Bucci, S., Bell, I. H., Kessing, L. V., Faurholt-Jepsen, M., Whelan, P., Carvalho, A. F., Keshavan, M., Linardon, J., & Firth, J. (2021). The growing field of digital psychiatry: Current evidence and the future of apps, social media, chatbots, and virtual reality. *World Psychiatry; Official Journal of the World Psychiatric Association (WPA)*, *20*(3), 318–335. doi:10.1002/wps.20883 PMID:34505369

Wedel, M., Bigné, E., & Zhang, J. (2020). Virtual and augmented reality: Advancing research in consumer marketing. *International Journal of Research in Marketing*, *37*(3), 443–465. doi:10.1016/j.ijresmar.2020.04.004

Wongkitrungrueng, A., & Suprawan, L. (2023). Metaverse meets branding: Examining consumer responses to immersive brand experiences. *International Journal of Human-Computer Interaction*, 1–20. doi:10.1080/10447318.2023.2175162

Xi, N., & Hamari, J. (2021). Shopping in virtual reality: A literature review and future agenda. *Journal of Business Research*, *134*, 37–58. doi:10.1016/j.jbusres.2021.04.075

Yaqoob, I., Salah, K., Jayaraman, R., & Omar, M. (2023). Metaverse applications in smart cities: Enabling technologies, opportunities, challenges, and future directions. *Internet of Things : Engineering Cyber Physical Human Systems*, *100884*, 100884. Advance online publication. doi:10.1016/j.iot.2023.100884

Yemenici, A. D. (2022). Entrepreneurship in the world of metaverse: Virtual or real? *Journal of Metaverse*, *2*(2), 71–82. doi:10.57019/jmv.1126135

Zakarneh, B., Annamalai, N., Alquqa, E. K., Mohamed, K. M., & Al Salhi, N. R. (2024). Virtual Reality and Alternate Realities in Neal Stephenson's—Snow Crash‖. *World Journal of English Language*, *14*(2), 244. doi:10.5430/wjel.v14n2p244

Zawish, M., Dharejo, F. A., Khowaja, S. A., Raza, S., Davy, S., Dev, K., & Bellavista, P. (2024). AI and 6G into the metaverse: Fundamentals, challenges and future research trends. *IEEE Open Journal of the Communications Society*, *5*, 730–778. doi:10.1109/OJCOMS.2024.3349465

Chapter 7
Metaverse:
Transforming the User Experience in the Gaming and Entertainment Industry

Pooja Swami
Chaudhary Devi Lal University, India

ABSTRACT

The concept of the metaverse is not new, as it dates back to 1992, but it is an interesting area that is receiving increased attention from researchers and marketers. This chapter provides insight into how the emerging virtual world of the metaverse is significantly enhancing the user experience in the gaming and entertainment industries by leveraging the latest technologies such as augmented reality (AR), virtual reality (VR), artificial intelligence (AI), blockchain technology, NFT, and others. This chapter aims to provide insight into the current developments in metaverse entertainment and gaming applications and how they will affect our user experience in the future. The approach used in this study is based on a comprehensive literature review on the subject of metaverse applications and their potential future in the gaming and entertainment industries. This chapter also discusses the various opportunities for the metaverse in the near future, as well as the challenges involved with it, such as privacy, security, and inclusivity.

INTRODUCTION

The next revolution in internet technology is "Metaverse". The metaverse can be defined as a network of interconnected virtual worlds, enabling real-time interaction between users and the digital environment. The term "metaverse" is derived from the fusion of the ancient Greek words "Meta" and "Verse." The word "verse" originates from the English term "universe," which signifies the whole universe and the word "meta" which comes from ancient Greek means both "after" and "beyond." So, this is a combination of terms meta and verse that make up the term "Metaverse," which emphasizes the fact that the virtual world is a post-real universe (Ergen, 2022). The metaverse originally is a concept from a science fiction novel Snow Crash written by an American writer Neal Stephenson which was published in 1992 and

DOI: 10.4018/979-8-3693-2607-7.ch007

today this concept has come into extensive usage in different spheres of various industries in the world via the development of technologies like virtual reality (VR), augmented reality (AR), extended reality, blockchain, and non-fungible tokens (NFTs) and its widespread application can be seen especially in the gaming and entertainment industry. These technologies facilitate in creating immersive, interactive, and innovative virtual environments, where users can engage in gaming, adventure, social interaction, and fun experiences. The metaverse is predominantly being leaded by the gaming and entertainment industries because it improves storytelling, encourages world-building by letting users customize their virtual environments, and encourages fan creativity by providing users with more control over the experiences and content they consume. As per a report from Exactitude Consultancy, the global metaverse gaming market is projected to grow from USD 90.58 Billion in 2023 to USD 874.36 Billion by 2030, with a compound annual growth rate (CAGR) of 38.25% during the projection period (Exactitude consultancy, n.d.). In the entertainment and media industry, the metaverse globally is expected to reach $221.7 billion by 2031, rising at a (CAGR) of 32.3%, as per a report published by Allied Market Research (Alliedmarketresearch., n.d.). With Metaverse's 3D capabilities, users can immerse themselves in a variety of media and entertainment activities. The literature appears to have presented an implications-based approach on a variety of aspects of the metaverse, with studies analyzing the transformational influence from institutional and societal perspectives, noting both challenges and unwanted impacts on users (Lee et al., 2021). The metaverse is an emerging subject for academics to research about, and this study provides a narrative about how the metaverse is a revolution in the gaming and entertainment industry. This chapter aims to bring insight into the applications of metaverse technologies in the gaming and entertainment industries, as well as how the metaverse is transforming the user experience in these industries and what implications it has for the future in terms of opportunities and challenges for the users and industries.

METAVERSE IN GAMING INDUSTRY

The term "metaverse" is used in the gaming industry to describe a collective virtual shared area that is created as a result of the interplay between the actual world and the virtual world. Inside the metaverse games, players have the opportunity to participate in a wide variety of activities, such as playing games, socializing with other players, creating and trading virtual assets and taking part in various types of engaging interactions (Oliveira & Cruz, 2023). Meta-gaming surpasses conventional gaming by providing a smooth and seamlessly integrated virtual world that extends across various games and experiences. The key elements of metaverse in gaming includes virtual economies with blockchain-based assets like non-fungible tokens (NFTs), content created by players, cross-platform interoperability and customized avatars for permanent identity. Gaming is becoming increasingly immersive, networked, and dynamic through the metaverse, which extends across games and platforms (Bhattacharya et al., 2023).

METAVERSE IN ENTERTAINMENT AND MEDIA INDUSTRY

In the context of the entertainment and media industry, the metaverse can be defined as the integration of advanced technologies such as virtual reality (VR), augmented reality (AR), blockchain, and artificial intelligence (AI) to provide users an immersive and stimulating environment that redefines the conventional definitions of entertainment. The introduction of virtual events and performances allows users to experience concerts and other events in a digital setting with actual artists (Baía Reis & Ashmore, 2022). Also, the immersive storytelling takes center stage with interactive stories that allow viewers to actively assess the story's progression. In virtual spaces, people can watch movies, TV shows, or live events together, making shared watching experiences possible. Virtual cinemas and theaters recreate the familiar experience of watching movies in traditional theatres while virtual museums and exhibitions provide a chance to explore the world of art, history, and culture through digital eyes (Baía Reis & Ashmore, 2022). Overall, the media and entertainment industry's metaverse represents a revolutionary change toward digital experiences that are more participatory, immersive, and linked which is influencing the content creation and its consumption.

META-GAMES ECOSYSTEM: UNDERSTANDING THE INTERCONNECTED VIRTUAL SPACE

Meta-games ecosystem is based on the fundamental structure that governs the metaverse's interconnected virtual spaces. In this context, a "meta-game" is core framework that includes different games, experiences, and interactions in the virtual environment. This ecosystem is created to allow seamless communication and interoperability between several virtual worlds, allowing players to move between them and engage with diverse content. As shown in figure 1 the metaverse gaming ecosystem consists of following components:

Avatar

A significant element that makes a virtual experience in the metaverse different from other digital platforms is the appearance of an avatar. An avatar is a visual representation of someone in a game or virtual world, serving as an alternative to the commonly known profile image. The avatar is a very authentic 360-degree representation that can convert the profile photograph into three-dimensional visuals, accompanied by remarkably human like expressions and gestures, so enhancing the whole experience (Kim et al., 2023). The avatar serves several purposes like as working, communicating, playing, designing clothes, trying them on, and shopping through different applications. It can even transfer virtual purchases made within the game into real-life products.

Presence

One of the first things a player feels is presence since the metaverse makes it possible to see the body parts, its movements, its facial expressions, and how it moves between psychological emotions as though the scene actually exists. "Presence" means a feeling of being physically present in a virtual environment. It refers to a player's sense of immersion and how connected and engaged they feel in the digital world (Voinea et al., 2022).

Homespace

Within the broader metaverse, a player's "Homespace" is their own unique, customized virtual environment or space where their avatar is located and where they can relax and rejuvenate. This space is

Figure 1. Metaverse gaming ecosystem

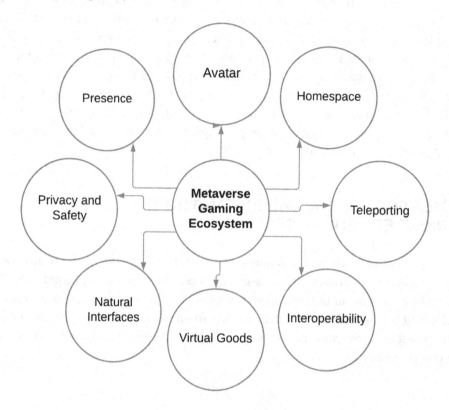

usually created according to the player's tastes and personality, giving them a spot to unwind, socialize, and engage in other activities (Macedo et al., 2022).

Teleporting

Teleporting means an avatar's ability to easily move between locations and places on a single click. The ability to teleport enables players to shop for goods and services across multiple stores and locations by simply clicking a particular button that transports them to a different space, enabling them to engage in the intended activities (Shahbaz Badr & De Amicis, 2023). This feature gives the avatar the power to jump from one exciting place to another making the whole experience fast, convenient and joyful.

Interoperability

In the context of metaverse games, interoperability means that players can move between and connect with different virtual worlds, platforms, and even across different metaverses keeping their digital presence intact throughout. It is designed to ensure that players can easily move between games and virtual universes by taking their digital items, avatars, and awards with them. This interoperability enables players to enter the metaverse from a variety of devices, including virtual reality setups, PCs, and gaming consoles, thereby ensuring a smooth experience (Li et al., 2023).

Virtual Goods

Virtual goods represent digital products or assets purchased, earned and used by players in metaverse games. Virtual goods include everything from virtual real estate and in-game currencies to fully customizable avatars, outfits, weapons and other accessories. Virtual goods are a key element of the gaming experience because they allow players to customize their avatars, express themselves, and engage in economic activities (Shen et al., 2021). Notably, these virtual products are purchased, sold, and traded in the metaverse with the use of blockchain technology.

Natural Interfaces

In metaverse games, natural interfaces are means of user interaction that imitate or match natural human movements, gestures, facial expressions or behaviors. The goal of these interfaces is to make the virtual gaming environment more immersive and intuitive. One of its example is tracking the eye movements of player that allows the game to respond to where the player is looking like aiming and selecting objects (Gao & Yu, 2023).

Privacy and Safety

Today, all electronic games are based on security and privacy features. This means that players can pick and choose who they play with and block others as required. Because these platforms are built on strong safety and security rules, players are always in a safe place. Besides these safety measures, many gaming platforms also have parental settings that allow parents limit their children's access to certain game content based on their age.

META-GAMES: THE APPLICATION OF METAVERSE IN GAMING INDUSTRY

The emergence of the metaverse signifies a revolutionary change in the digital interactions landscape, especially in the gaming industry. Beyond traditional gaming, the metaverse is an immersive, interconnected digital place for gamers where they can effortlessly travel from one virtual world to another. The following are the ways in which the integration of the metaverse into games is enhancing the gaming experience for players:

Immersive Gameplay

The metaverse fosters immersive gameplay through the integration of innovative technologies such as augmented reality, virtual reality, spatial computing, interlinked virtual environments, user-generated content and social interactions.

   Enhanced Virtual Environments. Metaverse environments can provide near-realistic physics, allowing for natural and intuitive interactions with objects and their surroundings. The players can climb rocks with grips that feel like real ones and use weapons that have the same weight and momentum (Shin, 2022). For example, A famous action role-playing game developer, CD Projekt is known for creating

"Cyberpunk 2077," an open-world game set in the future. The game's rich urban landscapes, dynamic weather, and day-night cycles all contribute to the game's realistic and immersive virtual environment.

Real time Interaction. Real-time interaction enables players to interact and have conversations with one another in a virtual environment. It is implemented by a variety of techniques, including voice chat, text messaging, and, in some cases, gestures or body language, depending on the amount of immersion offered by the game. Multiplayer games primarily rely on it as it enable players to coordinate strategies, share experiences, and communicate with one another in a virtual world, fostering a sense of connection and presence (Zhao et al., 2022).

Virtual Economies and In-Game Assets

In metaverse games, "virtual economies" and "in-game assets" mean the creation of monetary systems within virtual worlds, wherein the game's resources and virtual goods have monetary value and can be purchased, sold, and traded. It enables the players to engage in economic activities that resemble real-world market dynamics which is crucial for enhancing playing experience.

Tokenization of In-Game Items. To tokenize in-game items, metaverse games commonly make use of blockchain technology. Each item is transformed into a unique, marketable asset that is represented by a non-fungible token (NFT) ensuring ownership and exclusivity (Scheiding, 2023). For example, in the game "Cryptokitties," virtual cats are converted into NFTs that can be tokenized on the Ethereum blockchain. Each Cryptokitty is a separate digital asset with its traits and qualities. The blockchain safely records who owns the cats and their traits so players can buy, sell, and breed them on outside markets.

Economic Opportunities for Players. Many metaverse platforms allow players to create and trade content of their own which can involve virtual art and designs, personalized avatars, and in-game experiences. Players can earn money from their creativity by catering to the needs and wants of their virtual community. These virtual economies are designed to mimic real-world economic systems such as farming, crafting, and resource gathering are a few examples of activities that players may take part in to generate in-game wealth (Vidal-Tomás, 2022). In the case of "Decentraland," a blockchain-based virtual world, players can buy, sell, and develop their virtual land as well as make cryptocurrency by monetizing virtual experiences.

Cross-Platform Integration

Cross-platform integration in metaverse games enables players to access their gaming experiences across a variety of devices and platforms, including desktops, smartphones, tablets, and virtual setups.

Seamless Gaming Across Devices. Simply said, "seamless gaming across devices" means that players can move freely and continue playing on other devices as well. This feature ensures a seamless and continuous gaming experience by enabling users to play the same game on many platforms, access their in-game progress, and interact with the virtual world consistently (Rane et al., 2023). For example, Epic Games' "Fortnite" allows users to use the same account across multiple devices, including desktops, gaming consoles, and smartphones. The availability of this cross-platform functionality ensures a more consistent gaming experience.

Social Interaction and Community Building. The metaverse hosts virtual events, meetings, and in-game celebrations that players can join. These events offer opportunities to socialize, make new friends, and participate in community-driven activities in the virtual games. To facilitate player-to-player interaction in the metaverse, games have integrated real-time communication capabilities which includes voice chat, text messaging, and gestures which help build community. For example, Players in "VRChat" can create their avatars, discover user-generated worlds, and communicate with others in real time. Social hubs inside the game serve as gathering areas where people gather for events, conversations, or just to socialize.

METAVERTAINMENT: THE NEW ERA OF ENTERTAINMENT INDUSTRY

When we refer to "metavertainment" it is really just a combination of the words "metaverse" and "entertainment," and it defines an act of consuming entertainment within the metaverse itself. It includes a wide variety of entertainment activities that bring people together in a shared digital space by using augmented reality and virtual reality (VR) technologies. The rising urge for work-from-home and remote working technological advancements has played an important role in the sprawling of the metaverse in the entertainment industry (Ghryani et al., 2023). Furthermore, the metaverse's ability to connect people to a community also drives its rise in the entertainment sector. The following are some of the ways in which the users are enjoying immersive experiences from the application of metaverse into entertainment:

Immersive Cinematic Experiences

With the metaverse's ability to create immersive and interactive storylines, it has changed the whole experience of watching movies. In contrast to the 2D cinematic experience, where viewers would simply recline and watch a story being unfolding on screen, the metaverse brings a new dimension—an immersive one where viewers can even interact with characters and shape the storyline.

Virtual Movie Theatres and Interactive Films. When virtual movie theaters and interactive movies come together, they create a new kind of movie theater experience in the metaverse. In these new theatres, people put on virtual reality headsets and become immersed in a shared virtual movie theater, like "Bigscreen" (Vosmeer & Schouten, 2014). Here, they can not only watch movies on a big virtual screen, but they can also use avatars to talk to friends or other watchers in real time. For example, "Number One Player" and "Out of Control Player" are the quintessential "Metaverse" films of recent times. "Number One Player" generated a remarkable revenue of 1.4 billion US dollars at the box office during its release in March 2018. Also, "Out of Control Players" earned 150 million in its first week, creating significant buzz on various social media platforms (Chaintechsource, n.d.).

Virtual Concerts and Shows. The academic literature defines virtual concerts in different ways; some definitions include holographic concerts, livestream concerts and concerts that need VR technology. Here a virtual concert is defined as any kind of musical performance where the audience is immersed in a digital environment via the use of avatars. Most of these virtual concerts are found on blockchain technology, as in The Sandbox or Decentraland or on games such as in Fortnite, Second Life, Roblox or Minecraft (Yakura & Goto, 2020). Virtual shows in the metaverse have raised the bar for entertainment, giving fans exciting and thrilling experiences. An example worth mentioning is Travis Scott's virtual music concert in Fortnite which is one of the most popular video games in the world. The concert attracted more than 12 million live viewers worldwide and featured magnificent visuals and interactive sections making it a grand success (Stefanic, 2023).

Virtual Theme Parks and Attractions

Virtual theme parks are advanced digital recreations of traditional amusement parks into fictional or fantasy-like environments built in the metaverse. These parks are built on digital technologies to provide visitors with immersive and sensory-rich experiences. Users can experience a vast variety of rides, attractions, and themed locations in these virtual places all from the comfort of their homes (Marr, 2023).

Simulated Theme Park Experiences. Simulated theme parks attempt to replicate and provide the same adventurous experience as physical amusement parks in the real world. The goal is to recreate the feel of a physical theme park, filled with thrilling roller coaster rides, interactive elements, entertainment shows, and themed zones (Marr,2023). For example, Walt Disney Co. acquired a patent in 2021 for setting up virtual world simulator projecting three-dimensional pictures onto actual objects to engage with theme park tourists, making it easier to provide personalized interactive attractions for visitors across its theme parks. The company has 12 theme parks in several countries, including the United States, Paris, Japan, Hong-Kong and China (Blockchain Council, n.d.).

Virtual Reality Rides and Adventures. VR Adventures offers 4D simulators that enable players to engage in activities such as walking, climbing, exploring, and flying within virtual environments. Virtual rides provide thrilling stimulations that virtually imitate the sensations that are experienced while riding a roller coaster, driving a racing car or participating in other thrilling activities (Spence, 2021). Virtual reality (VR) or motion simulation allows users to experience the turns, twists and speeds that are related with the adventure that they have chosen to experience. When it comes to virtual rides and experiences, Triotech is the go-to creator. As a fully interactive motion simulator, their XD Dark Ride mixes motion seats, 3D graphics, and other interactive features to create an exciting ride(Triotech, n.d.).

Sports and Live Events in the Metaverse

The sporting world is a great place to test out the cutting-edge technologies and the metaverse has emerged as the latest frontier and a great number of businesses are competing to occupy that space. In a virtual sports space, players and fans can dress as virtual avatars, shop for and wear team gear, meet other supporters, have virtual celebrations, and obviously watch all the games and activities. With the use of multi-view camera technology, fans can actually access the field itself and stroll along the athletes or cheer for the team from various locations while watching the action.

Virtual Stadiums and Arenas. "Virtual stadiums" are simulated versions of real-life stadiums used for sporting events or other forms of entertainment in online games and other virtual worlds. These virtual stadiums imitate the look and feel of actual stadiums so that users can enjoy live entertainment like musical performances, sporting events, cheering up for their favorite players and more without leaving the comfort of their place (Capasa et al., 2022). The Manchester City soccer team created history by announcing the first-ever virtual recreation of Etihad Stadium in the Metaverse. It was out of world good news for soccer fans across the world because it made it possible for soccer supporters to watch live matches from their homes without going to the stadium (Duge, 2022).

Virtual Sports Tournaments and Competitions. Tournaments and competitions in virtual sports constitute sporting events in which players battle against one another in a variety of online games or e-sports titles inside a virtual environment where players often use digital avatars to compete against one another. Websites such as Twitch, YouTube Gaming, and others provide live coverage of several virtual sports competitions (Capasa et al., 2022). As a benefit of it, viewers are able to catch every moment of the matches as they happen, while analysts and experts enrich the coverage with their live commentary on the action. The FIFAe World Cup is an e-sports competition organized by FIFA and formerly in collaboration with EA Sports. Every tournament involves participants participating in matches in the most recent version of the FIFA association football video game series. With its open qualification style, millions of people may participate in the first online stages of the FIWC, making it the biggest online esports game according to Guinness World Records (Wikipedia, 2024).

OPPORTUNITIES AND FUTURE TRENDS OF METAVERSE IN GAMING AND ENTERTAINMENT INDUSTRY

In the gaming and entertainment industries, the metaverse offers a plethora of opportunities that promise to transform user experiences and market dynamics. The metaverse is changing the gaming and entertainment industry in many ways, including the way users interact with content, the prospects for economic growth, the rate of technology advancement, and the cultural and social dynamics at play.

- Metaverse gaming has a bright future. As technology advances, we can probably expect virtual worlds to become more complex, with better visuals and greater interactions powered by AI. These advancements will make virtual and real worlds even more identical, allowing for more immersive interactions. According to Gartner, metaverse technology will lead to a 25% increase in the serious gaming industry by 2025 (Gartner, 2022).
- NFTs, along with other digital assets, will play a crucial role in shaping the economic foundation of the gaming metaverse. To make it clear, the worldwide market for blockchain gaming is projected to see a significant surge, increasing from $4.6 billion in 2022 to $65.7 billion by 2027 (Meichler, 2023). Looking at these numbers, it is not tricky to predict that the upcoming era of gaming may be linked with non-fungible tokens (NFTs).
- The metaverse provides an important chance for gaming firms to broaden their monetization techniques beyond conventional sale of games and in-game transactions. If the metaverse development functions as an independent platform, games might be transformed into apps integrated inside that platform, rather than existing as independent products. Publishers might potentially create regular income by using subscription models and micropayments inside their metaverse games (A3Logics, 2023). As an example, gamers have the option to pay recurring monthly fees for deeply engaging MMO games or engage in frequent transactions to get virtual items.
- Customer spending on virtual concerts, events, and other forms of virtual entertainment is fueling the expansion of the metaverse economy. The fact that the metaverse can satisfy people's desire to feel connected to a community will continue to contribute to its popularity in the entertainment industry in the near future. It is more evident from the Statista's findings that from 2024 to 2030, the global market for Metaverse Live Entertainment will expand at a CAGR of 10.37%, reaching a value of 221.7 billion dollars by 2030 (Statista, 2024).
- Both the Metaverse and the entertainment industries will grow in the future to unprecedented heights which will be beyond human imagination in both their own right and in tandem. Meta Hollywood in 2023, stated that it will form a partnership with the Planet Hollywood group and Meta Hollywood organization to establish a revolutionary virtual studio in the metaverse patterned like the Hollywood backlot (Metavertainment, n.d.). This foundation of the Metaverse that

it satisfies people's desire to belong to a community, communicate with others, and share one's experiences will be a game-changer in the entertainment industry.

- Mega immersive live events are expected to grow in size and level of interaction in the years to come, becoming a significant source of revenue for artists and owners of virtual worlds while also providing fans with experiences that are one of its kind. Fans will be able to interact with their favorite artists in entirely new ways and the use of (NFTs) and cryptocurrency will minimize the need on the intermediaries. Not only this, artists will be able to communicate with fans directly and sell their music to them.

According to its forecast report, Gartner ranked the metaverse as one of the five most promising new technologies and trends for the future. According to Gartner, by 2026, nearly 25% of the population will spend at least an hour each day in the metaverse, and 30% of businesses will provide services or goods dedicated to the metaverse (Gartner, 2022). Although it is still in its beginning stages, the metaverse has great potential to play a pivotal role in the Internet's future.

CHALLENGES AND CONSIDERATIONS OF METAVERSE IN GAMING AND ENTERTAINMENT INDUSTRY

In a relatively short amount of time, Metaverse has established itself as a big cannon in the gaming and entertainment industries. While the metaverse promises boundless possibilities in these industries, it also comes with a set of unique challenges that need to be brought into light and addressed to harness the full potential of the metaverse. Table No.1 shows some multifaceted challenges faced by these industries while adapting to the metaverse.

In the upcoming years, the metaverse could totally transform how we meet, socialize, and do business in the digital age and to reach this stage, however, developers have to address these complicated set of challenges. These challenges can be resolved through collaboration, using new technologies like blockchain and opting for a user-friendly approach.

IMPLICATIONS OF THE STUDY

This study has significant implications for both metaverse users like players and content consumers as well as the content creators in these industries. For the users, the metaverse has the capability to provide interconnected virtual worlds at their fingertips which users can leverage to delve into diverse activities ranging from gaming adventures to virtual social gatherings, from attending live concerts in digital venues to participating in interactive storytelling experiences. The active users as well as the potential users should quickly adapt to this shift towards a more participatory and interconnected digital environment which can enhances their engagement and satisfaction. However, users should remain vigilant of challenges that comes with these virtual environments such as inclusivity and accessibility, privacy and data security which are crucial for maintaining trust and confidence among them. As active engagement of the users in this universe is of paramount importance, therefore it is suggested to the content creators to explore innovative storytelling techniques, leveraging the immersive capabilities of virtual reality (VR), augmented reality (AR), and other advanced technologies to captivate audiences in entirely new ways.

Table 1. Challenges and considerations in meta- gaming and entertainment industries

Challenges	Gaming Industry	Entertainment Industry
Technical Infrastructure	The metaverse demands robust technical infrastructure to support its immersive experiences that includes ensuring stable platforms, overcoming device accessibility issues, and optimizing for various devices which becomes the key hurdles in delivering seamless interactions.	Adapting existing entertainment content, such as movies and shows, to virtual and augmented reality (VR/AR) formats while maintaining high-quality visuals and storytelling poses a significant challenge.
Privacy and Security Concerns	Metaverse games frequently require players to create profiles and share personal information. Protecting sensitive data from unauthorized access, breaches, and cyberattacks is of grave concern.	Hosting virtual events within the metaverse such as concerts and shows raises concerns about security and unauthorized access. Ensuring that only authorized users can attend events and preventing potential disruptions, like virtual "gate-crashing," requires robust security measures.
Regulatory Landscape	Adapting to evolving regulations related to virtual economies, user safety, and digital transactions is crucial. Accordingly, game developers need to stay informed about legal requirements and compliance standards to operate within the regulatory framework.	The global metaverse presents jurisdictional law and regulation issues. The biggest challenge for metaverse entertainment platforms is to comply to different rules in different countries, making international law navigation effective.
Interoperability and Standards	Different gaming platforms use different technologies and frameworks in their ecosystems due to which achieving interoperability in meta-games becomes a challenge as game developers, platform operators, and technology vendors have to work alongside one another	Users often engage with a mix of VR and AR within the metaverse entertainment. Interoperability here means letting users switch between multiple entertainment forms while maintaining a consistent storyline and interface. It requires the complex task of standardizing approaches to content integration and presentation.
Ethical and Social Considerations	The game business faces the problem of handling concerns about potential addiction and excessive screen time. Game designers need to teach players how to play in a healthy way and include elements that encourage responsible gaming.	In virtual world, users engage in a wide range of behaviors, from socializing and collaborating to potentially engaging in inappropriate conduct. To prevent such unethical behavior such as harassment, bullying, or offensive interactions require robust moderation tools, reporting mechanisms, and community guidelines.

For this, the content creators should focus on creativity and individuality through providing customizable avatars, user-generated content, and virtual economies which provides users with greater control over their virtual experiences which helps in enriching their overall experience. As traditional boundaries between content consumption and creation have blurred, creators need to adapt themselves quickly at the forefront of a paradigm shift in content production and distribution. At last, it can be said that implications of the metaverse in the gaming and entertainment industry requires collaboration between both users and content creators to enhance the user experience while addressing challenges at the same time.

LIMITATIONS OF THE STUDY

This chapter have some limitations which can be addressed in further studies. First, it only considers two industries which are gaming and entertainment industries, so future studies involving more industries to study the impact of metaverse such as education, retail and e-commerce, tourism etc. will help in understanding the transformational change brought by this phenomenon in more depth. Second, this study is solely based on the existing literature available in context of metaverse which is secondary in nature completely based on the review of scholarly works, consultancy firm reports, trade publications, websites, books etc so it is suggested that future research should focus on developing more empirical studies that take into account the real opinions of users in terms of the extent to which metaverse has transformed their experience of content consumption and gaming in these industries. Also, this chapter studies this phenomenon from the lens of users or content consumers so the further studies can be studied from the point of view of the impact on other stakeholders as well such platform operators, service providers, content production and distribution house, influencers etc.

CONCLUSION

The recent development of the metaverse has sparked an increasing amount of academic discussion over its pros and cons and potential for redefining many industries. Even when the metaverse is still mostly at the conceptual stage, there are vast number of potential changes it might bring about for the gaming and entertainment industries. From immersive gaming environments to interactive storytelling and virtual events, the metaverse has opened up new possibilities for both players and users alike. Furthermore, the inception of the metaverse has brought about a significant transformation in the gaming industry, enabling players to become engrossed in richly developed virtual worlds and engage in novel collaborative interactions. Similarly, the entertainment sector has also used the metaverse to create immersive content and interactive experiences that respond to users' growing interests. As technology advances, we can expect to see even more imaginative uses of the metaverse specifically in these industries. The metaverse in near future can fundamentally alter how we play, consume, and interact with gaming and entertainment content, providing endless opportunities for innovation and exploration. This chapter highlights the need for interdisciplinary research that bridges the fields of gaming, entertainment, technology, and user experience design. By fostering collaboration between experts from different disciplines, we can better understand the complex dynamics of the metaverse and develop innovative solutions to address emerging challenges. By embracing the potential of the metaverse and addressing its challenges, we can unlock new possibilities for immersive and engaging user experiences that will shape the future of entertainment for years to come.

REFERENCES

A3Logics. (2023, May 18). How Metaverse Gaming Bought Revolution in Gaming Industry. *A3logics Blog*. https://www.a3logics.com/blog/metaverse-gaming-a-revolution-in-the-gaming-industry

Baía Reis, A., & Ashmore, M. (2022). From video streaming to virtual reality worlds: An academic, reflective, and creative study on live theatre and performance in the metaverse. *International Journal of Performance Arts and Digital Media*, *18*(1), 7–28. doi:10.1080/14794713.2021.2024398

Builders of Amusement Park Rides & Media-Based Attractions. (n.d.). Triotech. https://www.trio-tech.com/

Capasa, L., Zulauf, K., & Wagner, R. (2022). Virtual Reality Experience of Mega Sports Events: A Technology Acceptance Study. *Journal of Theoretical and Applied Electronic Commerce Research*, *17*(2), 2. doi:10.3390/jtaer17020036

Disney patents technology to focus on theme park in Metaverse—Blockchain Council. (n.d.). Blockchain. https://www.blockchain-council.org/news/disney-patents-technology-to-focus-on-theme-park-in-metaverse/

Ergen, I. (2022). *Design in Metaverse: Artificial Intelligence, Game Design, Style-Gan2 and More....* Allied Publishers.

FIFAe World Cup. (2024). Wikipedia. https://en.wikipedia.org/w/index.php?title=FIFAe_World_Cup&oldid=1195690321

Gao, X., & Yu, W. (2023). Innovative Thinking About Human-Computer Interaction in Interactive Narrative Games. In X. Fang (Ed.), *HCI in Games* (pp. 89–99). Springer Nature Switzerland. doi:10.1007/978-3-031-35930-9_7

Gartner Outlines Six Trends Driving Near-Term Adoption of Metaverse Technologies. (n.d.). Gartner. Retrieved February 6, 2024, from https://www.gartner.com/en/newsroom/press-releases/2022-09-13-gartner-outlines-six-trends-driving-near-term-adoptio

Gartner Predicts 25% of People Will Spend At Least One Hour Per Day in the Metaverse by 2026. (n.d.). Gartner. https://www.gartner.com/en/newsroom/press-releases/2022-02-07-gartner-predicts-25-percent-of-people-will-spend-at-least-one-hour-per-day-in-the-metaverse-by-2026

Ghryani, L., Sidiya, A. M., Almahdi, R., & Alzaher, H. (2023). The Future Metavertainment Application development. *2023 20th Learning and Technology Conference (L&T)*, 151–156. 10.1109/LT58159.2023.10092341

Kim, D. Y., Lee, H. K., & Chung, K. (2023). Avatar-mediated experience in the metaverse: The impact of avatar realism on user-avatar relationship. *Journal of Retailing and Consumer Services*, 73, 103382. doi:10.1016/j.jretconser.2023.103382

Li, T., Yang, C., Yang, Q., Lan, S., Zhou, S., Luo, X., Huang, H., & Zheng, Z. (2023). Metaopera: A Cross-Metaverse Interoperability Protocol. *IEEE Wireless Communications*, 30(5), 136–143. doi:10.1109/MWC.011.2300042

Macedo, C. R., Miro, D. A., & Hart, T. (2022). *The Metaverse: From Science Fiction to Commercial Reality—Protecting Intellectual Property in the Virtual Landscape. 31*(1).

Meichler, M. (2023, June 19). *The Future of NFTs: Is Gaming the Solution?* NFT Evening. https://nftevening.com/the-future-of-nfts-is-gaming-the-solution/

Metaverse Live Entertainment—Global | Market Forecast. (n.d.). Statista. https://www.statista.com/outlook/amo/metaverse/metaverse-live-entertainment/worldwide

Metaverse: The Revolution of the Sports World & Entire Life. (n.d.). ISPO. https://www.ispo.com/en/news-trends/metaverse-revolution-sports-world

Metavertainment: A Vision Into The World of The Metaverse and Entertainment. (n.d.). HackerNoon. https://hackernoon.com/metavertainment-a-vision-into-the-world-of-the-metaverse-and-entertainment

Oliveira, A., & Cruz, M. (2023). Virtually Connected in a Multiverse of Madness?—Perceptions of Gaming, Animation, and Metaverse. *Applied Sciences (Basel, Switzerland)*, 13(15), 15. doi:10.3390/app13158573

Rane, N., Choudhary, S., & Rane, J. (2023). *Metaverse for Enhancing Customer Loyalty: Effective Strategies to Improve Customer Relationship, Service, Engagement, Satisfaction, and Experience* (SSRN Scholarly Paper 4624197). doi:10.2139/ssrn.4624197

Scheiding, R. (2023). Designing the Future? The Metaverse, NFTs, & the Future as Defined by Unity Users. *Games and Culture*, *18*(6), 804–820. doi:10.1177/15554120221139218

Shahbaz Badr, A., & De Amicis, R. (2023). An empirical evaluation of enhanced teleportation for navigating large urban immersive virtual environments. *Frontiers in Virtual Reality*, *3*, 1075811. https://www.frontiersin.org/articles/10.3389/frvir.2022.1075811. doi:10.3389/frvir.2022.1075811

Shen, B., Tan, W., Guo, J., Zhao, L., & Qin, P. (2021). How to Promote User Purchase in Metaverse? A Systematic Literature Review on Consumer Behavior Research and Virtual Commerce Application Design. *Applied Sciences (Basel, Switzerland)*, *11*(23), 23. doi:10.3390/app112311087

Shin, D. (2022). The actualization of meta affordances: Conceptualizing affordance actualization in the metaverse games. *Computers in Human Behavior*, *133*, 107292. doi:10.1016/j.chb.2022.107292

Spence, C. (2021). Scenting Entertainment: Virtual Reality Storytelling, Theme Park Rides, Gambling, and Video-Gaming. *IPerception*, *12*(4), 20416695211034538. doi:10.1177/20416695211034538 PMID:34457231

Stefanic, D. (2023, December 7). Hosting Concerts and Shows in the Metaverse. *Hyperspace^mv - the Metaverse for Business Platform.* https://hyperspace.mv/metaverse-concerts-and-shows/

Vidal-Tomás, D. (2022). The new crypto niche: NFTs, play-to-earn, and metaverse tokens. *Finance Research Letters*, *47*, 102742. doi:10.1016/j.frl.2022.102742

Voinea, G. D., Gîrbacia, F., Postelnicu, C. C., Duguleana, M., Antonya, C., Soica, A., & Stănescu, R.-C. (2022). Study of Social Presence While Interacting in Metaverse with an Augmented Avatar during Autonomous Driving. *Applied Sciences (Basel, Switzerland)*, *12*(22), 22. Advance online publication. doi:10.3390/app122211804

Vosmeer, M., & Schouten, B. (2014). Interactive Cinema: Engagement and Interaction. In A. Mitchell, C. Fernández-Vara, & D. Thue (Eds.), *Interactive Storytelling* (Vol. 8832, pp. 140–147). Springer International Publishing., doi:10.1007/978-3-319-12337-0_14

Yakura, H., & Goto, M. (2020). Enhancing Participation Experience in VR Live Concerts by Improving Motions of Virtual Audience Avatars. *2020 IEEE International Symposium on Mixed and Augmented Reality (ISMAR)*, (pp. 555–565). IEEE. 10.1109/ISMAR50242.2020.00083

Zhao, Y., Jiang, J., Chen, Y., Liu, R., Yang, Y., Xue, X., & Chen, S. (2022). Metaverse: Perspectives from graphics, interactions and visualization. *Visual Informatics*, *6*(1), 56–67. doi:10.1016/j.visinf.2022.03.002

Chapter 8
Integration of the Metaverse in the Healthcare Industry:
A Catalyst for Profound Change

Sabyasachi Pramanik

https://orcid.org/0000-0002-9431-8751

Haldia Institute of Technology, India

ABSTRACT

This chapter explores the connection of the metaverse and healthcare, investigating whether this integration signifies a significant shift or is just a passing trend. The chapter begins by explaining the notion of the metaverse and its ramifications in the healthcare environment, setting the stage for the next discussion. The chapter examines the possible catalyst impact by exploring several options. This text discusses the potential of the metaverse to transform medical teaching, enhance telemedicine, enable therapeutic interventions, and promote worldwide collaborative networks in healthcare. This investigation aims to ascertain whether the metaverse has the capacity to revolutionize healthcare methodologies, improve patient treatment, and overcome geographical obstacles. However, there are significant obstacles that need to be addressed in order to successfully integrate the metaverse, as outlined in the next section. The chapter examines the long-term viability of the metaverse's influence on healthcare by analyzing technological complexities, ethical considerations, and barriers to adoption. The chapter showcases real-world case studies that illustrate how metaverse technologies have shown to be valuable and enduring in the healthcare industry, in contrast to the fleeting nature of fads. This supports the premise that the metaverse has the potential to go beyond being a temporary fad and establish a significant presence in healthcare procedures. By analyzing historical similarities, this chapter investigates whether the metaverse has the characteristics of long-lasting change or whether it is prone to being quickly outdated. As the chapter approaches its end, it presents a prospective view on the development of the metaverse in the healthcare sector. The text compiles the acquired insights from the investigation and provides a detailed assessment of whether the metaverse has the potential to be a powerful catalyst or a temporary trend in the field of healthcare. This chapter examines the possible impact of integrating the metaverse into healthcare, examining whether it will be a driving force for long-term change or a passing trend.

DOI: 10.4018/979-8-3693-2607-7.ch008

INTRODUCTION

Ensuring healthcare is crucial for promoting the holistic well-being of individuals globally, including their physical, social, and mental health. The primary objective of every healthcare system is to allocate its resources towards endeavors that promote, sustain, restore, and improve healthcare services. Furthermore, it plays a crucial role in promoting manufacturing and economic development inside a country, as well as advancing the evolution of interactive experiences. Due to extensive exposure to technology advancements aimed at enhancing communication between caregivers, patients, and relevant stakeholders, this sector has seen significant growth and transformation. The digital healthcare revolution has brought about substantial changes in the healthcare business (Chengoden, 2023).The use of internet and digital tools in healthcare have greatly influenced the dynamic between patients and physicians. This shift may be attributed to the utilization of technologies such as blockchain, augmented reality (AR), and virtual reality (VR). The healthcare sector has made rapid progress; however it continues to face some persistent challenges, such as the overwhelming weight of chronic diseases over extended periods, escalating costs, a growing elderly population, a scarcity of healthcare professionals, and limited availability of resources (Thomason, 2021). As a result of these significant issues, individuals increasingly need access to healthcare treatments inside the confines of their own residences. The COVID-19 pandemic has significantly burdened the worldwide healthcare sector, as well as the workforce, infrastructure, and supply chain management linked to it (Benrimoh, 2022). The COVID-19 pandemic has significantly accelerated transformation in the healthcare ecosystem, compelling players to consider the use of technological advancements in this business (Bansal, 2022).The post-pandemic period has resulted in significant transformative shifts in the healthcare sector. For example, the present cohort of consumers has started to actively engage in healthcare decision-making, leading to a keen embrace of virtual healthcare systems and associated digital innovations (Wiederhold, 2022).Furthermore, there has been a significant emphasis on the use of interoperable data and data analytics, along with unprecedented therapeutic partnerships. These collaborations have compelled governments, healthcare organizations, and other stakeholders to adjust and develop new approaches (Wiederhold, 2023).Nevertheless, there exist notable challenges that must be addressed in order to shape the future trajectory of the healthcare industry. The continually evolving requirements and aims of consumers (patients) serve as the primary catalyst for improvements in this discipline. Their main objectives are establishing digitally facilitated, readily available, and smooth patient-clinician contacts, ensuring the delivery of patient-centered treatments regardless of geographical barriers and socioeconomic divisions. Each patient's health journey is unique, and it is essential to acknowledge this, provide the appropriate services, and elevate each interaction to the standard of a personalized healthcare experience. To ensure maximum customer satisfaction, facilitate monitoring, monitor health status, and encourage adherence to prescriptions, it is essential to use cutting-edge digital tools and services. The need for organizations to provide interoperability across entities and uphold customers' confidence by the demonstration of reliability, openness, and empathy in their operations has intensified due to the rising willingness of healthcare consumers to disclose their sensitive data. Assumptions are guiding the transformation of service offerings and delivery channels, with the expectation that the emphasis will transition from healthcare to encompassing both health and well-being (Thomason, 2021).Therefore, the organizations advocate for the use of self-service apps for social assistance and education, along with virtual care, remote monitoring, digital diagnostics, decision support systems, and at-home prescription delivery systems. The integration of artificial intelligence, cloud computing, augmented reality, and virtual reality technologies has significantly transformed the healthcare ecosystem. This transformation has resulted in enhanced operational capacities, improved accessibility to services, and an enhanced experience for patients and clinicians (Chengoden, 2023). The merging of the metaverse, a complex digital dimension, with the healthcare domain is an intriguing intersection where advanced technology meets crucial healthcare requirements. This chapter explores the potential and uncertainties associated with incorporating the metaverse into healthcare. It considers whether the metaverse has the potential to significantly transform medical practices, education, and patient experiences, or if it is merely a passing technological trend without lasting influence (Tan, 2022). Through an examination of the metaverse's capacity to overcome geographical barriers, transform patient-provider relationships, and revolutionize medical education, our goal is to determine whether this emerging paradigm offers a solution for sustainable advancements in healthcare or simply aligns with passing technological fads (Bansal, 2022).

Global figures from the Metaverse indicate that the healthcare services industry is projected to increase from its present value of 5.06 billion dollars in 2021 to 71.97 billion dollars by 2030. This growth is estimated to occur at a compound annual growth rate (CAGR) of 34.8 percent throughout the forecast period of 2022 to 2030. North America is expected to surpass other countries in the Metaverse industry due to its high concentration of enterprises in this sector (Mohamed, 2023). In addition, their healthcare industry has a strong infrastructure that incorporates AR-VR technology, which has led to increased investment in AR-based software updates and high-quality hardware foundation (Bhattacharya, 2022).

THEORETICAL FRAMEWORK

The Theoretical Landscape of the Metaverse in Healthcare: Visualizing the Digital Transformation

The Metaverse is a digital realm that integrates features of social networking, online gaming, augmented reality, virtual reality, and crypto-currencies. The Metaverse is a network of interconnected virtual worlds that enables users to engage in social interactions, create and participate in gaming experiences, engage in professional activities, and engage in online shopping (Chengoden, 2023). A theoretical or developing interconnected online world with digitally enduring surroundings that users may enter using AR, VR, gaming consoles, mobile devices, or regular computers to engage in real-time interactions and experiences. The healthcare system in the Metaverse provides customized healthcare experiences that are interactive, immersive, and pleasant. Utilizing these technologies allows individuals to access innovative and more cost-effective means of delivering treatment, leading to enhanced patient results (Petrigna, 2022). The Metaverse leverages the Internet to provide an immersive virtual reality environment that replicates human emotions and movements. It encompasses the whole social and economic systems of both the real and virtual worlds. The technologies of the metaverse may assist medical staff in the precise planning and diagnosis of illnesses (Wang, 2022). In 2020, the neurosurgeons at Johns Hopkins Hospital used an Augmedics AR headgear during a surgical operation. The therapy included fusing six vertebrae in the patient's spine to alleviate persistent back pain using a transparent ocular display that displayed patients' anatomical views similar to X-ray vision (Sebastian, 2022). By using headsets and the Metaverse environment, the conversion of CT scans into 3D reconstructions enables enhanced preoperative surgical planning. Furthermore, this allows surgeons to meticulously examine, separate, and alter anatomical components in order to perform essential procedures. In addition, the metaverse devices amplify the effects of prescription drugs (Lee, 2022). For example, EaseVR is a medically prescribed device that utilizes virtual reality (VR) headgear and controllers to provide cognitive behavioral therapy to people suffering from back pain. These strategies facilitate the development of interoceptive awareness, induce profound relaxation, and enable adjustments in attention that specifically target the physiological components of pain. The intricate and challenging discipline of plastic surgery involves the rebuilding of many anatomical structures in the human body. Utilizing virtual reality (VR) in the Metaverse for plastic surgery is of utmost importance as it enables patients to see the potential impact of a genuine treatment on virtual avatars, hence enhancing their comprehension of the surgeon's proficiency (Sebastian, 2022).

Proficiency in human anatomy and the ability to use versatile, individually customizable gadgets with enhanced grasping skills are essential for operating in the Metaverse (Lee, 2022). The wide range of applications for this technology includes simple treatments and complex spinal surgery, as well as tumor removal. The radiology division of the metaverse has the capacity to unlock enhanced image visualization capabilities, enabling radiologists to see dynamic pictures with greater precision. The radiology division of the Metaverse has the capacity to unlock novel image visualization capabilities, enabling radiologists to examine dynamic images in a more comprehensive way, resulting in enhanced diagnosis and accurate decision-making (Koohang, 2023). Moreover, it would provide the opportunity for enhanced radiography education and the ability to collaborate as a group on three-dimensional medical images, even when located in different geographic regions. By utilizing superior immersive content and incorporating gamification elements, the healthcare metaverse has the potential to enhance patient involvement. It can assist clinicians in elucidating intricate concepts to patients, offer step-by-step demonstrations of medical procedures, and ensure patients adhere to their prescribed medication regimen. By incorporating the patient's vital signs, CT scans, medical records, and genetic test outcomes into a digital model that replicates the patient's anatomy and physiology, the use of digital twin solutions in the Metaverse will ensure that patients are well-informed and actively involved in their treatment. Patients have the ability to access their health information via a virtual dashboard. This allows them to interact with physicians, researchers, nutritionists, and other relevant parties in order to obtain personalized care and treatment (Petrigna, 2022). The current pandemic has spurred the need for remote healthcare services, and the Metaverse has the capacity to provide a superior experience compared to conventional telemedicine systems based on videoconferencing (Mejia, 2022). Patients have the ability to use augmented reality (AR) glasses to establish immediate voice and video connections with clinicians inside the Metaverse. AR technology enables responders to directly engage and transmit real-time emergency situations to distant physicians; facilitating prompt on-site treatment (Letafati, 2023). The metaverse has the potential to revolutionize the training and education of medical professionals. AR facilitates the demonstration of practical procedures rather than the dissemination of academic information. Esteemed universities are progressively using VR, AR, mixed reality (MR), and AI-based technologies to educate medical practitioners by simulating complex real-time procedures and imparting information about the cellular composition of the human body (Rahaman, 2022).

The Metaverse comprises state-of-the-art technology advancements such as blockchain, telepresence, augmented reality, and artificial intelligence (AI), which have a substantial influence on healthcare (Letafati, 2023).

Table 1. Technological paradigms reshaping healthcare: Applications and benefits

Technology	Description and Role in Healthcare	Applications and Benefits
Electronic Health Records (EHR)	Digitalized patient records and medical history. Centralized access for healthcare professionals.	Seamless sharing of patient data among healthcare providers.
Telemedicine	Remote medical consultations via digital platforms. Video and audio communication for diagnosis.	Improved access to medical care in remote areas, reduced travel for patients.
Mobile Health (mHealth)	Health-related services and information delivered via mobile devices.	Health monitoring, medication reminders and lifestyle tracking through apps.
Wearable Devices	Devices worn by individuals to track health and fitness data.	Real-time monitoring of vital signs, physical activity, and sleep patterns.
Internet of Things (IoT)	Interconnected devices for data exchange and automation	Remote monitoring of medical equipment, predictive maintenance, and real-time patient tracking.
Health Information Exchange (HIE)	Secure sharing of patient information among healthcare providers and organizations.	Coordinated care among different health care entities, reduced duplication of tests.
Artificial Intelligence (AI)	Machine learning algorithms for data analysis, prediction, and decision support.	Personalized treatment plans, medical image analysis, drug discovery.
Big Data Analytics	Processing and analyzing large volumes of healthcare data for insights.	Identifying health trends, population health management, disease prediction.
Remote Patient Monitoring	Continuous monitoring of patients outside of traditional healthcare settings.	Chronic disease management, early detection of health deterioration.
Blockchain	Secure and transparent data storage and transactions.	Secure sharing of patient records, maintaining data integrity.
Health Apps	Mobile applications for various health-related purposes.	Health tracking, medication reminders, mental health support.
Virtual Reality (VR) and Augmented Reality (AR)	Immersive experiences for medical training, therapy, and visualization.	Surgical simulations, medical education, pain management therapies.
Genomics and Personalized Medicine	Study of individual genetic makeup for personalized treatment.	Tailored treatment plans, targeted drug therapies, disease risk assessment.

A Comprehensive Investigation of Digital and smart Enabling Technologies That Are Transforming Healthcare

The combination of these technologies forms a complex and engaging metaverse in the healthcare field, providing inventive ways to enhance patient care, medical education, and overall healthcare experiences (Letafati, 2023).

The current digital and smart healthcare technologies play a crucial role in revolutionizing the healthcare industry. They enhance patient care, improve access to medical services, increase diagnostic accuracy, and promote tailored and efficient healthcare solutions (Lee, 2022).

Exploring the Potential Benefits and Opportunities of the Metaverse in the Healthcare Industry

The use of the Metaverse in healthcare offers a multitude of advantages and prospects that have the potential to completely transform the industry:

The Metaverse provides medical professionals with enhanced training by offering realistic and immersive surroundings. These environments enable professionals to practice operations, surgeries, and patient interactions in a risk-free digital setting. As a result, there is an enhancement in the acquisition of skills and preparedness (Chengoden, 2023).

Remote Consultations: Healthcare practitioners may provide virtual patient consultations and follow-ups, allowing access to medical competence irrespective of geographic location. This improves the quality of healthcare provided to patients, particularly those residing in distant or underprivileged regions (v, 2023).

Therapeutic Interventions: Virtual reality may be used for several therapeutic objectives, including pain mitigation, stress alleviation, and exposure treatment. These therapies possess the capacity to supplement conventional treatments and enhance patient outcomes (Song, 2022).

Patient Engagement: The Metaverse has the ability to include patients in their treatment programs by providing interactive instructional material, gamified exercises, and immersive experiences. This may result in improved patient compliance and enhanced health outcomes (Athar, 2023).

Rehabilitation and Physical Therapy: Customized virtual worlds may be designed for rehabilitation activities, encouraging patients to actively engage in their recuperation. This may expedite the process of healing and enhance the overall functioning results.

Collaborative Research: Researchers and medical experts may engage in virtual environments to examine intricate data, do simulations, and enhance medical research with more efficiency (Mozumder, 2022).

The Metaverse has the potential to democratize medical education via the provision of online courses, virtual workshops, and simulations. These resources provide flexible and easily accessible learning possibilities for students and professionals worldwide (Petrigna, 2022).

Support Communities: Online support groups and communities in the virtual world may bring together persons who are dealing with similar health issues, helping to alleviate feelings of loneliness and promoting emotional wellness.

Real-time Data Visualization: Augmented reality overlays may provide medical personnel immediate access to patient data, diagnostics, and treatment plans during operations, hence improving decision-making and accuracy.

The Metaverse has the potential to decrease healthcare expenditures by eliminating the need for in-person visits and hospital stays via remote consultations, virtual follow-ups, and preventative treatments (Ali, 2023).

Personalized Medicine: The Metaverse has the potential to streamline the incorporation of patient data, allowing for tailored treatment strategies that take into account unique medical backgrounds, genetic profiles, and reactions to various medications.

Innovative Treatment Approaches: The Metaverse's capacity for creativity enables the exploration of new treatment methods, such as using virtual environments for cognitive therapy and interventions in mental health (Ganapathy, 2022).

Health Data Tracking: Wearable devices and augmented reality (AR) interfaces have the capability to provide consumers immediate health data, encouraging self-awareness and proactive management of one's health.

Continuity of Care: Patients have the ability to retrieve medical information, data, and treatment plans in a durable virtual setting, guaranteeing uninterrupted care even during the switch between healthcare providers (Song, 2022).

The Metaverse fundamentally provides a means for revolutionizing healthcare by facilitating customized, immersive, and cooperative methods that may result in enhanced patient results, optimized processes, and a healthcare system that is more accessible and efficient (Bansal, 2022).

Analysis of the Metaverse's Impact on Healthcare: Is it a Transformative Force or Just a Passing Trend?

To determine whether the metaverse signifies a significant change or a temporary trend, it requires a thorough examination of many crucial factors (Bansal, 2022). The long-term sustainability of the system depends on its capacity to adapt to technological progress and meet the evolving demands of users in many sectors (Situmorang, 2023). Furthermore, it is of utmost importance to prioritize the resolution of ethical and privacy problems, particularly in highly sensitive industries like as healthcare (Marzaleh, 2022). The legitimacy of data use for enhanced treatment and protection of patient privacy relies on achieving a balance. Furthermore, the successful integration of the metaverse into current healthcare systems requires overcoming integration problems and technological constraints. Central to its continuous success are the key factors of ensuring compatibility, data security, and accessibility (Wang, 2022). Finally, by comparing it to other healthcare trends like EHRs and telemedicine, we may get an understanding of how lasting changes occur when they clearly improve patient care, simplify procedures, and adjust efficiently. Finally, the destiny of the metaverse hinges on its capacity to negotiate these intricacies, showcasing concrete worth and flexibility, finally establishing its position as either a passing trend or a groundbreaking metamorphosis in healthcare and other fields. Examining the notion of transformation vs fad within the metaverse framework, with specific emphasis on long-term sustainability, ethical and privacy issues, integration complexities, and similarities to past healthcare fads, unveils a nuanced viewpoint on the subject (Gupta, 2023).

Evaluating the long-term sustainability: The metaverse, a digital environment formed by the merging of physical and virtual reality, has gained considerable interest due to progress in augmented reality (AR), virtual reality (VR), and other immersive technologies. The long-term sustainability of the system relies on several aspects such as technical progress, user acceptance, and economic viability (Chengoden, 2023). The metaverse has the potential to revolutionize several sectors, such as healthcare, but its success relies on effectively addressing the practical requirements and desires of its users. Should the metaverse demonstrate significant use and maintain flexibility in response to changing requirements, it has the potential to become a revolutionary influence rather than a passing trend (Moztarzadeh, 2023).

Regarding Ethical and Privacy problems: Similar to every revolutionary technology, there are substantial ethical and privacy problems. Within the healthcare industry, these concerns are magnified as a result of the delicate nature of patient data and the possibility of security breaches (Petrigna, 2022). It is crucial to guarantee data security, get user permission, and implement adequate anonymization. Moreover, concerns emerge about the possibility of depersonalization in patient care and the ethical ramifications of integrating real and virtual medical procedures. Effectively addressing these issues will be essential for the metaverse to establish confidence and demonstrate its enduring worth (Moztarzadeh, 2023).

Overcoming technological obstacles is necessary to integrate the metaverse into healthcare (Bhugaonkar, 2022). It is crucial to have smooth compatibility across different virtual platforms, electronic health records (EHR) systems, medical equipment, and real-time patient data. It is crucial to have standardized protocols and APIs to ensure safe data flow. Furthermore, overcoming the challenge of providing accessibility to patients with diverse abilities and demographics is a major obstacle. Failure to adequately tackle these integration obstacles may result in the metaverse retaining its status as a specialized tool rather than a revolutionary trend in healthcare (Garavand, 2022).

Analyzing the Integration of Metaverse in Comparison to Previous Healthcare Trends: In order to determine if the metaverse signifies a substantial change or a passing trend, it is advantageous to draw comparisons with prior advancements in healthcare technology. Electronic health records (EHRs), tele-medicine, and wearable health gadgets, first met with doubt, have now become essential components of healthcare provision (Zhang, 2023). The success of these trends was propelled by their capacity to improve patient care, optimize processes, and adjust to changing demands. For the metaverse to be suc-cessful, it must show distinct benefits compared to current approaches and adapt as healthcare progresses (Song, 2022).

To ascertain whether the metaverse is a transformative force or a passing trend, a thorough assess-ment of its enduring sustainability, ethical implications, technological obstacles, and similarities to past healthcare patterns is necessary (Kim, 2023). The metaverse has the capacity to greatly influence healthcare by facilitating remote consultations, medical education, and treatment, among other uses (Yang, 2022). Nevertheless, the achievement of its goals relies on surmounting technological obstacles, tackling ethical considerations, and demonstrating its practical worth in the long run. It is of utmost importance to approach the integration of the metaverse into healthcare with a combination of hope and careful evaluation (Situmorang, 2023).

Exploring the Intersection of the Metaverse and Healthcare: Exemplary Cases and Optimal Approaches

The table presents a succinct summary of case studies, success stories, lessons learned, best practices, and case examples that demonstrate the beneficial impact of incorporating the Metaverse into healthcare. The "Case Studies" section features instances such as the use of virtual reality (VR) for pain treatment at Cedars-Sinai Medical Center and VR-based surgical training conducted by Osso VR. The "Success

Table 2. The use of metaverse in the healthcare industry has yielded notable achievements and exem-plary approaches

Case Studies	Success Stories and Best Practices	Case Examples: Positive Impact on Patient Outcomes
Cedars-Sinai Medical Center - VR Pain Management: Utilized virtual reality (VR) to reduce anxiety and pain perception during medical procedures.	**User-Centric Design:** Design virtual experiences with user-friendliness in mind.	**Virtual Physical Therapy for Seniors:** Improved mobility and quality of life through engaging VR-based physical therapy.
Osso VR - Surgical Training: Developed VR-based surgical training platform resulting in increased procedural accuracy and safety.	**Ethical Considerations:** Prioritize patient privacy and consent while exploring new applications.	**Pain Distraction for Pediatric Procedures:** Lowered anxiety and pain levels during procedures for pediatric patients using immersive virtual experiences.
Mayo Clinic - Virtual Patient Consultations: Implemented virtual consultations for remote patients, leading to better chronic condition management.	**Collaboration:** Engage multidisciplinary teams for comprehensive Metaverse solutions.	
Stanford Children's Health - Pediatric Rehabilitation: Enhanced pediatric rehabilitation with engaging virtual activities, resulting in improved motor skills.		

Stories and Best Practices" section highlights the importance of user-centric design, ethical concerns, and cooperation as crucial elements for achieving effective implementation. The column titled "Case Examples: Positive Impact on Patient Outcomes" showcases the positive effects of virtual physical therapy for elderly individuals and pain distraction strategies for pediatric operations. These interventions have resulted in increased patient mobility, decreased anxiety, and higher overall quality of life (Huang, 2023). Collectively, these observations demonstrate the revolutionary capacity of the Metaverse in the field of healthcare, emphasizing the significance of meticulous strategizing, ethical deliberations, and inventive methodologies. The case studies, success stories, lessons learned, and best practices exemplify the potential of integrating Metaverse technology in healthcare. They highlight the beneficial effects on patient outcomes, medical training, and overall patient care (Dogum, 2023).

Investigating the Future of Healthcare: Utilizing the Metaverse to Achieve Significant Real-World Effects

Based on the specific technologies used, such as augmented reality (AR), life logging, virtual reality (VR), and mirror world, the prospective uses of the Metaverse in healthcare may be categorized into four distinct groups (Usmani, 2022). Using an augmented reality (AR) T-shirt in an anatomy lab would allow students to vividly see the human body. Mirror world implementation involves the use of virtual mapping and modeling techniques to create an exact reproduction of the actual world, while also including essential environmental data. The present pandemic emergency has further enhanced the use of the Metaverse. People from distant locations participate and play in games inside a virtual reality platform known as the mirror world (Petrigna, 2022).Consequently, these state-of-the-art technologies provide more precise visualizations, understanding, and application of innovative techniques. Consequently, these state-of-the-art technologies provide more precise visualizations, understanding, and application of innovative techniques. The Metaverse provides a comprehensive visual representation of physical ailments and serves as an exceptionally effective tool for surgical training, promoting optimal collaboration and immersive experiences. Despite being in the experimental phase, the use of this technology has the potential to significantly benefit healthcare education and training. In contrast to the "handicraft workshop model," characterized by inconsistent diagnostic and treatment approaches among doctors and hospitals, the Metaverse significantly enhances the delivery of comprehensive healthcare (Wiederhold, 2022). Decisions in a scenario requiring comprehensive healthcare will rely on the guidance of the specialist and the results of the many Metaverse enabling technologies. The Metaverse has a wide range of medical applications, such as research, physical assessment, diagnosis, and insurance purposes (Curtis, 2023). Potential uses of the Metaverse that may gain popularity in the near future include virtual physiotherapy, virtual biopsy, virtual psychotherapy, and virtual alarm response. The act of obtaining and analyzing an image to characterize tissues is referred to as a virtual biopsy. Virtual physiotherapy may be used to provide guidance and instruction to patients undergoing rehabilitation, aiding them in their mobility and exercise routines (Nica, 2022).

Medical Diagnosis refers to the process of identifying a disease or condition in a patient based on their symptoms, medical history, and diagnostic tests.

Medical diagnosis is the systematic determination of a patient's medical state based on an analysis of their symptoms. The integration of the Metaverse in healthcare significantly enhances the precise identification of a patient's medical conditions via the use of advanced technologies such as augmented reality (AR), virtual reality (VR), extended digital twins, blockchain, 5G, and other similar innovations

(Turab, 2023). A research paper titled "Expert Consensus on the Metaverse in Medicine" was presented, elucidating the methods and rationale for implementing the Metaverse across many healthcare domains to provide comprehensive and superior healthcare services. The metaverse has the potential to enhance the current medical Internet of Things (IoT) by addressing its limitations in terms of human-computer interaction, connection, and integration with both the physical and virtual realms (Wiederhold, 2022).

Monitoring of Patients

The healthcare sector stands to gain significant advantages from the Metaverse due to the integration of telepresence, digital twinning, and blockchain technologies, namely in the realm of patient monitoring. Telemedicine, sometimes referred to as telepresence in medicine, is the practice of providing medical treatments remotely. During emergency situations, the use of patient simulators may be employed to assess the potential impact of therapies on real patients well in advance. Utilizing blockchain technology ensures the secure storage and sharing of medical data, safeguarding its integrity and minimizing potential risks (Petrigna, 2022).Efficient patient monitoring may be achieved when these three parts are carefully constructed to work together. The Metaverse provides a solution by integrating various technologies into a unified system. COVID-19 has prompted medical experts to explore the possibility of delivering high-quality healthcare remotely, using the combination of medical advice, phone calls, or video consultations with patients (Prasetyo, 2022).Advancements in the Metaverse have enabled the healthcare sector to generate virtual environments as needed and provide medical care to impoverished individuals, regardless of their distance from healthcare facilities (Bashir, 2023).

Medical Education

The Metaverse signifies a momentous shift in medical education. The forefront innovators in the field of medical education are using IoT, blockchain, AI, AR, and VR technologies to develop the Metaverse. The discussion revolved on the impact of AI, blockchain, and the Metaverse on healthcare. The blockchain's unique identifier tags facilitate the recognition of data throughout the blockchain-powered Metaverse (Sestino, 2023).The Metaverse is an AI and blockchain-powered digital virtual universe that surpasses the limitations of the physical world (Kahambing, 2023). These technologies facilitate medical students' ability to focus on the session, actively participate in the discussion, converse in depth, and engage with more pleasure, especially in the busy clinical environment. In the conventional method of teaching, the teacher would require the medical students to personally visit a patient, followed by presenting and discussing the relevant medical facts with the group of students. The advent of digital integration and 3D technology has brought about a substantial transformation in clinical training. Currently, a cohort of medical students is being introduced to a patient in a virtual reality setting. The authors proposed a hybrid approach that combines structural equation modeling and machine learning to predict users' intends to use the Metaverse for healthcare education (Han, 2023).

Medical Procedures

The metaverse is an essential medical technology, especially in the field of surgery. Presently, doctors use tools such as VR headsets and haptic gloves to replicate real surgical operations, hence enhancing preparedness and effectiveness in the operating room. Augmented reality (AR) may enhance the convenience of surgical operations by providing physicians easy access to data. Augmented reality (AR) enables surgeons to efficiently retrieve patient information by projecting 3D virtual representations onto the patient's body, without the need for physical interaction and with ease and speed (Chen, 2022). Within the Metaverse, educators and speakers have the capability to showcase intricate processes using three-dimensional representations. In addition, patients who have had surgery might obtain counseling services via the Metaverse, as suggested by Curtis (2023).

Medical Therapeutics and Theranostics

The branch of medicine that specifically focuses on the management and treatment of illnesses is often known as medical therapy. DTx, or digital therapeutics, refer to evidence-based therapeutic approaches within the field of digital medicine. According to the Digital Therapies Alliance, digital therapies are products that use high-quality software programs to provide evidence-based therapeutic interventions for the prevention, management, or treatment of medical disorders or diseases (Thomason, 2021).The use of the underlying technology has the potential to greatly transform the field of medicine via Metaverse participation in treatments and theranostics. A digital therapy, a kind of treatment that does not need the use of pharmaceutical drugs, is gaining importance in the healthcare sector (Situmorang, 2022).

Computer vision is a technology that can analyze, inspect, visualize, and comprehend pictures and movies (Mozumder, 2023).

The Convergence of the Metaverse With Healthcare Presents Several Challenges and Dynamic Trajectories

The table presents the obstacles and prospective paths for integrating the Metaverse into the healthcare sector. Regarding challenges, it tackles issues such as safeguarding patient data privacy and security, ethical considerations, ensuring fair access to services, training healthcare professionals, meeting technical infrastructure requirements, standardizing practices, obtaining regulatory approvals, implementing realistic simulation, integrating into existing workflows, and designing user experience. The future directions section proposes various strategies to bolster security measures, establish ethical guidelines, foster accessibility initiatives, offer professional training, enhance technical connectivity, establish interoperability frameworks, engage with regulatory bodies, invest in advanced simulation technologies, develop workflow integration solutions, and prioritize user-centric design principles (Thomason, 2021). The problems and directions highlight the intricate nature and possible advantages of incorporating the Metaverse into healthcare, while underlining the need of meticulous preparation, cooperation, and creativity to navigate this dynamic environment. The difficulties and future directions emphasize the potential advantages of integrating the Metaverse in healthcare. They also emphasize the need of thoughtful analysis, cooperation, and creativity in tackling the many problems that occur in this developing field (Curtis, 2023).

CONCLUSION

This chapter provides a comprehensive examination of the applications of the Metaverse in the field of healthcare. The current situation of digital healthcare and the need to embrace the Metaverse for healthcare

Table 3. Challenges and future directions in the synergy between metaverse and healthcare

Challenge	Description	Future Directions
Privacy and Security	Ensuring the protection of sensitive patient data and maintaining a secure environment in the virtual space.	Enhanced Security Measures: Developing robust encryption and authentication methods to safeguard patient information and maintain HIPAA compliance.
Ethical Concerns	Addressing potential ethical issues related to patient consent, data ownership, and the blurring of boundaries between virtual and real experiences.	Ethical Guidelines: Establishing clear ethical guidelines and standards for the use of the Metaverse in healthcare, addressing consent, data privacy, and virtual interactions.
Access and Equity	Ensuring equal access to Metaverse-based healthcare services for all individuals, regardless of their socioeconomic status or geographical location.	Accessibility Initiatives: Implementing initiatives to provide affordable VR/AR equipment and reliable internet access to underserved populations.
Training and Familiarity	Training healthcare professionals to effectively navigate and utilize Metaverse technologies for patient care and medical education.	Professional Training Programs: Developing specialized training programs and resources for healthcare professionals to proficiently use Metaverse tools and applications.
Technical Infrastructure	Establishing the necessary technical infrastructure to support seamless integration and real-time interactions within the Metaverse.	Improved Connectivity: Investing in high-speed internet connectivity and robust VR/AR hardware to ensure smooth experiences and minimize latency.
Standardization	Establishing industry-wide standards for interoperability, data exchange, and content creation within the healthcare Metaverse.	Interoperability Frameworks: Collaborating with technology companies to develop standardized protocols and APIs that enable seamless data sharing and collaboration across platforms.
Regulatory Approval	Navigating regulatory frameworks to ensure that Metaverse-based medical applications comply with existing healthcare regulations.	Regulatory Partnerships: Collaborating with regulatory agencies to develop guidelines that balance innovation with patient safety and privacy.
Realistic Simulation	Ensuring that virtual simulations accurately replicate real-world medical scenarios for effective training and treatment planning.	Advanced Simulation Technologies: Investing in AI-driven simulations and haptic feedback systems that replicate realistic physiological responses and patient interactions.
Integration Challenges	Integrating Metaverse tools seamlessly into existing healthcare workflows and electronic health record systems.	Workflow Integration Solutions: Collaborating with health IT companies to develop interfaces and integrations that allow for efficient data exchange between the Metaverse and existing systems.
User Experience	Designing user-friendly interfaces and intuitive interactions to ensure that healthcare professionals and patients can effectively navigate the Metaverse.	User-Centric Design: Employing human-centered design principles to create Metaverse applications that prioritize user experience, making them intuitive and easy to use.

are first outlined. Subsequently, an examination of the cutting-edge technologies now used in digital and smart healthcare frameworks is conducted, following the exploration of the enabling technologies of the Metaverse. Subsequently, the potential applications of the Metaverse in the healthcare industry became evident. Specifically, the focus is on the possible use of the Metaverse in medical diagnostics, patient monitoring, healthcare education, operations, medical treatments, and theranostics. Furthermore, current and future developments in the Metaverse for healthcare are emphasizing the use of blockchain, digital twins, and telemedicine. This analysis critically evaluates the obstacles that hinder the complete realization of the Metaverse's promise in the field of healthcare, while also considering its future prospects.

Enhancing the Healthcare Industry via the Metaverse: Key Recommendations

Several recommendations have been proposed to facilitate the secure implementation of the Metaverse in healthcare. Healthcare institutions and providers should have a proactive stance towards integrating the metaverse by devising strategies to seamlessly include it into their operations. First and foremost, it is essential to form interdisciplinary teams consisting of medical specialists, technologists, and user experience experts in order to develop efficient metaverse solutions. Furthermore, it is crucial to prioritize patient-centered care inside the metaverse. This entails guaranteeing that the virtual experience improves patient outcomes and engagement, while also protecting their privacy. Moreover, it will be crucial to provide comprehensive training to healthcare personnel in order to proficiently navigate and apply metaverse technologies. Implementing strong data security protocols and clear patient consent processes are essential for establishing confidence. Moreover, it will be crucial to engage in partnerships with technological allies in order to create compatible systems that can seamlessly connect with current electronic health records and medical equipment. Regarding study fields, exploring the influence of the metaverse on the relationships between patients and doctors, the effectiveness of therapeutic treatments, and the efficiency of medical training will provide useful insights for improving and optimizing its use in healthcare settings.

REFERENCES

Ali, S., Abdullah, Armand, T. P. T., Athar, A., Hussain, A., Ali, M., Yaseen, M., Joo, M.-I., & Kim, H.-C. (2023). Metaverse in healthcare integrated with explainable ai and blockchain: Enabling immersiveness, ensuring trust, and providing patient data security. *Sensors (Basel)*, *23*(2), 565. doi:10.3390/s23020565 PMID:36679361

Athar, A., Ali, S. M., Mozumder, M. A. I., Ali, S., & Kim, H. C. (2023, February). Applications and Possible Challenges of Healthcare Metaverse. In *2023 25th International Conference on Advanced Communication Technology (ICACT)* (pp. 328-332). IEEE. 10.23919/ICACT56868.2023.10079314

Bansal, G., Rajgopal, K., Chamola, V., Xiong, Z., & Niyato, D. (2022). Healthcare in metaverse: A survey on current metaverse applications in healthcare. *IEEE Access : Practical Innovations, Open Solutions*, *10*, 119914–119946. doi:10.1109/ACCESS.2022.3219845

Bashir, A. K., Victor, N., Bhattacharya, S., Huynh-The, T., Chengoden, R., Yenduri, G., Maddikunta, P. K. R., Pham, Q.-V., Gadekallu, T. R., & Liyanage, M. (2023). Federated Learning for the Healthcare Metaverse: Concepts, Applications, Challenges, and Future Directions. *IEEE Internet of Things Journal*, *10*(24), 21873–21891. doi:10.1109/JIOT.2023.3304790

Benrimoh, D., Chheda, F. D., & Margolese, H. C. (2022). The Best Predictor of the Future—The Metaverse, Mental Health, and Lessons Learned From Current Technologies. *JMIR Mental Health*, *9*(10), e40410. doi:10.2196/40410 PMID:36306155

Bhattacharya, P., Obaidat, M. S., Savaliya, D., Sanghavi, S., Tanwar, S., & Sadaun, B. (2022, July). Metaverse assisted telesurgery in healthcare 5.0: An interplay of blockchain and explainable AI. In *2022 International Conference on Computer, Information and Telecommunication Systems (CITS)* (pp. 1-5). IEEE. 10.1109/CITS55221.2022.9832978

Bhugaonkar, K., Bhugaonkar, R., & Masne, N. (2022). The trend of metaverse and augmented & virtual reality extending to the healthcare system. *Cureus*, *14*(9). doi:10.7759/cureus.29071 PMID:36258985

Chen Y. Lin W. Zheng Y. Xue T. Chen C. Chen G. (2022). Application of active learning strategies in metaverse to improve student engagement: An immersive blended pedagogy bridging patient care and scientific inquiry in pandemic. *Available at* SSRN 4098179. doi:10.2139/ssrn.4098179

Chengoden, R., Victor, N., Huynh-The, T., Yenduri, G., Jhaveri, R. H., Alazab, M., Bhattacharya, S., Hegde, P., Maddikunta, P. K. R., & Gadekallu, T. R. (2023). Metaverse for healthcare: A survey on potential applications, challenges and future directions. *IEEE Access : Practical Innovations, Open Solutions, 11*, 12765–12795. doi:10.1109/ACCESS.2023.3241628

Curtis, C., & Brolan, C. E. (2023). Health care in the metaverse. *The Medical Journal of Australia, 218*(1), 46. doi:10.5694/mja2.51793 PMID:36437589

Dogum, R., & Uribe, D. (2023). NFTs and Metaverse in Healthcare: What's the Big Opportunity? *Blockchain in Healthcare Today, 6*(1). doi:10.30953/bhty.v6.266

Ganapathy, K. (2022). Metaverse and healthcare: A clinician's perspective. *Apollo Medicine, 19*(4), 256–261.

Garavand, A., & Aslani, N. (2022). Metaverse phenomenon and its impact on health: A scoping review. *Informatics in Medicine Unlocked, 32*, 101029. doi:10.1016/j.imu.2022.101029

Gupta, O. J., Yadav, S., Srivastava, M. K., Darda, P., & Mishra, V. (2023). Understanding the intention to use metaverse in healthcare utilizing a mix method approach. *International Journal of Healthcare Management*, 1–12. doi:10.1080/20479700.2023.2183579

Han, B., Wang, H., Qiao, D., Xu, J., & Yan, T. (2023). Application of Zero-Watermarking Scheme Based on Swin Transformer for Securing the Metaverse Healthcare Data. *IEEE Journal of Biomedical and Health Informatics*. Advance online publication. doi:10.1109/JBHI.2021.3123936 PMID:37028374

Huang, H., Zhang, C., Zhao, L., Ding, S., Wang, H., & Wu, H. (2023). Self-Supervised Medical Image Denoising Based on WISTA-Net for Human Healthcare in Metaverse. *IEEE Journal of Biomedical and Health Informatics*. PMID:37216248

Kahambing, J. G. (2023). Metaverse, mental health and museums in post-COVID-19. *Journal of Public Health (Oxford, England), 45*(2), e382–e383. doi:10.1093/pubmed/fdad002 PMID:36680432

Kim, E. J., & Kim, J. Y. (2023). The metaverse for healthcare: Trends, applications, and future directions of digital therapeutics for urology. *International Neurourology Journal, 27*(Suppl 1), S3–S12. doi:10.5213/inj.2346108.054 PMID:37280754

Koohang, A., Nord, J. H., Ooi, K. B., Tan, G. W. H., Al-Emran, M., Aw, E. C. X., Baabdullah, A. M., Buhalis, D., Cham, T.-H., Dennis, C., Dutot, V., Dwivedi, Y. K., Hughes, L., Mogaji, E., Pandey, N., Phau, I., Raman, R., Sharma, A., Sigala, M., & Wong, L. W. (2023). Shaping the metaverse into reality: A holistic multidisciplinary understanding of opportunities, challenges, and avenues for future investigation. *Journal of Computer Information Systems, 63*(3), 735–765. doi:10.1080/08874417.2023.2165197

Lee, C. W. (2022). Application of metaverse service to healthcare industry: A strategic perspective. *International Journal of Environmental Research and Public Health, 19*(20), 13038. doi:10.3390/ijerph192013038 PMID:36293609

Lee, J., & Kwon, K. H. (2022). The significant transformation of life into health and beauty in metaverse era. *Journal of Cosmetic Dermatology*, *21*(12), 6575–6583. doi:10.1111/jocd.15151 PMID:35686389

Letafati, M., & Otoum, S. (2023). Digital Healthcare in The Metaverse: Insights into Privacy and Security. *arXiv preprint arXiv:2308.04438*.

Li, J. (2022). Impact of Metaverse cultural communication on the mental health of international students in China: Highlighting effects of healthcare anxiety and cyberchondria. *American Journal of Health Behavior*, *46*(6), 809–820. doi:10.5993/AJHB.46.6.21 PMID:36721290

Marzaleh, M. A., Peyravi, M., & Shaygani, F. (2022). A revolution in health: Opportunities and challenges of the Metaverse. *EXCLI Journal*, *21*, 791. PMID:35949490

Mejia, J. M. R., & Rawat, D. B. (2022, July). recent advances in a medical domain metaverse: Status, challenges, and perspective. In *2022 Thirteenth International Conference on Ubiquitous and Future Networks (ICUFN)* (pp. 357-362). IEEE. 10.1109/ICUFN55119.2022.9829645

Mohamed, E. S., Naqishbandi, T. A., & Veronese, G. (2023). Metaverse!: Possible Potential Opportunities and Trends in E-Healthcare and Education. [IJEA]. *International Journal of E-Adoption*, *15*(2), 1–21. doi:10.4018/IJEA.316537

Moztarzadeh, O., Jamshidi, M., Sargolzaei, S., Jamshidi, A., Baghalipour, N., Malekzadeh Moghani, M., & Hauer, L. (2023). Metaverse and Healthcare: Machine Learning-Enabled Digital Twins of Cancer. *Bioengineering (Basel, Switzerland)*, *10*(4), 455. doi:10.3390/bioengineering10040455 PMID:37106642

Mozumder, M. A. I., Armand, T. P. T., Imtiyaj Uddin, S. M., Athar, A., Sumon, R. I., Hussain, A., & Kim, H. C. (2023). Metaverse for Digital Anti-Aging Healthcare: An Overview of Potential Use Cases Based on Artificial Intelligence, Blockchain, IoT Technologies, Its Challenges, and Future Directions. *Applied Sciences (Basel, Switzerland)*, *13*(8), 5127. doi:10.3390/app13085127

Mozumder, M. A. I., Sheeraz, M. M., Athar, A., Aich, S., & Kim, H. C. (2022, February). Overview: Technology roadmap of the future trend of metaverse based on IoT, blockchain, AI technique, and medical domain metaverse activity. In *2022 24th International Conference on Advanced Communication Technology (ICACT)* (pp. 256-261). IEEE.

Nica, E. (2022). Virtual healthcare technologies and consultation systems, smart operating rooms, and remote sensing data fusion algorithms in the medical metaverse. *American Journal of Medical Research (New York, N.Y.)*, *9*(2), 105–120. doi:10.22381/ajmr9220227

Petrigna, L., & Musumeci, G. (2022). The metaverse: A new challenge for the healthcare system: A scoping review. *Journal of Functional Morphology and Kinesiology*, *7*(3), 63. doi:10.3390/jfmk7030063 PMID:36135421

Prasetyo, J. (2022). The Future of Post-Covid-19 Health Services using Metaverse Technology. *The Journal for Nurse Practitioners*, *6*(1), 93–99. doi:10.30994/jnp.v6i1.295

Qiu, C. S., Majeed, A., Khan, S., & Watson, M. (2022). Transforming health through the metaverse. *Journal of the Royal Society of Medicine*, *115*(12), 484–486. doi:10.1177/01410768221144763 PMID:36480946

Rahaman, T. (2022). Into the metaverse–perspectives on a new reality. *Medical Reference Services Quarterly*, *41*(3), 330–337. doi:10.1080/02763869.2022.2096341 PMID:35980623

Sebastian, S. R., & Babu, B. P. (2022). Impact of metaverse in health care: A study from the care giver's perspective. *International Journal of Community Medicine and Public Health*, *9*(12), 4613. doi:10.18203/2394-6040.ijcmph20223221

Sestino, A., & D'Angelo, A. (2023). My doctor is an avatar! The effect of anthropomorphism and emotional receptivity on individuals' intention to use digital-based healthcare services. *Technological Forecasting and Social Change*, *191*, 122505. doi:10.1016/j.techfore.2023.122505

Situmorang, D. D. B. (2022). "Rapid tele-psychotherapy" with single-session music therapy in the metaverse: An alternative solution for mental health services in the future. *Palliative & Supportive Care*, 1–2. PMID:36218066

Situmorang, D. D. B. (2023). Metaverse as a new place for online mental health services in the post-COVID-19 era: Is it a challenge or an opportunity? *Journal of Public Health (Oxford, England)*, *45*(2), e379–e380. doi:10.1093/pubmed/fdac159 PMID:36542106

Song, Y. T., & Qin, J. (2022). Metaverse and personal healthcare. *Procedia Computer Science*, *210*, 189–197. doi:10.1016/j.procs.2022.10.136

Suh, I., McKinney, T., & Siu, K. C. (2023, April). Current Perspective of Metaverse Application in Medical Education, Research and Patient Care. In Virtual Worlds, 2(2). MDPI.

Tan, T. F., Li, Y., Lim, J. S., Gunasekeran, D. V., Teo, Z. L., Ng, W. Y., & Ting, D. S. (2022). Metaverse and virtual health care in ophthalmology: Opportunities and challenges. *Asia-Pacific Journal of Ophthalmology*, *11*(3), 237–246. doi:10.1097/APO.0000000000000537 PMID:35772084

Thomason, J. (2021). Metahealth-how will the metaverse change health care? *Journal of Metaverse*, *1*(1), 13–16.

Turab, M., & Jamil, S. (2023). A Comprehensive Survey of Digital Twins in Healthcare in the Era of Metaverse. *BioMedInformatics*, *3*(3), 563–584. doi:10.3390/biomedinformatics3030039

Ullah, H., Manickam, S., Obaidat, M., Laghari, S. U. A., & Uddin, M. (2023). Exploring the Potential of Metaverse Technology in Healthcare: Applications, Challenges, and Future Directions. *IEEE Access : Practical Innovations, Open Solutions*, *11*, 69686–69707. doi:10.1109/ACCESS.2023.3286696

Usmani, S. S., Sharath, M., & Mehendale, M. (2022). Future of mental health in the metaverse. *General Psychiatry*, *35*(4), e100825. doi:10.1136/gpsych-2022-100825 PMID:36189180

Wang, G., Badal, A., Jia, X., Maltz, J. S., Mueller, K., Myers, K. J., Niu, C., Vannier, M., Yan, P., Yu, Z., & Zeng, R. (2022). Development of metaverse for intelligent healthcare. *Nature Machine Intelligence*, *4*(11), 922–929. doi:10.1038/s42256-022-00549-6 PMID:36935774

Wiederhold, B. K. (2022). Metaverse games: Game changer for healthcare? *Cyberpsychology, Behavior, and Social Networking*, *25*(5), 267–269. doi:10.1089/cyber.2022.29246.editorial PMID:35549346

Wiederhold, B. K. (2023). (Mental) Healthcare Consumerism in the Metaverse: Is There a Benefit? *Cyberpsychology, Behavior, and Social Networking*, *26*(3), 145–146. doi:10.1089/cyber.2023.29269. editorial PMID:36880891

Wiederhold, B. K., & Riva, G. (2022). Metaverse creates new opportunities in healthcare. *Ann. Rev. Cyber. Telemed*, *20*, 3–7.

Yang, Y., Siau, K., Xie, W., & Sun, Y. (2022). Smart health: Intelligent healthcare systems in the metaverse, artificial intelligence, and data science era. [JOEUC]. *Journal of Organizational and End User Computing*, *34*(1), 1–14. doi:10.4018/JOEUC.308814

Zhang, T., Shen, J., Lai, C. F., Ji, S., & Ren, Y. (2023). Multi-server assisted data sharing supporting secure deduplication for metaverse healthcare systems. *Future Generation Computer Systems*, *140*, 299–310. doi:10.1016/j.future.2022.10.031

Chapter 9
Navigating the Metaverse:
A Comprehensive Guide to Marketing, Branding, and Innovation

Harleen Pabla

(iD) https://orcid.org/0000-0001-5038-176X

I.K. Gujral Punjab Technical University, India

Harmeen Soch

(iD) https://orcid.org/0009-0008-4724-7314

I.K. Gujral Punjab Technical University, India

ABSTRACT

Delving into the dynamic intersections of augmented reality, artificial intelligence, blockchain, and spatial computing, this chapter offers strategic insights for brands seeking to establish a meaningful presence. From the evolution of brands in virtual environments to future trends, technological predictions and challenges, this chapter acts as a strategic roadmap. It addresses the needs of academic researchers, students, executives, and practitioners by synthesizing current research, offering practical applications, and proposing solutions. The chapter bridges the gap between theory and application, fostering a deeper understanding of the metaverse's impact on marketing, branding, and innovation. Aiming to be a valuable resource, the chapter equips a diverse audience with insights into the evolving metaverse landscape, providing a foundation for academic exploration and practical application.

INTRODUCTION

The late 1990s saw a significant disruption and radical transformation of strategic and operational practices due to the advent of the internet (Buhalis, 2003). Additionally, social media has reshaped how conventional marketing mix components are employed to engage with customers (Upadhyay et al., 2022). Nowadays, the metaverse combines advanced tech, changing consumer behavior and industry impacts. This chapter seeks to illuminate the intricate tapestry of these elements, offering a strategic compass for professionals, scholars and enthusiasts navigating the expansive landscape of the meta-

DOI: 10.4018/979-8-3693-2607-7.ch009

verse. According to Dwivedi et al., (2022), the metaverse holds the capability to expand the physical world by leveraging augmented and virtual reality technologies, enabling users to interact seamlessly in both real and simulated environments through the use of avatars and holograms. Virtual environments and immersive games like Second Life, Fortnite, Roblox and VRChat are considered precursors to the metaverse, providing valuable insights into the potential socio-economic impact of a fully operational, persistent and cross-platform metaverse.

As the metaverse transitions from a conceptual abstraction to a tangible reality, brands emerge as central players in an extraordinary transformation. The metaverse, with its immersive and interconnected attributes, disrupts traditional boundaries, opening unparalleled opportunities while simultaneously introducing unprecedented challenges. In this dynamic context, gaining a profound understanding of the metaverse's evolution becomes crucial for entities eager to leverage its transformative potential.

The metaverse, as a concept, has evolved from a speculative idea into a tangible and dynamic digital environment (Alessandrini & Rognoli, 2023). It is marked by its immersive nature, where individuals engage with a seamless blend of physical and virtual realities. This evolution dismantles the conventional constraints of space and time, offering brands a unique platform to redefine how they interact with consumers, present their products or services, and create brand experiences.

Brands now find themselves at the epicentre of this evolution, facing a landscape that demands adaptability, innovation, and a deep comprehension of the metaverse's intricacies (Wang, 2022). The immersive and interconnected nature of the metaverse opens new dimensions for brand-consumer interactions, challenging traditional marketing paradigms. Simultaneously, this transformative space introduces complexities and uncertainties that necessitate a strategic approach and a nuanced understanding of the evolving metaverse dynamics.

For those aiming to thrive in this new digital realm, recognizing the metaverse's evolution is not just a strategic choice but a fundamental necessity. It involves tracking the technological advancements, user behaviors and emerging trends within the metaverse ecosystem. Brands that stay attuned to these shifts position themselves to capitalize on the metaverse's transformative potential, forging meaningful connections with consumers and staying ahead in the ever-evolving landscape of digital innovation.

The central mission of this chapter is to provide a nuanced understanding of how marketing and branding adapt and thrive within the metaverse's immersive digital environment (Hollensen et al., 2022). By synthesizing a wealth of current research, industry best practices and emerging trends, this comprehensive guide aspires to equip a diverse readership with the insights necessary to navigate the complexities of the evolving metaverse landscape successfully.

Structured as a comprehensive guide, the subsequent sections of the chapter will unfold a narrative that commences with an exploration of the evolution of brands within the metaverse. Through the lens of case studies, early pioneers' strategies will be dissected, shedding light on creative approaches and innovative campaigns that have defined successful transitions into virtual spaces. The narrative will then transition to a consideration of the transformative benefits that marketing in the metaverse brings to both consumers and businesses, emphasizing the immersive and interconnected nature of these digital spaces.

EVOLUTION OF BRANDS IN THE METAVERSE

As the metaverse emerges as an innovative platform for brands to connect with consumers, businesses must reassess customer personas and journeys (Shen et al., 2021). In the burgeoning landscape of the metaverse, the evolution of brands stands as a testament to the transformative power of digital environments. As we delve into the metaverse's dynamic tapestry, it becomes evident that brands, once confined to traditional physical spaces and marketing paradigms, are undergoing a profound metamorphosis. In the evolution of brands within the metaverse, one crucial aspect is community building. Brands are leveraging the metaverse to foster and strengthen communities around their products or services in innovative ways (Dwivedi et al., 2022). This section serves as a comprehensive exploration into the journey of brands as they are building communities by navigating and redefining their identities within these immersive digital realms.

The metaverse represents a departure from conventional marketing avenues, compelling brands to adapt to a virtual ecosystem where consumer engagement transcends the limitations of physical spaces. In virtual worlds such as Second Life, Fortnite and Roblox, marketers are developing specialized locations where consumers can connect with one another and with the brand itself. These areas act as community engagement centres, allowing users to share their experiences, cooperate on initiatives, and connect with others who are interested in the brand. Fundamentally, the metaverse represents a transcendent domain that merges physical reality with digital virtuality, with the goal of enabling a robust and persistent multiuser experience (Mystakidis, 2022).

These early adopters navigated the uncharted territories of the metaverse, experimenting with novel approaches to brand representation. A critical aspect of this evolution lies in the strategic alignment of brand identity with the immersive nature of virtual environments (Messinger et al., 2009). Brands have not merely replicated their physical presence but have sought to establish a distinctive digital persona that resonates with the metaverse's unique dynamics.

Case studies illuminate the strategies employed by these early pioneers, offering insights into how established brands have successfully transitioned into virtual spaces. One notable trend is the cultivation of immersive brand experiences that go beyond traditional advertising. Virtual storefronts, interactive exhibits and experiential campaigns have become instrumental in shaping a brand's metaverse identity, fostering deeper connections with the digitally immersed consumer.

In the metaverse, brand evolution extends beyond visual representation to incorporate a sensory and interactive dimension. Brands are incorporating social aspects into their virtual experiences, enabling consumers to interact with one another in real time. Brands are leveraging augmented reality (AR) and virtual reality (VR) technologies to transcend the limitations of traditional mediums (Koohang et al., 2023). Through these technologies, consumers can not only witness but actively participate in brand narratives, creating a level of engagement that transcends the passive consumer experience of the physical world.

Furthermore, the metaverse facilitates a departure from linear storytelling, allowing brands to craft nonlinear and dynamic narratives that respond to user interactions (Durukal, 2022). This evolution in storytelling redefines the relationship between brands and consumers, as narratives become co-created in real-time within the virtual space (Davenport et al., 2020). Brands have become architects of experiences, constructing immersive narratives that invite consumers to explore, engage and contribute to the evolving brand story.

Crucially, the evolution of brands in the metaverse is marked by a paradigm shift in consumer-brand interactions. Traditional notions of one-way communication are replaced by a multidirectional dialogue, where consumers actively shape the brand's identity. The metaverse, with its social and interconnected nature, amplifies the significance of community engagement. Brands are cultivating communities within virtual spaces, where consumers not only consume but actively participate, share experiences, and contribute to the brand's evolving narrative (Mclean et al., 2018).

Amid this evolution, creativity has become the linchpin for brands seeking resonance in the metaverse. The ability to think beyond conventional boundaries, to innovate and experiment, has become a defining trait for brands thriving in these virtual landscapes. From gamified experiences to virtual events, brands are exploring avenues that extend beyond traditional marketing, pushing the boundaries of creativity to captivate and retain the attention of the digitally savvy consumer.

As brands evolve within the metaverse, a critical aspect of their transformation lies in the integration of authenticity. In the virtual realm, authenticity is not merely a buzzword but a cornerstone for building trust with consumers. Brands that successfully navigate this evolution strike a delicate balance between technological innovation and an authentic, human connection. This is not a departure from brand values but an elevation of these values within a digital context.

The evolution of brands in the metaverse is a dynamic and ongoing process. It is characterized by a departure from traditional marketing approaches, an embrace of immersive technologies and a redefinition of consumer-brand interactions. Early pioneers have paved the way, demonstrating that success in the metaverse requires a strategic alignment of brand identity with the unique dynamics of virtual environments. As brands continue to evolve, they are not merely adapting to the metaverse but actively shaping its contours, contributing to the ongoing narrative of this digital frontier. Few examples of brands that are building digital community are listed below:

1. Nike:
   ◦ Nike has ventured into the metaverse by creating virtual spaces within platforms like Roblox. In these spaces, users can explore Nike-branded environments, engage in virtual activities, and even purchase virtual Nike products for their avatars.
2. Decentraland and Atari:
   ◦ Decentraland is a virtual world built on blockchain technology, and Atari has collaborated with them to create a virtual casino within the metaverse. Users can visit this virtual casino, play games, and interact with the Atari brand in a digital space.
3. Gucci:
   ◦ Gucci has entered the metaverse by partnering with Arianee, a blockchain protocol, to create non-fungible tokens (NFTs) for its fashion items. This allows consumers to own digital representations of Gucci products in the virtual space.
4. Samsung:
   ◦ Samsung has explored the metaverse through partnerships with virtual reality platforms. The company has created VR experiences, allowing users to explore products and innovations in a virtual environment.
5. The Sandbox:
   ◦ The Sandbox is a virtual world and gaming platform that allows brands to create their virtual spaces. Several brands, including Atari, Binance, and The Smurfs, have acquired virtual land and engaged with users within The Sandbox.
6. Meta (formerly Facebook):
   ◦ Meta, the parent company of Facebook, has been actively investing in the development of the metaverse. Meta's CEO, Mark Zuckerberg, envisions a future where the company's plat-

forms are integral parts of the metaverse, facilitating social interactions, commerce, and virtual experiences.

7. Adidas:
   ◦ Adidas has explored the metaverse through partnerships and collaborations in virtual environments. In certain metaverse platforms, users can engage with Adidas-branded content and experiences.
8. Uniqlo:
   ◦ Uniqlo has used the Roblox platform to create a virtual store where users can explore and purchase digital versions of their clothing items for their avatars.
9. Luxury Fashion Houses:
   ◦ Several luxury fashion brands, such as Prada and Burberry, have explored the metaverse by incorporating virtual fashion shows and creating digital versions of their products for consumers to experience in virtual environments.
10. Lenskart:
    ◦ Lenskart, an Indian eyewear retailer, has experimented with augmented reality (AR) in its online shopping experience. While not strictly in the metaverse, AR is a technology often associated with virtual and augmented reality, providing users with interactive and engaging experiences.
11. Godrej Properties:
    ◦ Real estate developers in India, including Godrej Properties, have explored virtual reality (VR) to provide potential buyers with immersive virtual tours of properties. While not directly in the metaverse, these applications hint at the potential for real estate engagement within virtual environments.

BENEFITS FOR CONSUMERS AND BUSINESSES

For Consumers

In the metaverse, consumers find themselves immersed in an unprecedented era of experiential engagement. The benefits for consumers are manifold, fundamentally altering the way they interact with brands and consume products and services.

Immersive Shopping Experiences: Within the metaverse, consumers are no longer confined to the limitations of traditional online shopping. Immersive virtual environments allow users to explore digital storefronts, try on virtual representations of products, and engage with brands in ways that transcend the conventional boundaries of e-commerce. This immersive shopping experience brings an element of entertainment and interactivity, enhancing the overall enjoyment of the consumer journey.

In India, certain companies have adopted immersive shopping experiences in the metaverse. Titan, a well-known watch and jewellery manufacturer, has built a virtual showroom where customers can browse their newest collections and virtually try on various watches and jewellery items before making a purchase. This immersive experience not only improves the customer journey but also creates a feeling of elegance and exclusivity.

Similarly, Fabindia, a well-known Indian lifestyle brand, has entered the metaverse by building virtual places where users can explore their collection of ethnic fashion, home décor, and personal care goods.

These virtual surroundings allow visitors to see how Fabindia's items might fit into their homes or lives, improving their purchasing experience and developing a stronger relationship with the brand.

Personalization and Customization: Metaverse marketing enables a level of personalization and customization that surpasses traditional approaches. Brands can leverage data analytics and AI-driven technologies to understand individual preferences, offering tailored recommendations and content. This personalized approach creates a more intimate and meaningful connection between consumers and brands, fostering brand loyalty and a sense of exclusivity.

Netflix India leverages personalization algorithms to recommend personalized movie and TV show suggestions to its subscribers based on their viewing history and preferences. This customized approach not only enhances the user experience but also strengthens the bond between the consumer and the brand, fostering loyalty and retention.

Another example is Lenskart, an Indian eyewear brand, which offers virtual try-on services through its website and mobile app. By leveraging augmented reality (AR) technology, Lenskart allows users to virtually try on different frames and see how they look before making a purchase. This personalized experience not only helps users find the perfect pair of glasses but also enhances their overall shopping experience, leading to increased brand satisfaction and loyalty.

Community and Social Interaction: The metaverse is inherently social, providing consumers with opportunities to connect with like-minded individuals in virtual spaces. Virtual communities centered around specific interests or brands allow consumers to share experiences, recommendations, and feedback. This social dimension enhances the sense of belonging and community, making the consumer experience more dynamic and engaging (Rathore, 2017).

Indian brand leveraging the social dimension of the metaverse is BookMyShow, a leading online ticketing platform for movies, events, and live performances. BookMyShow has introduced virtual event spaces where users can connect with fellow movie buffs, discuss upcoming releases, and participate in virtual movie screenings and discussions. This virtual community enhances the overall movie-watching experience and strengthens the bond between users and the brand.

Access to Exclusive Content and Events: Consumers in the metaverse often gain access to exclusive virtual events and content that go beyond traditional marketing strategies. Brands can host virtual product launches, immersive storytelling experiences, and exclusive events that are accessible only within the metaverse. This exclusivity enhances brand desirability and incentivizes consumer participation.

OnePlus, a popular smartphone brand, hosted a virtual product launch event within the metaverse to unveil its latest smartphone model. This virtual event allowed consumers to experience the unveiling in a dynamic and immersive environment, complete with interactive elements and exclusive behind-the-scenes content. By offering this exclusive experience only within the metaverse, OnePlus generated excitement and anticipation among its fan base, enhancing the desirability of its new product.

Similarly, Red Bull, an energy drink brand known for its extreme sports and music events, hosted a virtual music festival within the metaverse. The festival featured performances by renowned artists, interactive gaming experiences, and exclusive meet-and-greet sessions with musicians—all accessible only to attendees within the virtual environment.

Enhanced Accessibility: One of the notable advantages for consumers in the metaverse is the breaking down of geographical barriers. Virtual environments enable consumers from around the globe to engage with brands and products seamlessly, transcending the limitations of physical location. This enhanced accessibility broadens market reach, allowing consumers to participate in a globalized marketplace.

Byju's, an Indian edtech company offering online learning solutions, has expanded its reach through virtual classrooms and educational experiences within the metaverse. By providing interactive learning environments accessible to students across different regions and time zones, Byju's ensures that education remains inclusive and accessible to all, regardless of geographical constraints. This approach not only broadens Byju's market reach but also democratizes access to quality education, empowering learners from diverse backgrounds.

For Businesses

The metaverse presents businesses with a myriad of opportunities to innovate their marketing strategies and connect with consumers in unprecedented ways. The benefits for businesses extend from global reach to data-driven insights and a redefined approach to brand innovation.

Global Reach and Market Expansion: Businesses operating in the metaverse enjoy the advantage of global reach, as virtual environments are accessible to a diverse and international audience. This globalized reach opens up new markets and opportunities for expansion, allowing businesses to tap into diverse consumer demographics and cultural contexts.

Paytm, India's leading digital payments platform, has ventured into the metaverse to offer virtual banking services and financial solutions to users worldwide. By providing virtual banking experiences accessible across borders, Paytm facilitates international transactions and financial management for its global user base. This global reach not only strengthens Paytm's position as a trusted financial services provider but also fosters financial inclusion and accessibility on a global scale.

Data-Driven Insights: Marketing in the metaverse generates a wealth of data on consumer behavior, preferences, and interactions. Businesses can leverage advanced analytics to gain data-driven insights that inform decision-making processes. This granular understanding of consumer behavior enables businesses to refine their marketing strategies, optimize product offerings, and deliver more targeted and effective campaigns.

Tata Consultancy Services (TCS), one of the largest IT services firms in India, harnesses data-driven insights from virtual interactions within the metaverse to drive digital transformation initiatives for its clients. By leveraging advanced analytics and machine learning algorithms, TCS helps businesses extract actionable insights from virtual data sources to optimize operations, improve customer experiences, and drive innovation.

Reliance Jio, a leading telecommunications company in India. Reliance Jio has utilized data analytics and insights from virtual interactions within its digital platforms to gain a deep understanding of consumer preferences and behaviors.

Cost-Effective Marketing: Virtual marketing campaigns within the metaverse often offer cost-effective alternatives to traditional advertising methods. Hosting virtual events, product launches, and interactive experiences can be more economical than organizing physical events, eliminating logistical constraints and reducing associated costs. This cost-effectiveness allows businesses to allocate resources more efficiently while reaching a wider audience.

Zomato, India's largest food delivery platform. Zomato has capitalized on the cost-effectiveness of virtual marketing campaigns by hosting virtual food festivals and culinary events within the metaverse. These virtual events provide a platform for restaurants and food vendors to showcase their offerings to a global audience without the need for physical infrastructure or logistical arrangements. By leveraging virtual experiences, Zomato effectively reduces marketing costs while amplifying its brand presence and engaging customers in innovative ways.

Brand Innovation and Differentiation: The metaverse serves as a playground for brand innovation and differentiation. Businesses that creatively leverage immersive technologies, augmented reality, and virtual reality can set themselves apart from competitors. The ability to create unique and memorable experiences within the metaverse contributes to building a distinct brand identity, fostering consumer engagement and loyalty.

Tanishq is India's largest jewellery brand. Tanishq has pioneered virtual try-on experiences in the metaverse, allowing clients to virtually try on jewellery pieces via its website and mobile application. Tanishq uses AR technology to let buyers to see how jewellery pieces would appear on them before making a purchase, improving the online buying experience and distinguishing itself from traditional jewellery merchants. Tanishq's unique strategy not only distinguishes it from competitors, but also strengthens its position as a forward-thinking and customer-centric brand in the Indian jewellery industry.

Adaptability to Changing Consumer Behavior: In the fast-paced landscape of the metaverse, businesses benefit from enhanced adaptability to changing consumer behaviors and preferences. The dynamic nature of virtual environments allows for rapid experimentation with marketing strategies, enabling businesses to stay agile and responsive to evolving consumer trends. This adaptability is crucial in a digital landscape characterized by continuous innovation.

Ola is a major transportation service provider in India. Ola has embraced the metaverse to develop its service offerings and adapt to shifting consumer patterns in the transportation industry. Ola improves the customer experience by using virtual and augmented reality technology into its smartphone app, resulting in tailored transportation options. Furthermore, Hindustan Unilever Limited (HUL), one of India's leading consumer products corporations, has shown agility in adapting to changing consumer preferences in the metaverse. HUL uses virtual worlds and immersive technology to engage customers in new ways and provide individualized brand experiences.

In essence, the metaverse serves as a transformative arena where the synergy between consumers and businesses is redefined. For consumers, the metaverse offers a playground of immersive experiences, personalization, and social interaction. Businesses, on the other hand, gain access to a globalized market, data-driven insights, and opportunities for creative brand innovation. As the metaverse continues to evolve, the reciprocal relationship between consumers and businesses within this digital frontier promises to reshape the landscape of commerce and consumer engagement in profound and exciting ways.

FUTURE TRENDS IN MARKETING IN THE METAVERSE

As we gaze into the crystal ball of the metaverse's future, one prominent trend that emerges is the rise of personalized and immersive advertising experiences. Personalization, a hallmark of modern marketing, is set to reach new heights within virtual environments. The metaverse's ability to capture and process vast amounts of user data creates an unprecedented opportunity for brands to deliver hyper-personalized content and interactions. From personalized virtual storefronts to tailored product recommendations based on real-time user behavior, marketing in the metaverse will transcend one-size-fits-all approaches, ensuring that each consumer's journey is a unique and tailored experience.

Another compelling trend on the horizon is the integration of artificial intelligence (AI) within metaverse marketing strategies. AI, coupled with machine learning algorithms, will play a pivotal role in understanding and predicting consumer preferences, behaviors, and trends. This intelligence will power chatbots, virtual assistants, and AI-driven content recommendations, enhancing user engagement and providing a seamless and responsive virtual experience. The metaverse, fuelled by AI, will not only adapt to user interactions but also proactively anticipate and fulfill consumer needs, blurring the lines between the physical and virtual realms.

The emergence of virtual influencers stands as a noteworthy trend that promises to redefine the influencer marketing landscape within the metaverse. These digital avatars, created and controlled by computer algorithms or human creators, have the potential to become powerful brand ambassadors within virtual spaces (Miao et al., 2022). Virtual influencers offer a unique advantage—they are not bound by the constraints of reality, enabling brands to craft personas that align perfectly with their metaverse presence. The rise of virtual influencers signals a shift towards a new era of brand partnerships, where the authenticity and relatability of virtual entities resonate with digitally native audiences.

The metaverse is also poised to usher in a new era of experiential marketing, leveraging the immersive capabilities of virtual reality (VR) and augmented reality (AR) technologies. Brands will increasingly invest in creating virtual events, immersive product launches, and interactive experiences that transcend traditional marketing formats. Virtual reality holds the potential to transport users to entirely new worlds, providing brands with a canvas to weave compelling narratives and create memorable experiences that linger long after the virtual encounter has ended. The metaverse, with its immersive technologies, will reshape the narrative from passive consumption to active participation, turning marketing into a dynamic and participatory venture.

Blockchain technology is set to play a pivotal role in shaping the future of metaverse marketing, particularly in the realm of virtual assets and non-fungible tokens (NFTs). NFTs, which represent ownership of unique digital assets, have already gained traction in the art and gaming sectors. In the metaverse, brands can leverage blockchain to create scarcity and authenticity, turning virtual goods and experiences into valuable commodities. Virtual real estate, limited edition digital products, and exclusive virtual events represented by NFTs offer a novel way for brands to engage with consumers and create a sense of digital ownership and exclusivity.

Moreover, the metaverse is poised to become a testing ground for the convergence of the digital and physical worlds through the Internet of Things (IoT). Smart devices and wearables will bridge the gap between the virtual and physical, enabling seamless integration of consumer experiences. From virtual try-on experiences that leverage augmented reality to smart products that communicate with their virtual counterparts, the metaverse will be a playground for brands to explore innovative ways of connecting the digital and physical aspects of consumer lifestyles.

As metaverse marketing evolves, the concept of the virtual showroom will gain prominence. Brands will increasingly leverage virtual spaces to showcase products, allowing consumers to explore and interact with items before making purchasing decisions. Virtual showrooms offer a dynamic and customizable environment where brands can experiment with visual aesthetics, product placements and storytelling, creating a captivating and immersive shopping experience that goes beyond the limitations of physical retail spaces.

Furthermore, the metaverse will foster new forms of social commerce, where the lines between social interaction and commerce blur seamlessly. Virtual social spaces will become marketplaces, enabling users to discover, discuss, and purchase products within the same digital environment. The metaverse's social fabric will give rise to shared shopping experiences, where friends and communities can collectively explore virtual storefronts, share recommendations, and make group purchases, mimicking the communal aspects of traditional retail experiences.

In conclusion, the future trends in metaverse marketing herald a new era of personalized, immersive, and technologically driven consumer interactions. From the rise of virtual influencers to the integration of AI, blockchain, and IoT, the metaverse is set to redefine how brands engage with their audiences. As these trends unfold, marketers and businesses must remain agile, continuously adapting their strategies to harness the full potential of the evolving metaverse landscape. The intersection of technology, consumer behavior, and innovation within the metaverse creates a canvas where the future of marketing is not just written but dynamically shaped by the collective experiences of users in these immersive digital realms.

PREDICTIONS FOR METAVERSE TECHNOLOGIES IN THE CONTEXT OF MARKETING

In forecasting the future trajectory of the metaverse and its integration with marketing, it becomes imperative to delve into the predictions surrounding emerging technologies that will shape this dynamic landscape. This section aims to illuminate the technological horizons that marketers should anticipate and strategically navigate for successful engagement within these immersive digital realms.

Augmented Reality (AR) and Virtual Reality (VR) Integration

A pivotal prediction for metaverse technologies lies in the continued integration and advancement of augmented reality (AR) and virtual reality (VR). These technologies will play a central role in reshaping consumer experiences within the metaverse. AR, with its ability to overlay digital information onto the physical world, will enhance real-time interactions, allowing users to seamlessly blend virtual and physical elements. VR, on the other hand, will continue to create immersive and alternate realities, transforming how users engage with brands and products.

VR technology generates immersive as well as alternate realities, transporting users to virtual surroundings (Rubio-Tamayo et al., 2017). In the context of marketing, the convergence of AR and VR is expected to revolutionize product visualization and virtual try-on experiences. Consumers will be able to interact with virtual representations of products in their physical spaces, enabling a more informed and personalized purchasing process. For example, AR could facilitate virtual "try before you buy" scenarios, allowing users to visualize how furniture, clothing, or cosmetics will appear in their own living environments. In marketing, VR enables businesses to develop immersive brand experiences such as virtual showrooms, product demos and interactive narrative campaigns (Zhang & Wen, 2023). Automotive businesses, for example, may employ VR to allow customers to virtually test drive automobiles or learn about new car features in a simulated setting. Similarly, travel companies may provide virtual tours of places or hotels, allowing prospective consumers to preview their experiences before booking.

Integration of Artificial Intelligence (AI) and Machine Learning (ML)

Artificial Intelligence pertains to technologies that empower machines to acquire knowledge, reason, and exhibit behavior akin to that of humans (De Bruyn et al., 2020). The predictive capabilities of artificial intelligence (AI) and machine learning (ML) are anticipated to be pivotal in enhancing user interactions and personalization within the metaverse. AI algorithms will analyze vast datasets generated by user behavior, preferences, and interactions, enabling marketers to deliver highly targeted and contextually relevant content. This predictive intelligence will extend beyond personalized recommendations to dynamically adapting virtual environments based on individual user preferences and behavior.

In marketing, AI-driven chatbots and virtual assistants will become integral components of user engagement within the metaverse. These intelligent entities will not only assist users in navigating virtual spaces but will also offer personalized product recommendations, answer queries, and provide a tailored and responsive brand experience. The predictive power of AI will elevate consumer interactions, creating a more immersive and user-centric metaverse.

Blockchain Technology and Non-Fungible Tokens (NFTs)

Blockchains can be defined as decentralized peer-to-peer databases or ledgers where information is stored in blocks, collectively shared among all network nodes (users), overseen by everyone, and without singular ownership or control (Shah & Shay, 2019). Blockchain technology, particularly through the use of non-fungible tokens (NFTs), is poised to redefine ownership, scarcity, and authenticity within the metaverse. NFTs represent unique digital assets, and their application extends from digital art to virtual real estate and branded collectibles. In the realm of marketing, NFTs will facilitate the creation of limited edition virtual products, exclusive experiences, and even ownership of virtual spaces within the metaverse.

Predictions suggest that NFTs will become a prominent mechanism for brands to establish digital ownership and rarity, fostering a sense of exclusivity and value for consumers (Seong et al., 2021). Virtual assets represented by NFTs will be tradable, collectible, and verifiable, offering a new dimension to consumer-brand interactions. Marketers will strategically leverage blockchain technology to enhance transparency, combat counterfeiting, and create unique opportunities for consumer engagement.

Extended Reality (XR)

The concept of Extended Reality (XR), encompassing AR, VR, and mixed reality (MR), is predicted to become a holistic and interconnected technological framework within the metaverse. XR will provide users with a continuum of experiences, seamlessly transitioning between virtual, augmented, and physical realities. This integration of XR technologies will amplify the depth and richness of consumer engagements within the metaverse, enabling a spectrum of immersive experiences.

In the marketing landscape, XR will be harnessed to create multi-dimensional campaigns that transcend traditional boundaries. For instance, XR technologies could enable users to interact with virtual brand ambassadors in augmented spaces, attend virtual events in mixed reality environments, or experience products in immersive virtual showrooms. The versatility of XR will redefine the storytelling potential for brands, allowing them to craft narratives that unfold across multiple layers of reality.

Internet of Things (IoT) Integration

The seamless integration of the Internet of Things (IoT) with the metaverse is a prediction that holds substantial potential for bridging the gap between the digital and physical worlds. IoT devices, ranging from smart wearables to connected home devices, will contribute to a more interconnected and responsive metaverse. Marketers will leverage data from these devices to gain insights into user behavior, preferences, and real-world interactions, enhancing the overall personalization of marketing strategies.

In the marketing context, IoT integration will enable dynamic and context-aware advertising. For example, smart home devices could trigger personalized virtual experiences based on user preferences, creating a highly tailored and responsive brand interaction. Marketers may acquire important insights into their customers' real-world actions and settings by using data from IoT devices such as smart wearables, linked home appliances and environmental sensors (Ferreira et al., 2021). This information may be utilized to provide highly targeted and relevant adverts or brand interactions based on consumers' individual requirements and interests.

Spatial Computing and 3D Experiences

Spatial computing, which involves the use of computer algorithms to interpret and respond to the spatial context of a user's environment, is predicted to play a pivotal role in shaping 3D experiences within the metaverse. This technology will enable a more intuitive and interactive engagement, allowing users to navigate virtual spaces with natural movements and gestures. As a result, marketing within the metaverse will transcend traditional 2D interactions, embracing a three-dimensional and spatially aware approach.

In marketing, spatial computing will enhance the creation of immersive and interactive 3D advertisements and environments (Scholz & Smith, 2016). Brands will design campaigns that respond to users' physical spaces, creating a sense of depth and presence within virtual landscapes. This shift towards spatial computing will redefine how brands conceptualize and deliver marketing content, fostering a more engaging and interactive metaverse experience.

CHALLENGES FOR BRANDS

Identity and Authenticity Concerns

One of the foremost challenges that brands face in the metaverse revolves around the preservation of identity and authenticity. Establishing and maintaining a consistent brand identity is inherently challenging in virtual environments where the boundaries between the real and digital worlds blur. Brands must navigate the risk of losing their authentic voice amidst the diverse and dynamic nature of the metaverse. The challenge lies in ensuring that the virtual representation aligns seamlessly with the brand's core values and resonates authentically with the diverse user base within these digital spaces.

One potential consequence of identity and authenticity concerns in the metaverse is the risk of damaging brand reputation and trust among consumers. If a brand's virtual representation deviates significantly from its real-world identity or fails to resonate authentically with users, it can lead to confusion and even backlash from customers.

Misinformation and Brand Dilution

The metaverse, like any digital realm, is susceptible to misinformation and brand dilution. In virtual environments where user-generated content flourishes, brands may find themselves contending with inaccurate representations, rumours or malicious activities that can tarnish their reputation. Maintaining control over the narrative and addressing misinformation becomes a critical challenge. Brands must develop robust strategies to monitor and respond swiftly to any false information circulating within the metaverse to safeguard their digital presence and reputation.

To address misinformation and brand dilution in the metaverse, brands can implement proactive measures such as establishing clear guidelines and policies for user-generated content within virtual platforms. Like, WhatsApp's recent advertisements emphasize the importance of not spreading and responding to fake news (Arora, 2020). By providing users with clear instructions on acceptable behavior and content standards, brands can minimize the risk of misinformation and maintain greater control over the narrative surrounding their brand.

Regulatory and Ethical Considerations

Navigating the metaverse entails grappling with a complex web of regulatory and ethical considerations. As virtual spaces become increasingly integrated with real-world economic activities, brands must navigate jurisdictional challenges, data protection regulations, and ethical dilemmas. Ensuring compliance with diverse regulatory frameworks across different regions poses a significant challenge, particularly as the metaverse operates on a global scale. Brands must proactively address these considerations to avoid legal complications and ethical controversies that could arise in the metaverse.

Failure to adhere to regulatory frameworks across different regions can result in costly legal battles, damage to brand reputation, and loss of consumer trust. Brands can implement robust compliance programs and governance structures to ensure adherence to relevant laws and ethical standards. This may involve appointing dedicated legal and compliance teams to oversee regulatory compliance and monitor changes in legislation and best practices within virtual environments.

User Privacy and Data Security

The metaverse's immersive experiences often require extensive user data collection to personalize interactions and enhance engagement. However, this pursuit of personalization raises significant concerns regarding user privacy and data security. Brands must grapple with the challenge of striking a delicate balance between providing tailored experiences and safeguarding user privacy. Implementing robust data protection measures, transparent data usage policies, and secure storage practices are imperative to mitigate the risks associated with potential data breaches or privacy infringements.

In the event of a data breach or privacy infringement, brands may face legal consequences, regulatory fines, and reputational damage, further exacerbating the fallout from inadequate data security practices. Brands can implement comprehensive privacy-by-design principles and security protocols throughout the development and deployment of virtual experiences.

Interoperability and Standardization

The metaverse is a diverse ecosystem comprising various platforms, virtual worlds, and technologies. The lack of interoperability and standardization across these diverse elements poses a formidable challenge for brands. Implementing cohesive and seamless marketing strategies requires navigating the fragmented nature of the metaverse, where each platform may have distinct technical specifications and user interfaces.

Without interoperable systems and standards, brands may struggle to maintain consistency in their messaging, branding, and user experiences, leading to disjointed interactions with consumers. Brands must invest in adaptable technologies and strategies that can traverse these varied virtual landscapes to ensure consistent and effective engagement.

User Experience and Accessibility

Ensuring a positive and inclusive user experience is a perennial challenge for brands venturing into the metaverse. Virtual environments must be designed with accessibility in mind, considering diverse user needs and capabilities. Brands must grapple with creating immersive experiences that are inclusive for users with disabilities, accommodating various interaction methods, and ensuring compatibility with a range of devices. Striking a balance between cutting-edge innovation and accessibility is crucial to prevent alienating segments of the audience and hindering the metaverse's potential for widespread adoption.

To address user experience and accessibility challenges in the metaverse, brands can prioritize inclusive design principles and accessibility standards throughout the development and deployment of virtual experiences. This may involve conducting user testing with individuals from diverse backgrounds and abilities to identify barriers and iterate on design improvements that enhance accessibility for all users.

Monetization and Revenue Models

While the metaverse presents expansive opportunities for brand engagement, determining effective monetization and revenue models remains a complex challenge. Brands must navigate the delicate balance between providing value to users and extracting value from virtual engagements. The metaverse's economic landscape is still evolving, and brands must experiment with innovative monetization strategies, such as virtual goods, experiences, or subscription models, while ensuring that users perceive these transactions as fair and beneficial.

By investing in unique virtual goods, exclusive experiences, and premium content, brands can create value propositions that resonate with users and justify monetization efforts. Additionally, brands should prioritize building long-term relationships with users based on trust and mutual benefit, rather than pursuing short-term revenue gains at the expense of user experience.

Talent and Skill Gaps

The dynamic and technologically sophisticated nature of the metaverse introduces a talent and skill gap challenge for brands. Crafting immersive and innovative virtual experiences requires expertise in emerging technologies, such as augmented reality, virtual reality, and blockchain. Recruiting and retaining professionals with the requisite skills to navigate this evolving landscape can be a significant hurdle. Brands must invest in talent development, training, and collaboration with skilled professionals to harness the full potential of the metaverse for marketing.

This limitation can hinder brands' ability to differentiate themselves in the competitive metaverse landscape and capitalize on the unique opportunities presented by virtual engagement. So, brands can leverage external expertise and collaboration with specialized agencies, freelancers, and consultants to fill talent gaps and access specialized skills and knowledge required for successful metaverse initiatives.

Integration With Traditional Marketing Channels

Harmonizing metaverse strategies with traditional marketing channels poses a challenge for brands seeking to maintain a cohesive and omnichannel presence. While the metaverse offers novel avenues for engagement, brands must integrate these efforts seamlessly with their existing marketing initiatives. Striking the right balance between virtual and physical marketing strategies, ensuring consistent messaging across platforms, and facilitating a unified brand experience are challenges that demand strategic alignment and coordination.

To address integration challenges between the metaverse and traditional marketing channels, brands can adopt a holistic approach that prioritizes strategic alignment and coordination across all touchpoints. Understanding how customers interact with a brand in both virtual and real contexts allow companies to improve their marketing efforts and increase engagement and conversion across all touchpoints.

User Adoption and Behavior Predictability

Predicting and influencing user adoption and behavior within the metaverse is inherently challenging. The metaverse is an evolving space where user preferences, trends, and platform popularity can shift rapidly. Brands must grapple with the challenge of staying ahead of evolving user behaviors, understanding emerging trends and adapting their strategies accordingly. Predicting how users will navigate and interact within virtual environments is a complex task that demands continuous monitoring, adaptability, and responsiveness.

If brands are unable to appropriately predict and adapt to changing user preferences and trends, they risk missing out on opportunities to successfully interact with people and achieve their marketing goals. This can lead to wasted costs, reduced brand awareness, and a loss of competitive edge in the continually changing metaverse market. To address the problems of user acceptance and predictability in the metaverse, marketers may employ data-driven strategies and analytics to acquire insights into user behavior patterns and trends. In addition, companies may interact with virtual communities and influencers in the metaverse to gather insights regarding user adoption and behavior.

POTENTIAL HURDLES

Consumers and businesses alike may face challenges while engaging in the metaverse. Consumers have a learning curve while traversing virtual environments and adopting immersive technology (Ipsita et al., 2022). For example, while virtual try-on technology provided by companies like as Lenskart allows customers to virtually put on glasses, certain users may struggle to adjust to the interface or encounter technological issues, resulting in disengagement.

Another challenge for customers is the question of privacy and data security in the metaverse. As virtual environments capture massive volumes of user data, questions arise about personal information security and potential data misuse (Pearce et al., 2013). For example, customers participating in virtual events offered by firms like Swiggy may be hesitant about revealing important information in the virtual realm.

In a similar way, companies encounter difficulties in adopting efficient marketing methods in the metaverse. One issue is the fight for customer attention in tangled virtual settings. For example, while staging virtual events might be cost-effective for businesses such as Zomato, recruiting and maintaining attendees in the face of several competing experiences can be difficult, affecting the event's performance and the brand's marketing initiatives.

Another challenge for corporations is assuring inclusion and accessibility in the metaverse. Because virtual experiences rely largely on technology, there is a danger of alienating sectors of the public that do not have access to the requisite gadgets or internet connectivity. Brands like as Tanishq, who provide virtual try-on experiences, may accidentally reject consumers who do not have access to appropriate devices, restricting their reach and potential customer base.

FUTURE RESEARCH DIRECTIONS

Consumer behaviors are undergoing fundamental shifts, progressively moving towards digital consumption (Shah & Murthi, 2021). In venturing into the metaverse for marketing endeavors, brands encounter a spectrum of challenges that demand nuanced strategies and careful navigation. One of the foremost hurdles lies in preserving the authenticity and identity of the brand within the dynamic and immersive nature of virtual environments. Striking a balance between the real and digital representations of a brand poses a formidable challenge, requiring a cohesive strategy that resonates authentically with the diverse audience populating the metaverse.

A significant concern arises in the form of misinformation and brand dilution within the user-generated content prevalent in virtual spaces. Brands must grapple with the risk of inaccurate representations, rumors or malicious activities that can swiftly tarnish their reputation. Vigilant monitoring and swift responses are imperative to address misinformation promptly, safeguarding the brand's integrity and maintaining a positive virtual presence.

Regulatory and ethical considerations add a layer of complexity to metaverse marketing. The global nature of virtual interactions necessitates careful adherence to diverse regulatory frameworks, data protection laws, and ethical standards. Navigating jurisdictional challenges while ensuring ethical practices becomes an ongoing challenge for brands operating within the metaverse, demanding a proactive approach to compliance and responsible digital conduct.

User privacy and data security present perennial challenges as brands strive to deliver personalized experiences. While the metaverse relies on extensive data collection to enhance user interactions, brands must delicately balance personalization with privacy concerns. Robust data protection measures and transparent policies are essential to mitigate risks associated with potential data breaches and to instill trust among users navigating virtual environments.

Interoperability and standardization pose technical challenges for brands seeking a cohesive metaverse presence. The fragmented nature of platforms, virtual worlds, and technologies within the metaverse demands adaptable strategies and technologies. Ensuring a seamless experience across diverse virtual landscapes requires brands to invest in flexible solutions capable of traversing the varied technical specifications of different platforms (Zaman et al., 2022).

Creating an inclusive and positive user experience is a multifaceted challenge. Metaverse platforms are employed to capture live events and broadcast them within the digital environment on the host networks (Khatri, 2022). So, brands must design virtual environments that are accessible to diverse user needs and capabilities, considering factors such as disabilities and varied interaction methods. Achieving a delicate balance between cutting-edge innovation and inclusivity is essential to prevent alienating segments of the audience and hindering widespread adoption of metaverse experiences.

Monetization and revenue models within the metaverse present a complex challenge for brands. Striking the right balance between providing value to users and extracting value from virtual engagements demands innovative approaches. The evolving economic landscape of the metaverse requires brands to experiment with novel monetization strategies while ensuring perceived fairness and mutual benefit.

Talent and skill gaps emerge as brands navigate the sophisticated technological requirements of the metaverse. Recruiting and retaining professionals proficient in emerging technologies, such as augmented reality and virtual reality, becomes a strategic imperative. Brands must invest in talent development and collaborations with skilled professionals to leverage the metaverse effectively for marketing.

Integrating metaverse strategies with traditional marketing channels is a coordination challenge for brands seeking a unified brand presence. Balancing virtual and physical marketing efforts, ensuring consistent messaging, and facilitating an omnichannel brand experience require strategic alignment and seamless integration.

Predicting and influencing user adoption and behavior within the metaverse presents an ongoing challenge. Rapid shifts in user preferences and emerging trends necessitate continuous monitoring, adaptability, and responsiveness from brands navigating the dynamic landscape of virtual interactions. Brands must stay ahead of evolving user behaviors to shape effective marketing strategies within the metaverse.

Future study might look at the ethical implications of data collecting tactics in the metaverse, as well as measures for protecting user privacy and data. Future study might look at concerns of diversity, inclusion, and representation in the metaverse, particularly in marketing and branding contexts. This involves investigating how virtual environments may be structured to promote diversity and inclusion, authentically reflect underrepresented cultures, and reduce the likelihood of repeating stereotypes or prejudices. Furthermore, researchers might investigate ways for building a sense of belonging and community among various user groups in virtual environments.

As the metaverse develops, there is a need for study on regulatory frameworks and governance systems to address ethical and social problems. This involves investigating the impact of government legislation, industry standards, and self-regulatory activities in encouraging ethical behavior and responsible practices in the metaverse.

CONCLUSION

Numerous major technology companies, including Meta (formerly Facebook), Microsoft and Nvidia Corporation, are allocating substantial financial investments to construct a digital universe aligned with the concept of the metaverse (Barrera & Shah, 2023). From healthcare and education to manufacturing and finance, digital technologies are transforming company models, processes and consumer experiences, resulting in increased agility, efficiency and competitiveness in a quickly changing global economy (Berkhout & Hertin, 2004). The delicate balance between personalization and user privacy underscores the ethical considerations inherent in metaverse marketing.

The metaverse has the potential to revolutionize many parts of our life, including as entertainment, education, social interaction and business (Damar, 2021). As virtual worlds grow more immersive and linked, they will open new possibilities for collaboration, creativity, and exploration, profoundly altering how we interact with digital information and one another. Interoperability challenges necessitate adaptable strategies to traverse diverse virtual landscapes seamlessly. Achieving inclusivity in user experience remains a constant pursuit, demanding brands to craft virtual environments that cater to diverse needs.

Monetization models, talent acquisition, and the integration of metaverse strategies with traditional channels require strategic foresight and flexibility.

In the current metaverse paradigm, a transformative fusion of augmented reality, artificial intelligence, blockchain and spatial computing is redefining the landscape, presenting a future where the interactions between consumers and digital spaces surpass the limitations of both physical and virtual realms. This convergence forms the foundation for a novel era of immersive and interconnected experiences. Bridging the digital gap and providing fair access to digital technologies are critical for achieving social inclusion, economic empowerment and sustainable development (Sharma, et al., 2016). Efforts to overcome the digital literacy, infrastructural, and affordability gaps will be critical in ensuring that all individuals and communities can fully engage in the digital economy and capitalize on the possibilities provided by technology breakthroughs.

REFERENCES

Alessandrini, L., & Rognoli, V. (2023). Introducing the material experience concept in the metaverse and in virtual environments. In *Connectivity and Creativity in times of Conflict*. Academia Press. doi:10.26530/9789401496476-057

Arora, M. (2020). Post-truth and marketing communication in technological age. In *Handbook of research on innovations in technology and marketing for the connected consumer*. IGI Global. doi:10.4018/978-1-7998-0131-3.ch005

Barrera, K. G., & Shah, D. (2023). Marketing in the Metaverse: Conceptual understanding, framework, and research agenda. *Journal of Business Research*, *155*, 113420. doi:10.1016/j.jbusres.2022.113420

Berkhout, F., & Hertin, J. (2004). De-materialising and re-materialising: Digital technologies and the environment. *Futures*, *36*(8), 903–920. doi:10.1016/j.futures.2004.01.003

Buhalis, D. (2003). eTourism: Information technology for strategic tourism management. Pearson education. Pearson Education Limited.

Damar, M. (2021). Metaverse shape of your life for future: A bibliometric snapshot. *Journal of Metaverse*, *1*(1), 1–8.

Davenport, T., Guha, A., Grewal, D., & Bressgott, T. (2020). How artificial intelligence will change the future of marketing. *Journal of the Academy of Marketing Science*, *48*(1), 24–42. doi:10.1007/s11747-019-00696-0

De Bruyn, A., Viswanathan, V., Beh, Y. S., Brock, J.-K.-U., & Von Wangenheim, F. (2020). Artificial Intelligence and Marketing: Pitfalls and Opportunities. *Journal of Interactive Marketing*, *51*, 91–105. doi:10.1016/j.intmar.2020.04.007

Durukal, E. (2022). Customer online shopping experience. *Handbook of Research on Interdisciplinary Reflections of Contemporary Experiential Marketing Practices*.

Dwivedi, Y. K., Hughes, L., Baabdullah, A. M., Ribeiro-Navarrete, S., Giannakis, M., Al-Debei, M. M., Dennehy, D., Metri, B., Buhalis, D., Cheung, C. M. K., Conboy, K., Doyle, R., Dubey, R., Dutot, V., Felix, R., Goyal, D. P., Gustafsson, A., Hinsch, C., Jebabli, I., & Wamba, S. F. (2022). Metaverse beyond the hype: Multidisciplinary perspectives on emerging challenges, opportunities, and agenda for research, practice and policy. *International Journal of Information Management, 66*, 102542. doi:10.1016/j.ijinfomgt.2022.102542

Ferreira, J. J., Fernandes, C. I., Rammal, H. G., & Veiga, P. M. (2021). Wearable technology and consumer interaction: A systematic review and research agenda. *Computers in Human Behavior, 118*, 106710. doi:10.1016/j.chb.2021.106710

Hollensen, S., Kotler, P., & Opresnik, M. O. (2022). Metaverse – the new marketing universe. *Journal of Business Strategy*.

Ipsita, A., Erickson, L., Dong, Y., Huang, J., Bushinski, A. K., Saradhi, S., & Ramani, K. (n.d.). Towards modeling of virtual reality welding simulators to promote accessible and scalable training. *2022 CHI Conference on Human Factors in Computing Systems*, (pp. 1–21). ACM. 10.1145/3491102.3517696

Khatri, M. (2022). Revamping the marketing world with metaverse–The future of marketing. *International Journal of Computer Applications, 975*(5), 8887. doi:10.5120/ijca2022922361

Koohang, A., Nord, J., Ooi, K., Tan, G., Al-Emran, M., Aw, E., Baabdullah, A., Buhalis, D., Cham, T., Dennis, C., Dutot, V., Dwivedi, Y., Hughes, L., Mogaji, E., Pandey, N., Phau, I., Raman, R., Sharma, A., Sigala, M., & Wong, L. (2023). Shaping the metaverse into reality: A holistic multidisciplinary understanding of opportunities, challenges, and avenues for future investigation. *Journal of Computer Information Systems, 63*(3), 735–765. doi:10.1080/08874417.2023.2165197

Mclean, G., Al-Nabhani, K., & Wilson, A. (2018). Developing a mobile applications customer experience model (MACE)- implications for retailers. *Journal of Business Research, 85*, 325–336. doi:10.1016/j.jbusres.2018.01.018

Messinger, P. R., Stroulia, E., Lyons, K., Bone, M., Niu, R. H., Smirnov, K., & Perelgut, S. (2009). Virtual worlds—past, present, and future: New directions in social computing. *Decision Support Systems, 47*(3), 204–228. doi:10.1016/j.dss.2009.02.014

Miao, F., Kozlenkova, I. V., Wang, H., Xie, T., & Palmatier, R. W. (2022). An emerging theory of avatar marketing. *Journal of Marketing, 86*(1), 67–90. doi:10.1177/0022242921996646

Mystakidis, S. (2022). *Metaverse. Encyclopedia, 2*(1).

Pearce, M., Zeadally, S., & Hunt, R. (2013). Virtualization: Issues, security threats, and solutions. *ACM Computing Surveys, 45*(2), 1–39. doi:10.1145/2431211.2431216

Rathore, B. (2017). Virtual consumerism: An exploration of e-commerce in the metaverse. *International Journal of New Media Studies, 4*(2), 61–69. doi:10.58972/eiprmj.v4i2y17.109

Rubio-Tamayo, J. L., Gertrudix Barrio, M., & García García, F. (2017). Immersive environments and virtual reality: Systematic review and advances in communication, interaction and simulation. *Multimodal Technologies and Interaction, 1*(4), 21. doi:10.3390/mti1040021

Scholz, J., & Smith, A. N. (2016). Augmented reality: Designing immersive experiences that maximize consumer engagement. *Business Horizons, 59*(2), 149–161. doi:10.1016/j.bushor.2015.10.003

Seong, S., Hoefer, R., & McLaughlin, S. (2021). NFT revolution [in Korean]. *The Quest.*

Shah, D., & Murthi, B. P. S. (2021). Marketing in a data-driven digital world: Implications for the role and scope of marketing. *Journal of Business Research, 125*, 772–779. doi:10.1016/j.jbusres.2020.06.062

Shah, D., & Shay, E. (2019). How and why artificial intelligence, mixed reality and blockchain technologies will change marketing we know today. Handbook of advances in marketing in an era of disruptions: Essays in honour of Jagdish N. Sheth. Sage. doi:10.4135/9789353287733.n32

Sharma, R., Fantin, A. R., Prabhu, N., Guan, C., & Dattakumar, A. (2016). Digital literacy and knowledge societies: A grounded theory investigation of sustainable development. *Telecommunications Policy, 40*(7), 628–643. doi:10.1016/j.telpol.2016.05.003

Shen, X., Zhang, Y., Tang, Y., Qin, Y., Liu, N., & Yi, Z. (2021). A study on the impact of digital tobacco logistics on tobacco supply chain performance: Taking the tobacco industry in Guangxi as an example. *Industrial Management & Data Systems, 122*(6), 1416–1452. doi:10.1108/IMDS-05-2021-0270

Upadhyay, Y., Paul, J., & Baber, R. (2022). Effect of online social media marketing efforts on customer response. *Journal of Consumer Behaviour, 21*(3), 554–571. doi:10.1002/cb.2031

Wang, I. (2022). *The Digital Mind of Tomorrow: Rethink, transform, and thrive in today's fast-changing and brutal digital world*. Digital Thinker.

Zaman, U., Koo, I., Abbasi, S., Raza, S. H., & Qureshi, M. G. (2022). Meet Your Digital Twin in Space? Profiling International Expat's Readiness for Metaverse Space Travel, Tech-Savviness, COVID-19 Travel Anxiety, and Travel Fear of Missing Out. *Sustainability (Basel), 14*(11), 6441. doi:10.3390/su14116441

Zhang, Z., & Wen, X. (2023). Physical or virtual showroom? The decision for omni-channel retailers in the context of cross-channel free-riding. *Electronic Commerce Research*, 1–27. doi:10.1007/s10660-022-09616-x

ADDITIONAL READINGS

Ball, M. (2020). *The Metaverse: What It Is. Where to Find It, Who Will Build It.* MatthewBall.

Buhalis, D., Lin, M. S., & Leung, D. (2022). Metaverse as a driver for customer experience and value co-creation: Implications for hospitality and tourism management and marketing. *International Journal of Contemporary Hospitality Management, 35*(2), 701–716. doi:10.1108/IJCHM-05-2022-0631

Hazan, E., Kelly, G., Khan, H., Spillecke, D., & Yee, L. (2022). Marketing in the metaverse: An opportunity for innovation and experimentation. *The McKinsey Quarterly.*

Hennig-Thurau, T., Aliman, N., Herting, A., Cziehso, G., Kübler, R., & Linder, M. (2022). *The value of real-time multisensory social interactions in the virtual-reality metaverse: Framework, empirical probes, and research roadmap.* Empirical Probes, and Research Roadmap.

Koohang, A., Nord, J., Ooi, K., Tan, G., & Al-Emran, M., & Wong, L. (2023). Shaping the metaverse into reality: Multidisciplinary perspectives on opportunities, challenges, and future research. *Journal of Computer Information Systems*. Advance online publication. doi:10.1080/08874417.2023.2165197

KEY TERMS AND DEFINITIONS

Artificial Intelligence (AI): Artificial intelligence refers to computer systems that can perform tasks that typically require human intelligence, such as problem-solving, learning, and decision-making.

Augmented Reality (AR): Augmented reality overlays digital information, such as images or data, onto the real-world environment, enhancing the user's perception of the physical world.

Extended Reality (XR): Extended reality is an umbrella term encompassing virtual reality (VR), augmented reality (AR), and mixed reality (MR), creating a spectrum of digital experiences that merge the virtual and physical worlds.

Internet of Things (IoT): The internet of things refers to the network of interconnected physical devices, such as household appliances or wearable gadgets, that can communicate and share data with each other over the internet.

Machine Learning (ML): Machine learning is a subset of artificial intelligence that involves algorithms and statistical models allowing computer systems to improve their performance on a specific task over time without explicit programming.

Non-Fungible Tokens (NFTs): Non-Fungible tokens are unique digital assets stored on a blockchain, certifying ownership and authenticity of a specific item, often used for digital art, collectibles, or virtual real estate.

Spatial Computing: Spatial computing refers to the use of computer algorithms to interpret and respond to the spatial context of a user's environment, enabling more intuitive and interactive digital experiences.

Virtual Reality (VR): Virtual reality creates a simulated digital environment that immerses users in a computer-generated reality, typically accessed through special equipment like VR headsets.

Chapter 10
The "Metaverse Society":
Transformative Effects of Metaverse on Society

Irfan Nawaz
ⓘ https://orcid.org/0000-0002-3817-2858
Ministry of Human Rights, Pakistan

Nazirullah
Universiti Sultan Zainal Abidin, Malaysia

Sabeeha Rahman
Alama Iqbal Open University, Islamabad, Pakistan

Alia Shaheen
Social Welfare and Baitul Mall, Pakistan

ABSTRACT

The term metaverse originated from the "Snow Crash" novel by Neal Stephenson in 1992. The term underwent massive evolution from a speculative concept into an immersive digital ecosystem. Technological advancement unveils the metaverse's potential in shaping the digital future more transformative and promising. The rapid growth of the metaverse extends beyond social interaction and entertainment. Metaverse has started contributing to education, commerce, and professional collaboration. The scope of this chapter is to provide a secondary analysis of the influence of metaverse in individual's lives and societal structures, using the embodied social presence theory and relying on key thematic areas (access and adoption; wellbeing; diversity and inclusion; sustainability; and empowerment) discussed by the World Economic Forum.

EMBODIED SOCIAL PRESENCE THEORY

The metaverse is a virtual environment where people may engage with one another in real-time via digital avatars. This area has been shown to be versatile, accommodating many activities such as gaming, com-

DOI: 10.4018/979-8-3693-2607-7.ch010

munication, marketing, education, and commerce (Garcia et al., 2023). These metaverse efforts emphasize that the success of this technology depends on its capacity to promote and allow social interaction inside the virtual realm efficiently. Therefore, it is crucial to have a thorough understanding of human behaviour and interaction in virtual environments. The chapter used theoretical framework and grounded the Embodied Social Presence Theory (Benosman, 2023). According to this theoretical paradigm, people's views of the virtual world they engage with are significantly impacted by their embodiment inside that space. Embodiment, in this sense, refers to the depiction of a user's tangible form inside a virtual setting.

Regarding telepresence, the physical body may be compared to the technology we use since both work as mediators between the mind and the outside world, facilitating communication and engagement. According to the notion, the way a person sees themselves as part of their surroundings may significantly affect how they think and interact with their environment. This, in turn, affects their degree of focus and involvement in shared activities and communication. There is empirical research that shows how virtual embodiment affects emotional reactivity to virtual stimuli. Enhancing emotional reactions is vital in several human-computer interaction applications. This need is ascribed to the substantial impact of emotions on cognitive processes and learning results. The virtual embodiment may enhance emotional involvement, leading to more profound and efficient learning experiences. This, in turn, can positively impact the acquisition and retention of information (Ghimire, 2023).

The Embodied Social Presence Theory emphasizes the significance of purposeful shared activities in fostering social engagement in virtual settings. Participating in community activities entails collaborating towards a shared objective, which cultivates a feeling of collective purpose and cooperation and aids in the development of a sense of interconnectedness, trust, and mutual comprehension among people. The collective encounter may provide the groundwork for more robust social connections (Bektas, 2023). These digital connections are essential in virtual worlds since they allow users to establish relationships with others and form communities in online surroundings. The virtual realm provides an exceptional medium for people from diverse geographical places, cultural backgrounds, and social circumstances to engage and build connections without being limited by physical distance. The presence of a feeling of inclusion and assistance from others might be especially crucial for persons who experience a sense of social isolation or detachment in their offline existence (Oh et al., 2023). However, users do not deliberately seek out human ties in a virtual environment; instead, these connections naturally develop. In addition to participating in shared activities, it is crucial for people to also participate in ordinary tasks and events that they would normally do with others in their offline daily lives (Zamanifard & Freeman, 2023). These activities foster a feeling of normality and familiarity among those who do not have any pre-existing offline connection.

To summarise, the Embodied Social Presence Theory had a dual impact on the creation of our metaverse: it affected the incorporation of avatar embodiment and facilitated the building of social relationships. Avatar embodiment enables users of the virtual realm to create and manipulate their digital identities, which function as a depiction of their selves inside the parallel setting. This implementation allows users to have a strong sense of possession and control over their avatars, hence enhancing their sensation of being fully present in the virtual environment. Simultaneously, cultivating social connections via ordinary activities provides metaverse users with chances to participate in cooperative endeavours together. The metaverse may foster social connections among individuals by offering shared activities and promoting a feeling of community and belonging inside the virtual realm.

Defining the Metaverse and its Core Features

This section elaborates the summarized concept of metaverse and its main components. Metaverse is a contemporary concept – intersecting virtual and physical realities – representing a collaborated virtual shared space with unique characteristics. Its key components include persistence, immersion, and interoperability. Persistence delineates that it maintains an enduring existence, enabling regular interaction and content production. Immersion offers user experience within digital environments. Interoperability emphasizes seamless connectivity between diverse virtual spaces and platforms. Overall, the metaverse boasts a dynamic digital economy, mirroring real-world economic principles involving the creation, exchange, and consumption of virtual goods and services.

A term metaverse originated from the "Snow Crash" novel by Neal Stephenson in 1992. The term underwent massive evolution from speculative concept into an immersive digital ecosystem. This digital concept further shaped by a multitude of technological growth that redefined the user interaction with virtual and augmented realities. Its key components include persistence, immersion, and interoperability (Stephenson, 2003). Persistence metaverse delineates that it maintains an enduring existence, enabling regular interaction and content production. The main example of persistence metaverse is Second Life and Decentraland that allows users to create and shape their virtual environments – using user-generated content persisting over time. It encourages users to leave lasting impact, promoting the sense of continuity and evolution. In addition, the Decentraland, based on blockchain, allows users to purchase, develop and trade virtual real estate, contributing to the metaverse's landscape in a way that endures over time (Weinberger, 2022).

The immersive part of the metaverse is vividly depicted through virtual reality (VR) technologies. For instance, Oculus Rift and HTC Vive offer multisensory experiences that shifts users into fully realized virtual realms. The immersion further advanced through games like Half-Life, Alyx, in which elements like visuals, spatial audio and interactive elements used to create an environment where users experience high sense of presence. This immersive quality is at the heart of the metaverse, creating a space where the boundaries between the physical and digital worlds are blurred (Wu et al., 2023).

The third key component of metaverse is the interoperability that traverse users into diverse virtual spaces. Cryptovoxels, a virtual world on the Ethereum blockchain, is the product of interoperability by encouraging users to shift their digital assets and identity across metaverse environments. This interconnectedness empowers users to explore a variety of experiences without being confined to a single platform, fostering a more expansive and connected metaverse (Damar, 2022).

Hardware component of metaverse is equally important. The examples of this are VR headsets (Meta Quest 2), Augmented Reality (AR) googles (Microsoft's HoloLens), increase the immersive experience of users' real world surrounded with virtual components. Thus, it blurs the links between physical and virtual world (Park & Kim, 2022). On the other hand, advanced algorithms and artificial intelligence (AI) is vital part of the software side of the metaverse. SpatialOS, a platform developed by Improbable, leverages cloud-based computing and AI to create expansive and persistent virtual worlds. These digital landscapes evolve through user interactions, regularly engaging and getting dynamic experience within the metaverse. This dynamic nature is essential for keeping the metaverse fresh, responsive, and adaptable to the ever-changing preferences and needs of its users (Gill et al., 2022).

Blockchain technology is an epitome of the metaverse. It offers digital ownership, secure transactions, and virtual economies. As discussed above, Decentraland, allows users to buy, sell and trade virtual real estate and other assets. It is a glare example of persistence, interoperability of blockchain within metaverse landscape. Rsoblox, a user-generated content platform, shows participatory aspect of the metaverse (Dziatkovskii et al., 2022). It encourages users to create games, virtual items, experiences, contributing to a dynamic environment. The participatory nature of the metaverse is further evident by Fortnite owned by Epic Games. This platform offers more advanced way of hosting events like virtual concerts, and film screenings, depicting the interoperability of experiences – attracting millions of users across metaverse (Ali et al., 2023).

The rapid growth of metaverse extends beyond social interaction and entertainment. It has started contributing to the education, commerce, and professional collaboration. The persistence nature of metaverse allows access to educational content, offers evolving learning experience. The digital platforms within metaverse opens new avenues for commerce, enables users to do cross-selling of products and services in entirely new way (Allam et al., 2022).

In a nutshell, the metaverse's key components—persistence, immersion, and interoperability—manifest in various forms across platforms. The metaverse is a multifaceted digital landscape continues to grow and redefine user-interaction with virtual world. The advancement of technology unveils the potential of metaverse in shaping digital future more transformative and promising.

Access and Adoption

In this section, scholarly analysis of the metaverse underpins the factors that influence its accessibility and adoption. A fundamental measuring scale is the level of digital literacy of the potential users to navigate the virtual environment in a meaningful way (Buana, 2023). Nevertheless, the presence of digital infrastructure and its robustness are critical in the geographical accessibility of the metaverse (Hu & Liu, 2022). In addition, affordability is another parameter in the accessibility of the metaverse because the economic position is associated with the user's purchasing power in specific geographical cohorts. Besides the regulatory framework, monitoring the metaverse affects the contours of its accessibility, considering the ethical and legal considerations. The notion of metaverse rapidly evolve as a digital ecosystem, offers novelty for human interactions and experiences. The impact of metaverse on social fabric and behaviours demanded through analysis of access and adoption within this digital landscape (Bacher, 2022).

Accessing to the metaverse is influenced by various factors. First of all, technological infrastructure is the foundation stone that ensures provision of high-speed internet connections, low-latency networks, and powerful computing devices. regions where internet infrastructure is advanced, embraced the metaverse seamlessly. On the other hand, regions where this infrastructure is not the level of adopting metaverse is lagging behind. This advantage creates a potential for digital divide between developed and less-developed countries. Secondly, access to metaverse also depends on economic conditions due to high-cost equipment involved in it. VR headsets, AR glasses, and advanced computing devices might be expensive, thus, limiting access to those who cannot afford. The economic disparity in specific socio-economic groups varies in access to the metaverse. Thirdly, digital literacy in navigating the technology stands another crucial factor in access to metaverse. A person equipped with operating complex digital environments can ensure meaningful engagement in the metaverse. Its reliance on advanced technologies and interfaces is likely to handle by a person with higher level of digital literacy (Kaufman et al., 2023).

In addition to access barriers, the adoption of metaverse is contingent to various factors including user experience, content development, and social interaction, the adoption shapes people experience in their social lives and daily activities (Henz, 2022). Metaverse has variety of platforms, offering diverse and unique user experiences such as virtual concerts, social events, etc (Morales-Fernández, 2024). What a user experiences in the virtual world contribute to the overall appeal of the metaverse. Then, number of platforms within metaverse offers users to create content. As seen in Roblox, users are empowered to create and share content – promoting sense of ownership and creativity (Ryu, 2024). This sense of owness encourages users to adopt the platform but also establishes a virtual community to offer an environment where users shape their digital experiences. Additionally, people are interacting with each other and enjoys the sense of ownership contributes towards building digital communities. This uniqueness promotes the adoption of metaverse for its novel experience. So, the communities whether they are related to education, business, gaming, IT, or real estate, are catalyst in adoption of metaverse through development of sense of belonging and shared experience. After that, adoption rate of metaverse also depends on its comp ability with existing business models, workspaces and meetings (Upadhyay et al., 2024). For instance, metaverse potentially integrates into business applications to offer seamless virtual meetings, virtual storefronts, and team building. The adoption of these technologies in a professional context is influenced by their efficacy in facilitating remote work, enhancing collaboration, and providing new avenues for business growth. Furthermore, socio-cultural acceptance of metaverse affects its adoption rate. Social attitude towards immersive technology particularly concerning privacy, ethics and physical-virtual world differentiation. As metaverse technologies become more deeply integrated into daily life, cultural acceptance and understanding will likely influence the pace and extent of adoption (Ball, 2022). Lastly, metaverse can pace its adoption through integration in education sector. This integration can offer virtual classrooms, interactive learning experiences, and customized learning environment. As educational institutions explore these possibilities, the metaverse becomes a valuable tool for learning and skill development (Garlinska et al., 2023). Such as, Garcia et al. (2022) suggested that virtual dietitian application still requires additional improvements, while metaverse applications have the potential to support dietitian applications in the modern society health sector.

The implications of metaverse access and adoption extend beyond individual experiences to shape the broader societal landscape. One of the most significant ramifications is the potential for a digital divide, wherein disparities in access to technology lead to digital exclusion. Bridging this gap requires targeted efforts to provide affordable hardware, internet connectivity, and comprehensive digital literacy programs. By addressing these factors, society can ensure a more inclusive metaverse that benefits a diverse range of individuals.

Well-Being

The modern digital landscape is dominated by a metaverse that offers an immersive user experience beyond the physical realm. This section will dissect the psycho-physical dimensions of metaverse users in the overarching concept of well-being. The metaverse allows users to transcend the limits of the physical world and get the immersive experience of digital environments. The notion of emersion potentially influences the cognitive process of humans and captivates their minds (Ud Din & Almogren, 2023). Furthermore, the experience of the metaverse is central to the more profound sense of presence, developing the incapability of distinction between the real and virtual world (Rahi et al., 2023). This phenomenon generates the debate about how users construct and shape identities within the metaverse. The metaverse users embodied themselves in digital incarnation (self-awareness, self-concept and self-philosophy) to envelop up their virtual experiences with a layer of physicality. In this context, it is crucial to examine self-perception, self-realization and interactions within the digital enclaves.

Metaverse is a virtual universe in which digital environments through customized avatars or digital representations of themselves. This nexus of virtual and physical world fades the differences in both worlds. Metaverse is a complicated aspect of metaverse engagement. For example, South Korea offers an example of how metaverse influences self-perception of users. The adoption of "Lost Ark", a virtual reality-based game, in 2018 took immersive experience to the different level. Just after its popularity, concerns raised about its addiction, compelled the South Korean Government to implement the "Shutdown Law" for tackling the potential negative effects of metaverse particularly on mental health. The law prohibits the children below the age of 16 years to play games in late-night hours. Such incidents trigger the delicate balancee between the allure of immersive virtual experiences and the need to safeguard mental wellbeing, particularly among younger users (Lee et al., 2024).

The discourse of self-realization in metaverse goes beyond mere visual representation. The virtual experience often grapples the users with blurred identity, authenticity, and complex intersection of virtual and physical enclaves. The nexus between self-perception and metaverse takes central place in understanding broader impact of metaverse on wellbeing (Zhou, 2023). This introspection has led to a profound re-evaluation of societal norms and expectations, challenging established notions of selfhood (Özkurt, 2023). Taking Japan as a case study, where "VRChat" platform offer users to create personalized avatars and engage in real-time conversations in digital landscape. Although VRChat promotes self-expression and creativity, yet it can trigger identity crisis in complex social dynamics. The dynamic canvas of metaverse is reflection of self-realization through provision of opportunities to individuals to explore various dimensions of their identities (Mantelli, 2021). This path of self-discovery intrigued with social expectations and explore alternative expressions of self. The mediation between self-realization and social exclusion is crucial and demands for careful examination of the self-realization through metaverse. This discovery of self-realization and potential negative affects generated scholarly debate within societal constructs and norms. The power for self-expressions of identity without cultural, gender and social limits can challenge self-realization of users. This reimagining of selfhood contributes to ongoing dialogues about inclusivity, acceptance, and the fluidity of identity in the digital age (Ambika et al., 2023).

Metaverse is mainly a platform offers social interaction in virtual world. Users interact, collaborate and form connections there. This interaction reflects the convergence of local cultural into global where individuals form connections and communities by transcending geographical boundaries. The collaborative nature of virtual environments fosters a sense of shared experience and collective creation, shaping digital societies that echo and sometimes challenge real-world structures (Nunes, 2023). In 2021, Chinese Government released "The White Paper on the Development of Virtual Economy" delineating detailed set of strategies to encourage growth of virtual economies within metaverse. This step positioned China at the forefront of the metaverse revolution. It also navigates the China's proactive approach towards embracing metaverse as a catalyst for economic growth within virtual spaces. On the other hand, it raised questions on balancing the economic growth and societal wellbeing within metaverse. The real challenge would be distribution of benefits equitably. The potential disparities may challenge the metaverse engagement and questions the inclusive growth through it (Zhang et al., 2021).

The hardest path in technological revolution is maintaining balance between technological innovation and ethical limits. Interaction opportunities inside metaverse raises concerns over privacy and ethical limits. When users embody themselves in digital avatars, the virtual space tied to one's virtual identity. Germany is a country with stringent data protection mechanism provides a contrasting example in the metaverse arena. In 2022, German government introduced "Digital Ethics Charter" to set guidelines for fostering ethical behaviour in digital landscape including metaverse. Emphasizing user privacy, consent, and the responsible use of emerging technologies, this initiative underscores Germany's commitment to ethical metaverse engagement. As users embody themselves in digital avatars, Germany's approach serves as a model for creating an ethical metaverse environment that aligns with societal expectations and respects individual autonomy. The ethical considerations and privacy beyond data protection encompasses broader questions about role of metaverse in wellbeing. While users scroll inside digital space, ethical norms are likely to compromise. Thus, digital citizenship framework can be the option to tackle the ethical crisis in virtual landscape (Becker et al., 2022).

As society navigates the evolving landscape of the metaverse, it is essential to consider the implications of self-embodiment on mental health, social dynamics, and privacy. By examining the experiences of different countries, policymakers, researchers, and communities can collaboratively develop frameworks that harness the potential benefits of the metaverse while mitigating risks and fostering a digital environment that enhances overall wellbeing. The exploration of self-perception, self-realization, and ethical considerations within the metaverse underscores the need for a holistic approach that prioritizes individual agency, societal values, and the collective wellbeing of users in this digital frontier.

Diversity and Inclusion

This section navigates cultural, moral, and ethical implications in the evolution of the metaverse. The deeper analysis will discuss the potential challenges and benefits concerning users' diversity and inclusion based on respect, tolerance, equity, and justice. Examples will be presented to illuminate how metaverse can catalyze the promotion or erosion of diversity and inclusion, manifesting through customization, collaboration, communication, and instances of discrimination. The moral and ethical debate of metaverse is central to the diverse identities, cultures, and communities. Metaverse navigates the perceptions that reinforce stereotypes and foster cultural understanding among societies (De Moor et al., 2023). It is a general misconception that the metaverse is devoid of cultural norms and values that challenge existing social constructions. The values and norms contextualize the ethical dimensions of the metaverse (Zallio & Clarkson, 2022). The users' protection rights and recognitions within virtual spaces, particularly privacy, consent, and digital citizenship, contour the ethical dimension of the metaverse. Potentially, the metaverse fosters an environment of respect and tolerance, emphasizing the diverse perspectives of a rich and tolerant metaverse ecosystem (Makarigakis et al., 2023). Equity, equality, and social justice are core values of the socially conscious from the perspective of the metaverse. However, it is crucial to underpin the power dynamics within this digital realm (Saka, 2023). It allows users to express individual identity. Regardless, the potential ambushes of reinforcing stereotypes arise from the metaverse, which is the question of modern literature, and this gap will be filled.

The vast digital realm of metaverse is an immersive experience for users that reshapes inclusivity and diversity. A thin line draws between inclusion and exclusion within metaverse (Gaurav, 2022). Metaverse is being used to ensure inclusion of the excluded groups. For instance, "VR for everyone" and "Accessible Metaverse Project" are few such initiatives, striving for enhancing accessibility for persons with disabilities in South Korea (Lee, 2023; Lee et al., 2023). Using advanced technologies, it provides users adaptive experiences, through accommodating them with various sensory needs, fostering the digital inclusion. Furthermore, virtual spaces have become the places where people can exchange cultural values, tradition beyond their geographical boundaries. Japan has taken initiative titled "Global Metaverse Cultural Festivals" to offer cross-cultural interactions within metaverse. It is a platform where users from the globe can share and celebrate their cultural heritage. Such initiatives are important pillars in promotion of tolerance, diversity and encourage sense of global community within metaverse (Bardhan, 2023).

Digital inclusion takes central place in inclusivity discourse. Digital Inclusion Initiative in Germany aims to address the economic disparities within metaverse. The program focuses on establishment of inclusive platforms through provision of accessibility to users from various socio-economic backgrounds. It encourages digital literacy and reducing financial barriers and building metaverse a place accessible to larger audience. The realization towards pivotal role of metaverse, tech companies is taking initiatives to make metaverse a place of human diversity (Bibri, 2022). In the United States, "Inclusive Metaverse Task Force" is an initiative to create digital environments that resonate with users from various cultural, ethnic, and gender backgrounds (Flannery, 2022).

On the other hand, the prevalence of metaverse is potentially exacerbating digital exclusion and disparities. The special programs, and premium features are only limited to those who can afford or living in developed countries, widening the existing digital divide between developed and non-developed countries. Such steps may inadvertently contribute to the metaverse where participation is stratified based on geographical location, financial position and social status (Calzada, 2023). Nevertheless, number of cases reported digital harassment and hate speech online. The anonymity offered by metaverse somehow leverage the users for discriminatory behaviour, hate speech and online harassment. However, efforts are being made to implement moderating tools, but the arduous nature of virtual spaces make it difficult to curb digital harassment and hate speech (Dwivedi et al., 2023).

As we navigate the evolving landscape of the metaverse, it is imperative to recognize that its impact on inclusion and diversity is nuanced. Positive initiatives in South Korea, Japan, hold the promise of creating a metaverse that embraces individuals of varied backgrounds, abilities, and perspectives. However, addressing negative consequences, particularly economic disparities and digital harassment, requires proactive measures globally to mitigate potential harms and ensure that the metaverse becomes a beacon of diversity rather than a platform that perpetuates existing inequalities.

Sustainability

In this portion of the chapter, debate of metaverse revolves around the consumption of resources and waste generation. The substantial energy footprint of metaverse activities becomes a focal point, raising pertinent concerns about ecological sustainability. The nature of the metaverse compels scientists to believe that it is a crucible for innovation – a catalyst to economic growth and the digital economy. It has the potential to optimize efficiency, bolster productivity, and accelerate the overall quality of user experience (Vlăduțescu & Stănescu, 2023). On the other hand, these prospects issued a clarion call for responsible consumption of energy to ensure a sustainable trajectory. It has potential for conservation through immersive virtual experiences, ensuring that digital processes are environmentally friendly, and managing digital consumption responsibly (Jauhiainen et al., 2022). The section will draw attention to the integration of the metaverse into our digital future through resource management, water consumption, and ensuring an ecologically conscious digital landscape.

As the metaverse becomes an increasingly integral part of our digital future, the need to integrate it responsibly into our global ecosystem takes center stage. This article explores the crucial intersection of the metaverse with resource management, with a focus on water consumption and the imperative to foster an ecologically conscious digital landscape. By examining specific initiatives taken by countries, we delve into the evolving narrative of sustainability in the metaverse.

The adaptability of metaverse also facilitates resource management particularly water management, and ecology conscious digital environment. The evolving landscape of metaverse offers efficient resource management. Let's take the example of Sweden's "Green Server Project" launched in 2021, which strives for optimizing server farms to reduce energy consumption and extending ecological footprints of metaverse. By embracing energy-efficient technologies and renewable energy sources, Sweden's initiative sets a precedent for responsible resource management in the digital realm (Pareliussen & Purwin, 2023). This is one such innovative stance affirming that the growth of metaverse can be possible without resource depletion. The world should understand the sustainable approach in adoption of metaverse particularly in advancement of technologies by reflecting interconnectedness between progress and climate stewardship (Mishra & Singh, 2023).

Besides, metaverse is contingent to water consumption with special reference to cooling systems of data centres (Lloyd Owen, 2021). Learning from the experience of Singapore "WaterSmart Guidelines" in 2022, which sets parameters for water efficiency in data centre through adoption of advanced cooling technologies and responsible water usage practices. Singapore's proactive stance underscores the importance of addressing water consumption as an integral component of ecologically conscious metaverse development (Laura, 2023) (Makarigakis et al., 2023).

This forward-thinking approach of Singapore's reiterates the importance of water as a precious resource and to lay the foundation of sustainable digital practices. In quest of ecologically conscious digital landscape, world should learn from exemplary initiatives taken by few of the countries and spearhead the agenda of sustainable digital practices. The world should foster sustainable metaverse development, focusing on responsible data management, recycling of electronic waster and adherence to circular economy principles. Germany's Green Pact Initiative set a precedent for nations who are struggling to balance technological advancements with climate stewardship (Dutu-Buzura, 2021).

The integration of the metaverse into our digital future is inseparable from responsible resource management and the cultivation of an ecologically conscious landscape. Initiatives from Sweden, Singapore, and Germany showcase diverse approaches to sustainability, highlighting the global commitment to mitigating the ecological impact of the metaverse. As we navigate the digital frontier, it is imperative to view the metaverse not only as a realm of technological innovation but also as a space where ecological responsibility and digital progress converge.

By learning from these initiatives, we can forge a path toward a metaverse that not only enriches our digital experiences but also nurtures the well-being of our planet. The lessons from Sweden, Singapore, and Germany collectively contribute to a narrative of sustainability, signaling that the metaverse's growth can be synonymous with environmental consciousness. As more countries embrace responsible practices, we move closer to a digital future where ecological considerations are not an afterthought but an integral part of the metaverse's evolution.

Empowerment

In this section, an analysis of empowerment in the context of the socio-political metaverse with a special focus on governance, ownership, agency, activism, and education will be presented. Further, how the metaverse brings empowerment in gender related to education (male and female) (Brahma et al., 2023). However, the governance structures within the metaverse, dissecting the questions of authority and control, will be examined in this section. The analysis will further elaborate on the concept of ownership considering digital property rights (virtual assets and spaces). The argument will be based on the capacity of the agency of metaverse users to exert influence to make autonomous choices (choice, voice, and influence) in digital realms. The available literature provided that the socio-political landscape of the metaverse encompasses user participation in virtual governance, creative expression, and mobilization of social causes. Grounded on this, this section contributes towards a greater understanding of the socio-political facets of the metaverse and how it contributes towards empowerment.

The rise of metaverse opens new avenues of governance structures. The adaptability of metaverse compel governments to shape the governance structure through metaverse. The prominent models, inspired by metaverse are Decentralized Governance Models, such as Blockchain systems. These models are key mechanism for empowering metaverse citizens through autonomy, inclusivity, and active participation in decision-making processes (Bibri et al., 2022). Such models allow users to decide on metaverse policies, assets and experiences. This decentralization also challenges the traditional authority structures, placing governance at the core of the community. For example, Estonian's has started its e-Residency Program which leverage blockchain for secure digital identities. This initiative shows Estonia's commitment to empowering citizens in the digital space. With this digital citizenship, decentralized finance (DeFi) models within metaverse such as Aave, and Compound, challenge the traditional narrative of need of conservative intermediaries for financial operations. In these platforms, users actively participate in shaping these decentralized protocols, impacting the governance of financial interactions within the metaverse (Lemos et al., 2022). Thus, decentralized governance models redefine the power dynamic within the metaverse, illustrating a departure from traditional hierarchical structures toward community-driven decision-making (Tan, 2021).

Virtual spaces allow users to shape their environment through customizable rules and regulations. This concept of user-generated governance within metaverse changed the notion of rule-setting and enforcement (Marinescu & Iordache, 2023). Metaverse has made the users architects of virtual spaces, setting up the norms that govern their interactions. This user-focused governance models promotes the sense of ownership and empowerment. The glare example of user-generated governance is Second Life (United States) where users shape their experience, establish property rights, and can create their own economic mechanisms. The success of such platforms showcases the viability and potential of user-generated governance structures in fostering empowerment (Hobson, 2024).

The growing authority of metaverse also raises questions about implications of corporate governance on digital citizenship. The real challenge is to create balance between corporate authority and user empowerment through his meaningful voice in decision-making processes within metaverse. China's exploration of the metaverse, exemplified by companies like Tencent and its virtual world initiatives, showcases the intertwining of corporate governance and digital citizenship. Understanding how this balance is navigated in a country with a strong corporate presence informs global conversations on metaverse governance. Corporate governance structures necessitate careful consideration to prevent the concentration of authority within a few entities, emphasizing the importance of equitable power distribution (Malerba, 2023).

The governance structure dominantly aimed for empowerment of users adds a layer of complexity for traditional governments. The expanding digital realms grabble countries with questions about limitation of governments and implementation of regulatory frameworks. Striking the right balance between preserving individual freedoms, empowerment and maintaining societal order requires innovative approaches to governance that acknowledge the unique challenges posed by the metaverse (Ud Din et al., 2023).

Germany took lead in data protection regulations and adopted holistic approach to balance innovation with privacy through systematic initiatives discussed above. In contrast, European Union has initiated deliberations on adopting stringent legal frameworks for regulating metaverse. However, it is important to understand that interplay between governmental authority and metaverse governance require adaptive regulatory frameworks that respect digital citizenship.

SUMMARY OF THE CHAPTER

The novelty of the chapter lies in the embedding aspects of metaverse in the society and its transformative effects on modern society, however, most of the literature focuses on the technological aspects of metaverse. The academic discussion surrounding the metaverse spans broad and fundamental topics. Every theme discussed in the chapter revealed a unique aspect of the metaverse's influence on society. This chapter focused on the issue of Access and Adoption, examining the various elements that influence the adoption of the metaverse. Specifically, it explored the impact of technological hurdles and concerns related to inclusivity. The concept of Wellbeing in context of metaverses opened up new avenues of research. Then, Diversity and Inclusion was examined through the lens of metaverse by considering aspects of representation, prejudice, and inclusion within virtual communities. Moreover, the concept of Sustainability revealed the environmental challenges associated with the metaverse, such as carbon footprints and energy usage. At the end of the chapter, the concept of Empowerment within the metaverse and its potential to empower individuals and communities was discussed in detail. The examination extended to digital citizenship, involvement in decision-making, and the democratization of virtual spaces. This thorough examination, grounded in the aforementioned principles and embodied social presence theory, this chapter provides a holistic comprehension of the potential societal ramifications of the metaverse. It will assist study scientists in having well-informed conversations about how to fairly incorporate the metaverse into people's life. In future, cultural dynamics within virtual communities (Abdulayeva et al., 2023), economic models (Abdulayeva et al., 2023), education (Darban, 2023), health (Garcia et al., 2022), security challenges (Mughal, 2018), environmental sustainability (Sudhakar, 2023), and human-robot interaction in virtual spaces (Sudhakar, 2023) represent additional promising areas for future research exploration, contributing to a comprehensive understanding of the evolving landscape of the Metaverse.

REFERENCES

Ali, M., Naeem, F., Kaddoum, G., & Hossain, E. (2023). Metaverse communications, networking, security, and applications: Research issues, state-of-the-art, and future directions. *IEEE Communications Surveys & Tutorials*. 10.1051/shsconf/202316400001

Allam, Z., Sharifi, A., Bibri, S. E., Jones, D. S., & Krogstie, J. (2022). The metaverse as a virtual form of smart cities: Opportunities and challenges for environmental, economic, and social sustainability in urban futures. *Smart Cities*, 5(3), 771–801. doi:10.3390/smartcities5030040

Ambika, A., Belk, R., Jain, V., & Krishna, R. (2023). The road to learning "who am I" is digitized: A study on consumer self-discovery through augmented reality tools. *Journal of Consumer Behaviour*, 22(5), 1112–1127. doi:10.1002/cb.2185

Bacher, N. (2022). *Metaverse Retailing* University of Pavia. https://www.researchgate.net/profile/Natalie-Bacher/publication/366441739_Metaverse_Retailing

Ball, M. (2022). *The Metaverse: And How it will Revolutionize Everything*. Liveright Publishing. doi:10.15358/9783800669400

Bardhan, A. (2023). Expansion of Space in Metaverse Communication and its Probable Impact. *Society Language and Culture: A Multidisciplinary Peer-Reviewed Journal*, (4), 30-36. https://www.society-languageculture.org

Becker, S. J., Nemat, A. T., Lucas, S., Heinitz, R. M., Klevesath, M., & Charton, J. E. (2022). A Code of Digital Ethics: Laying the foundation for digital ethics in a science and technology company. *AI & Society*, *38*(6), 2629–2639. doi:10.1007/s00146-021-01376-w

Bektas, H. (2023). *Revealing relevant factors impacting the viability of the metaverse by replacing online collaboration tools for business meetings* (Publication Number 60644) University of Twente]. https://essay.utwente.nl/96243/

Benosman, M. (2023). *Social Psychology in the Era of the Metaverse: An overview of recent studies*

Bibri, S. E. (2022). The social shaping of the metaverse as an alternative to the imaginaries of data-driven smart Cities: A study in science, technology, and society. *Smart Cities*, *5*(3), 832–874. doi:10.3390/smartcities5030043

Bibri, S. E., Allam, Z., & Krogstie, J. (2022). The Metaverse as a virtual form of data-driven smart urbanism: Platformization and its underlying processes, institutional dimensions, and disruptive impacts. *Computational Urban Science*, *2*(1), 2–22. doi:10.1007/s43762-022-00051-0 PMID:35974838

Brahma, M., Rejula, M. A., Srinivasan, B., Kumar, S., Banu, W. A., Malarvizhi, K., Priya, S. S., & Kumar, A. (2023). Learning impact of recent ICT advances based on virtual reality IoT sensors in a metaverse environment. *Measurement. Sensors*, *27*, 100754. doi:10.1016/j.measen.2023.100754

Buana, I. M. W. (2023). Metaverse: Threat or Opportunity for Our Social World? In understanding Metaverse on sociological context. *Journal of Metaverse*, *3*(1), 28–33. doi:10.57019/jmv.1144470

Calzada, I. (2023). Disruptive technologies for e-Diasporas: Blockchain, DAOs, data cooperatives, metaverse, and ChatGPT. *Futures*, *154*, 103258. doi:10.1016/j.futures.2023.103258

Damar, M. (2022). What the literature on medicine, nursing, public health, midwifery, and dentistry reveals: An overview of the rapidly approaching metaverse. *Journal of Metaverse*, *2*(2), 62–70. doi:10.57019/jmv.1132962

Darban, M. (2023). The future of virtual team learning: Navigating the intersection of AI and education. *Journal of Research on Technology in Education*, 1–17. doi:10.1080/15391523.2023.2288912

De Moor, K., Farias, M., Vinayagamoorthy, V., Daly, M., & Collingwoode-William, T. (2023). Diversity and Inclusion in Focus at ACM IMX'22 and MMSys' 22. *ACM SIGMultimedia Records*, *14*(3), 1–1. doi:10.1145/3630658.3630660

Dutu-Buzura, M. (2021). European Climate Pact–Framework for Information and Participation of the Public to the Climate Change Challenge. *Romanian Journal of Public Affairs*(3), 29-40. http://www. rjpa.ro/sites/

Dwivedi, Y. K., Kshetri, N., Hughes, L., Rana, N. P., Baabdullah, A. M., Kar, A. K., Koohang, A., Ribeiro-Navarrete, S., Belei, N., Balakrishnan, J., Basu, S., Behl, A., Davies, G. H., Dutot, V., Dwivedi, R., Evans, L., Felix, R., Foster-Fletcher, R., Giannakis, M., ... Yan, M. (2023). Exploring the Darkverse: A Multi-Perspective Analysis of the Negative Societal Impacts of the Metaverse. *Information Systems Frontiers*, 25(5), 2071–2114. doi:10.1007/s10796-023-10400-x PMID:37361890

Dziatkovskii, A., Hryneuski, U., Krylova, A., & Loy, A. C. M. (2022). Chronological Progress of Blockchain in Science, Technology, Engineering and Math (STEM): A Systematic Analysis for Emerging Future Directions. *Sustainability (Basel)*, 14(19), 12074. doi:10.3390/su141912074

Flannery, C. B. (2022). Philosophical and Practical Privacy in the Metaverse: A Case for Data Privacy Protection under the United States Constitution. *Cornell Journal of Law and Public Policy*, 32, 134–153. https://heinonline.org/

Gaurav, A. (2022). Metaverse and Globalization: Cultural Exchange and Digital Diplomacy. *Data Science Insights Magazine, 5*. https://insights2techinfo.com/

Ghimire, A. (2023). *AvatARoid: using a motion-mapped AR overlay to bridge the embodiment gap between robot and teleoperator in robot-mediated telepresence*. University of British Columbia.

Gill, S. S., Xu, M., Ottaviani, C., Patros, P., Bahsoon, R., Shaghaghi, A., Golec, M., Stankovski, V., Wu, H., Abraham, A., Singh, M., Mehta, H., Ghosh, S. K., Baker, T., Parlikad, A. K., Lutfiyya, H., Kanhere, S. S., Sakellariou, R., Dustdar, S., & Uhlig, S. (2022). AI for next generation computing: Emerging trends and future directions. *Internet of Things : Engineering Cyber Physical Human Systems*, 19, 100514. doi:10.1016/j.iot.2022.100514

Henz, P. (2022). The societal impact of the Metaverse. *Discover Artificial Intelligence*, 2(1), 19. doi:10.1007/s44163-022-00032-6

Hobson, A. (2024). Emergent Governance From Polycentric Order in Virtual Reality Social Spaces. In Law, Video Games, Virtual Realities (pp. 74-95). Routledge. https://doi.org/ doi:10.4324/9781003197805-5

Hu, Y., & Liu, C. (2022). The 'metaverse society': Beyond the discourse intrinsic potential and transformative impact. *Metaverse*, 3(2), 14. doi:10.54517/m.v3i2.2128

Jauhiainen, J. S., Krohn, C., & Junnila, J. (2022). Metaverse and Sustainability: Systematic Review of Scientific Publications until 2022 and Beyond. *Sustainability (Basel)*, 15(1), 346. doi:10.3390/su15010346

Kaufman, I., Horton, C., & Soltanifar, M. (2023). *Digital Marketing: Integrating Strategy, Sustainability, and Purpose*. Taylor & Francis. doi:10.4324/9781351019187

Laura, P. (2023). *A water smart city: Learning from Singapore*. https://www.beesmart.city/en/solutions/a-water-smart-city-learning-from-singapore

Lee, J.-W. (2023). The Future of Online Barrier-Free Open Space Cultural Experiences for People with Disabilities in the Post-COVID-19 Era. *Land (Basel)*, 13(1), 33. doi:10.3390/land13010033

Lee, M., Min, K. Z. L., & Kim, S.-H. (2024). Does the Experience of Using Metaverse Affect the Relationship between Social Identity, Psychological Ownership, and Engagement? *Proceedings of the 57th Hawaii International Conference on System Sciences*. University of Hawai.

Lee, S., Lee, Y., & Park, E. (2023). Sustainable Vocational Preparation for Adults with Disabilities: A Metaverse-Based Approach. *Sustainability (Basel)*, *15*(15), 12000. doi:10.3390/su151512000

Lemos, L., Ainse, D., & Faras, A. (2022). DAO meets the Estonian e-residency program: a stance from Synergy's blockchain-based open-source toolkit. Conference Proceedings of the STS Conference Graz 2022, Lloyd Owen, D. (2021). *Defining 'Smart Water'*. Wily Online Library. https://doi.org/10.1002/9781119531241.ch4

Makarigakis, A., Partey, S., Nagabhatla, N., De Lombaerde, P., Libert, B., Trombitcaia, I., Zerrath, E., Guerrier, D., Faloutsos, D., & Krol, D. (2023). *Regional Perspectives*. https://cris.unu.edu/sites/cris.unu.edu

Malerba, S. (2023). *Exploring the Potential of the Metaverse for Value Creation: An Analysis of Opportunities, Challenges, and Societal Impact, with a Focus on the Chinese Context* Ca' Foscari University of Venice. http://dspace.unive.it/bitstream/handle/10579/24277/890613-1281454

Mantelli, A. (2021). Learning Japanese through VR technology. The case of altspace VR. *Annali di Ca'Foscari. Serie Orientale*, *57*, 663–684. 10278/3742133/1/art-10.30687

Marinescu, I. A., & Iordache, D.-D. (2023). Exploring relevant technologies for simulating user interaction in Metaverse virtual spaces. *Romanian Journal of Information Technology & Automatic Control*, *33*(3), 129–142. doi:10.33436/v33i3y202310

Mishra, P., & Singh, G. (2023). Energy management systems in sustainable smart cities based on the internet of energy: A technical review. *Energies*, *16*(19), 6903. doi:10.3390/en16196903

Morales-Fernández, B. (2024). New Linguistic Spaces in Cyberculture: The Influence of the Metaverse on the Minifiction of Social Networks. In The Future of Digital Communication (pp. 27-38). CRC Press.

Mughal, A. A. (2018). Artificial Intelligence in Information Security: Exploring the Advantages, Challenges, and Future Directions. *Journal of Artificial Intelligence and Machine Learning in Management*, *2*(1), 22–34.

Nunes, C. C. (2023). *The Importance on Self-Expression Through Clothing and Fashion: A view on Digital Identity and Digital Fashion* Universidade Da Beira Interior. https://ubibliorum.ubi.pt/handle/10400.6/13583

Oh, H. J., Kim, J., Chang, J. J., Park, N., & Lee, S. (2023). Social benefits of living in the metaverse: The relationships among social presence, supportive interaction, social self-efficacy, and feelings of loneliness. *Computers in Human Behavior*, *139*, 107498. doi:10.1016/j.chb.2022.107498

Özkurt, M. (2023). *A Jungian Archetypal analysis of Earnest Cline's Ready Player One: quest for the Axis mMundi* Pamukkale University]. https://hdl.handle.net/11499/56004

Pareliussen, J., & Purwin, A. (2023). Climate policies and Sweden's green industrial revolution. *OECD Economics Department Working Papers*(1778), 1-48. https://doi.org/ doi:10.1787/18151973

Park, S.-M., & Kim, Y.-G. (2022). A metaverse: Taxonomy, components, applications, and open challenges. *IEEE Access: Practical Innovations, Open Solutions, 10*, 4209–4251. doi:10.1109/ACCESS.2021.3140175

Rahi, P., Sood, S. P., Dandotiya, M., Kalhotra, S. K., & Khan, I. R. (2023). Artificial Intelligence of Things (AIoT) and Metaverse Technology for Brain Health, Mental Health, and Wellbeing. In Contemporary Applications of Data Fusion for Advanced Healthcare Informatics (pp. 429-445). IGI Global. https://doi.org/ doi:10.4018/978-1-6684-8913-0.ch019

Ryu, S. (2024). Zepeto: Developing a Business Model for the Metaverse World.

Saka, E. (2023). Metaverse and Diversity. In *The Future of Digital Communication* (pp. 73–89). CRC Press., doi:10.1201/9781003379119-6

Stephenson, N. (2003). *Snow Crash: A Novel*. Spectra.

Sudhakar, M. (2023). Artificial Intelligence Applications in Water Treatment and Water Resource Assessment: Challenges, Innovations, and Future Directions. In Intelligent Engineering Applications and Applied Sciences for Sustainability (pp. 248-269). IGI Global.

Tan A. (2021). Metaverse Realities: A Journey Through Governance, Legal Complexities, and the Promise of Virtual Worlds. SSRN. https://doi.org/ doi:10.2139/ssrn.4393422

Ud Din, I., & Almogren, A. (2023). Exploring the psychological effects of Metaverse on mental health and well-being. *Information Technology & Tourism, 25*(3), 367–389. doi:10.1007/s40558-023-00259-8

Ud Din, I., Awan, K. A., Almogren, A., & Rodrigues, J. J. (2023). Integration of IoT and blockchain for decentralized management and ownership in the metaverse. *International Journal of Communication Systems, 36*(18), e5612. doi:10.1002/dac.5612

Upadhyay, U., Kumar, A., Sharma, G., Saini, A. K., Arya, V., Gaurav, A., & Chui, K. T. (2024). Mitigating Risks in the Cloud-Based Metaverse Access Control Strategies and Techniques. [IJCAC]. *International Journal of Cloud Applications and Computing, 14*(1), 1–30. doi:10.4018/IJCAC.334364

Vlăduțescu, Ș., & Stănescu, G. C. (2023). Environmental Sustainability of Metaverse: Perspectives from Romanian Developers. *Sustainability (Basel), 15*(15), 11704. doi:10.3390/su151511704

Weinberger, M. (2022). What Is Metaverse?—A Definition Based on Qualitative Meta-Synthesis. *Future Internet, 14*(11), 310. doi:10.3390/fi14110310

Wu, D., Yang, Z., Zhang, P., Wang, R., Yang, B., & Ma, X. (2023). Virtual-Reality Inter-Promotion Technology for Metaverse: A Survey. *IEEE Internet of Things Journal, 10*(18), 1–15. doi:10.1109/JIOT.2023.3265848

Zallio, M., & Clarkson, P. J. (2022). Designing the metaverse: A study on inclusion, diversity, equity, accessibility and safety for digital immersive environments. *Telematics and Informatics, 75*, 101909. doi:10.1016/j.tele.2022.101909

Zamanifard, S., & Freeman, G. (2023). A Surprise Birthday Party in VR: Leveraging Social Virtual Reality to Maintain Existing Close Ties over Distance. International Conference on Information, Zhang, W., Zhao, S., Wan, X., & Yao, Y. (2021). Study on the effect of digital economy on high-quality economic development in China. *PLoS One*, *16*(9), e0257365. doi:10.1371/journal.pone.0257365

Zhou, Z. (2023). Will the Metaverse Revolutionize the Narrative? *Critical Arts*, 1–15. doi:10.1080/02560046.2023.2282489

Chapter 11
Navigating the Metaverse in Business and Commerce:
Opportunities, Challenges, and Ethical Consideration in the Virtual World

Pooja Shukla

Amity University, Ranchi, India

Bhavna Taneja

(iD) https://orcid.org/0000-0002-5447-7758

Amity University, Ranchi, India

ABSTRACT

Trade and consumer interactions with goods and services could be drastically changed by the convergence of the metaverse and commerce. Blockchain technology is used in the metaverse to facilitate the production, ownership, and exchange of virtual products and digital assets. This opens up new business opportunities and includes digital stuff such as in-game items, digital art, virtual real estate, and other digital goods. The idea of " Metaverse" and the role played by Metaverse in business and commerce are intended to be explained in this chapter. The chapter aims to address the genesis, requirements, advantages, opportunities and challenges in the area of Metaverse . It also intends to highlight the ethical considerations and the actions necessary to make the associated practices robust, viable, and effective.

INTRODUCTION

A collaborative virtual shared space created by merging physical and virtual reality is called the "metaverse." The metaverse is a spatial computing platform built on blockchain technology that provides virtual experiences that either replace or replicate the real world and all its essential elements, including social interactions, currency, commerce, economy, and property (Gartner, 2022). The metaverse is a collection of three-dimensional virtual environments accessible via a headset, smartphone app, or the internet. The

DOI: 10.4018/979-8-3693-2607-7.ch011

metaverse's almost limitless possibilities and goals are currently making it the talk of the digital world. Due to its groundbreaking status in digital and technological discoveries, the metaverse is attracting a lot of investment. The digital and real worlds can coexist in this environment and have a major impact on key aspects of daily life. Essentially, it is a world of infinitely connected virtual communities where users can interact, create, and have fun using smartphone apps, augmented reality glasses, virtual reality headsets, and other technologies. It also covers other facets of the internet lifestyle, such as social networking and shopping.

Though the idea of the metaverse has existed for many years, the rebranding of "Meta" has brought it to the attention of the general public. By unveiling this rebranding, Meta—the "Big Tech" business that presently holds the largest interest in the Metaverse marketplace—signaled a major shift in its focus towards the creation of mixed, virtual, and augmented realities. It is reasonable to anticipate that when similar digital businesses pool their resources, future technology will influence how people live, work, and amuse themselves in urban life both locally and globally. Novelist Neal Stephenson is credited with popularizing the phrase "metaverse." His novel "Snow Crash" is widely regarded as the first to introduce the idea of the metaverse. The novel says that the metaverse consists of a virtual environment where users can communicate with one another in a common online space. It also states that the metaverse is a virtual environment that can be accessed with a virtual reality headset and used for social media, business, and entertainment purposes. The novel delves into the potential of virtual world and its potential societal implications, making it one of the first works of literature (Stephenson, 1992).

The idea of the metaverse has come to light as a revolutionary frontier in an era of unparalleled technical development, with the potential to drastically alter the business and commerce landscape. The Metaverse, which is described as a virtual shared space created by the fusion of permanent virtual world with digitally augmented physical reality, signifies a fundamental change in the way people interact, transact, and engage. People move between virtual worlds in the Metaverse with ease, taking part in activities that range from trade and education to social interactions and entertainment. Beyond the confines of actual life, this virtual environment presents countless options for creativity and discovery. The metaverse offers businesses the alluring possibility of breaking into new markets, establishing fresh connections with customers, and reinventing conventional business structures.

The metaverse opens a new floodgate of opportunities in the area of business and commerce (Swan, 2023). Developments in the field of information technology have added sophistication, leading to the development of innovative business models, products, and services. These business models, products, and services not only have the potential to upgrade the existing business paradigms but also to add new revenue streams. Using the metaverse, entrepreneurs and business houses can offer their goods and services to consumers across the globe. But despite the attraction of seemingly endless options, companies have to negotiate in a challenging and morally complex environment. Businesses that want to participate in the metaverse have to consider concerns about data security, privacy, and the morality of virtual interactions. The Metaverse will evolve into an extraordinarily comprehensive, extraordinarily transparent, and dynamically optimized system as the application scenarios mature. To make sure that the metaverse is an environment that promotes justice and fairness for all users, significant thought must be given to issues of accessibility, inclusion, and the digital divide.

REVIEW OF LITERATURE

Metaverse is a term that has acquired popularity, suggesting a revolutionary future where virtual worlds live in harmony with our daily lives Ball (2022). Metaverse aims to build a virtual world says Kim (2021), that is immersive, networked, and persistent. Social and economic connections, peer-to-peer communication, and even the ownership of virtual goods is made possible by this virtual reality (VR) and augmented reality (AR) environments.

Immersive 3D Environments

The metaverse is not one isolated, standalone platform. Popp & Cuțitoi, (2022) envisions an interconnected network of virtual spaces. It can be thought of as a collection of smoothly linked virtual worlds. Users can move freely between them with their avatars and possibly even their digital possessions. This persistence is important because the metaverse continues to exist and evolve even when certain users are not online.

Interconnectivity and Persistence

The metaverse does not exists in isolation. It is made up of network of interconnected virtual spaces. According to Moro-Visconti (2022), it is a collection of virtual worlds, seamlessly connected together. Users can without any hassle travel between them, carrying their avatars and potentially even their digital assets.

Social and Economic Interactions

The metaverse promotes social interaction and economic activity in addition to entertainment. Allam, et al., 2022, say that users can have meaningful conversations, build communities, work together on projects, and even take part in virtual economies. According to Kim et al., 2023, this can entail blending the boundaries between the real and virtual worlds by going to virtual conferences, concerts, or buying digital goods and services.

User-Generated Content and Ownership

Users are enabled to be creators rather than merely consumers by the metaverse. Chen, & Cheng (2022) say that a major part is played by user-generated content (UGC) -which enables people to create and modify their virtual environments and may even influence the metaverse's structure. Furthermore, Lee et al., 2022, reiterate that the establishment of safe and transparent digital ownership might be facilitated by ideas like blockchain technology, allowing people to trade and possess unique products or virtual land inside the metaverse.

Evolving and Unifying

The metaverse is an ever-evolving concept rather than a static one. Bolger (2021) says that it is always developing and improving its unique features and functionalities. Richter & Richter (2023) says that its flexible character makes it possible to incorporate new technologies and innovate continuously. In its perfect state, the metaverse also seeks to bring all the existing virtual experiences together into a single, coherent virtual environment.

Building Blocks of the Metaverse

The metaverse, an immersive virtual world, isn't just a futuristic concept anymore. It's actively being constructed with the help of various existing and emerging technologies. These technologies act as the foundation, laying the groundwork for the metaverse's functionalities and user experience. Let's delve into the key elements that hold this virtual space together.

Immersive Technologies - Virtual Reality (VR)

Han et al., 2022; Wu et al., 2023 say that by using headsets, virtual reality technology takes users into the center of the metaverse and creates fully replicated surroundings. These surroundings can be exact recreations of actual places or fanciful ones reveals.

Augmented Reality (AR)

Gattullo, et al., 2022 says that AR modifies the real world by superimposing digital components on top of it, unlike VR. This could provide a more integrated metaverse experience by enabling users to engage with the actual world and the virtual world at the same time states Popescu et al., 2022.

RESEARCH METHODOLOGY

The Study is basically exploratory in nature. The idea of " Metaverse" and the role played by Metaverse in business and commerce are intended to be explained in this study. The study aims to address the genesis, requirements, advantages, opportunities, and challenges in the area of Metaverse. It also intends to highlight the ethical considerations and the actions necessary to make the associated practices robust, viable, and effective. This study is based on data collected from the secondary sources. Relevant books, journals, periodicals, research papers, clippings and excerpts of newspapers, have been referred.

RESEARCH OBJECTIVES

- To study the technological foundation of the metaverse with reference to business and commerce
- To study the opportunities in the metaverse in the context of business and commerce.
- To explore challenges in applying the metaverse to business and commerce.
- To study ethical considerations in the metaverse concerning business and commerce.

TECHNOLOGICAL FOUNDATION OF METAVERSE

The metaverse, an immersive virtual world, is not just a futuristic concept anymore. It is actively being constructed with the help of various existing and emerging technologies. These technologies act as the foundation, laying the groundwork for the metaverse's functionalities and user experience. Let's delve into the key elements that hold this virtual space together:

Immersive Technologies

- **Virtual Reality (VR):** Han et al., 2022; Wu et al., 2023 say that by using headsets, virtual reality technology takes users into the center of the metaverse and creates fully replicated surroundings. These surroundings can be exact recreations of actual places or fanciful ones reveals.
- **Augmented Reality (AR):** Gattullo, et al., 2022 says that AR modifies the real world by superimposing digital components on top of it, unlike VR. This could provide a more integrated metaverse experience by enabling users to engage with the actual world and the virtual world at the same time states Popescu et al., 2022.

Connectivity and Infrastructure

- **Low-latency Networks:** The metaverse depends on smooth, instantaneous interactions. Low-latency, high-bandwidth networks are necessary to do this says Duong et al., 2023. Huynh et al., 2022 have expressed that to guarantee lag-free data flow and prevent interruptions, technologies like 5G and beyond will be required.
- **Cloud Computing:** Cloud computing will provide the massive volume of data and processing power needed for the metaverse says Xiang et al., 2023 . This makes it possible for data to be processed, stored, and delivered efficiently, which supports the seamless operation of the metaverse says Jiang et al., 2022.

Enabling Technologies

- **Artificial Intelligence (AI):** According to Huynh et al., 2023 artificial intelligence has a variety of functions in the metaverse,. Realistic avatars, virtual assistants, and even whole virtual worlds can be powered by it says Hwang, & Chien (2022). AI also can customize user interfaces, adjust to user preferences, and enhance the metaverse's general dynamic.
- **Blockchain Technology:** With this Blockchain Technology, digital ownership can be managed transparently and safely in the metaverse says Gadekallu et al., 2022. Users may trade and possess virtual commodities, land, and avatars via blockchain, which could lead to the creation of a virtual economy in the metaverse according to Jeon, et al., 2022.

User Interface and Interaction

- **Haptic Technologies:** Majerová, & Pera (2022) say that with the help of tactile feedback offered by these technologies, users can engage more realistically with the metaverse and feel virtual items . This has the potential to increase immersion and obfuscate the distinction between the real and virtual worlds.

- **Brain-computer interfaces (BCIs):** Though they are still in their infancy, BCIs have the power to completely change how people interact in the metaverse says Zhu, et al., 2023. In the future, these interfaces might make it possible to manage virtual environments more naturally and intuitively by using brain impulses rather than conventional controllers or keyboards.

Simply said, the metaverse is being shaped by several fundamental technologies. More breakthroughs and the incorporation of even more creative solutions are to be expected as development continues reiterates Abdelghafar et al., 2023. Beyond just being an incredible technological advancement, the metaverse can completely change the way people communicate, work, and even view the world. To appreciate both its present status and enormous promise for the future, one must have a solid understanding of its technological underpinnings.

OPPORTUNITIES IN THE METAVERSE FOR BUSINESS

The metaverse, an interconnected network of immersive virtual experiences, is rapidly gaining traction, stirring curiosity and excitement across industries. While its full potential remains under exploration, businesses in the realm of commerce stand to gain significant advantages from embracing this innovative frontier. Here are some key benefits of utilizing the metaverse for trade and business:

Redefining Customer Experiences

- **Immersion is King**: Businesses can offer fully immersive experiences on web platforms that are dynamic due to the metaverse says Erazo & Sulbarán (2022). Clients can experience product features in a virtual showroom, try on clothing in a 3D fitting room, or participate in interactive product presentations. This foster increased brand loyalty and confidence in the product. Zhou (2024) says that the metaverse enables the development and marketing of entirely new product categories. Companies can offer virtual apparel, accessories, or exclusive digital experiences for customers' avatars, creating a profitable source of income. especially for the expanding digital fashion and entertainment sectors.
- **Interactive Storytelling**: Yang (2023) says that this could include interactive product games, virtual tours of manufacturing plants, or behind-the-scenes looks at corporate culture. These interactions help businesses stand out by creating emotional connections with their customers says Deniz (2024).

  Boosting Customer Engagement

- **Virtually Connecting People**: Companies can host interactive concerts, seminars, and product debuts virtually, expanding their global audience and enhancing community engagement with customers, regardless of geographical constraints says Hamilton (2022).

- Öztürk & Hersono (2023) reveals that Companies can monetize virtual events by selling tickets, offering sponsorships, or introducing in-event advertising, allowing them to generate revenue while providing valuable experiences to their target audience.
- **Market Research Insights: According to** Barrera & Shah (2023) the metaverse provides valuable data on user behavior and preferences within the virtual world, allowing businesses to gain deeper customer insights and refine their marketing strategies accordingly.
- **Enhanced Customer Support**: Businesses can offer interactive and personalized customer support through virtual assistants says Rane, et al., 2023 or customer service representatives in the metaverse, providing a more efficient and satisfying experience for customers.
- **Gamification Power:** By incorporating gamification, companies can enhance the shopping experience, such as earning points for completing tasks, receiving virtual rewards, or participating in entertaining contests says Thomas et al., 2023. This increases customer retention and sales by making shopping more enjoyable and engaging.

Transforming Collaboration and Training

- **Virtual Workspaces:** Employees can collaborate in real-time on collaborative virtual workstations created through the metaverse, regardless of their geographical location, promoting enhanced teamwork, communication, and overall productivity says Popescu (2022).
- **Interactive Training Simulations:** Companies can create interactive training simulations using the metaverse, such as safety training, operating complex machinery, and rehearsing customer service scenarios, says Ljungholm (2022) offering a more effective and engaging learning environment compared to traditional methods.
- **Streamlined Financial Transactions:** The metaverse can facilitate secure and efficient financial transactions using digital currencies says Far et al., 2023. A person can seamlessly pay for virtual goods or services within the metaverse, simplifying transactions and potentially expanding financial inclusion.
- **Financial Literacy and Education:** The metaverse can offer innovative ways to promote financial literacy and education says Bremers (2023). Interactive simulations and immersive experiences can help individuals understand complex financial concepts in a more engaging and accessible manner.

While the metaverse is still evolving, and these advantages are yet to fully materialize, the potential for innovation and transformation is undeniable. Businesses that embrace the metaverse and strategically adapt their approaches stand to gain a significant competitive advantage in the future of commerce.

The metaverse presents a transformative opportunity for commerce and finance, offering exciting possibilities and requiring careful navigation. Collaboration, responsible development, and a focus on inclusivity are essential to realizing its full potential. By charting a course that prioritizes user needs, fosters trust, and adheres to ethical principles, businesses and stakeholders can help shape a future metaverse that benefits everyone and propels commerce and finance into a new era. **The below mentioned chart provides concise overview of opportunities the metaverse offers for businesses in terms of customer experiences, engagement, collaboration and financial transactions**.

Table 1. Opportunities and their descriptions

Sl No.	Opportunities	Description
1.	Redefining Customer Experiences	1. Offer fully immersive experiences on web platforms. 2. Develop and market new product categories.
2.	Interactive Storytelling	1. Create interactive product games. 2. Offer virtual tours and behind-the-scenes looks at corporate culture.
3.	Boosting Customer Engagement	1. Host interactive concerts, seminars, and product debuts virtually. 2. Monetize virtual events.
4.	Market Research Insights	1. Gain valuable data on user behaviour and preferences. 2. Refine marketing strategies accordingly.
5.	Enhanced Customer Support	1. Offer interactive and personalized customer support through virtual assistants.
6.	Gamification Power	1. Enhance the shopping experience with gamified elements.
7.	Transforming Collaboration	1. Enable real-time collaboration regardless of geographical location. 2. Create interactive training simulations.
8.	Streamlined Financial Transactions	1. Facilitate secure and efficient financial transactions using digital currencies.
9.	Financial Literacy and Education	1. Promote financial literacy and education through interactive simulations and immersive experiences.

Source: Original

NAVIGATING CHALLENGES IN APPLYING THE METAVERSE TO BUSINESS

The metaverse, an immersive virtual environment, promises to revolutionize interaction, communication, and business. While there are clear advantages for businesses, several significant obstacles hinder its broad use, such as accessibility limitations due to technology costs, privacy and security concerns, and potential ethical considerations. Navigating these challenges responsibly while embracing its potential will be key to unlocking the true advantages the metaverse offers for businesses and commerce.

Accessibility and Cost

- **Technological Hurdle:** Bag, et al., 2023 say that costly virtual reality equipment and fast internet connections are currently required to enter the metaverse, rendering a sizable percentage of the population less accessible This unfairly disadvantages businesses and may exclude a significant portion of their potential clientele.
- **Digital Divide:** The accessibility problem is exacerbated by the digital gap between those who have access to the required technology and those who do not says Gaurav (2023). Companies must explore ways to connect with more people who may not be able to fully engage with the metaverse yet.

Privacy and Security Concerns

- **Data Security Risks:** Utilizing the metaverse requires gathering and storing user data. To avoid security lapses and safeguard user privacy, Jaber (2022) says that businesses must establish strong data security protocols, including encryption and regular audits, and foster transparency and trust with clients around data usage.

- **Monetization and Ethical Dilemmas:** The metaverse opens opportunities for new schemes and exploitative practices says McCall, et al., 2022. Companies must create explicit policies and ethical monetization methods to protect consumers against online fraud and deceptive advertising.

Interoperability and Standardization

- **Fragmented Landscape**: The metaverse is currently not a single, cohesive platform. With multiple metaverse systems and inconsistent levels of interoperability, businesses might find it challenging to navigate this fragmented ecosystem says Earhart (2012) and Goldfield (2023), presenting issues with data portability, compatibility, and reaching cliens on various platforms.
- **Lack of Standardization:** The absence of standardized protocols and regulations creates uncertainty for businesses operating within the metaverse, hindering development and making it difficult to establish consistency across different virtual spaces says Hyun (2023).

While these challenges are significant, they are not insurmountable. By focusing on inclusivity, prioritizing security, and ethical practices, advocating for standardization, and upholding ethical principles and social responsibility, businesses can navigate the metaverse's challenges and unlock its potential for innovation and transformation in commerce.

ETHICAL CONSIDERATIONS

- **Addiction and Mental Health:** The immersive nature of the metaverse raises concerns about potential addiction and detrimental effects on mental health say Usmani et al., 2022. Companies should consider these concerns and prioritize user well-being in their design.
- **Social Responsibility:** The metaverse has significant implications for social responsibility. To provide all users with a positive and inclusive experience, businesses must address the possibility of discrimination, biased algorithms, and negative social interactions in the virtual world says Jones (2023)
- **Collaboration and Standardization:** According to Hyun (2023) Businesses, technology companies, and policymakers need to collaborate to establish standardized protocols and regulations for the metaverse. This ensures interoperability between platforms, fosters trust, and facilitates secure and ethical development.
- **Addressing Accessibility and Inclusivity:** Othman, et al., 2024 say that the metaverse risks can exacerbate existing inequalities if not developed with inclusivity in mind. Addressing accessibility limitations through affordable technology and alternative access points is crucial for ensuring participation of masses.
- **Prioritizing Ethical Considerations:** R Imamguluyev et al., 2023 say that businesses need to uphold ethical principles within the metaverse, focusing on data privacy, responsible advertising, and preventing harmful behaviours. This requires transparent data practices, user control over information, and robust safeguards against potential risks.

CONCLUSION

The metaverse represents a significant evolution in how we interact with digital environments, offering profound implications for business and commerce. As a spatial computing platform built on blockchain technology, the metaverse provides immersive virtual experiences that redefine customer interactions, boost engagement, and transform collaboration and training. By leveraging the metaverse, businesses can create innovative customer experiences, access valuable market insights, and streamline financial transactions, among other benefits.

To fully realize the metaverse's potential, it is vital to comprehend these essential features. It depicts an exciting future where work, pleasure, and communication are all made possible by the increased vagueness of borders between the physical and digital worlds. Although the metaverse is still in its infancy, its development has the potential to greatly influence the course of a new era in human experience and interaction. However, the adoption of the metaverse also presents challenges, including accessibility limitations, privacy and security concerns, and ethical considerations. Addressing these challenges requires collaboration, responsible development, and a focus on inclusivity to ensure that the metaverse benefits everyone and propels commerce and finance into a new era. To sum up, the metaverse experience in business and commerce is a symphony of possibilities, where opportunity and difficulty coexist together amidst the vastness of the digital universe. Here, in the exquisite interplay of creativity and engagement, companies stand on the brink of infinite possibilities, charged with the grave responsibility of negotiating the turbulent waters of ethical consideration. By means of cooperation, investigation, and a resolute dedication to equity and inclusivity, companies have the potential to unleash the metaverse's revolutionary potential and shape a future that glows brightly with digital potential.

Future Research Scope

Future research can further explore the role of the metaverse in achieving specific business sustainability goals and investigate regulatory landscapes and best practices for promoting its sustainable use in trade and commerce. By continuing to study and adapt to the evolving landscape of the metaverse, businesses can unlock its full potential and drive innovation in the digital economy.

REFERENCES

Abdelghafar, S., Ezzat, D., Darwish, A., & Hassanien, A. E. (2023). Metaverse for Brain Computer Interface: Towards New and Improved Applications. In *The Future of Metaverse in the Virtual Era and Physical World* (pp. 43–58). Springer International Publishing. doi:10.1007/978-3-031-29132-6_3

Allam, Z., Sharifi, A., Bibri, S. E., Jones, D. S., & Krogstie, J. (2022). The metaverse as a virtual form of smart cities: Opportunities and challenges for environmental, economic, and social sustainability in urban futures. *Smart Cities*, 5(3), 771–801. doi:10.3390/smartcities5030040

Bag, S., Rahman, M. S., Srivastava, G., & Shrivastav, S. K. (2023). Unveiling metaverse potential in supply chain management and overcoming implementation challenges: An empirical study. *Benchmarking*. Advance online publication. doi:10.1108/BIJ-05-2023-0314

Ball, M. (2022). *The metaverse: and how it will revolutionize everything*. Liveright Publishing. doi:10.15358/9783800669400

Barrera, K. G., & Shah, D. (2023). Marketing in the Metaverse: Conceptual understanding, framework, and research agenda. *Journal of Business Research, 155*, 113420. doi:10.1016/j.jbusres.2022.113420

Bolger, R. K. (2021). Finding holes in the metaverse: Posthuman mystics as agents of evolutionary contextualization. *Religions, 12*(9), 768. doi:10.3390/rel12090768

Bremers, L. P. Y. (2023). *Financial Inclusion in the Metaverse: Exploring the Relationship between Education and Attitude towards Cryptocurrencies* [Bachelor's thesis, University of Twente].

Chen, Y., & Cheng, H. (2022). The economics of the metaverse: A comparison with the real economy. *Metaverse, 3*(1), 19. doi:10.54517/met.v3i1.1802

Deniz, K. (2024). Metaverse and New Narrative: Storyliving in the Age of Metaverse. In The Future of Digital Communication (pp. 39-55). CRC Press.

Duong, T. Q., Van Huynh, D., Khosravirad, S. R., Sharma, V., Dobre, O. A., & Shin, H. (2023). From digital twin to metaverse: The role of 6G ultra-reliable and low-latency communications with multi-tier computing. *IEEE Wireless Communications, 30*(3), 140–146. doi:10.1109/MWC.014.2200371

Earhart, B. (2012). Reclaiming meaning across platforms: Fragmentation and expansion of the self. *Metaverse Creativity, 2*(2), 125–138. doi:10.1386/mvcr.2.2.125_1

Erazo, J., & Sulbarán, P. (2022). Metaverse: Above an immersion in reality. *Metaverse, 3*(2), 8. doi:10.54517/m.v3i2.2155

Far, S. B., Rad, A. I., & Asaar, M. R. (2023). Blockchain and its derived technologies shape the future generation of digital businesses: A focus on decentralized finance and the Metaverse. *Data Science and Management, 6*(3), 183–197. doi:10.1016/j.dsm.2023.06.002

Gadekallu, T. R., Huynh-The, T., Wang, W., Yenduri, G., Ranaweera, P., Pham, Q. V., & Liyanage, M. (2022). Blockchain for the metaverse: A review. *arXiv preprint arXiv:2203.09738*.

Gartner. (2022). Gartner Glossary: Metaverse. https://www.gartner.com/en/information-technology/glossary/metaverse

Gattullo, M., Laviola, E., Evangelista, A., Fiorentino, M., & Uva, A. E. (2022). Towards the evaluation of augmented reality in the metaverse: Information presentation modes. *Applied Sciences (Basel, Switzerland), 12*(24), 12600. doi:10.3390/app122412600

Gaurav, A. (2023). Metaverse and Globalization: Cultural Exchange and Digital Diplomacy, Data *Science Insights Magazine, Insights2Techinfo.*

Goldfield, C. C. (2023). THE NATIONAL SECURITY LANDSCAPE ISSUES OF THE METAUERSE. *Scitech Lawyer, 19*(2), 20–25.

Hamilton, S. (2022). Deep Learning Computer Vision Algorithms, Customer Engagement Tools, and Virtual Marketplace Dynamics Data in the Metaverse Economy. *Journal of Self-Governance and Management Economics, 10*(2), 37–51.

Han, D. I. D., Bergs, Y., & Moorhouse, N. (2022). Virtual reality consumer experience escapes: Preparing for the metaverse. *Virtual Reality (Waltham Cross)*, *26*(4), 1443–1458. doi:10.1007/s10055-022-00641-7

Huynh-The, T., Pham, Q. V., Pham, X. Q., Nguyen, T. T., Han, Z., & Kim, D. S. (2023). Artificial intelligence for the metaverse: A survey. *Engineering Applications of Artificial Intelligence*, *117*, 105581. doi:10.1016/j.engappai.2022.105581

Hwang, G. J., & Chien, S. Y. (2022). Definition, roles, and potential research issues of the metaverse in education: An artificial intelligence perspective. *Computers and Education: Artificial Intelligence*, *3*, 100082. doi:10.1016/j.caeai.2022.100082

Hyun, W. (2023, February). Study on standardization for interoperable metaverse. In *2023 25th International Conference on Advanced Communication Technology (ICACT)* (pp. 319-322). IEEE. 10.23919/ICACT56868.2023.10079642

Hyun, W. (2023, February). Study on standardization for interoperable metaverse. In *2023 25th International Conference on Advanced Communication Technology (ICACT)* (pp. 319-322). IEEE. 10.23919/ICACT56868.2023.10079642

Imamguluyev, R., Umarova, N., & Mikayilova, R. (2023, August). Navigating the Ethics of the Metaverse: A Fuzzy Logic Approach to Decision-Making. In *International Conference on Intelligent and Fuzzy Systems* (pp. 53-60). Cham: Springer Nature Switzerland. 10.1007/978-3-031-39777-6_7

Jaber, T. A. (2022). Security Risks of the Metaverse World. *International Journal of Interactive Mobile Technologies*, *16*(13).

Jeon, H. J., Youn, H. C., Ko, S. M., & Kim, T. H. (2022). Blockchain and AI Meet in the Metaverse. *Advances in the Convergence of Blockchain and Artificial Intelligence, 73*(10.5772).

Jiang, Y., Kang, J., Niyato, D., Ge, X., Xiong, Z., Miao, C., & Shen, X. (2022). Reliable distributed computing for metaverse: A hierarchical game-theoretic approach. *IEEE Transactions on Vehicular Technology*, *72*(1), 1084–1100. doi:10.1109/TVT.2022.3204839

Kim, J. (2021). Advertising in the metaverse: Research agenda. *Journal of Interactive Advertising*, *21*(3), 141–144. doi:10.1080/15252019.2021.2001273

Lee, C. T., Li, Z., & Shen, Y. C. (2024). Building bonds: An examination of relational bonding in continuous content contribution behaviors on metaverse-based non-fungible token platforms. *Internet Research*. Advance online publication. doi:10.1108/INTR-11-2022-0883

Ljungholm, D. P. (2022). Metaverse-based 3D visual modeling, virtual reality training experiences, and wearable biological measuring devices in immersive workplaces. *Psychosociological Issues in Human Resource Management*, *10*(1), 64–77. doi:10.22381/pihrm10120225

Majerová, J., & Pera, A. (2022). Haptic and biometric sensor technologies, spatio-temporal fusion algorithms, and virtual navigation tools in the decentralized and interconnected metaverse. *Review of Contemporary Philosophy*, *21*(0), 105–121. doi:10.22381/RCP2120227

McCall, R., Shell, J., Kacperski, C., Greenstein, S., Whitton, N., & Summers, J. (2022, October). Workshop on Social and Ethical Issues in Entertainment Computing. In *International Conference on Entertainment Computing* (pp. 429-435). Cham: Springer International Publishing.

Moro-Visconti, R. (2022). Metaverse: A Digital Network Valuation. In *The Valuation of Digital Intangibles: Technology, Marketing, and the Metaverse* (pp. 515–559). Springer International Publishing. doi:10.1007/978-3-031-09237-4_18

Mystakidis, S. (2022). Metaverse. [Key Characteristics of the metaverse]. *Encyclopedia, 2*(1), 486–497. doi:10.3390/encyclopedia2010031

Oh, H. J., Kim, J., Chang, J. J., Park, N., & Lee, S. (2023). Social benefits of living in the metaverse: The relationships among social presence, supportive interaction, social self-efficacy, and feelings of loneliness. *Computers in Human Behavior, 139*, 107498. doi:10.1016/j.chb.2022.107498

Othman, A., Chemnad, K., Hassanien, A. E., Tlili, A., Zhang, C. Y., Al-Thani, D., ... Altınay, Z. (2024). Accessible Metaverse: A Theoretical Framework for Accessibility and Inclusion in the Metaverse. *Multimodal Technologies and Interaction, 8*(3), 21. doi:10.3390/mti8030021

Öztürk, B., & Hersono, R. (2023). *Playing to Win: How Gamification Can Boost Customer Engagement and Turn Non-Fans into Brand Advocates.*

Popescu, G. H., Ciurlău, C. F., Stan, C. I., Băcănoiu, C., & Tănase, A. (2022). Virtual workplaces in the metaverse: Immersive remote collaboration tools, behavioral predictive analytics, and extended reality technologies. *Psychosociological Issues in Human Resource Management, 10*(1), 21–34. doi:10.22381/pihrm10120222

Popescu, G. H., Valaskova, K., & Horak, J. (2022). Augmented reality shopping experiences, retail business analytics, and machine vision algorithms in the virtual economy of the metaverse. *Journal of Self-Governance and Management Economics, 10*(2), 67–81.

Popp, J., & Cuţitoi, A. C. (2022). Immersive Visualization Systems, Spatial Simulation and Environment Mapping Algorithms, and Decision Intelligence and Modeling Tools in the Web3-powered Metaverse World. *Journal of Self-Governance and Management Economics, 10*(3), 56–72.

Rane, N., Choudhary, S., & Rane, J. (2023). Metaverse for Enhancing Customer Loyalty: Effective Strategies to Improve Customer Relationship, Service, Engagement, Satisfaction, and Experience. *Service, Engagement, Satisfaction, and Experience.*

Richter, S., & Richter, A. (2023). What is novel about the Metaverse? *International Journal of Information Management, 73*, 102684. doi:10.1016/j.ijinfomgt.2023.102684

Stephenson, N. (1992). Snow crash. *Futures, 26*(7), 798–800. doi:10.1016/0016-3287(94)90052-3

Swan, M. (2023). Metaverse Marketing: A Review and Research Agenda. *Journal of Marketing Management, 39*(3-4), 291–318.

Thomas, N. J., Baral, R., Crocco, O. S., & Mohanan, S. (2023). A framework for gamification in the metaverse era: How designers envision gameful experience. *Technological Forecasting and Social Change, 193*, 122544. doi:10.1016/j.techfore.2023.122544

Usmani, S. S., Sharath, M., & Mehendale, M. (2022). Future of mental health in the metaverse. *General Psychiatry*, *35*(4), e100825. doi:10.1136/gpsych-2022-100825 PMID:36189180

Van Huynh, D., Khosravirad, S. R., Masaracchia, A., Dobre, O. A., & Duong, T. Q. (2022). Edge intelligence-based ultra-reliable and low-latency communications for digital twin-enabled metaverse. *IEEE Wireless Communications Letters*, *11*(8), 1733–1737. doi:10.1109/LWC.2022.3179207

Wu, D., Yang, Z., Zhang, P., Wang, R., Yang, B., & Ma, X. (2023). Virtual-Reality Inter-Promotion Technology for Metaverse: A Survey. *IEEE Internet of Things Journal*, *10*(18), 15788–15809. doi:10.1109/JIOT.2023.3265848

Wynn, M., & Jones, P. (2023). New technology deployment and corporate responsibilities in the metaverse. *Knowledge (Beverly Hills, Calif.)*, *3*(4), 543–556.

Xiang, H., Zhang, X., & Bilal, M. (2023). A cloud-edge service offloading method for the metaverse in smart manufacturing. *Software, Practice & Experience*, spe.3301. doi:10.1002/spe.3301

Yang, S. (2023, April). Storytelling and user experience in the cultural metaverse. *Heliyon*, *9*(4), e14759. doi:10.1016/j.heliyon.2023.e14759 PMID:37035365

Zhou, Z. (2024). Will the Metaverse Revolutionize the Narrative? *Critical Arts*, 1–15.

Zhu, H. Y., Hieu, N. Q., Hoang, D. T., Nguyen, D. N., & Lin, C. T. (2023). A human-centric metaverse enabled by brain-computer interface: A survey. *arXiv preprint arXiv:2309.01848*.

Chapter 12
The Metaversal Shift:
A Bibliometric Analysis of Industry Transformation

Navneet Kaushal

Central University of Himachal Pradesh, India

Anshu Duhoon

Central University of Himachal Pradesh, India

ABSTRACT

Metaverse has emerged as an immersive digital environment, capturing widespread attention owing to its significant impact on industrial growth. This study aims to explain the evolution of research focused on the metatarsal shift in industries. This study offers a bibliometric analysis of industrial transformation research from 2007 to 2024. The finding shows a tremendous rise in publication over time. The objective of this analysis is to extract valuable insights and trends and to shed light on the key challenges and opportunities associated with digital transformation in the industrial sector. This study provides thorough coverage of existing literature on the implications of metaverse-enabled digital transformation for the industrial revolution and explores the interplay of various factors such as technology adoption, organizational culture, and strategic planning. The study contributes to understanding the ongoing discourse on digital transformation and its impact on the industrial landscape.

INTRODUCTION

The metaverse is emerging as a transformative trend across industries, promising to revolutionize how we interact, work, and play in digital environments. This virtual universe transcends traditional boundaries, offering immersive experiences where users can seamlessly navigate between virtual worlds, socialize with others, and engage in various activities (Dixon,2023). From gaming and entertainment to education and business, the metaverse presents boundless opportunities for innovation and collaboration. Companies are increasingly investing in metaverse technologies to create immersive virtual experiences and tap into new markets. As virtual reality (VR), augmented reality (AR), and other immersive technologies

DOI: 10.4018/979-8-3693-2607-7.ch012

advance, the metaverse is poised to become even more immersive and interconnected, blurring the lines between the physical and digital realms (Dwivedi et al.,2022).

The application of the metaverse spans across all industries, promising to revolutionize traditional business models and reshape the way to interact with digital environments. In entertainment, the metaverse offers immersive gaming experiences, interactive storytelling, and virtual events, enhancing engagement and expanding audience reach (Qi,2022). In education, it provides innovative learning environments, enabling interactive lessons, simulations, and virtual field trips that enhance student engagement and accessibility (Zonaphan et al.,2022). Within healthcare, the metaverse facilitates telemedicine, remote patient monitoring, and medical training simulations, improving access to care and enhancing medical education (Hancock,2022; Ali et al.,2023). In retail, it enables virtual stores, personalized shopping experiences, and social commerce, transforming the way consumers discover and purchase products (Abumalloh et al.,2023). In the tourism sector, it provides an avenue for cultural exchange, fostering connections between tourists and communities through shared culinary experiences with travelers and locals through common gastronomic interests (Gursoy et al., 2022). Religious tourism has always been an important aspect of the tourism industry (Kaushal et al., 2022a) and significantly contributes to the economic growth of the country (Kaushal et al., 2022b; Budovich, 2023). However, with the emergence of the metaverse, religious tourism has taken on a new dimension. It offers immersive virtual experiences that go beyond physical barriers, providing access to sacred sites and spiritual practices from all corners of the world (Ahmad et al., 2024).

The metaverse also has significant implications for communication and collaboration, enabling remote work, virtual meetings, and team collaboration in immersive digital environments (Bennett, 2022). Across industries, the metaverse fosters innovation, collaboration, and creativity, unlocking new opportunities for growth and advancement in the digital age (Mourtzis, 2023; Nabukalu & Wanjohi, 2023).

The metaverse catalyzes environmental stewardship by diminishing the necessity for extensive travel through remote work and virtual gatherings (Allam et al.,2022; Al-Emran,2023). Real-time data analytics within this digital domain empower industries with actionable insights, enabling agile decision-making and performance optimization. Small enterprises flourish in the accessible virtual marketplaces, expanding their global reach and catalyzing economic growth. Furthermore, collaborative research initiatives thrive as experts converge virtually to tackle complex challenges, propelling innovation forward (Bryda & Costa,2023). Ultimately, the symbiotic relationship between the metaverse and industry engenders a dynamic ecosystem characterized by creativity, progress, and shared prosperity.

Understanding the metaverse entails grasping a concept that transcends conventional virtual environments, constituting a collective digital universe interconnected through various digital spaces, experiences, and assets (Yang et al.,2024). At its essence, the metaverse is a persistent, shared, and immersive digital realm enabling real-time interaction for its users. Unlike disjointed online platforms, the metaverse aims for cohesion, allowing seamless navigation across diverse virtual worlds and experiences (Kadry,2022; Devlin,2023). A hallmark of the metaverse lies in its emphasis on user-generated content and creativity, empowering individuals to create, customize, and share digital assets, fostering a landscape of democratized content creation (Iden & Methlie,2012). Furthermore, the metaverse thrives on its social aspect, acting as a platform for socialization, collaboration, and community-building, mirroring real-world social dynamics. Additionally, it presents economic opportunities through virtual commerce, where users engage in buying, selling, and trading digital goods and services, propelling the emergence of a virtual economy. While the metaverse promises to revolutionize various aspects of human interaction, entertainment, and commerce, it also raises concerns regarding privacy, security, and digital rights in navigating this intricate digital realm (Bibri & Jagatheesaperumal, 2023). In summary, comprehending the metaverse involves recognizing it as a dynamic and multifaceted concept poised to reshape human engagement with digital technology, albeit with challenges requiring careful consideration to ensure its inclusivity, equity, and safety for all participants.

The literature on metaverse holds significance in all domains. Even though researchers and academics are paying attention to this topic, it still requires more development (Iqbal et al., 2023; Wider et al., 2023). The existing literature on metaverse has provided inconsistent findings, making it necessary to conduct a study that comprehends, examines, and identifies the central themes in this area. To tackle this issue, the current study employs a bibliometric review approach to address the following research questions:

(a) The publication trend over the period.
(b) Which countries made significant contributions to this field?
(c) What are the future avenues of this study?

The other sections of the paper are formulated as follows: The second section briefly discusses the literature review and the objectives of the study. The third section explains the research methodology. The fourth section is related to the analysis and interpretation of the data, and the last section discusses the conclusion and directions for future research.

REVIEW OF LITERATURE

The concept of Metaverse Shift, which explores the synergy between industry and the evolution of the metaverse, is a topic of growing interest and importance. Van Beers et al. (2007) provided insights into industrial symbiosis in heavy industrial regions such as Kwinana and Gladstone, highlighting the drivers, barriers, and trigger events for regional synergy initiatives. Corning (2013) discussed the role of functional synergy in evolution, suggesting a paradigm shift in understanding interdependent causal influences. Heracleous et al. (2019) examined NASA's capability evolution toward commercial space, showcasing the transition from a government-dominated to a commercially driven industry model. Shen et al. (2021) focused on promoting user purchases in the metaverse through a systematic literature review on consumer behavior research and virtual commerce application design. Li et al. (2021) analyzed the evolution of China's marine economic policy and the labor productivity growth momentum of its marine economy industries, emphasizing the structural shift effect caused by institutional changes. Hollensen et al. (2022) predicted the revolutionary impact of the Metaverse on various industries, including marketing, as the 3D version of the internet. Furthermore, Zhai et al. (2022) explored the educational metaverse as an innovative approach to high-quality education development and reshaping educational relationships. Buhalis et al. (2022) delved into the implications of the Metaverse for hospitality and tourism management and marketing, emphasizing customer experience and value co-creation. Mirza-Babaei et al. (2022) highlighted the relevance of games in the metaverse, proposing discussions on the future evolution of game research in this area. Continuing with these findings, Wang et al. (2022) presented a framework for constructing an Edu-metaverse ecosystem, leveraging new technologies like extended reality and artificial intelligence for learning environments. Garousi (2015) conducted a bibliometric analysis of the Turkish software engineering community. Muhuri et al. (2019) provided a detailed overview of Industry 4.0 through bibliometric analysis, and Furstenau et al. (2020) explored the link between sustainability and Industry 4.0. Goh et al. (2020) reviewed water utility benchmarking using bibliometric analysis. Sharma et al. (2021) discussed sustainable manufacturing and Industry 4.0, highlighting gaps in current knowledge. Chen et al. (2022) delved into the integration of Construction 4.0, Industry 4.0, and Building Information Modeling for sustainable building development within smart cities. Abbate et al. (2022) conducted a bibliometric literature review on the Metaverse, focusing on its implications for industry and society. Feng et al. (2022) analyzed the current status of Metaverse research through bibliometrics, while Rejeb et al. (2023) mapped out future research areas in the Metaverse field. Overall, these studies demonstrate the increasing interest in utilizing bibliometric analysis to understand trends, challenges, and opportunities in various industries, including software engineering, pharmaceuticals, sustainability, and the Metaverse. The integration of Industry 4.0 concepts with other disciplines, such as sustainable manufacturing and smart cities, is also a growing area of research (Yao et al.,2024). The Metaverse, in particular, is gaining attention for its potential impacts on industry and society, prompting further exploration and collaboration in this emerging field.

So, a literature-based study focusing on the synergy between industries and the evolution of the metaverse is imperative for advancing understanding in this emerging field and for contributing towards the development of robust theoretical frameworks, methodological approaches, and practical recommendations for navigating the evolving landscape of the metaverse and its intersection with industries.

RESEARCH METHODOLOGY

Prisma methodology, derived from the PRISMA (Preferred Reporting Items for Systematic Reviews and Meta-Analyses) framework commonly used in medical and health sciences, has been adapted for bibliometric analysis to ensure transparency, rigor, and reproducibility in research synthesis. In bibliometric analysis, PRISMA provides a structured approach to systematically identify, select, and synthesize relevant literature to answer specific research questions related to scholarly publications and citations (Moher et al., 2019). In the first step, a targeted search was conducted in the Scopus database by using two keywords: "Industry" AND "Metaverse". This database was selected because it is an extensive database and ensures that only the highest quality data are indexed through careful content selection and re-evaluation by an independent Content Selection and Advisory Board (Baas et al., 2020). This search resulted in 748 research articles. Then, only articles, conference papers, conference reviews, book chapters, and review papers were retained, which limits the number to 716. Thereafter, 31 research studies published in other than the English language were also excluded, and finally, 685 research articles were considered for further research (Figure 1). This review was limited only to the research articles because peer-reviewed articles are considered to have better quality than other forms such as book chapters, conference proceedings, etc. (Maier et al., 2020).

VOSviewer (Van Eck & Waltman, 2010) software has been used to create the visualization network. It presents bibliometric analysis in a way that is simple to understand (Van Eck & Waltman, 2011; Agbo et al., 2021; Duhoon & Singh, 2023).

Credibility of the Study

This study used bibliometric analysis to understand the synergy between the industry and metaverse. Bibliometric analysis is a quantitative method used to assess the impact and productivity of scholarly

Figure 1. PRISMA methodology
Source: Developed by Authors

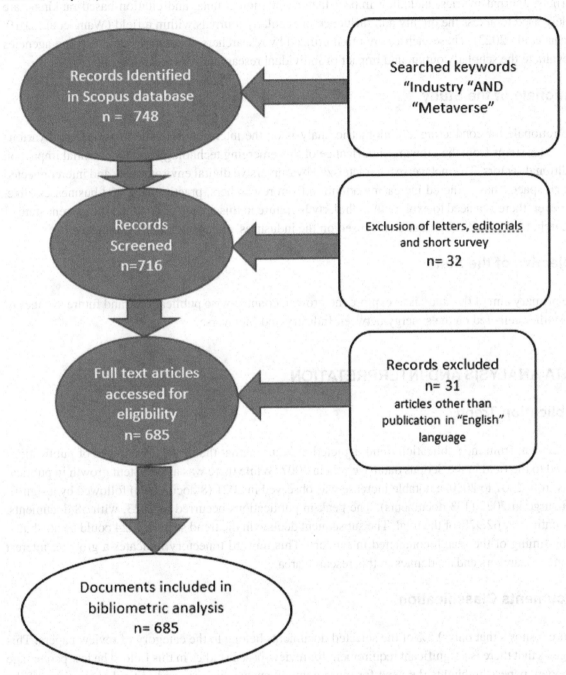

publications within a specific field or discipline (Ellegaard & Wallin,2015). It involves the systematic analysis of bibliographic data, such as citations, publication counts, authorship patterns, and journal impact factors, to gain insights into research trends, collaboration networks, and the influence of individuals, publications, or researchers.

Furthermore, bibliometric analysis can be applied to evaluate the productivity and impact of academic journals. Journal metrics, including impact factors, citation counts, and citation-based rankings, are widely used to assess the quality and influence of scholarly journals within a field (Wang et al., 2010; Cucari et al., 2023). These metrics are often utilized by researchers, institutions, and funding agencies to evaluate the scholarly output and impact of individual researchers or research groups.

Rationale of the Study

The rationale for conducting a bibliometric analysis on the intersection of the metaverse and various industries stems from the growing significance of this emerging technology and its potential impact on traditional sectors. The metaverse, characterized by immersive digital environments and interconnected virtual spaces, has garnered increasing attention from researchers, practitioners, and businesses alike. However, there is a need to explore the scholarly literature in this area to understand the current state of research, trends, and collaborations focused on the industries' engagement with the metaverse.

Objective of the Study

The primary aim of the study is to explore the growth, country-wise publications, and future avenues of the studies centered on the synergy between Industry and Metaverse.

DATA ANALYSIS AND INTERPRETATION

Publication Trend

It is evident from the publication trend depicted in Figure 2 that the initial appearance of publications related to the field in the Scopus database was in 2007. While there was a consistent growth in publications from 2007 to 2020, a notable increase was observed in 2021 (8 documents) followed by a significant surge in 2022 (133 documents). The peak in publications occurred in 2023, with 58 documents, accounting for 62.92% of the total. The subsequent decline in the trend seen in 2024 could be attributed to the timing of the search conducted in January. This upward trajectory indicates a growing interest among researchers and academics in this research area.

Documents Classification

Figure 3 shows that only 9.5% of the selected documents belong to the category of review papers. This suggests that there is a significant requirement for review-based studies in this field. The low percentage of review papers highlights the need for more comprehensive analyses and critical evaluations of the existing literature to gain a deeper understanding of the subject matter.

Figure 2. Publications growth
Source: Authors' compilation

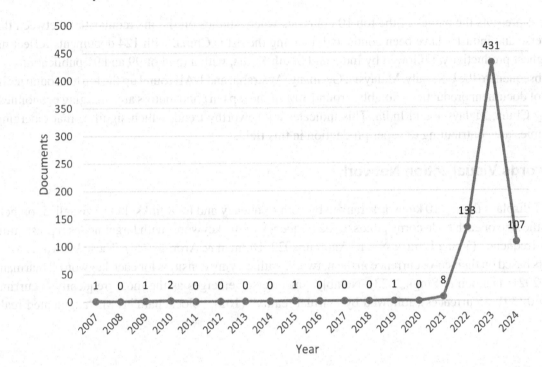

Figure 3. Documents by type
Source: Authors' compilation

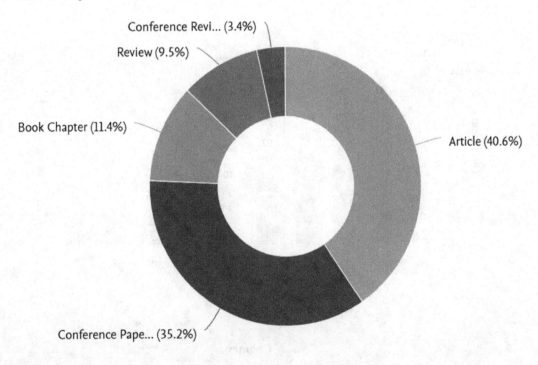

Country-wise publications

Figure 4 presents the names of the top 10 countries where studies on the interconnection between the metaverse and industry have been conducted. Leading the list is China, with 124 documents reflecting the highest productivity. Followed by India and South Korea, with a total of 99 and 91 publications.

Subsequent to the UK, Italy, Malaysia, Germany, Australia, and UAE round up the top ten countries in terms of document production. Notably, around 30% of the top ten contributors are emerging economies, namely China, Malaysia, and India. This indicates a noteworthy trend, which signifies that emerging economies are contributing to paper production in this field.

Keywords Visualization Network

Table 1 displays the top 10 keywords ranked by both frequency and total links. In the visualization network, the size of each node corresponds to the frequency of the keyword, with larger nodes representing higher frequency (Viana-Lora & Nel-lo-Andreu, 2022; Dhiman & Arora, 2024). These keywords form clusters based on their co-occurrence in the network, with varying densities for each keyword (Dharmani et al., 2021; Duhoon & Singh,2023). Notably, "metaverse" emerges as the most frequently occurring keyword (391 occurrences), followed by "virtual reality" (102), "blockchain" (68), "augmented real-

Figure 4. Top ten countries
Source: Authors' compilation

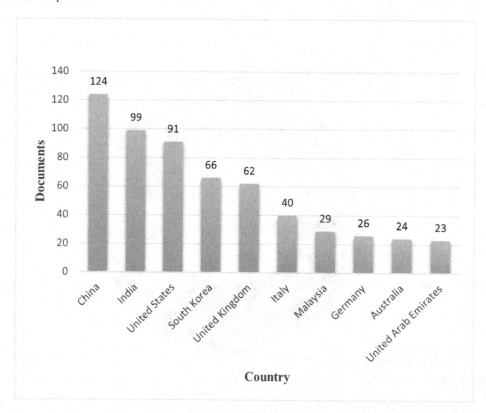

ity" (53), "artificial intelligence" (44), "extended reality" (32), "digital twin" (32), "healthcare" (23), "sustainability" (16), and "NFT"(16).

The authors' keywords are organized into six clusters (see Figure 5). The orange cluster is centered by metaverse and shows the correlation with other nodes "blockchain"," cryptocurrency"," NFT", "virtual worlds" and "Web 3". The red cluster highlights the proximity between "industry " and "sustainability," indicating a strong relationship compared to other keywords in the cluster, such as "5 G," "artificial intelligence", "building information modeling", "education", "IOT", "technology" and "tourism." The blue cluster is centered around "virtual reality" and "augmented reality" with other nodes like "avatars", "user experience" and "virtual world". In the green cluster, connections are observed among "digital twin", "federated learning", "internet of things", "security", and "training". Exploring the concept of "artificial intelligence", " the violet cluster encompasses research on "deep learning", "machine learning", "healthcare", and "IOT". Lastly, the light blue cluster elucidates the interconnections between "avatar", "gaming "and "virtual reality". The thickness of the links indicates the co-occurrence of keywords, reflecting similar research endeavors and highlighting areas that remain underexplored (Donthu et al., 2021a, b).

Figure 5. Keywords cluster map
Source: Authors' compilation

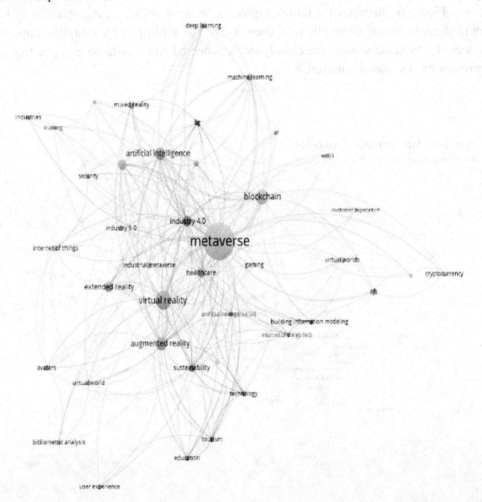

Table 1. Keyword clusters

Clusters	Total Links	Occurrences
Orange cluster	253	391
Blue cluster	32	102
Green cluster	20	32
Red cluster	19	31
Violet cluster	13	13
Light blue cluster	8	8

Source: Authors' compilation

Bibliographic Coupling

Bibliographic coupling serves as a method for science mapping, predicated on the idea that publications sharing references also share content similarities (Weinberg, 1974). Donthu et al. (2021a) and Zupic and Čater (2015) underscored the significance of bibliographic coupling, noting that it enables the grouping of publications into thematic clusters based on shared references. The graphical representation in Figure 6 illustrates the bibliographic network of authors, categorized into 12 clusters according to the intellectual connections in their work. The bibliographic coupling approach posits that papers citing the same sources are closely interconnected and should be grouped together in the visual representation's cluster solution.

Figure 6. Authors' bibliographic coupling
Source: Authors' compilation

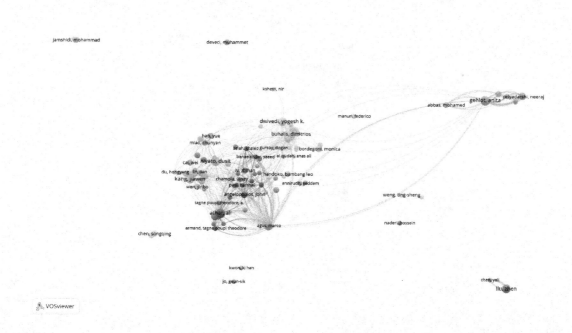

CONCLUSION

The bibliometric study on the synergy between industry and the evolution of the metaverse unveils a dynamic landscape characterized by rapid evolution and transformative shifts. Through year-wise analysis, it becomes evident how industries have progressed, marked by significant milestones and technological advancement. Keywords such as virtual reality, augmented reality, blockchain, and NFTs emerge as central themes, showcasing the key areas of industry engagement with the metaverse. These keyword clusters also show that the field of metaverse studies is predominantly focused on the healthcare industry in comparison to all other industries.

These findings hold implications for businesses, policymakers, investors, and consumers alike. Businesses can leverage insights for innovation and strategic positioning within the metaverse ecosystem, while policymakers may need to craft regulatory frameworks to support responsible development. Investors can identify promising investment opportunities, while consumers can make informed decisions about adoption and digital engagement.

However, despite these findings, bibliometric review-based study also has some limitations. Firstly, bibliometric analysis relies heavily on the availability and quality of data sources, which may not always capture the full breadth of industry-metaverse interactions (Wallin,2005). Additionally, while keywords provide valuable insights, they may not fully capture the complexity and nuances of emerging trends within the metaverse ecosystem. Furthermore, the study's focus on quantitative analysis may overlook qualitative aspects such as user experiences and cultural shifts, which are equally important in understanding industry-metaverse dynamics. Moreover, the rapidly evolving nature of both industries and the metaverse means that findings may quickly become outdated, requiring frequent updates to maintain relevance. This study's scope is limited to the Scopus database; the inclusion of other databases, such as EBSCO and Web of Science, can be used to enhance the importance of this field. However, despite these shortcomings, the study will be helpful to the researchers in acknowledging the earlier work and future directions in the field of metaverse.

While the metaverse presents innovative opportunities for industry research, challenges such as technological infrastructure constraints, accessibility and inclusivity issues, privacy and security concerns, ethical and societal implications, lack of standardization and regulation, digital divide disparities, and content quality and integrity issues need to be addressed. These limitations underscore the importance of a thoughtful and responsible approach to the development and deployment of the metaverse in industry, focusing on fostering inclusivity, safeguarding privacy and security, establishing standards and regulations, bridging digital divides, and ensuring the quality and integrity of virtual content (Raad & Rashid,2023). By addressing these limitations, researchers can maximize the potential of the metaverse while minimizing its risks and drawbacks in industry research. So, in the future, challenges related to their application can be explored to have a better understanding of metaverse applications.

REFERENCES

Abbate, S., Centobelli, P., Cerchione, R., Oropallo, E., & Riccio, E. (2022, April). *A first bibliometric literature review on Metaverse. In 2022 IEEE Technology and Engineering Management Conference.* TEMSCON EUROPE.

Abumalloh, R. A., Nilashi, M., Ooi, K. B., Wei-Han, G., Cham, T. H., Dwivedi, Y. K., & Hughes, L. (2023). The adoption of a metaverse in the retail industry and its impact on sustainable competitive advantage: The moderating impact of sustainability commitment. *Annals of Operations Research*, 1–42. doi:10.1007/s10479-023-05608-8

Agbo, F. J., Oyelere, S. S., Suhonen, J., & Tukiainen, M. (2021). Scientific production and thematic breakthroughs in smart learning environments: A bibliometric analysis. *Smart Learning Environments*, 8(1), 1–25. doi:10.1186/s40561-020-00145-4

Ahmad, M., Akram, M., & Ureeb, S. (2024). Exploring the Role of Metaverse in Promoting Religious Tourism. In *Service Innovations in Tourism: Metaverse, Immersive Technologies, and Digital Twin* (pp. 39–63). IGI Global. doi:10.4018/979-8-3693-1103-5.ch003

Al-Emran, M. (2023). Beyond technology acceptance: Development and evaluation of technology-environmental, economic, and social sustainability theory. *Technology in Society*, 75, 102383. doi:10.1016/j.techsoc.2023.102383

Ali, S., Abdullah, Armand, T. P. T., Athar, A., Hussain, A., Ali, M., Yaseen, M., Joo, M.-I., & Kim, H.-C. (2023). Metaverse in healthcare integrated with explainable ai and blockchain: Enabling immersiveness, ensuring trust, and providing patient data security. *Sensors (Basel)*, 23(2), 565. doi:10.3390/s23020565 PMID:36679361

Allam, Z., Sharifi, A., Bibri, S. E., Jones, D. S., & Krogstie, J. (2022). The metaverse as a virtual form of smart cities: Opportunities and challenges for environmental, economic, and social sustainability in urban futures. *Smart Cities*, 5(3), 771–801. doi:10.3390/smartcities5030040

Baas, J., Schotten, M., Plume, A., Côté, G., & Karimi, R. (2020). Scopus as a curated, high-quality bibliometric data source for academic research in quantitative science studies. *Quantitative Science Studies*, 1(1), 377–386. doi:10.1162/qss_a_00019

Bennett, D. (2022). Remote workforce, virtual team tasks, and employee engagement tools in a real-time interoperable decentralized metaverse. *Psychosociological Issues in Human Resource Management*, 10(1), 78–91. doi:10.22381/pihrm10120226

Bibri, S. E., & Jagatheesaperumal, S. K. (2023). Harnessing the potential of the metaverse and artificial intelligence for the internet of city things: Cost-effective XReality and synergistic AIoT technologies. *Smart Cities*, 6(5), 2397–2429. doi:10.3390/smartcities6050109

Bryda, G., & Costa, A. P. (2023). Qualitative research in digital era: Innovations, methodologies and collaborations. *Social Sciences (Basel, Switzerland)*, 12(10), 570. doi:10.3390/socsci12100570

Budovich, L. S. (2023). The impact of religious tourism on the economy and tourism industry. *Hervormde Teologiese Studies*, 79(1), 8607. doi:10.4102/hts.v79i1.8607

Buhalis, D., Lin, M. S., & Leung, D. (2022). Metaverse as a driver for customer experience and value co-creation: Implications for hospitality and tourism management and marketing. *International Journal of Contemporary Hospitality Management*, 35(2), 701–716. doi:10.1108/IJCHM-05-2022-0631

Chen, Y., Huang, D., Liu, Z., Osmani, M., & Demian, P. (2022). Construction 4.0, Industry 4.0, and Building Information Modeling (BIM) for sustainable building development within the smart city. *Sustainability (Basel)*, *14*(16), 10028. doi:10.3390/su141610028

Corning, P. A. (2013). Rotating the Necker cube: A bioeconomic approach to cooperation and the causal role of synergy in evolution. *Journal of Bioeconomics*, *15*(2), 171–193. doi:10.1007/s10818-012-9142-4

Cucari, N., Tutore, I., Montera, R., & Profita, S. (2023). A bibliometric performance analysis of publication productivity in the corporate social responsibility field: Outcomes of SciVal analytics. *Corporate Social Responsibility and Environmental Management*, *30*(1), 1–16. doi:10.1002/csr.2346

Devlin, M. (2023). *2035 AND BEYOND. A GUIDE TO THRIVING IN THE FUTURE WORKPLACE.: Unleash Your Potential in a Futuristic Career Landscape. Virtual Worlds, Skills Mastery, and Success.* Little Fish Big Impact.

Dharmani, P., Das, S., & Prashar, S. (2021). A bibliometric analysis of creative industries: Current trends and future directions. *Journal of Business Research*, *135*, 252–267. doi:10.1016/j.jbusres.2021.06.037

Dhiman, V., & Arora, M. (2024). How foresight has evolved since 1999? Understanding its themes, scope and focus. *Foresight*, *26*(2), 253–271. doi:10.1108/FS-01-2023-0001

Dixon, H. H. B. Jr. (2023). The Metaverse. *The Judges' Journal*, *62*(1), 36–38.

Donthu, N., Kumar, S., Mukherjee, D., Pandey, N., & Lim, W. M. (2021a). How to conduct a bibliometric analysis: An overview and guidelines. *Journal of Business Research*, *133*, 285–296. doi:10.1016/j.jbusres.2021.04.070

Donthu, N., Kumar, S., & Pandey, N. (2021). A retrospective evaluation of Marketing Intelligence and Planning: 1983–2019. *Marketing Intelligence & Planning*, *39*(1), 48–73. doi:10.1108/MIP-02-2020-0066

Duhoon, A., & Singh, M. (2023). Corporate Governance in Family Firms: A Bibliometric Analysis. *Management*, *1*, 22.

Duhoon, A., & Singh, M. (2023). Corporate tax avoidance: A systematic literature review and future research directions. *LBS Journal of Management & Research*, *21*(2), 197–217. doi:10.1108/LB-SJMR-12-2022-0082

Dwivedi, Y. K., Hughes, L., Baabdullah, A. M., Ribeiro-Navarrete, S., Giannakis, M., Al-Debei, M. M., Dennehy, D., Metri, B., Buhalis, D., Cheung, C. M. K., Conboy, K., Doyle, R., Dubey, R., Dutot, V., Felix, R., Goyal, D. P., Gustafsson, A., Hinsch, C., Jebabli, I., ... Wamba, S. F. (2022). Metaverse beyond the hype: Multidisciplinary perspectives on emerging challenges, opportunities, and agenda for research, practice, and policy. *International Journal of Information Management*, *66*, 102542. doi:10.1016/j.ijinfomgt.2022.102542

Ellegaard, O., & Wallin, J. A. (2015). The bibliometric analysis of scholarly production: How great is the impact? *Scientometrics*, *105*(3), 1809–1831. doi:10.1007/s11192-015-1645-z PMID:26594073

Feng, X., Wang, X., & Su, Y. (2024). An analysis of the current status of metaverse research based on bibliometrics. *Library Hi Tech*, *42*(1), 284–308. doi:10.1108/LHT-10-2022-0467

Furstenau, L. B., Sott, M. K., Kipper, L. M., Machado, E. L., Lopez-Robles, J. R., Dohan, M. S., Cobo, M. J., Zahid, A., Abbasi, Q. H., & Imran, M. A. (2020). Link between sustainability and industry 4.0: Trends, challenges, and new perspectives. *IEEE Access : Practical Innovations, Open Solutions*, 8, 140079–140096. doi:10.1109/ACCESS.2020.3012812

Garousi, V. (2015). A bibliometric analysis of the Turkish software engineering research community. *Scientometrics*, *105*(1), 23–49. doi:10.1007/s11192-015-1663-x

Goh, K. H., & See, K. F. (2021). Twenty years of water utility benchmarking: A bibliometric analysis of emerging interest in water research and collaboration. *Journal of Cleaner Production*, *284*, 124711. doi:10.1016/j.jclepro.2020.124711

Gursoy, D., Malodia, S., & Dhir, A. (2022). The metaverse in the hospitality and tourism industry: An overview of current trends and future research directions. *Journal of Hospitality Marketing & Management*, *31*(5), 527–534. doi:10.1080/19368623.2022.2072504

Hancock, K. (2022). Virtual Team Performance, Collaborative Remote Work, and Employee Engagement and Multimodal Behavioral Analytics in the Metaverse Economy. *Psychosociological Issues in Human Resource Management*, *10*(2), 55–70. doi:10.22381/pihrm10220224

Heracleous, L., Terrier, D., & Gonzalez, S. (2019). NASA's capability evolution toward commercial space. *Space Policy*, *50*, 101330. doi:10.1016/j.spacepol.2019.07.004

Hollensen, S., Kotler, P., & Opresnik, M. O. (2022). Metaverse–the new marketing universe. *The Journal of Business Strategy*, *44*(3), 119–125. doi:10.1108/JBS-01-2022-0014

Iden, J., & Methlie, L. B. (2012). The drivers of services on next-generation networks. *Telematics and Informatics*, *29*(2), 137–155. doi:10.1016/j.tele.2011.05.004

Iqbal, M. Z., & Campbell, A. G. (2023, October). Metaverse as tech for good: Current progress and emerging opportunities. In Virtual Worlds, 2(4), 326-342.

Kadry, A. (2022). The metaverse revolution and its impact on the future of advertising industry. *Journal of Design Sciences and Applied Arts*, *3*(2), 131–139. doi:10.21608/jdsaa.2022.129876.1171

Kaushal, N., Sharma, S., & Katoch, A. (2022a). The Satisfaction of Religious Tourists Visiting Shiva Circuit of Himachal Pradesh. *International Research Journal of Management Sociology & Humanities*, *13*(8), 11–19.

Kaushal, N., Sharma, S., & Katoch, A. (2022b). Problems and Challenges faced by Religious Tourists: A study of Religious Destinations of Himachal Pradesh. *International Journal of Commerce. Arts & Science*, *13*(8), 27–35.

Li, F., Xing, W., Su, M., & Xu, J. (2021). The evolution of China's marine economic policy and the labor productivity growth momentum of the marine economy and its three economic industries. *Marine Policy*, *134*, 104777. doi:10.1016/j.marpol.2021.104777

Maier, D., Maier, A., Aşchilean, I., Anastasiu, L., & Gavriş, O. (2020). The relationship between innovation and sustainability: A bibliometric review of the literature. *Sustainability (Basel)*, *12*(10), 4083. doi:10.3390/su12104083

Mirza-Babaei, P., Robinson, R., Mandryk, R., Pirker, J., Kang, C., & Fletcher, A. (2022, November). Games and the Metaverse. In *Extended abstracts of the 2022 annual symposium on computer-human interaction in play*. ACM. 10.1145/3505270.3558355

Moher, D., Liberati, A., Tetzlaff, J., & Altman, D. G. (2009). Preferred reporting items for systematic reviews and meta-analyses: The PRISMA statement. *Annals of Internal Medicine, 151*(4), 264–269. doi:10.7326/0003-4819-151-4-200908180-00135 PMID:19622511

Mourtzis, D. (2023). The Metaverse in Industry 5.0: A Human-Centric Approach towards Personalized Value Creation. *Encyclopedia, 3*(3), 1105–1120. doi:10.3390/encyclopedia3030080

Muhuri, P. K., Shukla, A. K., & Abraham, A. (2019). Industry 4.0: A bibliometric analysis and detailed overview. *Engineering Applications of Artificial Intelligence, 78*, 218–235. doi:10.1016/j.engappai.2018.11.007

Nabukalu, R., & Wanjohi, A. (2023). *Impact of Metaverse on Marketing Communication: A case study of the fashion industry*. Lulea University of Technology.

Qi, W. (2022). The Investment Value of Metaverse in the Media and Entertainment Industry. *BCP Business and Management, 34*, 279–283. doi:10.54691/bcpbm.v34i.3026

Raad, H., & Rashid, F. K. M. (2023). The Metaverse: Applications, Concerns, Technical Challenges, Future Directions and Recommendations. *IEEE Access : Practical Innovations, Open Solutions, 11*, 110850–110861. doi:10.1109/ACCESS.2023.3321650

Rejeb, A., Rejeb, K., & Treiblmaier, H. (2023). Mapping metaverse research: Identifying future research areas based on bibliometric and topic modeling techniques. *Information (Basel), 14*(7), 356. doi:10.3390/info14070356

Sharma, R., Jabbour, C. J. C., & Lopes de Sousa Jabbour, A. B. (2021). Sustainable manufacturing and industry 4.0: What we know and what we don't. *Journal of Enterprise Information Management, 34*(1), 230–266. doi:10.1108/JEIM-01-2020-0024

Shen, B., Tan, W., Guo, J., Zhao, L., & Qin, P. (2021). How to promote user purchase in metaverse? A systematic literature review on consumer behavior research and virtual commerce application design. *Applied Sciences (Basel, Switzerland), 11*(23), 11087. doi:10.3390/app112311087

Van Beers, D., Bossilkov, A., Corder, G., & Van Berkel, R. (2007). Industrial symbiosis in the Australian minerals industry: the cases of Kwinana and Gladstone.

Van Eck, N., & Waltman, L. (2010). Software survey: VOSviewer, a computer program for bibliometric mapping. *Scientometrics, 84*(2), 523–538. doi:10.1007/s11192-009-0146-3 PMID:20585380

Van Eck, N. J., & Waltman, L. (2011). Text mining and visualization using VOSviewer. arXiv preprint arXiv:1109.2058.

Viana-Lora, A., & Nel-lo-Andreu, M. G. (2022). Bibliometric analysis of trends in COVID- 19 and tourism. *Humanities & Social Sciences Communications, 9*(1), 173. doi:10.1057/s41599-022-01194-5

Wallin, J. A. (2005). Bibliometric methods: Pitfalls and possibilities. *Basic & Clinical Pharmacology & Toxicology*, *97*(5), 261–275. doi:10.1111/j.1742-7843.2005.pto_139.x PMID:16236137

Wang, M., Yu, H., Bell, Z., & Chu, X. (2022). Constructing an edu-metaverse ecosystem: A new and innovative framework. *IEEE Transactions on Learning Technologies*, *15*(6), 685–696. doi:10.1109/TLT.2022.3210828

Wang, M. H., Yu, T. C., & Ho, Y. S. (2010). A bibliometric analysis of the performance of Water Research. *Scientometrics*, *84*(3), 813–820. doi:10.1007/s11192-009-0112-0

Weinberg, B. H. (1974). Bibliographic coupling: A review. *Information Storage and Retrieval*, *10*(5–6), 189–196. doi:10.1016/0020-0271(74)90058-8

Wider, W., Jiang, L., Lin, J., Fauzi, M. A., Li, J., & Chan, C. K. (2023). Metaverse chronicles: A bibliometric analysis of its evolving landscape. *International Journal of Human-Computer Interaction*, 1–14. doi:10.1080/10447318.2023.2227825

Yang, L., Ni, S. T., Wang, Y., Yu, A., Lee, J. A., & Hui, P. (2024). Interoperability of the Metaverse: A Digital Ecosystem Perspective Review. *arXiv preprint arXiv:2403.05205*.

Yao, X., Ma, N., Zhang, J., Wang, K., Yang, E., & Faccio, M. (2024). Enhancing wisdom manufacturing as industrial metaverse for industry and society 5.0. *Journal of Intelligent Manufacturing*, *35*(1), 235–255. doi:10.1007/s10845-022-02027-7

Zhai, X., Chu, X., Wang, M., Zhang, Z., & Dong, Y. (2022). Education metaverse: Innovations and challenges of the new generation of Internet education formats. *Metaverse*, *3*(1), 13. doi:10.54517/met.v3i1.1804

Zonaphan, L., Northus, K., Wijaya, J., Achmad, S., & Sutoyo, R. (2022, November). Metaverse as a future of education: A systematic review. In *2022 8th International HCI and UX Conference in Indonesia (CHIuXiD)*, 1, 77-81). 10.1109/CHIuXiD57244.2022.10009854

Zupic, I., & Čater, T. (2015). Bibliometric methods in management and organization. *Organizational Research Methods*, *18*(3), 429–472. doi:10.1177/1094428114562629

ENDNOTES

[1] Research Associate, School of Commerce & Management Studies, Central University of Himachal Pradesh.

[2] Research Scholar, School of Commerce & Management Studies, Central University of Himachal Pradesh

Chapter 13
Transformation of Marketing Strategy by Metaverse in the Hospitality Industry Facing Crisis

Asik Rahaman Jamader

iD https://orcid.org/0000-0002-6938-5901

Pailan College of Management and Technology, India

Santanu Dasgupta

iD https://orcid.org/0000-0002-3060-4759

Pailan College of Management and Technology, India

Mushtaq Ahmad

The Neotia University, India

ABSTRACT

The hospitality industry is one of the largest manpower-driven industries and hence generates huge employment. Strategies evolved and applied till 2019 transformed greatly facing the crisis in 2020 to cope with the prevailing circumstances for sustenance. The use of technology came greatly into effect on the Metaverse. Hence a drastic change has taken place in hospitality marketing strategy using the Tourism Marketing Union Model (TMUM). People are becoming more and more technophiles, and desire to have as much data as possible before starting the tour hoping for a hindrance-free, comfortable, and enjoyable expedition. Therefore, a complete transformation occurred in every phase of the industry, especially in the marketing sector. Cost reduction and Time-saving became the aims of new strategies and for that, Metaverse Marketing Technology (MMT), influencer marketing, and targeting the right audience through Metaverse Visual Marketing are extensively used by marketers.

DOI: 10.4018/979-8-3693-2607-7.ch013

INTRODUCTION

Marketing is an important and inseparable part of every industry and there is no confusion in that. It supports the backbone of each and every sector by maximizing profit through well-planned and structured strategies (Ip et al., 2011). The hospitality industry is also no exception from it. It is the second-largest manpower-driven industry where marketing strategies play an important role. Marketing strategies that were applied till 2019 in the hospitality industry suddenly faced a crisis period due to COVID 19 pandemic and henceforth all the processes need to be restructured as the whole world started to live in the phase of 'new normal'. Till 2019 marketers used online and offline strategies to maximize the number of guests in the hospitality sector. But with the advent of a new normal phase, a 360-degree transformation took place in marketing strategies, instead of both online and offline, marketers focused totally on online-based strategies to target the customers. Different initiatives are taken into action to get the faith and loyalty of guests like – search engine optimization (SEO) and search engine marketing (SEM), boosting digital marketing (DM) platforms, and trying to increase customer satisfaction (CS) by posting more visual contents of hotels, content marketing (CM), etc (Law,et al., 2014). New generations and the Millennial found this online marketing process absolutely hassle-free, time-saving, and worthwhile for them, instead of other processes. Thus there is always a point of discussion whether only this new transformative strategy will be continued or alike before the crisis period, both online and offline strategies will be needed for the hospitality industry to survive in the future (Yoo,et al., 2011).

The travel and tourism sector offers an appropriate backdrop for examining the impact of advanced technology on relationship marketing since it is one of the businesses that have adopted information and communication technologies (ICT) most quickly. Buhalis claims that these innovations bring created additional growth plans for creating, developing, and commercialising client connections through a better comprehension of consumer needs as well as the fulfilment of their demands. Moreover, developments in integrated multimedia broadcasting, ICT, browser innovations, plus their confluence might effectively help to streamlining the procedure for obtaining and analyzing information related to consumers' particular requirements (Williams, A. 2006). In more detail, integrated multimedia television (iMTV) describes the growth of new communication networks that may deliver a variety of multimedia as well as World Wide Web applications. In contrast, Internet Protocol Multimedia Subsystem (IMS) is a promising technology that may be implemented in next smart phones & digitized broadcast networks to offer cutting-edge characteristics as well as additional communication services. To allow effective collection and analysis in tourism relationship marketing, this article offers a technological interaction model that elaborates on the convergence of IMS and iDTV systems (Wang, Y., & Qualls, W., 2007). The suggested system makes it easier for tourist businesses to follow individuals' choices but instead give clients greater economic benefit through personalised services since dynamic marketing strategy depends on clients' data. Because they would have a thorough understanding of the behaviour and preferences of their current or future clients, marketers will be able to base their judgments on marketing activities that are considerably greater expense. Statistical techniques, such as predicting visualization tools, are suggested in order to enable effective information analysis and processing and to best forecast future purchase trends (Pirnar, et al., 2010)

Changing Scenarios of Hospitality Marketing

The hospitality industry needs rigorous promotion and marketing to sustain itself in the ongoing competitive market. Current marketing scenarios possess a direct impact on marketing strategies. Till the year 2019, companies were following mixed strategies based on online and offline platforms like arranging and hosting various events (like exhibitions, and cultural programs) to promote the location and property, maximum discounts offered in off-seasons to attract guests, and happy hours announced in different outlets to provide guests the opportunity to taste and enjoy food and simultaneously hotels' also going to enjoy word of mouth through such events (DiPietro, et al., 2010). Except that online strategies also followed. But in the year 2020, India started facing a crisis due to the pandemic and people forcefully bound themselves at home to maintain the protocols required to sustain from Covid19 (Tuomi, et al., 2021). Therefore, a complete transformation took place in every phase of the industry, especially in the marketing sector. Cost reduction and Time-saving became the aims of new strategies and for that Mobile Marketing Technology, Influencers Marketing, and targeting the right audience through Visual Marketing are extensively used by marketers. Newer channels for interacting with target markets have emerged with the development of information technology (Inanc–Demir, M., & Kozak, M., 2019). Regardless of the type of organisation, digital marketing is now an essential component. The overwhelming importance of digital marketing has changed how businesses sell their products to current and future customers. In the hotel and tourist sectors, where clients have fast access to a wide range of information on the newest deals and greatest pricing, the need for content marketing is greater than ever (Damnjanović, et al., 2020). Nowadays, internet advertising is crucial to the success of any company in the hotel and tourist sector. Several of the earliest businesses to use digital marketing techniques were the hotel and tourist industry. Due in large part to the fact that the business largely offers experiences, this early adoption has also helped the sector to keep up with the most recent developments in digital promotion. In the past, the majority of customers in the hospitality and tourist industries used workstation as well as laptops to research locations and make reservations online. However, the business has recently seen a shift from PCs to mobile a device that has happened gradually but quickly (Leonidou, et al., 2013). This change has affected not just the aforementioned business but also digital use as a whole. Today's social media usage is shockingly different from what it was sometimes just few decades previously (Kuo, et al., 2017).

The said industry includes all the people, activities, and organizations involved in providing services for people on holiday, for example hotels, restaurants, and tour guides. Before the launch of digital marketing, the role of people who rendered these services was indispensable to the success of the business. The increasing number of mobile users, lowering prices of digital marketing services and rising effectiveness of social media strategies are a few of the multitude of reasons which has led to the widespread adoption of digital marketing strategies by the industry (Pappas, N., 2015). As such, there are modern-world start-ups coming up in the already highly saturated hospitality and tourism sector which are mobile-only. The entire industry is going mobile, quite literally. Since the invention of the internet, novel strategies for reaching target consumers with diverse services have emerged (Sigala, M. 2003). The fast growth of the internet has particularly impacted the travel and tourism sector as a whole. With the stroke of a mouse, users may compare prices for travel-related services from companies all around the world (Buhalis, D., & Sinarta, Y., 2019). The most important digital tasks to maintain are having a good website, having a presence on social media, using email marketing, being search engine optimised, and having a mobile-friendly website. Currently, internet advertising is upending sectors and altering how companies interact with their customers. The capacity of digital marketing to collect data regarding user activity as well as sustain a successful in real-time is the primary distinction between traditional and digital marketing. The upheaval in the tourist sector happened a few years ago and changed how services are delivered to customers. Market research is used in traditional marketing to gather data, which is then analysed to better understand the target consumers. The electronic nature of Internet technology offers a thorough and in-depth understanding of customer traits and behaviour in the electronic environment. The manner that company choices are made has changed as a result of this knowledge (Cline, R. S., 1999).

THE ARRIVAL OF THE INTERNET AND DIGITAL TRANSFORMATION FOR MARKETING GROW

The most significant development in marketing over the past three decades has been the widespread acceptance of the internet into daily life. When World Wide Web and Netscape Navigator were introduced, the number of individuals accessing the internet increased. Email gave way to search engines like Yahoo! and Google, as well as e-commerce websites like Amazon, as the number of users grew (Jamader, et al., 2019). This represented a gold mine for marketing. In addition to the conventional armoury of print, radio, and television commercials, email has emerged as a new outbound marketing weapon. While people could get the data, goods, plus services they wanted from the comfort of their homes thanks to search engines, new websites were being developed.

Big Data

Digital data was and is still being retained for all of this internet activity. The majority of text-based information that was "born digital" and is now known as big data was determined to be the sort of unique information that was created with the fastest rate of growth. Big data has made it feasible to follow behavioural patterns and trends, and its use in marketing is only going to grow. A number of businesses that specialise in utilising this technology have developed as advanced analytics branding has gained considerable traction (Das, et al., 2019).

Mobile Phones

Without mobile phones and tablets, wherever would we be? Advertising agencies are still catching up with the rapid growth of these new gadgets during the past ten years. Mobile phones are becoming the most popular digital device for browsing the internet, surpassing personal computers (Nayak, et al., 2022). Following the revolutionary launching of the iPhone, mobile phones did not reach the mainstream market until 2021. When we go at the present, we see that the UK alone has a smart phone ownership rate of more than 80%, with substantial rises in the percentage of 4G users and a quarter of subscribers not completing any conventional voice communication. Online and in our pockets, the world has changed. Where do we proceed from here, a combination of personalisation, accountability, as well as nimble advertising (Jamader, et al., 2021).

ACCESS TO INFORMATION THROUGH TELECOMMUNICATIONS IN DEVELOPMENT FOR MARKETING

With the help of control and, in certain circumstances, the opportunity to make purchases, interactive media in digital television systems transforms the viewer from a passive to an active participant. Interactive media, according to marketers, increases viewer engagement with the media and hence the content. It also makes it possible to display information in more visually appealing and engaging ways, and it is simple to update. In this regard, advancements in technology have already had an impact on one of the most often debated and used channels of interaction: marketing as well as its potential place on tv. Digital interactive television (iDTV), which invites users to enter a more specific tv environment as well as browse WebPages as well as other Internet-based applications, is one example of an evolutionary scientific progress (Sagayam, et al., 2022).

Based on a general interaction model, DTT networking architectures have been developed, allowing for the deployment of asymmetrical transmission of data between the service supplier as well as tele viewers. In these scenarios, upstream information transmitted is provided through a DVB-T channel, while reverse data traffic is transmitted by a variety of associated with positive (including such cell phone, cordless, or permanent connections). Such setups allow a phone company to offer digital television services that are both interactive and one-way. Another internet streaming services are TV programmes that use digital transmission standards. Interactive multimedia services also include video and audio on demand, Internet services including WWW access and e-mail, as well as videoconferencing on supply. But at the other extreme, modern machines and new services demand stringent quality and interactivity, since the previous generation of the Internet was primarily focused on the transportation of data to non-real demand service. Furthermore, in the upcoming years, it is anticipated that the demands for the supply of multimedia services would rise. There seems to be a significant tendency toward a common Internet architecture for services and applications. Customers in this situation appear to want open coverage to individualised immersive offerings on any platform (Jamader, 2022). New specifications for a future network infrastructure are brought about by this tendency. The Internet Protocol Part of the system, which was first developed to enable operators in offering cutting-edge services that will draw new customers, helps to meet this demand by bridging the gap between current traditional telecommunications and Internet applications. Using open standards that facilitate Internet-based network interfaces and fixed-mobile convergence, IMS is a fundamental network architecture that enables communication between servers and clients. IMS has a layered, functional improvement that controls how the information is handled as it travels across the infrastructure. It offers the system implementation necessary to deliver any video streaming to any mix of fixed and mobile end consumers. The creation of the IMS architecture established how applications connected with the fundamental broadband network as well as exchanged data.

By combining many telecommunications concepts into a comprehensive multimedia user experience, IMS-enabled TV systems support combination services and interaction. IMS was created in this environment to offer a private communication infrastructure with group communication, converting TV viewing from a social, participatory experience to a private, personal one. New customised TV experiences will be built specifically on presence and profile management (Jamader et al., 2023). The most accurate user profile, including their habits and wants, may be created by operators and their marketing teams. It can be quite useful for marketing purposes to have a single, uniform database that is based on the cellular world model with enhancements to fulfil iDTV unique demands.

THE TOURISM MARKETING UNION MODEL

Customer engagement relies on participatory contact to better understand the demands of Figure 1 shows a television broadcast interaction model that has been upgraded with IMS features. The suggested convergence paradigm makes it possible to gather data in real time from client sites. The IMS Module/ Database in Figure 1 houses this data, making it possible to properly serve clients and users. Modern technological developments may be the norm, allowing for an essential active interaction between the company and clients (Jamader, Chowdhary & Jha, 2023).

Throughout sequence for these two parties to work together and connect more effectively, integrating business systems through a unified platform is the first step in any corporate IT strategy. This allows customers to communicate and inform the authority's actual demands. Database analysis is the second element of this method (Das et al., 2022). The findings might serve as the foundation for algorithms designed to comprehend the wants of actual clients. Advances in iDTV, ICT, web applications, and their integration in this context should add greatly to automating and streamlining of collecting and analyzing the needed data that is essential in tourist Management (Jamader et al., 2023). Implementing the suggested strategy, Portfolio allows corporations to employ sarcastic retort marketing that cultivate relationships with consumers while also enabling user engagement via electronic content. To send used whenever to the network operator and enable the delivery of actual interactive services through iDTV systems, the use of an interaction channel is required, according to the generic interactivity model. to develop focused and effective advertising tactics, the marketing analysis step is necessary. In order to anticipate future probabilities and trends based on observed occurrences, marketers can undertake data analysis by utilising data mining techniques, such as predictive visual analytics. The suggested strategy incorporates a multi-perspective approach that integrates algorithms, predictive modelling, and reasoning based on domain expertise (Jamader, Das, & Acharya, 2022).

Figure 1. Tourism marketing union model (TMUM)

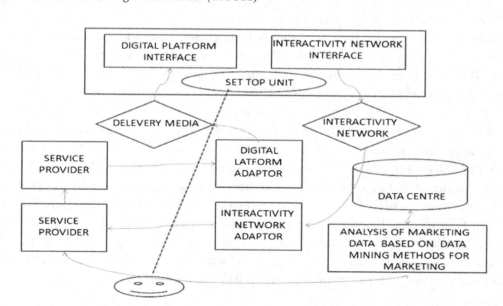

And as per the suggested strategy, collection of information will be analysed in an effort to improve consumer behaviour understanding and future purchase trends prediction. The suggested data mining approaches are utilised to determine channel strategy, product type, buying preferences, and regional market share. Then, to determine, for instance, whether novel merchandise should just be brought into the tourism industry, demographics, lifestyle factors, and purchasing behaviour are employed. Last but not least, behavioural metrics created using predictive analytics models may graphically display chosen marketing data and generate what-if scenarios to establish and confirm the proper pairings of new eco-tourism marketing. Prospective advanced analytic study often aims to make the overabundance of data inside an advantage. To make wise choices in circumstances where time is of the essence, decision-makers should be able to assess vast streams of information that are multidimensional, multi-source, and moment. People must be related to information data analysis in order to fully utilise the tremendous memory space as well as processing power of digital hardware while also bringing adaptability, imagination, as well as context to the procedure. A vitally essential of information visualization is that it enables judgement in the tourist industry to utilise sophisticated computer skills to speed up the discovery process while focusing all of their visuospatial resources on the data analysis.

Predictive visual analytics has replaced data warehousing and mining as the primary area of study for cutting-edge technology and innovation in our fast-paced world in order to handle all these challenges.

It would be simple to get the explanation by glancing at the individual in the seat next to you on the bus, by gazing up in the middle of the street, or by simply glancing about. If you do, you'll see that the individual sitting next to you is carrying a device, LED advertisements can be seen in the sky, and people are becoming more immersed in technology on a daily basis as you can see when you glance about. The majority of companies in the tourism sector are performing far better than those that aren't, according to actual data from numerous data. According to a latest studies, 3.2 billion people, or almost 50% of the world's population, are already smart phone subscribers.

CONCLUSION

This article goes into further detail on the research of IMS as a potential alternative that might be used in digitization and then the next systems, offering slightly up and additional benefit offerings. This work suggests a technological convergence model that might lead to a fresh research methodology usable in tourist Management, taking into consideration advancements in both scientific fields. Implementing the RM concept with a focus on creating high-quality relationships with customers and stakeholders is essential for competitiveness in the dynamic and uncertain economic environment of the hotel industry, which is characterised by tough competition and advanced requirement. Making sure visitors are happy is a certain method to keep loyal consumers and draw in new ones. The overarching goal of RM is to make it possible for marketers to keep track of the preferences of both current and future consumers in order to provide them with services that are more valuable overall. The suggested idea would make it possible for a more effective method of gathering and evaluating audience data information, which is essential for the best possible marketing outcomes. It might be the solution to one of the top goals on the wish lists of marketers: to advance toward one-to-one marketing contact with the target audience, capture their attention and interest, arouse their desire, and ultimately result in the compulsive or deliberate action of purchasing. Furthermore, the suggested machine learning techniques as well as internet applications improve the suggested research strategy by enabling, correspondingly, an appropriate way to analyse marketing data and an efficient way to automatically modify services for specific clients or market groups. Furthermore, the suggested machine learning techniques as well as internet applications improve the suggested research strategy by enabling, correspondingly, an appropriate way to analyse marketing data and an efficient way to automatically modify services for specific clients or market groups.

ACKNOWLEDGEMENTS

Funding: The Author declare that they do not have any funding or grant for the manuscript.

Conflict of Interest: The authors declare that they do not have any conflict of interests that influence the work reported in this paper

REFERENCES

Buhalis, D., & Sinarta, Y. (2019). Real-time co-creation and nowness service: Lessons from tourism and hospitality. *Journal of Travel & Tourism Marketing*, *36*(5), 563–582. doi:10.1080/10548408.2019.1592059

Cline, R. S. (1999). Hospitality 2000—the technology: Building customer relationships. *Journal of Vacation Marketing*, *5*(4), 376–386. doi:10.1177/135676679900500407

Damnjanović, V., Lončarić, D., & Dlačić, J. (2020). TEACHING CASE STUDY: Digital marketing strategy of Accor Hotels: shaping the future of hospitality. *Tourism and Hospitality Management*, *26*(1), 233–244.

Das, P., Jamader, A. R., Acharya, B. R., & Das, H. (2019, May). HMF Based QoS aware Recommended Resource Allocation System in Mobile Edge Computing for IoT. In *2019 International Conference on Intelligent Computing and Control Systems (ICCS)* (pp. 444-449). IEEE. 10.1109/ICCS45141.2019.9065775

DiPietro, R. B., & Wang, Y. R. (2010). Key issues for ICT applications: Impacts and implications for hospitality operations. *Worldwide Hospitality and Tourism Themes*, *2*(1), 49–67. doi:10.1108/17554211011012595

Inanc–Demir, M., & Kozak, M. (2019). Big data and its supporting elements: Implications for tourism and hospitality marketing. In *Big Data and Innovation in Tourism, Travel, and Hospitality* (pp. 213–223). Springer. doi:10.1007/978-981-13-6339-9_13

Ip, C., Leung, R., & Law, R. (2011). Progress and development of information and communication technologies in hospitality. *International Journal of Contemporary Hospitality Management*, *23*(4), 533–551. doi:10.1108/09596111111130029

Jamader, A. R. (2022). A Brief Report Of The Upcoming & Present Economic Impact To Hospitality Industry In COVID19 Situations. *Journal of Pharmaceutical Negative Results*, 2289–2302.

Jamader, A. R., Chowdhary, S., Jha, S. S., & Roy, B. (2023). Application of Economic Models to Green Circumstance for Management of Littoral Area: A Sustainable Tourism Arrangement. *SMART Journal of Business Management Studies*, *19*(1), 70–84. doi:10.5958/2321-2012.2023.00008.8

Jamader, A. R., Chowdhary, S., & Shankar Jha, S. (2023). A Road Map for Two Decades of Sustainable Tourism Development Framework. In Resilient and Sustainable Destinations After Disaster: Challenges and Strategies (pp. 9-18). Emerald Publishing Limited. doi:10.1108/978-1-80382-021-720231002

Jamader, A. R., Das, P., & Acharya, B. (2022). An Analysis of Consumers Acceptance towards Usage of Digital Payment System, Fintech and CBDC. *Fintech and CBDC (January 1, 2022)*.

Jamader, A. R., Das, P., Acharya, B., & Hu, Y. C. (2021). Overview of Security and Protection Techniques for Microgrids. In *Microgrids* (pp. 231–253). CRC Press. doi:10.1201/9781003121626-11

Jamader, A. R., Das, P., & Acharya, B. R. (2019, May). BcIoT: blockchain based DDoS prevention architecture for IoT. In *2019 International Conference on Intelligent Computing and Control Systems (ICCS)* (pp. 377-382). IEEE. 10.1109/ICCS45141.2019.9065692

Jamader, A. R., Immanuel, J. S., Ebenezer, V., Rakhi, R. A., Sagayam, K. M., & Das, P. (2023). Virtual Education, Training And Internships In Hospitality And Tourism During Covid-19 Situation. *Journal of Pharmaceutical Negative Results*, 286–290.

Kuo, C. M., Chen, L. C., & Tseng, C. Y. (2017). Investigating an innovative service with hospitality robots. *International Journal of Contemporary Hospitality Management, 29*(5), 1305–1321. doi:10.1108/IJCHM-08-2015-0414

Law, R., Buhalis, D., & Cobanoglu, C. (2014). Progress on information and communication technologies in hospitality and tourism. *International Journal of Contemporary Hospitality Management, 26*(5), 727–750. doi:10.1108/IJCHM-08-2013-0367

Leonidou, L. C., Leonidou, C. N., Fotiadis, T. A., & Zeriti, A. (2013). Resources and capabilities as drivers of hotel environmental marketing strategy: Implications for competitive advantage and performance. *Tourism Management, 35*, 94–110. doi:10.1016/j.tourman.2012.06.003

Nayak, D. K., Mishra, P., Das, P., Jamader, A. R., & Acharya, B. (2022). Application of Deep Learning in Biomedical Informatics and Healthcare. In *Smart Healthcare Analytics: State of the Art* (pp. 113–132). Springer. doi:10.1007/978-981-16-5304-9_9

Pappas, N. (2015). Marketing hospitality industry in an era of crisis. *Tourism Planning & Development, 12*(3), 333–349. doi:10.1080/21568316.2014.979226

Pirnar, I., Icoz, O., & Icoz, O. (2010). The new tourist: Impacts on the hospitality marketing strategies. *EuroCHRIE Amsterdam*, 25-28.

Das, P., Martin Sagayam, K., Rahaman Jamader, A., & Acharya, B. (2022). Remote Sensing in Public Health Environment: A Review. *Internet of Things Based Smart Healthcare: Intelligent and Secure Solutions Applying Machine Learning Techniques*, 379-397.

Sagayam, K. M., Das, P., Jamader, A. R., Acharya, B. R., Bonyah, E., & Elngar, A. A. (2022). DeepCOVIDNet [Detection of Chest Image Using Deep Learning Model.]. *COVID*, 19.

Sigala, M. (2003). Developing and benchmarking internet marketing strategies in the hotel sector in Greece. *Journal of Hospitality & Tourism Research (Washington, D.C.), 27*(4), 375–401. doi:10.1177/10963480030274001

Tuomi, A., Tussyadiah, I. P., & Stienmetz, J. (2021). Applications and implications of service robots in hospitality. *Cornell Hospitality Quarterly*, *62*(2), 232–247. doi:10.1177/1938965520923961

Wang, Y., & Qualls, W. (2007). Towards a theoretical model of technology adoption in hospitality organizations. *International Journal of Hospitality Management*, *26*(3), 560–573. doi:10.1016/j.ijhm.2006.03.008

Williams, A. (2006). Tourism and hospitality marketing: Fantasy, feeling and fun. *International Journal of Contemporary Hospitality Management*, *18*(6), 482–495. doi:10.1108/09596110610681520

Yoo, M., Lee, S., & Bai, B. (2011). Hospitality marketing research from 2000 to 2009: topics, methods, and trends. *International Journal of Contemporary Hospitality Management*.

Chapter 14
Unlocking the Potentials and Constraints of Metaverse Implementation in Manufacturing Firms

Mohammad Imtiaz Hossain

iD https://orcid.org/0000-0002-9637-3201

Multimedia University, Malaysia

Yasmin Jamadar

BRAC University, Bangladesh

Nurunnesa Begum Momo

BRAC University, Bangladesh

Nusrat Hafiz

BRAC University, Bangladesh

Rufaida Nurain Saiba

BRAC University, Bangladesh

ABSTRACT

This research investigates the potentials and constraints of metaverse technology within Malaysian manufacturing companies underpinned by the technology-organization-environment (TOE) theory. Firm size, firm age, annual revenue, and ownership structure were control variables. 240 questionnaire responses from Malaysian firms collected through convenience sampling techniques and analyzed by Smart-PLS software. The findings reveal technological limitations, poor diffusion through the network, lack of collaboration, and low perception of value by customers are significant constraints for the failure of metaverse technology implementation. The control variables did not evidence any impact on implementation. This study provides insights to metaverse technology developers and manufacturing practitioners besides theoretical contributions.

DOI: 10.4018/979-8-3693-2607-7.ch014

INTRODUCTION

Metaverse is a virtual world, which will compile virtual reality (VR) with augmented reality (AR), and will stabilize a link between the real world and a parallel virtual world for humans. The metaverse is poised to revolutionize various sectors by enhancing efficiency and reducing risks, especially in scientific experiments. For instance, businesses can leverage the metaverse to streamline tedious and hazardous tasks. A case in point is inventory management, which can be virtually automated, reducing the manual effort (Dwivedi et al., 2022). The metaverse also enables virtual property transactions.

In the realm of education, the metaverse offers immersive learning experiences, which experts argue are more effective than traditional audio-visual learning. This technology allows students to engage in realistic, risk-free learning and experimentation. Unlike the less interactive online education under Web 2.0, metaverse-based learning is highly interactive, facilitated by three-dimensional avatars. It also offers the flexibility of personalized learning schedules (Zhang, 2023).

Beyond business and education, the metaverse has significant implications for healthcare, tourism, and entertainment. It enables virtual travel to far-off places and enhances the realism of games, contributing to mental well-being. Therefore, the metaverse holds immense potential across sectors, promising risk reduction and economic growth.

Metaverse will have significance in both developed and developing countries, if they implement it after overcoming all challenges. It will be a new opportunity for businesses, they can earn more profit by showing their creativity in the virtual world. It will have virtual currency, assets, and the marketplace. Thus, it will be a new opportunity for the stakeholders to have benefits from businesses. Subsequently, manufacturing firms can do their work more smoothly with the help of it. For example: they can give training to their workers virtually and more interactively with the help of avatars. Moreover, multinational companies can run their business more effectively because it will mitigate the limitation of physical distance. Also, service industries like psychology and tourism can give their services more effectively by making the virtual experience more realistic through metaverse (Mourtzis, 2023). Besides, through it a diverse digital culture can be established, which will bring a collaborative new culture. In other words, it will bring more global connectivity through cross-cultural interactions.

While the metaverse offers numerous benefits, it also faces several implementation challenges. First, to create a realistic virtual experience, enhanced sensations are required. However, certain sensations, such as slipperiness, distinct aromas, and daylight, are more authentically experienced in the physical world. Therefore, these sensations need to be more naturally replicated in the metaverse, considering the multiple personas of human beings (Park & Kim, 2024). Nevertheless, the increased demand for high-powered technologies could negatively impact the environment, thereby undermining sustainability efforts.

Second, security and privacy are fundamental aspects of human life, and the potential for stored data and internet history to compromise these elements cannot be overlooked (Park & Kim, 2024). For example, Google Glass, despite being an innovative product, was discontinued due to privacy concerns. Moreover, legal regulations in the virtual world may differ from those in various countries, leading to potential conflicts. Cultural clashes may also arise in the metaverse. Finally, the global promotion and adoption of the metaverse present significant challenges. For instance, Google Glass was primarily used by financially stable individuals in developed countries. Consequently, individuals in developing and underdeveloped countries may require additional effort and training to adapt to this groundbreaking technology.

A collaborative digital environment that spans multiple dimensions, powered by a blend of Virtual Reality (VR), Augmented Reality (AR), and Mixed Reality (MR), holds the potential to deeply integrate the automotive and manufacturing sectors into the Metaverse. This industrial Metaverse could materialize through seamless integration of cyber-physical systems, digital twins, 5G-enabled AR, VR, and AI-driven computer vision, as well as low-latency remote control capabilities, among other technologies (Fernández-Caramés & Fraga-Lamas, 2024).

Within this industrial Metaverse, future factories would not only utilize AR/VR for on-site assistance and skills training but would also facilitate a virtual environment where individuals can work together, guided by AI algorithms to validate outcomes and rectify errors in real-time, eliminating the need for physical presence (Yao et al., 2024).

Moreover, various aspects of company operations including product design, development, trial production testing, operational management, and marketing, can be simulated and validated within this virtual ecosystem before implementation in the physical world.

Furthermore, blockchain technology could be leveraged to record decision-making processes and results, serving as a transparent basis for assessment and auditing across both virtual and physical realms (Zheng et al., 2022).

Being a developing country Malaysia began the journey with metaverse in various sectors, especially initiated with the gaming industry. As mentioned above Metaverse has a crucial role in the gaming industry. Furthermore, metaverse has not been implemented in the educational institutions but they are taking steps to start their journey with it. For instance- there are many articles where the authors proposed metaverse based education. Rahman et al. (2023) emphasized the importance of metaverse in education along with proposing a detailed figure of virtual classrooms to implement in the education sector of Malaysia. For instance, in Malaysia, the Arabic Learning Principles (ALP) were integrated with a 3D Metaverse platform to teach Arabic language skills to Muslim students (Basha, Khaleel, Mnaathr, & Rozinah, 2013). This platform included elements of traditional Arabic architecture found in mosques, allowing for congregational prayer, Quran recitation, supplication, and even the use of a compass to orient towards the Kaaba, among other features. Moreover, in the 4th industry revaluation (4IR) Malaysia already used some advanced technologies but they are not updated compared to other countries (Uddin, 2024). The reasons behind this are low education rate, lack of training, inadequate initiative and so on. Technology might cause unemployment in a short run but will create more job opportunities in the long run (Uddin, 2024). Therefore, Malaysia should adopt metaverse to boost its economy. Therefore, the journey of metaverse is not completely visible yet apart from the gaming industry and there are some prominent obstacles behind it.

Firstly, lack of knowledge, education and infrastructure are the barriers in the implementation of metaverse (Creed et al., 2024). Secondly, VR and AR and other accessories are very expensive (Mammadova, 2023), and these will be difficult for lot of firms specially SMEs to afford. Thirdly, cultural sensitivity will be another issue because metaverse is a global concept (Li, 2022), and alignment with other cultures will be a problem. Lastly, poor regulatory framework compared to other countries will hamper the privacy and security of its people, which will be a barrier. According to Ghobakhloo and Ching (2019), the utilization of high technology is observed in merely 37% of manufacturing enterprises, in contrast to a 20% prevalence within the service sector. These statistics underscore a deficiency in coordination and a proactive stance among stakeholders within the context of this nation. Creed et al. (2024) explored interaction barriers identifed across a spectrum of impairments including physical, cognitive, visual, and auditory disabilities, but no empirical quantitative study was conducted. Julian et al. (2023) mentioned the most common reason of concerns is data security and privacy. This response may reveal a lack of understanding rather than genuine concern (Seo et al., 2018). However, they also did not conduct any empirical study.

According to a tech trend survey conducted by Oppotus, it was found that 58% of respondents in Malaysia were aware of Augmented Reality (AR) (Statista, 2023). However, despite this awareness, the adoption rate of augmented reality and virtual reality (VR) among users in Malaysia is reported to be relatively low, standing at a penetration rate of only 38.2% (Statista, 2023). This discrepancy between awareness and adoption rates may suggest either a low level of acceptance of the technology or potentially subpar business performance in promoting and implementing AR and VR solutions in Malaysia. Numerous research studies have been conducted on subjects related to purchase intent, the interplay of cognition, affect, and conation, the roles of consumer control, and augmented reality, each employing various conceptual theories (Teo & Wong, 2023). However, there are limited studies to discuss the implementation challenges in Malaysian manufacturing industry.

The above discussion elaborates the crucial importance of metaverse in different sectors along with the challenges of its worldwide implication. However, this study focus on the challenges of implementing metaverse in manufacturing firms perspective. Wide and vast implication of metaverse is expected in the near future, and this study will help to predict the challenges in advance, which will help to overcome the challenges. This paper examines the influence of implementation challenges on failure to implement metaverse in manufacturing firms in Malaysia.

LITERATURE REVIEW AND HYPOTHESES DEVELOPMENT

Technology, Organization, and Environment (TOE) Framework

The Technology, Organization, and Environment (TOE) framework is a theoretical model that explains technology adoption in organizations. It describes how the process of adopting and implementing technological innovations are influenced by the technological context, organizational context, and environmental context (Wiangkham, & Vongvit, 2023). In the context of metaverse technologies, the TOE framework can be applied as follows:

Technological Context refers to the internal and external technologies relevant to the firm. In the case of metaverse technologies, it includes the existing infrastructure, the state of metaverse technology, and the firm's technological capabilities. For instance, a firm's technological limitations are among the most significant barriers to implementing metaverse technology.

Organizational Context pertains to the characteristics and resources of the organization. It includes aspects like the size of the organization, the amount of slack resources available, the level of centralization or formalization, managerial structure, and employee attitudes towards change. Factors such as traditional organizational culture, lack of stakeholder commitment, and low perception of value by customers can pose challenges to the adoption of metaverse technologies.

Environmental Context refers to the business environment in which the firm operates. It includes the industry setting, market size, competition, and the regulatory environment. Issues like lack of governance and standardization, and integration challenges can impact the implementation of metaverse technologies.

Therefore, the TOE framework provides a holistic perspective on the adoption and implementation of metaverse technologies in organizations, recognizing that both internal and external factors are important in shaping technology adoption and use. It helps in identifying potential barriers and developing suitable strategies for successful implementation.

Technological Limitations and the Failure to Implement Metaverse

Technological limitations are the challenges that are faced while using technological methods, tools, or systems. Modern people rely on technology but because of its limitations they face some obstacles (e.g., low quality, cost, time waste, risk, barriers in communication).There are different kinds of limitations, some are technical and some are human generated. For example: hacking, low-quality of bandwidth, lag etc. are the limitations. Some limitations can be eliminated through development but perception of the users is difficult to grasp. In the case of the metaverse, the boundaries between real life and virtual life will no longer exist through avatars. However, it will require vast amounts of energy and resources (Allam et al., 2022). For instance: short battery coverage of below 60 minutes was one of the limitations of revolutionary google glass (Millana et al., 2016). Besides, high powered internet is needed for implementing metaverse but in Malaysia many remote areas are lacking internet, where other countries are using 5G. However, according to the United States, the 5G network will hamper national security because the network is provided by the Chinese suppliers Huawei (Friis & Lysne, 2021). On the other hand, European countries have positive experience with 3G and 4G networks provided by Huawei, and they are preparing to adopt 5G (Friis & Lysne, 2021). Thus, the security of the 5G network is very contradictory among countries, and a high powered internet is required to implement metaverse. Thus, low speed internet and electricity issues will be a barrier in the implementation of metaverse. Therefore, the revolutionary metaverse has positive contributions along with some constraints, which will result in a failure to its implementation.

H1: Technological limitations have significant impact on the failure to implement metaverse

Lack of Governance and Standardization and the Failure to Implement

Revolutionary innovations developed, performed and implemented through some standardized framework and governance (Yang, 2023). Lack of governance and standardization causes corruption, discrimination and unfair policies. Also, it makes an impact on the sustainability and efficiency of the innovations. Equivalently, an adequate governance and standardization in the virtual world will bring equality, democracy, transparency and accountability (Allam et al., 2022). Many revolutionary innovations failed because they lacked governance and standardization. For example- one of the reasons behind the failure of the google glass was privacy and security concerns because through it users can record (Martinez-Millana et al., 2016). Likewise, metaverse will have privacy and security issues. Also, it will be challenging to make a standardized virtual law for all the countries because of different cultures, norms and laws (Allam et al., 2022). Thus, there will be cultural shock, and underdeveloped and developing countries might face pressure to adopt cultures and laws of the developing countries. Moreover, technical standards are needed to establish metaverse, and the compatible standards ensure adequate governance (Yang, 2023). In the introduction phase of metaverse, standardized frameworks are limited, and stakeholders are hoping to have appropriate standards for having security and compatibility in the virtual world (Yang, 2023). Therefore, lack of governance and standardization will be one of the reasons of the failure in metaverse implementation, and compatible, formulated and secure standards is needed to govern the virtual world successfully.

H2: Lack of governance and standardization has significant impact on the failure to implement metaverse

Integration Challenges and the Failure to Implement Metaverse

In the modern competitive era technology integration is more important and challenging than ever, and it is considered as a company's competitive advantage (Akpan et al., 2021). After intensive effort of the research & development (R&D) department, companies launch a technology but if they fail to integrate properly, they will not be able to fulfill the targeted goals. Furthermore, the product's life cycle is reduced compared to past decades because of the numerous technological developments, and cherish in the market companies need to bear challenges while integrating technologies. For instance: for seamless user experience Microsoft generated the windows 95 operating system, and while establishing it went through a lot of challenges (Akpan et al., 2021). Technological integration is complex compared to leadership, project management, and maintaining organizational structure. First reason behind it is technological integration is new and people are not familiar with it, and secondly companies select the wrong technology which causes them to face integration challenges. Subsequently, Metaverse is a revolutionary technology but companies need to choose wisely while using it and a wrong decision will cause them to face immense loss. From the above discussion we can conclude that individual companies face challenges while adopting technology but the metaverse will be adopted vastly by different companies. Therefore, the integration will be more challenging because of high power technology, cost, lack of training & awareness, cultural differences, and differences in laws, which might be the cause of the failure to implement metaverse.

H3: Integration challenges has significant impact on the failure to implement metaverse

Poor Diffusion Through the Network and the Failure to Implement Metaverse

The information, data, and innovation expand worldwide via the network diffusion (Al-Taie & Kadry, 2017). The diffusion process conducts through 3 steps, which are sender, receiver, and medium. Furthermore, through diffusion innovations spread so rapidly. For example, telephones took a few decades to become renowned in the USA, whereas people became aware of facebook in a few years because of good network structure. Similarly, in the modern era one of the revolutionary innovations of Google Company was its google glass but one of the reasons behind its failure was poor diffusion (Nunes & Filho, 2018). Moreover, the diffusion process of a network can be terminated, if the information is defective. This intervention can be a barrier for information spreading of a new product, and customers may lose their trust from the innovation (Al-Taie & Kadry, 2017). Subsequently, under metaverse all things will be virtual, and it will be a big change. Thus, strong network diffusion is mandatory to spread the innovation. For instance, as stated above, in 1992, Neal Stephenson first invented this word of metaverse in his science fiction but after around 3 and half decades people still are not familiar with the word. Therefore, poor diffusion is one of the limitations behind the lag of implementing a new innovation, and this will be a limitation of the implementation of the metaverse as well.

H4: Poor diffusion through the network has significant impact on the failure to implement metaverse

Traditional Organization Culture and the Failure to Implement Metaverse

Under traditional organizational culture the power goes to the upper management, and the organization maintains a chain of command like a pyramid. Here the main decisions come from the upper level (e.g., CEO), and then mid-level managers give instructions to meet the goals that were made by the upper level. It creates a stable work environment for the employees, and low risk associated with this type of culture. Whereas, modern organization culture has flexibility according to the need. Furthermore, generally in technological innovations the developing countries adopt lately, and the developed countries adopt fast because of their modern organizational culture (Dwivedi et al., 2022). Most organizations follow hierarchical or traditional culture in the developing and underdeveloped countries, and for this reason they are lacking behind adopting new changes (Dwivedi et al., 2022). For example: one of the reasons behind the collapse of the brand Nokia was traditional organizational culture, and this was an obstacle in its technological adoption (Peltonen, 2019). Therefore, Metaverse is a revolutionary technology which needs a lot of flexibility to adopt, and will be difficult to operate under the traditional organizational culture. In the modern era of technology organizations need to discard traditional culture, and should endorse modern culture to adopt innovative technology like metaverse.

H5: Traditional organization culture has significant impact on the failure to implement metaverse

Lack of Stakeholder Commitment and the Failure to Implement Metaverse

Stakeholders are directly or indirectly affected by the company's performance, and the stakeholders' commitment refers to the amount of involvement, support and dedication the stakeholders have for the company's success (Hossain et al., 2022). For the company's success, stakeholders' commitment plays an important role because it verifies whether the stakeholders are giving their time, effort, resources or not. Furthermore, according to some studies, lack of stakeholders' commitment leads to failure of the company's project (Hossain et al., 2022). Moreover, because of it, the organization faces many challenges, for example: dilemma in decision making, less support, misleading & misunderstanding, inflexibility, low motivation and so on. According to Bag et al. (2023), metaverse will play a vital role in the supply chain management but lack of stakeholders' commitment will be a big barrier in adopting it like any other new technology. In other words, a company's flexibility relies on how supportive the stakeholders are, and low support indicates low commitment which causes failure in the organization's project. Also, to implement metaverse a huge amount of expense needs to be borne by the stakeholders along with time, dedication and other resources (Bag et al., 2023). Moreover, an organization with low stakeholder commitment will not be able to run for a longer period because they will lose their guidance (Sheth, 2020). Therefore, stakeholders' commitment is crucial for adopting the metaverse.

H6: Lack of stakeholder commitment has significant impact on the failure to implement metaverse

Lack of Collaboration and the Failure to Implement Metaverse

Collaboration means when multiple stakeholders work together by sharing resources, knowledge, information, and other things to achieve a common goal (Hossain et al., 2022). Furthermore, collaborative works with good conflict or effective discussion between the team members will give a more optimal outcome, compared to individual work. However, maintaining collaboration is a most difficult task because people are different and their perceptions are different as well (Han, 2022). In consequence, teammates face the lack of collaboration, and to adopt any new changes a lot of collaboration is required in an organization. Subsequently, because of this issue the organizations face problems while implementing any new technology. Firstly, top management support is crucial for adopting a new technology (Hossain et al., 2024). Secondly, before collaborative technology adoption the companies need to ensure collaborative work practices in their organization. Similarly, the revolutionary metaverse needs stakeholders' collaboration to implement it worldwide because of its complexity, expensiveness, cultural differences, and lack of awareness. Thus, lack of collaboration while implementing metaverse will be one of the reasons behind its collapse.

H7: Lack of collaboration has significant impact on the failure to implement metaverse

Low Perceived Value by Customers and the Failure to Implement Metaverse

Perceived value refers to the monetary value that customers are willing to pay for a good or service (Sweeney & Soutar, 2001). Customer perceived value comes from two factors: the benefits that they get from the product, and the amount they pay for it. Higher perceived value means greater satisfaction compared to expectation, and the customers feel delighted during those scenarios. Furthermore, a perfect balance between expectation and actual benefit makes the customers satisfied. On the other hand, low perceived value indicates lower satisfaction compared to expectation, and during those situations the customer feels unsatisfied (Mainardes & Freitas, 2023). Subsequently, no product can be established for the long run without satisfying customers' perceived value. As stated above, metaverse has many limitations (e.g., security, high expense, technical issues, lack of awareness), and because of these limitations the customer might not feel the importance of metaverse. If the customers do not feel the worth of it, then there is no potential reason to establish it. For instance: Google glass was not nice-looking for some customers, and it was one of the reasons behind its failure (Martinez-Millana et al., 2016). Therefore, lack of awareness about metaverse or these above-mentioned limitations might cause low perceived value by the customers, which will make them dissatisfied. Eventually, dissatisfaction by the customers will be a cause of its failure.

H8 Low perceived value by customers has significant impact on the failure to implement metaverse

METHODOLOGY

The study applies positivism philosophy, quantitative survey method, cross-sectional time horizon and deductive approach. Data was collected through structured questionnaire to get more data in a quick time frame. The items were adapted from the previous studies and applied a five-point likert scale. Technological limitations (TL) four items, lack of governance and standardization (LGS) four items, integration challenges (IC) four items, poor diffusion through the network (PN) five items, traditional organization culture (TOC) three items, lack of stakeholder commitment (LSC) three items, lack of collaboration (LC) four items, low perception of value by customers (LVC) three items, and failure to metaverse technology implementation (FMTI) five items were adapted from Dwivedi et al. (2022), Mozumder et al. (2022), Queiroz et al. (2023).

Three (3) academicians and three (3) industry players checked the item's relevancy and quality. The sentence structures of the items were revised in accordance with the feedback provided by experts and

Figure 1. Conceptual framework

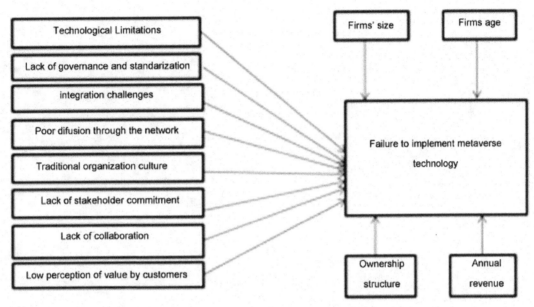

respondents. The researchers considered dropping few questions to ensure relevancy of the items with the context.

The study is of a cross-sectional nature as data was obtained at a singular point in time. A pilot study was performed consists 30 respondents. The unit of analysis was individuals consisting top and middle management officers including supervisors who have supreme knowledge about new technology implementation of the firms.

The non- probability sampling method and convenience sampling technique were employed as the sample frame was not available. By using the G-power software, based on the eight (8) predictors in this study's framework, 160 sample sizes are suggested (Figure 2). 245 responses were received after distributing questionnaire through a Google form link in various sources such as social media groups of manufacturer and email sending personally. 240 questionnaires were found usable for final analysis.

RESEARCH FINDINGS

Non-Response Bias (NRB) and Common Method Bias (CMB)

This study employs the Wallace & Cooke (1990) approach to examine NRB. NRB guarantees that the survey accurately reflects the desired study population. The researchers analysed the mean and standard deviation for the first 30 and final 30 respondents. They found no significant differences between the two groups, confirming the absence of NRB in the study.

Based on (Kock, 2015), if all VIFs in the inner model resulting from a full collinearity test are equal to or lower than 5.0, the model can consider free of CMB. The model is free from CMB because the VIFs are lower than 5.0 (Table 5).

Figure 2. Sample size determinations using G-power software

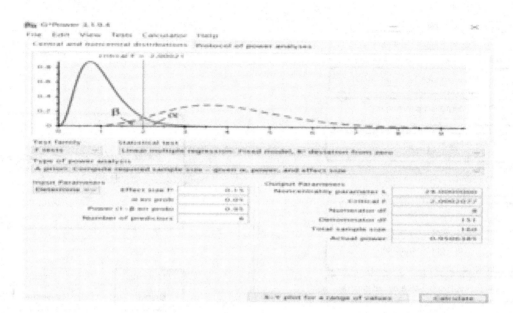

Demographics Data

Table 1 showed that majority of the responses received from Food, Beverage and Tobacco firms (75). Most of the companies are 1-10 years old (142), less than 50 employees (145) are working, annual revenue Not exceeding 10 million BDT (141) and Private-owned firms (179). Moreover, majority respondents are male (165), 26-31 years old (60), and Bachelor degree completed (83).

Measurement Model

Convergent Validity

Convergent validity, as defined by Bagozzi et al. (1981), pertains to the degree of correlation among multiple indicators or measures of the same construct. The calculation of the Average Variance Extracted (AVE) involves squaring the loading of each indicator on a construct and computing the mean value, following the approach outlined by Hair et al. (2019). Internal consistency, or reliability, is assessed using Cronbach's alpha coefficient, a measure introduced by Cronbach (1951) to evaluate the reliability of a set of survey items. Composite reliability, akin to Cronbach's alpha, serves as a gauge of internal consistency in scale items, as proposed by Netemeyer et al. (2003).

The outcomes presented in Table 2 demonstrate that all the items' except LGS and PN's Average Variance Extracted (AVE) values surpass the 0.5 thresholds recommended by Hair et al. (2019). Additionally, constructs except LGS's Cronbach's alpha and composite reliability exceed the 0.7 threshold, as suggested by Hair et al. (2019). These findings indicate that the measures exhibit acceptable reliability and high internal consistency, supporting the convergent validity of the study.

Table 1. Demographic data (n = 240)

Firms characteristics	Categories	Frequency
Type of firm	Food, Beverage and Tobacco	75
	Chemicals	14
	Fabricated metals	1
	Plastic	5
	Electrical & Electronics	29
	Machinery and Equipment	8
	Non-Metallic Mineral	6
	Transport, vehicle & equipment	8
	Rubber	3
	Basic metals	1
	Paper, printing and publishing	6
	Medical, precision and optical instruments, watches & clocks	6
	Textile, wearing apparel and leather	16
	Wood and wood products, excluding furniture	4
	Recycling	5
	Office, accounting and computing machinery	8
	Furniture	9
	Others	36
	Total	240
Firm age	Less than 1 year	17
	1 – 10 years	142
	11 - 20 years	41
	21-30 years	18
	Above 30 years	22
	Total	240
Firm size	Less than 50	145
	50–99	36
	100–299	17
	300–999	10
	1,000–1,999	11
	2,000–4,999	9
	5,000 or more	12
	Total	240
Annual revenue	Not exceeding 10 million BDT	141
	Between 11 -20 million BDT	49
	Between 21 - 30 million BDT	23
	Between 31 -40 million BDT	8
	More than 40 million BDT	19
	Total	240

continued on following page

Table 1. Continued

Firms characteristics	Categories	Frequency
Ownership structure	State-owned firms	25
	Private-owned firms	179
	Foreign-invested firms	36
	Total	240
Respondents characteristics	**Categories**	**Frequency**
Gender	Male	165
	Female	64
	Prefer not to say	11
Age	20- 25 years	42
	26 - 31 years	60
	32 - 37 years	47
	38-43 years	49
	More than 43 Years	42
Education	No formal education	12
	Vocational	7
	Foundation	6
	SPM	10
	STPM	3
	Diploma	42
	Bachelor	83
	Masters	63
	PhD	14

Discriminant validity

Fornell & Larcker (1981) criteria and Heterotrait-Monotrait (HTMT) ratio were applied to confirm discriminant validity. Table 3 demonstrates that the square root of AVE is higher than its correlation with other variables, confirming discriminant validity.

Henseler et al. (2015) proposed the HTMT method, which confirms discriminant validity between each pair of constructs if the correlation values are less than 0.90. Table 4 below shows that the HTMT values are below the threshold value, thus, discriminant validity established.

Structural Model Assessment

Hair et al. (2019) outlined a systematic approach comprising six steps for evaluating the structural model through Partial Least Squares Structural Equation Modeling (PLS-SEM). The initial phase involves addressing latent collinearity issues. Subsequently, the examination of the significance and relevance of relationships within the structural model is undertaken. This is followed by the assessment of the variance explained by the dependent variable (R^2), the effect size (f^2), and the predictive relevance (Q^2predict). Finally, an evaluation of the corresponding t-values of the path coefficients is conducted

Figure 3. The measurement model

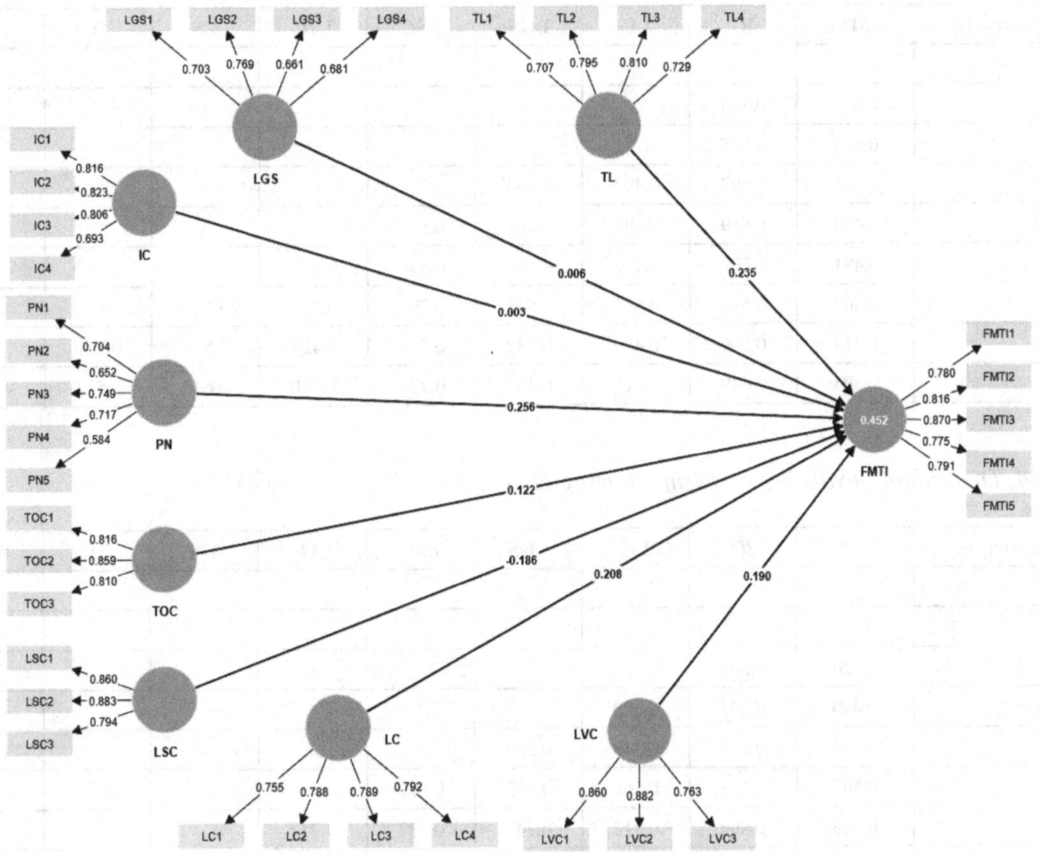

Table 2. Convergent validity

Constructs	Cronbach's alpha	Composite reliability	Average variance extracted
FMTI	0.866	0.903	0.651
IC	0.792	0.866	0.618
LC	0.788	0.862	0.610
LGS	0.668	0.797	0.496
LSC	0.802	0.883	0.717
LVC	0.784	0.875	0.700
PN	0.713	0.813	0.467
TL	0.758	0.846	0.580
TOC	0.773	0.868	0.687

through bootstrapping, employing 5,000 resamples with a two-tailed test at a significance level of 0.05. The results encompassing R^2, f^2, inner and outer model's Variance Inflation Factor (VIF), and Q^2predict are presented in Table 5 below.

Table 3. Discriminant validity assessment using Fornell and Larcker criteria

Constructs	FMTI	IC	LC	LGS	LSC	LVC	PN	TL	TOC
FMTI	0.807								
IC	0.483	0.786							
LC	0.525	0.545	0.781						
LGS	0.353	0.497	0.493	0.704					
LSC	0.434	0.659	0.598	0.403	0.847				
LVC	0.491	0.507	0.453	0.408	0.540	0.837			
PN	0.562	0.674	0.611	0.508	0.708	0.553	0.684		
TL	0.514	0.566	0.449	0.232	0.502	0.421	0.513	0.761	
TOC	0.505	0.689	0.611	0.453	0.721	0.510	0.643	0.522	0.829

Table 4. Discriminant validity assessment using Heterotrait-Monotrait (HTMT)

Constructs	FMTI	IC	LC	LGS	LSC	LVC	PN	TL	TOC
FMTI									
IC	0.577								
LC	0.626	0.688							
LGS	0.440	0.697	0.670						
LSC	0.513	0.828	0.749	0.552					
LVC	0.593	0.634	0.569	0.562	0.679				
PN	0.706	0.894	0.812	0.740	0.832	0.737			
TL	0.626	0.737	0.581	0.355	0.653	0.556	0.699		
TOC	0.608	0.879	0.783	0.637	0.814	0.649	0.862	0.686	

Table 5. Quality of the structural model

Endogenous Variables	R^2	Q^2predict	Exogenous Variables	f^2	VIF
FMTI	0.433	0.379	IC	0.000	2.639
			LC	0.040	2.001
			LGS	0.000	1.598
			LSC	0.022	2.846
			LVC	0.040	1.636
			PN	0.044	2.742
			TL	0.060	1.673
			TOC	0.010	2.736

The coefficient R^2 signifies the proportion of variance in the endogenous variable attributed to all exogenous variables. Ranging from 0 to 1, a higher R^2 indicates enhanced predictive accuracy. The conventional benchmarks for R^2 values categorize them as weak (0.25), moderate (0.50), and substantial

(0.75) levels of predictive accuracy (Hair et al., 2019). In this study, the model prediction exhibited close to moderate, as evidenced by an R^2 value of 0.433.

Assessing the effect size of predictor constructs using Cohen's f^2 (Cohen, 2013) provides insight into their relative impact on an endogenous construct. Cohen defines effect sizes as high (0.35), medium (0.15), and small (0.02) based on f^2 values. The current study's results, presented in Table 5, indicate small effect sizes for the exogenous variables.

The examination of collinearity in Table 5 reveals no multicollinearity concerns in the current study. Both inner model's Variance Inflation Factor (VIF) and outer model's VIF values fall below the threshold of 5.

In PLS version 4, Q^2-Predicts systematically remove and predict each data point of indicators within the reflective measurement model of the endogenous construct. This test evaluates the predictive capabilities of items related to endogenous variables in the structural model. As indicated in Table 5, a Q^2-Predict value exceeding 0 signifies the model's predictive capacity (Hair et al., 2019), establishing a higher level of predictive relevance in the study.

The researchers evaluated the association between constructs in the structural model based on the p-value and t-statistics value. The hypothesized relationship was perceived as significantly accepted when p values were less than 0.05 and T statistics were above 1.96 (Hair et al., 2019). Table 6 indicates that LC, LVC, PN, TL have a significant relationship with FMTI and IC, LGS, LSC, TOC have an insignificant relationship with FMTI.

Control Variables

Table 7 showed that firm age, firm size, annual revenue, ownership structure evidenced no influence in failure to metaverse technology implementation. Firm age, size, revenue, and ownership structure may not directly correlate with readiness to adopt emerging technologies like the metaverse. Malaysian manufacturing firms of varying ages, sizes, and revenue levels may demonstrate similar levels of readiness or resistance to adopting metaverse technology based on factors such as organizational culture, leadership vision, and technological capabilities.

While larger, more established firms have greater financial resources and organizational capacity, this does not necessarily translate into a greater willingness or ability to invest in metaverse technology implementation. Smaller or newer firms demonstrate agility and flexibility in adopting new technolo-

Table 6. Path coefficient result for hypotheses

Paths	Beta	T values	P values	Results
TL -> FMTI	0.235	2.995	0.003	Significant
LGS -> FMTI	0.006	0.091	0.927	Insignificant
IC -> FMTI	0.003	0.036	0.971	Insignificant
PN -> FMTI	0.256	2.840	0.005	Significant
TOC -> FMTI	0.122	1.262	0.207	Insignificant
LSC -> FMTI	-0.186	1.770	0.077	Insignificant
LC -> FMTI	0.208	2.716	0.007	Significant
LVC -> FMTI	0.190	2.121	0.034	Significant

Figure 4. The structural model

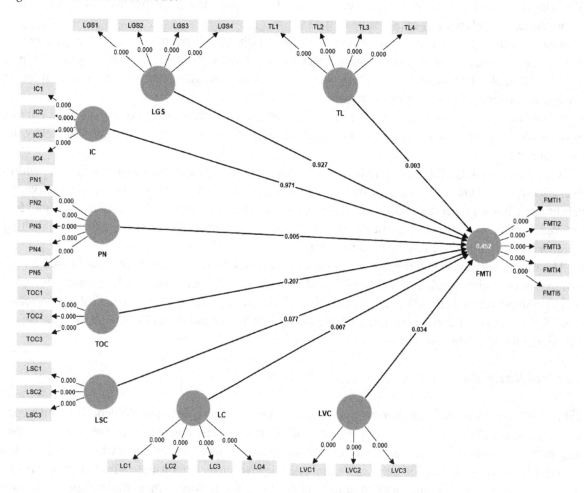

gies, while larger firms face internal barriers such as bureaucracy, inertia, or resistance to change (Polas et al., 2022).

The failure to implement metaverse technology in Malaysian manufacturing firms influenced more by external market dynamics and competitive pressures than internal firm characteristics. Factors such as market demand, industry trends, regulatory environment, and competitive landscape may play a more significant role in shaping technology adoption decisions and implementation outcomes (Hossain et al., 2023).

Table 7. Path coefficient result for control variables

Paths	Beta	T values	P values	Result
Firm age -> FMTI	-0.003	0.055	0.956	No influence
Firm size -> FMTI	-0.020	0.340	0.734	No influence
Annual revenue -> FMTI	0.065	1.060	0.289	No influence
Ownership structure -> FMTI	0.035	0.655	0.512	No influence

DISCUSSION

Result for hypothesis 1 evidenced that technological limitations have significant relationship with failure to metaverse technology implementation. The successful implementation of metaverse technology requires robust infrastructure, including high-speed internet connectivity, powerful hardware, and reliable servers. Technological limitations such as inadequate internet access, outdated hardware, or insufficient server capacity can hinder the performance and scalability of metaverse platforms, leading to user dissatisfaction and limited adoption (Wan et al., 2023). Metaverse technology often relies on interoperability across various devices, operating systems, and software applications. Technological limitations related to compatibility, such as platform-specific restrictions or lack of standardized protocols, can create barriers to seamless integration and interaction within the metaverse environment, undermining user experience and adoption. Technological limitations in implementing robust security measures, such as encryption, authentication, and data protection protocols, can compromise user trust and confidence in the safety and privacy of the metaverse environment, hindering adoption and usage (Dincelli & Yayla, 2022).

Result for hypothesis 2 evidenced that lack of governance and standardization has insignificant relationship with failure to metaverse technology implementation. Malaysian manufacturing firms may not be at the forefront of adopting advanced digital technologies like the metaverse due to various factors such as limited awareness, resource constraints, and focus on traditional manufacturing processes (Hossain et al., 2023). As a result, the absence of governance and standardization specific to metaverse technology may not directly contribute to implementation failures since these firms may not be actively pursuing such initiatives. Malaysian manufacturing firms prioritize investments in other areas of technology that are more directly related to their immediate business needs and objectives (Lada et al., 2023). For example, they may focus on upgrading production machinery, improving supply chain management systems, or implementing enterprise resource planning (ERP) software. In this context, the absence of governance and standardization for metaverse technology not be perceived as a critical factor affecting implementation success. Malaysia need to develop specific regulations or policies governing metaverse technology implementation in manufacturing firms (Ooi et al., 2023). While the absence of governance and standardization could potentially lead to challenges such as interoperability issues or data privacy concerns, the impact may be minimal if there are no explicit regulatory requirements or industry standards mandating compliance with metaverse technology.

Result for hypothesis 3 evidenced that integration challenges has insignificant relationship with failure to metaverse technology implementation. The current level of interconnectedness and digitalization in Malaysian manufacturing firms relatively low compared to firms in more advanced economies (Hossain et al., 2023). Consequently, the need for integrating metaverse technology with existing systems and processes may not be as pressing, and integration challenges may not be perceived as significant obstacles to implementation failure. The organizational readiness for digital transformation and innovation in Malaysia manufacturing firms vary. Some firms lack the internal capabilities and change management processes required to effectively integrate metaverse solutions into their operations (Lee et al., 2024). However, the impact of integration challenges on implementation failure can be limited if firms are not actively pursuing metaverse initiatives or if they are focusing on other technology priorities.

Result for hypothesis 4 evidenced that poor diffusion through the network has significant relationship with failure to metaverse technology implementation. Poor diffusion through the network implies that information about metaverse technology and its potential benefits may not reach key stakeholders within Malaysia manufacturing firms (Yao et al., 2024). If decision-makers, employees, and other relevant parties are unaware or do not fully understand the concept and value proposition of metaverse technology, they may be hesitant to invest resources or support its implementation. Inefficient diffusion through the network may result in a lack of knowledge sharing and collaboration among different departments or units within manufacturing firms. Without effective communication channels and mechanisms for sharing information about metaverse technology, opportunities for learning, experimentation, and innovation may be missed, leading to implementation failures.

Result for hypothesis 5 evidenced that traditional organization culture has insignificant relationship with failure to metaverse technology implementation. Malaysia manufacturing firms have a traditional organizational culture that prioritizes stability, hierarchy, and adherence to established practices (Adinew, 2023). However, if these firms have not yet embraced digital transformation or advanced technological solutions, the influence of traditional culture on metaverse technology implementation may be minimal. In such cases, failure to adopt metaverse technology may stem from factors unrelated to organizational culture, such as resource constraints or lack of awareness. While traditional organizational cultures value stability and continuity, they can also foster openness to innovation and adaptation. Malaysian manufacturing firms with a progressive mindset actively seek opportunities to leverage emerging technologies like the metaverse to enhance their operations and gain a competitive edge. In such organizations, traditional culture not impedes metaverse technology implementation but rather encourage exploration and experimentation. Organizations with a traditional culture can still demonstrate adaptability and flexibility in embracing new technologies. Malaysia manufacturing firms recognize the need to evolve and modernize their operations in response to changing market conditions, even if they maintain traditional cultural values. In such cases, organizational culture may not be a significant barrier to metaverse technology implementation.

Result for hypothesis 6 evidenced that lack of stakeholder commitment has insignificant relationship with failure to metaverse technology implementation. Stakeholders within Malaysian manufacturing firms may have limited awareness and understanding of metaverse technology and its potential applications. As a result, their lack of commitment may stem from a lack of familiarity with the technology rather than a deliberate resistance to its implementation. In such cases, failure to implement metaverse technology may be more closely linked to knowledge gaps or educational needs rather than stakeholder commitment. Malaysian manufacturing firms face resource constraints in terms of finances, technical expertise, and infrastructure (Lee et al., 2023). The lack of stakeholder commitment to metaverse technology implementation can be a reflection of these resource limitations rather than a fundamental opposition to the technology (Hossain et al., 2023). Stakeholders may be willing to support technology initiatives in principle but lack the resources to allocate towards implementation efforts. Stakeholder commitment to technology implementation can be influenced by competing organizational priorities and strategic objectives. Malaysian manufacturing firms may have limited capacity to invest in metaverse technology due to other pressing business needs or market challenges. In such cases, the lack of stakeholder commitment can be driven by strategic considerations rather than inherent resistance to the technology itself. Stakeholders may perceive metaverse technology as risky or uncertain, particularly if they are unfamiliar with its potential benefits and drawbacks.

Result for hypothesis 7 evidenced that the implementation of metaverse technology, a virtual world where users can communicate with each other in a computer-generated environment, can be significantly influenced by a lack of collaboration. A lack of collaboration can lead to technological limitations within an organization. Without effective collaboration, it can be challenging to overcome these limitations, which are among the most significant barriers to implementing metaverse technology (Bag et al., 2023).

Successful implementation of any new technology requires commitment from all stakeholders. This includes employees, management, and customers. If there is a lack of collaboration, it can be challenging to secure this commitment, which can lead to a failure in the implementation process.

Result for hypothesis 8 evidenced that low perception of value by customers has a significant relationship with failure to metaverse technology implementation. The success of any technology depends on its adoption by users. If customers perceive low value in the metaverse, they are less likely to use it, leading to low user adoption rates (Hadi et al., 2024). Businesses invest in new technologies like the metaverse expecting a return on their investment. If customers perceive low value, they are less likely to engage with the metaverse, affecting the ROI. Customer perception can influence the direction of innovation and development. If customers perceive low value, it may discourage further innovation and development in metaverse technology. If a company's metaverse implementation is perceived as low value by customers, it can negatively impact the company's brand reputation. Metaverse technology can provide a competitive advantage to businesses (Gauttier et al., 2024). However, if customers perceive low value, this advantage is diminished

Theoretical Implications

The current study extends Technology-Organization-Environment (TOE) theory. Investigating the constraints of implementing the metaverse allows for a deeper understanding of the technological characteristics specific to this innovative domain. The implementation of metaverse technology requires organizations to develop new capabilities, processes, and structures to leverage its potential effectively. Investigating the constraints of metaverse implementation within organizations sheds light on organizational readiness factors such as leadership support, change management practices, employee skills, and cultural alignment. Understanding how these organizational factors interact with the unique characteristics of the metaverse can provide valuable insights into the adoption process and implementation challenges. The metaverse operates within a dynamic and multifaceted environmental context that includes regulatory frameworks, industry standards, market dynamics, and societal trends. Investigating the constraints of metaverse implementation extends the TOE framework by exploring how external environmental factors influence adoption decisions and implementation strategies. This includes considerations such as legal and regulatory barriers, market competition, ecosystem partnerships, and user preferences, which shape the adoption trajectory of metaverse technologies within organizations.

Practical Implications

This study contributes in practice by highlighting the importance and significance of metaverse in different sectors (e.g., education, industry, entertainment) and identifying eight main barriers that can be faced while implementing metaverse. Although all the identified constraints are crucial, the findings provide some suggestions to focus on more on technological limitations, poor diffusion through the network, and lack of collaboration and low perception of value by customers.

Understanding the constraints can help managers develop more effective strategic plans for Metaverse implementation. By identifying barriers early on, managers can adjust their plans to mitigate risks and allocate resources more efficiently. Managers can allocate resources more effectively by understanding which constraints are most significant. This might involve investing in employee training, upgrading infrastructure, or partnering with external experts to overcome specific challenges. Identifying constraints allows managers to assess potential risks associated with Metaverse implementation and develop risk management strategies accordingly. This might involve creating contingency plans, securing insurance coverage, or implementing robust cybersecurity measures. Managers can use insights from examining constraints to inform their decisions about which Metaverse technologies to adopt. For example, if connectivity issues are identified as a significant constraint, managers might prioritize technologies that are less reliant on stable internet connections.

Implementing the Metaverse often requires significant changes in organizational culture, processes, and workflows. By understanding the constraints, managers can develop change management strategies to minimize resistance and facilitate smooth transitions. Organizations need to maintain flexible culture, rather than traditional culture. Subsequently, the stakeholders (e.g., customers, employees, suppliers) need to work together to adopt metaverse.

Furthermore, the IT facilities need to be more developed to mitigate technical problems, and network diffusion. Thus, the barriers of metaverse implementation can be diminished with a collaborative approach between stakeholders from different sectors, and it will make their work more efficient.

Limitations and Future Research Directions

Despite significant theoretical and empirical contributions, this study acknowledges a few limitations. First, a single survey method can cause CMB issues. However, statistical post-hoc procedures were taken into account to eradicate this issue. Secondly, this study examines a single counry (Malaysia) and single industry (Manufacturing). Service firms from other regions can be explored. Thirdly, this study used single method and cross-sectional quantitative survey. Other researchers can use comparative, qualitative, mixed or longitudinal studies to enhance generability. Other moderating or mediating variables, such as resource commitment, innovating behaviour of firms etc., can be considered with this model.

REFERENCES

Adinew, Y. (2023). A comparative study on motivational strategies, organizational culture, and climate in public and private institutions. *Current Psychology (New Brunswick, N.J.)*, 1–23.

Akpan, I. J., Soopramanien, D., & Kwak, D. H. (2021). Cutting-edge technologies for small business and innovation in the era of COVID-19 global health pandemic. *Journal of Small Business and Entrepreneurship*, *33*(6), 607–617. doi:10.1080/08276331.2020.1799294

Al-Taie, M. Z., & Kadry, S. (2017). Information Diffusion in Social Networks. In *Python for Graph and Network Analysis. Advanced Information and Knowledge Processing*. Springer. doi:10.1007/978-3-319-53004-8_8

Allam, Z., Sharifi, A., Bibri, S. E., Jones, D. S., & Krogstie, J. (2022). The metaverse as a virtual form of smart cities: Opportunities and challenges for environmental, economic, and social sustainability in urban futures. *Smart Cities*, *5*(3), 771–801. doi:10.3390/smartcities5030040

Bagozzi, R. P., Yi, Y., & Phillips, L. W. (1991). Assessing construct validity in organizational research. *Administrative Science Quarterly*, *36*(3), 421–458. doi:10.2307/2393203

Cohen, J., Cohen, P., West, S. G., & Aiken, L. S. (2013). *Applied multiple regression/correlation analysis for the behavioral sciences.* Routledge. doi:10.4324/9780203774441

Creed, C., Al-Kalbani, M., Theil, A., Sarcar, S., & Williams, I. (2024). Inclusive AR/VR: Accessibility barriers for immersive technologies. *Universal Access in the Information Society, 23*(1), 59–73. doi:10.1007/s10209-023-00969-0

Cronbach, L. J. (1951). Coefficient alpha and the internal structure of tests. *psychometrika, 16*(3), 297-334.

Dincelli, E., & Yayla, A. (2022). Immersive virtual reality in the age of the Metaverse: A hybrid-narrative review based on the technology affordance perspective. *The Journal of Strategic Information Systems, 31*(2), 101717. doi:10.1016/j.jsis.2022.101717

Dwivedi, Y. K., Hughes, L., Baabdullah, A. M., Ribeiro-Navarrete, S., Giannakis, M., Al-Debei, M. M., Dennehy, D., Metri, B., Buhalis, D., Cheung, C. M. K., Conboy, K., Doyle, R., Dubey, R., Dutot, V., Felix, R., Goyal, D. P., Gustafsson, A., Hinsch, C., Jebabli, I., & Wamba, S. F. (2022). Metaverse beyond the hype: Multidisciplinary perspectives on emerging challenges, opportunities, and agenda for research, practice and policy. *International Journal of Information Management, 66*, 102542. doi:10.1016/j.ijinfomgt.2022.102542

Fernández-Caramés, T. M., & Fraga-Lamas, P. (2024). Forging the Industrial Metaverse-Where Industry 5.0, Augmented and Mixed Reality, IIoT, Opportunistic Edge Computing and Digital Twins Meet. *arXiv preprint arXiv:2403.11312.*

Fornell, C., & Larcker, D. F. (1981). Evaluating structural equation models with unobservable variables and measurement error. *JMR, Journal of Marketing Research, 18*(1), 39–50. doi:10.1177/002224378101800104

Friis, K., & Lysne, O. (2021). Huawei, 5G and security: Technological limitations and political responses. *Development and Change, 52*(5), 1174–1195. doi:10.1111/dech.12680

Gauttier, S., Simouri, W., & Milliat, A. (2024). When to enter the metaverse: Business leaders offer perspectives. *The Journal of Business Strategy, 45*(1), 2–9. doi:10.1108/JBS-08-2022-0149

Ghobakhloo, M., & Ching, N. T. (2019). Adoption of digital technologies of smart manufacturing in SMEs. *Journal of Industrial Information Integration, 16*, 100107. doi:10.1016/j.jii.2019.100107

Hadi, R., Melumad, S., & Park, E. S. (2024). The Metaverse: A new digital frontier for consumer behavior. *Journal of Consumer Psychology, 34*(1), 142–166. doi:10.1002/jcpy.1356

Hair, J. F., Risher, J. J., Sarstedt, M., & Ringle, C. M. (2019). When to use and how to report the results of PLS-SEM. *European Business Review, 31*(1), 2–24. doi:10.1108/EBR-11-2018-0203

Han, E., Miller, M. R., Ram, N., Nowak, K. L., & Bailenson, J. N. (2022, May). Understanding group behavior in virtual reality: A large-scale, longitudinal study in the metaverse. In *72nd Annual International Communication Association Conference*, Paris, France.

Henseler, J., Ringle, C. M., & Sarstedt, M. (2015). A new criterion for assessing discriminant validity in variance-based structural equation modeling. *Journal of the Academy of Marketing Science, 43*(1), 115–135. doi:10.1007/s11747-014-0403-8

Hossain, M. I., Kumar, J., Islam, M. T., & Valeri, M. (2023). The interplay among paradoxical leadership, industry 4.0 technologies, organisational ambidexterity, strategic flexibility and corporate sustainable performance in manufacturing SMEs of Malaysia. *European Business Review*. doi:10.1108/EBR-04-2023-0109

Hossain, M. I., Ong, T. S., Tabash, M. I., & Teh, B. H. (2024). The panorama of corporate environmental sustainability and green values: Evidence of Bangladesh. *Environment, Development and Sustainability*, *26*(1), 1033–1059. doi:10.1007/s10668-022-02748-y

Hossain, M. I., San Ong, T., Teh, B. H., Said, R. M., & Siow, M. L. (2022). Nexus of Stakeholder Integration, Green Investment, Green Technology Adoption and Environmental Sustainability Practices: Evidence from Bangladesh Textile SMEs. *Pertanika Journal of Social Science & Humanities*, *30*(1). doi:10.47836/pjssh.30.1.14

Hossain, M. I., Teh, B. H., Dorasamy, M., Tabash, M. I., & Ong, T. S. (2023, May). Ethical Leadership, Green HRM Practices and Environmental Performance of Manufacturing SMEs at Selangor, Malaysia: Moderating Role of Green Technology Adoption. In *International Scientific Conference on Business and Economics* (pp. 85-104). Cham: Springer Nature Switzerland. 10.1007/978-3-031-42511-0_6

Julian, H. L. C., Chung, T., & Wang, Y. (2023). Adoption of Metaverse in South East Asia: Vietnam, Indonesia, Malaysia. In *Strategies and Opportunities for Technology in the Metaverse World* (pp. 196–234). IGI Global. doi:10.4018/978-1-6684-5732-0.ch012

Kock, N. (2015). Common method bias in PLS-SEM: A full collinearity assessment approach. [ijec]. *International Journal of e-Collaboration*, *11*(4), 1–10. doi:10.4018/ijec.2015100101

Lada, S., Chekima, B., Karim, M. R. A., Fabeil, N. F., Ayub, M. S., Amirul, S. M., Ansar, R., Bouteraa, M., Fook, L. M., & Zaki, H. O. (2023). Determining factors related to artificial intelligence (AI) adoption among Malaysia's small and medium-sized businesses. *Journal of Open Innovation*, *9*(4), 100144. doi:10.1016/j.joitmc.2023.100144

Lee, K. L., Teong, C. X., Alzoubi, H. M., Alshurideh, M. T., Khatib, M. E., & Al-Gharaibeh, S. M. (2024). Digital supply chain transformation: The role of smart technologies on operational performance in manufacturing industry. *International Journal of Engineering Business Management*, *16*, 18479790241234986. doi:10.1177/18479790241234986

Lee, K. L., Wong, S. Y., Alzoubi, H. M., Al Kurdi, B., Alshurideh, M. T., & El Khatib, M. (2023). Adopting smart supply chain and smart technologies to improve operational performance in manufacturing industry. *International Journal of Engineering Business Management*, *15*, 18479790231200614. doi:10.1177/18479790231200614

Li, J. (2022). Impact of Metaverse cultural communication on the mental health of international students in China: Highlighting effects of healthcare anxiety and cyberchondria. *American Journal of Health Behavior*, *46*(6), 809–820. doi:10.5993/AJHB.46.6.21 PMID:36721290

Mainardes, E. W., & Freitas, N. P. D. (2023). The effects of perceived value dimensions on customer satisfaction and loyalty: A comparison between traditional banks and fintechs. *International Journal of Bank Marketing*, *41*(3), 641–662. doi:10.1108/IJBM-10-2022-0437

Mammadova, A. (2023). *Digital big-bang Metaverse: opportunities and threats* [Master's thesis, Università Ca' Foscari Venezia]. http://dspace.unive.it/handle/10579/25766

Martinez-Millana, A., Bayo-Monton, J. L., Lizondo, A., Fernandez-Llatas, C., & Traver, V. (2016). Evaluation of Google Glass technical limitations on their integration in medical systems. *Sensors (Basel)*, *16*(12), 2142. doi:10.3390/s16122142 PMID:27983691

Mourtzis, D. (2023). The Metaverse in Industry 5.0: A Human-Centric Approach towards Personalized Value Creation. *Encyclopedia*, *3*(3), 1105–1120. doi:10.3390/encyclopedia3030080

Mozumder, M. A. I., Sheeraz, M. M., Athar, A., Aich, S., & Kim, H. C. (2022, February). Overview: Technology roadmap of the future trend of metaverse based on IoT, blockchain, AI technique, and medical domain metaverse activity. In *2022 24th International Conference on Advanced Communication Technology (ICACT)* (pp. 256-261). IEEE.

Netemeyer, R. G., Bearden, W. O., & Sharma, S. (2003). *Scaling procedures: Issues and applications.* sage publications.

Nunes, G. S., & Filho, E. J. M. A. (2018b). Consumer behavior regarding wearable technologies: Google Glass. *Innovation & Management Review*, *15*(3), 230–246. doi:10.1108/INMR-06-2018-0034

Ooi, K. B., Tan, G. W. H., Al-Emran, M., Al-Sharafi, M. A., Arpaci, I., Zaidan, A. A., ... Iranmanesh, M. (2023). The metaverse in engineering management: Overview, opportunities, challenges, and future research agenda. *IEEE Transactions on Engineering Management.*

Park, J., & Kim, N. (2024). Examining self-congruence between user and avatar in purchasing behavior from the metaverse to the real world. *Journal of Global Fashion Marketing*, *15*(1), 23–38. doi:10.1080/20932685.2023.2180768

Peltonen, T. (2019). Case Study 4: The Collapse of Nokia's Mobile Phone Business, Springer Books. In *Towards Wise Management* (pp. 163–188). Springer. doi:10.1007/978-3-319-91719-1_6

Polas, M. R. H., Jahanshahi, A. A., Kabir, A. I., Sohel-Uz-Zaman, A. S. M., Osman, A. R., & Karim, R. (2022). Artificial intelligence, blockchain technology, and risk-taking behavior in the 4.0 IR Metaverse Era: Evidence from Bangladesh-based SMEs. *Journal of Open Innovation*, *8*(3), 168. doi:10.3390/joitmc8030168

Queiroz, M. M., Wamba, S. F., Pereira, S. C. F., & Jabbour, C. J. C. (2023). The metaverse as a breakthrough for operations and supply chain management: Implications and call for action. *International Journal of Operations & Production Management*, *43*(10), 1539–1553. doi:10.1108/IJOPM-01-2023-0006

Rahman, K. R., Shitol, S. K., Islam, M. S., Iftekhar, K. T., & Pranto, S. A. H. A. (2023). Use of Metaverse Technology in Education Domain. *Journal of Metaverse*, *3*(1), 79–86. doi:10.57019/jmv.1223704

Seo, J., Kim, K., Park, M., Park, M., & Lee, K. (2018). An Analysis of Economic Impact on IOT Industry under GDPR. *Mobile Information Systems*, *2018*, 1–6. doi:10.1155/2018/6792028

Sheth, J. (2020). Business of business is more than business: Managing during the Covid crisis. *Industrial Marketing Management*, *88*, 261–264. doi:10.1016/j.indmarman.2020.05.028

Sweeney, J. C., & Soutar, G. N. (2001). Consumer perceived value: The development of a multiple item scale. *Journal of Retailing*, *77*(2), 203–220. doi:10.1016/S0022-4359(01)00041-0

Teo, K. S., & Wong, Y. W. (2023). *The determinants of Augmented Reality (AR) marketing affect purchase intention in the beauty and makeup industry among gen z in Malaysia* [Doctoral dissertation, UTAR].

Uddin, M. R. (2024). The role of the digital economy in Bangladesh's economic development. *Sustainable Technology and Entrepreneurship*, *3*(1), 100054. doi:10.1016/j.stae.2023.100054

Wallace, R. S. O., & Cooke, T. E. (1990). The diagnosis and resolution of emerging issues in corporate disclosure practices. *Accounting and Business Research*, *20*(78), 143–151. doi:10.1080/00014788.1990.9728872

Wan, X., Zhang, G., Yuan, Y., & Chai, S. (2023). How to drive the participation willingness of supply chain members in metaverse technology adoption? *Applied Soft Computing*, *145*, 110611. doi:10.1016/j.asoc.2023.110611

Wiangkham, A., & Vongvit, R. (2023). Exploring the Drivers for the Adoption of Metaverse Technology in Engineering Education using PLS-SEM and ANFIS. *Education and Information Technologies*, 1–28.

Yang, L. (2023). Recommendations for metaverse governance based on technical standards. *Humanities & Social Sciences Communications*, *10*(1), 1–10. doi:10.1057/s41599-023-01750-7

Yao, X., Ma, N., Zhang, J., Wang, K., Yang, E., & Faccio, M. (2024). Enhancing wisdom manufacturing as industrial metaverse for industry and society 5.0. *Journal of Intelligent Manufacturing*, *35*(1), 235–255. doi:10.1007/s10845-022-02027-7

Zhang, Q. (2023). Secure Preschool Education Using Machine Learning and Metaverse Technologies. *Applied Artificial Intelligence*, *37*(1), 2222496. doi:10.1080/08839514.2023.2222496

Zheng, Z., Li, T., Li, B., Chai, X., Song, W., Chen, N., & Li, R. (2022, December). Industrial metaverse: connotation, features, technologies, applications and challenges. In *Asian Simulation Conference* (pp. 239-263). Singapore: Springer Nature Singapore. 10.1007/978-981-19-9198-1_19

Chapter 15
Unleashing the Power of Research, Innovation, and Industry Impacts:
Exploring the Transformative Role of the Metaverse in Business and Commerce

Paramjeet Kumar
https://orcid.org/0000-0002-3824-2289
North Eastern Hill University, India

ABSTRACT

The notion of the metaverse has garnered substantial attention in recent years, captivating the imagination and piquing the interest of researchers, inventors, and industry executives alike. This chapter, "Unleashing the Power of Research, Innovation, and Industry Impacts: Exploring the Transformative Role of the Metaverse in Business and Commerce," seeks to investigate the potential of the metaverse and its impact on several facets of business and commerce. This proposal aims to examine the present patterns in metaverse research, which are influenced by applications that exploit the merging of interdisciplinary technologies. The advancement of developing technologies presents diverse prospects for the use of the metaverse in the realms of industry and commerce.

INTRODUCTION

The metaverse has garnered considerable interest in recent years, especially due to improvements in digital technology and the emergence of immersive virtual experiences. Although there have been limited surveys conducted on the metaverse, extant research may be classified into three primary domains: defining the metaverse, identifying the necessary conditions for its implementation and utilisation, and exploring the enabling technologies, applications, and problems associated with the metaverse (Ismail & Buyya, 2023). Within the initial category, scholars have concentrated their efforts

DOI: 10.4018/979-8-3693-2607-7.ch015

on precisely delineating the nature and characteristics of the metaverse. The metaverse, as determined in a comprehensive analysis of existing literature, is a virtual world that is immersive, synchronous, and persistent. It enables users, who are represented by avatars, to engage in interactions with both the environment and other users (source) (Ismail & Buyya, 2023). Conducting research in the metaverse is essential for fully realising its potential and comprehending its influential position in the realms of business and commerce.

UNDERSTANDING THE ROLE OF INNOVATION IN BUSINESS TRANSFORMATION

In the realm of business transformation, innovation assumes a pivotal role, and its importance is further magnified within the metaverse. The information systems literature has placed significant focus on the technical advancements of digital technologies and their influence on the value generated by businesses (Verhoef et al., 2021). Yet, to truly utilise the potential of the metaverse, it is crucial to investigate how innovation may propel change within this immersive digital realm. Research on innovation in the metaverse has concentrated on diverse facets, such as the advancement of fresh digital tools and technology, the establishment of unique business models, the investigation of untapped market prospects, and the improvement of user experiences. An area of innovation in the metaverse is the rise of Non-Fungible Tokens (NFTs) and virtual currency. NFTs have emerged as a favoured avenue for online businesses to delve into the metaverse, enabling the creation of distinctive digital assets and virtual advertising campaigns (Cui & Du, 2023). This novel methodology of asset ownership and digital transactions has the capacity to transform industries like as art, gaming, fashion, and others. Another domain of advancement inside the metaverse involves the progress of wearable devices. With the increasing prevalence of the metaverse, there is an anticipated surge in the sales of wearable devices. These devices, such as virtual reality headsets and augmented reality glasses, enhance users' experience in the metaverse by offering a more immersive and participatory environment. Moreover, the incorporation of artificial intelligence and machine learning technologies into the metaverse is also fueling innovation. These technologies has the capacity to improve personalisation, optimise user experiences, and offer vital insights for enterprises operating in the metaverse.

Exploring Industry Impacts Within the Metaverse

The metaverse possesses the capacity to profoundly influence several industries, revolutionising their operational methods and client interactions. The entertainment and media business is poised to undergo significant transformation due to the metaverse. The metaverse's immersive and interactive characteristics offer novel opportunities for storytelling, gaming, and content creation. By utilising the metaverse, entertainment and media organisations have the ability to craft distinctive and captivating encounters for their viewers, effectively erasing the boundaries between virtual and physical realms. As an illustration, virtual reality technology enables the streaming of live concerts and events, enabling individuals from different parts of the globe to engage in a collective experience. This not only broadens the scope of these events but also creates new sources of income through virtual ticket sales and virtual merchandising. Commerce is another industry that can derive advantages from the metaverse.

The Transformative Role of the Metaverse in Business and Commerce

The metaverse possesses the capacity to fundamentally transform the way businesses function and interact with their clientele. Smartphone firms aim to provide a competitive metaverse experience and take the lead in its development, in collaboration with Microsoft and Facebook. The competition in the smartphone market underscores the increasing acknowledgment of the metaverse as a powerful catalyst for change in the realms of business and commerce. As cutting-edge technologies like blockchain, augmented reality, virtual reality, artificial intelligence, 3D reconstruction, and the Internet of Things persistently fuel investment prospects in the metaverse, businesses in various sectors are increasingly adopting and supporting its growth. These industry participants acknowledge that the metaverse possesses the potential to generate fresh sources of income, improve client experiences, and stimulate innovation. For instance, in the realm of commerce, enterprises have the ability to establish virtual stores within the metaverse, enabling customers to navigate and buy things in a digital setting that replicates the actual shopping encounter. This not only creates more avenues for generating revenue but also offers organisations valuable data and insights regarding customer behaviour, preferences, and trends. In addition, the metaverse has the capability to enable virtual meetings and conferences, so eliminating the necessity for physical travel and decreasing expenses for organisations. The COVID-19 epidemic has greatly expedited the transition to virtual meetings and conferences, as organisations globally have had to adjust to distant work arrangements. The metaverse presents prospects for corporations to engage in collaborative efforts and foster innovation. Companies can utilise the collaborative virtual environment offered by consumer devices to enhance teamwork, foster innovation, and facilitate problem-solving.

Collaborative virtual environments in the metaverse facilitate the convergence of employees from various locations, utilising the immersive encounter to augment communication and production. In addition, the metaverse has the potential to stimulate innovation by offering a platform for conducting experiments and developing prototypes. Enterprises have the ability to experiment with novel ideas and concepts within a simulated setting, enabling faster and more economical iterations prior to applying modifications in the tangible realm. The metaverse plays a significant role in business and commerce, and this function is reinforced by advancements in artificial intelligence technologies. By incorporating AI computing into the metaverse, businesses may utilise virtual agents and clever algorithms to improve user experiences and increase immersion. These virtual agents have the capability to offer tailored suggestions, aid, and help to users within the metaverse, resulting in a more captivating and dynamic setting. They possess the ability to adjust to users' tastes and behaviours, predict their requirements, and offer immediate support. The degree of customisation and adaptability not only improves the user's experience but also creates opportunities for precise marketing and tailored advertising within the metaverse.

The Metaverse: A New Frontier for Business Innovation

The metaverse presents a novel opportunity for corporate innovation, enabling organisations to explore and use virtual environments to engage with customers, cooperate with partners, and enhance growth and competitiveness. The metaverse disrupts conventional business paradigms and creates novel prospects for research, innovation, and industry influence by erasing the distinctions between the physical and virtual realms. Businesses may optimise their utilisation of research, innovation, and industry impacts by effectively exploiting the possibilities of the metaverse. The metaverse empowers businesses to create immersive and interactive experiences that surpass the constraints of conventional online platforms by incorporating cutting-edge technologies like blockchain, augmented reality, virtual reality, artificial intelligence, 3D reconstruction, and the Internet of Things. Furthermore, the metaverse not only enhances customer experiences but also fundamentally changes the internal operations of enterprises. Through the establishment of virtual workspaces and collaboration platforms within the metaverse, enterprises may facilitate distant collaborations, enhance productivity, cultivate creativity and innovation, and overcome geographical limitations.

Driving Commercial Success Through Metaverse Integration

Incorporating the metaverse into business structures holds the capacity to propel economic triumph throughout diverse industries. Through the use of the metaverse, businesses can tap into untapped markets, expand their customer reach, and augment their brand's prominence. They have the ability to generate virtual showrooms and storefronts, enabling customers to engage with and buy products in immersive and engaging settings. This not only improves the overall customer purchasing experience but also yields vital data and insights for targeted marketing and product development. Through the examination of user behaviour and preferences within the metaverse, firms can customise their marketing campaigns to target certain client categories, providing individualised adverts and promotions. Moreover, the metaverse offers a medium for virtual events and conferences, allowing enterprises to engage with worldwide audiences without being limited by physical boundaries. This presents possibilities for enterprises to broaden their scope, allure international partners and customers, and cultivate collaboration on a worldwide level.

Metaverse: Shaping Future Commerce and Trade

The metaverse possesses the capacity to fundamentally transform the trajectory of commerce and trade in the future. The metaverse allows businesses to create distinctive and captivating experiences for their customers, thanks to its immersive and interactive characteristics. These experiences not only allure and maintain clients but also offer opportunity for businesses to distinguish themselves in a saturated market. Furthermore, the metaverse enables effortless amalgamation of physical and digital realms, hence fostering the development of groundbreaking business frameworks. As an illustration, the metaverse has the potential to facilitate businesses in providing virtual try-on experiences for products like apparel and cosmetics, enabling buyers to preview the appearance and fit of items before to making a purchase. This not only mitigates the likelihood of product returns and enhances consumer contentment, but also diminishes expenses linked to tangible inventory and retail premises. Moreover, the metaverse holds the capacity to completely transform supply chain management. Through the creation of a virtual depiction of the complete supply chain process, firms can enhance operational efficiency, minimise inefficiencies, and enhance transparency. This can result in expedited and more efficient procedures, hence decreasing expenses and enhancing overall efficiency.

Exploring the Metaverse's Potential in the Corporate World

The metaverse presents significant promise within the corporate realm, including prospects for research, innovation, and industry ramifications. The metaverse enhances user experience by digitising real-life encounters, resulting in improved efficiency and intuitiveness in professional tasks, as well as enhancing social interactions and leisure options (Dong & Liu, 2023). Moreover, the metaverse offers a cooperative digital setting that is crucial for creating immersive experiences of superior quality. Consumer devices are essential in facilitating this environment, as they play a pivotal role in enabling people to actively participate in the metaverse. The efficacy of research in the metaverse resides in its capacity to collect and scrutinise data derived from virtual encounters. These observations can be utilised to guide strategic choices, discern client patterns, and stimulate creativity. Furthermore, the metaverse provides a distinct platform for conducting experiments and creating prototypes. Businesses have the ability to experiment with novel concepts, goods, and services in a simulated setting prior to committing resources to actual execution. This not only decreases expenses but also mitigates risks linked to failure. The metaverse offers limitless opportunities for developing innovative business models.

Revolutionizing Industries Through Research and Innovation in the Metaverse

All industries have the opportunity to gain advantages from the revolutionary capabilities of the metaverse. The media and entertainment business is highly susceptible to upheaval. The metaverse enables media and entertainment organisations to develop captivating virtual experiences for their audiences. These experiences encompass a wide variety of activities, such as virtual concerts, live events, and interactive games, providing a heightened level of involvement and entertainment. The metaverse has the potential to bring significant advantages to the manufacturing industry. Manufacturers can enhance their manufacturing processes by utilising the metaverse to generate virtual simulations, enabling improved planning and optimisation with greater efficiency and effectiveness. The metaverse has the potential to revolutionise the medical and healthcare industries. Virtual reality simulations in the metaverse offer medical professionals the opportunity to engage in lifelike training scenarios, enabling them to refine their abilities and enhance their expertise inside a secure and regulated setting. Moreover, the metaverse holds the capacity to completely transform commerce. Within the metaverse, conventional physical stores can be converted into virtual storefronts, enabling customers to peruse and acquire things from the convenience of their residences. The metaverse enables e-commerce companies to provide customised shopping experiences by incorporating virtual reality technology, allowing users to virtually try on clothing and test products prior to making a purchase.

The Future of Business: Embracing the Metaverse for Sustainable Growth

Adopting the metaverse has the potential to foster sustainable expansion for enterprises through various means. To begin with, the metaverse enables enhanced efficiency and production. Through the utilisation of virtual simulations and immersive experiences, organisations have the ability to optimise operations, decrease expenses, and enhance overall efficiency. Manufacturers can utilise virtual simulations within the metaverse to evaluate and enhance their production processes, leading to increased operational efficiency. This can result in reduced expenses and enhanced productivity, hence fostering sustainable expansion. Furthermore, the metaverse presents novel avenues for generating income and exploring entrepreneurial prospects. By using the metaverse, firms can access untapped markets and develop cutting-edge offerings. Companies have the ability to generate virtual experiences and events that appeal to a worldwide audience, so extending their influence beyond the constraints of physical boundaries. This creates other sources of income and broadens the company's operations, decreasing dependence on conventional channels. Moreover, the metaverse promotes cooperation and originality. The metaverse fosters cross-disciplinary collaborations and idea exchange by providing a virtual platform for individuals and corporations to engage and collaborate. This fosters ingenuity and originality, resulting in the creation of novel products, services, and solutions capable of tackling intricate problems and satisfying ever-changing client demands. Through the utilisation of research, innovation, and industrial impacts, the metaverse have the capability to initiate profound transformations in business and commerce. Through harnessing the potential of research, organisations can discover significant insights and patterns that can guide their strategies and decision-making in the metaverse. Moreover, cultivating a culture of innovation within the organisation can stimulate experimentation and the creation of pioneering technologies and solutions in the metaverse. These innovations can have profound and extensive effects, not just within the organisation but also across many industries and sectors. Effectively utilising the capabilities of the metaverse necessitates adopting a conscientious stance towards technology. It is crucial for businesses to give utmost importance to ethical issues, data privacy, and security in the metaverse in order to safeguard user information and uphold confidence. Furthermore, it is crucial to prioritise inclusion and accessibility in order to guarantee that all individuals, irrespective of their background or skills, may fully access and benefit from the metaverse. The metaverse has significant potential to revolutionise industry and trade, but it also poses issues and considerations that need to be tackled. An essential obstacle in the metaverse revolves on the matter of social inclusion and justice. With the increasing prevalence of the metaverse, it is imperative to prioritise the protection and equitable access to opportunities and resources for vulnerable populations in this virtual realm. Another obstacle that arises is the requirement for interoperability and standardisation. As the metaverse progresses and grows, several platforms and technologies may arise, resulting in a fragmented environment. This can impede the smooth collaboration and communication between users and businesses functioning within the metaverse. In order to surmount these obstacles, it is imperative to engage in industrial collaboration and establish partnerships. Enterprises can collaborate to build shared standards and protocols that facilitate interoperability and guarantee a unified user experience across diverse platforms. The metaverse optimises work processes by digitising real-world experiences and providing a collaborative virtual environment that improves efficiency and intuitiveness, resulting in an immersive user experience. Additionally, it offers prospects for social engagement, amusement, and the investigation of virtual realms. The metaverse amalgamates technology, innovation, and industrial effects in a revolutionary manner. By doing research and fostering innovation, businesses have the ability to harness the full potential of the metaverse in order to fundamentally transform many facets of commerce. The metaverse provides organisations with fresh opportunities for customer involvement, product development, and marketing techniques. Through the utilisation of the metaverse, businesses can generate captivating and engaging encounters for their clientele, enabling them to navigate and examine items or services within a virtual environment prior to completing a transaction. This can result in heightened consumer satisfaction and loyalty. Moreover, the metaverse possesses the capacity to profoundly alter conventional supply chains and distribution models. Through the integration of virtual reality, augmented reality, and blockchain technology, businesses may optimise operations, minimise expenses, and expand their reach to a worldwide audience more effortlessly. In order to effectively harness the potential of research, innovation, and industrial effects in the metaverse, it is crucial to examine its revolutionary influence on business and commerce using a multidimensional strategy. This entails analysing the technological, social, and economic aspects of the metaverse and examining how they interconnect. Through an analysis of how industry leaders like Meta, Microsoft, Decentraland, and Nvidia implement metaverses, we may obtain vital knowledge about the practical uses and prospective advantages of the metaverse in the business sector.

REFERENCES

Cui, H., & Du, B. (2023, February 6). *The Theoretical Basis and Landing Strategy of the Metaverse Business Model*. IEEE. doi:10.3233/FAIA230010

Dong, H., & Liu, Y. (2023, May 1). *Metaverse Meets Consumer Electronics*. IEEE. doi:10.1109/MCE.2022.3229180

IsmailL.BuyyaR. (2023, August 21). Metaverse: A Vision, Architectural Elements, and Future Directions for Scalable and Realtime Virtual Worlds. https://arxiv.org/abs/2308.10559

Verhoef, P C., Broekhuizen, T., Bart, Y., Bhattacharya, A., Dong, J Q., Fabian, N E., & Haenlein, M. (2021, January 1). Digital transformation: A multidisciplinary reflection and research agenda. doi:10.1016/j.jbusres.2019.09.022

Chapter 16
Exploring Safe Hedging Options for Blockchain Assets in the Face of COVID–19–Induced Volatility

Himani Gupta
Jagannath International Management School, India

Rupinder Katoch
https://orcid.org/0000-0003-3191-7930
Lovely Professional University, India

Manisha Gupta
Sharda University, India

ABSTRACT

This chapter examines the transfer of daily volatility returns from one block-chain asset to another and hedging alternatives. The technique is based on adequately modelling of the dynamic conditional correlation of generalised autoregressive conditional heteroscedasticity (DCC GARCH) and the hedging ratio. The results reveal that the volatility spillover impact from Etherium to other block-chain assets exists both in the short and long run. There are also hedging possibilities available between the selected block-chain assets. This implies that, prior to investing, policymakers, regulators, and investors should be aware of volatility, spillover effects, and hedging alternatives in the constituent variables.

INTRODUCTION

Money systems have evolved greatly over the centuries. From barter to plastic money, there are a variety of different types of money. Throughout each era, technical developments, financial needs, and the equivalent efficiency of performing a transaction acted as the determinants of one money form's continuing

DOI: 10.4018/979-8-3693-2607-7.ch016

existence over another. Of today's world, there has been an increasing increase in international hostility toward the present monetary system, notably in the aftermath of the financial instability that enveloped financial markets from 2007 to 2009, resulting in catastrophic economic effects throughout the world. Bitcoin (the first cryptocurrency) was launched in 2009. As per its white paper, it sought to alter the world financial system fundamentally. Recently, the concept of bitcoin gained substantial public support as crowds began to use it for a variety of reasons, including the desire for a different monetary system that is less dependent on the present traditional one. Numerous other cryptocurrencies have benefited from this public interest, resulting in a considerable evolution of the cryptocurrency sector. The main point of contention in this issue is that virtual currency markets have no inherent worth and do not pay dividends, yet investors continue to invest and profit (Ozdemer, 2022).

Recent concerns and disagreement that has dogged the cryptocurrency market since creation, has evolved into one of the most important alternative investment venues in the financial market (Huynh et al., 2020). A keen interest in study on these themes has grown as a result of the recent quick rise in the price of cryptocurrencies such as Bitcoin, Ethereum, and Litecoin (Ozdemir, 2022). (Nakamoto, 2008) He first proposed the theories of Bitcoin, since then many investors have become interested in digital money, causing digital currency transactions to become more prominent in the business world and investing scene. Investors typically select hedging assets such as cryptocurrency to mitigate financial risk and lock in profits when financial markets become more volatile and risky.

According to Markarov & Schoar, 2020, the cryptocurrency market, which is regarded as a new class of assets, has attracted significant interest from academics, speculators, lawmakers, and authorities (Nasir et al., 2019; Kou et al., 2014). The intricacy of the cryptocurrency market may be explored from multiple angles, and the goal of our research is to build a network centered on crypto-currency information to track possible linkages, impacts, and hedging choices between different types of crypto-currencies. The World Health Organization reported corona virus, a pandemic in 2020. COVID-19 has a significant impact on practically all areas of the economy. This was the start of our research.

Throughout this COVID-19 problem, it is vital to know the cryptocurrency market dynamics, particularly the links between different cryptocurrencies. Financial advisors must adapt their asset mix to diversify risk if volatility is conveyed from one cryptocurrency to another during a crisis, and financial policymakers must adjust their rules to prevent the risk of contagion. (Caporin & Malik, 2020).

Numerous studies have concentrated on the impact of diversity, and have examined the best asset mix that may maximise returns while minimising volatility (Baur et al., 2018; Kajtazi & Moro, 2019; Urquhart & Zhang, 2019). Nonetheless, this study expands on past research in two areas. To begin, this study began with the top twenty cryptocurrencies, but owing to a lack of data availability and other precondition criteria, it has been condensed to only seven. During COVID 19, it compared the spillover effects of one crypto currency on another. Second, this study focused at the time variability in cryptocurrency diversification evaluations.

The study's uniqueness arises from the fact that, to the best of the author's knowledge, these cryptocurrencies have never been thoroughly examined for the purpose of analysing the spillover impact and hedging alternatives. These cryptocurrencies were chosen for the study because they are among the top twenty-five most widely traded cryptocurrencies, accounting for more than 90% of the total industry value.

The following is the outline of our paper. In part II, a literature review is given, and in section III, data and methods are presented. The empirical findings are reviewed in the next part, followed by the primary conclusion and policy proposal in the last section.

LITERATURE REVIEW

Our research is mostly connected to the previous studies, which seeks to comprehend the spillover impacts of multiple financial products on portfolio diversification (Ozdemir & Ozdemir, 2021; Gupta, 2023; Gupta,2024). Analyzing volatility and volatility spillover amongst stock prices, cryptocurrency, bonds etc. is a significant matter that has gained prominence in recent decades. Kuen & Hoong (1992) contrast three approaches. Specifically, the naïve technique, the exponentially weighted moving average, and the generalised autoregressive conditional heteroscedasticity (GARCH) model of volatility forecasting. Fowowe & Shaibu (2016) along with Zhang et al. (2019) concentrated on equities markets. Mensi et al. (2014), on the other hand, focused on the commodities market, Hoesli & Reka (2013) examined the real estate market, and Louzis (2015) examined the spillover effects in the money market. Numerous research has been carried during the last decade on the correlation between Bitcoin and financial markets, with the majority of findings indicating that Bitcoin is distinct from traditional investments such as stocks, monetary systems, commodity markets, debt securities, precious metals, crude oil, and other cryptocurrencies (Zhang et al., 2021)

Cryptocurrency is built on block chain technology, which allows for the safe movement of assets using cutting-edge cryptographic techniques; in certain circles, this technology has surpassed it as a financial instrument. According to Glaser et al. (2014), though cryptocurrencies are predominantly used as a capital invested, but now it can be utilised as a global currency as a result of huge corporations and other businesses deciding to use them for their payments. Additionally, it can be used as a tool for organizations to obtain funds through initial coin offerings. (Momtaz, 2021). Analyzing the market dynamics or effectiveness is a delicate investment outcome; the theory presupposes that financial markets reflect, whereas behavior finance theory contends that psychological factors significantly impact market prices. (Fama,1970; Madhavan, 2000: Barber & Odean,2008;Almansour, 2015; Almansour & Arabyat, 2017; Dyhrberg, 2016) assert that a market's informational efficiency, as well as its information structure, play a significant impact in the creation of pricing. Alvarez-Ramirez et al. (2018) and Jiang et al. (2018) stated that the bitcoin market's pricing and information systems are ineffective, which is considered inefficient. Because ineffective markets are extremely volatile, researchers focused on the bitcoin market's volatility. (Kim, 2017) Due to the high volatility, academics have focussed their efforts on the returns. Ardia et al. (2019) used time series data from 2011 to 2018 to examine the fluctuations in Bitcoin. Researcher discovered robust evidence that the GARCH model effectively estimates Bitcoin volatility. Katsiampa et al. (2019) looked at how three major cryptocurrencies (Bitcoin, Ethereum, and Litecoin) convey shock and volatility using the BEKKMGARCH model and discover bidirectional shock propagation among Bitcoin–Litecoin and Bitcoin–Ethereum pairs. Additionally, bidirectional volatility transmissions among Ethereum and Litecoin was also seen by Canh et al. (2019). By applying the DCC-MGARCH model, researcher examined the volatility dynamics of the seven largest cryptocurrencies and discover strong propagation of volatility between them. The GARCH in mean model is used by Liu & Tsyvinski (2021) to assess the degree of shock and volatility transmission across Bitcoin, Ethereum, and Litecoin. Beneki et al. (2019) explore the volatility transmission between Bitcoin and Ethereum using the BEKK-GARCH approach. They discover a one-way spillover of volatility from Ethereum to Bitcoin. Chu et al. (2017) analysed that there are seven cryptocurrencies with varying degrees of volatility.

Almansour & Inairat (2020) discovered the connection between exchange rates and Bitcoin returns, conducted a time-series study utilizing ARMA analysis, and discovered that exchange rates have a negligible effect. According to Qarni & Gulzar (2021), Bitcoin offers considerable portfolio diversification benefits for huge foreign currency holdings.

Previous research on several cryptocurrencies was already conducted. For example, Bariviera et al. (2018) analyze the 5-minute data of 12 cryptocurrencies with the help of complexity-entropy causality plane. It exhibit the same dynamics as ethereum, bitcoin and classic exhibit more determined stochastic dynamic forces.

In contrast, Jiang et al. (2018) exhibit more random walk-like behaviour. Notably, the efficacy of bitcoin futures as a hedge against other cryptocurrencies is contingent upon their correlation to bitcoin. According to Corbet et al. (2018b), litecoin, bitcoin, and ripple are all significantly related at varying intervals and so these linkages are momentary. Aslanidis et al. (2019) When applied to bitcoin and ripple, a generalized DCC class model yields similar conclusions, meaning that relationships between cryptocurrencies are favourable but changing over time. Cahn et al. (2019) demonstrate that shifts occur from more minor to more significant cryptocurrencies in terms of market capitalization and that the results from DCC-MGARCH model are suggestively significant.

As stated previously, our objective is to investigate the efficiency of hedging on bitcoin and other cryptocurrencies. Thus, it is worth noting that, while the price dynamics of bitcoin and other cryptocurrencies may appear to be relatively similar at first look, they may also exhibit distinct characteristics, particularly in a high-frequency context. As a result, bitcoin results cannot be directly transferred to further cryptocurrencies. In several ways, this work gives a perspective on the bitcoin nexus. First, we explore the cryptocurrency market association among the top seven cryptocurrencies using a time-varying dynamic conditional correlation test, which has the benefit of targeting causal periods throughout time. Second, unlike earlier research that focused on the causation between these two or three cryptocurrencies, our study examines the hedging alternatives available for investors especially portfolio managers in order to enhance returns.

RESEARCH METHODOLOGY

Data Collection

This study employed a total of twenty cryptocurrencies, however owing to the lack of a comprehensive data set, we are only able to study twelve of them i.e. BITCOIN, ETHEREUM, BNB, XRP, CARDANO, TERRA, BINANCE, DOGECOIN, POLYGONMATIC, CORONS, WRAPPED BITCOIN AND COSMOS. The sample spans January 1, 2020, to February 28, 2022, and includes 788 observations based on cryptocurrency data availability. Furthermore, because bitcoin trading is not limited to work days, the sample includes weekends. Because the cryptocurrencies were originally issued in domestic currencies, they were first transformed into return series (Gupta & Gupta,2023) using the formula: ln(Pt/Pt-1).

Econometrics Model

To evaluate our time series, we utilised R Studio, and we used ARCH and GARCH models to anticipate the cryptocurrency's volatility. The hedging ratio is estimated using a multivariate GARCH model. In financial data science, the modelling of conditional variance and conditional covariance matrices is crucial. As said by Bauwens et al. (2006), multivariate GARCH models may be divided into three types based on how the conditional covariance matrix is constructed. The Baba, Engle, Kraft, and Kroner (BEKK) GARCH model (Baba et al., 1991; Engle and Kroner,1995), Constant Conditional Correlation (CCC) GARCH model (Bollerslev, 1990), and Dynamic Conditional Correlation (DCC) GARCH model (Engle, 2002) are the three types of models. The general order of GARCH (p, q) is set to (1,1) to simplify the models. We used the DCC GARCH model in this research.

Multivariate DCC GARCH Model

In many empirical results, particularly in prior investigations, the assumption that conditional correlations are constant may appear implausible (for example: Manera et al.,2006). Engle (2002) and Tse & Tsui (2002) introduced a dynamic conditional correlation (DCC) model in order to make the conditional correlation matrix time dependent. Conditional mean and conditional variance are two elements of the DCC GARCH model.

Conditional Mean

The model's conditional mean equation is written as follows:

$$R_t = u + \gamma R_{t-1} + \varepsilon_t$$

with $\varepsilon_t = H_t^{1/2} \eta_t$

where $R_t = (R_t^s, R_{t-1}^0)'$ s the vector of cryptocurrency returns at time t, respectively.

γ = The impact of own lag and cross mean transmissions between various cryptocurrencies is measured using a 2×2 matrix of parameters.

ε_t = vector of error terms for the two series at time t,

η_t = a series of randomly distributed random errors that are spread separately and identically.

$H_t^{1/2}$ = the conditional variations of returns for several cryptocurrencies

Conditional Variance

The following are the features of the DCC-GARCH model:

$$H_t = D_t R_t D_t = p_{ijt} \sqrt{h_{iit} h_{jjt}}$$

Where, H_t is expressed as conditional variance co-variance matrix, R_t is a conditional correlation matrix in form of n x n matrix and D_t can be denoted as

$$D_t = diag(h_1 t_{1/2},..., h_1 /2nt).$$

Where D_t is a conditional standard deviation and h_{iit} is extracted to be univariate GARCH (1,1) model

$$R_t = (diag Q_t)^{-1/2} Q_t (diag Q_t)^{-1/2}$$

Where $Q_t = (1-\alpha-\beta) \bar{Q} + \alpha u_{t-1} u_{t-1} + \beta Q_{t-1}$ and it refers to a n x n symmetric positive definite matrix with $u_{it} = \varepsilon_{it} / \sqrt{h_{iit}}$, $\bar{Q}$ is the n x n unconditional variance matrix of u_t.

$\alpha + \beta$ are positive and their sum is less than one. Therefore, $\alpha \geq 0$, $\beta \geq 0$ and $\alpha + \beta < 1$.

The conditional correlation coefficient p_{ij} between two markets i and j is then calculated as follows:

$$p_{ij} = \frac{(1-\alpha-\beta)\bar{q}_{ij} + \alpha u_{i,t-1} u_{j,t-1} + \beta q_{ij,t-1}}{\left((1-\alpha-\beta)\bar{q}_{ii} + \alpha u_{i,t-1}^2 + \beta q_{ii,t-1}\right)^{1/2} \left((1-\alpha-\beta)\bar{q}_{jj} + a u_{j,t-1}^2 + \beta q_{jj,t-1}\right)^{1/2}}$$

Where p_{ij} refers to the element located in the ith row and j^{th} column of the symmetric positive definite matrix Q_t

Joint dccα measures the short span volatility between markets and joint dccβ measures the long span volatility impact of one market over another.

Hedge Ratio and Portfolio Weights

Hedging using DCC models that allow for time-dependent conditional correlations has been done in previous studies by Lai & Sheu (2011) and Lin & Yang (2006). Because the best hedge ratio is immediately estimated based on the variance and covariance projections, estimating multivariate volatility models with flexible dynamics is critical for cryptocurrencies hedging. We estimate optimum portfolio weights for chosen cryptocurrency-based portfolios as described by Kroner & Ng (1998).

$$W_{ij,t} = \frac{h_{jj,t-h_{ij,t}}}{h_{ii,t} - 2h_{ij,t} + h_{jj,t}}$$

Where if $W_{ij,t} < 0$, then consider it to be 0

If $W_{ij,t} > 1$, then consider it to be 1

The portfolio weights between two assets are denoted by $W_{ij,t}$. It represents the weight of first asset in a one dollar portfolio of two assets and weight of another asset is deoned by $1 - W_{ij,t}$. $h_{ij,t}$ stands for conditional covariance between two assets and $h_{ii,t}$ represents conditional variance of the particular asset.

We also compute the hedge ratio for various cryptocurrency portfolios since these ratios give investors with important information for hedging their portfolio risk (Toyoshima et al.,2013).

According to Kroner & Sultan (1993) hedge ratio can be represented as:

$$B_{ij,t} = \frac{h_{ij,t}}{h_{jj,t}}$$

Where $h_{ij,t}$ is covariance between asset i and asset j, where as $h_{jj,t}$ is variance of asset j.

EMPIRICAL RESULTS

Descriptive Statistics

The descriptive analysis of return series of selected crypto currency from 1st January 2020 to 27th February 2022 is depicted in table 1. The daily price return of 788 observations is taken. Figure 1 shows the change in closing price of selected crypto currency. Figure 2 depicts the returns of daily closing prices which is also known as volatility clustering. The lowest mean is of XRP i.e. 0.001676, whereas highest is of TERRA i.e. 0.007298. Over the time the maximum return is of BNB with 0.529243 and the minimum return is POLYGONMATIC with -0.714147. The reason can be that after every three months, the BNB repurchases its tokens with 20% of its earnings. The question now is why BNB purchased it again. BNB distributes its tokens to exchanges like Binance, where they are burnt and are no longer accessible. As a result of the token burning, the price rises. As an outcome, it will help BNB create a supply and demand gap, enhancing its value. Polygonmatic's negative returns are mostly attributable to the fact that, unlike BNB tokens, these tokens are only burnt once a year and in extremely small quantities. Polygonmatic deflation evolves over time, separating it from endless supply crypto. Standard deviation shows the volatility in the series. DOGECOIN demonstrates the greatest volatility of 0.097517 and BITCOIN demonstrates the least volatility of 0.04050 among all the variables which possess large variations. Dogecoin is a very volatile crypto market due to its meme currency qualities and ongoing backing from the Doge father, Elon Musk. The degree of volatility the crypto market is particularly high, with regular swings in cryptocurrency values that can result in profit or loss in crypto wallets. Elon Musk is the ultimate crypto influencer, with the ability to effectively regulate and mitigate the Dogecoin price in the crypto market volatility environment. DOGE tokens can frequently assist crypto investors that are interested in the meme cryptocurrency with real-world applications. On the other hand, Bitcoin is one of the market's few "physical assets" with no major revenue flow. This makes valuing it tough. Any analyst may compute any stock's "fair value," that could be deducted from cash flow and yield a specified return at the end of its life. Variance is the square of standard deviation. TERRA, DOGECOIN and POLYGONMATIC shows the positive skewness and all other variable shows the negative skewness. Negative skewness implies that there are chances of negative earnings to the investors. Kurtosis of DOGECOIN being the highest of 79.986163 and CARDANO being the lowest of 7.224901 among all variables. It shows that the values are too high. It also depicts that each variable under study is not normally distributed. It is further cross validated with the help of Jarque Berra Test. Thus, it strongly does not accept the null hypothesis with a significance threshold of 5%.

In time series analysis, stationarity of variables is more important than the normality of variables. Almost no time series data is normal but to do the analysis every time series data should be stationary. Furthermore, Phillip Perron (PP) Test and the Augmented Dicky Fuller (ADF) Test have been carried out to actually take a look at the stationarity of all twelve selected crypto currencies. The original price of the variables shows the stochastic trend which is shown if figure 1. ADF Test and PP Test also confirms that the original data has a unit root. So, the data is converted into return series. Return series is calculated as $r_t = \ln(p_t/p_{t-1})$, where p_t is a closing price at current time period and p_{t-1} is a closing price at previous day. Table 2 shows the result of stationarity of return series. ADF Test and PP Test confirms that the cryptocurrency return of selected variables are stationary at level i.e. I (0) at 1% level of significance. Thus, it strongly rejects the null hypothesis (series has unit root). It is also shown in figure 2.

Table 1. Descriptive statistics of daily returns of crypto currency

Variable	BITCOIN	ETHERIUM	BNB	XRP	CARDANO	TERRA	BINANCE	DOGECOIN	POLYGON MATIC	CORONS	WRAPPED BITCOIN	COSMOS
Mean	0.0021	0.0038	0.0041	0.0016	0.0041	0.0072	0.0022	0.0052	0.0058	0.0031	0.0020	0.0022
Median	0.0023	0.0049	0.0034	0.0013	0.0014	0.0017	0.0016	-0.0001	0.0028	0.0046	0.0022	0.0016
Maximum	0.1718	0.2307	0.5292	0.4446	0.2794	0.6409	0.2800	1.5162	0.4561	0.4490	0.1769	0.2801
Minimum	-0.4647	-0.5507	-0.5428	-0.5504	-0.5037	-0.4877	-0.5911	-0.5149	-0.7141	-0.4903	-0.4804	-0.5911
variance	0.0016	0.0028	0.0038	0.0047	0.0038	0.0068	0.0054	0.0095	0.0069	0.0036	0.0016	0.0054
Std dev	0.0405	0.05360	0.0617	0.0685	0.0622	0.0829	0.0741	0.0975	0.0834	0.0607	0.0408	0.0741
Skewness	-1.6193	-1.8758	-0.2396	-0.1691	-0.3468	0.8093	-0.8224	5.5171	0.0627	-0.2935	-2.0301	-0.8224
Kurtosis	16.7404	23.1315	18.0947	13.3076	7.2249	9.6998	8.5847	79.9861	11.0467	11.5103	25.1999	8.5847
Jarque-Bera	18133 (0.000)	9602.3 (0.00)	10822 (0.000)	5854.6 (0.000)	1742.1 (0.000)	3196.1 (0.000)	2525.6 (0.000)	215183 (0.00)	4033.1 (0.00)	4389.3 (0.000)	21513 (0.000)	2525.6 (0.000)
ADF Test	-8.3755 (0.01)	-8.2911 (0.01)	-7.1531 (0.01)	-8.1084 (0.01)	-7.8448 (0.01)	-7.762 (0.01)	-8.3585 (0.01)	-8.2535 (0.01)	-8.9606 (0.01)	-7.6223 (0.01)	-8.3856 (0.01)	-8.3585 (0.01)
PP test	-897.39 (0.01)	-898.17 (0.01)	-928.69 (0.01)	-826.65 (0.01)	-888.6 (0.01)	-888.11 (0.01)	-845.46 (0.01)	-778.7 (0.01)	-861.12 (0.01)	-937 (0.01)	-901.32 (0.01)	-845.46 (0.01)
ARCH-LM Test	15.862 (0.1976)	22.859 (0.0289)	62.733 (0.000)	36.034 (0.0003)	31.574 (0.0016)	55.659 (0.000)	17.861 (0.12)	16.812 (0.1568)	30.337 (0.002)	37.293 (0.002)	11.863 (0.4567)	17.861 (0.12)
Observations	788	788	788	788	788	788	788	788	788	788	788	788

Source: The Author

Figure 1. Original price series of variables
Source: The Author

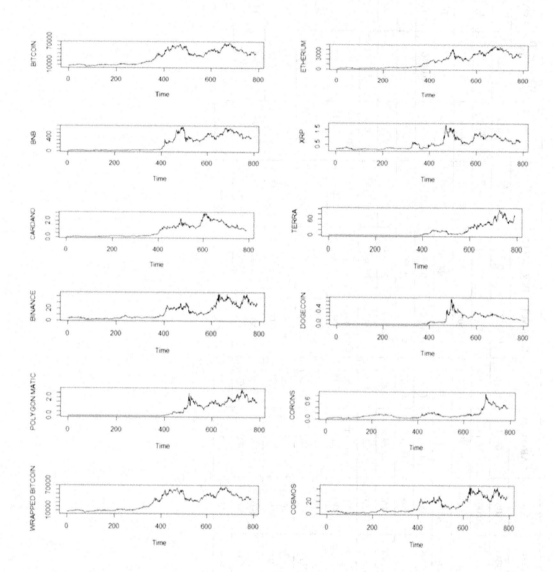

From Figure 2, it has been noticed that returns of almost all the cryptocurrency fell in first few days of COVID -19 news and there after all the returns realized negative as well as positive returns in cryptocurrency.The graphical representation gives us an idea about the behaviour of the series. It can be clearly observed that in every series huge fluctuations are accompanied by huge fluctuations, and minor are accompanied by minor, as shown in the figure 2.

ARCH Effect

Next step is to check the ARCH Effect in selected variables. GARCH model can only be applied if the three pre-requisite conditions are validated. The first and second condition is that the series should be

Figure 2. Return series of variables
Source: The Author

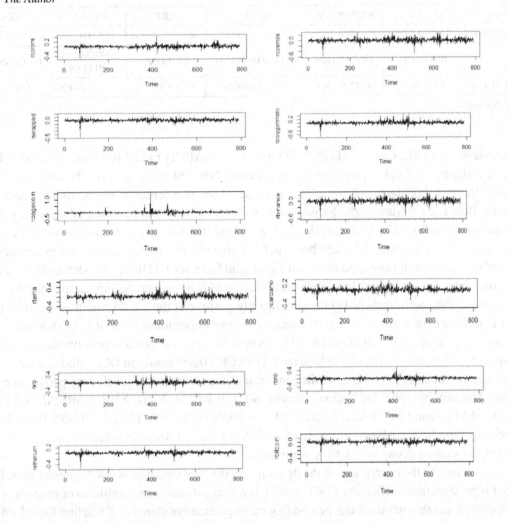

stationary and there should be volatility clustering. These two conditions are satisfied and shown in figure 2. The third condition is that there should be ARCH Effect in the series. To check the ARCH Effect we checked via LM Test. The outcomes of LM Test is shown in table 2. It shows that ETHERIUM, BNB, XRP, CARDANO, TERRA, POLYGONMATIC and CORONS have ARCH effect where as BITCOIN, NINANCE, GODECOIN, WRAPPEDBITCOIN and COSMOS does not have ARCH effect. So, our futher study will be with only those variables which have ARCH effect.

Results of Dynamic Conditional Correlation (DCC)

In this window spillover effect of ETHERIUM to BNB, XRP, CARDANO, TERRA, POLYGONMATIC and CORONS is discussed using Dynamic Conditional Correlation (DCC) model.It should be noted that the pattern of volatility clustering and ARCH effect is shown in figure 2 and table 2 for each selected crypto currency variable. The analysis is shown in table 3.Refering to the analysis mu,omega, alpha1and

Table 2. ARCH effect

Variable	BITCOIN	ETHERIUM	BNB	XRP	CARDANO	TERRA
ARCH-LM Test	15.862 (0.1976)	22.859 (0.0289)	62.733 (0.000)	36.034 (0.0003)	31.574 (0.0016)	55.659 (0.000)
Variable	BINANCE	DOGECOIN	POLYGON MATIC	CORONS	WRAPPED BITCOIN	COSMOS
ARCH-LM Test	17.861 (0.12)	16.812 (0.1568)	30.337 (0.002)	37.293 (0.002)	11.863 (0.4567)	17.861 (0.12)

Source: The Author

beta1 represents the ARCH term and GARCH term. DCC GARCH model is a variance model. In this omega is a variance intercept, alpha gives the information how volatility reacts to the new information. It tells us if there is short-term volatility. This is modeled on time series numbers from the past of the error terms. Beta is a measure of the long-term persistence of price swings that evaluates the effect of a disturbance on conditional correlation.Hence, we can say that beta explains the conditional volatility on its own lag. If, we see the alpha and beta coefficients individually for all the cryptocurrency, at a 5% level of significance, it is both positive and significant.Only for ETHERIUM,XRP and POLYGON-MATIC, the alpha term is insignificant indicating that there is no impact on short term volatility. In all of the variables, the coefficients of beta is significantly positive at the 1% threshold of significance . It suggests that there exist the long run persistence of its own conditional volatility. As shown in table 3 coefficient of alpha term (ARCH effect) in all the cryptocurrency variables is positive and smaller than their respective estimated coefficient of beta term(GARCH effect) values in DCC Model. It depicts that the variable own volatility persistence in the long- run is larger than its own volatility persistence in the short run . The sum of alpha and beta coefficient in ETHERIUM, BNB, XRP, CARDANO, TERRA, POLYGONMATIC and CORONS are 0.972799, 0.998935, 0.999, 0.921402, 0.967435, 0.961413 and 0.983866 respectively. It can be interpreted as CARDANO has fast decay in volatility persistence where as XRP has the slowest decay in volatility persistence.

Let's have a look at the coefficient of the dynamic conditional correlation (DCC) model now. Dcca1 and dccb1 represents the coefficient of DCC model. It reveals, if there is a short-term or long-term information spillover. In other words, it can be said that these parameters shows that whether the information of one variable is having the effect on another variable or not. And if, effect is there then that effect is for shorter period of time or for longer period. From table 3, it can be seen that dcca1 and dccb1 are significantly positive at 1% level of significance.It deduces that there can be a short-term and long-term effect of news of Ehereum on other variables.Hence ETHERIUM has a spillover effect on BNB,XRP,CARDANO,TERRA,POLYGONMATIC and CORONS. Dcca1 is 0.037236 which is positive and significant, indicates that information is spilling over or being transmitted in the short run from ETHERIUM to returns of other variables. Dccb1 is 0.937669 which is also positive and significant, indicates that the information is spilling over or being transmitted in the long run from ETHERIUM to returns of other variables. Because the sum of dcca1 and dccb1 is smaller than one, it is presumed that dynamic conditional correlation is mean reverting. Hence,cryptocurrencies are now causing quite a stir in the market. As is obvious, they have their own highs and lows depending on market conditions. However, there are variables that influence the value of cryptocurrencies. Cryptocurrencies, like any other money, derive their value through community participation. This might include coin demand, usefulness, and scarcity. In reality, the majority of cryptocurrencies emerge from private blockchain enterprises. As a result, the value of such cryptos will be determined by the company's perceived worth and project feasibility. The

Table 3. Results of DCC model

	Estimate	Std. Error	t value	Pr(>|t|)
[retherium].mu	0.0050	0.0017	3.0030	0.0027
[retherium].omega	0.0001	0.0001	1.6389	0.1012
[retherium].alpha1	0.1075	0.0636	1.6917	0.0907
[retherium].beta1	0.8653	0.0427	20.2730	0.0000
[rbnb].mu	0.0031	0.0015	2.0265	0.0427
[rbnb].omega	0.0001	0.0001	1.3451	0.1786
[rbnb].alpha1	0.1745	0.0723	2.4130	0.0158
[rbnb].beta1	0.8244	0.0583	14.1381	0.0000
[rxrp].mu	-0.0001	0.0020	-0.0391	0.9688
[rxrp].omega	0.0001	0.0001	0.6572	0.5110
[rxrp].alpha1	0.1005	0.0769	1.3065	0.1914
[rxrp].beta1	0.8985	0.0831	10.8073	0.0000
[rcardano].mu	0.0037	0.0020	1.8373	0.0662
[rcardano].omega	0.0004	0.0001	2.8687	0.0041
[rcardano].alpha1	0.1453	0.0555	2.6169	0.0089
[rcardano].beta1	0.7761	0.0496	15.6340	0.0000
[rterra].mu	0.0037	0.0027	1.3924	0.1638
[rterra].omega	0.0004	0.0003	1.2676	0.2050
[rterra].alpha1	0.1652	0.0643	2.5693	0.0102
[rterra].beta1	0.8022	0.0359	22.3204	0.0000
[rpolygonmatic].mu	0.0039	0.0023	1.6763	0.0937
[rpolygonmatic].omega	0.0004	0.0003	1.1632	0.2447
[rpolygonmatic].alpha1	0.1695	0.1055	1.6065	0.1082
[rpolygonmatic].beta1	0.7919	0.1180	6.7102	0.0000
[rcorons].mu	0.0041	0.0024	1.7327	0.0832
[rcorons].omega	0.0002	0.0001	1.9474	0.0515
[rcorons].alpha1	0.1850	0.0776	2.3847	0.0171
[rcorons].beta1	0.7989	0.0398	20.0849	0.0000
[Joint]dcca1	0.0372	0.0050	7.4659	0.0000
[Joint]dccb1	0.9377	0.0097	97.1501	0.0000

Source: The Author

effect of one cryptocurrency on another is a regular occurrence. This is what happened as a result of a major Bitcoin price fall in early 2018, which was followed by a reduction in the capitalization of all other cryptocurrencies at the same time. After Bitcoin, Ethereum is the most powerful cryptocurrency. Cryptocurrency exchange charts show that a reduction in Ethereum's price has an unavoidable influence on the exchange rates of BNB,XRP,CARDANO,TERRA,POLYGONMATIC, and CORONS. As a result, we may conclude that it may have an impact on the other cryptocurrencies under consideration.

The researcher next used the Sign Bias test to see if there was any asymmetry in the volatily. The p- value is found to be insignificant which confirms that asymmetry is not there.Therefore, asymmetry GARCH model were not applied.

The time varying conditional correlation calculated from DCC multivariate model between Etherium and BNB, Etherium and XRP, Etherium and Cardano, Etherium and Terra, Etherium and Polygonmatic & Etherium and Corons is depicted in figure 3. It is to be observed that the dynamic conditional correlation (DCC) among Etherium and BNB is all positive and more than 0.5. This suggests that portfolio can be diversified across these two cryptocurrencies data set. Similarly, the DCCs among Etherium and all sampled variables is also positive and more than 0.1 in all the cases.The DCC between each pair of cryptocurrency reach its lowest values around middle of the period i.e around January 2021. Thus,cross hedging is possible since all of the pairs have a positively correlated return movement.

Hedge Ratio and Portfolio Weight

We employ the estimates calculated from DCC GARCH model for portfolio creation and hedging methods in this section.

Hedge Ratios

To calculate the hedge ratio conditional volatility estimates generated from multivariate GARCH model are used.(Kroner & Sultan, 1993). In hedge ratio we have made the pair of two assets (one asset i and other asset j). In hedge ratio taking a long stake in a single asset might be risky so it can be offset by the short position of other asset. The hedge ratio between asset i and asset j can be calculated by:

Figure 3. Time varying conditional correlation from DCC model
Source: The Author

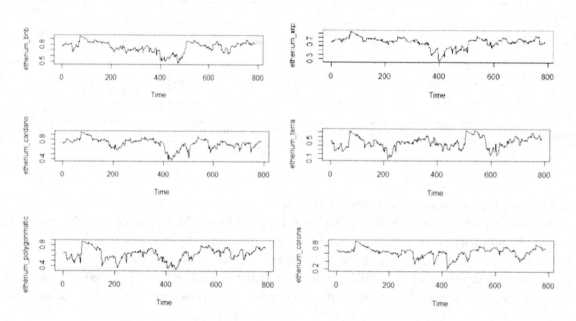

Figure 4. Graphs of hedge ratios
Source: The Author

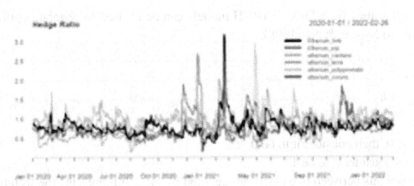

$$B_{ij,t} = \frac{h_{ij,t}}{h_{jj,t}}$$

Where $h_{ij,t}$ is covariance between asset i and asset j, where as $h_{jj,t}$ is variance of asset j. The hedge ratio of Etherium with all other variables is shown in figure 4. From figure 4, it can also be observed that there is lots of variation in all the hedge ratios. In Etherium/BNB, Etherium/XNP, Etherium/Terra and Etherium/Polygonmatic the maximum hedge ratio is observed at middle of the sample period i.e. in January 2021. Where as in the case of Etherium/Cardano the maximum hedge ratio is observed in the beginning of the sample period i.e. March 2020 and in case of Etherium/Corons the maximum hedge ratio is observed in the end of the sample period i.e. Januauary 2022.

Table 4 depicts the descriptive statistics of different pair of hedge ratio.The average hedge ratio of Etherium/BNB is 0.794,Etherium/XRP is 0.815, Etherium/Cardano is 0.8501, Etherium/Terra is 0.7088, Etherium/Polygonmatic is 0.9526 and Etherium/Corons is 0.7237. These are the important findings as it indicates that $1 long position of Etherium can be hedged for 79% with short position of BNB. Similarly, $1 long position of Etherium can be hedged for 81.5 percent with short position of XRP. The cheapest hedge is long Etherium and short Terra with 70.8 percent. The most expensive hedge is long Etherium and short Polygonmatic with the hedge ratio of 95.26 percent.From table 4 it is observed that all the hedge ratios are less than unity i.e.1.

Table 4. Hedge ratio (long/short) summary statistics

Variable	Mean ± SD	Min.	Max.
Etherium/BNB	0.794 ± 0.240	0.388	3.196
Etherium/XRP	0.815 ± 0.270	0.427	2.705
Etherium/Cardano	0.8501 ± 0.1673	0.369	1.500
Etherium/Terra	0.7088 ± 0.2625	0.1582	2.0446
Etherium/Polygonmatic	0.9526 ± 0.2358	0.3603	2.9503
Etherium/Corons	0.7237 ± 0.2123	0.1487	1.8552

Source: The Author

Portfolio Weights

The conditional volatilities from DCC GARCH models can be utilised to generate optimum portfolio weights, according to Kroner & Ng (1998).

$$W_{ij,t} = \frac{h_{jj,t-h_{ij,t}}}{h_{ii,t} - 2h_{ij,t} + h_{jj,t}}$$

Where if $W_{ij,t} < 0$, then consider it to be 0

If $W_{ij,t} > 1$, then consider it to be 1

The portfolio weights between two assets are denoted by $W_{ij,t}$. It represents the weight of first asset in a one dollar portfolio of two assets and weight of another asset is deoned by $1 - W_{ij,t}$. $h_{ij,t}$ stands for conditional covariance between two assets and $h_{ii,t}$ represents conditional variance of the particular asset.

Table 5 shows the descriptive summary of portfolio weights calculated with the help of DCC GARCH model. The average weights of Etherium/BNB is 0.51. This means that if you have a $1 portfolio, you should invest 51 percent in Etherium and 49 percent in BNB.Similarly, the average weight of Etherium/XRP indicates that 43 percent should be invested in Etherium and remaining 57 percent in XRP. The third weight of Etherium/Cardano gives us indication that only 29 percent should be invested in Etherium and 71 percent should be invested in Cardano. In the next pair of Etherium/Terra only 20 percent should be invested in Etherium and 80 percent in Terro. In addition, the average weight of Etherium/Polygonmatic portfolio shows that only 6 percent should be invested in Etherium and 94 percent in Polygonmatic. The last portfolio of Etherium/Corons shows that 43 percent should be invested in Etherium and 57 percent in Corons.

CONCLUSION AND POLICY IMPLICATIONS

As the level of investment in the cryptocurrency industry expands, it's critical to have a deeper grasp of how cryptocurrency values fluctuate. This research looks at the most popular aspects of volatility spill-over and hedging options between seven popular cryptocurrencies. It investigates correlations, volatility spillovers, and hedging options between cryptocurrency returns using multivariate GARCH models. The

Table 5. Summary statistics of portfolio weights

Variable	Mean ± SD	Min.	Max.
Etherium/BNB	0.51 ± 0.337	0	1
Etherium/XRP	0.43 ± 0.389	0	1
Etherium/Cardano	0.29 ± 0.336	0	1
Etherium/Terra	0.20 ± 0.213	0	1
Etherium/Polygonmatic	0.06 ± 0.159	0	1
Etherium/Corons	0.43 ± 0.289	0	1

Source: The Author

Dynamic Conditional Correlation (DCC) model was applied to daily returns of twelve common crypto-currencies from January 2020 to February 2022, validating the pre-condition for seven cryptocurrencies. Therefore, the study is continued with seven cryptocurrencies return. The researcher tried to find out the spillover effect from Ethereum to BNB,ERP, Cordano,Terra, Polygonmatic and Corons. The result indicates that there is spillover effect both in the short and the long run from Etherium to remaining six variables. This will aid portfolio managers and investors in recognising arbitrage possibilities in both markets owing to mispricing of cryptocurrency or extreme volatility at different times. Further, it is also observed that each of the six combinations has a positive correlation. It validates that the cross hedging is possible in all the pairs.

In the next step,hedge ratios propounded by Kroner & Sultan(1993) are calculated using the DCC-MGARCH model's conditional volatilities. With a short position in BNB, a $1 long position in Etherium may be hedged for 79 percent.Similarly, $1 long position of Etherium can be hedged for 81.5 percent with short position of XRP. The most cost-effective hedge is long Etherium and short Terra. The most pricey hedge is long Etherium and short Polygonmatic. This will support future academics in examining the volatility and optimum hedging strategy of various assets in more depth.For example, the constructed hedge ratio from DCC model recommend that $1 long investment in crude oil spot may be hedged with short in crude oil futures.(Tansuchat et al., 2010) This will also aid in identifying the different hedging and trading methods that these precius metal can employ (Lau et al., 2017). This will also assist banks and investors in hedging their exposure to these markets by utilising Bitcoin as a tool for diversity. (Brière et al.,2015)

Finally, the DCC model's conditional variances and covariances may be utilised to create optimum portfolio among returns of two cryptocurrency. In the first portfolio 51% should be invested in Etherium and 49% in BNB. The second portfolio can be with 43% of investment in Etherium and 57% in XRP. In the third portfolio 29% should be invested in Etherium and 71% in Cardano. The fourth portfolio average weights shows that 20% should be invested in Etherium and 80% in Terra. Fifth portfolio should be constructed with only 6% in Etherium and 94% in Polygomatic. The last portfolio of Etherium/Corons shows that 43 percent should be invested in Etherium and 57 percent in Corons.

The similar findings show that bitcoin could be utilised to hedge against the Financial Times Stock Exchange Index. In the near run, bitcoin may also be used as a hedge against the US currency(Dyhrberg, 2016). Klein et al. (2018) compare the gold and Bitcoin, discovering that the latter is positively correlated with negative swings in developed markets. Thus, there is a hedging options between gold and Bitcoin.Conlon et.al (2020)studied Bitcoin, Ethereum and Tether. According to their findings, Bitcoin and Ethereum are inappropriate for investment. Tether, on the other hand, is a secure investment. Such negative risk hedging characteristics, on the other hand, are not always present throughout time.

Our findings shows that there is hedging options among Ethereum and other variables. Furthermore, evaluating the interconnectedness of multiple markets, particularly cryptocurrencies, is critical for investors since it allows them to analyse and make appropriate judgments about portfolio diversification options. As a result, our research will be extremely useful for investors, speculators, and portfolio managers looking to diversify their risk.But before investing policy makers, regulators, in addition to investors must be aware of volatility and spillover effect in the constituent variables.

Our study, like many studies, has shortcomings. We could only analyse the initial and relatively brief effects of this pandemic on the dynamic connectivity between the key impacted cryptocurrencies due to the brief event time and the virus's shifting nature. Future studies should look at the long-term implications of the epidemic on cryptocurrency connectivity and compare it to other financial markets and commodities.

Declaration of Conflicting Interests

The authors declared no potential conflicts of interest with respect to the research, authorship and/or publication of this article.

Funding

The authors received no financial support for the research, authorship and/or publication of this article.

Data Availability

The datasets generated during and/or analysed during the current study are available from the corresponding author on reasonable request.

REFERENCES

Almansour, B. (2015). The impact of market sentiment index on stock returns: An empirical investigation on Kuala Lumpur Stock Exchange. *Journal of Arts, Science & Commerce, 6*(3).

Almansour, B. Y., & Arabyat, Y. A. (2017). Investment decision making among Gulf investors: Behavioural finance perspective. *International Journal of Management Studies, 24*(1), 41–71. doi:10.32890/ijms.24.1.2017.10476

Almansour, B. Y., & Inairat, M. (2020). The impact of exchange rates on bitcoin returns: Further evidence from a time series framework. *International Journal of Scientific & Technology Research, 9*(02), 4577–4581.

Ardia, D., Bluteau, K., & Rüede, M. (2019). Regime changes in Bitcoin GARCH volatility dynamics. *Finance Research Letters, 29*, 266–271. doi:10.1016/j.frl.2018.08.009

Aslanidis, N., Bariviera, A. F., & Martínez-Ibañez, O. (2019). An analysis of cryptocurrencies conditional cross correlations. *Finance Research Letters, 31*, 130–137. doi:10.1016/j.frl.2019.04.019

Baba, Y., Engle, R. F., Kraft, D. F., & Kroner, K. F. (1990). *Multivariate simultaneous generalized ARCH. Manuscript, University of California*. Department of Economics.

Balcilar, M., Bouri, E., Gupta, R., & Roubaud, D. (2017). Can volume predict Bitcoin returns and volatility? A quantiles-based approach. *Economic Modelling, 64*, 74–81. doi:10.1016/j.econmod.2017.03.019

Barber, B. M., & Odean, T. (2008). All that glitters: The effect of attention and news on the buying behavior of individual and institutional investors. *Review of Financial Studies, 21*(2), 785–818. doi:10.1093/rfs/hhm079

Bariviera, A. F., Zunino, L., & Rosso, O. A. (2018). An analysis of high-frequency cryptocurrencies prices dynamics using permutation-information-theory quantifiers. *Chaos (Woodbury, N.Y.)*, *28*(7), 075511. doi:10.1063/1.5027153 PMID:30070500

Baur, D. G., Dimpfl, T., & Kuck, K. (2018). Bitcoin, gold and the US dollar–A replication and extension. *Finance Research Letters*, *25*, 103–110. doi:10.1016/j.frl.2017.10.012

Bauwens, L., Laurent, S., & Rombouts, J. V. (2006). Multivariate GARCH models: A survey. *Journal of Applied Econometrics*, *21*(1), 79–109. doi:10.1002/jae.842

Bedoui, R., Braiek, S., Guesmi, K., & Chevallier, J. (2019). RETRACTED: On the conditional dependence structure between oil, gold and USD exchange rates: Nested copula based GJR-GARCH model. *Energy Economics*, *80*, 876–889. doi:10.1016/j.eneco.2019.02.002

Beneki, C., Koulis, A., Kyriazis, N. A., & Papadamou, S. (2019). Investigating volatility transmission and hedging properties between Bitcoin and Ethereum. *Research in International Business and Finance*, *48*, 219–227. doi:10.1016/j.ribaf.2019.01.001

Bollerslev, T. (1986). Generalized autoregressive conditional heteroskedasticity. *Journal of Econometrics*, *31*(3), 307–327. doi:10.1016/0304-4076(86)90063-1

Briere, M., Oosterlinck, K., & Szafarz, A. (2015). Virtual currency, tangible return: Portfolio diversification with bitcoin. *Journal of Asset Management*, *16*(6), 365–373. doi:10.1057/jam.2015.5

Chowdhury, A. (2016). Is Bitcoin the "Paris Hilton" of the currency world? Or are the early investors onto something that will make them rich? *Journal of Investing*, *25*(1), 64–72. doi:10.3905/joi.2016.25.1.064

Chowdhury, A., & Mendelson, B. K. (2013). Virtual currency and the financial system: the case of Bitcoin (No. 2013-09). Marquette University, Center for Global and Economic Studies and Department of Economics.

Chu, J., Zhang, Y., & Chan, S. (2019). The adaptive market hypothesis in the high frequency cryptocurrency market. *International Review of Financial Analysis*, *64*, 221–231. doi:10.1016/j.irfa.2019.05.008

Conlon, T., Corbet, S., & McGee, R. J. (2020). Are cryptocurrencies a safe haven for equity markets? An international perspective from the COVID-19 pandemic. *Research in International Business and Finance*, *54*, 101248. doi:10.1016/j.ribaf.2020.101248 PMID:34170988

Corbet, S., Hou, Y. G., Hu, Y., Oxley, L., & Xu, D. (2021). Pandemic-related financial market volatility spillovers: Evidence from the Chinese COVID-19 epicentre. *International Review of Economics & Finance*, *71*, 55–81. doi:10.1016/j.iref.2020.06.022

Dyhrberg, A. H. (2016). Bitcoin, gold and the dollar–A GARCH volatility analysis. *Finance Research Letters*, *16*, 85–92. doi:10.1016/j.frl.2015.10.008

Dyhrberg, A. H. (2016). Hedging capabilities of bitcoin. Is it the virtual gold? *Finance Research Letters*, *16*, 139–144. doi:10.1016/j.frl.2015.10.025

Engle, R. F. (1982). Autoregressive conditional heteroscedasticity with estimates of the variance of United Kingdom inflation. *Econometrica*, *50*(4), 987–1007. doi:10.2307/1912773

Engle, R. F., & Kroner, K. F. (1995). Multivariate simultaneous generalized ARCH. *Econometric Theory*, *11*(1), 122–150. doi:10.1017/S0266466600009063

Erdoğdu, A. (2017). The most significant factors influencing the price of gold: An empirical analysis of the US market. *Economics*, *5*(5), 399–406.

Fama, E. F. (1970). Efficient capital markets: A review of theory and empirical work. *The Journal of Finance*, *25*(2), 383–417. doi:10.2307/2325486

Fowowe, B., & Shuaibu, M. (2016). Dynamic spillovers between Nigerian, South African and international equity markets. *Inter Economics*, *148*, 59–80. doi:10.1016/j.inteco.2016.06.003

Glaser, F., Zimmermann, K., Haferkorn, M., Weber, M. C., & Siering, M. (2014). *Bitcoin-asset or currency? revealing users' hidden intentions. Revealing Users' Hidden Intentions (April 15, 2014)*. ECIS.

Gupta, H. (2023). Analysing volatility patterns in emerging markets: symmetric or asymmetric models? *Journal of Economic and Administrative Sciences*. doi:10.1108/JEAS-07-2023-0186

Gupta, H. (2024). Asymmetric Volatility in Stock Market: Evidence from Selected Export-based Countries. *The Indian Economic Journal*, *0*(0), 00194662241238598. doi:10.1177/00194662241238598

Gupta, H., & Gupta, A. (2023). Investor's behaviour to COVID-19 vaccine: An event study on health and pharmaceutical sector in India. *International Journal of Pharmaceutical and Healthcare Marketing*, *17*(4), 429–449. doi:10.1108/IJPHM-05-2022-0053

Hashim, S. L., Ramlan, H., Razali, N. H., & Nordin, N. Z. (2017). Macroeconomic variables affecting the volatility of gold price. [GBSE]. *Journal of Global Business and Social Entrepreneurship*, *3*(5), 97–106.

Hoesli, M., & Reka, K. (2013). Volatility spillovers, comovements and contagion in securitized real estate markets. *The Journal of Real Estate Finance and Economics*, *47*(1), 1–35. doi:10.1007/s11146-011-9346-8

Huynh, T. L. D., Nasir, M. A., Vo, X. V., & Nguyen, T. T. (2020). "Small things matter most": The spillover effects in the cryptocurrency market and gold as a silver bullet. *The North American Journal of Economics and Finance*, *54*, 101277. doi:10.1016/j.najef.2020.101277

Jiang, Y., Nie, H., & Ruan, W. (2018). Time-varying long-term memory in Bitcoin market. *Finance Research Letters*, *25*, 280–284. doi:10.1016/j.frl.2017.12.009

Kajtazi, A., & Moro, A. (2019). The role of bitcoin in well diversified portfolios: A comparative global study. *International Review of Financial Analysis*, *61*, 143–157. doi:10.1016/j.irfa.2018.10.003

Katsiampa, P., Corbet, S., & Lucey, B. (2019). High frequency volatility co-movements in cryptocurrency markets. *Journal of International Financial Markets, Institutions and Money*, *62*, 35–52. doi:10.1016/j.intfin.2019.05.003

Kim, Y. B., Lee, J., Park, N., Choo, J., Kim, J. H., & Kim, C. H. (2017). When Bitcoin encounters information in an online forum: Using text mining to analyse user opinions and predict value fluctuation. *PLoS One*, *12*(5), e0177630. doi:10.1371/journal.pone.0177630 PMID:28498843

Klein, T., Thu, H. P., & Walther, T. (2018). Bitcoin is not the New Gold–A comparison of volatility, correlation, and portfolio performance. *International Review of Financial Analysis, 59*, 105–116. doi:10.1016/j.irfa.2018.07.010

Kroner, K. F., & Sultan, J. (1993). Time-varying distributions and dynamic hedging with foreign currency futures. *Journal of Financial and Quantitative Analysis, 28*(4), 535–551. doi:10.2307/2331164

Kuen, T. Y., & Hoong, T. S. (1992). Forecasting volatility in the Singapore stock market. *Asia Pacific Journal of Management, 9*(1), 1–13. doi:10.1007/BF01732034

Lai, Y. S., & Sheu, H. J. (2011). On the importance of asymmetries for dynamic hedging during the subprime crisis. *Applied Financial Economics, 21*(11), 801–813. doi:10.1080/09603107.2010.539535

Lau, M. C. K., Vigne, S. A., Wang, S., & Yarovaya, L. (2017). Return spillovers between white precious metal ETFs: The role of oil, gold, and global equity. *International Review of Financial Analysis, 52*, 316–332. doi:10.1016/j.irfa.2017.04.001

Lien, D., & Yang, L. (2006). Spot-futures spread, time-varying correlation, and hedging with currency futures. *Journal of Futures Markets, 26*(10), 1019–1038. doi:10.1002/fut.20225

Liu, Y., & Tsyvinski, A. (2021). Risks and returns of cryptocurrency. *Review of Financial Studies, 34*(6), 2689–2727. doi:10.1093/rfs/hhaa113

Lodha, S. (2017). A Cointegration and Causation Study of Gold Prices, Crude Oil Prices and Exchange Rates. *IUP Journal of Financial Risk Management, 14*(3), 55–66.

Louzis, D. P. (2015). Measuring spillover effects in Euro area financial markets: A disaggregate approach. *Empirical Economics, 49*(4), 1367–1400. doi:10.1007/s00181-014-0911-x

Madhavan, A. (2000). Market microstructure: A survey. *Journal of Financial Markets, 3*(3), 205–258. doi:10.1016/S1386-4181(00)00007-0

Manera, M., McAleer, M., & Grasso, M. (2006). Modelling time-varying conditional correlations in the volatility of Tapis oil spot and forward returns. *Applied Financial Economics, 16*(07), 525–533. doi:10.1080/09603100500426465

Mensi, W., Hammoudeh, S., Nguyen, D. K., & Yoon, S. M. (2014). Dynamic spillovers among major energy and cereal commodity prices. *Energy Economics, 43*, 225–243. doi:10.1016/j.eneco.2014.03.004

Momtaz, P. P. (2021). The pricing and performance of cryptocurrency. *European Journal of Finance, 27*(4-5), 367–380. doi:10.1080/1351847X.2019.1647259

Nakamoto, S. (2008). Bitcoin: A peer-to-peer electronic cash system. *Decentralized business review*, 21260.

Ozdemir, H., & Ozdemir, Z. A. (2021). *A Survey of Hedge and Safe Havens Assets against G-7 Stock Markets before and during the COVID-19 Pandemic* (No. 14888). IZA Discussion Papers.

Özdemir, O. (2022). Cue the volatility spillover in the cryptocurrency markets during the COVID-19 pandemic: Evidence from DCC-GARCH and wavelet analysis. *Financial Innovation, 8*(1), 1–38. doi:10.1186/s40854-021-00319-0 PMID:35132369

Qarni, M. O., & Gulzar, S. (2021). Portfolio diversification benefits of alternative currency investment in Bitcoin and foreign exchange markets. *Financial Innovation*, 7(1), 1–37. doi:10.1186/s40854-021-00233-5

Šimáková, J. (2011). Analysis of the relationship between oil and gold prices. *The Journal of Finance*, *51*(1), 651–662.

Stoklasová, R. (2018). Short-term and Long-term relationships between Gold Prices and Oil Prices. *Scientific papers of the University of Pardubice. Series D. Faculty of Economics and Administration.*, *43*, 221–231.

TansuchatR.ChangC. L.McAleerM. (2010). Crude oil hedging strategies using dynamic multivariate GARCH. *Available at* SSRN 1531187. doi:10.2139/ssrn.1531187

Toraman, C., Basarir, C., & Bayramoglu, M. F. (2011). Effects of crude oil price changes on sector indices of Istanbul stock exchange. *European Journal of Economic and Political Studies*, *4*(2), 109–124.

Toyoshima, Y., Nakajima, T., & Hamori, S. (2013). Crude oil hedging strategy: New evidence from the data of the financial crisis. *Applied Financial Economics*, *23*(12), 1033–1041. doi:10.1080/09603107.2013.788779

Tse, Y. K., & Tsui, A. K. C. (2002). A multivariate generalized autoregressive conditional heteroscedasticity model with time-varying correlations. *Journal of Business & Economic Statistics*, *20*(3), 351–362. doi:10.1198/073500102288618496

Urquhart, A., & Zhang, H. (2019). Is Bitcoin a hedge or safe haven for currencies? An intraday analysis. *International Review of Financial Analysis*, *63*, 49–57. doi:10.1016/j.irfa.2019.02.009

Zhang, C., & Tu, X. (2016). The effect of global oil price shocks on China's metal markets. *Energy Policy*, *90*, 131–139. doi:10.1016/j.enpol.2015.12.012

Zhang, D., Lei, L., Ji, Q., & Kutan, A. M. (2019). Economic policy uncertainty in the US and China and their impact on the global markets. *Economic Modelling*, *79*, 47–56. doi:10.1016/j.econmod.2018.09.028

Zhang, X., Yu, L., Wang, S., & Lai, K. K. (2009). Estimating the impact of extreme events on crude oil price: An EMD-based event analysis method. *Energy Economics*, *31*(5), 768–778. doi:10.1016/j.eneco.2009.04.003

Zhang, Y. J., Bouri, E., Gupta, R., & Ma, S. J. (2021). Risk spillover between Bitcoin and conventional financial markets: An expectile-based approach. *The North American Journal of Economics and Finance*, *55*, 101296. doi:10.1016/j.najef.2020.101296

Chapter 17
Metaverse Metamorphosis:
Bridging the Gap Between Research Insights and Industry Applications

Manpreet Arora

iD https://orcid.org/0000-0002-4939-1992

School of Commerce and Management Studies, Central University of Himachal Pradesh, India

ABSTRACT

The incorporation of the metaverse into the world of business has brought about a significant and fundamental change, altering conventional frameworks and methods while presenting unparalleled prospects for expansion and creativity. This chapter examines the significant influence of the transformation of the metaverse on the worldwide economy, emphasising its ability to generate fresh prospects for work, labour, and employment. In addition, an attempt has been made to explore the economic consequences of the metaverse, encompassing the emergence of fresh sectors, markets, and sources of income, as well as the promotion of economic expansion and employment generation. This chapter examines the impact of the metaverse on economic development, innovation, and quality of life globally, highlighting its revolutionary capabilities. Furthermore, the author explores the significance of closing the divide between research discoveries and industrial implementations, highlighting the necessity of cooperation and information sharing to convert academic discoveries into tangible advancements that have a tangible effect on the real world. This chapter examines the impact of the metaverse on economic development, innovation, and quality of life globally.

INTRODUCTION

Artificial intelligence (AI) is crucial in multi-business contexts since it offers sophisticated analytics, automation, and decision-making abilities across diverse industries (Arora and Sharma; 2022). Whereas the metaverse has arisen as a powerful and game-changing force in the field of technology, with the potential to revolutionise our interactions with digital environments and each other. The metaverse fundamentally embodies the merging of virtual and physical realities, erasing the distinctions between the

DOI: 10.4018/979-8-3693-2607-7.ch017

digital and the tangible (Rathore & Arora, 2024). The metaverse differs from conventional virtual reality experiences by including a wide and linked network of virtual environments, allowing users to interact, create, and transact in real time (Narula, 2022; Bojic, 2022). The metaverse is characterised by its immersive quality, which allows users to feel fully present and have control within virtual surroundings. The metaverse allows users to utilise cutting-edge technologies like virtual reality, augmented reality, artificial intelligence, and blockchain to assume digital avatars, navigate virtual environments, and participate in various activities, including socialising, gaming, shopping, and education. This immersive experience has the capacity to transform the way we engage in work, leisure, and social interactions, surpassing the constraints of physical boundaries and temporal limits. Furthermore, the metaverse is not merely a static digital recreational area, but rather a vibrant and developing system propelled by user-created material and interactions. It encompasses the ideals of decentralisation and democratisation, giving individuals and communities the opportunity to build their own virtual experiences and economies. The metaverse provides a wide range of options for creativity, entrepreneurship, and innovation (Dhiman & Arora, 2024). It also includes virtual real estate, digital assets, virtual events, and entertainment. Nevertheless, the advent of the metaverse also gives rise to a multitude of intricate ethical, social, and economic inquiries that require meticulous examination. Concerns surrounding digital privacy, virtual identity, intellectual property rights, and algorithmic bias are becoming more relevant as the metaverse brings together virtual experiences and their real-world impacts. Moreover, the possibility of virtual addiction, social seclusion, and digital disparity emphasises the necessity for conscientious design and control to guarantee that the advantages of the metaverse are fairly distributed and available to everyone. The academia plays a crucial role in filling the knowledge gaps related to the metaverse and in advancing research, innovation, and policy formulation in this emergent domain. Academia can contribute to the responsible, equitable, and sustainable development of the metaverse by creating theoretical frameworks, analysing ethical and societal consequences, connecting academia with industry, promoting accessibility and inclusivity, and studying economic dynamics.

The incorporation of the metaverse into many industries, sectors, domains, and disciplines has the capacity to completely transform conventional processes, workflows, and experiences, while also resolving long-standing deficiencies. The benefits of utilising the metaverse are becoming more evident in several domains.

Within the field of education, the metaverse provides immersive and interactive learning environments that beyond the constraints of conventional classrooms. Students can actively participate in intricate ideas through practical simulations, computer-generated laboratories, and interactive instructional materials, promoting a more profound comprehension and long-term retention of knowledge. In addition, the metaverse promotes worldwide collaboration and provides access to educational resources, allowing learners from various backgrounds to connect and acquire knowledge from one another. The democratisation of education facilitates the elimination of geographical obstacles and socioeconomic inequities, thereby guaranteeing everyone access to high-quality education.

The metaverse has the potential to enhance patient care, medical training, and research in the field of healthcare. Virtual reality simulations enable medical students and professionals to engage in realistic settings to practise surgical operations and diagnostic skills, thereby minimising the requirement for expensive and time-consuming physical simulations. Telemedicine platforms that utilise augmented reality allow for remote consultations and diagnostics, hence increasing the availability of healthcare services in locations that lack sufficient access. In addition, the metaverse enables the exchange of data and cooperation among researchers, expediting the progress of novel treatments and therapies for diverse medical ailments. Looking further, the entertainment and gaming sectors have promptly adopted the metaverse, utilising its immersive features to develop fascinating experiences for users. Virtual reality gaming allows players to immerse themselves in imaginative realms, where they can actively engage with virtual characters, explore diverse settings, and partake in exhilarating quests. In addition, the metaverse erases the boundaries between gaming, socialising, and entertainment, offering possibilities for real-time events, virtual concerts, and interactive narrative encounters. The integration of entertainment and technology in this context improves user involvement and promotes a feeling of camaraderie among players, thus addressing the typical sense of seclusion found in conventional gaming encounters. Within the domain of business and commerce, the metaverse presents novel prospects for marketing, sales, and client interaction. Virtual showrooms and storefronts enable businesses to exhibit their products and services in immersive surroundings, offering customers a more captivating and interactive purchasing experience (Lee & Leonas, (2018); Violante, Vezzetti & Piazzolla, (2019); Hagtvedt & Chandukala, (2023); Erensoy et.al., (2022, December)). Virtual events and conferences allow companies to connect with a worldwide audience without the requirement of physical locations, resulting in cost savings and a reduced environmental footprint. In addition, the metaverse enables virtual collaboration and remote work, allowing teams to communicate across different physical locations and time zones, thus circumventing the limitations of typical office settings.

The metaverse provides architects, real estate developers, and urban planners with a potent instrument for visualising and modelling building designs and urban environments (Schumacher, 2022). Virtual reality walkthroughs enable clients to immerse themselves in architectural plans with intricate detail prior to the commencement of construction, thereby minimising expensive modifications and improving stakeholder involvement. In addition, virtual property tours allow potential buyers and renters to remotely examine real estate listings, thereby increasing market coverage and simplifying well-informed decision-making. The metaverse has the capacity to revolutionise the travel and tourism sector by providing virtual travel experiences that accurately replicate real-world destinations (Buhalis, Leung, & Lin, (2023); Um et.al., (2022, January); Gursoy, Malodia & Dhir, (2022); Volchek & Brysch, (2023, January); Go & Kang, (2023)). Virtual tourism platforms enable users to virtually see famous monuments, breathtaking natural wonders, and captivating cultural attractions without leaving their homes. These platforms offer a glimpse of other places and serve as a source of inspiration for future travel arrangements. Moreover, virtual travel experiences can accommodate persons with limited mobility or financial restrictions, hence enhancing travel accessibility and inclusivity. In the manufacturing sector, the metaverse offers opportunities for virtual prototyping, product design, and process optimization (Yao, et.al., 2024). Virtual reality simulations enable manufacturers to test product designs, manufacturing processes, and assembly lines in virtual environments, identifying potential issues and optimizing efficiency before physical production begins. Additionally, virtual collaboration platforms facilitate communication and collaboration among global teams, streamlining product development and reducing time-to-market. The metaverse offers novel opportunities for artistic and expressive endeavours across diverse creative sectors, including as art, music, film, and design (Baía Reis & Ashmore, (2022); Dionisio, et.al., (2013); Armitage, (2023); FREYERMUTH, (2022)). Virtual reality art galleries and immersive installations enable artists to exhibit their work in novel ways, reaching worldwide audiences and cultivating fresh modes of artistic expression. Virtual reality concerts and music festivals allow musicians to engage with listeners in immersive and interactive settings, surpassing the constraints of conventional live shows. Governments and public institutions have the ability to utilise the metaverse in order to enhance civic participation, public services, and governance (Allam, et.al., 2022). Virtual town halls and community forums facilitate global citizen participation in decision-making processes, hence enhancing transparency and accountability. In addition, virtual training simulations can enhance the preparedness and response capacities of government organisations and emergency responders by allowing them to practise and train for a range of scenarios, including natural disasters and public health emergencies.

The metaverse has the capacity to address enduring limitations in several businesses and sectors by offering immersive, interactive, and easily accessible solutions. The metaverse provides new solutions to solve the issues of the digital age, such as reducing geographical barriers in education and healthcare, enhancing user engagement in entertainment and gaming, and improving collaboration and productivity in business and commerce. As organisations and individuals further investigate the potential of the metaverse, the beneficial impacts are expected to increase, leading to a new era of interconnectedness, ingenuity, and advancement.

THE OPPORTUNITIES

The incorporation of the metaverse into the commercial world has fundamentally transformed the economic framework, providing many prospects for advancement, creativity, and success. The metaverse has revolutionised various industries and sectors by introducing a new era of connectivity, cooperation, and commerce. This transformation has had a significant impact on old business models and practices.

The metaverse has a profound influence on the corporate landscape by generating fresh prospects for work, labour, and employment. With the growing prevalence of virtual environments, various areas are witnessing the emergence of new jobs and job prospects; the prospects in gig economy are very bright (Arora & Singh, 2023). These include virtual reality creation, digital marketing, virtual event organising, and virtual commerce. The expansion of job options not only facilitates economic progress but also cultivates a climate of creativity and business initiative, stimulating general economic expansion and well-being. Furthermore, the metaverse presents unparalleled prospects for firms to access worldwide markets and enhance their clientele. E-commerce platforms, online marketplaces, and interactive shopping interfaces facilitate global business-customer interactions, surpassing limitations of distance and time. The extensive global presence not only enhances sales and revenue channels, but also facilitates cultural interchange and diversity, enhancing the commercial environment and promoting international collaboration and comprehension.

Moreover, the metaverse improves the efficiency and convenience of everyday activities for both companies and customers. Virtual collaboration solutions facilitate efficient cooperation among remote teams, allowing them to overcome geographical limitations and time restrictions. Virtual reality meetings, conferences, and training sessions provide immersive and interactive experiences that replicate real-world interactions, hence increasing productivity and engagement (Arora, 2024). Moreover, virtual assistants and AI-powered chatbots enhance the efficiency of customer care and support procedures by offering tailored guidance and promptly addressing inquiries.

The expansion of the metaverse also fosters economic development by generating new sectors, markets, and sources of income. The metaverse economy is primarily supported by virtual real estate, digital assets, and virtual currencies, which present many prospects for investment, speculation, and entrepreneurship. Entrepreneurial ventures contribute to a great deal towards economic development where digitalization is playing a pivotal role (Dhiman & Arora, 2024). Virtual events, entertainment experiences, and digital collectibles provide more opportunities for making money and generating revenue, stimulating economic activity and promoting job growth in many industries (Arora, Kumar & Valeri, 2023). The convergence of the metaverse and artificial intelligence (AI) offers unparalleled prospects for fostering sustainability and accelerating the attainment of the United Nations Sustainable Development Goals (SDGs). The metaverse can enhance resource management, minimise environmental impact, and expedite progress towards sustainable development goals by utilising virtual simulations, AI-powered analytics, and data-driven decision-making. Virtual reality training programmes can instruct individuals and organisations on sustainable practices, including the use of renewable energy, waste reduction, and conservation initiatives. Artificial intelligence algorithms have the capability to analyse extensive quantities of data obtained from virtual environments in order to enhance energy efficiency, transportation systems, and urban planning, resulting in the development of more sustainable and resilient cities. Furthermore, the metaverse facilitates telecommuting and virtual cooperation, so decreasing the necessity for physical transportation and travel, ultimately resulting in reduced carbon emissions and the alleviation of climate change. In addition, the widespread use of the metaverse and AI-powered technology presents novel employment prospects for achievement of SDGS in many sectors (Arora & Chandel, 2023). In various areas like AI coding, sustainability advisory, and digital advertising, it can promote fostering economic expansion and societal integration. By utilising the revolutionary capabilities of the metaverse and AI to advance sustainability and generate significant employment prospects, we can expedite the achievement of the Sustainable Development Goals (SDGs) and establish a more prosperous and fair future for everyone.

Ultimately, the transformation caused by the metaverse has fundamentally altered the entire landscape of business, opening up abundant possibilities for expansion, creativity, and success. The metaverse has the ability to greatly contribute to economic development and improve the quality of life for individuals and communities worldwide. It achieves this by introducing new job opportunities, increasing global markets, making living easier, and promoting economic growth. As businesses increasingly adopt the metaverse, we can anticipate a surge in invention, collaboration, and economic growth in the future.

ADDRESSING THE GAPS

The academic community plays a crucial role in influencing the discussion about the metaverse and in furthering our comprehension of its possible uses, consequences, and difficulties. Nevertheless, despite the growing interest and enthusiasm around this developing topic, there are certain deficiencies that academia must address in order to fully achieve the potential of the metaverse.

A notable deficiency exists in the theoretical underpinnings of the metaverse. Although there is a considerable amount of study on the technical elements of virtual reality, augmented reality, and related technologies, there is still a requirement for comprehensive theoretical frameworks that can assist us in understanding the metaverse as a complex socio-technical phenomenon. Academia can contribute by creating interdisciplinary methodologies that incorporate knowledge from disciplines such as sociology, psychology, anthropology, and communication studies to investigate the cultural, psychological, and social aspects of the metaverse. Another shortcoming lies in comprehending the ethical and societal ramifications of the metaverse. As virtual environments grow more integrated into our daily lives, it is essential to carefully analyse the ethical quandaries and societal repercussions that emerge. Topics such as digital privacy, virtual identity, digital inequality, and algorithmic prejudice necessitate meticulous examination and study. The academic community may have a significant impact by conducting empirical research, ethical investigations, and policy analysis to provide valuable insights for the responsible development and management of the metaverse.

Moreover, there exists a significant disparity in connecting the gap between academia and industry inside the dominion of the metaverse. Although academia frequently pioneers' advancements in knowledge and innovation, there can be a gap between academic research and industry practices. Academia may enhance collaboration and knowledge sharing with industry partners by implementing initiatives including collaborative research projects, industry-academic alliances, and technology transfer programmes. By closing this divide, academics can guarantee that research discoveries are converted into tangible implementations that yield societal benefits and stimulate economic expansion. Furthermore, there is a deficiency in effectively addressing the issues of accessibility and diversity inside the metaverse. With the increasing prevalence of virtual environments, it is crucial to guarantee their accessibility to individuals of diverse abilities and backgrounds. This encompasses the creation of user interfaces that are accessible to all users, the creation of technologies that aid individuals with disabilities, and the promotion of digital literacy and the enhancement of skills. Academia can take the lead in developing accessibility guidelines, conducting usability research, and advocating for inclusive design principles in the development of metaverse platforms and applications.

Ultimately, there exists a lack of comprehension of the economic workings of the metaverse. With the rise of virtual economies and digital marketplaces, it is crucial to create strong economic models and frameworks to effectively analyse and comprehend these phenomena. This encompasses the examination of virtual currencies, digital assets, virtual property rights, and the rise of novel business models and sources of income. Academia may make valuable contributions to the metaverse economy by doing empirical research, performing economic analysis, and evaluating policies. These efforts can provide valuable information for decision-making and regulation in this emerging field.

Academicians have multiple obstacles when it comes to bridging the divide between research discoveries and industry applications.

Differing Objectives and Timelines

Academia and industry can have divergent objectives and deadlines. Academia places importance on meticulous research and extensive examination of theoretical ideas, whereas industry prioritises practical resolutions and immediate results. The misalignment between academia and industry partners might pose challenges for researchers in adapting their results to meet the specific needs and limitations of the sector.

Access to Resources and Infrastructure

Scholars may encounter constraints when it comes to getting the resources and infrastructure required to transform their research into concrete applications. Industries frequently have access to specialised equipment, technology, and money that may not be easily accessible in university environments. The scarcity of resources might impede the progress and execution of research-based solutions in practical situations.

Intellectual Property and Commercialization

The presence of intellectual property rights and the need to consider commercialization might pose substantial obstacles in connecting academia and industry. Scholars may encounter difficulties in navigating the intricate realm of patents, licencing agreements, and commercialization channels, particularly when working along with corporate partners. Successfully managing the simultaneous goals of achieving high academic standards and turning research findings into profitable products necessitates skillful negotiating and meticulous strategic planning.

Communication and Collaboration

Efficient communication and collaboration between academia and industry are crucial for closing the divide between research findings and practical implementations in the business world. Nevertheless, disparities in communication methods, anticipated outcomes, and corporate cultures might impede cooperation. Academics should actively interact with industry stakeholders, establish connections, and effectively communicate their research findings in a manner that aligns with industry requirements and priorities.

Risk Aversion and Institutional Barriers

The existing institutional frameworks and motivators inside academia could unintentionally impede the willingness to take risks and engage in innovative practices. The prioritisation of publishing metrics, tenure criteria, and academic reputation may discourage academics from engaging in practical research and collaborating with industries. To overcome these institutional impediments, it is necessary to obtain support from academic institutions and to change towards acknowledging and incentivizing interdisciplinary collaboration and tangible real-world outcomes.

Interdisciplinary Collaboration and Knowledge Integration

Facilitating the connection between research findings and practical implementation in many industries often necessitates the collaboration of experts from different disciplines and the integration of their knowledge. Nevertheless, multidisciplinary research poses difficulties as a result of disciplinary silos, communication impediments, and divergent techniques. Academics should proactively pursue chances for interdisciplinary collaboration, utilise a range of views, and incorporate insights from other fields to effectively tackle difficult real-world issues.

Insufficient Practical Experience

Academicians may have a limited understanding of the real-world issues and limitations encountered by industry professionals due to their lack of firsthand experience in industry settings. Lacking practical experience, academics may face difficulties in formulating research answers that are genuinely relevant and applicable to real-life situations.

Cultural Differences

Cultural disparities exist between academia and industry, characterised by contrasting cultural environments, encompassing divergent values, conventions, and expectations. The presence of cultural disparities can impede cooperation and effective communication, resulting in misinterpretations and disputes.

Academics should be aware of these cultural distinctions and strive to establish trust and rapport with industry collaborators.

Technology Transfer and Commercialization Processes

The technology transfer and commercialization processes involve the transfer of technology from academic institutions to the industry and the conversion of research outputs into commercial products. These processes can be intricate and need a significant amount of time. Academics may have insufficient knowledge and skills to efficiently traverse these processes, resulting in delays and inefficiencies. Engaging with technology transfer offices and industry specialists can assist academics in overcoming these obstacles and optimising the influence of their research.

Resistance to Change

Resistance to change, whether it occurs in academia or industry, can hinder attempts to connect research findings with practical applications in the business world. Academics may face opposition from colleagues or administrators who are doubtful of multidisciplinary collaboration or commercialization endeavours. Likewise, individuals involved in the sector may be hesitant to embrace novel technologies or methods that question established norms. To overcome this resistance, it is necessary to have robust leadership, efficient communication, and a dedication to innovation and advancement.

Sustainability and Scalability

Academicians have the difficulty of ensuring the long-term viability and ability to expand research-driven solutions. Although academic research may produce encouraging outcomes in controlled environments, implementing these ideas on a larger scale to address the requirements of industry and society as a whole can be difficult. When developing research-driven solutions for industry applications, academicians must take into account variables such as cost-effectiveness, scalability, and long-term viability.

Ethical and Social Considerations

Academicians must confront ethical and societal considerations when applying research results to industry. Research-based solutions can potentially lead to unforeseen repercussions or ethical issues that require thorough examination and resolution. Scholars must carefully and honestly address these ethical and social factors, ensuring that their research has a beneficial impact on society as a whole.

In order to connect research findings with practical applications in industry, academics must cross a multifaceted terrain of institutional, cultural, and practical obstacles. Through promoting collaboration, communication, and interdisciplinary involvement, academics can surmount these obstacles and make valuable contributions to the creation and execution of research-based solutions that have significant effects on both industry and society.

CONCLUSION

To summarise, the metaverse signifies a fundamental change in our understanding and engagement with digital technology, presenting extraordinary possibilities as well as difficulties. As we begin this process of transforming the metaverse, it is crucial to approach it with a discerning and reflective mindset, ensuring that we balance creativity with ethical considerations and uphold the ideals of inclusivity, diversity, and sustainability. The complete use of the metaverse's potential to establish a more linked, immersive, and fair digital future can only be achieved through cooperative endeavours and careful management. Ultimately, the rise of the metaverse signifies a fundamental change in how we engage with digital technology, presenting unparalleled opportunities as well as notable obstacles. As we begin this transforming journey, it is crucial to approach the metaverse with a thoughtful and introspective perspective, acknowledging both its possibilities and its drawbacks.The metaverse has the potential to profoundly transform multiple facets of human existence, encompassing domains such as education, healthcare, entertainment, and business. The immersive and linked nature of this technology provides unprecedented prospects for creativity, collaboration, and invention. However, fully harnessing the capabilities of the metaverse necessitates thoughtful examination of the ethical, societal, and economic consequences. It is imperative to give priority to inclusivity, diversity, and sustainability while creating and implementing metaverse technologies, with the aim of ensuring that they have a positive impact on individuals and communities worldwide. Through promoting collaboration, communication, and cooperation among academia, industry, and government, we may effectively navigate the intricacies of the metaverse and utilise its revolutionary potential for the betterment of society.

Moreover, as we explore into the potentialities of the metaverse, it is imperative that we maintain a watchful eye on its potential hazards and difficulties. Topics such as digital privacy, virtual identity, economic injustice, and cultural homogenization necessitate careful examination and aggressive measures to address them. To overcome these obstacles and ensure the growth of the metaverse is proactive and ethical, we may construct a digital future that is interconnected, immersive, and equitable for everyone. In order for the metaverse to reach its maximum capabilities, it is essential for there to be a collaborative endeavour and responsible management. By engaging in cooperative efforts, fostering cross-disciplinary discussions, and exhibiting principled guidance, we have the ability to mould the metaverse into a catalyst for beneficial transformation, propelling advancements, financial expansion, and societal advancement in the future. Furthermore, as we explore the intricacies of the metaverse, it is crucial to sustain a harmonious equilibrium between groundbreaking advancements and ethical deliberations. Although the metaverse presents enticing prospects for innovation and progress, it is crucial to be aware of the potential repercussions that may arise from uncontrolled growth. Concerns like as the protection of data privacy, the presence of algorithmic bias, and the problem of digital addiction necessitate careful monitoring and regulation to protect the rights and welfare of users. By giving precedence to ethical values and adopting a human-centered design approach, we can guarantee that the metaverse will augment rather than diminish our quality of life.

Furthermore, prioritising inclusivity and accessibility is crucial in fully harnessing the capabilities of the metaverse. In our pursuit of the new digital era, it is crucial that we work towards closing the gap between those who have access to digital resources and those who do not. By giving priority to inclusivity and accessibility, we may construct a metaverse that accurately mirrors the wide range and depth of human experience.

Moreover, cultivating a culture of sustainability is crucial in constructing a metaverse that is both groundbreaking and conscientious towards the environment and society. The creation and functioning of virtual environments necessitate substantial energy and resources, and unregulated expansion could have adverse effects on the environment and worsen pre-existing inequities. Through the adoption of sustainable design methods, the reduction of carbon footprints, and the promotion of responsible consumption and production, we can lessen the negative environmental effects of the metaverse and guarantee its contribution to a more sustainable future for future generations.

To summarise, the metaverse offers a significant chance to redefine our engagement with digital technology and create our digital destiny. By adopting a thoughtful and introspective approach to the metaverse, emphasising moral issues, advocating for inclusivity and accessibility, and cultivating a sustainable culture, we may utilise its revolutionary potential to establish a more interconnected, immersive, and fair digital era. By engaging in cooperative endeavours and practicing accountable governance, we can unleash the complete capabilities of the metaverse and establish a path towards a more promising future for everyone.

REFERENCES

Allam, Z., Sharifi, A., Bibri, S. E., Jones, D. S., & Krogstie, J. (2022). The metaverse as a virtual form of smart cities: Opportunities and challenges for environmental, economic, and social sustainability in urban futures. *Smart Cities, 5*(3), 771–801. doi:10.3390/smartcities5030040

Armitage, J. (2023). Rethinking haute couture: Julien Fournié in the virtual worlds of the metaverse. *French Cultural Studies, 34*(2), 129–146. doi:10.1177/09571558221109708

Arora, M. (2024). Virtual Reality in Education: Analyzing the Literature and Bibliometric State of Knowledge. *Transforming Education with Virtual Reality*, 379-402.

Arora, M., & Chandel, M. (2023). SDGs and Skill Development: Perspectivizing future insights for the tourism industry. In Springer international handbooks of education (pp. 1–20). Springer. doi:10.1007/978-981-99-3895-7_26-1

Arora, M., Kumar, J., & Valeri, M. (2023). Crises and Resilience in the Age of Digitalization: Perspectivations of Past, Present and Future for tourism industry. In Emerald Publishing Limited eBooks. doi:10.1108/978-1-83797-166-420231004

Arora, M., & Sharma, R. L. (2022). Artificial intelligence and big data: Ontological and communicative perspectives in multi-sectoral scenarios of modern businesses. *Foresight, 25*(1), 126–143. doi:10.1108/FS-10-2021-0216

Arora, M., & Singh, S. (2023). Women's empowerment through entrepreneurship in emerging economies. In Advances in logistics, operations, and management science book series (pp. 205–223). IGI Global. doi:10.4018/979-8-3693-0111-1.ch011

Baía Reis, A., & Ashmore, M. (2022). From video streaming to virtual reality worlds: An academic, reflective, and creative study on live theatre and performance in the metaverse. *International Journal of Performance Arts and Digital Media, 18*(1), 7–28. doi:10.1080/14794713.2021.2024398

Bojic, L. (2022). Metaverse through the prism of power and addiction: What will happen when the virtual world becomes more attractive than reality? *European Journal of Futures Research, 10*(1), 22. doi:10.1186/s40309-022-00208-4

Buhalis, D., Leung, D., & Lin, M. (2023). Metaverse as a disruptive technology revolutionising tourism management and marketing. *Tourism Management, 97*, 104724. doi:10.1016/j.tourman.2023.104724

Dhiman, V., & Arora, M. (2024). Current State of Metaverse in Entrepreneurial Ecosystem: A Retrospective Analysis of Its Evolving Landscape. In Exploring the Use of Metaverse in Business and Education (pp. 73-87). IGI Global. doi:10.4018/979-8-3693-5868-9.ch005

Dhiman, V., & Arora, M. (2024). Exploring the linkage between business incubation and entrepreneurship: Understanding trends, themes and future research agenda. LBS Journal of Management & Research/ LBS. *Journal of Management Research.* doi:10.1108/LBSJMR-06-2023-0021

Dionisio, J. D. N., Iii, W. G. B., & Gilbert, R. (2013). 3D virtual worlds and the metaverse: Current status and future possibilities. *ACM Computing Surveys, 45*(3), 1–38. doi:10.1145/2480741.2480751

Erensoy, A., Mathrani, A., Schnack, A., Zhao, Y., Chitale, V. S., & Baghaei, N. (2022, December). Comparing Customer Behaviours: Immersive Virtual Reality Store Experiences versus Web and Physical Store Experiences. In *2022 IEEE Asia-Pacific Conference on Computer Science and Data Engineering (CSDE)* (pp. 1-7). IEEE. 10.1109/CSDE56538.2022.10089288

Freyermuth, G. S. (2022). Vegas, Disney, and the Metaverse. *Studies of Digital Media Culture, 14*, 17.

Go, H., & Kang, M. (2023). Metaverse tourism for sustainable tourism development: Tourism agenda 2030. *Tourism Review, 78*(2), 381–394. doi:10.1108/TR-02-2022-0102

Gursoy, D., Malodia, S., & Dhir, A. (2022). The metaverse in the hospitality and tourism industry: An overview of current trends and future research directions. *Journal of Hospitality Marketing & Management, 31*(5), 527–534. doi:10.1080/19368623.2022.2072504

Hagtvedt, H., & Chandukala, S. R. (2023). Immersive retailing: The in-store experience. *Journal of Retailing, 99*(4), 505–517. doi:10.1016/j.jretai.2023.10.003

Lee, H., & Leonas, K. (2018). Consumer experiences, the key to survive in an omni-channel environment: Use of virtual technology. *Journal of Textile and Apparel, Technology and Management, 10*(3).

Narula, H. (2022). *Virtual Society: The Metaverse and the New Frontiers of Human Experience.* Crown Currency.

Rathore, S., & Arora, M. (2024). Sustainability Reporting in the Metaverse: A Multi-Sectoral Analysis. In Exploring the Use of Metaverse in Business and Education (pp. 147-165). IGI Global. doi:10.4018/979-8-3693-5868-9.ch009

Schumacher, P. (2022). The metaverse as opportunity for architecture and society: Design drivers, core competencies. *Architectural Intelligence, 1*(1), 11. doi:10.1007/s44223-022-00010-z PMID:35993030

Um, T., Kim, H., Kim, H., Lee, J., Koo, C., & Chung, N. (2022, January). Travel Incheon as a metaverse: smart tourism cities development case in Korea. In *ENTER22 e-Tourism Conference* (pp. 226–231). Springer International Publishing. doi:10.1007/978-3-030-94751-4_20

Violante, M. G., Vezzetti, E., & Piazzolla, P. (2019). How to design a virtual reality experience that impacts the consumer engagement: The case of the virtual supermarket. [IJIDeM]. *International Journal on Interactive Design and Manufacturing*, *13*(1), 243–262. doi:10.1007/s12008-018-00528-5

Volchek, K., & Brysch, A. (2023, January). Metaverse and tourism: From a new niche to a transformation. In *ENTER22 e-Tourism Conference* (pp. 300–311). Springer Nature Switzerland. doi:10.1007/978-3-031-25752-0_32

Yao, X., Ma, N., Zhang, J., Wang, K., Yang, E., & Faccio, M. (2024). Enhancing wisdom manufacturing as industrial metaverse for industry and society 5.0. *Journal of Intelligent Manufacturing*, *35*(1), 235–255. doi:10.1007/s10845-022-02027-7

Compilation of References

A3Logics. (2023, May 18). How Metaverse Gaming Bought Revolution in Gaming Industry. *A3logics Blog*. https://www.a3logics.com/blog/metaverse-gaming-a-revolution-in-the-gaming-industry

Abbate, S., Centobelli, P., Cerchione, R., Oropallo, E., & Riccio, E. (2022, April). *A first bibliometric literature review on Metaverse. In 2022 IEEE Technology and Engineering Management Conference*. TEMSCON EUROPE.

Abdelghafar, S., Ezzat, D., Darwish, A., & Hassanien, A. E. (2023). Metaverse for Brain Computer Interface: Towards New and Improved Applications. In *The Future of Metaverse in the Virtual Era and Physical World* (pp. 43–58). Springer International Publishing. doi:10.1007/978-3-031-29132-6_3

Abrash, M. (2021, Dec 11-16). Creating the Future: Augmented Reality, the next Human-Machine Interface. *IEEE International Electron Devices Meeting*. IEEE International Electron Devices Meeting (IEDM), San Francisco, CA. 10.1109/IEDM19574.2021.9720526

Abumalloh, R. A., Nilashi, M., Ooi, K. B., Wei-Han, G., Cham, T. H., Dwivedi, Y. K., & Hughes, L. (2023). The adoption of a metaverse in the retail industry and its impact on sustainable competitive advantage: The moderating impact of sustainability commitment. *Annals of Operations Research*, 1–42. doi:10.1007/s10479-023-05608-8

Acevedo Nieto, J. (2022). Una introducción al metaverso: conceptualización y alcance de un nuevo universe. *adComunica*, (24), 41-56. doi:10.6035/adcomunica.6544

Adinew, Y. (2023). A comparative study on motivational strategies, organizational culture, and climate in public and private institutions. *Current Psychology (New Brunswick, N.J.)*, 1–23.

Afrashtehfar, K. I., & Abu-Fanas, A. S. H. (2022). Metaverse, Crypto, and NFTs in Dentistry. *Education Sciences*, *12*(8), 538. https://www.mdpi.com/2227-7102/12/8/538. doi:10.3390/educsci12080538

Agarwal, R., & Prasad, J. (2000). The role of e-commerce success factors in customer satisfaction. *Journal of the Academy of Marketing Science*, *28*(1), 18–25. doi:10.1177/0092070300281002

Agbo, F. J., Oyelere, S. S., Suhonen, J., & Tukiainen, M. (2021). Scientific production and thematic breakthroughs in smart learning environments: A bibliometric analysis. *Smart Learning Environments*, *8*(1), 1–25. doi:10.1186/s40561-020-00145-4

Ahmad, M., Akram, M., & Ureeb, S. (2024). Exploring the Role of Metaverse in Promoting Religious Tourism. In *Service Innovations in Tourism: Metaverse, Immersive Technologies, and Digital Twin* (pp. 39–63). IGI Global. doi:10.4018/979-8-3693-1103-5.ch003

Ahn, S. J., Kim, J., & Kim, J. (2022). The future of advertising research in virtual, augmented, and extended realities. *International Journal of Advertising*, 1–9. doi:10.1080/02650487.2022.2137316

Akpan, I. J., Soopramanien, D., & Kwak, D. H. (2021). Cutting-edge technologies for small business and innovation in the era of COVID-19 global health pandemic. *Journal of Small Business and Entrepreneurship*, *33*(6), 607–617. doi:10.1080/08276331.2020.1799294

Al-Adwan, A. S., Li, N., Al-Adwan, A., Abbasi, G. A., Albelbis, N. A., & Habibi, A. (2023). Extending the Technology Acceptance Model (TAM) to Predict University Students' Intentions to Use Metaverse-Based Learning Platforms. *Education and Information Technologies*, *28*(11), 15381–15413. doi:10.1007/s10639-023-11816-3 PMID:37361794

Albayati, H. (2024). Investigating undergraduate students' perceptions and awareness of using ChatGPT as a regular assistance tool: A user acceptance perspective study. *Computers and Education: Artificial Intelligence*, *6*, 100203. doi:10.1016/j.caeai.2024.100203

Al-Emran, M. (2023). Beyond technology acceptance: Development and evaluation of technology-environmental, economic, and social sustainability theory. *Technology in Society*, *75*, 102383. doi:10.1016/j.techsoc.2023.102383

Alessandrini, L., & Rognoli, V. (2023). Introducing the material experience concept in the metaverse and in virtual environments. In *Connectivity and Creativity in times of Conflict*. Academia Press. doi:10.26530/9789401496476-057

Alexandrova, E., & Poddubnaya, M. (2023). Metaverse in fashion industry development: applications and challenges. *E3S Web of Conferences*, *420*, 06019. doi:10.1051/e3sconf/202342006019

Al-Ghaili, A. M., Kasim, H., Al-Hada, N. M., Hassan, Z. B., Othman, M., Tharik, J. H., Kasmani, R. M., & Shayea, I. (2022). A review of Metaverse's definitions, architecture, applications, challenges, issues, solutions, and future trends. *IEEE Access : Practical Innovations, Open Solutions*, *10*, 125835–125866. doi:10.1109/ACCESS.2022.3225638

Ali, M., Naeem, F., Kaddoum, G., & Hossain, E. (2023). Metaverse communications, networking, security, and applications: Research issues, state-of-the-art, and future directions. *IEEE Communications Surveys & Tutorials*. 10.1051/shsconf/202316400001

Ali, M., Naeem, F., Kaddoum, G., & Hossain, E. (2023). Metaverse communications, networking, security, and applications: Research issues, state-of-the-art, and future directions. *IEEE Communications Surveys and Tutorials*, 1. doi:10.1109/COMST.2023.3347172

Ali, S., Abdullah, Armand, T. P. T., Athar, A., Hussain, A., Ali, M., Yaseen, M., Joo, M.-I., & Kim, H.-C. (2023). Metaverse in healthcare integrated with explainable ai and blockchain: Enabling immersiveness, ensuring trust, and providing patient data security. *Sensors (Basel)*, *23*(2), 565. doi:10.3390/s23020565 PMID:36679361

Allam, Z., Sharifi, A., Bibri, S. E., Jones, D. S., & Krogstie, J. (2022). The Metaverse as a virtual form of smart Cities: Opportunities and challenges for environmental, economic, and social sustainability in urban futures. *Smart Cities*, *5*(3), 771–801. doi:10.3390/smartcities5030040

Almansour, B. (2015). The impact of market sentiment index on stock returns: An empirical investigation on Kuala Lumpur Stock Exchange. *Journal of Arts, Science & Commerce, 6*(3).

Almansour, B. Y., & Arabyat, Y. A. (2017). Investment decision making among Gulf investors: Behavioural finance perspective. *International Journal of Management Studies*, *24*(1), 41–71. doi:10.32890/ijms.24.1.2017.10476

Almansour, B. Y., & Inairat, M. (2020). The impact of exchange rates on bitcoin returns: Further evidence from a time series framework. *International Journal of Scientific & Technology Research*, *9*(02), 4577–4581.

Al-Taie, M. Z., & Kadry, S. (2017). Information Diffusion in Social Networks. In *Python for Graph and Network Analysis. Advanced Information and Knowledge Processing*. Springer. doi:10.1007/978-3-319-53004-8_8

Alzayat, A., & Lee, S. H. M. (2021). Virtual products as an extension of my body: Exploring hedonic and utilitarian shopping value in a virtual reality retail environment. *Journal of Business Research*, *130*, 348–363. doi:10.1016/j.jbusres.2021.03.017

Ambika, A., Belk, R., Jain, V., & Krishna, R. (2023). The road to learning "who am I" is digitized: A study on consumer self-discovery through augmented reality tools. *Journal of Consumer Behaviour*, *22*(5), 1112–1127. doi:10.1002/cb.2185

Ardia, D., Bluteau, K., & Rüede, M. (2019). Regime changes in Bitcoin GARCH volatility dynamics. *Finance Research Letters*, *29*, 266–271. doi:10.1016/j.frl.2018.08.009

Aria, M., & Cuccurullo, C. (2017). Bibliometrix: An R-tool for comprehensive science mapping analysis. *Journal of Informetrics*, *11*(4), 959–975. doi:10.1016/j.joi.2017.08.007

Ariel Gendler, M. (2023). De la cibernética al metaverso: Una genealogía de características, transparencias y opacidades algorítmicas. *Disparidades. Revista de Antropologia*, *78*(1), e001b. doi:10.3989/dra.2023.001b

Armitage, J. (2023). Rethinking haute couture: Julien Fournié in the virtual worlds of the metaverse. *French Cultural Studies*, *34*(2), 129–146. doi:10.1177/09571558221109708

Arora, M. (2024). Virtual Reality in Education: Analyzing the Literature and Bibliometric State of Knowledge. *Transforming Education with Virtual Reality*, 379-402.

Arora, M., & Chandel, M. (2023). SDGs and Skill Development: Perspectivizing future insights for the tourism industry. In Springer international handbooks of education (pp. 1–20). Springer. doi:10.1007/978-981-99-3895-7_26-1

Arora, M., & Rathore, S. (2023). Sustainability Reporting and Research and Development in Tourism Industry: A Qualitative Inquiry of Present Trends and Avenues. In International Handbook of Skill, Education, Learning, and Research Development in Tourism and Hospitality (pp. 1-17). Singapore: Springer Nature Singapore. doi:10.1007/978-981-99-3895-7_33-1

Arora, M., & Singh, S. (2023). Women's empowerment through entrepreneurship in emerging economies. In Advances in logistics, operations, and management science book series (pp. 205–223). IGI Global. doi:10.4018/979-8-3693-0111-1.ch011

Arora, M., Dhiman, V., & Sharma, R. L. (2023). Exploring the Dimensions of Spirituality, Wellness and Value Creation amidst Himalayan Regions Promoting Entrepreneurship and Sustainability. *Journal of Tourismology*. doi:10.26650/jot.2023.9.2.1327877

Arora, M., Kumar, J., & Valeri, M. (2023). Crises and Resilience in the Age of Digitalization: Perspectivations of Past, Present and Future for tourism industry. In Emerald Publishing Limited eBooks. doi:10.1108/978-1-83797-166-420231004

Arora, M. (2020). Post-truth and marketing communication in technological age. In *Handbook of research on innovations in technology and marketing for the connected consumer* (pp. 94–108). IGI Global., doi:10.4018/978-1-7998-0131-3.ch005

Arora, M. (2024). Virtual Reality in Education Analyzing the literature and bibliometric state of knowledge. In *Transforming Education with Virtual Reality* (pp. 379–402). Wiley. doi:10.1002/9781394200498.ch22

Arora, M., & Sharma, R. L. (2022). Artificial intelligence and big data: Ontological and communicative perspectives in multi-sectoral scenarios of modern businesses. *Foresight*, *25*(1), 126–143. doi:10.1108/FS-10-2021-0216

Arpacı, İ., & Bahari, M. (2023). Investigating the role of psychological needs in predicting the educational sustainability of Metaverse using a deep learning-based hybrid SEM-ANN technique. *Interactive Learning Environments*, 1–13. doi:10.1080/10494820.2022.2164313

Arya, V., Sambyal, R., Sharma, A., & Dwivedi, Y. K. (2023). Brands are calling your AVATAR in Metaverse-A study to explore XR-based gamification marketing activities & consumer-based brand equity in virtual world. *Journal of Consumer Behaviour*. doi:10.1002/cb.2214

Ashmore, D., & Venz, S. (2023). *A brief history of Web 3.0*. Forbes Advisor. Retrieved May 20th, 2023 from https://www.forbes.com/advisor/au/investing/cryptocurrency/what-is-web-3-0/

Aslanidis, N., Bariviera, A. F., & Martínez-Ibañez, O. (2019). An analysis of cryptocurrencies conditional cross correlations. *Finance Research Letters*, *31*, 130–137. doi:10.1016/j.frl.2019.04.019

Athar, A., Ali, S. M., Mozumder, M. A. I., Ali, S., & Kim, H. C. (2023, February). Applications and Possible Challenges of Healthcare Metaverse. In *2023 25th International Conference on Advanced Communication Technology (ICACT)* (pp. 328-332). IEEE. 10.23919/ICACT56868.2023.10079314

Azuma, R. T. (1997). A Survey of Augmented Reality. *Presence (Cambridge, Mass.)*, *6*(4), 355–385. doi:10.1162/pres.1997.6.4.355

Baas, J., Schotten, M., Plume, A., Côté, G., & Karimi, R. (2020). Scopus as a curated, high-quality bibliometric data source for academic research in quantitative science studies. *Quantitative Science Studies*, *1*(1), 377–386. doi:10.1162/qss_a_00019

Baba, Y., Engle, R. F., Kraft, D. F., & Kroner, K. F. (1990). *Multivariate simultaneous generalized ARCH. Manuscript, University of California*. Department of Economics.

Bacher, N. (2022). *Metaverse Retailing* University of Pavia. https://www.researchgate.net/profile/Natalie-Bacher/publication/366441739_Metaverse_Retailing

Bagozzi, R. P., Yi, Y., & Phillips, L. W. (1991). Assessing construct validity in organizational research. *Administrative Science Quarterly*, *36*(3), 421–458. doi:10.2307/2393203

Bag, S., Rahman, M. S., Srivastava, G., & Shrivastav, S. K. (2023). Unveiling metaverse potential in supply chain management and overcoming implementation challenges: An empirical study. *Benchmarking*. Advance online publication. doi:10.1108/BIJ-05-2023-0314

Bag, S., Srivastava, G., Bashir, M. M. A., Kumari, S., Giannakis, M., & Chowdhury, A. H. (2022). Journey of customers in this digital era: Understanding the role of artificial intelligence technologies in user engagement and conversion. *Benchmarking*, *29*(7), 2074–2098. doi:10.1108/BIJ-07-2021-0415

Baía Reis, A., & Ashmore, M. (2022). From video streaming to virtual reality worlds: An academic, reflective, and creative study on live theatre and performance in the metaverse. *International Journal of Performance Arts and Digital Media*, *18*(1), 7–28. doi:10.1080/14794713.2021.2024398

Balcilar, M., Bouri, E., Gupta, R., & Roubaud, D. (2017). Can volume predict Bitcoin returns and volatility? A quantiles-based approach. *Economic Modelling*, *64*, 74–81. doi:10.1016/j.econmod.2017.03.019

Bale, A. S., Ghorpade, N., Hashim, M. F., Vaishnav, J., Almaspoor, Z., & Agostini, A. (2022). A comprehensive study on Metaverse and its impacts on humans. *Advances in Human-Computer Interaction, 2022*, 1-11. *Article, 3247060*. Advance online publication. doi:10.1155/2022/3247060

Ball, M. (2022). *The Metaverse: And How it Will Revolutionize Everything*. Liveright Publishing. doi:10.15358/9783800669400

Bamodu, O., & Ye, X. (2013). Virtual Reality and Virtual Reality System Components. *Advanced Materials Research*, *765-767*, 1169–1172. doi:10.4028/www.scientific.net/AMR.765-767.1169

Bansal, G., Rajgopal, K., Chamola, V., Xiong, Z., & Niyato, D. (2022). Healthcare in metaverse: A survey on current metaverse applications in healthcare. *IEEE Access : Practical Innovations, Open Solutions, 10,* 119914–119946. doi:10.1109/ACCESS.2022.3219845

Barber, B. M., & Odean, T. (2008). All that glitters: The effect of attention and news on the buying behavior of individual and institutional investors. *Review of Financial Studies, 21*(2), 785–818. doi:10.1093/rfs/hhm079

Bardhan, A. (2023). Expansion of Space in Metaverse Communication and its Probable Impact. *Society Language and Culture: A Multidisciplinary Peer-Reviewed Journal,* (4), 30-36. https://www.societylanguageculture.org

Bariviera, A. F., Zunino, L., & Rosso, O. A. (2018). An analysis of high-frequency cryptocurrencies prices dynamics using permutation-information-theory quantifiers. *Chaos (Woodbury, N.Y.), 28*(7), 075511. doi:10.1063/1.5027153 PMID:30070500

Barrera, K. G., & Shah, D. (2023). Marketing in the Metaverse: Conceptual understanding, framework, and research agenda. *Journal of Business Research, 155,* 113420. doi:10.1016/j.jbusres.2022.113420

Bashir, A. K., Victor, N., Bhattacharya, S., Huynh-The, T., Chengoden, R., Yenduri, G., Maddikunta, P. K. R., Pham, Q.-V., Gadekallu, T. R., & Liyanage, M. (2023). Federated Learning for the Healthcare Metaverse: Concepts, Applications, Challenges, and Future Directions. *IEEE Internet of Things Journal, 10*(24), 21873–21891. doi:10.1109/JIOT.2023.3304790

Baskaran, K. (2023). Customer Experience in the E-Commerce Market Through the Virtual World of Metaverse. In *Handbook of Research on Consumer Behavioral Analytics in Metaverse and the Adoption of a Virtual World* (pp. 153–170). IGI Global. doi:10.4018/978-1-6684-7029-9.ch008

Baur, D. G., Dimpfl, T., & Kuck, K. (2018). Bitcoin, gold and the US dollar–A replication and extension. *Finance Research Letters, 25,* 103–110. doi:10.1016/j.frl.2017.10.012

Bauwens, L., Laurent, S., & Rombouts, J. V. (2006). Multivariate GARCH models: A survey. *Journal of Applied Econometrics, 21*(1), 79–109. doi:10.1002/jae.842

BBC. (2021). *Ariana Grande sings in Fortnite's metaverse.* BBC. https://www.bbc.com/news/av/technology-58146042

Becker, S. J., Nemat, A. T., Lucas, S., Heinitz, R. M., Klevesath, M., & Charton, J. E. (2022). A Code of Digital Ethics: Laying the foundation for digital ethics in a science and technology company. *AI & Society, 38*(6), 2629–2639. doi:10.1007/s00146-021-01376-w

Bedoui, R., Braiek, S., Guesmi, K., & Chevallier, J. (2019). RETRACTED: On the conditional dependence structure between oil, gold and USD exchange rates: Nested copula based GJR-GARCH model. *Energy Economics, 80,* 876–889. doi:10.1016/j.eneco.2019.02.002

Bektas, H. (2023). *Revealing relevant factors impacting the viability of the metaverse by replacing online collaboration tools for business meetings* (Publication Number 60644) University of Twente]. https://essay.utwente.nl/96243/

Beneki, C., Koulis, A., Kyriazis, N. A., & Papadamou, S. (2019). Investigating volatility transmission and hedging properties between Bitcoin and Ethereum. *Research in International Business and Finance, 48,* 219–227. doi:10.1016/j.ribaf.2019.01.001

BenMabrouk, H. S., Sassi, S., Soltane, F., & Abid, I. (2024). Connectedness and portfolio hedging between NFTs segments, American stocks and cryptocurrencies Nexus. *International Review of Financial Analysis, 91,* 102959. doi:10.1016/j.irfa.2023.102959

Bennett, D. (2022). Remote workforce, virtual team tasks, and employee engagement tools in a real-time interoperable decentralized metaverse. *Psychosociological Issues in Human Resource Management, 10*(1), 78–91. doi:10.22381/pihrm10120226

Bennett, E. E., & McWhorter, R. R. (2022). Dancing in the paradox: Virtual human resource development, online teaching, and learning. *Advances in Developing Human Resources, 24*(2), 99–116. doi:10.1177/15234223221079440

Benosman, M. (2023). *Social Psychology in the Era of the Metaverse: An overview of recent studies*

Benrimoh, D., Chheda, F. D., & Margolese, H. C. (2022). The Best Predictor of the Future—The Metaverse, Mental Health, and Lessons Learned From Current Technologies. *JMIR Mental Health, 9*(10), e40410. doi:10.2196/40410 PMID:36306155

Berglund, Å. F., Gong, L., & Li, D. (2018). Testing and validating Extended Reality (xR) technologies in manufacturing. *Procedia Manufacturing, 25*, 31–38. doi:10.1016/j.promfg.2018.06.054

Berkhout, F., & Hertin, J. (2004). De-materialising and re-materialising: Digital technologies and the environment. *Futures, 36*(8), 903–920. doi:10.1016/j.futures.2004.01.003

Berlo, Z. M. C., Reijmersdal, E. A., & Eisend, M. (2021). The Gamification of Branded Content: A Meta-Analysis of Advergame Effects. *Journal of Advertising, 50*(2), 179–196. doi:10.1080/00913367.2020.1858462

Bhattacharya, P., Obaidat, M. S., Savaliya, D., Sanghavi, S., Tanwar, S., & Sadaun, B. (2022, July). Metaverse assisted telesurgery in healthcare 5.0: An interplay of blockchain and explainable AI. In *2022 International Conference on Computer, Information and Telecommunication Systems (CITS)* (pp. 1-5). IEEE. 10.1109/CITS55221.2022.9832978

Bhattacharya, P., Saraswat, D., Savaliya, D., Sanghavi, S., Verma, A., Sakariya, V., Tanwar, S., Sharma, R., Raboaca, M. S., & Manea, D. L. (2023). Towards Future Internet: The Metaverse Perspective for Diverse Industrial Applications. *Mathematics, 11*(4), 941. doi:10.3390/math11040941

Bhugaonkar, K., Bhugaonkar, R., & Masne, N. (2022). The trend of metaverse and augmented & virtual reality extending to the healthcare system. *Cureus, 14*(9). doi:10.7759/cureus.29071 PMID:36258985

Bibri, S. E. (2022). The social shaping of the metaverse as an alternative to the imaginaries of data-driven smart Cities: A study in science, technology, and society. *Smart Cities, 5*(3), 832–874. doi:10.3390/smartcities5030043

Bibri, S. E., Allam, Z., & Krogstie, J. (2022). The Metaverse as a virtual form of data-driven smart urbanism: Platformization and its underlying processes, institutional dimensions, and disruptive impacts. *Computational Urban Science, 2*(1), 24. doi:10.1007/s43762-022-00051-0 PMID:35974838

Bibri, S. E., & Jagatheesaperumal, S. K. (2023). Harnessing the potential of the metaverse and artificial intelligence for the internet of city things: Cost-effective XReality and synergistic AIoT technologies. *Smart Cities, 6*(5), 2397–2429. doi:10.3390/smartcities6050109

Bidar, M. (2022). *Companies race to build "digital twins" in the metaverse.* CBS News. https://www.cbsnews.com/news/metaverse-amazon-bmw-lockheed-martin-adobe-digital-twin/

Billewar, S. R., Jadhav, K., Sriram, V. P., Arun, D. A., Mohd Abdul, S., Gulati, K., & Bhasin, D. N. K. K. (2022). The rise of 3D E-Commerce: The online shopping gets real with virtual reality and augmented reality during COVID-19. *World Journal of Engineering, 19*(2), 244–253. doi:10.1108/WJE-06-2021-0338

Bojic, L. (2022). Metaverse through the prism of power and addiction: What will happen when the virtual world becomes more attractive than reality? *European Journal of Futures Research, 10*(1), 22. doi:10.1186/s40309-022-00208-4

Boletsis, C. (2017). The New Era of Virtual Reality Locomotion: A Systematic Literature Review of Techniques and a Proposed Typology. *Multimodal Technologies and Interaction*, *1*(4), 24. doi:10.3390/mti1040024

Bolger, R. K. (2021). Finding holes in the metaverse: Posthuman mystics as agents of evolutionary contextualization. *Religions*, *12*(9), 768. doi:10.3390/rel12090768

Bollerslev, T. (1986). Generalized autoregressive conditional heteroskedasticity. *Journal of Econometrics*, *31*(3), 307–327. doi:10.1016/0304-4076(86)90063-1

Bonetti, F., Warnaby, G., & Quinn, L. (2018). Augmented Reality and Virtual Reality in Physical and Online Retailing: A Review, Synthesis and Research Agenda. In T. Jung & M. C. tom Dieck (Eds.), *Augmented Reality and Virtual Reality: Empowering Human, Place and Business* (pp. 119–132). Springer International Publishing., doi:10.1007/978-3-319-64027-3_9

Bousba, Y., & Arya, V. (2022). Let's connect in metaverse. Brand's new destination to increase consumers' affective brand engagement & their satisfaction and advocacy. *Journal of Content. Community & Communication*, *15*(8), 276–293. doi:10.31620/JCCC.06.22/19

Boyack, K. W., & Klavans, R. (2014). Including cited non-source items in a large-scale map of science: What difference does it make? *Journal of Informetrics*, *8*(3), 569–580. doi:10.1016/j.joi.2014.04.001

Brahma, M., Rejula, M. A., Srinivasan, B., Kumar, S., Banu, W. A., Malarvizhi, K., Priya, S. S., & Kumar, A. (2023). Learning impact of recent ICT advances based on virtual reality IoT sensors in a metaverse environment. *Measurement. Sensors*, *27*, 100754. doi:10.1016/j.measen.2023.100754

Bremers, L. P. Y. (2023). *Financial Inclusion in the Metaverse: Exploring the Relationship between Education and Attitude towards Cryptocurrencies* [Bachelor's thesis, University of Twente].

Briere, M., Oosterlinck, K., & Szafarz, A. (2015). Virtual currency, tangible return: Portfolio diversification with bitcoin. *Journal of Asset Management*, *16*(6), 365–373. doi:10.1057/jam.2015.5

Brown, D. (2021). "What is the 'metaverse'? Facebook says it's the future of the Internet. *The Washington Post*.

Bruni, R., Piccarozzi, M., & Caboni, F. (2023). Defining the Metaverse with challenges and opportunities in the business environment. *Journal of Marketing Theory and Practice*, 1–18. Advance online publication. doi:10.1080/10696679.2023.2273555

Bryda, G., & Costa, A. P. (2023). Qualitative research in digital era: Innovations, methodologies and collaborations. *Social Sciences (Basel, Switzerland)*, *12*(10), 570. doi:10.3390/socsci12100570

Buana, I. M. W. (2023). Metaverse: Threat or Opportunity for Our Social World? In understanding Metaverse on sociological context. *Journal of Metaverse*, *3*(1), 28–33. doi:10.57019/jmv.1144470

Budovich, L. S. (2023). The impact of religious tourism on the economy and tourism industry. *Hervormde Teologiese Studies*, *79*(1), 8607. doi:10.4102/hts.v79i1.8607

Buhalis, D. (2003). eTourism: Information technology for strategic tourism management. Pearson education. Pearson Education Limited.

Buhalis, D., Leung, D., & Lin, M. (2023). Metaverse as a disruptive technology revolutionising tourism management and marketing. *Tourism Management*, *97*, 104724. doi:10.1016/j.tourman.2023.104724

Buhalis, D., Lin, M. S., & Leung, D. (2022). Metaverse as a driver for customer experience and value co-creation: Implications for hospitality and tourism management and marketing. *International Journal of Contemporary Hospitality Management, 35*(2), 701–716. doi:10.1108/IJCHM-05-2022-0631

Buhalis, D., O'Connor, P., & Leung, R. (2023). Smart hospitality: From smart cities and smart tourism towards agile business ecosystems in networked destinations. *International Journal of Contemporary Hospitality Management, 35*(1), 369–393. doi:10.1108/IJCHM-04-2022-0497

Buhalis, D., & Sinarta, Y. (2019). Real-time co-creation and nowness service: Lessons from tourism and hospitality. *Journal of Travel & Tourism Marketing, 36*(5), 563–582. doi:10.1080/10548408.2019.1592059

Builders of Amusement Park Rides & Media-Based Attractions. (n.d.). Triotech. https://www.trio-tech.com/

Burlington. (2021). *Searching for utopia: from dinosaurs to the metaverse.* Burlington. https://www.burlington.org.uk/archive/editorial/searching-for-utopia-from-dinosaurs-to-the-metaverse

Cali, U., Kuzlu, M., Karaarslan, E., & Jovanovic, V. (2022). *Opportunities and Challenges in Metaverse for Industry 4.0 and Beyond Applications.* IEEE 1st Global Emerging Technology Blockchain Forum - Blockchain and Beyond, (IGETblockchain), Irvine, CA. https://doi.org/ doi:10.1109/iGETblockchain56591.2022.10087104

Calzada, I. (2023). Disruptive Technologies for e-Diasporas: Blockchain, DAOs, Data Cooperatives, Metaverse, and ChatGPT. *Futures, 154*, 103258. doi:10.1016/j.futures.2023.103258

Calzone, N., Sileo, M., Mozzillo, R., Pierri, F., & Caccavale, F. (2023). Mixed Reality Platform Supporting Human-Robot Interaction. Advances on Mechanics, Design Engineering and Manufacturing IV, Cham. doi:10.1007/978-3-031-15928-2_102

Capasa, L., Zulauf, K., & Wagner, R. (2022). Virtual Reality Experience of Mega Sports Events: A Technology Acceptance Study. *Journal of Theoretical and Applied Electronic Commerce Research, 17*(2), 2. doi:10.3390/jtaer17020036

Cappannari, L., & Vitillo, A. (2022). XR and Metaverse Software Platforms. *Roadmapping Extended Reality: Fundamentals and Applications*, 135-156. doi:10.1002/9781119865810.ch6

Carew, A. (2022). A whole new world: Metaverse as fairytale in Belle. *Metro*(212), 92-97. https://search.informit.org/doi/abs/10.3316/informit.938183067792285

Carter, M., & Egliston, B. (2023). What are the risks of Virtual Reality data? Learning Analytics, Algorithmic Bias and a Fantasy of Perfect Data. *New Media & Society, 25*(3), 485–504. doi:10.1177/14614448211012794

Chaudhary, M., Jaswal, N., & Sohal, A. (2023). Demystifying the Relationship Between Emotional Intelligence and Leadership Effectiveness: Focusing on Mental Health and Happiness. In AI and Emotional Intelligence for Modern Business Management (pp. 113-133). IGI Global. doi:10.4018/979-8-3693-0418-1.ch008

Chaves, A. (2023). *O que é Web 5.0 e qual a diferença da web3?* Be(in)Crypto. https://br.beincrypto.com/aprender/o-que-e-web-5-0/

Cheng, R. Z., Wu, N., Chen, S. Q., & Han, B. (2022, Mar 12-16). Reality check of metaverse: A first look at commercial social virtual reality platforms. *2022 IEEE Conference on Virtual Reality and 3D User Interfaces Abstracts and Workshops.* IEEE. 10.1109/VRW55335.2022.00040

Chengoden, R., Victor, N., Huynh-The, T., Yenduri, G., Jhaveri, R. H., Alazab, M., Bhattacharya, S., Hegde, P., Maddikunta, P. K. R., & Gadekallu, T. R. (2023). Metaverse for healthcare: A survey on potential applications, challenges and future directions. *IEEE Access : Practical Innovations, Open Solutions, 11*, 12765–12795. doi:10.1109/ACCESS.2023.3241628

Cheng, X. U. (2023). From Fiction to Reality: Harnessing the Power of Imaginative Narratives to Shape the Future of the Metaverse. *Journal of Metaverse, 3*(2), 108–120. doi:10.57019/jmv.1277525

Chen, H., Duan, H., Abdallah, M., Zhu, Y., Wen, Y., Saddik, A. E., & Cai, W. (2023). Web3 Metaverse: State-of-the-art and vision. *ACM Transactions on Multimedia Computing Communications and Applications, 20*(4), 1–42. doi:10.1145/3630258

Chen, N. C. (2024). Analysis on the Development of the Meta Universe to the Generation of Electronic Games from the Perspective of Media Convergence. *Computer-Aided Design and Applications.*

Chen, X., Li, H., Zhao, J., & Li, H. (2022). Security and privacy issues in the metaverse: A survey. *ACM Computing Surveys, 55*(2), 1–41.

Chen, Y., & Cheng, H. (2022). The economics of the metaverse: A comparison with the real economy. *Metaverse, 3*(1), 19. doi:10.54517/met.v3i1.1802

Chen, Y., Huang, D., Liu, Z., Osmani, M., & Demian, P. (2022). Construction 4.0, Industry 4.0, and Building Information Modeling (BIM) for sustainable building development within the smart city. *Sustainability (Basel), 14*(16), 10028. doi:10.3390/su141610028

ChenY.LinW.ZhengY.XueT.ChenC.ChenG. (2022). Application of active learning strategies in metaverse to improve student engagement: An immersive blended pedagogy bridging patient care and scientific inquiry in pandemic. *Available at* SSRN 4098179. doi:10.2139/ssrn.4098179

Chen, Z. S. (2023). Beyond Reality: Examining the Opportunities and Challenges of Cross-Border Integration between Metaverse and Hospitality Industries. *Journal of Hospitality Marketing & Management, 32*(7), 967–980. doi:10.1080/19368623.2023.2222029

Chowdhury, A., & Mendelson, B. K. (2013). Virtual currency and the financial system: the case of Bitcoin (No. 2013-09). Marquette University, Center for Global and Economic Studies and Department of Economics.

Chowdhury, A. (2016). Is Bitcoin the "Paris Hilton" of the currency world? Or are the early investors onto something that will make them rich? *Journal of Investing, 25*(1), 64–72. doi:10.3905/joi.2016.25.1.064

Chu, J., Zhang, Y., & Chan, S. (2019). The adaptive market hypothesis in the high frequency cryptocurrency market. *International Review of Financial Analysis, 64*, 221–231. doi:10.1016/j.irfa.2019.05.008

Cipresso, P., Giglioli, I. A. C., Raya, M. A., & Riva, G. (2018). The Past, Present, and Future of Virtual and Augmented Reality Research: A Network and Cluster Analysis of the Literature. *Frontiers in Psychology, 9*, 2086. doi:10.3389/fpsyg.2018.02086 PMID:30459681

Clement, J. (2022). *In what type of projects does your company invest in the metaverse?* Statista. https://www.statista.com/statistics/1302200/metaverse-project-investment-businesses/

Clement, J. (2023). *Video game industry - statistics & facts.* Statista. https://www.statista.com/topics/868/video-games/#topicOverview

Cline, R. S. (1999). Hospitality 2000—the technology: Building customer relationships. *Journal of Vacation Marketing, 5*(4), 376–386. doi:10.1177/135676679900500407

Cobo, M. J., López-Herrera, A. G., Herrera-Viedma, E., & Herrera, F. (2011). Science mapping software tools: Review, analysis, and cooperative study among tools. *Journal of the American Society for Information Science and Technology, 62*(7), 1382–1402. doi:10.1002/asi.21525

Cohen, J., Cohen, P., West, S. G., & Aiken, L. S. (2013). *Applied multiple regression/correlation analysis for the behavioral sciences*. Routledge. doi:10.4324/9780203774441

Conlon, T., Corbet, S., & McGee, R. J. (2020). Are cryptocurrencies a safe haven for equity markets? An international perspective from the COVID-19 pandemic. *Research in International Business and Finance, 54*, 101248. doi:10.1016/j.ribaf.2020.101248 PMID:34170988

Corbet, S., Hou, Y. G., Hu, Y., Oxley, L., & Xu, D. (2021). Pandemic-related financial market volatility spillovers: Evidence from the Chinese COVID-19 epicentre. *International Review of Economics & Finance, 71*, 55–81. doi:10.1016/j.iref.2020.06.022

Corning, P. A. (2013). Rotating the Necker cube: A bioeconomic approach to cooperation and the causal role of synergy in evolution. *Journal of Bioeconomics, 15*(2), 171–193. doi:10.1007/s10818-012-9142-4

Creed, C., Al-Kalbani, M., Theil, A., Sarcar, S., & Williams, I. (2024). Inclusive AR/VR: Accessibility barriers for immersive technologies. *Universal Access in the Information Society, 23*(1), 59–73. doi:10.1007/s10209-023-00969-0

Cronbach, L. J. (1951). Coefficient alpha and the internal structure of tests. *psychometrika, 16*(3), 297-334.

Cucari, N., Tutore, I., Montera, R., & Profita, S. (2023). A bibliometric performance analysis of publication productivity in the corporate social responsibility field: Outcomes of SciVal analytics. *Corporate Social Responsibility and Environmental Management, 30*(1), 1–16. doi:10.1002/csr.2346

Cui, H., & Du, B. (2023, February 6). *The Theoretical Basis and Landing Strategy of the Metaverse Business Model*. IEEE. doi:10.3233/FAIA230010

Curtis, C., & Brolan, C. E. (2023). Health care in the metaverse. *The Medical Journal of Australia, 218*(1), 46. doi:10.5694/mja2.51793 PMID:36437589

Daimiel, G. B., Estrella, E. C. M., & Ormaechea, S. L. (2022). Analysis of the use of advergaming and metaverse in Spain and Mexico. *Revista Latina De Comunicacion Social, 80*(80), 155–178. doi:10.4185/RLCS-2022-1802

Damar, M. (2021). Metaverse shape of your life for future: A bibliometric snapshot. *Journal of Metaverse, 1*(1), 1–8.

Damar, M. (2022). What the literature on medicine, nursing, public health, midwifery, and dentistry reveals: An overview of the rapidly approaching metaverse. *Journal of Metaverse, 2*(2), 62–70. doi:10.57019/jmv.1132962

Damnjanović, V., Lončarić, D., & Dlačić, J. (2020). TEACHING CASE STUDY: Digital marketing strategy of Accor Hotels: shaping the future of hospitality. *Tourism and Hospitality Management, 26*(1), 233–244.

Darban, M. (2023). The future of virtual team learning: Navigating the intersection of AI and education. *Journal of Research on Technology in Education*, 1–17. doi:10.1080/15391523.2023.2288912

Das, P., Martin Sagayam, K., Rahaman Jamader, A., & Acharya, B. (2022). Remote Sensing in Public Health Environment: A Review. *Internet of Things Based Smart Healthcare: Intelligent and Secure Solutions Applying Machine Learning Techniques*, 379-397.

Das, P., Jamader, A. R., Acharya, B. R., & Das, H. (2019, May). HMF Based QoS aware Recommended Resource Allocation System in Mobile Edge Computing for IoT. In *2019 International Conference on Intelligent Computing and Control Systems (ICCS)* (pp. 444-449). IEEE. 10.1109/ICCS45141.2019.9065775

Davenport, T., Guha, A., Grewal, D., & Bressgott, T. (2020). How artificial intelligence will change the future of marketing. *Journal of the Academy of Marketing Science, 48*(1), 24–42. doi:10.1007/s11747-019-00696-0

Davis, A., Khazanchi, D., Murphy, J., Zigurs, I., & Owens, D. (2009). Avatars, People, and Virtual Worlds: Foundations for Research in Metaverses. *Journal of the Association for Information Systems, 10*(2), 90–117. doi:10.17705/1jais.00183

Davis, F. D. (1989). Perceived usefulness, perceived ease of use, and user acceptance of information technology. *Management Information Systems Quarterly, 13*(3), 319–340. doi:10.2307/249008

Davis, F. D., Bagozzi, R. P., & Warshaw, P. R. (1989). User acceptance of computer technology: A comparison of two theoretical models. *Management Science, 35*(8), 982–1003. doi:10.1287/mnsc.35.8.982

De Bruyn, A., Viswanathan, V., Beh, Y. S., Brock, J.-K.-U., & Von Wangenheim, F. (2020). Artificial Intelligence and Marketing: Pitfalls and Opportunities. *Journal of Interactive Marketing, 51*, 91–105. doi:10.1016/j.intmar.2020.04.007

De Moor, K., Farias, M., Vinayagamoorthy, V., Daly, M., & Collingwoode-William, T. (2023). Diversity and Inclusion in Focus at ACM IMX'22 and MMSys' 22. *ACM SIGMultimedia Records, 14*(3), 1–1. doi:10.1145/3630658.3630660

Deniz, K. (2024). Metaverse and New Narrative: Storyliving in the Age of Metaverse. In The Future of Digital Communication (pp. 39-55). CRC Press.

Devlin, M. (2023). *2035 AND BEYOND. A GUIDE TO THRIVING IN THE FUTURE WORKPLACE.: Unleash Your Potential in a Futuristic Career Landscape. Virtual Worlds, Skills Mastery, and Success.* Little Fish Big Impact.

Dharmani, P., Das, S., & Prashar, S. (2021). A bibliometric analysis of creative industries: Current trends and future directions. *Journal of Business Research, 135*, 252–267. doi:10.1016/j.jbusres.2021.06.037

Dhiman, V., & Arora, M. (2023). How foresight has evolved since 1999? Understanding its themes, scope and focus. *foresight.* doi:10.1108/FS-01-2023-0001

Dhiman, V., & Arora, M. (2024). Current State of Metaverse in Entrepreneurial Ecosystem: A Retrospective Analysis of Its Evolving Landscape. In Exploring the Use of Metaverse in Business and Education (pp. 73-87). IGI Global. doi:10.4018/979-8-3693-5868-9.ch005

Dhiman, V., & Arora, M. (2024). *Exploring the linkage between business incubation and entrepreneurship: understanding trends, themes and future research agenda.* LBS Journal of Management & Research., doi:10.1108/LBSJMR-06-2023-0021

Dickey, M. D. (1999). *3D virtual worlds and learning: an analysis of the impact of design affordances and limitations in active worlds, blaxxun interactive, and onlive! Traveler; and a study of the implementation of active worlds for formal and informal education.* [Doctoral dissertation, The Ohio State University].

Dincelli, E., & Yayla, A. (2022). Immersive virtual reality in the age of the Metaverse: A hybrid-narrative review based on the technology affordance perspective. *The Journal of Strategic Information Systems, 31*(2), 101717. doi:10.1016/j.jsis.2022.101717

Dinev, T., & Hart, P. J. (2006). An empirical examination of the deLone and McLean model of information systems success. *Management Information Systems Quarterly, 30*(3), 691–721.

Dionisio, J. D. N., Iii, W. G. B., & Gilbert, R. (2013). 3D virtual worlds and the metaverse: Current status and future possibilities. *ACM Computing Surveys, 45*(3), 1–38. doi:10.1145/2480741.2480751

DiPietro, R. B., & Wang, Y. R. (2010). Key issues for ICT applications: Impacts and implications for hospitality operations. *Worldwide Hospitality and Tourism Themes, 2*(1), 49–67. doi:10.1108/17554211011012595

Disney patents technology to focus on theme park in Metaverse—Blockchain Council. (n.d.). Blockchain. https://www.blockchain-council.org/news/disney-patents-technology-to-focus-on-theme-park-in-metaverse/

Dixon, H. H. B. Jr. (2023). The Metaverse. *The Judges' Journal, 62*(1), 36–38.

Dobre, C., Milovan, A. M., Dutu, C., Preda, G., & Agapie, A. (2021). The Common Values of Social Media Marketing and Luxury Brands. The Millennials and Generation Z Perspective. *Journal of Theoretical and Applied Electronic Commerce Research, 16*(7), 2532–2553. doi:10.3390/jtaer16070139

Dogum, R., & Uribe, D. (2023). NFTs and Metaverse in Healthcare: What's the Big Opportunity? *Blockchain in Healthcare Today, 6*(1). doi:10.30953/bhty.v6.266

Dong, H., & Liu, Y. (2023, May 1). *Metaverse Meets Consumer Electronics.* IEEE. doi:10.1109/MCE.2022.3229180

Dong, Y., Sharma, C., Mehta, A., & Torrico, D. D. (2021). Application of augmented reality in the sensory evaluation of yogurts. *Fermentation (Basel, Switzerland), 7*(3), 147. doi:10.3390/fermentation7030147

Donthu, N., Kumar, S., Mukherjee, D., Pandey, N., & Lim, W. M. (2021). How to conduct a bibliometric analysis: An overview and guidelines. *Journal of Business Research, 133*, 285–296. doi:10.1016/j.jbusres.2021.04.070

Donthu, N., Kumar, S., & Pandey, N. (2021). A retrospective evaluation of Marketing Intelligence and Planning: 1983–2019. *Marketing Intelligence & Planning, 39*(1), 48–73. doi:10.1108/MIP-02-2020-0066

Duhoon, A., & Singh, M. (2023). Corporate Governance in Family Firms: A Bibliometric Analysis. *Management, 1*, 22.

Duhoon, A., & Singh, M. (2023). Corporate tax avoidance: A systematic literature review and future research directions. *LBS Journal of Management & Research, 21*(2), 197–217. doi:10.1108/LBSJMR-12-2022-0082

Duong, T. Q., Van Huynh, D., Khosravirad, S. R., Sharma, V., Dobre, O. A., & Shin, H. (2023). From digital twin to metaverse: The role of 6G ultra-reliable and low-latency communications with multi-tier computing. *IEEE Wireless Communications, 30*(3), 140–146. doi:10.1109/MWC.014.2200371

Durukal, E. (2022). Customer online shopping experience. *Handbook of Research on Interdisciplinary Reflections of Contemporary Experiential Marketing Practices.*

Dutta, D., Srivastava, Y., & Singh, E. (2023). Metaverse in the tourism sector for talent management: A technology in practice lens. *Information Technology & Tourism, 25*(3), 331–365. doi:10.1007/s40558-023-00258-9

Dutu-Buzura, M. (2021). European Climate Pact–Framework for Information and Participation of the Public to the Climate Change Challenge. *Romanian Journal of Public Affairs*(3), 29-40. http://www.rjpa.ro/sites/

Dwivedi, Y. K., Hughes, L., Baabdullah, A. M., Ribeiro-Navarrete, S., Giannakis, M., Al-Debei, M. M., Dennehy, D., Metri, B., Buhalis, D., Cheung, C. M. K., Conboy, K., Doyle, R., Dubey, R., Dutot, V., Felix, R., Goyal, D. P., Gustafsson, A., Hinsch, C., Jebabli, I., & Wamba, S. F. (2022). Metaverse beyond the hype: Multidisciplinary perspectives on emerging challenges, opportunities, and agenda for research, practice and policy. *International Journal of Information Management, 66*, 102542. doi:10.1016/j.ijinfomgt.2022.102542

Dwivedi, Y. K., Kshetri, N., Hughes, L., Rana, N. P., Baabdullah, A. M., Kar, A. K., Koohang, A., Ribeiro-Navarrete, S., Belei, N., Balakrishnan, J., Basu, S., Behl, A., Davies, G. H., Dutot, V., Dwivedi, R., Evans, L., Felix, R., Foster-Fletcher, R., Giannakis, M., ... Yan, M. (2023). Exploring the Darkverse: A Multi-Perspective Analysis of the Negative Societal Impacts of the Metaverse. *Information Systems Frontiers, 25*(5), 2071–2114. doi:10.1007/s10796-023-10400-x PMID:37361890

Dwivedi, Y. K., Kshetri, N., Hughes, L., Slade, E. L., Jeyaraj, A., Kar, A. K., Baabdullah, A. M., Koohang, A., Raghavan, V., Ahuja, M., Albanna, H., Albashrawi, M. A., Al-Busaidi, A. S., Balakrishnan, J., Barlette, Y., Basu, S., Bose, I., Brooks, L., Buhalis, D., ... Wright, R. (2023). "So what if ChatGPT wrote it?" Multidisciplinary perspectives on opportunities, challenges and implications of generative conversational AI for research, practice and policy. *International Journal of Information Management, 71*, 102642. doi:10.1016/j.ijinfomgt.2023.102642

Dyhrberg, A. H. (2016). Bitcoin, gold and the dollar–A GARCH volatility analysis. *Finance Research Letters*, *16*, 85–92. doi:10.1016/j.frl.2015.10.008

Dyhrberg, A. H. (2016). Hedging capabilities of bitcoin. Is it the virtual gold? *Finance Research Letters*, *16*, 139–144. doi:10.1016/j.frl.2015.10.025

Dziatkovskii, A., Hryneuski, U., Krylova, A., & Loy, A. C. M. (2022). Chronological Progress of Blockchain in Science, Technology, Engineering and Math (STEM): A Systematic Analysis for Emerging Future Directions. *Sustainability (Basel)*, *14*(19), 12074. doi:10.3390/su141912074

Earhart, B. (2012). Reclaiming meaning across platforms: Fragmentation and expansion of the self. *Metaverse Creativity*, *2*(2), 125–138. doi:10.1386/mvcr.2.2.125_1

Efendioğlu, İ. H. (2023). The Effect Of Information About Metaverse On The Consumer's Purchase Intention. *Journal of Global Business and Technology*, *19*(1), 63–77.

Ellegaard, O., & Wallin, J. A. (2015). The bibliometric analysis of scholarly production: How great is the impact? *Scientometrics*, *105*(3), 1809–1831. doi:10.1007/s11192-015-1645-z PMID:26594073

Enache, M. C. (2022). Metaverse Opportunities for Businesses. *Annals of the University Dunarea de Jos of Galati: Fascicle: I. Economics & Applied Informatics*, *28*(1), 67–71. Advance online publication. doi:10.35219/eai15840409246

Engage. (2024). *Engage Studio*. EngageVR. https://engagevr.io/engage-studio/

Engle, R. F. (1982). Autoregressive conditional heteroscedasticity with estimates of the variance of United Kingdom inflation. *Econometrica*, *50*(4), 987–1007. doi:10.2307/1912773

Engle, R. F., & Kroner, K. F. (1995). Multivariate simultaneous generalized ARCH. *Econometric Theory*, *11*(1), 122–150. doi:10.1017/S0266466600009063

Erazo, J., & Sulbarán, P. (2022). Metaverse: Above an immersion in reality. *Metaverse*, *3*(2), 8. doi:10.54517/m.v3i2.2155

Erdoğdu, A. (2017). The most significant factors influencing the price of gold: An empirical analysis of the US market. *Economics*, *5*(5), 399–406.

Erensoy, A., Mathrani, A., Schnack, A., Zhao, Y., Chitale, V. S., & Baghaei, N. (2022, December). Comparing Customer Behaviours: Immersive Virtual Reality Store Experiences versus Web and Physical Store Experiences. In *2022 IEEE Asia-Pacific Conference on Computer Science and Data Engineering (CSDE)* (pp. 1-7). IEEE. 10.1109/CSDE56538.2022.10089288

Ergen, I. (2022). *Design in Metaverse: Artificial Intelligence, Game Design, Style-Gan2 and More....* Allied Publishers.

Fahimnia, B., Sarkis, J., & Davarzani, H. (2015). Green supply chain management: A review and bibliometric analysis. *International Journal of Production Economics*, *162*, 101–114. doi:10.1016/j.ijpe.2015.01.003

Fama, E. F. (1970). Efficient capital markets: A review of theory and empirical work. *The Journal of Finance*, *25*(2), 383–417. doi:10.2307/2325486

Faraboschi, P., Frachtenberg, E., Laplante, P., Milojicic, D., & Saracco, R. (2022). Virtual worlds (Metaverse): From skepticism, to fear, to immersive opportunities. *Computer*, *55*(10), 100–106. doi:10.1109/MC.2022.3192702

Far, S. B., Rad, A. I., & Asaar, M. R. (2023). Blockchain and its derived technologies shape the future generation of digital businesses: A focus on decentralized finance and the Metaverse. *Data Science and Management*, *6*(3), 183–197. doi:10.1016/j.dsm.2023.06.002

Fazio, G., Fricano, S., Iannolino, S., & Pirrone, C. (2023). Metaverse and tourism development: Issues and opportunities in stakeholders' perception. *Information Technology & Tourism*, *25*(4), 507–528. doi:10.1007/s40558-023-00268-7

Feng, X., Wang, X., & Su, Y. (2024). An analysis of the current status of metaverse research based on bibliometrics. *Library Hi Tech*, *42*(1), 284–308. doi:10.1108/LHT-10-2022-0467

Fernández-Caramés, T. M., & Fraga-Lamas, P. (2024). Forging the Industrial Metaverse-Where Industry 5.0, Augmented and Mixed Reality, IIoT, Opportunistic Edge Computing and Digital Twins Meet. *arXiv preprint arXiv:2403.11312*.

Ferreira, J. J., Fernandes, C. I., Rammal, H. G., & Veiga, P. M. (2021). Wearable technology and consumer interaction: A systematic review and research agenda. *Computers in Human Behavior*, *118*, 106710. doi:10.1016/j.chb.2021.106710

FIFAe World Cup. (2024). Wikipedia. https://en.wikipedia.org/w/index.php?title=FIFAe_World_Cup&oldid=1195690321

Flannery, C. B. (2022). Philosophical and Practical Privacy in the Metaverse: A Case for Data Privacy Protection under the United States Constitution. *Cornell Journal of Law and Public Policy*, *32*, 134–153. https://heinonline.org/

Fornell, C., & Larcker, D. F. (1981). Evaluating structural equation models with unobservable variables and measurement error. *JMR, Journal of Marketing Research*, *18*(1), 39–50. doi:10.1177/002224378101800104

Fowowe, B., & Shuaibu, M. (2016). Dynamic spillovers between Nigerian, South African and international equity markets. *Inter Economics*, *148*, 59–80. doi:10.1016/j.inteco.2016.06.003

Freyermuth, G. S. (2022). Vegas, Disney, and the Metaverse. *Studies of Digital Media Culture*, *14*, 17.

Friis, K., & Lysne, O. (2021). Huawei, 5G and security: Technological limitations and political responses. *Development and Change*, *52*(5), 1174–1195. doi:10.1111/dech.12680

Furstenau, L. B., Sott, M. K., Kipper, L. M., Machado, E. L., Lopez-Robles, J. R., Dohan, M. S., Cobo, M. J., Zahid, A., Abbasi, Q. H., & Imran, M. A. (2020). Link between sustainability and industry 4.0: Trends, challenges, and new perspectives. *IEEE Access : Practical Innovations, Open Solutions*, *8*, 140079–140096. doi:10.1109/ACCESS.2020.3012812

Fu, Y. C., Li, C. L., Yu, F. R., Luan, T. H., Zhao, P. C., & Liu, S. (2023). A Survey of Blockchain and Intelligent Networking for the Metaverse. *IEEE Internet of Things Journal*, *10*(4), 3587–3610. doi:10.1109/JIOT.2022.3222521

Gadekallu, T. R., Huynh-The, T., Wang, W., Yenduri, G., Ranaweera, P., Pham, Q. V., & Liyanage, M. (2022). Blockchain for the metaverse: A review. *arXiv preprint arXiv:2203.09738*.

Ganapathy, K. (2022). Metaverse and healthcare: A clinician's perspective. *Apollo Medicine*, *19*(4), 256–261.

Gao, X., & Yu, W. (2023). Innovative Thinking About Human-Computer Interaction in Interactive Narrative Games. In X. Fang (Ed.), *HCI in Games* (pp. 89–99). Springer Nature Switzerland. doi:10.1007/978-3-031-35930-9_7

Gao, Z., & Braud, T. (2023). VR-driven museum opportunities: Digitized archives in the age of the metaverse. *Artnodes*, *0*(32). Advance online publication. doi:10.7238/artnodes.v0i32.402462

Garavand, A., & Aslani, N. (2022). Metaverse phenomenon and its impact on health: A scoping review. *Informatics in Medicine Unlocked*, *32*, 101029. doi:10.1016/j.imu.2022.101029

Garousi, V. (2015). A bibliometric analysis of the Turkish software engineering research community. *Scientometrics*, *105*(1), 23–49. doi:10.1007/s11192-015-1663-x

Gartner Outlines Six Trends Driving Near-Term Adoption of Metaverse Technologies. (n.d.). Gartner. Retrieved February 6, 2024, from https://www.gartner.com/en/newsroom/press-releases/2022-09-13-gartner-outlines-six-trends-driving-near-term-adoptio

Gartner Predicts 25% of People Will Spend At Least One Hour Per Day in the Metaverse by 2026. (n.d.). Gartner. https://www.gartner.com/en/newsroom/press-releases/2022-02-07-gartner-predicts-25-percent-of-people-will-spend-at-least-one-hour-per-day-in-the-metaverse-by-2026

Gartner. (2022). Gartner Glossary: Metaverse. https://www.gartner.com/en/information-technology/glossary/metaverse

Gasmi, A., & Benlamri, R. (2022). Augmented reality, virtual reality and new age technologies demand escalates amid COVID-19. In *Novel AI and Data Science Advancements for Sustainability in the Era of COVID-19* (pp. 89–111). Academic Press. doi:10.1016/B978-0-323-90054-6.00005-2

Gattullo, M., Laviola, E., Evangelista, A., Fiorentino, M., & Uva, A. E. (2022). Towards the evaluation of augmented reality in the metaverse: Information presentation modes. *Applied Sciences (Basel, Switzerland)*, *12*(24), 12600. doi:10.3390/app122412600

Gaurav, A. (2022). Metaverse and Globalization: Cultural Exchange and Digital Diplomacy. *Data Science Insights Magazine, 5.* https://insights2techinfo.com/

Gaurav, A. (2023). Metaverse and Globalization: Cultural Exchange and Digital Diplomacy, Data *Science Insights Magazine, Insights2Techinfo.*

Gauttier, S., Simouri, W., & Milliat, A. (2024). When to enter the metaverse: Business leaders offer perspectives. *The Journal of Business Strategy*, *45*(1), 2–9. doi:10.1108/JBS-08-2022-0149

Ghimire, A. (2023). *AvatARoid: using a motion-mapped AR overlay to bridge the embodiment gap between robot and teleoperator in robot-mediated telepresence.* University of British Columbia.

Ghobakhloo, M., & Ching, N. T. (2019). Adoption of digital technologies of smart manufacturing in SMEs. *Journal of Industrial Information Integration*, *16*, 100107. doi:10.1016/j.jii.2019.100107

Ghryani, L., Sidiya, A. M., Almahdi, R., & Alzaher, H. (2023). The Future Metavertainment Application development. *2023 20th Learning and Technology Conference (L&T)*, 151–156. 10.1109/LT58159.2023.10092341

Gill, S. S., Xu, M., Ottaviani, C., Patros, P., Bahsoon, R., Shaghaghi, A., Golec, M., Stankovski, V., Wu, H., Abraham, A., Singh, M., Mehta, H., Ghosh, S. K., Baker, T., Parlikad, A. K., Lutfiyya, H., Kanhere, S. S., Sakellariou, R., Dustdar, S., & Uhlig, S. (2022). AI for next generation computing: Emerging trends and future directions. *Internet of Things : Engineering Cyber Physical Human Systems*, *19*, 100514. doi:10.1016/j.iot.2022.100514

Glaser, F., Zimmermann, K., Haferkorn, M., Weber, M. C., & Siering, M. (2014). *Bitcoin-asset or currency? revealing users' hidden intentions. Revealing Users' Hidden Intentions (April 15, 2014).* ECIS.

Goel, A. K., Bakshi, R., & Agrawal, K. K. (2022). Web 3.0 and Decentralized Applications. *Materials Proceedings*, *10*(1), 8. https://www.mdpi.com/2673-4605/10/1/8

Go, H., & Kang, M. (2022). Metaverse tourism for sustainable tourism development: Tourism Agenda 2030. *Tourism Review*, *78*(2), 381–394. doi:10.1108/TR-02-2022-0102

Goh, K. H., & See, K. F. (2021). Twenty years of water utility benchmarking: A bibliometric analysis of emerging interest in water research and collaboration. *Journal of Cleaner Production*, *284*, 124711. doi:10.1016/j.jclepro.2020.124711

Goldfield, C. C. (2023). THE NATIONAL SECURITY LANDSCAPE ISSUES OF THE METAUERSE. *Scitech Lawyer*, *19*(2), 20–25.

Golf-Papez, M., Heller, J., Hilken, T., Chylinski, M., de Ruyter, K., Keeling, D. I., & Mahr, D. (2022). Embracing falsity through the metaverse: The case of synthetic customer experiences. *Business Horizons*, *65*(6), 739–749. doi:10.1016/j.bushor.2022.07.007

Guan, J., Morris, A., & Irizawa, J. (2023). *Extending the Metaverse: Hyper-Connected Smart Environments with Mixed Reality and the Internet of Things*. 30th IEEE Conference Virtual Reality and 3D User Interfaces (IEEE VR), Shanghai. 10.1109/VRW58643.2023.00251

Gupta, H. (2023). Analysing volatility patterns in emerging markets: symmetric or asymmetric models? *Journal of Economic and Administrative Sciences*. doi:10.1108/JEAS-07-2023-0186

Gupta, H. (2024). Asymmetric Volatility in Stock Market: Evidence from Selected Export-based Countries. *The Indian Economic Journal*, *0*(0), 00194662241238598. doi:10.1177/00194662241238598

Gupta, H., & Gupta, A. (2023). Investor's behaviour to COVID-19 vaccine: An event study on health and pharmaceutical sector in India. *International Journal of Pharmaceutical and Healthcare Marketing*, *17*(4), 429–449. doi:10.1108/IJPHM-05-2022-0053

Gupta, O. J., Yadav, S., Srivastava, M. K., Darda, P., & Mishra, V. (2023). Understanding the intention to use metaverse in healthcare utilizing a mix method approach. *International Journal of Healthcare Management*, 1–12. doi:10.1080/20479700.2023.2183579

Gupta, R., & Singh, S. (2022). Network infrastructure for the metaverse: Requirements and challenges. *IEEE Internet of Things Journal*, *9*(12), 13298–13310.

Gursoy, D., Malodia, S., & Dhir, A. (2022). The metaverse in the hospitality and tourism industry: An overview of current trends and future research directions. *Journal of Hospitality Marketing & Management*, *31*(5), 527–534. doi:10.1080/19368623.2022.2072504

Hackl, C. (2020). The Metaverse is coming and it's a very big deal. *Forbes*. https://www.forbes.com/sites/cathy-hackl/2020/07/05/the-metaverse-is-coming--its-a-very-big-deal/

Hadi, R., Melumad, S., & Park, E. S. (2024). The Metaverse: A new digital frontier for consumer behavior. *Journal of Consumer Psychology*, *34*(1), 142–166. doi:10.1002/jcpy.1356

Hagtvedt, H., & Chandukala, S. R. (2023). Immersive retailing: The in-store experience. *Journal of Retailing*, *99*(4), 505–517. doi:10.1016/j.jretai.2023.10.003

Hair, J. F., Risher, J. J., Sarstedt, M., & Ringle, C. M. (2019). When to use and how to report the results of PLS-SEM. *European Business Review*, *31*(1), 2–24. doi:10.1108/EBR-11-2018-0203

Hajjami, O., & Park, S. (2023). Using the metaverse in training: Lessons from real cases. *European Journal of Training and Development*. Advance online publication. doi:10.1108/EJTD-12-2022-0144

Hamilton, S. (2022). Deep Learning Computer Vision Algorithms, Customer Engagement Tools, and Virtual Marketplace Dynamics Data in the Metaverse Economy. *Journal of Self-Governance and Management Economics*, *10*(2), 37–51.

Hamza, R., & Pradana, H. (2022). A survey of intellectual property rights protection in big data applications. *Algorithms*, *15*(11), 418. doi:10.3390/a15110418

Han, B., Wang, H., Qiao, D., Xu, J., & Yan, T. (2023). Application of Zero-Watermarking Scheme Based on Swin Transformer for Securing the Metaverse Healthcare Data. *IEEE Journal of Biomedical and Health Informatics*. Advance online publication. doi:10.1109/JBHI.2021.3123936 PMID:37028374

Hancock, K. (2022). Virtual Team Performance, Collaborative Remote Work, and Employee Engagement and Multimodal Behavioral Analytics in the Metaverse Economy. *Psychosociological Issues in Human Resource Management, 10*(2), 55–70. doi:10.22381/pihrm10220224

Han, D.-I. D., Bergs, Y., & Moorhouse, N. (2022). Virtual reality consumer experience escapes: Preparing for the meta-verse. *Virtual Reality (Waltham Cross), 26*(4), 1443–1458. doi:10.1007/s10055-022-00641-7

Han, E., Miller, M. R., DeVeaux, C., Jun, H., Nowak, K. L., Hancock, J. T., Ram, N., & Bailenson, J. N. (2023). People, places, and time: A large-scale, longitudinal study of transformed avatars and environmental context in group interaction in the metaverse. *Journal of Computer-Mediated Communication, 28*(2), zmac031. doi:10.1093/jcmc/zmac031

Han, E., Miller, M. R., Ram, N., Nowak, K. L., & Bailenson, J. N. (2022, May). Understanding group behavior in virtual reality: A large-scale, longitudinal study in the metaverse. In *72nd Annual International Communication Association Conference*, Paris, France.

Harley, D. (2022). "This would be sweet in VR": On the discursive newness of virtual reality. *New Media & Society, 17*, 14614448221084655. doi:10.1177/14614448221084655

Hashim, S. L., Ramlan, H., Razali, N. H., & Nordin, N. Z. (2017). Macroeconomic variables affecting the volatility of gold price. [GBSE]. *Journal of Global Business and Social Entrepreneurship, 3*(5), 97–106.

Hennig-Thurau, T., Aliman, D. N., Herting, A. M., Cziehso, G. P., Linder, M., & Kübler, R. V. (2023). Social interactions in the metaverse: Framework, initial evidence, and research roadmap. *Journal of the Academy of Marketing Science, 51*(4), 889–913. doi:10.1007/s11747-022-00908-0

Henseler, J., Ringle, C. M., & Sarstedt, M. (2015). A new criterion for assessing discriminant validity in variance-based structural equation modeling. *Journal of the Academy of Marketing Science, 43*(1), 115–135. doi:10.1007/s11747-014-0403-8

Henz, P. (2022). The societal impact of the Metaverse. *Discover Artificial Intelligence, 2*(1), 19. doi:10.1007/s44163-022-00032-6

Heracleous, L., Terrier, D., & Gonzalez, S. (2019). NASA's capability evolution toward commercial space. *Space Policy, 50*, 101330. doi:10.1016/j.spacepol.2019.07.004

Hester, A. J., Hutchins, H. M., & Burke-Smalley, L. A. (2016). Web 2.0 and Transfer: Trainers' Use of Technology to Support Employees' Learning Transfer on the Job. *Performance Improvement Quarterly, 29*(3), 231–255. doi:10.1002/piq.21225

Hobson, A. (2024). Emergent Governance From Polycentric Order in Virtual Reality Social Spaces. In Law, Video Games, Virtual Realities (pp. 74-95). Routledge. https://doi.org/ doi:10.4324/9781003197805-5

Hoesli, M., & Reka, K. (2013). Volatility spillovers, comovements and contagion in securitized real estate markets. *The Journal of Real Estate Finance and Economics, 47*(1), 1–35. doi:10.1007/s11146-011-9346-8

Hollebeek, L. D., Clark, M. K., Andreassen, T. W., Sigurdsson, V., & Smith, D. (2020). Virtual reality through the customer journey: Framework and propositions. *Journal of Retailing and Consumer Services, 55*, 102056. doi:10.1016/j.jretconser.2020.102056

Hollensen, S., Kotler, P., & Opresnik, M. O. (2022). Metaverse – the new marketing universe. *Journal of Business Strategy*.

Hollensen, S., Kotler, P., & Opresnik, M. O. (2022). Metaverse–the new marketing universe. *The Journal of Business Strategy, 44*(3), 119–125. doi:10.1108/JBS-01-2022-0014

Horng, S. M., & Wu, C. L. (2020). How behaviors on social network sites and online social capital influence social commerce intentions. *Information & Management, 57*(2), 103176. doi:10.1016/j.im.2019.103176

Hossain, M. I., Teh, B. H., Dorasamy, M., Tabash, M. I., & Ong, T. S. (2023, May). Ethical Leadership, Green HRM Practices and Environmental Performance of Manufacturing SMEs at Selangor, Malaysia: Moderating Role of Green Technology Adoption. In *International Scientific Conference on Business and Economics* (pp. 85-104). Cham: Springer Nature Switzerland. 10.1007/978-3-031-42511-0_6

Hossain, M. I., Kumar, J., Islam, M. T., & Valeri, M. (2023). The interplay among paradoxical leadership, industry 4.0 technologies, organisational ambidexterity, strategic flexibility and corporate sustainable performance in manufacturing SMEs of Malaysia. *European Business Review*. doi:10.1108/EBR-04-2023-0109

Hossain, M. I., Ong, T. S., Tabash, M. I., & Teh, B. H. (2024). The panorama of corporate environmental sustainability and green values: Evidence of Bangladesh. *Environment, Development and Sustainability, 26*(1), 1033–1059. doi:10.1007/s10668-022-02748-y

Hossain, M. I., San Ong, T., Teh, B. H., Said, R. M., & Siow, M. L. (2022). Nexus of Stakeholder Integration, Green Investment, Green Technology Adoption and Environmental Sustainability Practices: Evidence from Bangladesh Textile SMEs. *Pertanika Journal of Social Science & Humanities, 30*(1). doi:10.47836/pjssh.30.1.14

Huang, H., Zhang, C., Zhao, L., Ding, S., Wang, H., & Wu, H. (2023). Self-Supervised Medical Image Denoising Based on WISTA-Net for Human Healthcare in Metaverse. *IEEE Journal of Biomedical and Health Informatics.* PMID:37216248

Huang, W., Leong, Y. C., & Ismail, N. A. (2024). The influence of communication language on purchase intention in consumer contexts: The mediating effects of presence and arousal. *Current Psychology (New Brunswick, N.J.), 43*(1), 658–668. doi:10.1007/s12144-023-04314-9

Huang, Y., Wu, S., & Zhao, X. (2021). The metaverse for business: Opportunities and challenges. *Journal of Management Information Systems, 38*(3), 1089–1111.

Hu, Y., & Liu, C. (2022). The 'metaverse society': Beyond the discourse intrinsic potential and transformative impact. *Metaverse, 3*(2), 14. doi:10.54517/m.v3i2.2128

Huynh, T. L. D., Nasir, M. A., Vo, X. V., & Nguyen, T. T. (2020). "Small things matter most": The spillover effects in the cryptocurrency market and gold as a silver bullet. *The North American Journal of Economics and Finance, 54,* 101277. doi:10.1016/j.najef.2020.101277

Huynh-The, T., Gadekallu, T. R., Wang, W. Z., Yenduri, G., Ranaweera, P., Pham, Q. V., da Costa, D. B., & Liyanage, M. (2023). Blockchain for the metaverse: A Review. *Future Generation Computer Systems, 143,* 401–419. doi:10.1016/j.future.2023.02.008

Huynh-The, T., Pham, Q. V., Pham, X. Q., Nguyen, T. T., Han, Z., & Kim, D. S. (2023). Artificial intelligence for the metaverse: A survey. *Engineering Applications of Artificial Intelligence, 117,* 105581. doi:10.1016/j.engappai.2022.105581

Hwangbo, H., Kim, E. H., Lee, S. H., & Jang, Y. J. (2020). Effects of 3D virtual "try-on" on online sales and customers' purchasing experiences. *IEEE Access : Practical Innovations, Open Solutions, 8,* 189479–189489. doi:10.1109/ACCESS.2020.3023040

Hwang, G. J., & Chien, S. Y. (2022). Definition, roles, and potential research issues of the metaverse in education: An artificial intelligence perspective. *Computers and Education: Artificial Intelligence, 3,* 100082. doi:10.1016/j.caeai.2022.100082

Hyun, W. (2023, February). Study on standardization for interoperable metaverse. In *2023 25th International Conference on Advanced Communication Technology (ICACT)* (pp. 319-322). IEEE. 10.23919/ICACT56868.2023.10079642

Iden, J., & Methlie, L. B. (2012). The drivers of services on next-generation networks. *Telematics and Informatics*, *29*(2), 137–155. doi:10.1016/j.tele.2011.05.004

Imamguluyev, R., Umarova, N., & Mikayilova, R. (2023, August). Navigating the Ethics of the Metaverse: A Fuzzy Logic Approach to Decision-Making. In *International Conference on Intelligent and Fuzzy Systems* (pp. 53-60). Cham: Springer Nature Switzerland. 10.1007/978-3-031-39777-6_7

Immersive Virtual Reality. (2008). In B. Furht (Ed.), *Encyclopedia of Multimedia* (pp. 345–346). Springer US., doi:10.1007/978-0-387-78414-4_85

Inanc–Demir, M., & Kozak, M. (2019). Big data and its supporting elements: Implications for tourism and hospitality marketing. In *Big Data and Innovation in Tourism, Travel, and Hospitality* (pp. 213–223). Springer. doi:10.1007/978-981-13-6339-9_13

Ip, C., Leung, R., & Law, R. (2011). Progress and development of information and communication technologies in hospitality. *International Journal of Contemporary Hospitality Management*, *23*(4), 533–551. doi:10.1108/09596111111130029

Ipsita, A., Erickson, L., Dong, Y., Huang, J., Bushinski, A. K., Saradhi, S., & Ramani, K. (n.d.). Towards modeling of virtual reality welding simulators to promote accessible and scalable training. *2022 CHI Conference on Human Factors in Computing Systems*, (pp. 1–21). ACM. 10.1145/3491102.3517696

Iqbal, M. Z., & Campbell, A. G. (2023, October). Metaverse as tech for good: Current progress and emerging opportunities. In Virtual Worlds, 2(4), 326-342.

IsmailL.BuyyaR. (2023, August 21). Metaverse: A Vision, Architectural Elements, and Future Directions for Scalable and Realtime Virtual Worlds. https://arxiv.org/abs/2308.10559

Jaber, T. A. (2022). Security Risks of the Metaverse World. *International Journal of Interactive Mobile Technologies*, *16*(13).

Jackson, R. (2023). *Young users favor immersive media over social media. Why it matters?* TipRanks. https://www.nasdaq.com/articles/young-users-favor-immersive-media-over-social-media.-why-it-matters

Jamader, A. R., Chowdhary, S., & Shankar Jha, S. (2023). A Road Map for Two Decades of Sustainable Tourism Development Framework. In Resilient and Sustainable Destinations After Disaster: Challenges and Strategies (pp. 9-18). Emerald Publishing Limited. doi:10.1108/978-1-80382-021-720231002

Jamader, A. R., Das, P., & Acharya, B. (2022). An Analysis of Consumers Acceptance towards Usage of Digital Payment System, Fintech and CBDC. *Fintech and CBDC (January 1, 2022)*.

Jamader, A. R. (2022). A Brief Report Of The Upcoming & Present Economic Impact To Hospitality Industry In COVID19 Situations. *Journal of Pharmaceutical Negative Results*, 2289–2302.

Jamader, A. R., Chowdhary, S., Jha, S. S., & Roy, B. (2023). Application of Economic Models to Green Circumstance for Management of Littoral Area: A Sustainable Tourism Arrangement. *SMART Journal of Business Management Studies*, *19*(1), 70–84. doi:10.5958/2321-2012.2023.00008.8

Jamader, A. R., Das, P., & Acharya, B. R. (2019, May). BcIoT: blockchain based DDoS prevention architecture for IoT. In *2019 International Conference on Intelligent Computing and Control Systems (ICCS)* (pp. 377-382). IEEE. 10.1109/ICCS45141.2019.9065692

Jamader, A. R., Das, P., Acharya, B., & Hu, Y. C. (2021). Overview of Security and Protection Techniques for Microgrids. In *Microgrids* (pp. 231–253). CRC Press. doi:10.1201/9781003121626-11

Jamader, A. R., Immanuel, J. S., Ebenezer, V., Rakhi, R. A., Sagayam, K. M., & Das, P. (2023). Virtual Education, Training And Internships In Hospitality And Tourism During Covid-19 Situation. *Journal of Pharmaceutical Negative Results*, 286–290.

Jana, K. (2023, June 17). Metatext and metaverse. *The Telegraph Online.*

Jauhiainen, J. S., Krohn, C., & Junnila, J. (2022). Metaverse and Sustainability: Systematic Review of Scientific Publications until 2022 and Beyond. *Sustainability (Basel)*, *15*(1), 346. doi:10.3390/su15010346

Jeon, H. J., Youn, H. C., Ko, S. M., & Kim, T. H. (2022). Blockchain and AI Meet in the Metaverse. *Advances in the Convergence of Blockchain and Artificial Intelligence, 73*(10.5772).

Jeon, Y. A. (2022). Reading Social Media Marketing Messages as Simulated Self Within a Metaverse: An Analysis of Gaze and Social Media Engagement Behaviors within a Metaverse Platform. *Proceedings - 2022 IEEE Conference on Virtual Reality and 3D User Interfaces Abstracts and Workshops, VRW 2022*. IEEE. 10.1109/VRW55335.2022.00068

Jeong, H., Yi, Y., & Kim, D. (2022). An innovative e-commerce platform incorporating metaverse to live commerce. *International Journal of Innovative Computing, Information, & Control*, *18*(1), 221–229. doi:10.24507/ijicic.18.01.221

Jiang, Y., Kang, J., Niyato, D., Ge, X., Xiong, Z., Miao, C., & Shen, X. (2022). Reliable distributed computing for metaverse: A hierarchical game-theoretic approach. *IEEE Transactions on Vehicular Technology*, *72*(1), 1084–1100. doi:10.1109/TVT.2022.3204839

Jiang, Y., Nie, H., & Ruan, W. (2018). Time-varying long-term memory in Bitcoin market. *Finance Research Letters*, *25*, 280–284. doi:10.1016/j.frl.2017.12.009

Joy, A., Zhu, Y., Pena, C., & Brouard, M. (2022). Digital future of luxury brands: Metaverse, digital fashion, and non-fungible tokens. *Strategic Change*, *31*(3), 337–343. doi:10.1002/jsc.2502

Julian, H. L. C., Chung, T., & Wang, Y. (2023). Adoption of Metaverse in South East Asia: Vietnam, Indonesia, Malaysia. In *Strategies and Opportunities for Technology in the Metaverse World* (pp. 196–234). IGI Global. doi:10.4018/978-1-6684-5732-0.ch012

Ju, N., & Lee, K. H. (2021). Perceptions and resistance to accept smart clothing: Moderating effect of consumer innovativeness. *Applied Sciences (Basel, Switzerland)*, *11*(7), 3211. doi:10.3390/app11073211

Jungherr, A., & Schlarb, D. B. (2022). The extended reach of game engine companies: how companies like epic games and unity technologies provide platforms for extended reality applications and the Metaverse. *Social Media + Society*, *8*(2), 12. doi:10.1177/20563051221107641

Jung, T. M., Cho, J. S., Han, D. I. D., Ahn, S. J., Gupta, M., Das, G., Heo, C. Y., Loureiro, S. M. C., Sigala, M., Trunfio, M., Taylor, A., & Dieck, M. C. T. (2024). Metaverse for service industries: Future applications, opportunities, challenges and research directions. *Computers in Human Behavior*, *151*, 108039. Advance online publication. doi:10.1016/j.chb.2023.108039

Kaddoura, S., & Al Husseiny, F. (2023). The rising trend of Metaverse in education: Challenges, opportunities, and ethical considerations. *PeerJ. Computer Science*, *9*, e1252. doi:10.7717/peerj-cs.1252 PMID:37346578

Kadry, A. (2022). The metaverse revolution and its impact on the future of advertising industry. *Journal of Design Sciences and Applied Arts*, *3*(2), 131–139. doi:10.21608/jdsaa.2022.129876.1171

Kahambing, J. G. (2023). Metaverse, mental health and museums in post-COVID-19. *Journal of Public Health (Oxford, England), 45*(2), e382–e383. doi:10.1093/pubmed/fdad002 PMID:36680432

Kajtazi, A., & Moro, A. (2019). The role of bitcoin in well diversified portfolios: A comparative global study. *International Review of Financial Analysis, 61*, 143–157. doi:10.1016/j.irfa.2018.10.003

Katsiampa, P., Corbet, S., & Lucey, B. (2019). High frequency volatility co-movements in cryptocurrency markets. *Journal of International Financial Markets, Institutions and Money, 62*, 35–52. doi:10.1016/j.intfin.2019.05.003

Kaufman, I., Horton, C., & Soltanifar, M. (2023). *Digital Marketing: Integrating Strategy, Sustainability, and Purpose.* Taylor & Francis. doi:10.4324/9781351019187

Kaushal, N., Sharma, S., & Katoch, A. (2022a). The Satisfaction of Religious Tourists Visiting Shiva Circuit of Himachal Pradesh. *International Research Journal of Management Sociology & Humanities, 13*(8), 11–19.

Kaushal, N., Sharma, S., & Katoch, A. (2022b). Problems and Challenges faced by Religious Tourists: A study of Religious Destinations of Himachal Pradesh. *International Journal of Commerce. Arts & Science, 13*(8), 27–35.

Keller, K. L. (2001). *Building Customer-Based Brand Equity: A Blueprint for Creating Strong Brands* (01-107). (Working Paper). M. S. Institute. http://anandahussein.lecture.ub.ac.id/files/2015/09/article-4.pdf

KevinsJ. (2022) Metaverse as a New Emerging Technology: An Interrogation of Opportunities and Legal Issues: Some Introspection (SSRN paper 4050898). doi:10.2139/ssrn.4050898

Khatri, M. (2022). Revamping the marketing world with metaverse–The future of marketing. *International Journal of Computer Applications, 975*(5), 8887. doi:10.5120/ijca2022922361

Kim, D., Lee, H. K., & Chung, K. (2023). Avatar-mediated experience in the metaverse: The impact of avatar realism on user-avatar relationship. *Journal of Retailing and Consumer Services, 73*, 103382. doi:10.1016/j.jretconser.2023.103382

Kim, E. J., & Kim, J. Y. (2023). The metaverse for healthcare: Trends, applications, and future directions of digital therapeutics for urology. *International Neurourology Journal, 27*(Suppl 1), S3–S12. doi:10.5213/inj.2346108.054 PMID:37280754

Kim, J. (2021). Advertising in the Metaverse: Research Agenda. *Journal of Interactive Advertising, 21*(3), 141–144. doi:10.1080/15252019.2021.2001273

Kim, J., Hwang, L., Kwon, S., & Lee, S. (2022). Change in Blink Rate in the Metaverse VR HMD and AR Glasses Environment. *International Journal of Environmental Research and Public Health, 19*(14), 8551. https://www.mdpi.com/1660-4601/19/14/8551. doi:10.3390/ijerph19148551 PMID:35886402

Kim, M., Oh, J., Son, S., Park, Y., Kim, J., & Park, Y. (2023). Secure and Privacy-Preserving Authentication Scheme Using Decentralized Identifier in Metaverse Environment. *Electronics (Basel), 12*(19), 4073. doi:10.3390/electronics12194073

Kim, Y. B., Lee, J., Park, N., Choo, J., Kim, J. H., & Kim, C. H. (2017). When Bitcoin encounters information in an online forum: Using text mining to analyse user opinions and predict value fluctuation. *PLoS One, 12*(5), e0177630. doi:10.1371/journal.pone.0177630 PMID:28498843

Kim, Y., Park, J., & Sohn, D. (2022). Understanding user acceptance of the metaverse: Integrating the technology acceptance model and the flow theory. *Journal of Information Technology Management, 13*(2), 357–377.

Klein, T., Thu, H. P., & Walther, T. (2018). Bitcoin is not the New Gold–A comparison of volatility, correlation, and portfolio performance. *International Review of Financial Analysis, 59*, 105–116. doi:10.1016/j.irfa.2018.07.010

Kock, N. (2015). Common method bias in PLS-SEM: A full collinearity assessment approach. [ijec]. *International Journal of e-Collaboration*, *11*(4), 1–10. doi:10.4018/ijec.2015100101

Koohang, A., Nord, J. H., Ooi, K. B., Tan, G. W. H., Al-Emran, M., Aw, E. C. X., Baabdullah, A. M., Buhalis, D., Cham, T. H., Dennis, C., Dutot, V., Dwivedi, Y. K., Hughes, L., Mogaji, E., Pandey, N., Phau, I., Raman, R., Sharma, A., Sigala, M., & Wong, L. W. (2023). Shaping the Metaverse into Reality: A Holistic Multidisciplinary Understanding of Opportunities, Challenges, and Avenues for Future Investigation. *Journal of Computer Information Systems*, *63*(3), 735–765. doi:10.1080/08874417.2023.2165197

Kraus, S., Kanbach, D. K., Krysta, P. M., Steinhoff, M. M., & Tomini, N. (2022). Facebook and the creation of the metaverse: Radical business model innovation or incremental transformation? *International Journal of Entrepreneurial Behaviour & Research*, *28*(9), 52–77. doi:10.1108/IJEBR-12-2021-0984

Kroner, K. F., & Sultan, J. (1993). Time-varying distributions and dynamic hedging with foreign currency futures. *Journal of Financial and Quantitative Analysis*, *28*(4), 535–551. doi:10.2307/2331164

Kuen, T. Y., & Hoong, T. S. (1992). Forecasting volatility in the Singapore stock market. *Asia Pacific Journal of Management*, *9*(1), 1–13. doi:10.1007/BF01732034

Kumar, M. (2024). Virtual Reality in Education: Analyzing the Literature and Bibliometric State of Knowledge. In *Transforming Education with Virtual Reality* (pp. 379-402). Wiley Online Library.

Kumawat, V., Dhaked, R., Sharma, L., & Jain, S. (2020). Evolution of Immersive Technology. *Journey of Computational Reality*.

Kuo, C. M., Chen, L. C., & Tseng, C. Y. (2017). Investigating an innovative service with hospitality robots. *International Journal of Contemporary Hospitality Management*, *29*(5), 1305–1321. doi:10.1108/IJCHM-08-2015-0414

Lada, S., Chekima, B., Karim, M. R. A., Fabeil, N. F., Ayub, M. S., Amirul, S. M., Ansar, R., Bouteraa, M., Fook, L. M., & Zaki, H. O. (2023). Determining factors related to artificial intelligence (AI) adoption among Malaysia's small and medium-sized businesses. *Journal of Open Innovation*, *9*(4), 100144. doi:10.1016/j.joitmc.2023.100144

Lai, Y. S., & Sheu, H. J. (2011). On the importance of asymmetries for dynamic hedging during the subprime crisis. *Applied Financial Economics*, *21*(11), 801–813. doi:10.1080/09603107.2010.539535

Lan, Y. J. (2024). 3D immersive scaffolding game for enhancing Mandarin learning in children with ADHD. *Journal of Educational Technology & Society*.

Lau, M. C. K., Vigne, S. A., Wang, S., & Yarovaya, L. (2017). Return spillovers between white precious metal ETFs: The role of oil, gold, and global equity. *International Review of Financial Analysis*, *52*, 316–332. doi:10.1016/j.irfa.2017.04.001

Laura, P. (2023). *A water smart city: Learning from Singapore*. https://www.beesmart.city/en/solutions/a-water-smart-city-learning-from-singapore

Law, R., Buhalis, D., & Cobanoglu, C. (2014). Progress on information and communication technologies in hospitality and tourism. *International Journal of Contemporary Hospitality Management*, *26*(5), 727–750. doi:10.1108/IJCHM-08-2013-0367

Lazaroiu, G., Androniceanu, A., Grecu, I., Grecu, G., & Neguriță, O. (2022). Artificial intelligence-based decision-making algorithms, Internet of Things sensing networks, and sustainable cyber-physical management systems in big data-driven cognitive manufacturing. *Oeconomia Copernicana*, *13*(4), https://doi.org/. doi:1047-1080

Lee, H., & Leonas, K. (2018). Consumer experiences, the key to survive in an omni-channel environment: Use of virtual technology. *Journal of Textile and Apparel, Technology and Management*, *10*(3).

Lee, C. T., Ho, T. Y., & Xie, H. H. (2023). Building brand engagement in metaverse commerce: The role of branded non-fungible toekns (BNFTs). *Electronic Commerce Research and Applications*, *58*, 101248. Advance online publication. doi:10.1016/j.elerap.2023.101248

Lee, C. T., Li, Z., & Shen, Y. C. (2024). Building bonds: An examination of relational bonding in continuous content contribution behaviors on metaverse-based non-fungible token platforms. *Internet Research*. Advance online publication. doi:10.1108/INTR-11-2022-0883

Lee, C. W. (2022). Application of metaverse service to healthcare industry: A strategic perspective. *International Journal of Environmental Research and Public Health*, *19*(20), 13038. doi:10.3390/ijerph192013038 PMID:36293609

Lee, J., & Kwon, K. H. (2022). The significant transformation of life into health and beauty in metaverse era. *Journal of Cosmetic Dermatology*, *21*(12), 6575–6583. doi:10.1111/jocd.15151 PMID:35686389

Lee, J., Park, H., & Song, J. (2023). Safety assessment of augmented reality and virtual reality in the metaverse: A review. *International Journal of Occupational Safety and Health*, ●●●, 1–10.

Lee, J.-W. (2023). The Future of Online Barrier-Free Open Space Cultural Experiences for People with Disabilities in the Post-COVID-19 Era. *Land (Basel)*, *13*(1), 33. doi:10.3390/land13010033

Lee, K. L., Teong, C. X., Alzoubi, H. M., Alshurideh, M. T., Khatib, M. E., & Al-Gharaibeh, S. M. (2024). Digital supply chain transformation: The role of smart technologies on operational performance in manufacturing industry. *International Journal of Engineering Business Management*, *16*, 18479790241234986. doi:10.1177/18479790241234986

Lee, K. L., Wong, S. Y., Alzoubi, H. M., Al Kurdi, B., Alshurideh, M. T., & El Khatib, M. (2023). Adopting smart supply chain and smart technologies to improve operational performance in manufacturing industry. *International Journal of Engineering Business Management*, *15*, 18479790231200614. doi:10.1177/18479790231200614

Lee, M., Min, K. Z. L., & Kim, S.-H. (2024). Does the Experience of Using Metaverse Affect the Relationship between Social Identity, Psychological Ownership, and Engagement? *Proceedings of the 57th Hawaii International Conference on System Sciences*. University of Hawai.

Lee, S., Lee, Y., & Park, E. (2023). Sustainable Vocational Preparation for Adults with Disabilities: A Metaverse-Based Approach. *Sustainability (Basel)*, *15*(15), 12000. doi:10.3390/su151512000

Lee, Y., Kim, J., & Lee, Y. (2012). The role of perceived realism and trust in the continued usage of virtual worlds. *Computers in Human Behavior*, *28*(2), 346–352.

Lemos, L., Ainse, D., & Faras, A. (2022). DAO meets the Estonian e-residency program: a stance from Synergy's blockchain-based open-source toolkit. Conference Proceedings of the STS Conference Graz 2022, Lloyd Owen, D. (2021). *Defining 'Smart Water'*. Wily Online Library. https://doi.org/10.1002/9781119531241.ch4

Leonidou, L. C., Leonidou, C. N., Fotiadis, T. A., & Zeriti, A. (2013). Resources and capabilities as drivers of hotel environmental marketing strategy: Implications for competitive advantage and performance. *Tourism Management*, *35*, 94–110. doi:10.1016/j.tourman.2012.06.003

Letafati, M., & Otoum, S. (2023). Digital Healthcare in The Metaverse: Insights into Privacy and Security. *arXiv preprint arXiv:2308.04438*.

Liberatore, M. J., & Wagner, W. P. (2021). Virtual, mixed, and augmented reality: A systematic review for immersive systems research. *Virtual Reality (Waltham Cross)*, *25*(3), 773–799. doi:10.1007/s10055-020-00492-0

Lien, D., & Yang, L. (2006). Spot-futures spread, time-varying correlation, and hedging with currency futures. *Journal of Futures Markets*, *26*(10), 1019–1038. doi:10.1002/fut.20225

Li, F., Xing, W., Su, M., & Xu, J. (2021). The evolution of China's marine economic policy and the labor productivity growth momentum of the marine economy and its three economic industries. *Marine Policy*, *134*, 104777. doi:10.1016/j.marpol.2021.104777

Li, H., Li, Z., & Zhang, X. (2021). Understanding users' acceptance of the metaverse: An extended UTAUT model and empirical test. *International Journal of Information Management*, *59*, 102495.

Li, H., & Zhang, Y. (2021). Data integration challenges and technologies in the metaverse. *IEEE Access : Practical Innovations, Open Solutions*, *9*, 149696–149709.

Li, J. (2022). Impact of Metaverse cultural communication on the mental health of international students in China: Highlighting effects of healthcare anxiety and cyberchondria. *American Journal of Health Behavior*, *46*(6), 809–820. doi:10.5993/AJHB.46.6.21 PMID:36721290

Li, J. J. (2024). Virtual Currency and Smart Financial Management in Immersive Online Games in the Metaverse Environment. *Computer-Aided Design and Applications*.

Lin, C. C., & Huang, Y. (2022). The impact of metaverse technology on human resource development: A review of the literature. *Journal of Human Resources Development*, *41*(4), 599–618.

Lindstrom, M. (2009). *Buy.ology: A ciência do Neuromarketing*. Gestão Plus.

Lin, H. (2019). The acceptance of virtual worlds: A meta-analysis. *Computers in Human Behavior*, *93*, 113–122.

Li, T., Yang, C., Yang, Q., Lan, S., Zhou, S., Luo, X., Huang, H., & Zheng, Z. (2023). Metaopera: A Cross-Metaverse Interoperability Protocol. *IEEE Wireless Communications*, *30*(5), 136–143. doi:10.1109/MWC.011.2300042

Liu, Y., & Tsyvinski, A. (2021). Risks and returns of cryptocurrency. *Review of Financial Studies*, *34*(6), 2689–2727. doi:10.1093/rfs/hhaa113

Ljungholm, D. P. (2022). Metaverse-based 3D visual modeling, virtual reality training experiences, and wearable biological measuring devices in immersive workplaces. *Psychosociological Issues in Human Resource Management*, *10*(1), 64–77. doi:10.22381/pihrm10120225

Lodha, S. (2017). A Cointegration and Causation Study of Gold Prices, Crude Oil Prices and Exchange Rates. *IUP Journal of Financial Risk Management*, *14*(3), 55–66.

Lombart, C., Millan, E., Normand, J. M., Verhulst, A., Labbé-Pinlon, B., & Moreau, G. (2020). Effects of physical, non-immersive virtual, and immersive virtual store environments on consumers' perceptions and purchase behavior. *Computers in Human Behavior*, *110*, 106374. doi:10.1016/j.chb.2020.106374

Louzis, D. P. (2015). Measuring spillover effects in Euro area financial markets: A disaggregate approach. *Empirical Economics*, *49*(4), 1367–1400. doi:10.1007/s00181-014-0911-x

Lowood, H. E. (2022). *virtual reality*. Encyclopedia Britannica. https://www.britannica.com/technology/virtual-reality

Lv, Z., Qiao, L., Li, Y., Yuan, Y., & Wang, F. Y. (2022). BlockNet: Beyond reliable spatial Digital Twins to Parallel Metaverse. *Patterns (New York, N.Y.)*, *3*(5), 100468. doi:10.1016/j.patter.2022.100468 PMID:35607617

Macedo, C. R., Miro, D. A., & Hart, T. (2022). *The Metaverse: From Science Fiction to Commercial Reality—Protecting Intellectual Property in the Virtual Landscape. 31*(1).

Maden, A., & Yücenur, G. N. (2024). Evaluation of sustainable metaverse characteristics using scenario-based fuzzy cognitive map. *Computers in Human Behavior*, *152*, 108090. doi:10.1016/j.chb.2023.108090

Madhavan, A. (2000). Market microstructure: A survey. *Journal of Financial Markets*, *3*(3), 205–258. doi:10.1016/S1386-4181(00)00007-0

Maier, D., Maier, A., Aşchilean, I., Anastasiu, L., & Gavriş, O. (2020). The relationship between innovation and sustainability: A bibliometric review of the literature. *Sustainability (Basel)*, *12*(10), 4083. doi:10.3390/su12104083

Mainardes, E. W., & Freitas, N. P. D. (2023). The effects of perceived value dimensions on customer satisfaction and loyalty: A comparison between traditional banks and fintechs. *International Journal of Bank Marketing*, *41*(3), 641–662. doi:10.1108/IJBM-10-2022-0437

Majerová, J., & Pera, A. (2022). Haptic and biometric sensor technologies, spatio-temporal fusion algorithms, and virtual navigation tools in the decentralized and interconnected metaverse. *Review of Contemporary Philosophy*, *21*(0), 105–121. doi:10.22381/RCP2120227

Makarigakis, A., Partey, S., Nagabhatla, N., De Lombaerde, P., Libert, B., Trombitcaia, I., Zerrath, E., Guerrier, D., Faloutsos, D., & Krol, D. (2023). *Regional Perspectives*. https://cris.unu.edu/sites/cris.unu.edu

Malerba, S. (2023). *Exploring the Potential of the Metaverse for Value Creation: An Analysis of Opportunities, Challenges, and Societal Impact, with a Focus on the Chinese Context* Ca' Foscari University of Venice. http://dspace.unive.it/bitstream/handle/10579/24277/890613-1281454

Mammadova, A. (2023). *Digital big-bang Metaverse: opportunities and threats* [Master's thesis, Università Ca' Foscari Venezia]. http://dspace.unive.it/handle/10579/25766

Mancuso, I., Petruzzelli, A. M., & Panniello, U. (2023). Digital business model innovation in metaverse: How to approach virtual economy opportunities. *Information Processing & Management*, *60*(5), 103457. doi:10.1016/j.ipm.2023.103457

Manera, M., McAleer, M., & Grasso, M. (2006). Modelling time-varying conditional correlations in the volatility of Tapis oil spot and forward returns. *Applied Financial Economics*, *16*(07), 525–533. doi:10.1080/09603100500426465

Mantelli, A. (2021). Learning Japanese through VR technology. The case of altspace VR. *Annali di Ca'Foscari. Serie Orientale*, *57*, 663–684. 10278/3742133/1/art-10.30687

Marinescu, I. A., & Iordache, D.-D. (2023). Exploring relevant technologies for simulating user interaction in Metaverse virtual spaces. *Romanian Journal of Information Technology & Automatic Control*, *33*(3), 129–142. doi:10.33436/v33i3y202310

Martinez-Millana, A., Bayo-Monton, J. L., Lizondo, A., Fernandez-Llatas, C., & Traver, V. (2016). Evaluation of Google Glass technical limitations on their integration in medical systems. *Sensors (Basel)*, *16*(12), 2142. doi:10.3390/s16122142 PMID:27983691

Marzaleh, M. A., Peyravi, M., & Shaygani, F. (2022). A revolution in health: Opportunities and challenges of the Metaverse. *EXCLI Journal*, *21*, 791. PMID:35949490

Massaro, M. (2023). Digital transformation in the healthcare sector through blockchain technology. Insights from academic research and business developments. *Technovation*, *120*, 102386. doi:10.1016/j.technovation.2021.102386

Maurizio Unali, G. C. (2024). Towards a Virtual Museum of Ephemeral Architecture: Methods, Techniques and Semantic Models for a Post-digital Metaverse. In M. R. Andrea Giordano, Beyond Digital Representation. Springer Nature Switzerland.

McCall, R., Shell, J., Kacperski, C., Greenstein, S., Whitton, N., & Summers, J. (2022, October). Workshop on Social and Ethical Issues in Entertainment Computing. In *International Conference on Entertainment Computing* (pp. 429-435). Cham: Springer International Publishing.

Mclean, G., Al-Nabhani, K., & Wilson, A. (2018). Developing a mobile applications customer experience model (MACE)-implications for retailers. *Journal of Business Research, 85*, 325–336. doi:10.1016/j.jbusres.2018.01.018

Meichler, M. (2023, June 19). *The Future of NFTs: Is Gaming the Solution?* NFT Evening. https://nftevening.com/the-future-of-nfts-is-gaming-the-solution/

Mejia, J. M. R., & Rawat, D. B. (2022, July). recent advances in a medical domain metaverse: Status, challenges, and perspective. In *2022 Thirteenth International Conference on Ubiquitous and Future Networks (ICUFN)* (pp. 357-362). IEEE. 10.1109/ICUFN55119.2022.9829645

Mensi, W., Hammoudeh, S., Nguyen, D. K., & Yoon, S. M. (2014). Dynamic spillovers among major energy and cereal commodity prices. *Energy Economics, 43*, 225–243. doi:10.1016/j.eneco.2014.03.004

Messinger, P. R., Stroulia, E., Lyons, K., Bone, M., Niu, R. H., Smirnov, K., & Perelgut, S. (2009). Virtual worlds—past, present, and future: New directions in social computing. *Decision Support Systems, 47*(3), 204–228. doi:10.1016/j.dss.2009.02.014

Metaverse Live Entertainment—Global | Market Forecast. (n.d.). Statista. https://www.statista.com/outlook/amo/metaverse/metaverse-live-entertainment/worldwide

Metaverse: The Revolution of the Sports World & Entire Life. (n.d.). ISPO. https://www.ispo.com/en/news-trends/metaverse-revolution-sports-world

Metavertainment: A Vision Into The World of The Metaverse and Entertainment. (n.d.). HackerNoon. https://hackernoon.com/metavertainment-a-vision-into-the-world-of-the-metaverse-and-entertainment

Miao, F., Kozlenkova, I. V., Wang, H., Xie, T., & Palmatier, R. W. (2022). An emerging theory of avatar marketing. *Journal of Marketing, 86*(1), 67–90. doi:10.1177/0022242921996646

Mirza-Babaei, P., Robinson, R., Mandryk, R., Pirker, J., Kang, C., & Fletcher, A. (2022, November). Games and the Metaverse. In *Extended abstracts of the 2022 annual symposium on computer-human interaction in play*. ACM. 10.1145/3505270.3558355

Mishra, P., & Singh, G. (2023). Energy management systems in sustainable smart cities based on the internet of energy: A technical review. *Energies, 16*(19), 6903. doi:10.3390/en16196903

Mittal, G., & Bansal, R. (2023). Driving Force Behind Consumer Brand Engagement: The Metaverse. In Cultural Marketing and Metaverse for Consumer Engagement (pp. 164-181). IGI Global. doi:10.4018/978-1-6684-8312-1.ch012

Mogaji, E. (2023). Metaverse influence on transportation: A mission impossible? *Transportation Research Interdisciplinary Perspectives, 22*, 100954. doi:10.1016/j.trip.2023.100954

Mogaji, E., Dwivedi, Y. K., & Raman, R. (2024). Fashion marketing in the metaverse. *Journal of Global Fashion Marketing, 15*(1), 115–130. doi:10.1080/20932685.2023.2249483

Mohamed, E. S., & Naqishbandi, T. A. (2023). Metaverse! Possible Potential Opportunities and Trends in E-Healthcare and Education. *International Journal of E-Adoption, 15*(2), 1–21. doi:10.4018/IJEA.316537

Moher, D., Liberati, A., Tetzlaff, J., & Altman, D. G. (2009). Preferred reporting items for systematic reviews and meta-analyses: The PRISMA statement. *Annals of Internal Medicine, 151*(4), 264–269. doi:10.7326/0003-4819-151-4-200908180-00135 PMID:19622511

Momtaz, P. P. (2021). The pricing and performance of cryptocurrency. *European Journal of Finance, 27*(4-5), 367–380. doi:10.1080/1351847X.2019.1647259

Morales-Fernández, B. (2024). New Linguistic Spaces in Cyberculture: The Influence of the Metaverse on the Minifiction of Social Networks. In The Future of Digital Communication (pp. 27-38). CRC Press.

Moro-Visconti, R. (2022). Metaverse: A Digital Network Valuation. In *The Valuation of Digital Intangibles: Technology, Marketing, and the Metaverse* (pp. 515–559). Springer International Publishing. doi:10.1007/978-3-031-09237-4_18

Mourtzis, D. (2023). The Metaverse in Industry 5.0: A Human-Centric Approach towards Personalized Value Creation. *Encyclopedia*, *3*(3), 1105–1120. doi:10.3390/encyclopedia3030080

Moztarzadeh, O., Jamshidi, M., Sargolzaei, S., Jamshidi, A., Baghalipour, N., Malekzadeh Moghani, M., & Hauer, L. (2023). Metaverse and Healthcare: Machine Learning-Enabled Digital Twins of Cancer. *Bioengineering (Basel, Switzerland)*, *10*(4), 455. doi:10.3390/bioengineering10040455 PMID:37106642

Mozumder, M. A. I., Sheeraz, M. M., Athar, A., Aich, S., & Kim, H. C. (2022, February). Overview: Technology roadmap of the future trend of metaverse based on IoT, blockchain, AI technique, and medical domain metaverse activity. In *2022 24th International Conference on Advanced Communication Technology (ICACT)* (pp. 256-261). IEEE.

Mozumder, M. A. I., Armand, T. P. T., Imtiyaj Uddin, S. M., Athar, A., Sumon, R. I., Hussain, A., & Kim, H. C. (2023). Metaverse for Digital Anti-Aging Healthcare: An Overview of Potential Use Cases Based on Artificial Intelligence, Blockchain, IoT Technologies, Its Challenges, and Future Directions. *Applied Sciences (Basel, Switzerland)*, *13*(8), 5127. doi:10.3390/app13085127

Mughal, A. A. (2018). Artificial Intelligence in Information Security: Exploring the Advantages, Challenges, and Future Directions. *Journal of Artificial Intelligence and Machine Learning in Management*, *2*(1), 22–34.

Muhuri, P. K., Shukla, A. K., & Abraham, A. (2019). Industry 4.0: A bibliometric analysis and detailed overview. *Engineering Applications of Artificial Intelligence*, *78*, 218–235. doi:10.1016/j.engappai.2018.11.007

Munn, N., & Weijers, D. (2023). The real ethical problem with metaverses. *Frontiers in Human Dynamics*, *5*, 1226848. doi:10.3389/fhumd.2023.1226848

Mystakidis, S. (2022). *Metaverse. Encyclopedia*, *2*(1).

Mystakidis, S. (2022). Metaverse. [Key Characteristics of the metaverse]. *Encyclopedia*, *2*(1), 486–497. doi:10.3390/encyclopedia2010031

Nabukalu, R., & Wanjohi, A. (2023). *Impact of Metaverse on Marketing Communication: A case study of the fashion industry*. Lulea University of Technology.

Naderi, H., & Shojaei, A. (2023). Digital twinning of civil infrastructures: Current state of model architectures, interoperability solutions, and future prospects. *Automation in Construction*, *149*, 104785. doi:10.1016/j.autcon.2023.104785

Nakamoto, S. (2008). Bitcoin: A peer-to-peer electronic cash system. *Decentralized business review*, 21260.

Narula, H. (2022). *Virtual Society: The Metaverse and the New Frontiers of Human Experience*. Crown Currency.

NathK. (2022). Evolution of the Internet from Web 1.0 to Metaverse: The Good, The Bad and The Ugly. TechRxiv. doi:10.36227/techrxiv.19743676

Nayak, D. K., Mishra, P., Das, P., Jamader, A. R., & Acharya, B. (2022). Application of Deep Learning in Biomedical Informatics and Healthcare. In *Smart Healthcare Analytics: State of the Art* (pp. 113–132). Springer. doi:10.1007/978-981-16-5304-9_9

Nazma, R. B., & Devi, R. (2023). Sustainable Development Using Green Finance and Triple Bottom Line: A Bibliometric Review. *Management*, *1*, 22. doi:10.1177/ijim.231184138

Needleman, S. E. (2021). The Amazing Things You'll Do in the 'Metaverse' and What It Will Take to Get There. *The Wall Street Journal*.

Netemeyer, R. G., Bearden, W. O., & Sharma, S. (2003). *Scaling procedures: Issues and applications*. sage publications.

Netemeyer, R. G., Bearden, W. O., & Sharma, S. (2003). *Scaling procedures: Issues and applications*. Sage publications.

Nevelsteen, K. J. L. (2018). Virtual world, defined from a technological perspective and applied to video games, mixed reality, and the Metaverse. *Computer Animation and Virtual Worlds, 29*(1), 22, Article e1752. doi:10.1002/cav.1752

Neves, J., Bacalhau, L. M., & Santos, V. (2024). *A Systematic Review on the Customer Journey Between Two Worlds: Reality and Immersive World*. Marketing and Smart Technologies.

Ng, D. T. K. (2022). What is the metaverse? Definitions, technologies and the community of inquiry. *Australasian Journal of Educational Technology, 38*(4), 190–205. doi:10.14742/ajet.7945

Nica, E. (2022). Virtual healthcare technologies and consultation systems, smart operating rooms, and remote sensing data fusion algorithms in the medical metaverse. *American Journal of Medical Research (New York, N.Y.), 9*(2), 105–120. doi:10.22381/ajmr9220227

Novak, K. (2022). Introducing the Metaverse, Again! *TechTrends, 66*(5), 737–739. doi:10.1007/s11528-022-00767-0

Nunes, C. C. (2023). *The Importance on Self-Expression Through Clothing and Fashion: A view on Digital Identity and Digital Fashion* Universidade Da Beira Interior. https://ubibliorum.ubi.pt/handle/10400.6/13583

Nunes, G. S., & Filho, E. J. M. A. (2018b). Consumer behavior regarding wearable technologies: Google Glass. *Innovation & Management Review, 15*(3), 230–246. doi:10.1108/INMR-06-2018-0034

Nuñez, J., Krynski, L., & Otero, P. (2024). The metaverse in the world of health: The present future. Challenges and opportunities. *Archivos Argentinos de Pediatria, 122*(1). doi:10.5546/aap.2022-02942.eng PMID:37171469

Oh, H. J., Kim, J., Chang, J. J., Park, N., & Lee, S. (2023). Social benefits of living in the metaverse: The relationships among social presence, supportive interaction, social self-efficacy, and feelings of loneliness. *Computers in Human Behavior, 139*, 107498. doi:10.1016/j.chb.2022.107498

Olaleye, S. (2023). The Bibliometric Commingling of Metaverse and Non-fungible Tokens in Marketing. In J. R. Reis, Marketing and Smart Technologies. Springer Nature Singapore.

Oliveira, A., & Cruz, M. (2023). Virtually Connected in a Multiverse of Madness?—Perceptions of Gaming, Animation, and Metaverse. *Applied Sciences (Basel, Switzerland), 13*(15), 15. doi:10.3390/app13158573

Oliveira, C. M. (2023). *Humantech Marketing: o marketing molecular e humano*. Conjuntura Actual Editora.

Ooi, K. B., Tan, G. W. H., Al-Emran, M., Al-Sharafi, M. A., Arpaci, I., Zaidan, A. A., ... Iranmanesh, M. (2023). The metaverse in engineering management: Overview, opportunities, challenges, and future research agenda. *IEEE Transactions on Engineering Management*.

Ooi, K., Tan, G. W., Aw, E. C., Cham, T., Dwivedi, Y. K., Dwivedi, R., Hughes, L., Kar, A. K., Loh, X., Mogaji, E., Phau, I., & Sharma, A. (2023). Banking in the metaverse: A new frontier for financial institutions. *International Journal of Bank Marketing, 41*(7), 1829–1846. doi:10.1108/IJBM-03-2023-0168

Orr, E. (2022). The Metaverse Can Create A Boundless Healthcare Experience. *Forbes*. https://www.forbes.com/sites/forbestechcouncil/2022/01/26/the-metaverse-can-create-a-boundless-healthcare-experience/?sh=1b21c0ab2340

Othman, A., Chemnad, K., Hassanien, A. E., Tlili, A., Zhang, C. Y., Al-Thani, D., ... Altınay, Z. (2024). Accessible Metaverse: A Theoretical Framework for Accessibility and Inclusion in the Metaverse. *Multimodal Technologies and Interaction, 8*(3), 21. doi:10.3390/mti8030021

Ozdemir, H., & Ozdemir, Z. A. (2021). *A Survey of Hedge and Safe Havens Assets against G-7 Stock Markets before and during the COVID-19 Pandemic* (No. 14888). IZA Discussion Papers.

Özdemir, O. (2022). Cue the volatility spillover in the cryptocurrency markets during the COVID-19 pandemic: Evidence from DCC-GARCH and wavelet analysis. *Financial Innovation, 8*(1), 1–38. doi:10.1186/s40854-021-00319-0 PMID:35132369

Özkurt, M. (2023). *A Jungian Archetypal analysis of Earnest Cline's Ready Player One: quest for the Axis mMundi* Pamukkale University]. https://hdl.handle.net/11499/56004

Öztürk, B., & Hersono, R. (2023). *Playing to Win: How Gamification Can Boost Customer Engagement and Turn Non-Fans into Brand Advocates.*

Pachouri, V., Singh, R., Gehlot, A., Pandey, S., Akram, S. V., & Abbas, M. I. (2024). Empowering sustainability in the built environment: A technological Lens on industry 4.0 Enablers. *Technology in Society, 76*, 102427. doi:10.1016/j.techsoc.2023.102427

Panda, T. K. (2022). In the world of Metaverse. *NMIMS Management Review, 30*(03), 03-05. doi:10.53908/NMMR.300210

Papagiannidis, S., Pantano, E., See-To, E. W., Dennis, C., & Bourlakis, M. (2017). To immerse or not? Experimenting with two virtual retail environments. *Information Technology & People, 30*(1), 163–188. doi:10.1108/ITP-03-2015-0069

Pappas, N. (2015). Marketing hospitality industry in an era of crisis. *Tourism Planning & Development, 12*(3), 333–349. doi:10.1080/21568316.2014.979226

Pareliussen, J., & Purwin, A. (2023). Climate policies and Sweden's green industrial revolution. *OECD Economics Department Working Papers*(1778), 1-48. https://doi.org/ doi:10.1787/18151973

Park, S., & Kim, S. (2022). Identifying world types to deliver gameful experiences for sustainable learning in the Metaverse. *Sustainability, 14*(3), 14. doi:10.3390/su14031361

Park, A., Wilson, M., Robson, K., Demetis, D., & Kietzmann, J. (2023). Interoperability: Our exciting and terrifying Web3 future. *Business Horizons, 66*(4), 529–541. doi:10.1016/j.bushor.2022.10.005

Park, H., Ahn, D., & Lee, J. (2023). Towards a Metaverse Workspace: Opportunities, Challenges, and Design Implications. In *Proceedings of the 2023 CHI Conference on Human Factors in Computing Systems* (pp. 1-20). ACM. 10.1145/3544548.3581306

Park, J., & Kim, N. (2024). Examining self-congruence between user and avatar in purchasing behavior from the metaverse to the real world. *Journal of Global Fashion Marketing, 15*(1), 23–38. doi:10.1080/20932685.2023.2180768

Park, S. M., & Kim, Y.-G. (2022). A Metaverse: Taxonomy, Components, Applications, and Open Challenges. *IEEE Access : Practical Innovations, Open Solutions, 10*, 4209–4251. doi:10.1109/ACCESS.2021.3140175

Pearce, M., Zeadally, S., & Hunt, R. (2013). Virtualization: Issues, security threats, and solutions. *ACM Computing Surveys, 45*(2), 1–39. doi:10.1145/2431211.2431216

Pellas, N., Mystakidis, S., & Kazanidis, I. (2021). Immersive Virtual Reality in K-12 and Higher Education: A systematic review of the last decade scientific literature. *Virtual Reality (Waltham Cross), 25*(3), 835–861. doi:10.1007/s10055-020-00489-9

Peltonen, T. (2019). Case Study 4: The Collapse of Nokia's Mobile Phone Business, Springer Books. In *Towards Wise Management* (pp. 163–188). Springer. doi:10.1007/978-3-319-91719-1_6

Pérez, J., Castro, M., & López, G. (2023). Serious Games and AI: Challenges and Opportunities for Computational Social Science. *IEEE Access : Practical Innovations, Open Solutions*, *11*, 62051–62061. doi:10.1109/ACCESS.2023.3286695

Periyasami, S., & Periyasamy, A. P. (2022). Metaverse as future promising platform business model: Case study on fashion value chain. *Businesses*, *2*(4), 527–545. doi:10.3390/businesses2040033

Petrigna, L., & Musumeci, G. (2022). The metaverse: A new challenge for the healthcare system: A scoping review. *Journal of Functional Morphology and Kinesiology*, *7*(3), 63. doi:10.3390/jfmk7030063 PMID:36135421

Pirnar, I., Icoz, O., & Icoz, O. (2010). The new tourist: Impacts on the hospitality marketing strategies. *EuroCHRIE Amsterdam*, 25-28.

Pizzi, G., Scarpi, D., Pichierri, M., & Vannucci, V. (2019). Virtual reality, real reactions?: Comparing consumers' perceptions and shopping orientation across physical and virtual-reality retail stores. *Computers in Human Behavior*, *96*, 1–12. doi:10.1016/j.chb.2019.02.008

Podmurnyi, S. (2022). Business Insights On The Opportunity For The Educational Metaverse. *Forbes*. https://www.forbes.com/sites/forbestechcouncil/2022/08/05/business-insights-on-the-opportunity-for-the-educational-metaverse/?sh=240d59874a3f

Polas, M. R. H., Jahanshahi, A. A., Kabir, A. I., Sohel-Uz-Zaman, A. S. M., Osman, A. R., & Karim, R. (2022). Artificial intelligence, blockchain technology, and risk-taking behavior in the 4.0 IR Metaverse Era: Evidence from Bangladesh-based SMEs. *Journal of Open Innovation*, *8*(3), 168. doi:10.3390/joitmc8030168

Popescu, G. H., Ciurlău, C. F., Stan, C. I., Băcănoiu, C., & Tănase, A. (2022). Virtual workplaces in the metaverse: Immersive remote collaboration tools, behavioral predictive analytics, and extended reality technologies. *Psychosociological Issues in Human Resource Management*, *10*(1), 21–34. doi:10.22381/pihrm10120222

Popescu, G. H., Valaskova, K., & Horak, J. (2022). Augmented reality shopping experiences, retail business analytics, and machine vision algorithms in the virtual economy of the metaverse. *Journal of Self-Governance and Management Economics*, *10*(2), 67–81.

Popp, J., & Cuțitoi, A. C. (2022). Immersive Visualization Systems, Spatial Simulation and Environment Mapping Algorithms, and Decision Intelligence and Modeling Tools in the Web3-powered Metaverse World. *Journal of Self-Governance and Management Economics*, *10*(3), 56–72.

Prasetyo, J. (2022). The Future of Post-Covid-19 Health Services using Metaverse Technology. *The Journal for Nurse Practitioners*, *6*(1), 93–99. doi:10.30994/jnp.v6i1.295

Proelss, J., Sévigny, S., & Schweizer, D. (2023). GameFi: The perfect symbiosis of blockchain, tokens, DeFi, and NFTs? *International Review of Financial Analysis*, *90*, 102916. doi:10.1016/j.irfa.2023.102916

Profumo, G., Testa, G., Viassone, M., & Ben Youssef, K. (2024). Metaverse and the fashion industry: A systematic literature review. *Journal of Global Fashion Marketing*, *15*(1), 131–154. doi:10.1080/20932685.2023.2270587

Qarni, M. O., & Gulzar, S. (2021). Portfolio diversification benefits of alternative currency investment in Bitcoin and foreign exchange markets. *Financial Innovation*, *7*(1), 1–37. doi:10.1186/s40854-021-00233-5

Qiu, C. S., Majeed, A., Khan, S., & Watson, M. (2022). Transforming health through the metaverse. *Journal of the Royal Society of Medicine*, *115*(12), 484–486. doi:10.1177/01410768221144763 PMID:36480946

Qi, W. (2022). The Investment Value of Metaverse in the Media and Entertainment Industry. *BCP Business &amp. Management, 34*, 279–283. doi:10.54691/bcpbm.v34i.3026

Queiroz, M. M., Wamba, S. F., Pereira, S. C. F., & Jabbour, C. J. C. (2023). The metaverse as a breakthrough for operations and supply chain management: Implications and call for action. *International Journal of Operations & Production Management, 43*(10), 1539–1553. doi:10.1108/IJOPM-01-2023-0006

Raad, H., & Rashid, F. K. M. (2023). The Metaverse: Applications, Concerns, Technical Challenges, Future Directions and Recommendations. *IEEE Access : Practical Innovations, Open Solutions, 11*, 110850–110861. doi:10.1109/AC-CESS.2023.3321650

Rad, A. I., & Far, S. B. (2023). SocialFi transforms social media: An overview of key technologies, challenges, and opportunities of the future generation of social media. *Social Network Analysis and Mining, 13*(1), 42. doi:10.1007/s13278-023-01050-7

Rahaman, T. (2022). Into the metaverse–perspectives on a new reality. *Medical Reference Services Quarterly, 41*(3), 330–337. doi:10.1080/02763869.2022.2096341 PMID:35980623

Rahi, P., Sood, S. P., Dandotiya, M., Kalhotra, S. K., & Khan, I. R. (2023). Artificial Intelligence of Things (AIoT) and Metaverse Technology for Brain Health, Mental Health, and Wellbeing. In Contemporary Applications of Data Fusion for Advanced Healthcare Informatics (pp. 429-445). IGI Global. https://doi.org/ doi:10.4018/978-1-6684-8913-0.ch019

Rahman, K. R., Shitol, S. K., Islam, M. S., Iftekhar, K. T., & Pranto, S. A. H. A. (2023). Use of Metaverse Technology in Education Domain. *Journal of Metaverse, 3*(1), 79–86. doi:10.57019/jmv.1223704

Rajan, A., Nassiri, N., Akre, V., Ravikumar, R., Nabeel, A., Buti, M., et al. (2018). *Virtual Reality Gaming Addiction.* Fifth HCT Information Technology Trends (ITT).

Rana, J., Gaur, L., Singh, G., Awan, U., & Rasheed, M. I. (2022). Reinforcing customer journey through artificial intelligence: A review and research agenda. *International Journal of Emerging Markets, 17*(7), 1738–1758. doi:10.1108/IJOEM-08-2021-1214

Rane, N., Choudhary, S., & Rane, J. (2023). *Metaverse for Enhancing Customer Loyalty: Effective Strategies to Improve Customer Relationship, Service, Engagement, Satisfaction, and Experience* (SSRN Scholarly Paper 4624197). doi:10.2139/ssrn.4624197

Rane, N., Choudhary, S., & Rane, J. (2023). Metaverse for Enhancing Customer Loyalty: Effective Strategies to Improve Customer Relationship, Service, Engagement, Satisfaction, and Experience. *Service, Engagement, Satisfaction, and Experience.*

Rathore, S., & Arora, M. (2024). Sustainability Reporting in the Metaverse: A Multi-Sectoral Analysis. In Exploring the Use of Metaverse in Business and Education (pp. 147-165). IGI Global. doi:10.4018/979-8-3693-5868-9.ch009

Rathore, B. (2017). Virtual consumerism: An exploration of e-commerce in the metaverse. *International Journal of New Media Studies, 4*(2), 61–69. doi:10.58972/eiprmj.v4i2y17.109

Rauschnabel, P. A., Babin, B. J., tom Dieck, M. C., Krey, N., & Jung, T. (2022). What is augmented reality marketing? Its definition, complexity, and future. *Journal of Business Research, 142*, 1140–1150. doi:10.1016/j.jbusres.2021.12.084

Rejeb, A., Rejeb, K., & Treiblmaier, H. (2023). Mapping metaverse research: Identifying future research areas based on bibliometric and topic modeling techniques. *Information (Basel), 14*(7), 356. doi:10.3390/info14070356

Richter, S., & Richter, A. (2023). What is novel about the Metaverse? *International Journal of Information Management, 73*, 102684. doi:10.1016/j.ijinfomgt.2023.102684

Rogers, E. M. (2003). *Diffusion of innovations.* Simon and Schuster.

Romano, B., Sands, S., & Pallant, J. I. (2021). Augmented reality and the customer journey: An exploratory study. *Australasian Marketing Journal, 29*(4), 354–363. doi:10.1016/j.ausmj.2020.06.010

Rosenblum, L., & Cross, R. (1997). Challenges in Virtual Reality. In *In Visualization and Modelling.* Academic Press.

Rubio-Tamayo, J. L., Gertrudix Barrio, M., & García García, F. (2017). Immersive environments and virtual reality: Systematic review and advances in communication, interaction and simulation. *Multimodal Technologies and Interaction, 1*(4), 21. doi:10.3390/mti1040021

Ryu, S. (2024). Zepeto: Developing a Business Model for the Metaverse World.

Sagayam, K. M., Das, P., Jamader, A. R., Acharya, B. R., Bonyah, E., & Elngar, A. A. (2022). DeepCOVIDNet [Detection of Chest Image Using Deep Learning Model.]. *COVID,* 19.

Saka, E. (2023). Metaverse and Diversity. In *The Future of Digital Communication* (pp. 73–89). CRC Press., doi:10.1201/9781003379119-6

Sandal, M. M., Taner, T., Firat, B. B., Ünal, H. T., Ulucan, S., & Mendı, A. F. Ö, Ö., & Nacar, M. A. (2023, 8-10 June 2023). *WEB 3.0 Applications and Projections. 2023 5th International Congress on Human-Computer Interaction, Optimization and Robotic Applications (HORA).* IEEE. 10.1109/HORA58378.2023.10156728

Schauman, S., Greene, S. K., & Korkman, O. (2023). Sufficiency and the dematerialization of fashion: How digital substitutes are creating new market opportunities. *Business Horizons, 66*(6), 741–751. doi:10.1016/j.bushor.2023.03.003

Scheiding, R. (2023). Designing the Future? The Metaverse, NFTs, & the Future as Defined by Unity Users. *Games and Culture, 18*(6), 804–820. doi:10.1177/15554120221139218

Schlemmer, E., & Backes, L. (2015). The metaverse: 3D digital virtual worlds. In *Learning in Metaverses: Co-Existing in Real Virtuality* (pp. 48–81). IGI Global., doi:10.4018/978-1-4666-6351-0.ch003

Schnack, A., Wright, M. J., & Elms, J. (2021). Investigating the impact of shopper personality on behaviour in immersive Virtual Reality store environments. *Journal of Retailing and Consumer Services, 61,* 102581. doi:10.1016/j.jretconser.2021.102581

Scholz, J., & Smith, A. N. (2016). Augmented reality: Designing immersive experiences that maximize consumer engagement. *Business Horizons, 59*(2), 149–161. doi:10.1016/j.bushor.2015.10.003

Schumacher, P. (2022). The metaverse as opportunity for architecture and society: Design drivers, core competencies. *Architectural Intelligence, 1*(1), 11. doi:10.1007/s44223-022-00010-z PMID:35993030

Sebastian, S. R., & Babu, B. P. (2022). Impact of metaverse in health care: A study from the care giver's perspective. *International Journal of Community Medicine and Public Health, 9*(12), 4613. doi:10.18203/2394-6040.ijcmph20223221

Seo, J., Kim, K., Park, M., Park, M., & Lee, K. (2018). An Analysis of Economic Impact on IOT Industry under GDPR. *Mobile Information Systems, 2018,* 1–6. doi:10.1155/2018/6792028

Seong, S., Hoefer, R., & McLaughlin, S. (2021). NFT revolution [in Korean]. *The Quest.*

Sestino, A., & D'Angelo, A. (2023). My doctor is an avatar! The effect of anthropomorphism and emotional receptivity on individuals' intention to use digital-based healthcare services. *Technological Forecasting and Social Change, 191,* 122505. doi:10.1016/j.techfore.2023.122505

Shah, D., & Shay, E. (2019). How and why artificial intelligence, mixed reality and blockchain technologies will change marketing we know today. Handbook of advances in marketing in an era of disruptions: Essays in honour of Jagdish N. Sheth. Sage. doi:10.4135/9789353287733.n32

Shahbaz Badr, A., & De Amicis, R. (2023). An empirical evaluation of enhanced teleportation for navigating large urban immersive virtual environments. *Frontiers in Virtual Reality, 3*, 1075811. https://www.frontiersin.org/articles/10.3389/frvir.2022.1075811. doi:10.3389/frvir.2022.1075811

Shah, D., & Murthi, B. P. S. (2021). Marketing in a data-driven digital world: Implications for the role and scope of marketing. *Journal of Business Research, 125*, 772–779. doi:10.1016/j.jbusres.2020.06.062

Sharma, R., Fantin, A. R., Prabhu, N., Guan, C., & Dattakumar, A. (2016). Digital literacy and knowledge societies: A grounded theory investigation of sustainable development. *Telecommunications Policy, 40*(7), 628–643. doi:10.1016/j.telpol.2016.05.003

Sharma, R., Jabbour, C. J. C., & Lopes de Sousa Jabbour, A. B. (2021). Sustainable manufacturing and industry 4.0: What we know and what we don't. *Journal of Enterprise Information Management, 34*(1), 230–266. doi:10.1108/JEIM-01-2020-0024

Shen, B., Tan, W., Guo, J., Zhao, L., & Qin, P. (2021). How to promote user purchase in metaverse? A systematic literature review on consumer behavior research and virtual commerce application design. *Applied Sciences (Basel, Switzerland), 11*(23), 11087. doi:10.3390/app112311087

Shen, X., Zhang, Y., Tang, Y., Qin, Y., Liu, N., & Yi, Z. (2021). A study on the impact of digital tobacco logistics on tobacco supply chain performance: Taking the tobacco industry in Guangxi as an example. *Industrial Management & Data Systems, 122*(6), 1416–1452. doi:10.1108/IMDS-05-2021-0270

Sheth, J. (2020). Business of business is more than business: Managing during the Covid crisis. *Industrial Marketing Management, 88*, 261–264. doi:10.1016/j.indmarman.2020.05.028

Shi, J., Mo, X., & Sun, Z. (2012). Content validity index in scale development. *Zhong nan da xue xue bao. Yi xue ban= Journal of Central South University. Medical Science, 37*(2), 152–155.

Shin, D. (2022). The actualization of meta affordances: Conceptualizing affordance actualization in the metaverse games. *Computers in Human Behavior, 133*, 107292. doi:10.1016/j.chb.2022.107292

Sigala, M. (2003). Developing and benchmarking internet marketing strategies in the hotel sector in Greece. *Journal of Hospitality & Tourism Research (Washington, D.C.), 27*(4), 375–401. doi:10.1177/10963480030274001

Silitonga, D., Rohmayanti, S. A. A., Aripin, Z., Kuswandi, D., Sulistyo, A. B., & Juhari. (2024). Edge Computing in E-commerce Business: Economic Impacts and Advantages of Scalable Information Systems. *EAI Endorsed Transactions on Scalable Information Systems, 11*(1). Advance online publication. doi:10.4108/eetsis.4375

Šimáková, J. (2011). Analysis of the relationship between oil and gold prices. *The Journal of Finance, 51*(1), 651–662.

Siponen, M., & Vance, A. (2010). User trust in information systems: A critical review of the literature. *Management Information Systems Quarterly, 34*(2), 339–368.

Situmorang, D. D. B. (2022). "Rapid tele-psychotherapy" with single-session music therapy in the metaverse: An alternative solution for mental health services in the future. *Palliative & Supportive Care*, 1–2. PMID:36218066

Situmorang, D. D. B. (2023). Metaverse as a new place for online mental health services in the post-COVID-19 era: Is it a challenge or an opportunity? *Journal of Public Health (Oxford, England), 45*(2), e379–e380. doi:10.1093/pubmed/fdac159 PMID:36542106

Slater, M., & Sanchez-Vives, M. V. (2016). Enhancing our lives with immersive virtual reality. *Frontiers in Robotics and AI*, *3*, 74. doi:10.3389/frobt.2016.00074

Smith, A. H., & Shakeri, M. (2022). The future's not what It used to be: Urban wormholes, simulation, participation, and planning in the Metaverse. *Urban Planning*, *7*(2), 214–217. doi:10.17645/up.v7i2.5893

Smith, J., & Jones, A. (2023). The metaverse: A potential game-changer for industries. *Journal of Emerging Technologies*, *12*(3), 45–62.

Solomon, P. R. (2018). Neuromarketing: Applications, Challenges and Promises. *Biomedical Journal of Scientific & Technical Research*, *12*(2). doi:10.26717/BJSTR.2018.12.002230

Song, Y. T., & Qin, J. (2022). Metaverse and personal healthcare. *Procedia Computer Science*, *210*, 189–197. doi:10.1016/j.procs.2022.10.136

Sowmya, G., Chakraborty, D., Polisetty, A., Khorana, S., & Buhalis, D. (2023). Use of metaverse in socializing: Application of the big five personality traits framework. *Psychology and Marketing*, *40*(10), 2132–2150. doi:10.1002/mar.21863

Spence, C. (2021). Scenting Entertainment: Virtual Reality Storytelling, Theme Park Rides, Gambling, and Video-Gaming. *IPerception*, *12*(4), 20416695211034538. doi:10.1177/20416695211034538 PMID:34457231

Stefanic, D. (2023, December 7). Hosting Concerts and Shows in the Metaverse. *Hyperspace^{mv} - the Metaverse for Business Platform*. https://hyperspace.mv/metaverse-concerts-and-shows/

Stephenson, N. (1992). Snow Crash (Spectra, Ed.). Bantam Books.

Stephenson, N. (1992). *Snow Crash*. Bantam Books.

Stephenson, N. (1992). Snow crash. *Futures*, *26*(7), 798–800. doi:10.1016/0016-3287(94)90052-3

Stephenson, N. (1992). *Snow Crash: A Novel*. Bantam Books.

Stoklasová, R. (2018). Short-term and Long-term relationships between Gold Prices and Oil Prices. *Scientific papers of the University of Pardubice. Series D. Faculty of Economics and Administration.*, *43*, 221–231.

Sudhakar, M. (2023). Artificial Intelligence Applications in Water Treatment and Water Resource Assessment: Challenges, Innovations, and Future Directions. In Intelligent Engineering Applications and Applied Sciences for Sustainability (pp. 248-269). IGI Global.

Suh, I., McKinney, T., & Siu, K. C. (2023, April). Current Perspective of Metaverse Application in Medical Education, Research and Patient Care. In Virtual Worlds, 2(2). MDPI.

Sullivan, C., & Tyson, S. (2023). A global digital identity for all: The next evolution. *Policy Design and Practice*, *6*(4), 433–445. doi:10.1080/25741292.2023.2267867

Sung, E., Kwon, O., & Sohn, K. (2023). NFT luxury brand marketing in the metaverse: Leveraging blockchain-certified NFTs to drive consumer behavior. *Psychology and Marketing*, *40*(11), 2306–2325. doi:10.1002/mar.21854

Sutherland, K. E., & Barker, R. (2023). The Future of Transmedia Brand Storytelling and a Model for Practice. In Transmedia Brand Storytelling: Immersive Experiences from Theory to Practice (pp. 247-271). Singapore: Springer Nature Singapore. doi:10.1007/978-981-99-4001-1_12

Swan, M. (2023). Metaverse Marketing: A Review and Research Agenda. *Journal of Marketing Management*, *39*(3-4), 291–318.

Sweeney, J. C., & Soutar, G. N. (2001). Consumer perceived value: The development of a multiple item scale. *Journal of Retailing*, 77(2), 203–220. doi:10.1016/S0022-4359(01)00041-0

Taçgın, Z., & Dalgarno, B. (2021). Building an Instructional Design Model for Immersive Virtual Reality Learning Environments. In *Designing* (pp. 20–47). Deploying, and Evaluating Virtual and Augmented Reality in Education. doi:10.4018/978-1-7998-5043-4.ch002

TanA. (2021). Metaverse Realities: A Journey Through Governance, Legal Complexities, and the Promise of Virtual Worlds. SSRN. https://doi.org/ doi:10.2139/ssrn.4393422

TansuchatR.ChangC. L.McAleerM. (2010). Crude oil hedging strategies using dynamic multivariate GARCH. *Available at* SSRN 1531187. doi:10.2139/ssrn.1531187

Tan, T. F., Li, Y., Lim, J. S., Gunasekeran, D. V., Teo, Z. L., Ng, W. Y., & Ting, D. S. (2022). Metaverse and virtual health care in ophthalmology: Opportunities and challenges. *Asia-Pacific Journal of Ophthalmology*, 11(3), 237–246. doi:10.1097/APO.0000000000000537 PMID:35772084

Taylor, S. E., & Todd, P. A. (1995). Understanding information technology use as a process: A conceptual model of user acceptance and use. *Management Information Systems Quarterly*, 19(4), 197–217.

Teo, K. S., & Wong, Y. W. (2023). *The determinants of Augmented Reality (AR) marketing affect purchase intention in the beauty and makeup industry among gen z in Malaysia* [Doctoral dissertation, UTAR].

Thomas, N. J., Baral, R., Crocco, O. S., & Mohanan, S. (2023). A framework for gamification in the metaverse era: How designers envision gameful experience. *Technological Forecasting and Social Change*, 193, 122544. Advance online publication. doi:10.1016/j.techfore.2023.122544

Thomason, J. (2021). Metahealth-how will the metaverse change health care? *Journal of Metaverse*, 1(1), 13–16.

Tlili, A., Huang, R., & Kinshuk, K. (2023). Metaverse for climbing the ladder toward 'Industry 5.0' and 'Society 5.0'? *Service Industries Journal*, 43(3–4), 260–287. doi:10.1080/02642069.2023.2178644

Toraman, C., Basarir, C., & Bayramoglu, M. F. (2011). Effects of crude oil price changes on sector indices of Istanbul stock exchange. *European Journal of Economic and Political Studies*, 4(2), 109–124.

Toraman, Y., & Geçit, B. B. (2023). User acceptance of metaverse: An analysis for e-commerce in the framework of technology acceptance model (TAM). *Sosyoekonomi*, 31(55), 85–104. doi:10.17233/sosyoekonomi.2023.01.05

Tornatzky, L. G., & Fleischer, M. (1990). *The process of technological innovation*. Lexington Books.

Torous, J., Bucci, S., Bell, I. H., Kessing, L. V., Faurholt-Jepsen, M., Whelan, P., Carvalho, A. F., Keshavan, M., Linardon, J., & Firth, J. (2021). The growing field of digital psychiatry: Current evidence and the future of apps, social media, chatbots, and virtual reality. *World Psychiatry; Official Journal of the World Psychiatric Association (WPA)*, 20(3), 318–335. doi:10.1002/wps.20883 PMID:34505369

Toyoshima, Y., Nakajima, T., & Hamori, S. (2013). Crude oil hedging strategy: New evidence from the data of the financial crisis. *Applied Financial Economics*, 23(12), 1033–1041. doi:10.1080/09603107.2013.788779

Trevor, A. (2022). *Metaverso 360 - La guida più completa su Metaverse e investimenti, web 3.0, NFT, DeFi, augmented reality (AR), cryptoassets, digital real estate e future networking*. Independently published.

Tse, Y. K., & Tsui, A. K. C. (2002). A multivariate generalized autoregressive conditional heteroscedasticity model with time-varying correlations. *Journal of Business & Economic Statistics*, 20(3), 351–362. doi:10.1198/073500102288618496

Tuomi, A., Tussyadiah, I. P., & Stienmetz, J. (2021). Applications and implications of service robots in hospitality. *Cornell Hospitality Quarterly*, *62*(2), 232–247. doi:10.1177/1938965520923961

Turab, M., & Jamil, S. (2023). A Comprehensive Survey of Digital Twins in Healthcare in the Era of Metaverse. *BioMedInformatics*, *3*(3), 563–584. doi:10.3390/biomedinformatics3030039

Ud Din, I., & Almogren, A. (2023). Exploring the psychological effects of Metaverse on mental health and well-being. *Information Technology & Tourism*, *25*(3), 367–389. doi:10.1007/s40558-023-00259-8

Ud Din, I., Awan, K. A., Almogren, A., & Rodrigues, J. J. (2023). Integration of IoT and blockchain for decentralized management and ownership in the metaverse. *International Journal of Communication Systems*, *36*(18), e5612. doi:10.1002/dac.5612

Uddin, M. R. (2024). The role of the digital economy in Bangladesh's economic development. *Sustainable Technology and Entrepreneurship*, *3*(1), 100054. doi:10.1016/j.stae.2023.100054

Ullah, H., Manickam, S., Obaidat, M., Laghari, S. U. A., & Uddin, M. (2023). Exploring the Potential of Metaverse Technology in Healthcare: Applications, Challenges, and Future Directions. *IEEE Access : Practical Innovations, Open Solutions*, *11*, 69686–69707. doi:10.1109/ACCESS.2023.3286696

Um, T., Kim, H., Kim, H., Lee, J., Koo, C., & Chung, N. (2022, January). Travel Incheon as a metaverse: smart tourism cities development case in Korea. In *ENTER22 e-Tourism Conference* (pp. 226–231). Springer International Publishing. doi:10.1007/978-3-030-94751-4_20

Upadhyay, U., Kumar, A., Sharma, G., Saini, A. K., Arya, V., Gaurav, A., & Chui, K. T. (2024). Mitigating Risks in the Cloud-Based Metaverse Access Control Strategies and Techniques. [IJCAC]. *International Journal of Cloud Applications and Computing*, *14*(1), 1–30. doi:10.4018/IJCAC.334364

Upadhyay, Y., Paul, J., & Baber, R. (2022). Effect of online social media marketing efforts on customer response. *Journal of Consumer Behaviour*, *21*(3), 554–571. doi:10.1002/cb.2031

Urquhart, A., & Zhang, H. (2019). Is Bitcoin a hedge or safe haven for currencies? An intraday analysis. *International Review of Financial Analysis*, *63*, 49–57. doi:10.1016/j.irfa.2019.02.009

Usmani, S. S., Sharath, M., & Mehendale, M. (2022). Future of mental health in the metaverse. *General Psychiatry*, *35*(4), e100825. doi:10.1136/gpsych-2022-100825 PMID:36189180

Van Beers, D., Bossilkov, A., Corder, G., & Van Berkel, R. (2007). Industrial symbiosis in the Australian minerals industry: the cases of Kwinana and Gladstone.

Van Eck, N. J., & Waltman, L. (2011). Text mining and visualization using VOSviewer. arXiv preprint arXiv:1109.2058.

Van Eck, N., & Waltman, L. (2010). Software survey: VOSviewer, a computer program for bibliometric mapping. *Scientometrics*, *84*(2), 523–538. doi:10.1007/s11192-009-0146-3 PMID:20585380

Van Huynh, D., Khosravirad, S. R., Masaracchia, A., Dobre, O. A., & Duong, T. Q. (2022). Edge intelligence-based ultra-reliable and low-latency communications for digital twin-enabled metaverse. *IEEE Wireless Communications Letters*, *11*(8), 1733–1737. doi:10.1109/LWC.2022.3179207

Vemula, S. (2020). Leveraging VR/AR/MR and AI as Innovative Educational Practices for "iGeneration" Students. In Handbook of Research on Equity in Computer Science in P-16 Education (pp. 265-277). doi:10.4018/978-1-7998-4739-7.ch015

Venkatesh, V., Brown, S. A., & Bala, H. (2013). Bridging the qualitative-quantitative divide: Guidelines for conducting mixed methods research in information systems. *Management Information Systems Quarterly, 37*(1), 21–54. doi:10.25300/MISQ/2013/37.1.02

Venkatesh, V., & Davis, F. D. (2000). A theoretical extension of the technology acceptance model: Four longitudinal field studies. *Management Science, 46*(2), 186–204. doi:10.1287/mnsc.46.2.186.11926

Venkatesh, V., Morris, M. G., Davis, G. B., & Davis, F. D. (2003). User acceptance of information technology: Toward a unified view. *Management Information Systems Quarterly, 27*(3), 425–478. doi:10.2307/30036540

Verhoef, P C., Broekhuizen, T., Bart, Y., Bhattacharya, A., Dong, J Q., Fabian, N E., & Haenlein, M. (2021, January 1). Digital transformation: A multidisciplinary reflection and research agenda. doi:10.1016/j.jbusres.2019.09.022

Viana-Lora, A., & Nel-lo-Andreu, M. G. (2022). Bibliometric analysis of trends in COVID- 19 and tourism. *Humanities & Social Sciences Communications, 9*(1), 173. doi:10.1057/s41599-022-01194-5

Vidal-Tomás, D. (2022). The new crypto niche: NFTs, play-to-earn, and metaverse tokens. *Finance Research Letters, 47*, 102742. doi:10.1016/j.frl.2022.102742

Vidal-Tomás, D. (2023). The illusion of the metaverse and meta-economy. *International Review of Financial Analysis, 86*, 102560. doi:10.1016/j.irfa.2023.102560

Vig, S. (2023). Preparing for the New Paradigm of Business: The Metaverse. *Foresight and STI Governance (Foresight-Russia till No. 3/2015), 17*(3), 6-18. doi:10.17323/2500-2597.2023.3.6.18

Villalonga-Gómez, C., Ortega-Fernández, E., & Borau-Boira, E. (2023). Fifteen years of metaverse in Higher Education: A systematic literature review. *IEEE Transactions on Learning Technologies, 16*(6), 1057–1070. doi:10.1109/TLT.2023.3302382

Violante, M. G., Vezzetti, E., & Piazzolla, P. (2019). How to design a virtual reality experience that impacts the consumer engagement: The case of the virtual supermarket. [IJIDeM]. *International Journal on Interactive Design and Manufacturing, 13*(1), 243–262. doi:10.1007/s12008-018-00528-5

Vlăduțescu, Ș., & Stănescu, G. C. (2023). Environmental Sustainability of Metaverse: Perspectives from Romanian Developers. *Sustainability (Basel), 15*(15), 11704. doi:10.3390/su151511704

Voinea, G. D., Gîrbacia, F., Postelnicu, C. C., Duguleana, M., Antonya, C., Soica, A., & Stănescu, R.-C. (2022). Study of Social Presence While Interacting in Metaverse with an Augmented Avatar during Autonomous Driving. *Applied Sciences (Basel, Switzerland), 12*(22), 22. Advance online publication. doi:10.3390/app122211804

Volchek, K., & Brysch, A. (2023, January). Metaverse and tourism: From a new niche to a transformation. In *ENTER22 e-Tourism Conference* (pp. 300–311). Springer Nature Switzerland. doi:10.1007/978-3-031-25752-0_32

Volvo. (2022). *The Volvoverse: Volvo Cars launches first car in the metaverse.* Volvo. https://www.volvocars.com/au/news/technology/The-Volvoverse/

Vosmeer, M., & Schouten, B. (2014). Interactive Cinema: Engagement and Interaction. In A. Mitchell, C. Fernández-Vara, & D. Thue (Eds.), *Interactive Storytelling* (Vol. 8832, pp. 140–147). Springer International Publishing., doi:10.1007/978-3-319-12337-0_14

Wallace, R. S. O., & Cooke, T. E. (1990). The diagnosis and resolution of emerging issues in corporate disclosure practices. *Accounting and Business Research, 20*(78), 143–151. doi:10.1080/00014788.1990.9728872

Wallin, J. A. (2005). Bibliometric methods: Pitfalls and possibilities. *Basic & Clinical Pharmacology & Toxicology*, *97*(5), 261–275. doi:10.1111/j.1742-7843.2005.pto_139.x PMID:16236137

Wang, G., Badal, A., Jia, X., Maltz, J. S., Mueller, K., Myers, K. J., Niu, C., Vannier, M., Yan, P., Yu, Z., & Zeng, R. (2022). Development of metaverse for intelligent healthcare. *Nature Machine Intelligence*, *4*(11), 922–929. doi:10.1038/s42256-022-00549-6 PMID:36935774

Wang, I. (2022). *The Digital Mind of Tomorrow: Rethink, transform, and thrive in today's fast-changing and brutal digital world*. Digital Thinker.

Wang, M. H., Yu, T. C., & Ho, Y. S. (2010). A bibliometric analysis of the performance of Water Research. *Scientometrics*, *84*(3), 813–820. doi:10.1007/s11192-009-0112-0

Wang, M., Yu, H., Bell, Z., & Chu, X. (2022). Constructing an edu-metaverse ecosystem: A new and innovative framework. *IEEE Transactions on Learning Technologies*, *15*(6), 685–696. doi:10.1109/TLT.2022.3210828

Wang, Y., & Qualls, W. (2007). Towards a theoretical model of technology adoption in hospitality organizations. *International Journal of Hospitality Management*, *26*(3), 560–573. doi:10.1016/j.ijhm.2006.03.008

Wanick, V., & Stallwood, J. (2022). *Brand storytelling, gamification, and social media marketing in the "Metaverse": a case study of The Ralph Lauren winter escape.*

Wan, X., Zhang, G., Yuan, Y., & Chai, S. (2023). How to drive the participation willingness of supply chain members in metaverse technology adoption? *Applied Soft Computing*, *145*, 110611. doi:10.1016/j.asoc.2023.110611

Wedel, M., Bigné, E., & Zhang, J. (2020). Virtual and augmented reality: Advancing research in consumer marketing. *International Journal of Research in Marketing*, *37*(3), 443–465. doi:10.1016/j.ijresmar.2020.04.004

Weinberg, B. H. (1974). Bibliographic coupling: A review. *Information Storage and Retrieval*, *10*(5–6), 189–196. doi:10.1016/0020-0271(74)90058-8

Weinberger, M. (2022). What Is Metaverse?—A Definition Based on Qualitative Meta-Synthesis. *Future Internet*, *14*(11), 310. doi:10.3390/fi14110310

Wiangkham, A., & Vongvit, R. (2023). Exploring the Drivers for the Adoption of Metaverse Technology in Engineering Education using PLS-SEM and ANFIS. *Education and Information Technologies*, 1–28.

Wider, W., Jiang, L., Lin, J., Fauzi, M. A., Li, J., & Chan, C. K. (2023). Metaverse chronicles: A bibliometric analysis of its evolving landscape. *International Journal of Human-Computer Interaction*, 1–14. doi:10.1080/10447318.2023.2227825

Wiederhold, B. K. (2022). Metaverse games: Game changer for healthcare? *Cyberpsychology, Behavior, and Social Networking*, *25*(5), 267–269. doi:10.1089/cyber.2022.29246.editorial PMID:35549346

Wiederhold, B. K. (2023). (Mental) Healthcare Consumerism in the Metaverse: Is There a Benefit? *Cyberpsychology, Behavior, and Social Networking*, *26*(3), 145–146. doi:10.1089/cyber.2023.29269.editorial PMID:36880891

Wiederhold, B. K., & Riva, G. (2022). Metaverse creates new opportunities in healthcare. *Ann. Rev. Cyber. Telemed*, *20*, 3–7.

Williams, A. (2006). Tourism and hospitality marketing: Fantasy, feeling and fun. *International Journal of Contemporary Hospitality Management*, *18*(6), 482–495. doi:10.1108/09596110610681520

Wongkitrungrueng, A., & Suprawan, L. (2023). Metaverse meets branding: Examining consumer responses to immersive brand experiences. *International Journal of Human-Computer Interaction*, 1–20. doi:10.1080/10447318.2023.2175162

Wong, L. W., Tan, G. W. H., Ooi, K. B., & Dwivedi, Y. K. (2023). Metaverse in hospitality and tourism: A critical reflection. *International Journal of Contemporary Hospitality Management*. doi:10.1108/IJCHM-05-2023-0586

World Commission on Environment and Development (WCED). (1987). *Our Common Future (Brundtland Report)*. United Nations. https://sustainabledevelopment.un.org

Wu, C. H., & Liu, C. Y. (2023). Educational Applications of Non-Fungible Token (NFT). *Sustainability (Basel)*, *15*(1), 7. Advance online publication. doi:10.3390/su15010007

Wu, D., Yang, Z., Zhang, P., Wang, R., Yang, B., & Ma, X. (2023). Virtual-Reality Inter-Promotion Technology for Metaverse: A Survey. *IEEE Internet of Things Journal*, *10*(18), 1–15. doi:10.1109/JIOT.2023.3265848

Wynn, M., & Jones, P. (2023). New technology deployment and corporate responsibilities in the metaverse. *Knowledge (Beverly Hills, Calif.)*, *3*(4), 543–556.

Xiang, H., Zhang, X., & Bilal, M. (2023). A cloud-edge service offloading method for the metaverse in smart manufacturing. *Software, Practice & Experience*, spe.3301. doi:10.1002/spe.3301

Xi, N., & Hamari, J. (2021). Shopping in virtual reality: A literature review and future agenda. *Journal of Business Research*, *134*, 37–58. doi:10.1016/j.jbusres.2021.04.075

Xu, M., Ng, W. C., Lim, W. Y. B., Kang, J., Xiong, Z., Niyato, D., Yang, Q., Shen, X. S., & Miao, C. (2022). A Full Dive into Realizing the Edge-enabled Metaverse: Visions, Enabling Technologies, and Challenges. *IEEE Communications Surveys and Tutorials*, *1*. doi:10.1109/COMST.2022.3221119

Yakura, H., & Goto, M. (2020). Enhancing Participation Experience in VR Live Concerts by Improving Motions of Virtual Audience Avatars. *2020 IEEE International Symposium on Mixed and Augmented Reality (ISMAR)*, (pp. 555–565). IEEE. 10.1109/ISMAR50242.2020.00083

Yang, L., Ni, S. T., Wang, Y., Yu, A., Lee, J. A., & Hui, P. (2024). Interoperability of the Metaverse: A Digital Ecosystem Perspective Review. *arXiv preprint arXiv:2403.05205*.

Yang, F. X., & Wang, Y. (2023). Rethinking Metaverse Tourism: A Taxonomy and an Agenda for Future Research. *Journal of Hospitality & Tourism Research (Washington, D.C.)*. doi:10.1177/10963480231163509

Yang, L. (2023). Recommendations for metaverse governance based on technical standards. *Humanities & Social Sciences Communications*, *10*(1), 1–10. doi:10.1057/s41599-023-01750-7

Yang, Q., Al Mamun, A., Hayat, N., Salleh, M. F. M., Jingzu, G., & Zainol, N. R. (2022). Modelling the mass adoption potential of wearable medical devices. *PLoS One*, *17*(6), e0269256. doi:10.1371/journal.pone.0269256 PMID:35675373

Yang, S. (2023, April). Storytelling and user experience in the cultural metaverse. *Heliyon*, *9*(4), e14759. doi:10.1016/j.heliyon.2023.e14759 PMID:37035365

Yang, Y., Siau, K., Xie, W., & Sun, Y. (2022). Smart health: Intelligent healthcare systems in the metaverse, artificial intelligence, and data science era. [JOEUC]. *Journal of Organizational and End User Computing*, *34*(1), 1–14. doi:10.4018/JOEUC.308814

Yao, X., Ma, N., Zhang, J., Wang, K., Yang, E., & Faccio, M. (2024). Enhancing wisdom manufacturing as industrial metaverse for industry and society 5.0. *Journal of Intelligent Manufacturing*, *35*(1), 235–255. doi:10.1007/s10845-022-02027-7

Yaqoob, I., Salah, K., Jayaraman, R., & Omar, M. (2023). Metaverse applications in smart cities: Enabling technologies, opportunities, challenges, and future directions. *Internet of Things : Engineering Cyber Physical Human Systems*, *23*, 100884. doi:10.1016/j.iot.2023.100884

Yemenici, A. D. (2022). Entrepreneurship in the world of metaverse: Virtual or real? *Journal of Metaverse*, *2*(2), 71–82. doi:10.57019/jmv.1126135

Yilmaz, M., O'Farrell, E. & Clarke, P. (2023). Examining the training and education potential of the metaverse: results from an empirical study of next generation SAFe training. *Journal of Software: Evolution and Process*. doi:10.1002/smr.2531

Yoo, M., Lee, S., & Bai, B. (2011). Hospitality marketing research from 2000 to 2009: topics, methods, and trends. *International Journal of Contemporary Hospitality Management*.

Yu, X., & Fang, B. (2020). *Cybersecurity challenges and opportunities in the metaverse*. Research Gate.

Yu, F., Jian, S., Shen, C., Xue, W., & Fu, Y. (2022). On the Issue of "Digital Human" in the context of digital transformation. In *2022 International Conference on Culture-Oriented Science and Technology (CoST)* (pp. 258-262). IEEE. 10.1109/CoST57098.2022.00060

Zainurin, M. Z. L., Masri, M. H., Besar, M. H. A., & Anshari, M. (2023). Towards an understanding of metaverse banking: A conceptual paper. *Journal of Financial Reporting and Accounting*, *21*(1), 178–190. doi:10.1108/JFRA-12-2021-0487

Zakarneh, B., Annamalai, N., Alquqa, E. K., Mohamed, K. M., & Al Salhi, N. R. (2024). Virtual Reality and Alternate Realities in Neal Stephenson's—Snow Crash‖. *World Journal of English Language*, *14*(2), 244. doi:10.5430/wjel.v14n2p244

Zallio, M., & Clarkson, P. J. (2022). Designing the metaverse: A study on inclusion, diversity, equity, accessibility and safety for digital immersive environments. *Telematics and Informatics*, *75*, 101909. doi:10.1016/j.tele.2022.101909

Zamanifard, S., & Freeman, G. (2023). A Surprise Birthday Party in VR: Leveraging Social Virtual Reality to Maintain Existing Close Ties over Distance. International Conference on Information, Zhang, W., Zhao, S., Wan, X., & Yao, Y. (2021). Study on the effect of digital economy on high-quality economic development in China. *PLoS One*, *16*(9), e0257365. doi:10.1371/journal.pone.0257365

Zaman, U., Koo, I., Abbasi, S., Raza, S. H., & Qureshi, M. G. (2022). Meet your digital twin in space? Profiling international expat's readiness for metaverse space travel, Tech-Savviness, COVID-19 travel anxiety, and travel fear of missing out. *Sustainability (Basel)*, *14*(11), 6441. doi:10.3390/su14116441

Zawish, M., Dharejo, F. A., Khowaja, S. A., Raza, S., Davy, S., Dev, K., & Bellavista, P. (2024). AI and 6G into the metaverse: Fundamentals, challenges and future research trends. *IEEE Open Journal of the Communications Society*, *5*, 730–778. doi:10.1109/OJCOMS.2024.3349465

Zhai, X., Chu, X., Wang, M., Zhang, Z., & Dong, Y. (2022). Education metaverse: Innovations and challenges of the new generation of Internet education formats. *Metaverse*, *3*(1), 13. doi:10.54517/met.v3i1.1804

Zhang, C., & Tu, X. (2016). The effect of global oil price shocks on China's metal markets. *Energy Policy*, *90*, 131–139. doi:10.1016/j.enpol.2015.12.012

Zhang, D., Lei, L., Ji, Q., & Kutan, A. M. (2019). Economic policy uncertainty in the US and China and their impact on the global markets. *Economic Modelling*, *79*, 47–56. doi:10.1016/j.econmod.2018.09.028

Zhang, Q. (2023). Secure Preschool Education Using Machine Learning and Metaverse Technologies. *Applied Artificial Intelligence*, *37*(1), 2222496. doi:10.1080/08839514.2023.2222496

Zhang, T., Shen, J., Lai, C. F., Ji, S., & Ren, Y. (2023). Multi-server assisted data sharing supporting secure deduplication for metaverse healthcare systems. *Future Generation Computer Systems*, *140*, 299–310. doi:10.1016/j.future.2022.10.031

Zhang, X., Yu, L., Wang, S., & Lai, K. K. (2009). Estimating the impact of extreme events on crude oil price: An EMD-based event analysis method. *Energy Economics*, *31*(5), 768–778. doi:10.1016/j.eneco.2009.04.003

Zhang, Y. J., Bouri, E., Gupta, R., & Ma, S. J. (2021). Risk spillover between Bitcoin and conventional financial markets: An expectile-based approach. *The North American Journal of Economics and Finance*, *55*, 101296. doi:10.1016/j.najef.2020.101296

Zhang, Z., & Wen, X. (2023). Physical or virtual showroom? The decision for omni-channel retailers in the context of cross-channel free-riding. *Electronic Commerce Research*, 1–27. doi:10.1007/s10660-022-09616-x

Zhao, Y., Jiang, J., Chen, Y., Liu, R., Yang, Y., Xue, X., & Chen, S. (2022). Metaverse: Perspectives from graphics, interactions and visualization. *Visual Informatics*, *6*(1), 56–67. doi:10.1016/j.visinf.2022.03.002

Zheng, Z., Li, T., Li, B., Chai, X., Song, W., Chen, N., & Li, R. (2022, December). Industrial metaverse: connotation, features, technologies, applications and challenges. In *Asian Simulation Conference* (pp. 239-263). Singapore: Springer Nature Singapore. 10.1007/978-981-19-9198-1_19

Zhou, Z. (2023). Will the Metaverse Revolutionize the Narrative? *Critical Arts*, 1–15. doi:10.1080/02560046.2023.2282489

Zhu, H. Y., Hieu, N. Q., Hoang, D. T., Nguyen, D. N., & Lin, C. T. (2023). A human-centric metaverse enabled by brain-computer interface: A survey. *arXiv preprint arXiv:2309.01848*.

Zonaphan, L., Northus, K., Wijaya, J., Achmad, S., & Sutoyo, R. (2022, November). Metaverse as a future of education: A systematic review. In *2022 8th International HCI and UX Conference in Indonesia (CHIuXiD)*, 1, 77-81). 10.1109/CHIuXiD57244.2022.10009854

Zupic, I., & Čater, T. (2015). Bibliometric methods in management and organization. *Organizational Research Methods*, *18*(3), 429–472. doi:10.1177/1094428114562629

Zyda, M. (2022). Let's rename everything "the Metaverse!". *Computer*, *55*(3), 124–129. doi:10.1109/MC.2021.3130480

About the Contributors

Jeetesh Kumar is Head (a) of Research at the Faculty of Social Sciences and Leisure Management, Senior Lecturer at the School of Hospitality, Tourism and Events, Associate Director for Information Management & Documentation at the Centre for Research and Innovation in Tourism (CRiT), and Hub Leader of the "Responsible Tourism for Inclusive Economic Growth" Sustainable Tourism Impact Lab at Taylor's University, Malaysia.

Manpreet Arora, a Senior Assistant Professor of Management at the Central University of Himachal Pradesh, Dharamshala, India, brings over twenty-two years of rich teaching experience. She holds academic accolades including a Ph.D. in International Trade, an M.Phil, a gold medalist and several other academic distinctions from Himachal Pradesh University, Shimla. Dr. Arora's diverse research interests encompass Accounting, Finance, Strategic Management, Entrepreneurship, Qualitative Research and Microfinance. She works on Mixed methods research. Noteworthy for guiding doctoral research and delving into Microfinance, Entrepreneurship, Behavioral Finance and Corporate Reporting, she has presented at numerous seminars, delivering talks on various academic subjects across multiple universities and colleges. An accomplished academic, she has an impressive publication record, having authored over 30 papers in esteemed national and international journals listed in Scopus, WOS and Category journals, alongside contributing to fifty-five book chapters in publications by reputed publishers like Emerald, Routledge, CABI, Springer Nature, AAP, Wiley and more. Her commitment to management research is evident through the editing of six books. She is presently working in the area of Metaverse. Her impactful contributions showcase a multifaceted professional excelling in academia, research, and social advocacy.

Erkol Bayram is currently an Associate Professor in the School of tourism and hotel management, department of tour guiding, University of Sinop, Sinop, Turkey. Dr. Erkol Bayram has worked as an internal trainer and teacher in the tour guiding arena. Her doctorate is in Tourism Management from the Sakarya University, Turkey, and she completed her dissertation research on Tour Guiding in Turkey. Her core subjects are Tourism, tour guiding, tourism policy and Planning, women studies. Erkol Bayram has also worked as a professional tour guide in the tourism sector. The editor has many book chapters in the international arena and published her books as an editor in the national arena. She also has many book chapters under IGI GLOBAL related women, tourism and management studies. She has been invited for many talks/lectures/ panel discussions by different Universities.

Kausar Alam is working as an Assistant Professor of Accounting at BRAC Business School, BRAC University. He completed PhD from Universiti Putra Malaysia (UPM). His research interests are accounting, Shariah governance, institutional theory, Islamic banking, legitimacy theory, corporate governance, integrated reporting, working capital management, and qualitative research. His research works were published in APE, MDE, JAAR, ARA, Pacific Accounting Review, JIABR, AJAR, JPA, and QROM.

Lara Sofia Mendes Bacalhau holds a Ph.D. in Management - Specialization in Marketing and Strategy from the Faculty of Economics of the University of Porto (FEP-UP), where she also completed a Master's degree in Data Analysis and Decision Support Systems. This master's degree allowed her to combine her previous degrees, a Bachelor's degree in Mathematics - Teaching Branch of the Faculty of Science and Technology of the University of Coimbra and a Bachelor's degree in Business Management and a degree in Accounting and Auditing - via Business Management at the Coimbra Higher Institute of Accounting and Administration of the Polytechnic Institute of Coimbra (ISCAC | Coimbra Business School - IPC). She has other complementary training, including an MBA in Digital Marketing, a Postgraduate Diploma in Information Technology and Multimedia Communication, and a Training Course for Trainers to Obtain Specialization in Gender Equality. Lecturer at ISCAC since 2003, she has always been teaching in Marketing, Business Management, Accounting, and Taxation areas. In addition, she is also a lecturer/trainer at the Viseu School of Technology and Management of the Polytechnic Institute of Viseu (ESTGV-IPV), Coimbra Business School Executive, Institute for Employment and Vocational Training (IEFP), and ISLA Santarém. This teaching experience has led her to teach various undergraduate, master's, postgraduate and short courses. In addition to teaching, she was a member of the Direction of the Marketing and International Business Bachelor Degree (2013-April 2021) and is currently the director of this course. She is also a member of the Direction of the corresponding Master's Degree (2020-present). She was co-coordinator of the Preparation Workshops for the Certified Accountants Bar Exam (2016-2022). She is a researcher in the areas of Marketing (Branding, Digital Marketing, Social Media Marketing, E-commerce, and Relationship Marketing) and Business Management. She participates in national and international research projects. She is a peer reviewer and co-author of scientific publications in conference proceedings, book chapters, and journals. She is also a Certified Accountant.

Himani Gupta is an Associate Professor at JIMS, New Delhi, India. She has numerous research paper published in ABDC, SCOPUS and WOS listed journals. She has authored various books on accounts, finance and tax. She has completed projects from NHRC and ICSSR. She has won various research awards in conferences. She has uploaded various research and subject related videos on her YouTube channel. She has also taken many webinars/FDPs on econometrics (time series), finance, accounting and indirect taxes.

Manisha Gupta is working as an Associate Professor in Sharda University. She has various research paper published in ABDC, SCOPUS and WOS listed Journals.

Nusrat Hafiz, serving as the Assistant Professor of Entrepreneurship and International Business at BRAC Business School, is committed to driving impactful change. Armed with a Ph.D. from Putra Business School (AACSB Accredited), her outstanding research contribution has garnered her "quality journal publication awards" in multiple categories, recognizing her as one of the top contributors to Q1 journals. She possesses a decade's worth of experience in academia and half a decade of corporate exposure, complemented by her deep-rooted family values and unwavering work ethics. Dr. Hafiz's teaching philosophy prioritizes pragmatic approaches, while her research interests span strategic management, organizational sustainability, women's empowerment, digitalization and innovation, dynamic capabilities and social entrepreneurship. Her personal slogan, "Empowering Students, Every Step of the Way," embodies her commitment to student-centricity.

Mohammad Imtiaz Hossain is a PhD Fellow and Graduate research assistant (GRA) at Multimedia University, Malaysia. He pursued MSc in Business Economics from the School of Business and Economics, Universiti Putra Malaysia (UPM), Malaysia [AACSB & EQUIS accredited]. He has completed Bachelor in Business Management from Binary University, Malaysia and Diploma in Business from Mahsa Prima International College, Malaysia. His research interests include sustainability, SME, entrepreneurship, ambidexterity, leadership, technology adoption, tourism, service quality, human resource management, innovation, and many other interdisciplinary areas. Mr. Imtiaz has published numerous scholarly articles in Web of science, ABDC, Scopus, ERA, Google scholar and other indexed journals. Additionally, he is also serving as a reviewer for some prominent journals.

Tariqul Islam, a Ph.D. student in Hospitality and Tourism at Taylor's University, Malaysia. He holds a Master of Science (by research) in Tourism from Universiti Putra Malaysia, Malaysia. He graduated with distinction in Airlines, Tourism, and Hospitality from Lovely Professional University, India. Tariqul has published several research articles in ABDC- listed and Scopus-indexed journals and presented the findings of his research at various national and international conferences. His area of research includes consumer behaviour and technology adoption.

Yasmin Jamadar is currently serving as an Assistant Professor (Finance) at the BRAC Business School (BBS), BRAC University (BRACU). She is involved actively in teaching, supervision, research, development of new curricula and courses at the undergraduate and postgraduate levels. Before joining BRACU, she worked as a lecturer (Accounting & Finance) at Alfa University College, Malaysia. Dr. Yasmin obtained her Doctor of Philosophy (PhD) in Finance from the School of Business and Economics, Universiti Putra Malaysia (UPM) [AACSB & EQUIS accredited] and she graduated on time (GOT). She also served as an academic mentor at SBE, UPM. Moreover, as an invited member, she participated and contributed to the peer review process for EQUIS accreditation and AACSB re-accreditation of SBE, UPM. She achieved several merit and full bright scholarships throughout her academic career. Her research areas include corporate finance, corporate governance, accounting, sustainability, Insider trading, and earnings management. Her publications have appeared in various international refereed journals indexed in the Chartered Association of Business Schools (ABS), Web of Science (WoS), Australian Business Deans Council (ABDC) and Scopus. Additionally, Dr. Yasmin is also serving as a reviewer for some prominent journals including the Journal of Islamic Accounting and Business Research; Investment analyst; and Managerial and Decision Economics to name a few. She is a certified expert on STATA, Eviews, and SPSS software. She presented papers at several international conferences in UK, Malaysia, UAE, and Bahrain. Her corporate experience includes working as a business development executive in Nascenia IT, Bangladesh. She has also engaged in different social and professional development activities.

Asik Rahaman Jamader is working as an Assistant Professor in the department of Hospitality & Hotel Administration at Pailan College of Management & Technology, Kolkata, India, also he is the Corporate Advisory Board Member of the Smart Journal of Business Management Studies indexed by Emerging Sources Citation Index (ESCI) - Web of Science (Clarivate Analytics) with 5.748 Impact factor. His research interest is in Hospitality and innovative Technique implemented in Hospitality Industry. He is a scientist by having 23 numbers of International granted patents & 12 numbers of registered and published national & International patents also have a good number of authored Book/Book Chapters publications, including some SCOPUS/SCIE/ESCI/WOS publications. Recently he joined as an Ad Hoc reviewer of the International Journal of Business Intelligence Research (IJBIR), IGI Global publishing indexed by WOS and Scopus.

Rupinder Katoch is working as a Professor in Lovely Professional University. She has various research paper published in ABDC, SCOPUS and WOS listed Journals.

Nrnnesa Begum Momo is an undergraduate student at BRAC Business School, BRAC University, Bangladesh.

Jana Neves has a master's degree in marketing and international business at Coimbra Business School, specializing in Marketing strategies, international business dynamics, and consumer behavior. Prior academic achievements include a Bachelor's degree in Applied Communication from Lusofona University - Porto Center, focusing on communication theories, Marketing, and media studies. Practical expertise was gained as a Cisco Certified Network Associate through the Cisco Networking Academy, where skills in networking principles and system security were developed. Complementing the academic background, a three-year Informatic Internship at Lusofona University - Porto provided opportunities to offer technical support and perform system maintenance. Currently engaged in research in marketing and technology, with a focus on Digital Marketing strategies, E-commerce, and the integration of technology in Marketing campaigns. Furthermore, continuous knowledge enhancement is pursued through online courses, particularly in Data Analysis, Digital Marketing, and emerging technologies.

Harleen Pabla is a researcher in the field of marketing, whose expertise spans various areas including brand experience, consumer behavior, the metaverse, artificial intelligence, sustainability and the aviation sector. Her work has been published in prestigious international journals recognized by respected bodies like the Web of Science (WoS), Australian Business Deans Council (ABDC) and Scopus.

Sbyasachi Pramanik is a professional IEEE member. He obtained a PhD in Computer Science and Engineering from Sri Satya Sai University of Technology and Medical Sciences, Bhopal, India. Presently, he is an Associate Professor, Department of Computer Science and Engineering, Haldia Institute of Technology, India. He has many publications in various reputed international conferences, journals, and book chapters (Indexed by SCIE, Scopus, ESCI, etc). He is doing research in the fields of Artificial Intelligence, Data Privacy, Cybersecurity, Network Security, and Machine Learning. He also serves on the editorial boards of several international journals. He is a reviewer of journal articles from IEEE, Springer, Elsevier, Inderscience, IET and IGI Global. He has reviewed many conference papers, has been a keynote speaker, session chair, and technical program committee member at many international conferences. He has authored a book on Wireless Sensor Network. He has edited 8 books from IGI Global, CRC Press, Springer and Wiley Publications.

Rfaida Nurain Saiba is an undergraduate student at BRAC Business School, BRAC University, Bangladesh.

Aiesh Kumar Sharma is a Research Scholar at Mittal School of Business, Lovely Professional University, Phagwara, Punjab, India. His research interests are digital marketing, social media marketing, search engine marketing, remarketing, data analytics, artificial intelligence, machine learning, and the applications of technology in business.

Rhul Sharma is a highly accomplished professor of marketing with over 14 years of experience in academia. He has a PhD in marketing and has published over 15 articles in high-quality journals in the field. Dr Sharma's research interests include consumer behaviour, business analytics and digital marketing. In addition to his research, Dr Sharma is also a highly sought-after resource person in various faculty development programmes.

Menu Sharma is currently working as an Associate Professor and Head of the Department of Public Administration at the Assam Royal Global University, Guwahati, Assam. She has 19 years of teaching experience. She has supervised the research work of 10 doctoral scholars and 16 M.Phil Scholars. She has presented 60 research papers at international and national conferences/seminars in India. She has attended and completed 20 faculty development programs/refresher programs/orientation programs/workshops. Her 46 research papers have been published in national and international journals. Her 17 chapters in edited books have been published. She is a life member of the Indian Institute of Public Administration, New Public Administration Society of India, Indian Political Science Association, Indian Political Economy Association, Indian Public Administration Association, Agricultural Economics and Social Science Research Association (AESSRA), Indian Association for Women's Studies. She has supervised 10 doctoral research work and 16 M.Phil research work, She is supervising 5 doctoral research work.

Hreen Soch is a Professor of Marketing at the Department of Management and Hospitality, I.K. Gujral Punjab Technical University, Kapurthala, India. Her research interests focus on customer relationship management, adoption of mobile technologies, scale development and validation, customer loyalty, service recovery and brand experience. She has published articles in various national and international journals like Journal of Asia Business Studies, Journal of Indian Business Research, Journal of Services Research, Global Business Review, Journal of Global Marketing and Journal of Air Transport Management.

Bana Taneja has a doctorate in Management and an MBA specializing in marketing and finance. She has over 18 years of teaching experience In premium institutes like Xiss, Xaviers College Ranchi, Birsa Agricultural University, etc. Presently she is associated with Amity University Jharkhand. She has several publications to her name. Dr. Taneja is an active Rotarian and is presently on the board of directors of the Rotary Club of Ranchi. She is a Pranic healer.

Rajesh Verma is Sr. Dean & Professor of Strategy at Mittal School of Business (NIRF, Government of India Ranking #32; ACBSP, USA Accredited), Lovely Professional University, Punjab, India. His research & teaching interests entail areas like Business Models, Strategic Management & Political Marketing.

Index

A

Applications 2, 6, 12, 17-22, 24-25, 27-28, 33, 39-42, 44, 57, 60, 65, 74-75, 77-78, 91, 102, 106, 110-112, 114-117, 132-133, 137, 139-142, 144, 146, 150, 164, 168, 171, 177, 181, 192, 194, 207, 211, 214, 217-220, 222, 239-240, 245-247, 260, 275, 280, 282

Artificial Intelligence (AI) 4, 41, 57, 63, 78, 85, 115-116, 132, 153, 155, 166, 169, 187, 244, 275, 279

Augmented Reality (AR) 1, 6, 25, 44, 57, 63, 65, 85, 93-96, 107, 115-116, 124, 130, 132, 134-135, 137-139, 148, 150-151, 154-155, 166, 169, 185-187, 197, 224-226, 246

Avatars 1, 3, 10, 13, 16, 19-20, 25, 30, 32, 37-38, 68, 77-78, 97-98, 116, 118-122, 125, 128, 132, 147, 149-150, 154, 167-168, 172-173, 185, 187-188, 205, 224, 227, 248, 276

B

Bibliometric Analysis 29, 76, 80-81, 87-91, 93, 98-100, 197, 199-200, 202, 207-212

Bitcoin 4, 27-28, 32-33, 39, 255-257, 260, 263, 265, 269-274

Blockchain 3-4, 7-8, 11, 16, 19-23, 26, 28, 30-34, 37, 40-41, 57, 63, 65, 77, 85-86, 93, 106, 108, 115-116, 119-124, 126, 130, 132, 137-138, 140-143, 146, 149, 154-156, 159, 163, 165-167, 169, 176, 178-179, 181, 183, 185, 187, 192-194, 204-205, 207-208, 221, 225, 245, 249-250, 253-254, 264, 276

Branding 10, 114, 146-147, 159, 162, 216

Business 1, 4, 17-18, 20, 22-24, 30-32, 34, 36-37, 39-40, 44, 59-60, 63, 65, 70-73, 75, 77, 83, 85, 88, 90-91, 95, 102-103, 110-111, 113-114, 124, 128, 130, 162-165, 171, 178, 181, 183-184, 186, 188, 190, 192-193, 195, 197-198, 209-211, 215, 218, 220, 224, 226, 239-240, 242-253, 255, 271-275, 277-283, 285

C

Commerce 5-11, 19, 22, 68, 72, 85-86, 94, 96, 98-99, 106, 108-109, 112-113, 126, 128, 150, 153-154, 165, 167-168, 170, 183-184, 186, 188-192, 198-199, 210-212, 247-253, 270, 275, 277-278

Concept Transformation 213

Constraints 13, 30, 57, 70, 97, 109, 135, 147, 152, 154, 188, 207, 223, 227, 239-242, 250, 252, 276-277, 280

Consumer Behavior 24, 113, 128, 146, 152-153, 155, 199, 211, 243, 245

Consumer Shift 93, 99, 101

Cryptocurrencies 3, 33, 41, 193, 255-259, 264-266, 268-271

Customer Engagement 93, 95, 98-101, 188, 193, 195, 218

Customer Experience 65, 93-94, 99, 101, 106, 111, 153, 164-165, 199, 208

D

DCC GARCH 254, 258, 264, 266, 268

Decentralized Autonomous Organizations (DAOs) 12, 25

Digital 1-9, 11-14, 16-18, 21-22, 24-26, 28-33, 35-40, 42, 44-45, 62-65, 67, 69-73, 75-77, 79, 85, 89, 91-92, 94-95, 97-99, 106, 108-111, 113-115, 117-124, 126, 130-135, 137-140, 142-144, 146-150, 152-158, 161-163, 165-190, 192-193, 195-199, 202, 205, 207-208, 212, 214-217, 219-221, 224-225, 239-240, 243-251, 253, 255, 276, 278-280, 283-285

Digital Divide 167, 170-171, 174, 184, 190, 207

Digital Identity 13, 24-25, 180

Digital Transformation 1, 22, 64, 92, 131, 146, 152, 197, 216, 239-240, 253

E

E-Commerce 1, 4, 47, 58, 77, 93-104, 106-112, 114, 125, 150, 164, 216, 251, 278

Economic Development 64, 69-70, 72, 130, 182, 246, 275, 278-279

Engagement 4, 6, 8-11, 13, 15-16, 21-22, 25, 29, 48-50, 63, 65, 77, 79, 88, 93-95, 97-98, 100-101, 109-111, 113, 124, 128, 134, 141-142, 148, 150, 153-160, 165, 168, 170, 172-173, 180, 188-189, 192-193, 195, 198-199, 202, 207-208, 210, 217-218, 252, 278, 283-284, 286

Entertainment 2, 9, 11, 23, 30, 40, 44, 66, 95, 115-117, 121-128, 150, 162, 167, 170, 184-185, 188, 195, 197-198, 211, 224, 241, 248, 251, 276-278, 283

Environmental Sustainability 62, 64, 67, 69, 72, 177, 181, 244

Ethical Considerations 2, 14, 16, 21, 25, 129, 136, 139, 158, 161-162, 173, 183, 186, 190-192, 283

Extended Reality (XR) 1, 4, 7, 18, 156, 166

F

Future Trends 17, 107, 123, 146, 153, 155

G

Gacha model 27, 33

Gamification 5-6, 8-10, 18, 24-25, 93, 97-98, 110, 132, 189, 195

H

Healthcare 2, 12, 22-23, 28, 40, 63, 67-68, 72, 77, 101, 103, 129, 131-145, 162, 181, 198, 205, 207-208, 221, 224, 244, 251, 272, 276, 278, 283

Hedging 41, 254-255, 257, 259, 266, 268-269, 271, 273-274

Hospitality industry 66, 213-215, 220-221

Human Resources 60, 76-77, 79-83, 85-90

Human-Computer Interaction (HCI) 25

I

Immersive Realities 4-6, 8-9

Industrial Revolution 63, 180, 197

Industry Impacts 146, 247-249

Innovation 1, 11, 30-31, 60, 62, 65, 67, 70, 72, 74, 76, 79, 85-86, 96, 110, 113, 126, 146-147, 149, 152-153, 155, 159, 161, 165, 172, 174-176, 189, 191-192, 197-198, 207, 210, 219-220, 228, 239-

242, 244-245, 247-253, 273-276, 280, 282-283

Integration of Metaverse 44, 88, 100, 129, 136, 163

Intention to Use 43-50, 57-58, 142, 144

Interdisciplinary Technologies 247

Internet of Things (IoT) 63-64, 138, 154, 156, 166

Interoperability 12-14, 16, 22-23, 26, 44, 116-118, 127, 130, 139, 158, 161-162, 169-170, 191, 212, 239, 252

M

Machine Learning (ML) 63, 155, 166

Malaysia 43, 57-58, 103, 167, 204, 223, 225-227, 239-240, 242, 244, 246

Manufacturing 2, 18-19, 43-46, 51, 57-58, 61, 63, 66, 68, 72, 83, 91, 130, 162, 188, 196, 200, 211-212, 223-226, 237-240, 242-244, 246, 251, 277, 286

Marketing Strategy 213-214, 220-221

Metaverse 1-50, 57-75, 77-83, 85-104, 106-129, 131-145, 148-155, 157-168, 170-182, 184-200, 202, 204-205, 207-213, 223-230, 237-253, 275-280, 283-286

Mixed Reality (MR) 4, 6, 63, 96, 132, 156, 166, 225

Multiplayer Real-Time Virtual World 27

N

Non-Fungible Tokens (NFTs) 3, 7, 26, 65, 116, 123, 149, 154, 156, 166, 248

P

Patterns 22, 66, 77, 80, 87-88, 93, 98-100, 109-110, 136, 153, 160, 201, 216, 247, 251-252, 272

Portfolio Weights 254, 259, 268

Q

Qualitative Analysis 62

R

Research 1-2, 10, 15-22, 24-25, 27, 31, 39-41, 44-45, 48-50, 58-61, 63-66, 68-69, 72-74, 76-77, 79-83, 85-94, 97-104, 106, 109-114, 116, 125-126, 128, 134, 137-138, 142-144, 146-147, 161, 163-166, 168, 177-178, 186, 189, 192-195, 197-202, 205, 207-212, 215-216, 219-223, 226, 228, 231, 242-243, 245-249, 251-253, 255-258, 268-272, 275-276, 280-282, 285

Review 17-18, 21, 23-24, 27-29, 41-42, 45, 59-60,

74, 77, 85, 88-91, 95, 100, 102, 111, 113-115, 125, 128, 142-143, 164, 179-180, 185, 193-195, 199-200, 202, 207, 209-212, 221, 226, 243-245, 255-256, 270-274, 285
Roblox Gaming Platform 27, 32

S

Social Implications 167
Social Inclusion 62, 64, 68, 72-73, 163, 252
Spatial Computing 1, 5, 93, 119, 146, 157, 163, 166, 183, 192
Stereoscopes 31
Sustainable Development Goals 62-67, 70-71, 73, 279

T

Tourism 2, 20, 25, 40, 63-65, 74, 83, 89-90, 125, 163, 165, 181, 198-199, 205, 208, 210-211, 213-215, 218-222, 224, 277, 284-286
Transformative Role 247, 249

U

Ultima Online 32
Unified Theory of Acceptance 43, 47, 57
User experience 12, 25, 45, 115-116, 125-126, 139, 141, 151, 159, 161-162, 169-171, 174, 186-187, 196, 205, 217, 228, 239, 251-252

V

Virtual 1-22, 24-42, 44-45, 47-50, 57, 59-60, 62-74, 76-79, 85-86, 88-91, 94-101, 106-132, 134-139, 141, 143-144, 146-147, 149, 151, 153-195, 197-199, 202, 204-205, 207-211, 221, 223-228, 240, 242-243, 247-251, 253, 255, 271, 275-280, 283-286
Virtual Environments 1-2, 5-7, 11-16, 26, 32, 40, 44, 48, 50, 63, 71, 78-79, 85, 88, 93, 95-98, 100, 106, 109-110, 116, 119, 122, 124, 128, 134, 138, 146-153, 156-163, 168-169, 172, 183, 185, 188, 198, 249, 276-280, 284
Virtual Games 34, 115, 120
Virtual Reality (VR) 1, 6, 26, 29, 34, 44, 57, 63, 65, 85, 93-96, 107, 115-116, 121-122, 124, 129-130, 132, 135-137, 148, 150, 154-155, 166, 169, 185-187, 197, 224-226
Virtual Realms 4, 6, 79, 99-101, 138, 154, 163, 169, 249, 252

W

World Wide Web 31, 214, 216

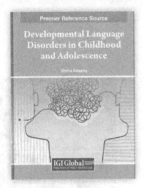

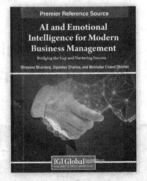

 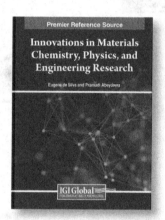 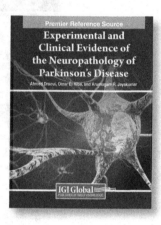 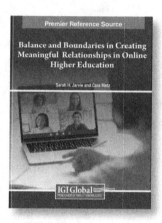

Printed in the United States
by Baker & Taylor Publisher Services

Printed in the United States
by Baker & Taylor Publisher Services